International Economics

4th Edition

L. Alan Winters

London and New York

First published 1991
by Harper Collins Academic

Reprinted 1992
by Routledge
11 New Fetter Lane, London EC4P 4EE

Simultaneously published in the USA and Canada
by Routledge
a division of Routledge, Chapman and Hall, Inc.
29 West 35th Street, New York, NY 10001

© 1991 L. Alan Winters

Typeset in 10/11pt Baskerville by
Columns Design and Production Services Ltd.
Printed and bound in Great Britain by
Bell & Bain, Thornliebank, Glasgow

British Library Cataloguing in Publication Data

A catalogue record for this book is available from the British Library.

ISBN 0–415–08426–1

Library of Congress Cataloging-in-Publication Data

A catalogue record for this book is available from the Library of Congress.

Contents

Contents

Contents

TO MEG
VICKI AND CATEY

Preface to the First Edition

This book aims at meeting the oft-repeated demand by teachers and students for a modern textbook to cover the elements of modern international economics at a level appropriate to a second or third year undergraduate course, in which the student might or might not wish to specialize intensively in international economics. My object is to produce a book containing the body of knowledge with which every aspiring graduate in economics ought to be familiar, and which will at the same time provide a groundwork text upon which those who wish to specialize in international economics at postgraduate level might be able to build. For the benefit of the latter, I have indicated throughout the text the lines along which the advanced student should develop his more specialized reading – although I hope that *all* students will refuse to be content with reading this one book.

I also have in mind that a large number of intelligent people, whether university students or not, are seriously interested in a wide range of problems in international economics. In my work as an occasional extra-mural lecturer I have been most impressed by the keen desire of many people in all walks of life to become more fully acquainted with problems of the world economy. Accordingly I have tried to write this book in such a way that intelligent laymen, who have little grounding in formal economic analysis, will find their way about it without undue difficulty.

In writing a textbook it is difficult to make full acknowledgement to all the people who have played a part, directly or otherwise, in its writing. As an economist who has always been especially interested in international economic problems, I owe a debt to a large number of scholars who have influenced my thinking; notably Professors James Meade and Harry Johnson, and Dr W. M. Corden. On particular points I have tried to make full acknowledgement in text and notes; if there has been any omission, I trust the oversight will be forgiven. I feel that it is also appropriate to place on record the enormous debt (intellectual and personal) which I owe to Professor James Meade. My debt to James Meade as a scholar should be apparent from the following pages. My debt to him as a teacher and one-time supervisor is even more profound.

Part of the pleasure I have derived from writing this book has been due to the help received from a large number of people. Indeed it has seemed at times a truly co-operative endeavour. I am especially grateful to those who read through and commented upon the first draft, either in whole or in part. I would like to record my thanks to my colleagues at the University of Salford, Dr Wolfgang Brassloff and Mr Peter Lomas. With Dr Brassloff I spent many hours discussing the basic framework of the book, as well as the final draft. For penetrating criticism on content I am especially indebted to Dr W. M. Corden, Nuffield Reader in International Economics at the University of Oxford, Mr Dudley Peake of the University College of North Wales, Bangor, Professor D. J. Coppock of the University of Manchester, and Mr David Robertson of the University of Reading. I also showed the draft to one of my ex-students at Salford, Miss Margaret Smith. As representing the consumer interest, Margaret Smith's comments were invaluable and, I hope, have made the book a little more acceptable to the undergraduate reader. My Secretary Miss Margaret Parker has typed and retyped seemingly endless drafts with fortitude and patience; in the closing stages of the work she has been helped by Miss Pauline Bolger of Salford University and also by Mrs Callaghan and Mrs Parker. I am grateful to Mr Reginald Oliver, who prepared the diagrams for the press. As with every piece of work I have attempted I owe a great debt to my wife, Margaret, and family who not only helped in drawing up the tables and checking facts and figures, but also provided the encouragement which every writer requires. Finally, I must thank Mr Charles A. Furth, of Allen and Unwin, who not only suggested that I should write this book but who has been a model of patience and kindliness in seeing this work completed.

SIDNEY WELLS

University of Salford   *November 1968*

Preface to the Revised Edition

Few textbooks stand the test of time as well as Sidney Wells' *International Economics* has. First published in 1969, and slightly revised by Dr E. W. Brassloff in 1973, it has been a leading introduction to international economics for fifteen years. Much has changed over these years, however, both in international economics and in the international economy, and it has now become necessary to make further and more drastic revisions. It has been my honour and pleasure to carry out this task.

The present edition has been completely rewritten in the course of revision. In some places this was quite inevitable, because the nature of the analysis has changed since the late 1960s. Thus, for example, the discussion of flexible exchange rates, macro-economic policy, the oil price and developments in the International Monetary Fund could not have been other than entirely new. In other instances I have chosen to rewrite the original text to take account of more recent analytical research and changes in emphasis. Thus, I adopt a different approach to the Heckscher–Ohlin theory of trade, and devote a chapter to modern theories of trade based on technology and on imperfect competition. Finally, I have increased the emphasis on testing economic hypotheses. In part this reflects my own interests, but mainly it arises from changes in the general approach to economics over the last decade.

Such drastic revision has, inevitably, had some cost – especially as the new edition is no longer than the original. First, some of the controversies of the 1960s have died a natural death; for example, the problem of sterling features only briefly, and then as an issue of recent economic history. Second, there is somewhat less space devoted to institutional matters than previously. Third, the discussion of international economic integration has been shortened, as have, fourth, certain issues in development economics. These contractions have been made reluctantly, but given the availability of alternative textbooks and the size constraints on the present edition I hope they do not do too much violence to Wells' original intentions. While the differences just noted are considerable, the new edition is still a direct descendant of Wells' *International Economics*. It bears the same overall structure, it fulfils the same purposes, it presents many of the same arguments and it has the same flavour of applied, as opposed to purely abstract, economics.

In preparing this edition, I have drawn extensively on the goodwill of my friends. Among those to whom I am most grateful for advice are Alan Armstrong, John Beath, David Demery and Partha Sen of the University of Bristol and Oli Havrylyshyn of George Washington University, who read and commented upon various draft chapters, and William Shaw of the World Bank, and John Black of the University of Exeter who read and commented on the complete draft. To the last, in particular, I owe a great debt. His help covered every aspect of the book, from its structure to its preparation for printing, and that his advice was not always taken is due only to my own stubbornness and indolence. The burdens of typing were shared by Karen Adams, Mary Harthan, Vicky Sugui and Janet Wright, with super-human patience and efficiency, while the figures were excellently traced by Carrie Pharoah. I am most grateful to all of them. The proposal that I should make this revision came from Nicholas Brealey of George Allen & Unwin, who has been helpful and patient throughout its gestation. Naturally none of these people, nor my employers, bear any responsibility for the book's views or shortcomings.

My final debt of gratitude is to my family. My daughters, Vicki and Catey, have always been solicitous as to the book's progress, and have been very tolerant of the absences and preoccupations that authorship seems to involve. My wife, Meg, has been all these things, as well as a willing partner in proof-reading and preparing the manuscript. She has been sympathetic and supportive throughout the endeavour, and without her I doubt that it would have been completed.

The University of Bristol
and
The World Bank

L. ALAN WINTERS
March 1984

Preface to the Fourth Edition

I have been gratified by the success of the third edition of *International Economics* and flattered by the request to update it. This process has been more extensive than I anticipated and has resulted in several significant changes to the book. All the material on the Heckscher–Ohlin model of international trade is now collected into two consecutive chapters and that on factor mobility into one. Substantial new sections have been provided on: trade under imperfect competition, world trade patterns, non-tariff barriers, strategic trade policy, the completion of the European internal market, the political economy of protection, trade and development, foreign exchange markets, the US budget deficit, the Euro-capital markets, and the debt crisis. Reductions have been made to the treatment of North Sea oil and the history of international monetary affairs. In addition, every chapter has been given sections on key concepts and questions for review, and several include case-studies to illustrate the practical aspects of international economics.

Despite these changes I hope that the book maintains its original flavour of applied economics grounded jointly in theory and empirical research. A sound appreciation of theory – albeit rarified and abstract – is the necessary starting point for economic analysis, but it must be supplemented by empirical testing and quantification. I continue to be disturbed by the scarcity of first-rate empirical work in international economics and hope that this book will help to fire a few students' enthusiasm to undertake that most difficult of tasks. I also hope that the book dissolves the common misapprehension among students that policy economics is applied and empirical while 'pure' economics is abstract and theoretical. Positive theory needs empirical testing before it is useful, while economic policy must be based on the best of economic and econometric theory. Indeed, especially if the underlying theory has been tested previously, the discussion of economic policy may be entirely theoretical.

In preparing the new edition I have benefited from comments from John Black, Ted Gardener, Andre Sapir, Stephen Smith, John Thornton, Roy Trinder and an anonymous referee.

Elena Ellis, Sue James and Meg Winters have cheerfully undertaken the typing of my appalling manuscript and Meg Winters has also undertaken proof-reading and other editorial tasks. Tony Griffiths drew the new figures. I am most grateful to them all. Finally, I must re-express my gratitude for the support I received from my family, Meg, Vicki and Catey.

University of Wales, Bangor   L. ALAN WINTERS
University of Birmingham   *1990*

Acknowledgements

I am grateful to the following for permission to reproduce their copyright material:

  The American Economic Association and Professor P. Isard (Figure 20.2)

  Cambridge University Press (Table 19.3)

  Chapman and Hall Publishing Co. (Table 19.2)

  Gower Publishing Co. Ltd (Table 16.1)

  The International Monetary Fund (Tables 19.4 and 26.2)

  Lloyds Bank Ltd (Table 18.2)

  The Morgan Bank (Table 29.2)

  North Holland Publishing Co. (Tables 18.3 and 19.1)

  The Organization for Economic Co-operation and Development (Tables 18.1 and 19.5)

  The Editor of the *Southern Economic Journal* (Table 8.3)

  The Trade Policy Research Centre (Table 8.1 – extracted from Table 1 of an article by Hugh Corbet, 'The Importance of Being Earnest about Further GATT Negotiations', which appeared in the September 1979 number of *The World Economy*, the quarterly journal of the Trade Policy Research Centre, London.

1 Introduction – Why, What and How

1.1 WHY INTERNATIONAL ECONOMICS?

Why do we need textbooks on international economics? What differentiates economic transactions between countries from those that take place within a country? Are economic principles relating to the international economy different from those appropriate to a single country? What is special about international economics to justify separate theories, courses and examination papers?

In many ways it is neither necessary nor desirable for the student to make a hard and fast distinction in her mind between problems in general economics and those in international economics. Indeed, the greater the number of links that she can find between general economic theory and the special field of international economics, the better will she understand both. My hope is that as she works through this book the reader will constantly relate what she learns to the broad body of general economic theory with which she is already familiar – or becoming familiar.

There are nevertheless several reasons for the development of a distinctive branch of economics dealing with problems of the international economy. Some of these reasons are practical, some pedagogic. Perhaps the most obvious justification for a separate study arises from the barriers between countries that prevent the completely free movement of goods, persons and capital. These barriers may be political, social or linguistic, as well as economic. Barriers that are primarily economic take the form of customs duties, direct trade restrictions or exchange controls. Sometimes the impediments are more subtle, taking the form of elaborate customs procedures, packaging requirements, health regulations and 'mixing' regulations that require the use of a given minimum quantity of a domestically produced raw material in conjunction with an imported product. Such trade barriers are rarely important enough to impede the flow of trade *within* a country; but, to the extent that they are important *between* countries, they give rise to a number of problems that form part of the study of international economics.

The nineteenth-century classical economist believed that the immobility of factors of production between countries, as contrasted with their mobility within a country, was the most important distinguishing feature of international trade. This view is now outmoded and it is widely realised that factors do move extensively between countries (and sometimes sluggishly within a country). None the less, it still remains true that restrictions, legal or otherwise, on inter-country factor movements are much more widespread than internal barriers and that the prevalence of these restrictions has important economic consequences.

Another justification for a special book on international economics is that there are differences between countries in their currency systems. The mere existence of different currencies is in itself of minor significance. For example, if the value of one currency in terms of another is rigidly fixed and a citizen of one country can freely convert his currency into that of any other country, the fact that one country uses pounds while another uses dollars matters little. In reality, however, differences in currencies often reflect more fundamental differences in economic systems and policies. In the world in which we live, the value of one currency in terms of another does change – in some cases frequently, in others only at rare intervals. Every time a change takes place, or indeed looks as if it *might* take place, a number of economic issues arise. Nor are all currencies equally acceptable: some are widely used in international trade, others are virtually inconvertible into any other currency. This consideration itself gives rise to a further set of economic problems.

Another factor is that economic conditions and policies are likely to differ more markedly between countries than within a country. For example, demand may be high in Britain when the money supply is rising rapidly; as a result Britons are likely to purchase more goods from France – or perhaps take more and longer holidays in that country. This will be reflected either in a depreciation of sterling, as Britons sell sterling to obtain the francs with which to buy French goods, or in a British balance of payments deficit, as existing British stocks of francs are run down by expenditure in France. Each of these outcomes has further consequences and each, at times, has been considered a major economic problem to be solved by policy-makers.

Such questions do not arise within a country. The residents of a *region* might very well 'import' more from other regions than they 'export' to them, but no balance of payments problem would become apparent. This is because all regions use the same currency and, as they share a common banking system, the flow of funds from the deficit to the surplus region takes the form of a transfer of balances between banks of the same country, or even between branches of the same bank. Accordingly there is little danger of a region losing all its means of payments; wealth is merely transferred from one region to the other.

This is not to deny that differences in income employment and economic activity can grow up between regions of one country – compare, for example, North-East and South-East England – but just to argue that the symptoms are different. So too, however, are the cures. The regions of any one country face pretty much the same monetary and fiscal policies. Slight differences may exist in micro-economic incentives – for example, development grants to stimulate investment in depressed regions – but broadly they inhabit the same economic environment. Between countries, on the other hand, policies can vary immensely: the relative prices of two countries' monies (and outputs) can vary through exchange rate changes; interest rates can vary; the balance between private and public provision of services can vary; and so on.

These different 'menus' of policy really stem from a further fundamental difference between international and inter-regional trade. The former involves partners from different *sovereign* states; the latter does not. The central government typically determines regional policy for its regions and does so with a view to the national, rather than the strictly regional, interest. In international trade, two national governments are potentially involved, each defining policy in terms of the welfare of its own residents rather than those of the world as a whole. Most prominent among the results of this difference in policy environments is the ability to make income transfers between two transactors. Inter-regional transfers occur all the time and are frequently not even explicitly measured; for example, Londoners' tax bills finance Ulster's unemployment benefit with little or no political problem. International

2

transfers are politically much more difficult to effect – witness the unpopularity of foreign aid flows and the constant squabbling over Britain's contribution to the European Community's budget. Thus not only do policies vary more between countries than within them, but their fundamental directions differ: inter-regional trade falls within one jurisdiction, international trade falls under two.

Finally, geographical considerations also give rise to a number of special economic problems best dealt with under the umbrella of international trade theory. Countries differ in size and resource endowment. They often have their own transport systems with differences in transport, tariffs, and freight regulations.

1.2 ISSUES IN INTERNATIONAL ECONOMICS

Having argued why international economics should be treated as a separate subject, we now briefly identify some of the issues it considers. Tables 6.1–6.5 describe the patterns of world trade:

● Why has the value of world trade increased twenty-fold over thirty years?
● How much is due to changes in price and how much to changes in quantities?
● Why did the share of fuels double?
● What are the consequences of such large changes?
● Why has service trade increased five-fold since 1970?
● What are the NICs and why are they so successful?
● Is the Japanese economy unfairly closed to foreign goods?

Turning to British trade:

● Why has trade reoriented so strongly towards Europe?
● Why does the UK both import and export cars?
● Why has the UK share of world manufactured exports fallen so rapidly?

Similarly, for other countries:

● Why have countries like Singapore, Korea and Taiwan been able to more than double their share of world manufactured exports?
● Will China, Morocco, Bangladesh or Zambia be able to do the same?
● Is the USA turning into a primary commodity exporter?

Among the more general questions surrounding international trade:

● Why has the share of world output traded internationally increased from 8.5 per cent in 1950 to 16 per cent in 1980?
● Why do some countries have surpluses of exports over imports and others the reverse? Does this matter, and can anything be done about it?
● Why do some firms build factories abroad?
● How does one country's macro-economic policy affect another's economic performance?
● Why do exchange rates fluctuate so much; or rather, do exchange rates fluctuate 'so much'?
● Why do countries hold reserves of foreign currencies?
● What constitutes international money?
● What are Euro-dollars?

3

If these questions seem rather dry, international economics also has very many policy problems. For example:

- Should Britain curtail her imports of clothes from Asia, or of cars from Japan?
- Does Britain gain economically from membership of the EC?
- Should international migration be encouraged or discouraged?
- Should the multinationals be controlled?
- What will be the consequences of completing the European internal market in 1992?
- Does protection allow industries to become technically efficient?
- Should short-term capital flows ('hot money') be taxed or banned?
- Should exchange rates be fixed?
- Should the International Monetary Fund be strengthened?
- Should developing countries' debts be re-scheduled or written off?
- Would it pay such countries to repudiate their debts?

All of these questions and many more are the subject matter of international economics. Some have straightforward answers, some are controversial, and some seem, frankly, quite intractable. The purpose of this book is not so much to present a list of answers as to introduce the student to the ways and means by which economists analyse these questions. Plenty of them will be resolved in this process, but, more importantly, at the end of the course the student will be equipped to pose and answer new questions for herself.

1.3   ON STUDYING INTERNATIONAL ECONOMICS

Having treated the 'why' and 'what' of international economics, we now consider the 'how'. This section is not an essay in economic method, but it does introduce certain important ideas that will clarify the nature of the arguments made below.

Positive and normative economics

First, we distinguish throughout the book between *positive* and *normative* economics. The former deals with how the world is, the latter with how it ought to be. Statements of positive economics are, at least in principle, susceptible to test, by confronting them with 'the facts'. Normative statements, on the other hand, while obviously having factual dimensions, also add value judgements. Ultimately, disagreements over normative issues cannot be settled by fact alone, for it is possible for people to agree entirely about the facts of two situations but still to differ as to which is preferable.

International economics encompasses both the positive and normative approaches – often, in the past, without separating the two very clearly. For example, Ricardo's comparative advantage theory of international trade serves both to predict patterns of trade (a positive aspect) and to show the benefits of free trade over protection (a normative aspect). Below, however, we aim to keep the distinction clear, and also to resolve positive (testable) issues before letting normative or judgemental factors loose on a question.

Theory and refutation

The purposes of positive economics are to understand and predict economic phenomena. In order to do this, we generally need to organise our information according to some guiding principle – what we might loosely call a theory.

4

Typically, theories are rather abstract and unrealistic, but by concentrating on one crucial aspect of the question in hand they shed light on practical issues. The role of assumption in economic theorising is to allow this concentration on crucial aspects in a rigorous fashion by stripping away distracting details. To be useful, however, a theory must bear some relation to known facts. Thus the phenomenon being explained must be real and observable, and the predictions made by the theory broadly correct. Unfortunately in economics many more theories exist than have been adequately tested; we shall frequently encounter cases below where many possible explanations exist for a phenomenon but where the empirical job of deciding how well each describes the world has not yet been completed.

In devising an economic theory, we presuppose that certain assumed features of the world are true, and from these deduce predictions about economic behaviour. The assumptions really define the theory. They come in two basic types: assumptions about unobservables (e.g. that consumers maximise utility), and strategic simplifications, which, while not literally true, facilitate analysis without fundamentally altering the predictions. The latter obviously depend on the circumstances, but a typical example would be assuming perfect competition. Neither type of assumption is open to direct testing – the first for obvious reasons and the second because it cannot be known beforehand whether a particular simplification will make a theory's predictions unrealistic or not. Thus, in order to see whether a theory is likely to be useful, we have to test its predictions.

The procedure is as follows. A specific hypothesis is formed; it makes specific assumptions (A) and from them logically deduces predictions about observable phenomena (P). Provided the assumptions (A) are sufficient to guarantee the outcome (P), A can be tested by observing whether or not P occurs. Observation can only *reject* A with certainty, however; it can never prove beyond doubt that assumptions A *are* true (justified), because one can never exclude the possibility that some other set of circumstances might actually have given rise to P. Thus, observing 'not-P' tells us that 'not-A' is true, but observing P tells us only that A *could be* true. We should proceed, therefore, by a series of hypotheses and rejections, the body of theory extant at any time being merely those assumptions that appear useful and that have not yet been rejected. Theory is just the best tool kit we happen to have at any point of time; there is nothing absolute, or even provenly 'true', about it.

Indeed, economists frequently have to use theory that they know does not predict certain phenomena well, but if it is the best available it may survive even though various refutations of its predictions exist. It is in these circumstances that disagreements arise and normative considerations slip in. Without universal agreement on what constitutes sufficient grounds for rejecting a theory, or on what the trade-off between 'usefulness' and 'refutation' should be, economists tend to favour those positive theories that best fit their normative preconceptions. (This is not unique to economics, or even to social science. For example, witness the way scientific groups lined up over the issue of whether or not lead in petrol was a serious health hazard: those with broader 'environmental interests' said it was; those concerned with industrial growth said it was not.)

Statistical testing

Nearly all testing of predictions in economics involves the use of statistics, and this further complicates matters. Nothing can be measured with perfect accuracy and, in economics, variables are always subject to shocks and

5

changes other than those of interest to a particular theory. Thus, for instance, while theory might suggest that a particular parameter, say β, should have the value zero, an estimate of β, say $\hat{\beta}$, 'close to' zero would not be sufficient grounds for rejecting that view. The crucial question, of course, is what constitutes 'close to'.

Imagine that we could conduct hundreds of independent tests of the hypothesis that $\beta = 0$, under circumstances in which $\beta = 0$ were actually true. We could then work out a range within which, say, 95 per cent of the estimates of β would fall under these circumstances. (All this can be done theoretically – we do not actually have to do the tests.) Now consider the one test we actually have conducted, which has produced the estimate $\hat{\beta}$. If $\hat{\beta}$ falls inside the 95 per cent range we have just calculated, we accept (do not reject) the hypothesis that $\beta = 0$, whereas if it falls outside the range we reject the hypothesis. Clearly in the latter case we have a 5 per cent chance of rejecting the hypothesis when it is actually true, because 5 per cent of the estimates will lie outside the range even when $\beta = 0$. Thus we say that we are '95 per cent confident' that $\beta \neq 0$, or alternatively that we have rejected the hypothesis $\beta = 0$ 'at 5 per cent significance'. Clearly, the chances of mistakenly rejecting $\beta = 0$ could be reduced to 1 per cent by calculating the range to include 99 per cent of the estimates when the hypothesis is true; this would be referred to as testing 'at 1 per cent significance'.

The range that includes 99 per cent of the estimates obviously exceeds that including 95 per cent, and sometimes these ranges can be so large as to be almost useless. For example, an estimated range for a price elasticity of -15 to $+5$ would be useless for almost any purpose. Behaviour is qualitatively different according to whether the actual elasticity is greater than or less than zero, but the quoted range would never allow us to reject the hypothesis that the elasticity was zero in favour of that saying it was negative. Thus the level of significance of a test has to be chosen carefully to balance the chances of wrongly rejecting the hypothesis against those of failing correctly to identify cases where it does not hold.

Economists frequently report estimates of parameters of interest along with their 'standard errors'. The latter are used in constructing the critical ranges for conducting hypothesis tests. Suppose we wish to test whether parameter β takes the value m; let $\hat{\beta}$ be our estimate and s its standard error. At 5 per cent significance, the acceptance range is $(m \pm 1.96\,s)$ and at 1 per cent $(m \pm 2.58\,s)$. If $\hat{\beta}$ lies outside these ranges we reject the hypotheses at 5 per cent and 1 per cent significance, respectively. Sometimes we talk of a parameter 'being significant at 5 per cent'; this means that it is significantly different from zero at 5 per cent significance, namely that $\hat{\beta}$ lies outside the range $\pm 1.96\,s$.[1]

Conclusion on method

Thus we see that positive economics should ideally proceed by a series of hypotheses and refutations. A suggestion (hypothesis) is advanced that relates particular observable phenomena to unobservable assumptions in a logically water-tight fashion. Assuming the hypothesis is true, we ask what range the observables would have in the real world, given our imperfect methods of measurement and the presence of other shocks. If our actual observations fall within this range, the hypothesis is tentatively accepted, whereas if they fall outside it is rejected. After several such tests, and with a view to the usefulness (power) of the hypothesis and the available alternatives, the hypothesis is incorporated into the body of theory or rejected completely.

There is room for ambiguity and disagreement about what constitutes sufficient grounds for rejection of a hypothesis, but otherwise the procedure outlined seems fairly objective and straightforward. This is not to claim, however, that positive economics is entirely 'value-free'. Unfortunately, normative considerations do sometimes influence the strength of the rejection criteria applied. More importantly, they also influence the set of questions asked and the hypotheses tested in the first place. The latter is quite unavoidable and all that one can hope is that, given the hypotheses, objective and scientific procedures are used to evaluate them, and that value judgements are consciously made and explicitly reported.

**Some
terminology**

Below we shall frequently talk of a *model* of some economic process. A model is really no more than a theory; it is a simplified and small-scale replica of reality – the nature of the simplification being dictated by the theory and made concrete in the model by assumptions about economic behaviour.

Another term frequently encountered is *regression equation* or *regression*. This is a technique econometricians use to measure the relationship between certain economic variables and another particular variable of interest: thus, to explain the demand for shoes, we might regress the quantity sold on incomes and the relative prices of shoes and other goods. Regression coefficients record the effect that a determining variable (e.g income) has on the variable of interest (demand); there is typically one coefficient per determining variable. Interest is focused on the regression coefficients first as a measure of the quantitative effect that one variable has on another, and second to test whether or not that effect could reasonably be supposed to be zero. For the latter task, we use the estimate of the regression coefficient β and its standard error (s) in the way just described, and test whether or not β (the 'true' effect of the determining variable) could be zero.

1.4 ABOUT THIS BOOK

**The
approach**

This book provides an introduction to the main aspects of international economics. It presents the theory in an accessible form and tries wherever possible to provide empirical evidence and applications to back up that theory. Compared with the first edition, less space is devoted to institutional details – describing how things work – and more to the testing and evaluation of alternative theoretical approaches. Thus the emphasis is shifted somewhat towards international economics as an intellectual discipline, and away from the international economy as a phenomenon. The reader will none the less still find much on the latter to interest her.

A corollary of including more empirical work is that there is a greater air of uncertainty about this book than in most others. Economic theory appears very confident in its descriptions of causes and consequences, and a theoretical explanation can always be found for any causal observation we happen to make. When we systematically confront theory with data, however, its shortcomings are clearly visible, and it becomes obvious that we should, in fact, be rather tentative about most of our claims, both positive and normative. This does not mean that economics is not useful (after all, the errors in weather forecasts do not lead us to reject meteorology as a useful discipline), but it does call for a certain modesty and caution on the part of economists. By illustrating this fact, this book is merely being realistic.

The use of mathematics in the text is very slight. Mathematical symbols are occasionally useful as a form of notational shorthand, but very rarely is there any manipulation. The predominant mode of argument is verbal, supported and illustrated by graphs. This tends to make the analysis slightly less precise than mathematics would allow, but it certainly does not make it simple-minded. Several of the arguments presented are quite sophisticated and need to be read slowly and several times over. This almost certainly applies to section 1.3, which you have just read, and which is among the most difficult of the book.

Each chapter includes a selected and annotated Further Reading. The references given will allow you to follow up various points from the text more deeply or in different directions. Except in the few cases noted, the arguments should be accessible to the student who has successfully worked through the relevant chapter of this book, although for the empirical papers further study may be required to master the econometric techniques used. The latter, however, are not essential in order to understand the main economic content of the results. It is not necessary to read every reference; rather you should be guided by the notes provided.

The chapters conclude with Key Concepts and Questions for Review. The Key Concepts are a set of buzz-words designed to stimulate recollection of the material covered. In every case the student should ask herself how the key concept fits into the argument of the chapter and to which ideas it is related. The Questions for Review may form the basis of discussion, written work or, for the solitary student, reflection. They vary from merely asking for a well-ordered repetition of the chapter material to requiring significant extensions of that material. Every student should attempt at least some of the questions. Finally, several chapters contain case-studies. These are a fundamental part of the book; they seek to apply the ideas covered to particular issues. Some deal with economic statistics and others with hypothesis tests, but most are concerned with economic policy in the real world.

The plan
The book is organised along the lines of Marshall's disinction between the 'pure' and the 'monetary' branches of international trade theory. As an expository device this distinction has much to commend it, for it helps in relating international trade to other fields of economics. Pure theory is concerned with real as opposed to monetary magnitudes, its subject matter being the theory of value or price in an international context. Tariff theory, and such questions as the determination of the pattern of international trade and the effects of economic growth, fall within its purview. International monetary economics, on the other hand, is concerned with the theory of money and employment in an international setting; it deals with such problems as balance of payments equilibria, exchange rates, the transmission of business fluctuations between countries, the demand for international reserves and the Euro-dollar market.

Part I of this book deals with pure theory. It starts with the positive theory of international trade, examining various explanations for the existence and the pattern of trade. Chapters 2–6 take us from Ricardo's theory of comparative advantage through to modern theories based on technological mastery and differentiated products. In the course of these chapters the benefits of international trade are introduced, but these are not treated formally until Chapter 7. Chapters 8 and 9 introduce tariffs and non-tariff restrictions on international trade. They deal with positive aspects of these questions, including, in the latter case, a description of many of the interferences to international trade that are possible. Chapters 10 and 11 consider the normative arguments for and against protection in both industrial and developing economies, and Chapter 12 examines how tariffs are actually set in the real world. Chapter 13 deals with the formation of customs unions, in which groups of countries abolish tariffs on their mutual trade and harmonise their other economic policies. This is illustrated in Chapter 14, which discusses the European Communities (the EC). Chapter 15 considers international trade and economic growth, including issues of economic development, while Chapter 16 looks at international factor migration. After a brief general introduction it deals mostly with multinational companies.

Monetary aspects of the international economy are the subject of Parts II and III. Part II deals basically with a single country in a monetary world. Chapter 17 introduces the concepts of the balance of payments and the exchange rate. Chapters 18 and 19 deal with the effects of national income and prices on the balance of payments, while Chapters 20 and 21 integrate international and domestic aspects of macro-economics. Chapters 22 and 23 are devoted to the determinants of exchange rates – an area of very rapid development in contemporary international economics. Chapter 24 asks how macro-economic policy should be conducted in an open economy and Chapter 26 whether, all things considered, fixed or floating exchange rates are preferable. Chapter 25 pulls these various analyses together into two case-studies: the discovery of North Sea oil and the USA's huge public budget deficit.

Part III shifts attention to global monetary issues. Chapter 27 deals with the demand for reserves of international money, while Chapter 28 considers the supply. It takes a historical perspective, taking us from a discussion of the nineteenth-century gold standard through the era of fixed exchange rates to the present 'non-system' of floating rates and potential debt crises. The role of institutions such as the International Monetary Fund and Special Drawing Rights (SDRs) is considered closely. Chapter 29 offers an analysis of the Euro-markets, while Chapter 30 covers the international monetary system and the developing countries. The latter is mainly concerned with the debt crisis.

It is hoped that the reader who perseveres through this book will feel at the end that, although she has learnt something, she has still a vast amount more to learn. At best a textbook should be like an iceberg, showing but a fraction of the vast bulk of material that makes up the whole study. If, after working through it, the student comes to regard this book as an introduction to an exciting field of economic science, and feels moved to acquaint herself at first hand with some of the more detailed and more distinguished texts, then its writing will have been abundantly worthwhile.

FURTHER READING

References will be introduced as appropriate below, but we mention here two sets of survey articles which cover the ground in this book at a more advanced level: *Dornbusch and Frenkel* (1979) and *The Handbook of International Economics* (*Jones and Kenen*, 1983). A useful introduction to economic methodology is *Blaug* (1980), while the use of statistics for hypothesis testing and estimation will be covered by any elementary statistics textbook; see, for example, *Yeomans* (1968).

NOTE

1 These are the values for large samples. Where only small samples of data are available the ranges are somewhat larger. They also refer to tests of the hypothesis $\beta = 0$ against the alternative $\beta \neq 0$. Where we wish to test it against, say $\beta > m$, the acceptance region is below $(m + 1.64\,s)$ at 5 per cent and below $(m + 2.33\,s)$ at 1 per cent. That is, we do not reject $\beta = m$ in favour of $\beta > m$, if β is positive and below $(m + 1.64\,s)$ or if it takes any negative value.

Part I

2 Comparative Costs and International Trade

The pure theory of international trade encompasses the determinants of trade and its consequences, the methods of controlling trade and their consequences, and the interaction between international trade and other real aspects of the economy. Our first five chapters deal almost exclusively with the positive analysis of the causes of trade. The principal question posed is why country A exports good X while country B exports good Y. Or to be more concrete: why have Japanese electronic goods swept the world; why must India import food; why has Britain switched from being a net exporter of manufactures to being a net importer?

The chapters start with the earliest and simplest of trade theories – the classical or Ricardian theory – and progress through neo-classical analysis to recent work. Ricardo, writing in 1817, attributed trade to differences in countries' ability to produce different goods: one produced one good relatively cheaply, the other another good. The differences arose from differences in labour productivity but were not otherwise explained; presumably they lay in variations in countries' natural environments or available technologies. Although Ricardo's is a positive theory of trade (an explanation), he was arguably more interested in normative issues. The theory emerged from his battle to repeal the Corn Laws, and he used it to demonstrate the superiority of free trade over autarky (no trade). This chapter also examines this aspect of Ricardo's writing, although a full treatment of trade and economic welfare is postponed until Chapter 7.

Chapters 3 and 4 present the neo-classical theory of international trade. This is primarily incorporated in the Heckscher–Ohlin theory, which explains countries' differing abilities in different goods by reference to differences in their endowments of factors of production. Thus it offers some justification for Ricardo's differing labour productivities, because in different countries labour has different quantities of other factors with which to combine. The Heckscher–Ohlin theory is still the dominant mode of thought within international trade theory and it underlies much of the normative analysis and extensions of later chapters.

The next chapter deals with modern trade theory. On the one hand this re-emphasises technology, but seeks to explain it further than Ricardo did, and on the other it stresses the role of product differentiation in international trade. The latter is a new, and apparently fruitful, area of research that incorporates imperfect competition into international trade theory and offers some explanation for 'intra-industry' trade. This phenomenon – of countries simultaneously both importing and exporting very similar goods – is virtually impossible to explain with earlier trade theory, which depends only on differences in costs of production to generate trade.

2.1 SOME TOOLS OF ANALYSIS

Before embarking on the Ricardian model, we need to explore a few basic tools of analysis. International economics is not a separate subject but a single

13

branch of the general subject of economics. Thus the international economist uses the same tools of analysis and terminology as other economists. In particular, for questions of international trade we use techniques familiar from micro-economics, welfare economics and general equilibrium analysis. The brief introduction that follows may be pursued in any micro-economics textbook – for example, Lancaster (1969), or Russell and Wilkinson (1979). Throughout this chapter we shall assume that perfect competition and perfect information rule in all markets. We shall also generally limit ourselves to considering just two goods.

Consumption

We start by considering a single consumer, assuming that his preferences over the goods he consumes can be represented by a series of *indifference curves*, as in Figure 2.1. The slope of an indifference curve, which is always negative, is known as the *marginal rate of substitution* (MRS) between the two goods (X and Y). It tells us how much Y the consumer must be offered in return for a unit of X if his welfare is to remain unchanged.

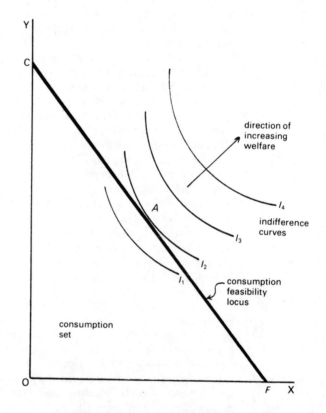

Figure 2.1 Consumer equilibrium

The consumer makes his choice over a set of possible consumption choices defined by his income and the prices of the goods. This set is known as the *consumption set* and its outermost frontier as the *consumption feasibility locus*. The latter shows the maximum of X available for any consumption of Y, and vice versa. Suppose the consumer has income 20 and that the prices of X and Y

14

are 2 and 1 per unit respectively. He can buy 10X or 20Y or any mixture just exhausting his income. These mixtures are shown by line *CF* in Figure 2.1 – hence area O*CF* is the consumption set and *CF* the consumption feasibility locus. The slope of *CF* is given by the price ratio, because it shows how much Y could be added to consumption in return for one X.

The consumer will always aim to be on his highest indifference curve. This will be where an indifference curve just touches the consumption feasibility set – such as at *A* in Figure 2.1. Note how the marginal rate of substitution equals the price ratio ($MRS = P$). This is necessary if the consumer is actually maximising welfare. (Imagine a position where $MRS = 3$ and $P = 2$. How could we raise welfare?)

Production

We assume that a country's stock of factors of production is fixed, but that all can be used in producing either X or Y; we also assume that firms maximise their profits, which implies minimising costs for any level of production. The *marginal cost* of X is the (minimum) cost of producing an additional unit of X, and similarly for Y. The *marginal rate of transformation* (*MRT*) is the rate at which the marginal unit of X can be transformed into Y. This is merely the ratio of their marginal costs. It may also be thought of as the marginal opportunity cost of Y in terms of X – i.e. how much X has to be forgone in order to raise Y-output by one unit.

Given the factors of production, technology and the assumptions of efficiency and full employment, we can calculate the whole range of possible combinations of output. This is known as the *production set*, and its frontier is the *production possibility frontier* or the *transformation frontier*. The latter shows the maximum X available given output of Y, and vice versa. The *MRT* is the slope of the transformation frontier – check that you know why. If firms are maximising profits, the equilibrium values of *MRT* and the price ratio (Y per X) must be equal. (If $MRT = 3$ and $P = 2$ producers would seek to transform X into Y, obtaining 3Y per X, and then sell these at 2Y for 1X to obtain a profit of $\frac{1}{2}$X. Such a position cannot be an equilibrium since there is an incentive to increase Y-output.) The only exception to this equality is where one good is not being produced. Y will not be produced whenever $MRT < P$, because then producing a unit of Y uses up more resources (X) than can be purchased by selling it.

Equilibrium

For a closed economy – one that undertakes no international trade – consumption is limited to what can be produced locally: thus the production set becomes the consumption set. Hence Figure 2.1 could be reinterpreted to represent the equilibrium of a closed economy with preferences *I* (we ignore the problems of adding different people's preferences, for now) and production possibility frontier *CF*. Since, from above, $MRS = P$ and $MRT = P$, the marginal rate of substitution, the marginal rate of transformation and the price ratio will all be equal in full equilibrium.

2.2 ABSOLUTE AND COMPARATIVE COSTS

Absolute advantage

The seed of modern international trade theory comes from Adam Smith (1776). His concern with the division of labour as a means of increasing efficiency is well known and he generalised this to specialisation between trades and between countries:

It is the maxim of every prudent master of a family, never to attempt to make at home what it will cost him more to make than buy. The tailor does not attempt to make his own shoes, but buys them from the shoemaker. The shoemaker does not attempt to make his own clothes but employs a tailor. The farmer attempts to make neither the one nor the other, but employs those different artificers. All of them find it for their interest to employ their whole industry in a way in which they have some advantage over their neighbours, and to purchase with a part of its produce, or what is the same thing, with the price of part of it, whatever else they have occasion for.

What is prudence in the conduct of every private family, can scarce be folly in that of a great kingdom. If a foreign country can supply us with a commodity cheaper than we ourselves can make it, better buy of them with some part of the produce of our own industry, employed in a way in which we have some advantage. (1961 reprint, p. 424.)

Thus countries trade, and should trade, in order to acquire their consumption more cheaply. They buy abroad when foreign prices are below domestic ones. Prices are the immediate determinant of trade, and, although much of what follows below delves behind relative prices, this basic fact should never be forgotten.

Smith also argued that, by extending the market, international trade allows greater specialisation and division of labour than would otherwise be possible. It therefore offers scope for additional gain by reducing costs below their autarky levels. This is a separate argument from the pure trade argument of the quotation, and is held over until Chapter 5 below.

To make the pure trade example more concrete, suppose we have only two goods (food and cloth) and two countries (Britain and America). Further assume that transport is costless and that labour, which is mobile between industries, is the only factor of production. Assume that the labour requirements for each good and country are as follows:

Labour per unit of output in	Britain	America
Food	5	3
Cloth	2	6

In the absence of trade – that is, under *autarky* – prices will reflect labour requirements. So, if wages are the same in the two countries, Britain will be the cheaper source of cloth and America cheaper for food. Hence, when trade first opens, Britain will export cloth and import food.

Trade can increase economic welfare in both countries. Suppose that under autarky each country has 60 units of labour in each industry. Britain's production (and, under autarky, consumption) is 12 of food and 30 of cloth – write this as (12,30) – whilst America's is (20,10). World production is (32,40). Now redistribute labour such that America has 120 workers in food and Britain has 120 in cloth. World production becomes (40,60), so that, by specialising and trading, each country can consume its autarky bundle and there is still some of each product left over. Each country could thus raise its consumption of each good, and assuming more of each good is better than less, the trading outcome *could* allow both countries to increase their welfare. Thus, not only can *absolute advantage* describe international trade patterns, but it can also provide the rationale to prescribe their implementation as a means to raising economic welfare.

Comparative advantage The example above worked very conveniently. Britain was the least-cost producer of cloth and America the least-cost producer of food, and the opportunities for trade were obvious enough. What, however, if one country – Britain, say, – were more efficient in the production of both goods? Absolute advantage would suggest that both goods should be purchased from Britain, but this could not be a long-term solution, because Britain would not wish to buy anything from America in return. Writing some forty years after Smith, Ricardo (1817) was the first economist to analyse this situation formally, with his justly famous law of comparative advantage.

Suppose our matrix of labour requirements were:

Labour per unit of output in	*Britain*	*America*
Food	5	6
Cloth	2	12

Although Britain now requires less labour than America in both industries, this does not preclude profitable trade. Previously we used money prices and wage rates to compare the efficiencies of the two economies; now we use relative prices and barter. In Britain under autarky 1 unit of food trades for $2\frac{1}{2}$ units of cloth – each is equivalent to five men's output. (The *relative price* of food and cloth depends only on the relative labour inputs provided that (i) both goods are produced and (ii) labour productivity is independent of the level of output in each industry. We assume the former, and the latter is implied by our simple numbers above.) Similarly, in America 1 unit of food trades for a $\frac{1}{2}$ unit of cloth – both the product of six men.

When we open trade between America and Britain, the different relative prices provide scope for profitable trade. For example, if American relative prices prevailed in the trading world, a Briton owning 1 unit of food could swap it in Britain for $2\frac{1}{2}$ units of cloth and then, selling these in America, realise 5 units of food – an overall profit of 4 units of food. Similarly, if British prices prevailed, an American entrepreneur initially employing twelve men to produce 1 unit of cloth could switch to producing 2 units of food, and, selling these in Britain, receive 5 units of cloth – again a profitable trade. At intermediate relative prices, both countries would gain, although not by as much as in the examples given.

An alternative view of international trade is as a form of technical innovation. By increasing the choice of methods for transforming food and cloth, it cannot harm society (the new method need not be used), and may benefit it if the new method is an improvement on the old. Clearly for Britain, international trade offering 2 food for 1 cloth is a substantial improvement over the autarkic possibility of $\frac{2}{5}$ food for 1 cloth. Hence Britons will seek to obtain food by switching factors of production from food to cloth and then transforming the resulting cloth into food through international trade, rather than by using the factors directly in food production. For Americans, the opposite incentive would apply. Thus, each country shifts towards the good in which it has a *comparative advantage*. Britain is comparatively more efficient in cloth than in food, whereas America is more efficient (less inefficient) in food: Britain requires $\frac{5}{6}$th of the American inputs in food but only $\frac{1}{6}$th in cloth.

In this simple example, the law of comparative advantage states that country A will export good F if and only if

$$\frac{l_F^A}{l_F^B} < \frac{l_C^A}{l_C^B} \qquad (2.1)$$

where l_j^i is the input requirement for good j in country i. In the 'two-by-two' model, (2.1) may also be expressed as

$$\frac{l_F^A}{l_C^A} < \frac{l_F^B}{l_C^B} \tag{2.2}$$

which implies that A exports the good for which its input requirements are relatively lower compared with those of country B.

The gains from trade

We shall illustrate the gains from trade geometrically in this case. The left panel of Figure 2.2(A) shows Britain's production possibility frontier assuming she has, as before, 120 labourers (DH). If all produce cloth, 60 units are available. As they are switched from cloth to food, 5 cloth are lost for each 2 food gained, until ultimately just 24 food are available. Under autarky the production set is also the consumption set, so consumers as a group will choose some point on DH as the final consumption and production equilibrium, say J. The corresponding production possibility frontier (GC) for America is shown on the right, also assuming 120 labourers. It is smaller than Britain's because America is absolutely less efficient than Britain.

Now open trade: Britain concentrates on cloth production and America on food. Suppose, for now, that each specialises entirely, so that British production shifts to D and American to C. For Britain, DF shows the consumption possibilities of production at D if she can trade at America's autarkic prices. Its slope is one-half, indicating America's willingness to transform any $\frac{1}{2}$ cloth into 1 food. Thus it would be possible for Britain to consume anywhere along DF, which clearly dominates its autarky consumption locus. Correspondingly, if America specialises and can still trade at British autarky prices, she has a 'trading' consumption feasibility locus of EC, which again dominates her autarky possibilities.

Observe how the possibility of gains from trade depends on trade occurring at a price ratio other than the country's own autarky ratio. This is obvious enough: if foreigners transformed goods at the same rate as locals, there would be no reason to trade abroad rather than at home. None the less it is important. Note also that it would not be possible simultaneously for Britain to trade at American prices and for America to trade at British prices. In full equilibrium, the two trading price ratios must be the same, because the two countries are at opposite ends of the same transaction. The determination of this common trading price and of the final production and consumption points are considered in the next section.

2.3 SPECIALISATION AND THE TERMS OF TRADE

The building blocks

While Figure 2.2(A) illustrates the potential for welfare gains from trade, it does not fully define the final trading equilibrium in terms of either the final price ratio or the final production and consumption points. To examine these questions we shall assume that all people in both countries have identical, homothetic, preferences.[1] This allows us to aggregate preferences in each country into a single 'national social welfare function' and then to combine these into a single world welfare function. These functions may be represented

18

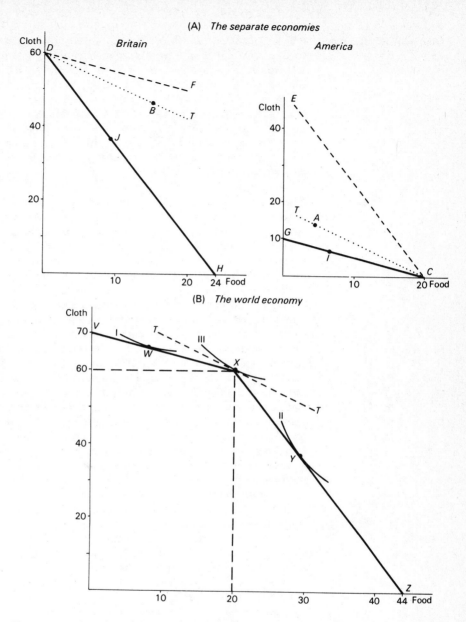

Figure 2.2 Two trading economies – constant costs. (A) The separate economies. (B) The world economy

by families of indifference curves, which behave just like individual preferences, and we assume that society, like individuals, seeks to attain the highest indifference curve possible. (Further details of the aggregation of preferences appear in Chapter 7 below.)

We shall also combine the individual country production structures to describe a single (world) economy with two techniques for transforming food into cloth – one British and one American. Combining the two transformation curves in Figure 2.2(A), we can construct the world transformation curve in part (B) of the figure. If both countries produce only food, output is (44,0).

These are shown as points V and Z. Now suppose that, starting from V, some food is desired: if it is produced in Britain $2\frac{1}{2}$ cloth must be surrendered, whereas in America the price is only $\frac{1}{2}$ cloth. Hence, moving from V, world output is maximised if America switches from cloth to its comparative advantage good, food. This continues until America is entirely specialised in food. World production is then given by point X, i.e. (20,60). If still more food is required, we must then use the less efficient technique – Britain – surrendering $2\frac{1}{2}$ cloth per food unit: this takes us along XZ towards Z. Hence VXZ represents the *world transformation schedule* of food for cloth, *assuming that the most efficient techniques are used.*

The terms of trade

The 'terms of trade' is just another expression for the relative price of one good in terms of another, although it is usually reserved for cases where the two goods originate from different countries. As before, prices are determined by the maximisation of welfare over the feasible consumption set. Here this exercise is conducted on a world scale, confronting the world transformation function with the world preference function.

We consider three alternative positions for the world indifference curves. If demand is strongly oriented towards cloth – giving indifference curves of family I – equilibrium occurs at W. Here, Britain is entirely specialised in cloth but America produces both goods. The world price ratio is determined by the slope of the social indifference curve at equilibrium, and at W this equals the American rate of transformation, because America is the marginal producer. That is, to obtain 1 extra unit of cloth, 2 units of American food must be surrendered, because Britain has no resources not already devoted to cloth. In this circumstance, the world price ratio equals the American autarky price ratio. Britain gains from trade (she can trade along DF in Figure 2.2(A)) but America on the other hand gains nothing, since both foreign trade and switching factors between industries offer the same rate of transformation of food for cloth. Clearly this would apply wherever the tangency between the indifference curve and transformation surface occurred between V and X.

An equivalent case is social indifference curve II – which produces equilibrium Y. Here, America specialises and gains, but, with the terms of trade at Britain's autarky price ratio, Britain does not.

The more interesting case is indifference curve III. Here, both countries specialise and the world terms of trade are determined by the slope of the indifference curve at point X (the slope of TT). It is clear that this could lie anywhere between the slope of VX (America's autarky price ratio) and XZ (Britain's autarky price ratio). Within these limits, the terms of trade are determined solely by the shape of the indifference curve – i.e. the pattern of demand.

Assuming equilibrium at X, and terms of trade TT, British and American consumption possibilities are shown in Figure 2.2(A) as DT and CT respectively (DT, CT and TT are all parallel). The final terms of trade differ from both autarky price ratios and hence both countries benefit from trade. The final consumption baskets for each country lie along DT and CT respectively and, given our assumption of identical homothetic preferences, they must contain goods in the same proportions as the world equilibrium X. They are thus points A and B. Britain produces at D and consumes at B, selling cloth for food, while America produces at C and consumes at A, trading from C to A, trading from C to A, which precisely matches Britain's trade from D to B.

The world production point X arises at any terms of trade between the two autarky price ratios. This does not mean that the terms of trade are irrelevant however, for they determine the distribution of the gains from trade. Suppose that tastes change from our previous equilibrium so that food becomes more highly valued. People will surrender more cloth per unit of food, so the terms of trade line becomes steeper. Hence both DT and CT become steeper: the former, pivoting on D, leads to a contraction of the British consumption set, while the latter, pivoting on C, expands the American consumption set. Thus a shift in a country's terms of trade in favour of its exports (i.e. a rising relative price of exports) increases its economic welfare.

Specialisation

Let us summarize these results. In the simple Ricardian two-by-two model either:

(i) just one country specialises and gains from trade. The terms of trade settle at the other (non-specialising) country's autarky price ratio and that country gains nothing by trade; or

(ii) both countries specialise and both gain by trade. The terms of trade depend on demand patterns, but must lie between the two autarky price ratios.

Which of these outcomes occurs depends on both the size and efficiency of the countries and on demand patterns. Given the latter, the smaller a country's output the greater the probability that it specialises. (In Figure 2.2, the smaller America's output, the closer would X be to the upright axis and the greater the chance that the highest of any family of indifference curves would be tangent to XZ rather than to VX). Thus it seems that large or efficient countries have less to gain through trade than small countries, since trade is less likely to expand their consumption sets.[2]

If this seems somewhat counter-intuitive, it is because the model does not fully reflect reality. In order to produce the outcomes described, we must have perfectly competitive good and factor markets and the government must not intervene at all in international trade. Large countries, however, are often felt to gain from trade because they have market power: by threatening to withdraw from or hinder trade they (or their large companies) can threaten to damage small partners, and hence appropriate some of the latter's gains to themselves.

Money and prices

Most international trade theory uses barter theory as we have just done, but before proceeding we should at least assure ourselves that there is a consistent story of money and absolute prices to accompany it. Return to the table of labour requirements on p. 17 above. If both British and American workers earn 1 unit of local currency per day, that table also represents *local currency* prices under autarky. Suppose initially that when trade is opened the exchange rate is £1 = $1. No one would wish to buy American goods, so there would be no demand for dollars, but everyone would be trying to get pounds in order to buy British goods. Hence the pound would tend to rise in value – say to £1 = $2. At this price America is the cheaper source of food and Britain the cheaper source of cloth, and, by following absolute prices, trade would also fall into the comparative advantage pattern.

The equilibrium exchange rate will be determined so that, given local currency wages, each country is absolutely the cheaper for its comparative advantage good and there is only one price for each good. This, in fact, amounts to determining the terms of trade, because once the terms of trade are set, as in Figure 2.2(B), so too is the exchange rate. At X, for example, terms of trade of 1 food to $1\frac{1}{2}$ cloth imply an exchange rate of £1 = \$2. (American food costs \$6, or £3, per unit; British cloth £2.) At equilibrium W, however, the terms of trade are 1 food to $\frac{1}{2}$ cloth – the American autarky ratio. This requires an exchange rate of £1 = \$6 so that British and American cloth are both £2 per unit and food is £1 per unit.

Hence, underlying the comparative advantage analysis is a monetary analysis that shows how, with people buying from the cheapest source and with the exchange rate flexible, the required trade patterns come about. Note in passing that in this model wages differ between countries: labour in the more efficient country receives higher wages and consumption.

2.4 FURTHER ANALYSIS OF THE RICARDIAN MODEL

The previous two sections have sketched a complete model of world trade based on Ricardo's seminal law of comparative advantage. This analysis underlies nearly all later trade theory, and to facilitate our study of this we now look more deeply at the model, in terms other than Ricardo's.

The assumptions

International trade takes place because goods are available more cheaply from abroad than at home. Ricardo's model explains the pattern of trade by relating prices to certain fundamental features of the economies concerned. This requires several assumptions:

(i)   There is only one factor of production – labour.

(ii)   Its productivity – i.e. the production technology – differs between countries, but no explanation is give for these technological differences.

(iii)   Labour is perfectly mobile between industries within a country but perfectly immobile between countries.

(iv)   There are constant returns to scale in each industry – i.e. unit costs are independent of the level of output.

(v)   There are no impediments to trade such as tariffs or transport costs.

Assumptions (iii) and (iv) ensure that each country's transformation curve between cloth and food is a straight line. The rate of transformation is quite independent of the composition of output – e.g. it is always 1 food for $\frac{1}{2}$ cloth for America. Hence there is only one price ratio consistent with the production of both goods – in America this is 2 cloth for 1 food; any other price ratio causes producers to specialise, because then 1 unit of labour can earn more money in one branch than the other. Thus, labour productivities determine costs (rates of transformation), which determine the direction of trade when it occurs. In Ricardo's model, therefore, the assumptions ensure that the direction of trade is determined solely by comparative labour productivities.

As with nearly all trade theory, the immediate cause of the direction of trade is relative prices. Ricardo's assumptions determine relative prices by relative labour productivities; other theories postulate other determinants, but the basic approach remains the same. This section and the next chapters now consider relaxing Ricardo's assumptions and extending his model.

Opportunity costs

Ricardo expressed his theory in terms of the labour theory of value – labour was the only factor of production. This was an expositional convenience rather than a statement of fact, but it nevertheless took many years for trade theory to escape from this strait-jacket. The latter was accomplished by Haberler (1936), who re-expressed the theory in terms of *opportunity costs*. The opportunity cost of good X is the amount of good Y that has to be surrendered in order to obtain a unit of X. In Ricardo's theory this transformation occurs by shifting labour from one industry to another, so opportunity costs are naturally defined in terms of relative labour productivities. However, it is obvious that a similar concept would apply even when there were several factors of production. Provided that these general opportunity costs were constant, the whole of the above theory would follow without change. We need merely treat the labour requirements on p. 17 above as being requirements for general bundles of factors, with lower requirements indicating greater efficiency. However, with more factors, costs are unlikely to be constant, and we shall see in Chapter 3 how this affects trade theory.

Demand

The Ricardian theory is a supply theory of international trade: it is differences in supply conditions that give rise to the possibilities of trade, and trade occurs even when, as above, demand conditions are identical across countries. This is not to dismiss demand, however, for it explains much of the detail of the final outcome. In any case, the analysis may be completed without the assumption of identical demand without any fundamental differences (see, for example, our first edition, Chapter 4, or Chacholiades, 1981).

Many goods and countries

One obvious shortcoming of our theory is its unrealistic two-by-two nature. This might be justified on pedagogic grounds, but in fact multi-dimensional trade theory is much more complex and ambiguous in its results than the simple models. This book will not present any such analysis, leaving it to more advanced texts, but we shall summarise some of the results and point out – where necessary – the dangers of simply extrapolating from the two-by-two case.

Consider first a model with two countries but many goods. We can establish a chain of comparative advantage, similar to equation (2.1), that ranks goods ($i = 1 \ldots n$) by country A's comparative advantage. Thus

$$\frac{l_1^A}{l_1^B} \leq \frac{l_2^A}{l_2^B} \leq \ldots \leq \frac{l_i^A}{l_i^B} \leq \ldots \leq \frac{l_n^A}{l_n^B}, \tag{2.3}$$

which states that, of all goods, good 1 requires the least inputs in A relative to B, and so on. The two-by-two theory generalises in an obvious fashion here: A will produce and export goods to the left (where its advantage is greatest) and B will export those to the right. At most, one good could be produced in both countries – where the labour input ratio equals the terms of trade. The precise point at which the chain is 'broken', whether there is a common good, and the terms of trade all depend, as before, on the structure of demand as well as of productivities.

Next consider many countries ($j = 1 \ldots m$) but only two goods. Again a chain exists, but now like (2.2):

$$\frac{l_F^1}{l_C^1} \leq \frac{l_F^2}{l_C^2} \leq \ldots \leq \frac{l_F^j}{l_C^j} \leq \ldots \leq \frac{l_F^m}{l_C^m}. \tag{2.4}$$

This states that country 1 has the greatest comparative advantage (efficiency) in food relative to cloth, etc. The chain will again be broken by demand, but if country j exports food so too will every country to the left of it in (2.4). At most, one country produces both goods, and, if it does, the world terms of trade equal its autarky ratio and it gains nothing by trade. Note also that nothing here determines bilateral trade links (i.e. who exports to whom); only total exports are determined. This case can be analysed geometrically as in Figure 2.2(B). The only difference is that the world transformation surface has a face (straight section) for each country, with faces (countries) ordered as in (2.4).

The generalisation to many countries *and* many goods is more complex, but roughly speaking the chain concept persists. Each country will tend to specialise, producing several goods only if world relative prices equal its autarky price ratio. Similarly there will be only a limited number of cases of two countries producing the same good. In this particular case, then, multi-dimensional trade theory does bear a strong resemblance to the simple model.

Trade impediments

In a two-country model, trade impediments that involve only extra costs – for example, tariffs and transport costs as opposed to subsidies – can change the point at which the chain of comparative advantage is broken, but not reverse the ordering of goods within it. For example, B's tariffs may prevent A from exporting good 1 in chain (2.3), and thereby oblige it to export good i, where in the absence of tariffs i would have been imported. However, they cannot change the fact that all A's imports must lie to the right of its exports in chain (2.3); in the example quoted, good 1 would merely become non-traded. Similarly, transport costs can insert a band of non-traded goods into chain (2.3) but again not mix up the ordering of imports and exports; if a round-trip costs 10 per cent of the value of trade (that is, swapping £100 of exports for £100 of imports costs £10), there will be a band of goods covering a 10 per cent range of relative productivities in (2.3) that will be non-traded. However, A will still export from the goods to the left of the band and import from those to the right. Thus, while with only two countries trade impediments might complicate the results, they do not fundamentally reverse them.

Once the model is generalised to many countries and many goods, however, or to allow for traded intermediate goods (inputs into the production of other goods), trade impediments can destroy the chains of comparative advantage. Hence, while the basic notions of comparative advantage certainly still help to explain trade patterns in these more realistic cases, totally specific and unambiguous predictions about who exports what are not always possible.

2.5 TESTING RICARDIAN THEORY

We have spent much effort exploring the implications of various assumptions in the Ricardian model. In the end this is helpful only if it enhances our understanding of the world we inhabit: ultimately our models must have some link with reality. The intuitive connection is clear enough, but to be confident of the model's usefulness we need the firmer evidence of proper econometric studies. The Ricardian theory was first formally tested by MacDougall (1951) – 134 years after its inception!

MacDougall considered the UK's and the USA's trade in 1937. Since

UK–US bilateral trade was distorted by tariffs and was small relative to their total trade, he generalised the Ricardian theory to argue that a country with a comparative advantage in some good would have a relatively large share of third-country markets in that good. Strictly, the theory states that generally only one country will export any good, so that comparative advantage will be associated with 100 per cent shares and disadvantage with 0 per cent shares. However, if we allow for transport costs, differences in quality, etc., MacDougall's assertion seems reasonable. (Nevertheless, observe that having several exporters for any good is already sufficient to refute simple Ricardian trade theory!)

Using data for twenty-five manufactured products, MacDougall found that the UK/US export ratio to third markets was strongly negatively related to both the ratio of UK to US physical labour requirements and the ratio of UK to US labour costs. This seems to confirm the basic thrust of the theory: where productivity is comparatively high so too are exports. Interestingly, however, MacDougall found that, where UK and US labour costs were roughly equal, exports were not equal but rather the UK's were more than twice the USA's. This he attributed to the UK's reputation for high quality and to Imperial Preference.

These results have been broadly corroborated on many different industries and years (see Bhagwati, 1964), although through time the extent of the UK's advantage in the equal-cost case has been declining. In fact, MacDougall's basic results have never really been challenged. Bhagwati (1964) has, however, seriously challenged their interpretation on theoretical and empirical grounds.

Theoretically he objected (a) that Ricardo said nothing about third-country markets (we have dismissed this above), and (b) that, while for any one good a relative cheapening of UK supplies by 10 per cent may increase the UK share by, say, x per cent, it does not follow, when comparing two goods one of which has a lower UK/US cost relative by 10 per cent, that the relatively less costly good will have an x per cent higher market share. That depends on the goods' demand curves. Nevertheless, by lumping all goods into the same cross-section regression equation. MacDougall is implicitly assuming that a given cost advantage translates into the same market share benefit for all goods. This is plainly not precisely true and can only be countered by observing that, theory notwithstanding, the results have received sufficient support for us to accept the approach as a reasonable approximation.

On empirical grounds, Bhagwati's criticism is also interesting. The causal chain of the Ricardian theory runs from labour costs to autarky prices to the direction of trade. Given the imperfections in trade that we postulated above, however, *post-trade* prices in each country should partly reflect autarky prices (imperfections prevent US and UK prices being wholly equalised). Hence we would expect correlations between relative (post-trade) export prices and export shares – which MacDougall found – and also between relative costs and relative prices. Bhagwati, however, could find no evidence of the latter and therefore argued that, since the causal chain could not be established, the Ricardian theory should be rejected even though its ultimate prediction appeared to be corroborated. Certainly we must suspect predictions whose mechanisms are not explicable, but in this case the bulk of the Ricardian theory may be salvaged.

Schematically the argument may be presented thus:

The solid lines represent the 'traditional' causal chain. Link (a) could not be established empirically, but links (b) and (c) were empirically justified. So, to justify the Ricardian theory, we need essentially to establish a causal explanation for (c) that does not depend on (a). Suppose different industries earn different rates of profit – owing possibly to different degrees of monopoly or capital costs. Prices may then be independent of labour costs, but costs are still important because the lower are costs the higher are export profits and hence the greater is the incentive to export. Thus, with independent prices, industries with comparative cost advantages will still export relatively more owing to the stronger incentives to supply exports. This breaks with the Ricardian model discussed above by introducing an additional element of costs, but in Ricardo's other writing profits are fully recognised and may differ between industries except in the very longest of runs.

To conclude, therefore, while the specific predictions of Ricardian trade theory are not supported by the data – especially the prediction of almost complete specialisation – the general tenor of the results is that comparative advantage can explain broad trade patterns and that relating comparative advantage to relative labour requirements (or costs) is not grossly misleading.

FURTHER READING

Our first edition gives a brief historical sketch of classical trade theory (Chapter 2): the classic reference is *Viner* (1937). Among alternative textbook introductions to trade theory the best are *Caves and Jones* (1981) and *Lindert and Kindleberger* (1982), who follow a similar scheme to ourselves, and *Findlay* (1970a), who is rather different. *Bhagwati* (1964) is authoritative and also very interesting (although not entirely correct) on empirical testing, whilst *MacDougall* (1951) is a magnificent example of applied economics. *Jones* (1976) considers expanding the two-by-two model. Most of these references will be more accessible after you have read Chapter 3 below.

Among more advanced treatments of the subjects of this chapter are *Chipman* (1966), and also *Dixit and Norman* (1980) and *Deardorff* (1979, 1980) who make use of the techniques of revealed preference and duality in considering multi-dimensional trade theory. Duality is introduced by *Mussa* (1979) as well as by Dixit and Norman.

KEY CONCEPTS

consumption set	transformation frontier
MRS, MRT	absolute advantage
comparative advantage	gains from trade
specialisation	terms of trade
opportunity costs	chain of comparative advantage

QUESTIONS FOR REVIEW

2.1 'Every country has comparative advantage in something.' Explain carefully why. Suppose a country's exchange rate appreciated by 100 times, making all its prices 100 times higher relative to world prices. What would happen to its comparative advantage?

2.2 Country A can produce 50 units of X *or* 20 of Y *or* any linear combination bounded by these amounts. Country B can produce 80 units of X *or* 80 units of Y *or* any linear combination. All consumers consume X and Y in proportion 5X and 3Y. Find output, consumption and prices under autarky and with free trade and, in the latter, the pattern of trade. If both countries have 20 workers, what are their wages in the two countries in terms of X? (A graphical solution would be adequate.)

2.3 Theory suggests that the USA gains nothing from trade with Nepal, but that Nepal gains a lot. Why? What factors might explain the common impression that large countries gain most from trade?

2.4 What are the assumptions of the Ricardian model? Which do you think are crucial in the sense that their removal affects the results significantly? Which extensions to the Ricardian model are the most necessary?

NOTES

1 Homotheticity implies that the proportions in which people consume the two goods do not vary with total consumption expenditure.

2 This conclusion is reinforced if market size influences efficiency (by allowing more internal specialisation), because then large countries have less need of trade to reap economies of scale than do smaller countries.

3 International Trade and Factor Endowments: (A) The Heckscher–Ohlin Theory

This chapter develops the analysis of Chapter 2 along neo-classical lines. First, it relaxes the assumption of constant costs, showing how international trade under increasing costs will rarely involve complete specialisation. Second, it develops a rationale for increasing costs and for differences in comparative productivity in terms of countries' differing endowments of factors of production. This is the Heckscher–Ohlin model of trade, and it is examined in some detail, both in itself and in its implications for factor rewards and patterns of output. The analysis is continued in the next chapter, which deals with a particular variant of the model and with empirical tests of Heckscher–Ohlin.

3.1 INTERNATIONAL TRADE WITH INCREASING COSTS

Section 2.1 introduced the tools required for exploring neo-classical trade theory, but one vital extension is required. Our discussion of the transformation function was predicated upon constant relative labour costs: labour requirements per unit of output were fixed and constant in each industry and consequently the marginal rate of transformation of food for cloth was constant regardless of the pattern of production. Thus the transformation curve was a straight line. In section 2.4 we reinterpreted the transformation curve in terms of opportunity costs, allowing for many factors of production, but we still clung to constant costs. We now relax that assumption.

Increasing costs In this and most subsequent chapters we shall assume that industries face increasing costs: as the output of cloth rises, successive units cost more to produce. In opportunity cost terms, as cloth (food) output increases, successive increments require the surrender of increasing amounts of food (cloth); the marginal rate of transformation of cloth into food falls as cloth output rises. This implies that the transformation curve is bowed outwards away from the origin. The slope will still be negative – implying that more food always entails less cloth – but it will change from being relatively shallow at high cloth outputs (low MRT) to being relatively steep at low cloth outputs. Figure 3.1 below shows a typical example.

Before we discuss possible causes of increasing costs we must define some terminology. We use decreasing, constant or increasing *returns to scale* to describe how costs change when *all* factors of production are increased proportionately – that is, when the technique of production (the relative inputs of the factors) is unchanged but the scale of the enterprise is increased. On the other hand we use diminishing, constant or increasing *marginal returns* to refer to the increase in output available by adding an extra unit of just one factor. In this case technique does change, because the relative factor inputs have altered. In neo-classical trade theory we usually assume *constant returns to scale* but *diminishing marginal returns to each factor*.

We mention three possible causes of increasing costs. First, some factors may be better suited to cloth production and others to food: as we shift more from food to cloth, we increasingly move factors with a high output of food into cloth where they have low productivity. Second, there may be some wholly specific factors of production, limited to particular industries: for example, coal mines are limited to coal production. If these are fixed in supply, as we draft more of the mobile factors into an industry, these factors encounter diminishing marginal returns, and hence cannot match their productivity in other industries. Third, industries may require homogeneous and mobile factors in different proportions. Thus, when both goods are produced in quantity, factors can be allocated between industries to exploit their different requirements of different factors, but under complete specialisation the producing industry must accept the factor proportions endowed on the country. However, this is the crux of the Heckscher–Ohlin theorem, and so discussion is postponed until the next section.

International equilibrium

With the exception of the curved transformation curve, the analysis of international trade proceeds precisely as in Chapter 2; it is summarised in Figure 3.1. The two national tranformation frontiers are shown as DH and GC and the autarkic equilibria as J and I respectively. Note that in autarky, Britain, which still has a comparative advantage in cloth, has a relatively lower price for cloth than America. This is evident from the slope of the transformation curve ($MRT = P$), which is steeper at J than at I.

In part (B) of the figure, the world transformation curve is constructed by adding the outputs of the two countries, assuming that both face the same price ratio and therefore that both have the same marginal rate of transformation. (This is clearly a condition for maximising world output. If America's MRT exceeded Britain's, say $3C = 1F$ and $2C = 1F$ respectively, it would pay to switch a unit of American food output to cloth, yielding 3 cloth, while increasing British food output by 1 unit, sacrificing only 2 cloth.) The addition of transformation curves is effected practically by inverting one of the national curves and sliding it along the other, keeping the two sets of axes parallel. The origin of the former then traces out the world transformation curve. (Because the two curves are just touching at their point of contact, they have there the same slopes of MRTs.) This operation is sketched in Figure 3.1(B).

If the MRT takes a common value for both America and Britain, that same value must also apply to the world as a whole, for transformation must occur in either America or Britain. Hence the slope of the world transformation curve at any point equals the slopes of the national curves at the points that just add up to give that world point. This is illustrated in Figure 3.1(B). World preferences define X as the maximum welfare point on the world transformation curve VXZ, and the terms of trade as TT. Production at X requires the national curves to be positioned as shown and national production to be at point L for Britain and K for America. The national curves at these points both have slope $T'T'$, which is the same as slope TT.

With production at L and K and terms of trade $T'T'$, each country can consume anywhere along the lines $T'T'$ in Figure 3.1(A); but, given our assumption of identical preferences, the shares of the goods in total consumption must be identical and hence the final outcomes are given by A and B respectively. Clearly these outcomes dominate the autarky points. Britain trades cloth for food to get from production point L to consumption point B, while America makes the precisely opposite trade to get from K to A.

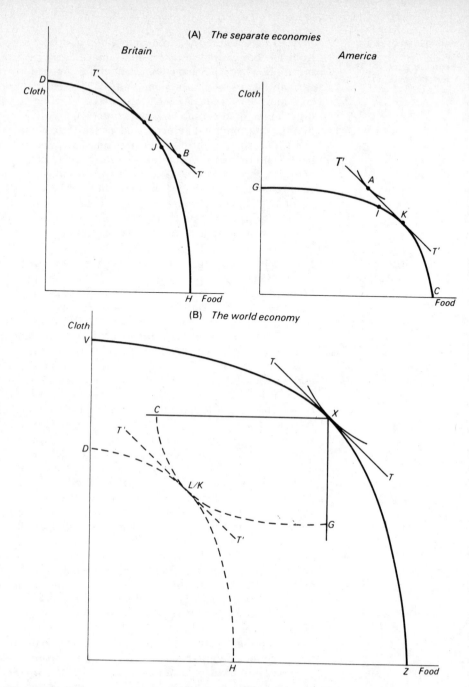

Figure 3.1 Two trading economies. (A) The separate economies. (B) The world economy

International trade has two effects on each economy: it increases the output of one good (the comparative advantage good) and increases consumption of the other. This reflects the price changes induced by trade. In Britain, the relative price of cloth rises, which encourages production and diverts consumption: with a higher price producers can afford to produce more cloth despite the fact that this raises opportunity costs, while the lower relative price for food forces food production to be cut back in order to reduce opportunity costs in line with prices.

The most important difference between this model and the Ricardian outcome is that here we no longer have complete specialisation. With increasing costs America can produce a little cloth at the same price as Britain can produce a lot. Hence both American and British cloth producers can coexist; there will just be more of the latter. The cause of trade then is not merely costs, but that, at any given level of cost (price), one country can produce relatively more of a good than the other. That is, their transformation curves differ in shape. This recognition of incomplete specialisation is clearly a big gain in realism.

3.2 THE HECKSCHER–OHLIN THEORY

The neo-classical theory of international trade reaches its apotheosis in the Heckscher–Ohlin theory. Initiated by Eli Heckscher in 1919 in an article in Swedish, it first became widely recognised with the publication of Ohlin (1933). Since then it has been massively researched, refined and formalised, probably way beyond what its original authors would have accepted.

Heckscher and Ohlin asked *why* productivities differed across countries; why transformation possibilities differed. Ricardo said technology differed, but they argued that countries' abilities varied with their endowments of different factors of production. Hence America, with her huge prairies, was well equipped to produce food, while Britain, with abundant labour, was better at manufacturing. This argument has great intuitive force – and it is a short step from production to trade. Provided demand patterns do not differ much between countries, the *Heckscher-Ohlin theorem* of trade states: *countries will export those goods whose production is relatively intensive in the factors with which they are well endowed*. The rest of this chapter explores and formalises this sensible observation.

The assumptions

The Heckscher–Ohlin approach (H–O) stresses the role of factor endowments. When we formalise it into a theorem, we wish to isolate this feature as the only possible cause of international trade and to examine its consequences. This implies not that it is *actually* the only cause of trade, but that it is interesting to know how the world would look if it were.

The H–O theorem may be shown to be true under a set of seven assumptions. The first two isolate endowments as the cause of trade:

(i)   Consumption is determined by identical, homothetic, preferences (as we assumed above).
(ii) Technology is identical across countries.

The next two restrict the technology in important respects:

(iii) The production functions for each good exhibit constant returns to scale but diminishing marginal returns to any single factor.
(iv)   Goods differ in their requirements of different factor inputs. If one good requires relatively more labour than another at one set of factor prices, it does so at all sets of factor prices. This is known as the exclusion of 'factor-intensity reversals' and it allows us to identify the labour-intensive product unambiguously.

31

The next two assumptions describe economic behaviour:

(v)   Perfect competition exists in all factor and product markets.
(vi) There are no impediments to trade, such as tariffs or transport costs, but the migration of factors of production is quite impossible.

The final assumption imposes restrictions on the world:

(vii) There are just two factors, two goods and two countries. The factors are homogeneous within countries, identical between them, and fixed in supply.

The role that these assumptions play will become clearer as the proof proceeds, but we can note here that they have different status. Assumptions (i) and (ii) are necessary to pose the question 'what does factor-endowment-related' trade look like?' Assumptions (iii)–(v) are critical: (v) ensures the equality of prices and costs, and of prices and marginal utilities in consumption; (iv) allows us to identify *the* labour-intensive good technically, i.e. regardless of any economic phenomenon; and (iii) is central to the translation of price signals into quantity changes – its absence would not necessarily reverse the pattern of trade but it would make it impossible to prove that the H–O result always rules.

Commodity and factor prices

We start our proof by introducing a new tool of analysis – the *isoquant*. An isoquant is drawn on a graph with quantities of factors on the axes; it connects all combinations of the two factors that could produce a given output of a particular good. There is a separate isoquant for each level of output. Figure 3.2 shows isoquants for two goods. Their shape – convex to the origin – derives from the assumption of diminishing marginal returns: as labour replaces capital, increasing amounts are required to substitute for successive units of capital.

Constant returns to scale define the relationship between isoquants. It implies that doubling all inputs doubles outputs with no change in technique. Hence the isoquant for 2 units of output is just an expanded version of that for 1 unit. An important feature of the expansion is that, as we move out along any ray from the origin (like OD in Figure 3.2), each successive isoquant has the same slope as we cross it; the isolation for 1 million units, say, looks just like that for 1 unit with the scale on the axes multiplied by 1 million. Hence the whole of the production technology for a good can be summarised by the shape of a single isoquant.

Figure 3.2 shows representatives of two sets of isoquants: for cloth (C) – the more capital-intensive – and for food (F). It also shows a budget-line for firms buying factors in the factor markets. Given factor prices, line AB represents all the bundles of factors purchasable for, say, £1. Clearly its slope is the factor price ratio: it shows how much extra capital could be bought by purchasing 1 less unit of labour. Profit-maximising firms will always produce the maximum possible for £1 and hence will produce on the isoquant that is just tangential to the budget line. This defines the factor intensities of their production methods. Thus cloth producers will produce 4 cloth for £1 using K_C of capital and L_C of labour, while food producers will produce 2 food using K_F and L_F.

Under perfect competition, costs equal prices. If we know that the cost of producing 4C equals that of producing 2F, we also know that their prices must be equal (£1), and hence we know the commodity price ratio – 2 cloth

Figure 3.2 Production conditions for two goods

per 1 unit food. Thus Figure 3.2 shows how we can move from a given factor price ratio (the slope of AB) to a unique commodity price ratio. In fact, we can also work backwards. If the commodity price ratio were given, such that 2 cloth traded for 1 food, we know from the competitiveness assumptions that both must cost the same. The isoquants 4C and 2F must therefore be tangential to the same budget-line, and a little experimentation will show that AB is the only possible line that is tangential to both. Once AB is drawn, however, the factor price ratio is known from its slope. Hence, under the assumptions given, there is a unique one-for-one relationship between factor prices and commodity prices. Any lowering of the relative price of labour lowers the relative price of the labour-intensive good. (Check this by flattening AB in Figure 3.2. If the new line is still tangential to 2F, it must be tangential to a cloth isoquant below 4, and 1 food would now trade for less than 2 cloth.)

We can see these links algebraically as follows. Perfect competition ensures that prices equal costs: hence

$$P_F = a_{FL}w + a_{FK}r$$
$$P_C = a_{CL}w + a_{CK}r$$

(3.1)

where P_F and P_C are food and cloth prices, w and r are wages and capital rentals, and a_{ij} ($i = F,C$; $j = L,K$) are the inputs of factor j per unit of output i. These equations define the factor price to commodity price link. Clearly, however, (3.1) may be rewritten to show w and r as functions of P_F, P_C and the a_{ij}, and this defines the reverse link. Provided the a_{ij} satisfy certain conditions (derived from the H–O assumptions), the latter is unique.

33

Suppose the world comprised two identical countries. In autarky each would have the same equilibrium – say that in Figure 3.2. There would be no scope for trade between them since commodity prices would be identical. Now grant one country – America (A) – an increased supply of labour, holding (for now) everything else constant. With constant commodity prices, factor prices are constant, and constant factor prices imply unchanged techniques of production (points X and Y in Figure 3.2). So how could the extra labour be absorbed into the American economy? Not by giving a little to each industry, because that would change their techniques of production, but by increasing the output of food and decreasing that of cloth. Reducing cloth output releases factors in bundles of K_C capital and L_C labour (remember the technique of production is given); however, food will absorb them in proportions K_F and L_F. Hence, for every K_C of capital taken on by food producers, considerably more than L_C of labour will be required and these workers will be found from the pool of 'new' labour.

This argument is due to Rybczynski (1955) and may be summarised as saying that, under the assumptions enumerated above (including frozen commodity prices), the country better endowed with labour will produce absolutely more food (the labour-intensive good) and absolutely less cloth (capital-intensive).

We assumed identical preferences across countries. Thus the extra food will be consumed only if its price falls relative to cloth. This in turn reduces the relative price of labour, as we saw above; so, with extra labour, complete equilibrium in America actually requires relatively lower wages, lower food prices and greater food output than in Britain. Obversely, of course, Britain is now capital-abundant relative to America and she will have relatively low capital rentals, low cloth prices and high cloth output.

Finally, suppose we now open trade between America and Britain. With different relative prices there is now scope for profitable trade, and it takes the form predicted by the H–O theorem: Britain, which is capital-abundant, exports cloth (the capital-intensive good) and America (labour-abundant) exports food (labour-intensive).

To explore the final world equilibrium we note that the H–O assumptions guarantee that transformation curves are bowed outwards and that they differ between countries (see Appendix). The capital-abundant country's curves is biased towards cloth production and, at any commodity price ratio, entails its producing a higher ratio of cloth to food than the other country. Thus the world and national equilibria are just as in Figure 3.1, and all the previous conclusions follow.

The validity of Heckscher–Ohlin depends crucially on the absence of factor-intensity reversals. Figure 3.3 illustrates how the theorem breaks down if this is violated. Suppose food technology gives much greater opportunities for the substitution of labour for capital than cloth technology. The food isoquants will be relatively straight (indicating a wide range of possible input bundles), those for cloth strongly curved. The difficulty is that under these circumstances there are two factor price ratios (represented by AB and DE) consistent with a single commodity price ratio (4C:2F). Furthermore, at one ratio cloth is capital-intensive (DE), whereas at the other ratio food is. If America's trading equilibrium is DE and Britain's AB, Heckscher–Ohlin trade is impossible, because America's labour-intensive good and Britain's capital-intensive good are the same!

Figure 3.3 Factor-intensity reversals

Our proof of the Heckscher–Ohlin theorem also depended on both goods actually being produced (if not, the factor budget line *AB* could not be drawn). This is not strictly required for the trade theorem, but it is necessary for the extensions that we explore below.

We held demand patterns constant over countries to emphasise the role of factor endowment differences. Although this is not entirely necessary, the H–O theorem can in fact be overturned if demand patterns differ substantially. If the capital-abundant country's demand is sufficiently strongly biased towards capital-intensive goods, it will have higher autarky prices for both capital and the capital-intensive good than the other country. Hence it will import them when trade occurs. This has led some economists to define a country's abundant factor as that for which its autarky price is relatively lower, rather than our physical definition, and, in this form, demand cannot upset the theorem for it has already been taken into account.

We should also note that all the results here are of a comparative static nature. We have compared the full equilibria of the world economy under trade and autarky. We have done nothing to discuss the actual transition from autarky to trade or the effects of the growth in the supply of one of the factors.

Multi-dimensional Heckscher–Ohlin

Generalising the Heckscher–Ohlin model beyond the two dimensions has proved very tricky, partly because it is difficult even to define factor intensity if there are more than two factors. However, some results have emerged recently. Neary (1985) shows that some questions can be tackled by grouping factors and good into two groups each. Jones (1974) considered a small trading economy in a multi-good, two-factor world. (A small country has no influence over world prices.) The country imports most goods, producing just the one or two that maximimise the value of its national output at the given world prices. With many goods, the ones produced will frequently lie in the middle of the list of goods ordered by capital intensity, hence the country will import goods both more and less capital-intensive than its exports. Jones

35

showed that, the greater the small country's capital abundance, the more capital-intensive will be the goods it actually produces. Clearly such complete specialisation is unrealistic, but this result does warn us that exports will not always be uniformly either more or less capital-intensive than imports.

Returning to a multi-country model with large countries, the following results have been obtained:

- A country's net exports of a good (exports *minus* imports) are negatively correlated with the difference between its autarky price and the world price for that good. That is, on average countries export those goods that they produce relatively cheaply, but not necessarily every one of them.
- If differences in countries' factor endowments are small, each country will export goods intensive in its relatively abundant factors, provided 'intensive' and 'abundant' are defined in a particular fashion. For large endowment differences, however, the most that can be said is that, if factor prices are not equalised across countries, there will be a correlation between net exports and the intensive use of abundant factors. The 'small' difference case is a precise, but not very relevant generalisation of H–O; the latter 'statistical' result is weaker but potentially more useful.

3.3   THREE COROLLARIES OF HECKSCHER–OHLIN

We have just derived the Heckscher–Ohlin theorem that countries export the goods intensive in their abundant factors. In the course of doing so we have set the scene for proving three other theorems that illustrate the power and scope, if not the realism, of the Heckscher–Ohlin approach to trade policy.

Factor price equalisation

Figure 3.2 and its associated analysis showed that there is a unique relationship between factor prices and commodity prices in equilibrium. Provided that both goods are produced in both economies, international trade ensures the equality of goods prices in the two economies, and thus, through this unique link, the equality of factor prices! The importance of both goods being produced – an eighth assumption:

(viii)   incomplete specialisation –

is evident from Figure 3.2. If one of the sets of isoquants did not exist because there was no production it would be impossible to define the tangent *AB*.

This remarkable result, which was first due to Samuelson (1948, 1949), suggests that in a Heckscher–Ohlin world no factor of production would have any incentive to migrate. Not only is this an important issue practically, but it has also become one of the hallmarks of the Heckscher–Ohlin theorem. It is worthwhile, therefore, to rehearse the steps of the arguments in a slightly different form.

First we show that factor price equalisation (FPE) is consistent with international equilibrium, which requires equal goods prices in the two countries – from assumption (vi) – and thus equal costs of production. Assumption (v) ensures prices equal costs, while assumption (viii) ensures that both goods are produced at finite cost in both countries. If factor prices are identical, so too will be techniques of production, because technique depends only on the factor price ratio – assumptions (ii)–(v). Thus, with equal factor prices and identical techniques, costs of production will be equalised, and the proposition is established.

36

We now show that international equilibrium cannot exist without FPE. Starting from the equilibrium just defined, let us slightly increase wages in country A. This will raise the costs of the labour-intensive product more than the other, and thus increase A's relative price of the former. But with B's prices unchanged this would not be consistent with international equilibrium. This argument generalises to other factor price differences between countries, and so we have established that factor price equalisation is necessary for full equilibrium.

We can give more flesh to this argument using Samuelson's own geometric analysis, Figure 3.4(A) shows the relationships between relative factor rewards (wages and rentals), factor intensities and relative goods prices. The lower quadrant shows for each good the optimum capital/labour ratio (k) for any given factor price ratio. Assumptions (iii) and (v) ensure that each factor price ratio is associated with a unique factor input ratio in each industry: assumption (v) ensures that factors are paid their marginal products, while, in assumption (iii), constant returns to scale ensure that the size of the industry does not affect input proportions, and diminishing marginal returns ensure that, as the input of one factor rises, its marginal product (and reward) falls while that of the other factor rises. Thus each input ratio is associated with a unique ratio of marginal products and thus of factor rewards. Assumption (iii) means that these relationships hold in both countries. As previously, cloth is the more capital-intensive at each factor price ratio – satisfying assumption (iv).

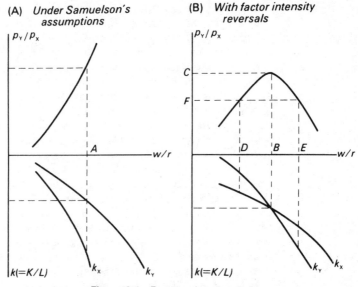

Figure 3.4 Factor price equalisation

The upper quadrant plots relative goods prices. At factor prices A, techniques of production are determined in the lower quadrant, and thus relative goods prices may be determined. Now suppose wages were slightly higher than at A. Food, employing relatively more labour, will suffer more than cloth and thus the price ratio p_F/p_C will increase as shown. Similar arguments plot out the whole of the function between relative good and factor prices, and hence, as we saw above, the relationship is monotonic and single-valued. Thus common prices under international trade entail common factor prices.

Specialisation and factor-intensity reversals

Figure 3.4 also illustrates how factor-intensity reversals can upset factor price equalisation. In part (B), food is labour-intensive at low wage–rental ratios but capital-intensive at high ratios. (Food shows greater substitution between factors than cloth.) At factor price ratio B, factor intensities are identical between industries and the goods price ratio is given by C. Now consider a lower factor price ratio (D). Food uses relatively more of the cheaper factor than cloth and thus must have a relatively lower price than at C. Similarly, however, at a higher factor price ratio (E): food also uses more of the relatively cheaper factor and thus has a lower price here as well. Hence, with factor-intensity reversals, a given goods price ratio (F) may be consistent with two different factor price ratios. Thus FPE is not assured, although neither is it ruled out.

The significance of non-specialisation is also evident from Samuelson's analysis. Suppose country A specialised in cloth; the cloth sector would be required to employ A's total endowment of labour and capital: its factor intensity would be fixed exogenously by A's endowments. Given our technology assumptions, however, a given factor intensity is uniquely linked to a particular factor price ratio, and so A's factor price ratio would be determined also. Now suppose the price of cloth rose relatively. Country B may respond as in our analysis above, with rewards to cloth's intensive factor rising, but A cannot do so. It earns more for its export good, to be sure, but its factor price *ratio* cannot change, because cloth still uses exactly the same combination of factors as before.

In terms of Figure 3.4(A), given the price ratio p_F/p_C, the food industry requires factors in proportion G while food requires them in proportion H. If the country's endowments lie within this range, factors can be fully employed by a mixture of the two industries, but, if they lie outside it, output will be specialised on to only one good and the wage–rental ratio will be determined by the appropriate k-schedule at the endowment ratio. The range G–H is known as the *cone of diversification* – so called because if the ratios G and H were plotted on Figure 3.2 they would describe a cone emanating from the origin.

It may seem strange that, in discussing factor prices, factor supplies (endowments) have been hardly mentioned. They enter indirectly, however, because, through their influence on the countries' transformation frontiers, they determine both the world prices of goods and, via the cone of diversification, each country's degree of specialisation. The only circumstance where endowments do not matter is for a non-specialised small country: with fixed world prices, the country's factor price ratio is entirely insensitive to endowment changes, unless the latter are so great as to induce specialisation.

It is also noteworthy that, under the strict assumptions necessary for factor price equalisation, there would be no incentive for international factor mobility. Thus international trade and international factor mobility would be substitutes; either would be sufficient to maximise world output. We return to factor mobility in Chapter 15 below.

Generalisations

Factor price equalisation is one of the hallmarks of the Heckscher–Ohlin model and has thus been one of the first issues to be investigated in any attempted generalisation. With more factors than goods equalisation is unlikely because equations such as (3.1) have more unknowns than equations. With equal numbers, or more goods than factors, FPE must occur except when specialisation intervenes, and even then it is possible. With more goods than factors there would seem to be a greater chance of some goods not being produced in some countries – see Jones' model (pp. 35–6), where each country produces only two out of many goods – but Dixit and Norman (1980) show that, in general, increasing the number of goods neither necessarily increases nor necessarily decreases the chances of FPE.

The Rybczynski theorem

In proving the Heckscher–Ohlin theorem, we have already used Rybczynski's basic result. A country with relatively large endowments of capital will produce relatively larger quantities of the capital-intensive good at any given set of prices. The Rybczynski theorem extends this result to consider the impact of *changing* the factor endowments of a small open economy. A small open economy faces given commodity prices, and from the previous subsection we know that this implies constant factor prices and techniques of production. Thus if, for example, the endowment of labour increased, the only way of absorbing it would be to increase output of the labour-intensive good. Moreover, in order to release the capital for the new labour to work with at the fixed factor proportions, output of the capital-intensive good must be reduced. Rybczynski's theorem states that an increase in the endowment of one factor of production increases absolutely the output of the good intensive in that factor and reduces absolutely output of the other good.

The Stolper–Samuelson theorem

The Rybczynski theorem links quantities of factors to quantities of goods. The Stolper–Samuelson (1941) theorem is its dual, and links goods prices to factor prices. The analysis surrounding Figures 3.2 and 3.4 showed the unique link from relative goods prices to relative factor prices. Stolper–Samuelson goes one better and shows that a rise in the price of one good raises absolutely the real reward of the factor intensive in that good and reduces absolutely that of the other.

To prove the Stolper–Samuelson result we first need to consider the determinants of wages and capital rentals. Firms demand factors in order to produce goods and sell them. If they maximise profits, they will go on purchasing labour so long as the cost per unit – i.e. the wage – is below the revenue earned by selling that unit's produce. This revenue comprises the physical output derived by employing the extra unit of labour – its marginal physical productivity (MPP_L) – multiplied by the price of output. Hence, in equilibrium, the wage equals the marginal revenue productivity, or, in symbols, for labour in industry i:

$$w_L = p_i MPP^i_L. \tag{3.2}$$

Alternatively (3.2) can be written as

$$\frac{w_L}{p_i} = MPP^i_L, \tag{3.3}$$

which states that the real wage in terms of output i is just labour's marginal physical productivity in that industry. Analogous reasoning can show that capital (or any other factor) will be paid its marginal product. A convenient feature of constant returns to scale technologies is that if every factor is paid its marginal product output is just exhausted. Thus, given that assumption,

39

the marginal productivity theory entirely explains income distribution between factors. For concreteness, assume that the price of the labour-intensive good, food, rises.[1] This increses the output of food and decreases that of cloth, and both labour and capital move from cloth to food. Imagine initially that factor prices do not change; neither industry then changes its factor proportions, so cloth would shed factors in ratio 1 L : 1 K, say, while food (the labour-intensive industry) would recruit them in ratio 2 L : 1 K, say. Clearly this would generate an excess demand for labour, raising its relative price. This in turn encourages *both* industries to economise on labour, hence *in both industries* the labour/capital ratio falls. Now, given diminishing marginal returns – assumption (iii) – this raises labour's MPP and reduces capital's. (Each unit of capital has less labour to work with.) However, from (3.3) we know that, with rising MPP_L in each industry, labour's wage in terms of each good must have risen. Hence, no matter what combination of food and cloth labour buys, the real wage must be higher than previously. The opposite applies to capital: a falling MPP_k reduces the rental in terms of each good and hence also in terms of any conceivable consumption basket.

If the real wage increases in terms of both goods, its proportionate rise in money terms must exceed that of either price. Conversely, the rise in the capital's money rental (a fall is just a negative rise) must be less than either price change. Using ˆ to denote proportionate changes, we have the ordering:

$$\hat{r} < \hat{p}_C < \hat{p}_f < \hat{w}. \tag{3.4}$$

Trade changes relative prices and hence absolute factor rewards. Under H–O, opening trade raises the relative price of the good intensive in the abundant factor and thus benefits that factor and harms the other. Intuitively, under autarky the scarce factor can reap the rewards of its scarcity, but trade allows the country to circumvent that scarcity by importing the factor's services from abroad (albeit already embodied in goods). Thus, trade erodes that factor's scarcity rents. Notice that in this analysis labour and capital have opposing interests in the opening and closing of trade, but all labour has identical interests, as does all capital.

Generalising the Rybczynski and Stolper–Samuelson results to a multi-dimensional context is difficult, but some results are feasible, especially if we assume that there are more goods than factors so that factor price equalisation occurs. For changes that do not induce specialisation we know that:

● a general set of commodity price changes will raise the price of at least one factor in terms of all goods and lower that of at least one other factor;
● a general set of commodity price changes will, on average, raise the prices of the factors used most intensively by the commodities whose prices have risen relatively;
● a general change in factor endowments will raise the output of at least one good relative to all endowments and reduce the output of at least one other good; and
● a general change in factor endowments will, on average, induce the largest increase in output in those goods using most intensively the factors whose endowments have increased most.

FURTHER READING

The analysis of general transformation curves was introduced by *Haberler* (1936). It, and the basic Heckscher–Ohlin model, may be pursued in the texts recommended for Chapter 2. Additional references on the latter include *Samuelson* (1949), *Jones* (1956) and *Lancaster* (1957); *Ohlin* (1933) – the classic reference – is also stimulating. On multi-dimensional versions, *Deardorff* (1982) and *Dixit and Woodland* (1982) are excellent although difficult, whilst Jones' results are best described in *Caves and Jones* (1981).

The classic references on factor price equalisation are *Samuelson* (1948 and, especially, 1949). *Dixit and Norman* (1980) treat the issue excellently, including multi-dimensional cases, but they concentrate on necessary rather than sufficient conditions for equalisation, and their treatment is rather technical. *Samuelson* (1981) offers a fascinating overview of the question, including discussion of Heckscher's and Ohlin's views. *Stolper and Samuelson* (1941) and *Rybczynski* (1955) are interesting in the original and *Bhagwati and Srinivasan* (1983) gives a useful unifying treatment.

Some of this literature will be more accessible after you have read Chapter 4.

KEY CONCEPTS

increasing costs	concave transformation curve
factor intensity	factor endowments
non-specialisation	factor price equalisation
factor-intensity reversals	Rybczynski theorem
Stolper–Samuelson theorem	Heckscher–Ohlin theorem

QUESTIONS FOR REVIEW

3.1 Describe carefully why the transformation curve in a $(2 \times 2 \times 2)$ model will be concave from below if goods have different factor intensities. Note any assumptions you make.

3.2 Describe the roles of the standard assumptions in deriving the Stolper–Samuelson result.

3.3 Which of the standard theorems of this chapter are robust with respect to complete specialisation? Why?

3.4 What effects might the immigration of labour have on the UK's production and trade? Would anyone be adversely affected by such immigration?

APPENDIX: THE SHAPE OF THE TRANSFORMATION CURVE

Imagine our economy is endowed with 200 units of capital (200K) and 100 of labour (100L), and that the maximum possible output of food is 100F and of cloth 100C. The straight-line transformation curve of Chapter 2 showed that, if labour (then the only factor) were split equally between industries, output would be (50F, 50C), because constant returns to scale ensures that halving *all* factors just halves output. However, we can actually do better than this. So far, both industries have the same capital/labour ratio, so we are operating at some point like Z in Figure 3.2. Inspection of Figure 3.2, however, shows that, by shifting a little labour from cloth to food and a little capital from food to cloth (to reach points V and W, say), we can actually increase output of both goods. At its middle the transformation curve allows more of each output than the straight line – hence it is bowed outwards.

The bias of the capital-abundant country's transformation curve towards the capital-intensive good is obvious enough. In Figure 3.2, a country with endowment X could produce 4C but less than 2F, whereas one with endowment Y could produce 2F but less than 4C.

NOTE

1 We talk loosely of prices rising. In fact we are strictly comparing two economies identical in every respect except in that one has a higher price for one good than the other.

4 International Trade and Factor Endowments: (B) Specific Factors and Empirical Tests

This chapter continues the analysis of the last in two distinct directions. First, it varies the time-scale of the Heckscher–Ohlin model, considering both the very long run, during which the capital stock varies with rates of national investment, and the very short run, in which capital cannot be switched between sectors. Second, it considers the empirical evidence surrounding the Heckscher–Ohlin and its corollary theorems.

4.1 HECKSCHER–OHLIN IN THE LONG AND SHORT RUNS

Heckscher–Ohlin is a comparative static theory. It compares two worlds each with two countries. In one the countries are (and always have been and will be) under autarky, whereas in the other they trade. The theory describes the equilibrium in the latter, using data from the former. Unfortunately, the real world is not like this, and to be useful we have to be sure that H–O will translate into real time. This is far from certain and is actually very complex, but we consider here two minor aspects, both relating to capital. Heckscher–Ohlin assumes that factors of production are homogeneous, identical across countries, fixed in supply and applicable in both (all) industries. This section varies the last two assumptions.

The very long run For periods of five–ten years it may be reasonable to assume that countries' relative rankings in capital abundance do not change. For longer periods, however, this is not realistic. Both population and capital stocks are then subject to change, and, if they change in response to other economic phenomena, these phenomena will ultimately determine international trade patterns, via their effects on factor supplies.

We can illustrate this with respect to capital. The capital stock changes through investment, and, in the long run, investment equals savings. Thus the ultimate determinant of capital abundance, and hence of trade, is differences in the level of savings. If we have two countries identical except for their propensity to save (reflecting their desire to postpone consumption for the future), eventually the higher saver will become relatively capital abundant and export the capital-intensive good.

The short run We now focus on the applicability of capital in both industries. If this is to occur in real time, capital must be immediately and costlessly transferable between industries. This is plainly unrealistic – buses cannot change into computers over-night – and so we now look at a model in which capital is specific to the industry in which it was first installed.

Our model has three factors of production – food capital (K_F), cloth capital (K_C) and labour. This makes it extremely unlikely that factor prices and commodity prices will be uniquely linked, because the equations corresponding to (3.1) become

$$P_F = a_{FL}w + a_{FK}r_F$$
$$P_C = a_{CL}w + a_{CK}r_C$$

(4.1)

where r_F and r_C are the rentals of the specific capitals. These two equations cannot be rearranged to express the three factor prices as functions of the commodity prices and a_{ij} alone. This means we cannot determine the direction of trade in the same way as we did above.

In fact it is rather complex to predict trade patterns unambiguously. At a simple level, however, imagine the two countries have equal amounts of labour and food capital. Trade will then be determined by endowments of cloth capital, with the better-endowed country exporting cloth. Clearly a similar argument could be made for food capital. Now suppose capital endowments are equal but labour endowments unequal. The labour-abundant country will then use more labour in both industries, but, relatively speaking, labour will be concentrated in the labour-intensive industry, because this industry can absorb more labour without dramatic declines in its productivity. Since both countries have identical capital stocks, the labour-abundant country produces relatively more of the labour-intensive good and hence exports it when trade ocurs. The difficulties in predicting trade patterns arise when endowments differ in more complex ways: for example, if one country has relatively more labour (tending to raise food output) and relatively little food capital (tending to reduce it). Here the outcome depends on the precise shapes of the production functions and we cannot make any generalisations.

Despite the difficulty of predicting trade patterns, however, the specific factors model has clear implications for the corollary theorems of the Heckscher–Ohlin model. First, we have just seen that factor price equalisation is no longer assured; now we consider the Stolper–Samuelson theorem. Imagine that the economy has settled in a perfect equilibrium in which the returns to the two stocks of capital are equalised, and that it then experiences a change in the terms of trade. The initial equilibrium is illustrated by the solid lines in Figure 4.1, which describes the allocation of labour between the two industries. MRP_F shows the marginal revenue product of labour in the food sector at each level of labour input measured from the left-hand origin, O. MRP_C shows the marginal revenue product of labour in cloth measured from the right-hand origin O'. The distance OO' reflects the economy's total endowment of labour. In equilibrium the marginal revenue products are equal to each other and also to the wage rate, w_0, so that initially OL_0 of labour works in the food sector and L_0O' in the cloth sector. Now imagine that the price of food rises. This shifts the marginal revenue product in food up to MRP'_F and raises the money wage rate to w_1. But what happens to real wages and to the returns on capital?

As labour shifts into the food industry, each unit of food capital has more labour to work with, so that its marginal physical product increases; as we saw in section 3.3, this increases its return measured in terms of food. As before, letting ^ denote percentage changes, this means that $\hat{r}_F > \hat{p}_F$. By analogous reasoning the marginal productivity of cloth capital falls, implying that $\hat{r}_C < \hat{p}_C$. Labour, on the other hand, experiences the opposite changes, so that $\hat{w} < \hat{p}_F$ and $\hat{w} > \hat{p}_C$. Hence overall we have

$$\hat{r}_F > \hat{p}_F > \hat{w} > \hat{p}_C > \hat{r}_C.$$

(4.2)

The specific factor in the industry whose price has risen gains absolutely: its money return rises more than any price. The other specific capital loses

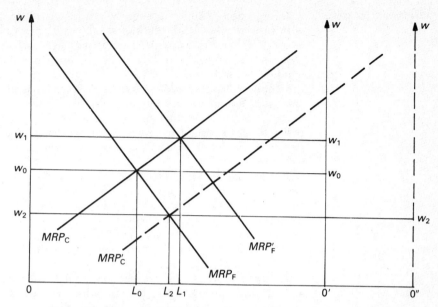

Figure 4.1 The specific factors model – an increase in labour supply

absolutely. The wage change is intermediate, however, and the real wage change could go either way. If labour consumes mostly cloth, real wages rise, whereas if it consumes mostly food they fall.

Just as in equation (3.4) above the change in the price of a good is sandwiched betwen the changes in the prices of the factors it uses. This is because costs are a mixture of both factor prices (both factors are used in positive amounts), and prices equal costs. hence at either end of chains like these a factor price change must be found. It also implies that specific factors will tend to change more in price than mobile factors.

The basic observation that some factor must be at the extremes of the list of price changes such as (4.2) generalises to any dimensionality; it is sometimes known as the *magnification* effect. For any single price change, at least one factor must gain and another lose, and completely specific factors will be so affected by changes in the price of 'their' good.

This highlights a notable contrast between the specific factors model and the Heckscher–Ohlin model proper. Whereas in the latter all units of capital have identical interests in opening trade or in changes in the terms of trade, in the former owners of different capital equipment have opposite interests.

There are also Rybczynski-type results for the specific factors model. First, suppose that an injection of food capital occurs. This raises MRP_F, as in Figure 4.1, and allows the food industry to bid labour away from cloth because, with more capital available, its marginal product of labour is increased. The transfer of labour reduces factor inputs in the cloth sector, reducing absolutely the level of output in accordance with the Rybczynski theorem. There is, however, one difference. In the mobile capital Heckscher–Ohlin model, the injection of capital left factor rewards unchanged provided that specialisation did not result. Here, on the other hand, factor price equalisation does not apply and the capital injection benefits labour and harms *both* forms of capital as capital/labour ratios fall in both sectors.

An injection of labour is slightly more complex; it is analysed in Figure 4.1 with broken lines. With additional labour we have to expand the horizontal axis to OO″ and measure MRP_C relative to O″ rather than O′. This makes it clear that an injection of labour drives down the wage to w_2, and increases employment in both industries. (The increase in labour is O′O″, which equals the rightward shift in MRP_C, but employment in food increases by only L_0L_2). Increased employment, coupled with fixed capital stocks, reduces labour's marginal physical product and increases capital's, so that real wages fall while real returns to capital increase. Again we note the contrast with the mobile capital model in which small changes in endowment did not typically change factor rewards.

The specific factor model may be taken in its own right or as a short-run version of the Heckscher–Ohlin model, referring to periods over which capital cannot be reallocated. In longer runs, capital moves by having net depreciation or scrapping in one industry and net investment in the other. In this case, H–O considerations determine full equilibria, as in Chapter 3, and the model differs from H–O only when something changes. Consider briefly the transition from autarky to free trade for a small country. The world price ratio (which is unaffected by whether a small country trades) is shown as TT or $T'T'$ in Figure 4.2. The country's long-run transformation curve is given by AB; but in the short run, given the capital allocation, it is less easy to transform cloth into food, so the short-run curve (DE) lies inside AB except at J, the autarkic equilibrium. The two curves correspond at J because there the short-term, fixed, allocation of capital is just that required for long-run maximum output. When trade is opened, labour is reallocated, moving production from J to K. Then, through time, as capital gradually moves, DE expands out to AB and production expands out to L. As this occurs, consumption first jumps from J to M and then expands gradually to N.

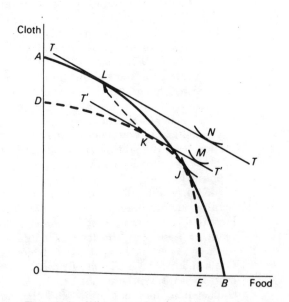

Figure 4.2 Adjustment from autarky to free trade

In some cases a factor may suffer from a change in the short run but benefit in the long run. For example, in Figure 4.2 all capital owners benefit from the opening up of trade because the relative price of the capital-intensive good, cloth, is increased. In the short run, however, owners of food capital suffer as the cloth industry bids labour away from them in the move from J to K. Thus the combination of short-term capital specificity and long-term capital mobility offers economists a much richer explanation of real-world phenomena than either can in isolation.

4.2 TESTING THE HECKSCHER–OHLIN THEOREM

In its simple form, Heckscher–Ohlin gives one easily tested prediction: factor prices will be equalised across countries. This is manifestly false, so the simple version must immediately be rejected. Nevertheless, it is worth asking why factor price equalisation fails and by how much, for it is still possible that factor prices have been moved towards equality (this is difficult to test, for we cannot observe autarky prices), and that trade satisfies the H–O pattern. Economists have therefore subjected H–O to a series of direct tests. These have usually involved comparing the factor contents of a bundle of imports and a bundle of exports. This is a slightly weaker form of the theorem than we examined, but it is more easily generalisable to many dimensions. Our results above clearly entail that the capital-abundant country's exports will embody more capital than its imports.

The Leontief paradox The first thorough test of the Heckscher–Ohlin theory was Leontief (1954), which considered US trade in 1947. Leontief used an input–output table (which shows the inputs required in producing a unit of each output in the economy) to calculate the factor inputs for a typical $1m. of US exports and for a tyical $1m. of local substitutes for US imports. The input–output tables allowed him to include not only labour and capital at the last stage of production, but also that embodied in inputs to that stage, and in inputs to inputs, etc. For example, the labour input to cars included not only assembly workers, but also workers who produced the glass and the steel used, and those who produced the coal to make the steel, and so on. Assuming that the USA was the most capital-abundant country in 1947, H–O predicts that US exports should embody relatively more capital to labour than import subsidies. In fact his results showed the opposite:

	Requirements per typical $1m. worth of:		
	Exports	Import substitutes	Import/export ratio
Capital ($,000, 1947 prices)	2,551	3,091	1.212
Labour (man-years)	182	170	0.932
Capital/labour ratio	13.99	18.18	

Responses to Leontief Leontief's findings were catalytic. They generated huge volumes of research aimed variously at undermining their statistical basis, at modifying H–O to 'dissolve' the paradox, and at seeking further explanations of trade. Chapter 5 deals with the last category as well as presenting some further empirical results: here we briefly consider the other responses and their consequences for the theory itself.

Leontief's reaction to his results was that American labour was more efficient than world labour – by a factor of three – and hence that the USA was labour-abundant in terms of 'efficiency units' if not in actual workers. Therefore, perhaps there was no paradox at all. This is entirely *ad hoc*. There is no reason to suppose that higher US efficiency resides only or even mainly in labour rather than capital, or that a factor of three was justified. It is hardly a satisfactory explanation, although it would save H–O intact.

A related explanation, of which we shall see more below, is that by merely counting heads Leontief ignored workers' skills – their *human capital*. If this were added to physical capital, US exports would probably prove to be capital-intensive. However, theorists have questioned whether the two forms of capital are really perfectly substitutable, and statistical tests have suggested that human capital is better treated as a third factor determining trade. In fact, human capital appears to be the USA's relatively abundant factor and is prominent in her export composition. That labour and human capital were joint inputs (complements) in production could explain Leontief's results, although only at the expense of introducing extra factors into H–O.

Another factor that similarly helps explain the paradox is natural resources. Vanek (1959) showed that US imports were much more natural-resource-intense than her exports, suggesting that the USA is short of such resources. Further, he suggested, capital and natural resources are complementary, so that importing resources necessarily entails importing capital. Several researchers have repeated Leontief's exercise excluding resource-based industries and found that the paradox disappears. This appears to reconcile H–O and the Leontief paradox, although the treatment of natural resources as factors of production usable in any industry (as H–O factors are) is very unrealistic. This result is therefore better interpreted as saying that certain obvious commodities fall outside the H–O framework.

A more threatening explanation of the paradox was that factor-intensity reversals were prevalent. This would just destroy the H–O theory. Minhas (1963) found different degrees of substitutability between labour and capital in different industries, which shows that reversals must occur at some point. However, Bhagwati (1969b, ch. 1, Addendum) showed that, of 210 possible reversals, only 18 occurred between the US and India's factor price ratios, where the USA has approximately the highest wage/rental ratio and India the lowest. Hence, as a practical explanation, factor-intensity reversals are probably not important, which is fortunate for H–O.

A telling statistical point was made by Leamer (1980). He showed that, even when H–O holds for balanced trade, we cannot say for unbalanced trade which factor will be relatively stronger in imports or exports. However, even for unbalanced trade the production basket of goods will always use more of the abundant factor than the consumption basket. Re-examining US trade for 1947 (when the USA had a large export surplus) Leamer found production more capital-intensive than consumption, and hence concluded that there is no paradox.

Various other explanations for the Leontief paradox have been suggested, although subsequent research has not supported them. They include: that US consumption is biased towards capital-intensive goods – the evidence, if anything, suggests an opposite bias; that trade impediments distort trade – but Deardorff (1982) showed that, provided subsidies are not dominant, distortions cannot reverse trade patterns; that Leontief should have considerd only immediate (direct) factor inputs rather than total inputs via the input–output table – again Deardorff (1983) has shown the opposite; and that Leontief should have considered not capital stock but the flow of capital services used, i.e. taking into account the rate of capacity utilisation – this is wrong because the rate of utilisation is an endogenous economic variable and thus cannot be the fundamental determinant of trade. The stock of capital, on the other hand, is assumed quite exogenous.

Extending Heckscher–Ohlin

Of the explanations offered above for Leontief's paradox, the most promising are natural resources and human capital. Natural resources cannot really be fitted into the Heckscher–Ohlin framework because they are not transferable between industries; resource-based industries have, therefore, usually been omitted in later exercises. Human capital may be treated either as affecting technology or as an additional factor within a known and common technology. The former view, which is explored in Chapter 5, holds that technology is basically 'embodied' in the skills of its designers and controllers; here we briefly examine the latter view, despite our opinion that it is the inferior interpretation.

Baldwin (1971) considered the factor content of US trade in 1962 for a large range of factors, including many different levels and types of human capital. He found that US exports were intensive relative to imports in: labour measured in man-years (confirming Leontief), more highly educated labour, more highly paid labour (pay and skills are positively related), and particularly engineers and scientists. Excluding natural resource industries nearly eliminates the paradox in man-years, and emphasises the differences between exports and imports for the other measures. This suggests that H–O has some role in non-resource-based trade.

Stern and Maskus (1981) also extended Leontief, but using a single measure of human capital based on rates of pay – assuming the higher the wage the more skilled the employee. For 1958 they confirmed the paradox, but found that imports embodied only 80 per cent of the human capital of exports, the figure falling to 66 per cent if resource industries were excluded. For 1972, however, the paradox disappeared – imports appearing to be relatively labour-intensive compared with exports – but simultaneously the net exports of human capital declined sharply, with imports and exports being roughly similar in their intensities. This could be reconciled with H–O if in 1958 the USA were relatively well endowed with skilled labour, but less so in 1972. This accords with casual observation – Japan and Western Europe have caught up rapidly in education and technology over the period – but of course it would have to be confirmed by careful measurement before these results could constitute a full test of H–O. Stern and Maskus also estimated the factor content of production and consumption, as recommended by Leamer, and found them almost identical for all three factors. This removes the paradox, but at the expense of leaving H–O explaining virtually nothing at all.

Usually more favourable to H–O are tests of developing countries' trade. Havrylyshyn (1984), for example, showed that for a sample of developing countries both the physical and human capital intensities of imports exceeded those of production, which, in turn, exceeded those of exports. He attributed the clearer results here to the greater differences between developing countries and their major markets (the industrial countries) than between different industrial countries in their mutual trade. As we shall see, however, not all developing industrial country trade displays H–O features.

49

Commodity results

More direct than the factor content of trade, we could just examine whether the commodities exported by a capital-abundant country are capital-intensive. This is normally done by regressing trade flows or net exports (exports minus imports) for each good on various measures of the good's factor intensity. We would expect US net trade to be positively correlated with capital intensity (i.e. she exports more of the capital-intensive commodities).

Multiple regression allows us to consider many factors simultaneously, so these regression tests generally consider several different trade theories at once. We shall examine them in Chapter 5, but note here that they do shed some light on Heckscher–Ohlin. In a series of regressions, Baldwin (1971) found US net exports negatively related to capital intensity – thus confirming the Leontief paradox by a quite different route. He also found some evidence of the positive role of human skills. This was strongly confirmed by Stern and Maskus (1981), who found net exports related positively to human capital inputs and negatively to crude labour and physical capital inputs in every year from 1958 to 1976.

UK trade

The attraction of testing trade theories on early US data is that the USA could be presumed to be at the extreme of factor endowments, being more capital-abundant (physical and human) than any other country. Hence her exports to any and all countries would, in theory, be capital-intensive. For intermediate countries, however, the position is less clear, as we saw above: exports are concentrated in one area of the factor-intensity spectrum, and imports will normally lie on either side of that area. Hence total export *versus* total import tests are unlikely to be fruitful. This probably accounts for the growing agnosticism of US tests (other countries now have similar endowments), and for the lack of factor-based tests for other countries.

Baldwin (1979) calculated the factor content for many countries' total trade in the early 1960s. He found UK imports embodying much more capital than exports and the opposite for many developing countries. Katrak (1982) considered the years 1968, 1972 and 1978, finding that exports and imports had similar capital intensities at first but that by 1978 exports were 4 per cent more intense. This was accompanied by a slight fall between 1968 and 1972 in their skill intensity, although Britain still appeared to be a substantial net exporter of inputs of skilled labour.

More detailed results for the 1970s are found in Smith *et al.* (1983). This regression study included many variables, but UK trade performance was persistently related negatively to capital/labour ratios and positively to human capital intensity (in which professional and technical manpower were the dominant aspect). These results applied strongly to UK trade with developing countries (the UK imported capital-intensive goods, confirming Baldwin's view) but less so to trade with the EC. The latter appears to be largely independent of factor considerations, probably because UK and European factor endowments are so similar.

A difficulty with all the foregoing tests is that while the H–O model relates three phenomena – trade patterns, factor intensity and factor endowments – the tests refer to only two. For example, Leontief considered only trade and intensity measures, leaving abundance to be handled informally at the end. Bowen, Leamer and Sveikauskas (1987), on the other hand, sought to relate all three phenomena formally. They showed that in an H–O model with equal numbers of factors and goods a country's net exports of a factor's services (i.e. the factors used to produce its bundle of net exports) will equal its relative endowments of that factor: specifically that

$$(F_{ki}/E_{kw})/G_i = [(E_{ki}/E_{kw})/G_i] - 1, \qquad (4.3)$$

where

F_{ki} is the content of factor k embodied in country i's bundle of exports;
E_{ki} is country i's endowment of factor k;
E_{kw} is world endowment of factor k; and
G_i is country i's share of world GDP.

Thus, $(E_{ki}/E_{kw})/G_i$ measures whether country i has more factor k relative to the world than it has of factors in general, the relative general endowment being captured by i's share of total world factor rewards, i.e. its share of world income or GDP.

Using data for twelve factors and twenty-seven countries, Bowen *et al.* calculated separate estimates of the right- and left-hand sides of equation (4.3) and asked how well they match up. The answer is not very well – for example, in only 61 per cent of the 324 possible matches are the signs of the two sides the same. The authors then went on to try to locate the source of the failure of H–O by exploring the discrepancies thrown up by (4.3). They found mild support for the view that, while consumption patterns are common across countries (assumption (i) in section 3.2 above), technology differs by a simple multiplicative factor between countries.

Bowen *et al.*'s results should certainly give us pause for thought about the H–O model, but they do not necessarily invalidate the factor endowments approach entirely. First, as the authors concluded, the difficulties of accurately measuring trade, let alone endowments and intensities, makes it very difficult to draw any firm conclusions at all. Second, less highly structured tests suggest that endowments play a very significant role, albeit in a more sophisticated fashion than H–O admits. For example, Leamer (1984) found that factor endowments broadly defined explain a large amount of observed trade (see pages 75–7 below), while Balassa and Bauwens (1988) found a strong tendency for capital-endowed countries to export capital-intensive manufactures. Thus Bowen *et al*'s rejection of H–O probably owes more to the subsidiary 'supporting' assumptions made to derive clean theoretical results than to the irrelevance of factor endowments *per se*.

Testing the corollaries

A final problem of the tests outlined above is that they do not specify clear alternative hypotheses against which to measure H–O. One exception to this is an elegant test of the Stolper-Samuelson theorem by Magee (1980). Unlike the H–O case, the specific factors model allows labour and capital in an industry to have similar interests in the opening of trade while capitals in different industries have different interests. Consider a rise in the price of food in equation (4.2) holding constant the price of cloth: $\hat{p}_C = 0$, so $\hat{r}_F > \hat{w} > 0$ and both factors gain from the price rise of food. Hence both labour and capital would be likely to support protection for food, whereas cloth capitalists would oppose it. Magee considered the attitudes of US labour and capital towards protection in their own industries. Of twenty-one industries, he found nineteen had labour and capital displaying the same preferences over protection; he also found that labour split $3:1$ in favour of protection and capital $2:1$ in favour. Both results tend to support the specific factor model over H–O, although with the proviso that both labour and capital are industry specific.

51

D

FURTHER READING

Findlay (1970b) considers trade in the very long run. The short-run and specific factors model is covered by *Jones* (1971), *Mayer* (1974) and *Neary* (1978). *Neary* (1985) considers general adjustment problems in a broad but accessible fashion, while *Grossman* (1983) looks at models intermediate to perfect and zero factor mobility. *Caves and Jones* (1981) and *Bhagwati and Srinivasan* (1983) offer alternative textbook treatments.

The Leontief paradox is admirably surveyed by *Bhagwati* (1964, 1969a), *Findlay* (1970a) and *Baldwin* (1971), and at a higher level by *Stern* (1975) and *Deardorff* (1983). The empirical references of the text and also *Leamer* (1974) should be consulted, and more empirical works on various countries may be located in the surveys. All these references, however, will be more accessible when you have read Chapter 5.

KEY CONCEPTS

specific factors
short-run transformation curve
human capital
magnification effect

capital accumulation and trade
Leontief paradox
factor content of trade

QUESTIONS FOR REVIEW

4.1 What is the appropriate time-frame for using the Heckscher–Ohlin to predict trade patterns?

4.2 Describe the short-run implications of the immigration of labour.

4.3 The specific factors model suggests quite different interests in the opening of international trade from the Heckscher–Ohlin model. How are they different? How can the difference help us to identify the more appropriate model?

4.4 In what sense is the 'Leontief paradox' no paradox at all?

4.5 Does the empirical evidence refute the Heckscher–Ohlin model? Does it refute the role of factor abundance in determining trade patterns?

5 Modern Trade Theory

The Leontief paradox generated several responses among trade economists. We have examined above the statistical arguments and the minor modifications to Heckscher–Ohlin. We now consider the most constructive response – the development of new theories. These primarily hinge around technology, and are treated in section 5.1. Section 5.2 considers how economies of scale and the degree of monopoly influence trade patterns, and section 5.3 develops them further into theories of differentiated trade. These sections explain the phenomenon of 'intra-industry' trade – the simultaneous import and export of the same good – which is quite beyond traditional theory.

5.1 TECHNOLOGY THEORIES OF INTERNATIONAL TRADE

The theories of this section return to Ricardo's basic approach, but pay more attention to the factors determining technology. Basically it is *changing* technology that determines trade, so we are moving from equilibrium to disequilibrium theories.

The imitation gap In Ricardo's static model, technology differed between countries for ever. In Posner's (1961) imitation gap theory, technological differences are seen as temporary and part of a dynamic process, with technology constantly evolving through a series of inventions and innovations. Immediately after inventing a new good, a country has a comparative advantage in, and hence exports, that good. Its advantage persists until its partners have, by one means or another, acquired the new technology themselves, at which time trade will no longer be necessary. Trade occurs to the extent that the *imitation gap* exceeds the *demand gap*. The *demand gap* is the time taken for a good invented in one country to be demanded in others, while the *imitation gap* is the time required for one country's invention to become producible elsewhere. Clearly these gaps depend on many factors and will differ between commodities.

This technology theory could give rise to two sorts of trade. Even if both countries A and B are equally adept at making inventions, there is likely to be trade between them, for invention is partly a random process. A's lead in one field will be balanced by B's in another, possibly closely related, field. Trade between richer countries often takes this form, and only if technological advance were to stop entirely would it disappear.

The alternative trade pattern arises if A is persistently more dynamic than B. Then A always exports modern or advanced goods and B pays for them with (lower-priced) standard goods. As time progresses, modern goods become standard (e.g. motor cars), but A is always technically in advance of B and earning monopoly rents on its new products. Country A may be the more dynamic for a number of reasons, which we discuss below, but technological leads, once gained, can be self-perpetuating. This is likely if the development of technology is linear, in that one must have mastered the use of one level of technology before one can invent the next. This seems plausible for many

53

goods, especially if the pressure for, and basic germ of innovation comes from the users rather than the designers of technology, as Rothwell (1980) suggested.

Failure can also be self-reinforcing. For example, B's disadvantage in high-value modern goods might result in persistent balance of payments crises and lower incomes, and, if this discourages investment in research and development and in high technology industries, B becomes caught in a vicious circle of failure and (relative) decline. Britain is sometimes held to be in this position relative to West Germany and Japan, and something of this nature clearly characterises trade between rich countries ('the North') and poor ('the South') (Balogh, 1963).

Economic dynamism

Crucial to the technology approach to trade is the question of what causes innovation. Obviously luck has some role, but there must also be systematic factors. Since technological advances have to be sought rather than merely falling from the sky, we are basically asking why some countries undertake more (or better) research and development (R&D) than others.

First, institutions may differ: for example, strong patent laws may encourage R&D (because one can reap the benefits of an innovation oneself), and so too may favourable tax laws.

Second, a country may be well endowed with the factors required for R&D. These include scientists and engineers and their equipment and, since R&D is an investment, sufficient savings to finance their activities. (Very poor countries may be unable to afford to divert people from immediate production into uncertain investment tasks like R&D.) The supply of skilled manpower depends on earlier decisions about educational investment and is clearly related to the supply of human capital in general that we discussed in section 4.2.

Third, innovators need a market for their output. They need to know what the market wants and the institutional arrangements for supplying and selling those things. The market also needs to be large and rich, since new goods are frequently costly, and the innovators need to be assured of access to it before beginning their research projects. All these reasons suggest that rich countries will be the principal sources of innovation.

The product cycle

Innovation may occur in the rich OECD countries, but this does not explain why production should. Could not innovators set up their factories in the countries where conditions – e.g. resources, factors of production – are best suited to producing their goods? Posner did not answer this question, but Hirsch (1967) and Vernon (1966) did. They argued that the factors required for a good vary through its life-time. Initially, as new goods are being developed and first sold, there is considerable uncertainty over both their production and marketability. This must be met by flexibility, which requires considerable inputs of skilled labour (Hirsch) and proximity to the market in order to receive and respond to customer reactions (Vernon). Since these are the same factors as stimulate innovation, there is a locational link between innovation and production: new goods will be produced and exported by the rich and large economies.

As the product matures, its basic technology and functional specification become standardised (although peripheral product differentiation may still be rife), making flexibility less important. World demand grows, making large-scale production feasible, and production costs become significant – especially if, as is usual, other, similarly endowed, countries are able to imitate the innovation. These changes tend to shift comparative advantage away from innovating countries, which are typically high-cost locations, towards other relatively wealthy, capital-abundant, countries. Hence physical capital replaces human capital as the intensive factor, and the innovating country may well switch from exporting to importing the good.

The final stage occurs when (if) technology and specification become wholly standardised and universally known. This often allows production to be broken down into a number of relatively unskilled tasks, and certainly stimulates competition and pressure to reduce costs. Thus comparative advantage finally shifts to the low-wage, labour-abundant developing countries, which eventually become net exporters.

The last two stages of this cycle are less clearly defined than the first in practice, but it is clear that the cycle could help to explain the pattern of US trade, since the USA was, during the 1950s and 1960s, the archetypal innovator. Note that with international investment the whole of the cycle could take place under the auspices of a single firm. Note also that, whereas in Posner's theory countries' endowments (of knowledge) changed, in the product cycle it is the good that changes its input requirements. The later stages of cycle correspond closely to the Heckscher–Ohlin theory, and, in the absence of innovation, trade would settle down to a Heckscher–Ohlin pattern.

Testing the technology theories

Although one would not expect technology to explain all international trade, the theories of this section have a strong intuitive appeal. Empirical evidence backs this up in an informal way, but the difficulties of actually measuring technological advantage are likely always to preclude convincing results. The most direct evidence comes from case studies of particular industries. Wells (1969) provided several examples of innovations in consumers' durable goods (TVs, washing machines, etc.) spreading outwards from the USA, with the subsequent reversal of US trade patterns. But perhaps most striking is the semi-conductor, or transistor, industry (Tilton, 1971, especially ch. 2). Invented in the USA, semi-conductor production spread to Western Europe and Japan over the 1950s and 1960s. Since then, while production has spread more slowly, the use of semi-conductors in consumer goods has very largely shifted from the West to the rapidly developing nations of South-East Asia. A similar process now appears to be affecting silicon-chip technology, which was initiated by the USA but has been rapidly taken over in commercial use by the Far East. In this case, however, current developments and applications are as advanced in Japan as in the USA, which suggests that leadership can change hands over time. How far these results generalise – or rather, what proportion of goods actually exhibit product cycle developments – is not clear, but it is probably not very great.

More formal econometric evidence on technology theories requires proxies for technological leadership. Two main ones exist: research and development effort (input into technology) and patents (part of the output). These are usually included in regression equations (along with a number of other variables) to explain the country composition of trade in particular goods or the commodity composition of a particular country's trade.

Of the former type is Soete (1981). For each of forty product groups he related OECD countries' export performance to their shares of patents in the industry, population, distance from world markets and capital abundance. The last factor appeared unimportant, but the others were generally

55

significant. For about three-quarters of Soete's groups, a country's export performance was positively related to its share of patents. Those goods where patents did not affect trade were standardised goods such as textiles, basic chemicals and food, while those where they had strongest effects were the technological industries such as aircraft, weapons, office equipment and scientific instruments.

Country studies include Stern and Maskus (1981), who found US industries' net exports positively related to both their ratio of R&D to value-added (R&D intensity) and the share of scientists and engineers in total employment, and Baldwin (1971), who also found the latter useful.

R&D as a factor of production

A distinction should be made between two different approaches to technology and innovativeness. Ignoring certain conceptual problems, we might treat innovativeness, or R&D, as akin to a factor of production. A country cannot, for example, expect to achieve long-run success in electronic engineering except through a series of innovations and developments. Hence countries well endowed with R&D inputs have a comparative advantage in this industry and the analysis of Chapter 3 carries through. In this view, given their endowments, countries have no discretion over their comparative advantage. Posner's approach, however, implies no such restriction: what matters is being more advanced than your competitors; implicitly, countries can specialise in any industry provided they generate sufficient innovations. In the former case, trade responds to the R&D intensity of particular goods (R&D-abundant countries export R&D-intensive goods). In the latter case, it is the gap between countries in any particular good that is important; although equal amounts of R&D by two partners will generate trade – because the countries will discover different things – the greater one country's lead in R&D the greater its net exports.

Hughes (1986) attempted to separate these two causal chains by relating UK export performance by industry to both the industry's R&D intensity and the gap between UK and competitors's R&D in that industry. Both hypotheses received some support, but the 'factor' approach appeared to be the stronger. A similar test is found in Katrak (1973). He related US/UK relative exports to human capital intensity and the US/UK R&D gap; again human capital seemed more important. In a further development of this test, Katrak (1982) examined the factor content of UK trade, treating scientists in R&D and scientists in other activities as separate factors. Neither really reflected technological gaps, but the former emphasised innovation whereas the latter emphasised skilled production. In the event, UK exports in 1972 contained 20 per cent more of each factor than UK imports, which is consistent with the UK's relatively skill-abundant position, but does not identify whether UK advantage lies in skilled production or in innovation.

Summary

Technological differences and changes can explain much international trade in manufactured goods. While goods are relatively young we expect them to be exported by the country of innovation. Thereafter trade may cease as knowledge is diffused, or reversed as knowledge is replaced by factor endowments as the principal determinant of trade. The fact that one innovation frequently leads to another means that innovations tend to originate in just a few countries, but, as Western Europe and Japan gradually gain on the USA, we see that changes in relative dynamism can occur. There are at least two channels through which research and development is translated into export advantage and it is not yet clear which, if either, is dominant. Nor is it really clear why some countries seem to be so much more dynamic than others. Thus, we are not yet in a position to develop very formal models of technology akin to the Heckscher–Ohlin theory.

5.2 ECONOMIES OF SCALE AND IMPERFECT COMPETITION

External economies of scale

An obvious motive for international trade is the exploitation of economies of scale. Trade opens up the prospect of larger markets and hence reduces unit costs. If we have two countries and two industries each with economies of scale there are clearly profits and social benefits to be earned by specialisation. If the scale economies are strong, the transformation curve will actually curve inwards, and the analysis is just an extreme version of that of Figure 2.2.

As before, trade patterns will be determined by relative prices. If trade is opened from a position of autarky, each country exports its relatively cheap good and, by thus increasing output, further reduces its relative price of that good. If demand is identical between countries, pre-trade prices reflect comparative advantage and specialisation follows the obvious pattern. If, however, demand is biased strongly enough to give countries relatively low prices in their 'non-advantage' goods, each will specialise in the 'wrong' good. Trade will still be preferable to autarky, but not as beneficial as if comparative advantage determined specialisation.

A similar case can arise if countries differ in size and industries differ in the extent of their economies of scale. Here the larger country will have a relatively lower autarky price for the 'scale-good' regardless of comparative advantage, and so specialisation could again be incorrect. Under completely free trade, however, the smaller country, observing that it could now capture the whole of the world market in the scale-good, would have an incentive to switch to that good wholesale. Whether this actually occurs depends on the precise working of the price mechanism, but if we introduce transport costs and trade impediments it seems unlikely. Hence we are left with a presumption that large economies will specialise in goods with greater economies of scale.

This argument has received some empirical support, Katrak (1973) found the USA specialised in scale-goods relative to the UK, and Hufbauer (1970) found countries' exports of scale-goods positively correlated with their size. On the other hand, Baldwin (1971) found no role for scale in the US trade figures, and Smith *et al.* (1983) found only dubious evidence for the UK. Note, however, that as a middle-sized market among OECD countries it is not clear whether to expect a positive or negative relationship for the UK.

Monopoly

The previous paragraphs assumed implicitly that the existence of economies of scale was compatible with perfect competition. This requires that the economies be external to the firm – that no firm can reduce its own costs by increasing output, but that increases in national output reduce national costs. We now relax that assumption and allow external economies to affect market structure by reducing the number of firms that can exist in an industry. At an intuitive level we explore the issue by thinking about a monopolistic exporter. We then consider a formal model of trade in oligopolistic industries.

A monopolist tries to exploit his home market by forcing up price; this increases the likelihood of imports coming in. Similarly, if he is obliged (legally) to charge the same at home and abroad, he may choose not to sell on the (competitive) world market because that would force him to charge less in his monopolistic market at home. Furthermore, monopoly is often associated with general inefficiency – X-inefficiency – which harms trade performance. All these arguments suggest that net exports will be lower for monopolised industries. Against them must be set the facts that exporting involves fixed costs (setting up dealerships, etc.) and also greater risks than home sales, both of which tend to preclude small firms from exporting. However, in most industries firms reach an efficient exporting size well before they attain very high concentration.

Evidence on the effects of concentration on trade is mixed, but Utton and Morgan (1983) suggest some support for views expressed above, at least for labour-intensive industries.

Empirically there are two separate elements to the measurement of economies of scale. First the extent to which scale reduces costs and second whether or not the minimum efficient scale (MES) for a firm is large or small relative to the market size. For example, that costs halve as firm size doubles is of hardly any consequence if there is room for, say, 1,000 firms at MES. Pratten (1971) estimated that, from a sample of twenty-seven industries in the 1960s, MES exceeded half the British market for nine: dyes, rolled steel products, cars, aircraft, machine tools, turbo generators, electric motors, electronic capital goods and plastics. However, of these only dyes, aircraft, electric motors and plastics had cost increases of over 10 per cent by operating at half MES. At the other extreme, costs at half MES were higher by 15 per cent and 25 per cent in bread and cement respectively, but there was room for at least 100 and 200 MES firms respectively. Other evidence – e.g. Hufbauer (1970) – broadly confirms these results on wider samples, so we must conclude that economies of scale are likely to be a significant factor in the determination of international trade.

Reciprocal dumping

We now consider a simple but formal model of international trade in oligopolistic industries. Recent research has shown that oligopolies (industries with only a few firms) can generate two-way, or *intra-industry*, trade, and that such trade may be either strongly beneficial or harmful according to the circumstances.

To illustrate this case we consider the so-called 'reciprocal dumping' model of Brander and Krugman (1983). Imagine that good X is produced by just two firms, firm A located in country A and firm B in country B. Each firm realises its interdependence with the other, but assumes for convenience that it may take the other's level of output as fixed regardless of what it chooses to do itself. This assumption stems from the earliest work on oligopoly – Cournot (1838) – and is known as Cournot behaviour. It is obviously rather extreme but it may have empirical relevance and is, anyway, the easiest case to analyse.

Let the demand curve for X in country A be written in inverse form as $P_A = f(X_A)$, where P_A, the price in A, is expressed as a function of X_A, the quantity consumed; by definition, $X_A = X_A^A + X_A^B$, where X_A^A is X supplied to market A by firm A and X_A^B that supplied by firm B. Firm A earns revenue $R_A^A = P_A X_A^A$ from sales in A, and will maximise its profits by equating its perceived marginal revenue and marginal costs in that market. Assuming that the latter are constant at level C_A^A, A's profit-maximisation condition is

$$C_A^A = \frac{dR_A^A}{dX_A^A} = P_A + X_A^A \frac{dP_A}{dX_A}\left(\frac{\widetilde{dX_A}}{dX_A^A}\right). \tag{5.1}$$

The right-hand side of (5.1) tells us that supplying an extra unit of X_A^A increases total revenue by the price, P_A, less the expected effect of the reduction in price on all existing sales (X_A^A); the latter effect is represented by the product of the effect of increased total supply on price and the expected effect of increased X_A^A on total supply, X^A. The latter, $\widetilde{dX_A}/dX_A^A$, is known as the *conjectural variation*, and under the Cournot assumption it is unity, because X_A^B is assumed by firm A to be constant. By simple manipulation the former, dP_A/dX_A, equals $P_A/\epsilon X_A$, where ϵ is the elasticity of demand for X_A (ϵ is a negative number). Then, substituting into (5.1), we have

$$C_A^A = P_A\left[1 + \frac{s_A^A}{\epsilon}\right], \tag{5.2}$$

where s_A^A is firm A's share of sales in market A.

Equation (5.2) tells us first that price exceeds marginal cost, because s_A^A/ϵ is always negative, and, second, that the extent of the difference depends on firm A's market share – the greater its share, the greater its monopoly power and the greater its mark-up over marginal costs. This is a standard result, but for our purposes it is most useful to invert it and say that, given the price, the higher are A's costs the lower its market share.

There will be a similar equation for firm B's supplies to market A.

$$C_A^B = P_A\left[1 + \frac{s_A^B}{\epsilon}\right], \tag{5.3}$$

from which it is plain that, given their assumptions about each other's behaviour, there is room for both firms to supply market A at the common price, P_A. Moreover, if, as is plausible, B's costs of supplying that market exceed A's – say, because of transport costs – there is still room for them both, provided that B has the smaller market share. A's larger market share means that it has lower marginal revenue than B because, although an extra unit supplied by either of them has the same depressing effect on price, this effect hits A's revenue harder than B's because A has a larger existing volume of sales on which the price has fallen.

A perfectly symmetrical analysis could be made of country B's market, and so it is clear that good X – which we have assumed perfectly homogeneous – can flow simultaneously both from A to B and from B to A; i.e. there is two-way trade. Such trade obviously wastes transport resources, but it is not necessarily economically harmful because it has a pro-competitive effect. Suppose that international trade were banned: each firm would immediately be transformed into a monopolist in its own market, its market share would be one, and, as equation (5.2) shows, given costs, price would rise from, say, $C_A^A(1 + s_A^A/\epsilon)^{-1}$ to $C_A^A(1 + 1/\epsilon)^{-1}$. This increase in monopoly power imposes losses on consumers and on the economy as a whole. The gains from trade in this simple world clearly depend on the trade-off between transport costs and the pro-competitive effects.

The reciprocal dumping model may be generalised in a number of directions. The most obvious is to increase the number of firms. Since this will tend to reduce each firm's share, it will tend to make the industry more competitive, i.e. to reduce the mark-up over costs. A particular case of many firms will be where each country has one firm but there are many countries. In the absence of international trade there will be domestic monopoly, as above, but when trade is introduced, instead of shifting to a duopoly, the industry will become an oligopoly, and price will fall to something like $C_A^A(1 + 1/n\epsilon)^{-1}$, where n is the number of firms each with a share of $1/n$. That is, if international trade admits several competitors rather than just one, its pro-competitive effect will be correspondingly greater.

The model can also be extended to allow the products supplied by A and B to differ somewhat and to allow for slightly different assumptions about rivals' behaviour. If firm A expects B to copy its production decision, $\widetilde{dX_A}/dX_A^A$ would be 2, for example, and if it expects B to compensate for them by moving in the opposite direction, $\widetilde{dX_A}/dX_A^A < 1$. These changes obviously alter equations (5.2) and (5.3), but the basic ideas follow through. Although varying $\widetilde{dX_A}/dX_A^A$ misses a lot of the subtlety of oligopolistic interactions, it does allow different approaches to oligopoly and the degree of competition to be modelled crudely.

5.3 PRODUCT DIFFERENTIATION AND INTRA-INDUSTRY TRADE

All our previous discussion of trade theory has focused on supply – comparative costs or market structure. We now consider demand. It is clear from Chapters 2 and 3 that differences in patterns of demand could generate international trade. Indeed they could be quite an important explanation of world trade if, as Hunter and Markusen (1988) suggest, demand patterns shift predictably with levels of development. We shall not pursue this issue here, however, but rather consider a different aspect of demand: the demand for variety – the fact that different consumers like different varieties of basic goods. If anything prevents all possible varieties of a good from being produced locally, it is likely that international trade will occur and that it will be beneficial. Moreover, such trade will typically be two-way or *intra-industry trade* (IIT) as consumers in each country buy varieties from the other. This observation has given rise to a plethora of theoretical and empirical work over the last two decades, which forms the basis of this section. We start by examining the phenomenon of intra-industry trade, and then move on to the various explanations of it.

Intra-industry trade

Intra-industry trade is the simultaneous export and import of basically the same good – for example, Britain and Germany trading Mercedes and Jaguars with each other. It is usually measured as the proportion of total trade accounted for by 'overlapping' exports and imports. Hence if exports are £100 and imports £60, £120 of trade 'overlaps' (£60 of imports and £60 of exports) and £40 does not: IIT would thus be 75 per cent. Formally, the most common measure of IIT for any good i is:

$$B_i = \frac{(X_i + M_i) - |X_i - M_i|}{(X_i + M_i)} \cdot 100\% \tag{5.4}$$

where X and M are exports and imports, and $|x|$ is the absolute value of x. $(X + M)$ is total trade, while $|X - M|$ is the degree of non-overlap, i.e. the extent that trade is unbalanced. Observe that the measure does not depend on the sign of the trade imbalance, just its size.

For perfect *inter-industry trade*, where trade flows just one way, $B = 0\%$. For example, if we only export a good, $X + M = |X - M| = X$, so the top of (5.4) is zero. For perfect *intra-industry trade*, $B = 100\%$: trade is balanced, $X = M$, so $|X - M| = 0$. Between these extremes, high Bs indicate a greater degree of IIT. Observe that B is a relative measure: we could double both X and M without altering it.

Aggregation So far we have avoided defining good i or, equivalently, saying how similar items must be to be treated as varieties of the same good rather than separate goods. This is an arbitrary and largely unresolved issue. Clearly if we define goods so precisely that any good can be produced in only one country (e.g. German lager is a different good from Dutch lager), IIT is impossible, which is not helpful. But neither should we go to the other extreme and, say, define manufactures as a single good, for then exporting aircraft in return for rubber ducks would look like IIT, which is just silly.

As disaggregation proceeds to finer levels, measured IIT declines, because surpluses on one good will no longer be offset by deficits on another. For example, suppose we have two types of car, 1 and 2; let $X_1 = 100$, $M_1 = 60$, $X_2 = 60$ and $M_2 = 100$. The separate IIT measures are both 75 per cent, suggesting the car industry has 75 per cent IIT. However, if we combine the two types into a single aggregate called 'cars', $X_c = 160$ and $M_c = 160$, and the industry now appears to have 100 per cent intra-industry trade.

Official classifications of international trade are based on the Standard International Trade Classification (SITC), now in its second revision, SITC (R2). The classification is numerical, with more digits indicating greater detail: this is evident in Table 5.1, which describes part of the UK classification. Even at its finest level the SITC does not define homogeneous groups, but data are rarely analysed at this level. More common are data at the '3' or '4-digit level', which roughly accord with industries.

Grubel and Lloyd (1975), in a pioneering book, examined the effect of aggregation on Australia's measured IIT in 1968–9. Averaging over all trade

Table 5.1 An example of the UK international trade classification

		Number of categories at this level in SITC (R2)
SECTION 7	MACHINERY AND TRANSPORT EQUIPMENT	10
Division 71	Power Generating Machinery and Equipment	63
Group 713	Internal combustion piston engines, and parts thereof	233
Sub-group 713.3	Internal combustion engines, marine propulsion	786
Heading 713.31	– outboard	1,832[a]
Code[b] 84061000	of cylinder capacity 325 cm^3 or less	
84061200	of cylinder capacity more than 325 cm^3	c. 10,000

Sources: United Nations (1981); Customs and Excise, *Guide to the Classification for Overseas Trade Statistics* (1983).
Notes:
[a] Total of all 5-digit and undivided 4-digit sub-groups.
[b] This level is specific to UK statistics.

flows, they found it fell from 43 per cent at 1-digit level, through 20 per cent (3-digits), 15 per cent (4-digits) to 6 per cent at 7-digit level. Greenaway and Milner (1983), examining UK trade in 1977, found average IIT of 69 per cent for chemicals at the 3-digit level, declining to 67 per cent (4-digits) to 53 per cent at 5-digits. Similar patterns emerged for other UK manufacturing groups. IIT has grown over recent years: Grubel and Lloyd found the average of 3-digit measures for OECD countries rising from 36 per cent in 1959 to 48 per cent by 1967. It also shows considerable variation over countries: 69 per cent for the UK, 65 per cent for France, 46 per cent for Germany, 49 per cent for the USA, and 21 per cent for Japan in 1967 at the 3-digit level (Grubel and Lloyd, 1975).

Although there clearly are measurement problems, these figures all suggest that intra-industry trade is not a mere statistical artefact. We therefore now turn to the economics of it.

Homogeneous goods

We saw above that reciprocal dumping can generate IIT in perfectly homogeneous goods. It is also possible in a few other minor cases. First *entrepôt* trade: when goods are shipped in bulk to Rotterdam, and then re-shipped to Germany or Switzerland, this appears as Dutch IIT if the goods pass through Dutch customs. This is especially likely if, for example, Dutch industry repacks the goods into retail sizes in the process. Second *seasonality*: Britain imports apples in January and exports them in September; hence over a year IIT appears. This is a problem of temporal, rather than commodity, aggregation. Similarly, *transport costs* can produce IIT along extended national boundaries. For instance, if masons buy stone from the nearest quarry, it may be that at the southern end of the Franco-German border a French firm serves parts of both countries, whereas in the north a German firm does.

Differentiated goods

These arguments cannot explain the recorded quantities of IIT, however. For this we must turn to the theory of differentiated products. Within what we commonly define as a good there will be scope for minor variations, which differentiate one variety of the good from another without going beyond the bounds of the same basic good. Differentiation may be largely cosmetic, relying on brand images (e.g. soap powder), or functional, where specifications differ (e.g. pocket calculators). Either way, we merely assume – entirely realistically – that different varieties are demanded by consumers. This may be because all of them like some variety (e.g. theatre tickets), or because individuals differ in their requirements (e.g. the demand for cars).

There are two ways that demand for variety can generate international trade. The first, and less realistic, assumes that different varieties require different factor proportions in production (Finger, 1975; Falvey, 1981). Hence the whole exercise becomes like Heckscher–Ohlin, each country producing the varieties most suiting its endowments. This amounts to arguing that IIT is just an aggregation problem with varieties incorrectly grouped into goods so that 'the same good' seems to have several production technologies. Apart from its intuitive implausibility, this approach cannot account for the strong growth of IIT over time.

The second approach appeals to economies of scale in the production of varieties. Thus the most efficient way of supplying the varieties demanded in a trading world is by specialisation in varieties and subsequent two-way trade. There have been several recent formalisations of this approach, but all make the two crucial assumptions that demand exists for many varieties and that this cannot be efficiently met locally because of economies of scale. In all these models, product differentiation leads to imperfect competition among producers – usually monopolistic competition where firms face downward-sloping demand curves but free entry to the industry competes profits down to normal levels.

In any such economy, variety must be traded off against cost. Not every conceivable variety can be produced, because that would involve too great a loss of economies of scale,[1] whereas producing just one variety at huge scale would do too much violence to tastes. Imagine that this trade-off has been made in each of America and Britain, resulting in n_A and n_B varieties respectively. Now open trade (ignoring transport costs). If the American and British varieties are identical, there is an immediate gain by pooling the production of each at one site and reaping the scale economies. If none of the varieties is identical, consumers in each country now have $(n_A + n_B)$ varieties to choose from, which also raises welfare. In fact, the final equilibrium will probably be somewhere in between. Some varieties will be displaced by very similar foreign rivals, but the final number will exceed n_A and n_B. Foreign trade, therefore, is likely to raise welfare by both increasing choice and reducing costs.

There have been several formalisations of these ideas recently. While the resulting models do not add much to the intuition of the previous paragraph, they are useful in providing the building blocks for further analysis, identifying the crucial determinants and features of such trade, and permitting the quantification of the various effects. The simplest formal introduction is Krugman (1979).

Monopolistic competition (a) Krugman

In order to make the analysis tractable, Krugman assumes particular functional forms for his various relationships. These assumptions can be important to the results, and although generalisations of Krugman's assumptions are usually feasible, we stick with his simple forms for illustrative purposes. He proceeds by asking what an autarkic economy would look like with a monopolistically competitive sector; he then asks what it would look like if it were twice the size. The latter concept corresponds to the world economy with free and costless trade between two of the previously autarkic economies.

Assume that all consumers have the utility function

$$u = \sum_{i=1}^{n} c_i^{\theta} \qquad 0 < \theta < 1, \tag{5.5}$$

where c_i is consumption on the ith variety of the basic good. (5.5) shows that utility is raised by either increasing any c_i or increasing n. We can also show that, if the price and consumption of each good are the same (that is, if $p_i = p$ and $c_i = c$, all i – so-called symmetry assumption), then utility will be increased by an x per cent increase in n even if it entails an x per cent reduction in the consumption level of each good. That is, consumers will maximise their welfare by maximising their variety. Among other things, this ensures that each form will produce a unique variety: it never pays to copy a rival.

Assume that each good has an identical production function, using a single factor of production, labour:

$$l_i = \alpha + \beta x_i, \tag{5.6}$$

where x_i is output and l_i labour input. Given the wage rate, w, the fixed cost component α ensures that average costs fall as x_i rises (wl_i/x_i falls), but marginal costs are constant at βw. The symmetry assumption ensures that in equilibrium $l_i = 1$ and $x_i = x$, all i.

Equation (5.6) gives rise to two equilibrium conditions. First, each firm has some monopoly power because it produces a unique variety; thus it equates marginal cost and marginal revenue, so that

$$p(1 - 1/\epsilon) = \beta w, \tag{5.7}$$

where we have dropped the subscript because of the symmetry assumption, and ϵ is the elasticity of demand for each individual variety. This is just equation (5.2) again, but with each variety having 100 per cent of its own market.

Second, we assume that new firms will enter production until there are no more profits to be gained from doing so. This zero profit condition requires the equality of average costs and revenues, viz.

$$px = (\alpha + \beta x) w. \tag{5.8}$$

Equations (5.7) and (5.8) define the final equilibrium of the economy. It is best seen by deriving the relationships they imply between real prices (p/w) and per capita consumption (c):

$$p/w = \frac{\beta\epsilon}{\epsilon - 1} \tag{5.7a}$$

$$p/w = \beta + \frac{\alpha}{Lc}, \tag{5.8a}$$

where the elasticity of demand depends on c (it is *assumed* to fall), and where output (x) of any variety equals the product of population (L) and per capita consumption (c). Figure 5.1 plots those two relationships and shows the equilibrium. In addition, we assume full employment,

$$L = \sum l_i = nl,$$

so that from (5.6) the number of varieties is seen to be

$$n = \frac{L}{\alpha + \beta x} = \frac{L}{\alpha + \beta Lc}. \tag{5.9}$$

Suppose now that L – the size of the economy – were increased. Locus (5.7) in Figure 5.1 would be unaffected, but locus (5.8) would shrink inwards to (5.8') – to maintain a given real price, c must fall as L rises. The new equilibrium entails lower real prices $(p/w)'$ and lower per capita consumption of each variety, c'. However, because (p/w) has fallen, Lc must have risen (see equation 5.8a), so that output of each variety has risen. Moreover from (5.9) a rise in L and a fall in c implies a rise in n (the denominator rises less than proportionately to L, first because α is constant and second because c falls). Thus the increase in L benefits consumers by reducing real prices (p/w) and increasing variety.

Under autarky, home consumers live in an economy of size L. If this economy trades freely with another of size L^* they then live in an economy of size $(L + L^*)$ with all its attendant advantages. Each consumer will obtain more varieties, but the total number of varieties in the world will decrease, as

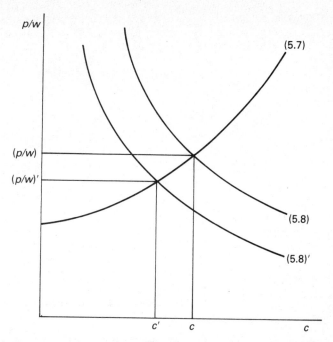

Figure 5.1 Krugman's model with monopolistic competition

the output of each surviving variety is increased. (Prior to trade, home consumers could not consume foreign varieties.)

Monopolistic competition (b) Lancaster

A peculiar feature of the Krugman model is its assumption that every consumer likes some of every product. This means that variety is desirable in and of itself, and that all of society can agree that it is a good thing. An alternative approach, which is more convincing for some goods, is that varieties differ in particular dimensions and that consumers differ over their preferred varieties; cars, for example, fall into this category. This approach to differentiation stems from Lancaster's (1966) work on product characteristics and has been translated into international trade terms by Lancaster (1980) and Helpman (1981). It is more complex than Krugman's approach and rather more ambiguous in its conclusions. Consequently it has been used rather less in the literature.

The easiest conceptualisation of the Lancaster model is in terms of distance. Imagine that consumers live around a circle and that there are four producers located equi-distantly around the circle – see Figure 5.2, with four producers located at A_0, A_3, etc. Each consumer buys one unit of the good and buys from his nearest producer in order to minimise transport costs. Some consumers are lucky, e.g. those at 3 o'clock in Figure 5.2, because they have zero costs, others less so, e.g. those at 4 o'clock. Now imagine that there were six producers located at B_0, B_2, etc. On average, transport costs are less than previously, so that society as a whole gains but some consumers are worse off, e.g. those at 3 o'clock.

If we can translate product variety into this simple distance analogy (with transport costs representing the cost of not getting one's favourite variety), we can see that international trade is beneficial on average but potentially

65

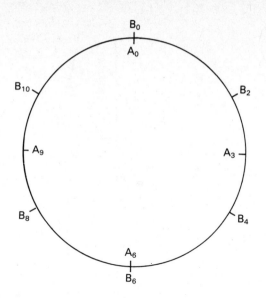

Figure 5.2 The location of producers – Lancaster

harmful to some consumers. Moreover, if we are to implement the model we need to know how many varieties are produced (which is possible, but complex) and where on the circle they are. If the latter distribution is random, balanced IIT is likely to result – a consumer's preferred variety is as likely to be foreign as domestic. If, however, different countries have comparative advantage over certain ranges of the circle, more complex patterns can emerge. For example, suppose that international trade introduces new varieties only at 3 o'clock. The local producers at A_3 may be forced out of business and those at A_0 and A_6 may lose custom, but, provided none of them relocates, the producer at A_9 is unaffected.

Unfortunately the intuitive appeal of Lancaster's analysis has only very recently been exploited empirically. Hocking (1980) observed that different countries produced cars with different characteristics, but Levinsohn and Feenstra (1990) were the first to exploit this information to identify competing models. They examined 137 types of car on sale in the USA. Using data on the cars' various characteristics (e.g. horsepower) and the values that consumers put on them, Levinsohn and Feenstra identified the competition for each model. No car was free of competitors and most had between four and eight. From a trade theorist's perspective their most interesting conclusion was that competition did not correlate at all closely with nationality: Japanese cars, for example, did not cluster particularly closely in one region of the characteristic space.

Both approaches can easily be integrated with the earlier supply models of trade to explain both inter- and intra-industry trade. Suppose food production is subject to constant returns to scale, while cloth has both economies of scale and product differentiation. Factor endowments determine the basic food/cloth specialisation, but within cloth there may be IIT. If factor endowments are very different, Heckscher–Ohlin inter-industry trade will predominate, with the world consuming only those varieties of cloth that Britain produces. If they are similar, however, IIT dominates, with America exporting food and some varieties of cloth in return for many other varieties of cloth from Britain. IIT in cloth will thus exist, but net trade (exports minus imports) will reflect traditional comparative advantage. The extent of IIT in cloth clearly depends on the similarity of factor endowments. Helpman (1987) shows that trade among fourteen industrial countries does indeed reflect the hypothesis.

Other factors

Another possible determinant of IIT is per capita income. So far the varieties of a good that a country produces have been assumed to be purely random. However this is not very plausible. Domestic producers have a competitive edge in their own markets because they avoid transport costs and tariffs, and they will maximise the benefits of this by producing those varieties that have the largest domestic markets. Hence, assuming production conditions are identical across the world, countries will produce to satisfy local tastes, and have large shares of their home markets. A major determinant of tastes is income: the rich demand (and can pay for) better goods. When we allow trade, therefore, it is likely that rich consumers will buy more varieties imported from other rich countries than of those from poor countries. The more similar two countries' per capita incomes, the more, *ceteris paribus*, they will trade varieties with each other (Linder, 1961). This too is confirmed by Helpman's tests.

The last two paragraphs suggest why virtually all intra-industry trade occurs between the rich OECD countries, and also, since these economies appear to have converged since 1950, why such trade has grown in importance. A further explanation of the latter comes from Barker's (1977) *variety hypothesis*. Roughly speaking, foreign varieties are available to consumers only if they pay the premium due to transport costs, etc. At relatively low incomes they choose to avoid this, making do with local varieties, but, as incomes rise, increasing numbers can afford to pay the premium to obtain the (imported) varieties that suit them best. The ratio of imported units to domestic units consumed thus rises with income. This offers one explanation of why the income elasticity of demand for imports exceeds unity; that is, why imports typically grow faster than income.

Yet a further reason advanced for the growth of IIT is the dismantling of tariff barriers. Industrial adjustment is probably easier with intra- rather than inter-industry specialisation, because shifts within an industry probably involve smaller changes in factor demands. Hence Hufbauer and Chilas (1974) suggest that governments have deliberately biased tariff reductions towards IIT, which has involved reducing tariffs mainly on the goods traded between rich countries. A striking example of the potency of mutual tariff reductions between rich countries was the huge growth of mutual IIT following the formation of the European Economic Community.

Empirical evidence on intra-industry trade

Intra-industry trade generated considerable activity among applied economists in the 1970s and 1980s, mostly devoted to explaining industries' differences in IIT in terms of industry characteristics. Two major problems existed. First, there was little theoretical guidance on what to expect, although this is gradually being resolved, as we saw above. Second, many of the causes thought to be important are poorly, if at all, measurable. Consequently, results have varied according to the proxies chosen for the various effects. We briefly examine three major studies.

Caves (1981), examined IIT among thirteen OECD nations in 1970, on ninety-four SITC 3-digit goods. He related it to measures of product heterogeneity, product differentiation, scale economies, integrated production, foreign direct investment and trade barriers. The first three have been justified above as necessary conditions for intra-industry trade. However, Caves introduced some interesting refinements to those arguments. First he argued that, while 'technical' product differentiation will stimulate intra-industry trade (as above), 'brand-image' differentiation may hinder it because brand images do not travel. This is supported by his data: factors like R&D that suggest technical differentiation had positive influence, while factors like advertising expenditure reduced IIT. Second, while some economies of scale are necessary for IIT, greater rather than lesser economies hinder IIT because they confine production to a few countries. Product heterogeneity, on the other hand, clearly stimulates trade. Foreign direct investment is the ownership of factories in one country by firms in another. This is a substitute for trade, especially if trade is determined by technology, because it takes production rather than goods to the market. It is countered, however, by the international integration of production, which causes multinational companies to shift semi-finished goods between factories, and possibly to produce different varieties of output in different countries. The negative influence appears to dominate. Trade barriers might be expected to hinder trade, but overall little evidence emerges of this.

Marvel and Ray (1987) also found economies of scale and consumer product differentiation negatively related to the extent of IIT. Rather it is goods which are used in a wide variety of industrial processes or that are made to order that show most IIT, probably because these factors increase the scope for specialisation in producing varieties. Marvel and Ray also confirmed the relationship between IIT and trade policy, but argued that it is IIT which stimulates trade liberalisation (or prevents the growth of protection) rather than vice versa. Finally, at a broader level, Havrylyshyn and Civan (1983) found strong evidence that across countries the extent of IIT increases with per capita income. In particular, it is low for developing countries – even the relatively industrialised ones.

FURTHER READING

The technology theories of trade are expounded well in the original references given in the text. An excellent early work is *Vernon* (1970), especially the seminal empirical paper by *Hufbauer* (1970), which has underlain so much later research. Subsequent results are summarised by *Deardorff* (1983). Additional useful references include *Hirsch* (1975), *Walker* (1979), *Aquino* (1981), *Hughes* (1986) and *Greenhalgh* (1990). Early work on economies of scale and international trade includes *Melvin* (1969), *Panagariya* (1980), *Markusen and Melvin* (1981) and *Ethier* (1982, 1983).

Models with imperfect competition are surveyed in *Helpman* (1983) and *Helpman and Krugman* (1985), although neither is easy. In addition to those in the text, other important references are *Dixit and Norman* (1980), *Lancaster* (1980, 1982), *Krugman* (1981) and *Venables* (1984). Accessible introductions include *Greenaway* (1985), and *Greenaway and Milner* (1986). The latter deals with all aspects of IIT including empirical estimates. Among the latter we note additionally to the text *Loertscher and Wolter* (1980) and *Balassa and Bauwens* (1987).

KEY CONCEPTS

imitation gap	product cycle
human capital	external economies of scale
reciprocal dumping	pro-competitive trade
Cournot equilibrium	product differentiation
product characteristics	SITC
intra-industry trade	desire for variety

QUESTIONS FOR REVIEW

5.1 Are trade patterns explained by absolute or relative levels of R&D?

5.2 Does the distinction between external and internal economies of scale matter in predicting trade patterns?

5.3 Distinguish between the two approaches to modelling the demand for variety. Give examples of goods or services appropriate to each.

5.4 How might the similarity of levels of income stimulate trade? Contrast your model with the effects of income similarity in the Heckscher–Ohlin model.

5.5 How does trade theory account for the following data:

		Number ('000)	Value (£m.)
Exports of cars in 1975:	Japan to UK	124.81	112.20
	UK to Japan	1.98	4.39

(*Source*: *Annual Statement of Trade*, vol. IV, 1975)

NOTE

1 Strictly, this is inevitable only if (i) there are very many varieties for which some demand exists, and (ii) the economies of scale arises at least partly from fixed costs associated with producing any single variety.

6 Trade Theory: An Overview

This chapter pulls together the trade theory of the last four chapters. It starts by briefly describing some of the main features of world trade, including international trade in services. This is followed by a section using trade theories to explain these (and other) features, which shows that, while factor endowments are useful in this regard, they are not, by themselves, sufficient. Lastly, the chapter asks why the Heckscher–Ohlin theory has survived so many empirical refutations.

6.1 PATTERNS OF INTERNATIONAL TRADE

The growth of world trade

Before we leave the theory of international trade we should pause briefly to consider the phenomenon itself. Tables 6.1 and 6.2 summarise the commodity and country composition of world trade from 1955 to 1985, the latest year available. The most obvious feature is its huge growth. In part this reflects inflation – prices measured in US dollars have roughly quadrupled since 1950 – but there is also evidently very substantial real growth. The latter stems both from a rapid growth of world output (even allowing for the slump around 1980) and a strong increase in openness – the proportion of a country's output that is traded. The theories of Chapter 5 offer one explanation of why growth and openness increase together, but in truth the changes in Tables 6.1 and 6.2 are probably more readily explained by other phenomena. First, openness was recovering from exceptionally low levels to more normal values. The slump and protectionism of the 1920s and 1930s reduced the share of output traded by 40 per cent and it fell further during the Second World War. It was 1975 before openness regained its level of the beginning of the century. Second, significant reductions in the cost of transport and communication have stimulated trade, as, too, has the rise in the price of oil over the 1970s – industrial countries had to increase exports to pay for higher-priced oil (see Chapter 25 below).

Table 6.1 The composition of world exports, 1955–85

	1955	1960	1965	1970	1975	1980	1985
Total (US$b.)	94.0	128.3	187.2	315.3	876.7	2,012.7	1,929.5
Shares in total (%)							
Food products	21.8	19.4	18.2	14.7	13.2	11.1	10.3
Agricultural raw materials	12.9	10.8	7.8	5.8	3.9	3.8	3.2
Crude metals and minerals	3.7	3.9	3.3	3.4	2.4	2.1	1.7
Fuels	11.0	9.9	9.6	9.3	19.4	24.0	18.4
Manufactures	49.0	54.8	58.5	64.9	59.4	57.3	62.6
of which:							
Chemicals	5.0	5.9	6.5	7.1	7.0	7.4	8.0
Machinery	18.1	21.7	24.6	28.8	28.0	25.6	30.4
Others	25.9	27.2	27.4	29.0	24.4	24.3	24.2
Unclassified	1.6	1.2	2.6	1.9	1.7	1.7	3.8

Source: UNCTAD, *Handbooks on International Trade and Development*.

Table 6.2 The geographical structure of world exports, 1955–85

	1950	1955	1960	1965	1970	1975	1980	1985
Total (US$b.)	60.7	94.0	128.3	187.2	315.2	876.7	2,012.7	1,929.5
Shares in total (%)								
Developed market economies	61.1	64.5	66.8	68.8	71.3	66.0	63.0	65.4
of which:								
USA	16.7	16.4	15.9	14.5	13.7	12.3	11.0	10.6
EC (9)	26.8	30.4	32.6	34.4	35.7	34.0	32.9	31.8
Japan	1.4	2.1	3.2	4.5	6.1	6.4	6.4	9.1
Developing market economies	30.8	25.5	21.5	19.6	17.9	24.3	28.2	24.0
of which:								
Oil exporters	7.2	8.1	7.5	7.1	6.7	14.1	16.9	n.a.
Manufactures exporters	6.9	4.2	3.3	2.9	3.0	3.2	4.2	n.a.
Least developed	1.5	1.3	1.1	0.9	0.7	0.4	0.4	n.a.
Socialist economies	8.1	10.0	11.7	11.6	10.6	9.8	8.8	15.1

n.a. not available.
Source: As for Table 6.1.

Within the general growth there is clearly a stumble between 1980 and 1985. This partly reflects declining trade volumes over 1980–2, but it also arises from a statistical artefact. In 1985 the US dollar was unrealistically overvalued relative to other currencies: thus trade denominated in other currencies was relatively undervalued when converted into dollars for aggregation into a world total. (Part II below will explain these phenomena in more detail.)

Within the detail of the tables, the huge rise in the relative shares of fuels and oil-exporting countries is plain. Fuel trade has increased strongly, but, more important, over the period 1973–87 its price was very high by historical standards: with demand for fuels relatively price inelastic in the medium run, high prices imply high expenditure. In fact, since 1985 oil prices have slumped and, while fuel imports have continued to grow in volume terms, their share of the total imports of industrial countries has fallen from 26 per cent in 1980, through 20 per cent in 1985 and 12 per cent in 1986, to 9 per cent in 1988. Thus the swing in the fuel share in Table 6.1 reflects pricing issues and market power rather than changes in comparative advantage that are the subject of trade theory.

The NICs and the NECs

Putting oil aside, manufactures display the most growth. They have accounted for a steadily rising share of non-fuel trade, with the strongest rises being in sophisticated goods such as chemicals and machinery. The pattern of supply has also changed. As Europe recovered from the war its share increased rapidly, but after 1960 Japan became the most dynamic group, followed by the newly industrialised countries (NICs) in the 1970s and the new exporting countries (NECs) in the 1980s. In all three cases, manufactured exports blossomed as countries followed their comparative advantage, starting with simple labour-intensive goods and gradually evolving into capital- and then knowledge-intensive exports.

The precise set of countries included in the NICs varies from source to source, but certainly South Korea, Taiwan, Hong Kong, Singapore, Spain, Portugal, Yugoslavia and Brazil would be included. They achieved spectacular rates of growth of manufactured exports – for example, 12 per cent per year over 1965–84 – and by 1985 provided about 10 per cent of industrial countries' total manufactured imports. For some commodities and countries the NICs now supply over half of total imports and account for over 10 per cent of total consumption of the good concerned – e.g. textiles and clothing and communication equipment. As they have developed, the NICs have also rapidly upgraded their export bundle: in 1964 textiles and clothing accounted for 18 and 32 per cent of their total manufactured exports, respectively; by 1985 these shares had fallen to 4 and 19 per cent respectively, with office machinery, telecommunications equipment and electrical machinery having expanded from virtually nothing to account for 6, 10 and 11 per cent respectively. On the strength of this export growth – often achieved in the face of significant trade barriers in industrial country markets – the NICs, especially those in the Far East, have experienced very rapid income growth.

The NICs' spectacular growth subsided somewhat over the 1980s. As we have seen, they faced growing competition in simple manufactures and moved on towards the supply of capital- and skill-intensive goods. They were displaced in the growth stakes by the new exporting countries (NECs or second-tier exporters) such as Colombia, Morocco, Thailand and Malaysia. These countries, like Japan and the NICs before them, expanded rapidly by providing cheap labour-intensive manufactures.

The final observation on Tables 6.1 and 6.2 concerns primary commodities and developing countries. Neither the volumes nor the prices of primary commodities were very buoyant over the period 1955–85. We shall discuss this phenomenon further in Chapter 15 below, but note here that it has resulted in rapidly falling shares for primaries and the countries supplying them. The latter include the least-developed group (the world's forty poorest nations) but also middle- and some high-income countries, e.g. Canada, Australia and the USA.

The direction of trade

Table 6.3 shows bilateral trade links in 1988. Our theory is not generally very informative about the direction of trade, but several features are worth noting in this table. First, intra-Western European trade is huge relative to other flows: this reflects the integration of the European economies – the European Community (EC) and the European Free Trade Association (EFTA) – and the high level of intra-industry trade between the relatively small but affluent European economies. Second, the Eastern Trading Bloc trades more with Europe and the developing world than with Japan and the USA; this reflects both geography and politics. Third, Japan is relatively dependent on imports from developing countries; these are imports of primaries, especially oil, rather than of manufactures, although by the end of the 1980s Japanese imports from East Asian developing countries had become quite large. Fourth, Japan trades

Table 6.3 The direction of merchandise trade, 1988 (US$b.)

			Importer		
Exporter	North America	Japan	Western Europe	Developing countries	Eastern Trading Bloc
North America	151	45	99	116	12
Japan	97	—	57	85	14
Western Europe	113	25	906	149	47
Developing countries	166	72	138	143	39
Eastern Trading Bloc	7	11	56	49	145

Source: Gatt, *International Trade 88–89*.

more heavily with North America than with Western Europe, while Western European trade is slightly biased towards the developing world. Fifth, Japan has surpluses with every trading bloc, but especially with North America; 1988 was not, then, an equilibrium year, for equilibrium would require each bloc to be in overall balance.

Services

Tables 6.1–6.3 refer only to international trade in goods – visible or merchandise trade – but trade in services is also important. The service accounts of the balance of payments – the only comprehensive source of data on service trade – include investment income (essentially factor payments for capital), transfers, official transactions and commercial services.[1] They include: the shipment of goods, passenger services, port services, travel and other private services, including labour income earned abroad by temporary migrants, royalties, licence fees, brokerage and consultancy fees, etc. Service trade has grown strongly since 1970, but expecially 'other private services' – see Table 6.4. Commercial services exports are roughly one-quarter the size of total merchandise exports. There is no reason why countries should have balanced service accounts – and they do not, as Table 6.5 shows. Among the 'big six', Germany and Japan are major net importers and France and the UK major exporters.

Table 6.4 World exports of commercial services, 1970 and 1987

| | Value (US$b.) | | Share in exports of commercial services (%) | |
	1970	1987	1970	1987
Shipment	14	66	22	13
Passenger services	3	30	5	6
Port services	8	57	13	11
Travel	18	150	29	30
Other private services and income	20	201	31	40
Commercial services	64	505	100	100

Source: GATT, International Trade 88–89.

Table 6.5 The major traders of commercial services, 1987 ($USb.)

	Exports	Imports
USA	56	56
France	53	43
UK	43	33
West Germany	41	64
Italy	33	26
Japan	28	52

Source: GATT, International Trade 88–89.

6.2 CAN TRADE THEORY EXPLAIN TRADE PATTERNS?

Explaining
trade in goods

The previous section noted some of the major features of world trade. The crucial question is whether theory is useful in explaining them. We have four broad theories of the pattern of international trade: three based on supply conditions – the Ricardian, Heckscher–Ohlin and technology theories – and one on demand. They clearly have different implications, and so we should briefly try to reconcile them. Two approaches are possible.

First, we could seek a general theory for all trade either based on a combination of the theories, or using just the one that best fits the evidence. This is an empirical question, and it underlies several of the regression studies mentioned in Chapter 4. Leamer (1974) distinguished three groups of variables determining trade performance:

- 'state of development' variables – GDP and population;
- 'resistance' variables – tariffs, distance from markets; and
- 'resource' variables – capital intensity, R&D, education levels and electricity use (a proxy for industrial sophistication).

Using a sample of many countries and industries, he found that trade dependence (the ratio of imports to GDP) is best explained by the development variables, with resource explanations coming a poor third. This, of course, refers to the amount of trade and not its composition, but it lends support to the economies of scale/Linder approach to trade. Among the (insignificant) resource effects, R&D coupled with the factor-intensity variables perform best. Looking at net exports, however, resources (especially R&D) become the predominant factor. These results tend to suggest a role for both traditional and modern approaches. Hirsch (1975) and Aquino (1981) reached similar conclusions. Leamer (1984), on the other hand, suggested a strong role for factor endowments (see case-study 6.1).

The second approach is more catholic. It recognises the strengths of each theory within its own sphere of influence, allowing each to explain the direction of trade of certain goods. This is potentially fruitful provided two puzzles are solved: first, how are goods allocated to theories – intuition is probably sufficient in most cases; and, second, which theories dominate in cases of conflict – this is largely unresolved, but we return to it below.

Following Hufbauer (1970) and Hirsch (1974) we might identify three classes of goods – each with a different source of comparative advantage:

- *Ricardo* goods are allocated over countries on the basis of production conditions. They include natural resource industries – oil, coal, wheat, – and simple processing industries based on materials – e.g. food processing and non-ferrous metal refining. Comparative advantage generally lies with developing countries because they are at less disadvantage in this sphere than in other types of trade.
- *Heckscher-Ohlin* goods comprise mainly 'foot-loose' manufactures. These have well-established technologies and no essential specific factors; they are free to migrate around the world in search of ideal factor endowments. Examples include: textiles, ferrous metals and building materials. Comparative advantage goes with factor endowments, as we saw in Chapter 3, and we may expect such trade to be relatively important between developing and developed countries.
- *Technological goods* emanate from the most developed nations. Their production is characterized by sophisticated, rapidly developing, non-transferable technologies, and, in the product cycle view, by proximity to large and affluent markets. Obvious examples include aircraft and computers. In some cases they will mature into Heckscher–Ohlin goods, but some are likely to remain constantly in this category.

74

CASE-STUDY 6.1: COMPARATIVE ADVANTAGE IN MANUFACTURES

One of the most comprehensive studies of the relationship between factor endowments and international trade is by Leamer (1984). It is based on the Heckscher–Ohlin theory but tests a broader and looser model: in particular Leamer includes many natural resource 'factors' and does not explicitly consider the factor intensities of different industries. On the other hand, he does exploit the H–O prediction that both countries' net exports of particular goods and their levels of income will be linearly related to their factor endowments.

Leamer tests this model on data from sixty countries (twenty industrial, forty developing) referring approximately to 1958 and 1975, distinguishing ten aggregates of goods and eleven of factors. Six of the goods are resource-based, and are explained by the presence of the corresponding resources. Four, however, refer to manufactures. In order of increasing sophistication, they are:

labour-intensive goods,
capital-intensive goods,
machinery, and
chemicals.

The eleven factor groups are:

1	Capital	7	Humid-climate land (A) e.g. California
2	Professional or technical workers		
3	Literate non-professional workers	8	Humid-climate land (B) e.g. Michigan
4	Illiterate workers		
5	Tropical land	9	Coal
6	Dry-climate land	10	Minerals
		11	Oil

As Leamer notes, most of us would expect the first three or four to provide the principal positive contributions to comparative advantage in manufacturing goods.

The pattern of manufactured trade in 1975 is shown in Table 6.6. Leamer refers to this as a ladder of development; only the 'rogue' exporter of chemicals – Jamaica – appears to belie this interpretation, and she turns out to be exporting very simple chemicals. Moreover, the transition between 1958 and 1975 (not shown here) also supports a developmental interpretation – there is a general drift up the table, with notable jumps for the larger industrial countries and some of the NICs. Thus it appears that comparative advantage is explained not only by random factor endowments but by the evolution of endowments during the process of development. Physical and human capital accumulation are the most obvious signs of such evolution.

Leamer's linear model can explain quite a large proportion of the inter-country variance of net exports for each good. However, the likely errors of observation are so severe that the data alone cannot distinguish adequately between alternative hypotheses without being supplemented by prior information. Combining the two sources of information yields the set of explanations given in Table 6.7.

In 1958 the major net exporters of labour-intensive manufactures were the industrial countries, including the USA and Germany, but subsequently a

Table 6.6 Patterns of manufacturing trade, 1975 (sign of net exports of manufactured aggregates; + denotes exports exceed imports)

Aggregates[a]				Countries[b]
7	8	9	10	
−	−	−	+	Netherlands
−	−	+	+	Switzerland, United States*
−	+	+	+	Germany*, United Kingdom*
−	−	+	−	Sweden*
+	+	+	+	France, Japan*
+	+	−	+	Belgium–Luxembourg
+	+	+	−	Italy
+	+	−	−	Austria, India, Korea*, Spain*
+	−	−	−	Brazil*, Columbia*, Cyprus*, Denmark, Egypt*, Finland*, Greece*, Hong Kong, Israel, Malta*, Philippines, Portugal, Sierra Leone,[c] Thailand*, Turkey*, Yugoslavia
−	−	−	−	Afghanistan,[c] Argentina, Australia, Brunei,[c] Burma,[c] Canada, Chile*[c], Costa Rica, Dominican Republic, Ecuador,[c] El Salvador,[c] Ghana, Honduras, Iceland, Indonesia, Ireland, Libya, Malaysia, Mauritius,[c] Mexico*[c], New Zealand, Nigeria, Norway, Panama, Paraguay*, Peru, Singapore, Sri Lanka
−	−	−	+	Jamaica

Notes:
[a] The aggregates are defined as follows:
   7 Labour-intensive manufactures
   8 Capital-intensive manufactures
   9 Machinery
  10 Chemicals.
[b] Asterisk indicates a shift up the table since 1958.
[c] Based on 1972 data.
Source: Leamer (1984).

Table 6.7 The main factors explaining countries' net trade in manufactures

	Main explanatory factors	
	Main positive effects	Main negative effects
	1958	
Labour-intensive manufactures	Professional labour, literate labour, illiterate labour	Capital, illiterate labour, 'Michigan', oil
Capital-intensive manufactures	Professional labour, literate labour	Capital, illiterate labour, 'Michigan', oil
Machinery	Professional labour, coal	Capital, literate labour, illiterate labour, 'Michigan'
Chemicals	Capital, professional labour, coal	Literate labour, oil
	1975	
Labour-intensive manufactures	Literate labour	Professional labour, oil
Capital-intensive manufactures	Literate labour, illiterate labour, capital	Professional labour, oil
Machinery	Capital	Professional labour, oil
Chemicals	Capital, professional labour	Literate labour 'California', oil

Source: Leamer (1984).

mixture of NICs and poorer industrial countries took over (Italy, Hong Kong, Korea, Japan and Spain being the top five). These changes indicate changes in the sources of comparative advantage. An interesting shift is that of professional labour from having a mildly positive influence on exports of labour-intensive goods in 1958 to having a negative one in 1975. This probably relates to the rise of the NICs and the NECs, and the possibility that multinational companies can split research and production activities geographically. The most consistent results on labour-intensive goods are the importance of skilled labour and the disadvantages implied by oil and 'Michigan-type' land. Capital-intensive manufactures are much more the province of the established industrial countries, although Korea, one of the NICs, was the fourth largest net exporter relative to GDP in 1975. The notable factors behind this trade are the positive role of skilled labour in both years and the reversal of the importance of physical capital (capital) and human capital (professional labour) between 1958 and 1975. Whereas in 1958 knowledge appeared to matter, by 1975 the critical factor was physical equipment, human capital having led countries off in other directions. This shift could again reflect the role of the multinationals, and also the rapid accumulation of capital in the NICs where it can substitute for human capital.

Net trade in machinery shows a similar set of determinants to capital-intensive goods, except for a surprising positive link with coal in 1958. Chemicals net exports are also associated with the presence of coal but in addition show links with capital and professional labour, which stimulate exports, and with literate labour and oil, which curtail them. This pattern is consistent with chemicals being the most sophisticated of the goods aggregates. Both machinery and chemical net exports are dominated by the established industrial countries, and both are reasonably well explained by the simple linear model.

Overall Leamer's study suggests that, whereas in 1958 highly skilled (professional) labour was the predominant factor inducing net exports of manufactures, by 1975 it had been displaced by capital and skilled (literate) labour, in all cases except chemicals. The study also suggests that, while we need to relax the strict Heckscher–Ohlin model, the factor endowments approach to comparative advantage can explain much of the pattern of international trade in manufactures. Moreover its predictions seem quite plausible, for it appears consistent with a ladder of development, it can cope with the emergence of the NICs, and it can explain the shifting importance of different industrial countries.

Within the last two categories we might also distinguish sub-groups of goods where product variety is particularly important, and thus where intra-industry trade may be expected. Motor vehicles would be a Heckscher-Ohlin example of this, and photographic equipment a technological-trade example.

Table 6.8 classifies various countries' trade into these groups. It illustrates industrial countries' comparative advantage in technological products and developing countries' advantage in Ricardian goods. The Heckscher–Ohlin category is equally represented in both groups' trade, and in UK exports and imports, but of course, within the category, labour- and capital-intensive goods will figure differently. In the UK case, at least, exports and imports appear to be roughly equal in the 'variety' sub-categories.

Table 6.8 Patterns of trade, 1980 (%[a])

Region	Ricardo goods	Class of goods[b] Heckscher–Ohlin goods		Technological goods	
		Standard	Differentiated	Standard	Differentiated
World exports	39	22	8	22	3
Industrial countries' exports	23	24	12	31	4
Developing countries' exports	60	25	1	7	1
UK exports	25	22	8	34	5
UK imports	41	21	8	24	4

Notes:
[a] Percentages do not sum to 100 because certain categories of trade are excluded from the classification.
[b] Classification derived from Hufbauer and Chilas (1974).
Source: World Bank Trade System.

Hirsch (1974) conducted a similar analysis on a country level. For 1968–71 he found the USA very strong in technology goods (even labour-intensive ones), and fairly strong in Ricardian goods; the EC weak in Ricardian goods but moderately strong in the others; and Japan very weak in Ricardian goods but very strong in Heckscher–Ohlin goods. Evidence since then in Heller (1976) and Katrak (1982) suggests that Japan is moving into technological goods while Britain is, relatively, moving out of them into capital-intensive Heckscher–Ohlin goods.

An interesting contrast to these results is found in Hufbauer and Chilas (1974). They examined inter-regional trade and specialisation within the USA, which, they argued, is similar to world trade but without any artificial barriers. There they found Heckscher–Ohlin specialisation the greatest; they argued that this is not repeated in world trade because trade barriers have been erected especially to avoid the rigours of free inter-industry trade.

Services again

Services have again been left until last. In general we would expect exactly the same set of factors to determine service trade as goods trade. For example, in shipping and aviation one country may provide services to another quite independently of the ownership of the goods transported. Shipping exports probably require cheap labour most of all; capital is very mobile and so does not really influence the national ownership of production facilities. In financial services, technological and scale-economy factors are important and so the imperfectly competitive models become useful. Tourism could fall into any category: Ricardian if people travel for ski-ing, beaches, etc.; Heckscher–Ohlin if the attractions are based on levels of personal service; and technological if visitors seek specialist conference centres or skills like theatre or concerts. Some confirmation of these views may be found in Sapir and Lutz (1981).

While services respond briefly to comparative advantage there are, however, potential complications in defining advantage. For example, suppose that a management-abundant country, A, provides managers to country B, which produces a management-intensive good for export to A. B, the less management-abundant country, appears to be violating Heckscher–Ohlin, but in fact what is happening is that A is exporting its abundant factor directly in return for goods. (See Melvin, 1989.) Similarly, problems of asymmetric information – the fact that buyers cannot ascertain the quality of a service (e.g. the security of their deposits in a bank) – can pull trade patterns away from a simple comparative costs pattern.

The persistence of Heckscher–Ohlin

Science proceeds by refutation. Theories make assumptions and develop from them logically necessary predictions. If these predictions are correct, the theory is not proven, because there may have been other causes; if they are wrong, however, the theory is refuted, because if the conclusion must follow from the assumptions, the absence of the conclusion must indicate the inapplicability of at least one assumption. Obviously one does not throw away theories after just one refutation, but one might ask why, after so many refutations (see especially section 4.2), Heckscher–Ohlin will not lie down and die.

First, H–O has a great intuitive appeal: 'surely', its proponents say, 'trade must tend to make use of "surplus" factors, and import the fruits of scarce ones. Hence, even if we cannot go all the way to Samuelson's factor-price equalisation, there must be some tendency towards it.'

Second, H–O is magnificently powerful; it is one of the most powerful theories of all economics. With 'a few assumptions' it takes us from observations of factor endowments, through to the structure of production and trade, factor prices, commodity prices, the effects of factor growth, and the distribution of income. Compare this with the limited scope of the other theories. H–O thus provides a much more fertile field for exploring the effects of tariffs, etc.

Third, if we wish to have a general theory of trade (as opposed to several), H–O is still a good candidate, at least if we admit human capital, as for example Leamer (1984) and Baldwin (1971) have shown. Certainly the product cycle and Ricardian approaches seem no stronger as *universal* theories.

Fourth, there is continuing argument about the validity of the refutations. We saw in section 4.2 that the most likely explanations of Leontief's paradox did not strike at the very heart of H–O. Moreover, proponents have argued that existing tests are so distorted by trade barriers, changing conditions and imperfect information that they do not constitute a fair test of a static theory of free trade. Deardorff (1982) has dismissed the first of these complaints, and the last two amount to complaining that 'the world doesn't fit our theory'. Change and imperfections are a fact of life and, if a theory cannot function, even as a broad tendency, in their presence, one can question its worth.

The fifth reason for H–O's survival concerns economics in general. Neo-classical general equilibrium economics concentrates on the question of efficient allocation in a static framework with basically free markets. H–O fits happily into this framework, so it benefits from being part of a larger 'research programme', receiving results from elsewhere in the programme and proceeding within a received framework. This framework defines the 'permissible' questions and, by precluding awkward questions, speeds progress on less awkward ones. For instance, it is entirely within the mainstream to try to extend the dimensionality of H–O, but not to question whether it makes sense to aggregate capital into a single unit. Hence H–O is really the international trade manifestation of a broader programme, and lives and dies with that programme. What factors control the growth of programmes is a complex and contentious issue, but one cannot help observing that neo-classical economic theory runs very close to the West's prevailing political orthodoxy.

Where does all this leave us? Heckscher–Ohlin is a useful tool for international economists, and it provides considerable insight into the workings of market economies. It should, however, be handled with care. It does not directly explain much of the world around us and it is not applicable

79

to all components of trade. Hence, although we shall make some use of it below, we should beware of taking its predictions too literally or of being drawn into the minutiae of what is at best only a broad brush approximation to the real world.

FURTHER READING

Trade patterns are best explored directly in the statistical sources, e.g. UNCTAD's *Handbooks in International Trade and Development* and GATT's *International Trade* annuals. The latter offer a commentary, which for 1988/9 included material on services. Useful summary discussions include *Winters* (1984a, 1989a) and *OECD* (1987a). The particularities of service trade are discussed in *Hindley and Smith* (1984) and *Ryan* (1988). The link between trade theory and fact is best made by the text references – especially *Hirsch* (1974) and *Leamer* (1984). *Blaug* (1980) and *de Marchi* (1976) consider the persistence of Heckscher–Ohlin.

KEY CONCEPTS

openness	valuation of trade in dollars
NICs and NECs	ladder of development
Ricardo goods	Heckscher–Ohlin goods
technology goods	

QUESTIONS FOR REVIEW

6.1 How does one explain the growing openness of the world economy?

6.2 What arguments can be adduced for there being a ladder of development or series of stages of comparative advantage through which nearly all countries pass?

6.3 Is it useful to distinguish between Ricardo, Heckscher–Ohlin and technology goods? Why? Contrast the classification in this chapter with that in OECD (1987a, Chapter 7).

6.4 Are there *practical* alternatives to Heckscher–Ohlin? What are their advantages and disadvantages?

NOTE

1 Balance of payments accounts are discussed in Chapter 17 below.

7 International Trade and Welfare

The previous chapters dealt with the causes of international trade, and also touched briefly upon its consequences for welfare: because trade increased the set of consumption possibilities, it was held to be beneficial. This chapter formalises this argument a little further. It considers the conditions that must be met to ensure beneficial trade and introduces some tools for the analysis of economic welfare. These tools include community indifference curves – which summarise society's preferences – and the general theory of second best – which cautions us against applying our simple models to the real world too glibly. These are issues of *normative* or *prescriptive* economics, rather than of positive analysis such as has occupied us so far.

The results of this chapter are put to use in the next seven chapters as we examine the impact of commercial policy. For centuries economists have been asked whether protecting domestic industry from foreign competition is economically advantageous. Chapters 8 and 9 introduce the simple analysis of tariffs and non-tariff barriers respectively, while Chapters 10 and 11 further develop the welfare implications of protection. Chapter 12 considers the political economy of protection – why and how protection is introduced – and, finally, Chapters 13 and 14 look at the economics of customs unions such as the European Economic Community.

7.1 THE CASE FOR FREE TRADE

We saw above how free trade (trade with no impediments) enlarged the feasible consumption set for a community; from that, we concluded that free trade was beneficial. The gains from trade contained both a *production* component – which increased world output through greater specialisation – and a *consumption* component – which arose because consumption and production points could differ. For a single country (say, Britain in Figure 3.1), trade changes production in order to maximise the value of output at world prices (at prices $T'T'$, L represents the maximum value of any production combination). Consumption changes in order to take advantage of the new relative prices offered by trade (with budget-line $T'T'$, B maximises utility). We now briefly re-examine the assumptions underlying this argument.

Production Consider the maximisation of the value of output. The mechanism presupposed perfect competition (very many small producers) and perfect information. Each producer took the price (P_i) he faced as exogenously given – nothing he could do individually could affect the price – and maximised his profits by producing at a level where marginal costs (MC) equalled price. Since for each good $P_i = MC_i (i = X, Y)$, overall we have

$$P = \frac{P_X}{P_Y} = \frac{MC_X}{MC_Y} = MRT \tag{7.1}$$

where P is the relative price of X in terms of Y and MRT the marginal rate of

81

transformation of Y into X. This is the condition from section 2.1 for maximising the value of output.

There are two areas where this chain might break down. First, the costs faced by producers may not accurately reflect the costs faced by society. This may be because of ignorance (producers do not know their own costs accurately) or taxes and subsidies on factors of production. It may also be because of *externalities* – costs or benefits that one economic activity imposes on another, other than via the price mechanism. For instance, cloth production may involve pumping soot into the atmosphere, the costs of which fall on everyone, not just cloth producers. Hence the social *MC* of cloth will exceed private *MC* and private decisions will not ensure that (7.1) holds for social costs. A positive externality might be that, in producing food, farmers cultivate the countryside in a way that pleases the community at large by providing pleasant country walks. In this case private *MC* exceeds social *MC*.

The second possible break-down concerns the failure of price to equal marginal costs. The most obvious example is of a *monopoly* that exploits its market power by restricting output so that marginal revenue (which is below price) equals marginal costs. Second, taxes on output drive a wedge between price and marginal costs. Third, in increasing returns industries, marginal costs are below average costs (*AC*) because each additional unit reduces the cost of all previous units. Hence $P = MC$ will not cover costs, so, unless the government supports such firms, the market must set $P \geqslant AC > MC$.

If free trade is to maximise the value of output, none of these problems, which are known as *distortions*, must arise: a fairly tall order for the real world.

All this analysis assumes that firms carefully and informedly minimise costs. It is often suggested, however, that in the absence of foreign competition firms become lazy and do not actually operate on their production frontiers. This seems particularly likely for monopolists, and has been called *X-inefficiency* by Leibenstein (1966). In this case, opening free trade will raise the value of output not only through specialisation, but also by pushing production out onto the transformation curve. This 'salutary jolt' was frequently advanced as a reason for Britain joining the EEC, and for the completion of the European internal market in 1992.

Consumption

A similar set of arguments applies to consumption. Taking prices as given, consumers consume until their marginal utility from a good is proportional to its price, with the same factor or proportionality for each good. Hence

$$P = \frac{P_X}{P_Y} = \frac{MU_X}{MU_Y} = MRS \qquad (7.2)$$

where *MRS* is the marginal rate of substitution. We saw in Chapter 2 how (7.2) maximised welfare for an individual. Just as before, externalities can separate private and social utility, and taxes and monopsony (market power for buyers) can separate prices and marginal utilities.

A further benefit of free trade concerns variability. International trade breaks the dependence of consumption on local production. Hence, if food output is variable – because the weather varies – one can compensate somewhat by importing in times of shortage and exporting in times of plenty. Clearly one cannot avoid all the consequences of output fluctuations, because income fluctuates with output, but some smoothing is possible. This assumes, of course, that world output does not fluctuate as much as domestic output, but this seems reasonable given that for most commodities the world comprises many producers operating under varying conditions. It is improbable that all will, say, suffer drought at the same time.

This sort of 'smoothing trade' represents a rescheduling of food consumption relative to production. Trade provides the means both of swapping cloth for food, and thus of spreading a shortfall of food over the whole basket of consumption, and also of converting food today into food tomorrow, so that shortfalls may be spread out over a number of years. All that is required for the latter is that countries be able to have an excess of imports over exports in some periods and the opposite in others; that is, the trade can be temporarily unbalanced. Although most of our pure theory in Part I of this book concerns balanced trade, this ability to reschedule consumption should not be ignored as a source of gain.

Pareto efficiency

So far we have not asked in what sense – if any – free trade maximises world welfare. It seems obvious enough from Figure 3.1, but that case is restricted by having identical tastes in both countries. We therefore now consider a broader case and show that free trade (under all the foregoing assumptions) is *Pareto optimal*. A division of welfare between countries is Pareto optimal if one country can be made better off only by making at least one other worse off. In other words: there is no way of making every country better off, or of raising one's welfare, holding all the others' constant. This is clearly agnostic on the question of distribution; writing W_i for i's welfare ($W_A = 60$, $W_B = 60$) and ($W_A = 1$, $W_B = 119$) could both be Pareto optimal distributions. However, it does seem to provide a reasonable *minimum* condition for the allocation of income to maximise world welfare.

The necessary conditions for Pareto optimality between countries are easily established. First, no rearrangement of production among countries must be able to produce more of one good without resulting in less of the other. Otherwise, additional output could be 'freely' produced, potentially raising every country's welfare. As we saw in section 3.1, this entails the equality of MRTs across countries. (If Britain's MRT were $3Y:2X$ and America's $3Y:1X$, we could increase X-output by letting America produce 1 unit less and letting Britain convert the resulting $3Y$ into $2X$. The only limit to this is that both countries produce both goods.) Similarly with consumption: assuming each country has a national welfare function (see section 7.2 below), output can only be optimally allocated if the MRSs for each country are identical. (Check this by an analogy to the production case.) Finally, again as we saw above, these (common) MRSs and MRTs must be equal.

Free trade is able to meet these conditions simply, because under utility and profit maximisation MRSs and MRTs are set equal to the price ratio, and with free trade there is just one world price ratio. Hence free trade is Pareto optimal: no country could be made better off under free trade without some other country suffering. Note, however, that this says nothing about the distribution of welfare between countries, and neither does it imply that free trade is necessarily optimal for any single country. The latter is the subject of the next few chapters.

A *Pareto improvement* is any change that benefits one party without harming any other. From the definition of optimality, it is always possible to make a Pareto improvement from any point that is not Pareto optimal.

Uncertainty

The introduction of uncertainty changes many aspects of economic theory, and trade theory is no exception. The last but one subsection noted the smoothing properties of trade but implicitly only under conditions in which future fluctuations were known. Under uncertainty, trade could conceivably be harmful, as the following highly simplfied example shows.

Imagine two countries each of which has an industry – manufacturing – whose output is certain, and another – fishing – with uncertain yields. Suppose that both countries fish the same seas, which yield a fixed crop of fish, so that if country A has a good year country B has a correspondingly bad one. Assume also that utility functions are such that each year consumers in each country spend fixed sums on manufactures and on fish. This ensures that, if there is no trade, fishermen in each country have perfect income stability, because any shortfall in fish supplies in their country is off-set by a price increase of the same proportion. If the two countries trade, however, the world price of fish is constant because world supply is fixed and demands are constant. This makes fishermen's incomes variable, which makes them worse off and may cause some of them to leave the industry. The exodus raises the price of fish. Thus consumers face two off-setting effects when trade is opened: they are better off because they no longer face fluctuating fish prices, but are worse off because the average price of fish has risen. If the latter effect dominates, trade is Pareto inferior to autarky because both producers and consumers are made worse off.

The crucial element of this story is the incompleteness of markets: fishermen are not able to insure themselves against output and price fluctuations. Under autarky, the special assumption about consumption allows the fish market to double as an insurance market because incomes are guaranteed, but when trade occurs it is as if a previously existing insurance market had been closed. The loss of this implicit market can dominate the benefits of international trade.

This example – due to Newbery and Stiglitz (1984) – warns us that we must be careful of drawing welfare conclusions in circumstances where full insurance markets do not exist. However, in many cases – for example, when equity in firms is internationally traded – substitutes may be found for insurance markets, hence rehabilitating our basic results; in many other cases the complications are genuine, but the imperfections due to missing markets are small enough to ignore. Moreover, the difficulties that missing insurance markets cause with unrestricted trade are often just as bad when trade is restricted. Hence the practial importance of the Newbery–Stiglitz results should not be overstated.

7.2   COMMUNITY INDIFFERENCE AND SOCIAL WELFARE

Identical preferences

So far we have assumed that all members of a community have identical and homothetic utility functions. Homotheticity implies that the shares of different goods in consumption expenditure are determined only by relative prices and not by income; thus, as income changes (holding prices constant), expenditure on each good changes by the same proportion. Now, since everyone in the country faces the same prices, they all consume goods in the same proportion. Total consumption of each good is, therefore, just its proportion times total expenditure. Under these circumstances we can combine individual preferences into a single set of *community indifference curves* that summarises the choices society will make between goods when faced with any (social) consumption set. These are drawn with goods on the axes, and will look just like an individual's indifference curves; in particular, they will not intersect.

Such community indifference curves will not, however, tell us how well off each member of society is. Shifting £100 from man A to man B leaves society at the same point on the same indifference curve because, by assumption, A and B will spend the £100 identically. (This is the reason that the aggregation is possible.) Thus, while international trade may be socially desirable, it need not necessarily benefit every member of society. With the present assumptions, however, we know that if trade puts society onto a higher community indifference curve, everybody *could* be made better off if income were suitably redistributed. (For example, give each person the same proportion of national income before and after trade.) Hence trade is *potentially* Pareto improving and is actually Pareto improving if the redistributions are made. Of course, redistribution has to be done in such a way as to maintain the crucial equalities $MRT = P = MRS$, which rules out commodity and factor taxes, and also, if we consider the trade-off between work and leisure, income taxes. (Income tax reduces the return to working – money – relative top leisure – watching TV, say.) This leaves us with so-called 'lump-sum taxes', which shift income between individuals independently of how they earn or spend it. These, of course, are virtually unknown in the real world and they are a slender reed on which to proclaim the optimality of free trade. None the less, that is what economists tend to do.[1]

Differing preferences

Now suppose that preferences differ between individuals: community indifference curves can still be drawn, but they may intersect. The reason is that society's 'preferences', as exhibited in its behaviour, reflect the distribution of income. If people who like claret receive most of the national income, claret is 'highly valued' by society in the sense that, at any price ratio, relatively much will be bought. On the other hand, if beer drinkers receive most income, claret will be relatively less highly valued. Given a particular endowment of beer and claret, more beer is required to compensate for the loss of one bottle of claret under the first distribution of income than under the second. At that point, the slopes of the two community indifference curves differ, and so they intersect.

Intersecting indifference curves make welfare comparisons virtually impossible. Preferring A to B on one set of curves is quite consistent with preferring B to A on another. (Try this in a diagram yourself.) Since opening trade shifts the distribution of income, it is possible that, whereas opening trade looks beneficial with pre-trade distribution, autarky looks preferable with post-trade distribution. This arises because some people gain from trade while other lose. However, it may be proved that (under all the assumptions of section 7.1) free trade is *potentially* preferable to autarky in the sense that there is some distribution of income under free trade that leaves everyone at least as well off as under autarky (Samuelson, 1962). This is because free trade allows society to reach a point where more of *every* good is available than under autarky (see Figure 3.1). Then everyone can be made better off regardless of preferences, for they can be offered their autarky bundle plus something extra. Society may not actually choose such a point in the absence of government intervention, but its existence is sufficient to show that trade could be beneficial. (In normative economics, the ability to get more of every good is frequently used as the sufficient criterion for defining a potentially beneficial change.)

The social welfare function

We have shown that free trade is potentially Pareto improving, and can always be made actually so by the requisite redistribution. If we stick rigidly to Pareto criteria, we can recommend free trade only if that redistribution is made. This is too restrictive, however, because such redistribution is rare, and yet countries constantly make economic decisions on trade vs. autarky. They do so by means of their governments' views about income distribution, and, provided these views are stable, we can use them to choose, as it were, between different families of community indifference curves. Either we can assume that the government always acts to keep income distribution in its favoured form and hence that only one family of community indifference curves ever applies, or we can assume that it evaluates all individuals' baskets of consumption in terms of a single *social welfare function* that uniquely orders all possible outcomes. The social welfare function reflects both efficiency – for example, to maximise welfare everybody's MRSs must be the same – and distribution – for example, more equality is preferable to less. Stringent conditions must be satisfied if the social welfare function is to be 'well behaved' and reflect individual welfare (by well-behaved we mean that it behaves like an individual utility function). It nevertheless provides the best, albeit inadequate, means of representing the collective welfare judgements that are necessary for normative trade theory. Henceforth we shall normally assume that each country has a well-behaved social welfare function and that societies, through their governments, act to maximise this.

Revealed preference

An alternative approach to the welfare effects of trade is based on Samuelson's theory of revealed preference. If a consumer chooses bundle M when bundle N is also available, he reveals that he prefers M to N. Hence if we observe that, at some set of prices, this consumer chooses N, we know that M must be infeasible – that is, M must cost more than N at that set of prices. Continuing this argument, any *voluntary* change in the quantities consumed which increases the value of consumption at an initial set of prices is potentially welfare improving, because the original bundle was available but was rejected in favour of a new one. A corollary on the production side of the economy is that, given factor endowments, the bundle of goods produced at a particular set of goods and factor prices must be at least as valuable as any other feasible bundle of goods. Total factor payments are the same for all bundles because both endowments and factor prices are the same; hence profits are maximised by maximising the value of output.

These two relationships are frequently encountered in normative trade theory and we illustrate them with a simple proof of the benefits of free trade based on Smith (1982). Writing p_i for the price of good i, w_j for the wage of factor j, v_j for the economy's stock of factor j, and x_i for the output of good i chosen at prices p_i and v_j, the producers' corollary above tells us that

$$\sum_i p_i x_i^0 - \sum_j w_j v_j \leq \sum_i p_i x_i - \sum_j w_j v_j = 0, \tag{7.3}$$

where x_i is the chosen output of i and x_i^0 some other output. The optimal output vector at prices p_i and w_j yields zero profits if we assume perfect competition – hence the last equality. Balanced trade at given world prices, π_i, means that net imports, z_i, must satisfy

$$\sum_i \pi_i z_i = 0. \tag{7.4}$$

The value of demand and supply must be equal in any feasible equilibrium, and so, with c_i as consumption of i $(c_i = x_i + z_i)$,

$$\sum p_i \, c_i = \sum p_i \, x_i + \sum p_i \, z_i$$
$$= \sum w_j \, v_j + \sum \pi_i \, z_i + \sum \tau_i \, z_i$$
$$= \sum w_j \, v_j + \sum \tau_i \, z_i, \tag{7.5}$$

where τ is the difference between local prices (p_i) and world prices (π_i).

The steps of (7.5) may be repeated for any other feasible output combination denoted by superscript ^{0}:

$$\sum p_i \, c_i^0 = \sum p_i \, x_i^0 + \sum p_i \, z_i^0$$
$$\leqslant \sum w_j \, v_j + \sum \tau_i \, z_i^0 \tag{7.6}$$

where the value of trade has been decomposed as before and the inequality arises from the left-hand side of (7.3). Now let ^{0} denote autarky, so that all $z_i^0 \equiv 0$ by definition, and let the basic (unsuperscripted) situation represent free trade, so that all $\tau_i = 0$. Subtracting (7.5) from (7.6) yields

$$\sum p_i \, c_i^0 \leqslant \sum p_i \, c_i. \tag{7.7}$$

This tells us that at free trade prices the economy *could* generate the autarky consumption bundle c_i^0, because it costs less than the bundle actually chosen. However, since c_i^0 is not chosen, we conclude that the free trade bundle is preferred. This conclusion accords with the results given in Chapters 2 and 3 above, but we repeat it here to illustrate an important method of analysis.

7.3 SECOND BEST

Some people – for reasons entirely beyond the author's ken – enjoy drinking tomato juice with Worcester sauce and a glacé cherry. If they find, however, that one day no tomato juice is available, we would not expect them to drink just Worcester sauce with a cherry! So it is in economics. If conditions x, y and z must be satisfied to obtain full optimality, it does not follow that, given the absence of x, achieving y and z will still take us closest to optimality. This conclusion is known as the general theory of second best.

Consider the argument of free trade in section 7.1. The *first-best* solution (the full optimum) involved having no externalities, taxes or monopoly. But suppose there were an externality leading to the over-production of good X. The *second-best* solution, assuming that the externality could not be removed, would, fairly obviously, be to impose a tax on X to cut its production back a little. Another example concerns establishing free trade areas between a few nations. Suppose country A's imports from a low-cost producer, B, face tariffs, whereas those from a high-cost source, C, face none, and that consequently A imports only from C. First best would be to abolish all tariffs, but, if that were impossible, a uniform tariff on all imports might be preferable to the supposed situation, for it would allow A to benefit from B's comparative advantage, which had previously been hidden by the tariff.

Observe carefully that we say 'might'. Second best merely states that achieving $(n-1)$ of the optimality conditions *may not* be the best possible position in the absence of the nth. Nor does it state that, in the absence of one optimality condition, we cannot rank positions with respect to the remainder; in general we can (see especially Chapter 10). It merely says that we must examine each case on its merits, and not necessarily expect one optimality condition to be unaffected by the failure of another.

Given the obvious prevalence of distortions and market imperfections in the real world, one might ask why so much attention is paid to the conditions of the first-best position of free trade. First, free trade is the easiest case to analyse and it provides a useful theoretical benchmark. Second, and less important, it provides, given its assumptions, an ideal – a clear position relative to which everything else is second best. Third, the existence of distortions does not automatically invalidate the free-trade prescriptions. We still have to identify the areas where policy will actually be beneficial in countering unavoidable distortions, and then to administer it efficiently. Thus, free trade may, in fact, prove quite a robust policy prescription for an open economy.

FURTHER READING

The best introduction to the welfare analysis of trade is *Findlay* (1970a, chs 2 and 6), who builds on *Samuelson*'s (1962) classic paper. *Bhagwati* (1964) provides an excellent survey and summary. More detailed treatments of welfare economics in general include *de V. Graaff* (1957), *Little* (1957) or *Winch* (1971) – which are welfare texts – or *Meade* (1951), *Bator* (1957) or *Layard and Walters* (1978, chs 1 and 2). The classic references on second best are *Meade* (1951) and *Lipsey and Lancaster* (1956). Analysis eschewing community indifference maps includes *Dixit and Norman* (1980), who cover all the topics of this chapter, and *Smith* (1982), who is excellent on the gains from trade.

KEY CONCEPTS

marginal conditions	externalities
uncertainty	missing markets
community indifference curves	social welfare function
revealed preference	income distribution and demand
second best	

QUESTIONS FOR REVIEW

7.1 Discuss carefully how free trade ensures the attainment of the marginal conditions for Pareto efficiency.

7.2 Appraise the validity of Pareto efficiency as a goal for international trade policy.

7.3 Using community indifference curves show how induced changes in the distribution of income can confuse the assessment of economic policy. How do revealed preference and social welfare function analyses deal with this problem?

7.4 Think of five examples where policies which might be harmful in isolation could be welfare improving if introduced in a distorted economy.

NOTE

1   Even lump-sum taxes will distort economic behaviour if they apply any systematic criterion in determining tax rates. Thus, even with them, it is difficult to see how systematic redistribution is possible. In fact, Smith (1982) and Dixit and Norman (1986) show that much of trade theory follows through without lump-sum taxes, provided that other taxes are suitably chosen. Although they are clearly not so determined in fact, this possibility brings trade results much nearer to actual application.

8 Methods of Protection: (A) Tariffs

This chapter analyses tariffs as a tool of economic policy. It starts by considering a tariff on a single good, tracing both its positive and normative (welfare) effects in both partial and general equilibrium. Section 8.2 shows how a tariff is equivalent to the joint imposition of a consumption tax and a production subsidy, while section 8.3 distinguishes betwen *nominal* protection – the extent to which a tariff raises the price of a final good – and *effective* protection – the extent to which the tariff structure raises the returns to the factors producing a good. Section 8.4 considers tariffs under imperfect competition and shows that the pro-competitive effect of free trade could be one of its greatest virtues. The final section considers the measurement and history of tariffs and their effects. It presents detailed data on UK protection via tariffs and taxes and also assesses certain estimates of the welfare effects of protection.

8.1 TARIFFS – A SIMPLE ANALYSIS

A tariff is an amount of money paid by an importer to the government to allow him to bring goods into the country. It may be levied in two different ways. A *specific duty or tariff* is levied per unit quantity of imports: e.g. £1 per gallon on whisky. It is independent of the price of the initial import, although of course the final (imported) price will include the tariff. An *ad valorem tariff*, on the other hand, is levied per unit value of imports: e.g. 65 per cent on chewing tobacco. This clearly depends on the price of imports. Administratively this is a great advantage in times of inflation, because it is 'inflation linked'. For most purposes, the two are equivalent, although specific duties provide the importer some incentive to import dearer but better goods, because then the duty represents a smaller percentage of the final value.

A single good   We start by analysing the impact of a tariff on a single good, holding everything else constant. We assume that the good accounts for only a minute proportion of total expenditure, so that any change in its price has a negligible effect on the general purchasing power of money or real income. Suppose good X is produced domestically by a competitive industry with supply curve $S_h S_h$ in Figure 8.1. Assume that an identical good may be imported, also with a rising supply curve. The latter is not shown in the figure, but combined with home supply let it imply a total supply curve of SS: this shows the price required to bring forth any particular overall supply. With demand curve DD and free trade, price is p_f and total quantity q_f; local supplies are h_f (the value of $S_h S_h$ at p_f) and imports are $(q_f - h_f)$.

Now introduce a specific tariff t. To bring forth any level of imports, the landed (tariff-inclusive) price must rise by t, allowing the price indicated by SS to be paid to the foreign seller and t to the government. Thus the 'effective' foreign supply curve will rise by t and, adding $S_h S_h$ for domestic supplies, will produce a new total supply curve $S_h S'S'$. The new equilibrium has internal

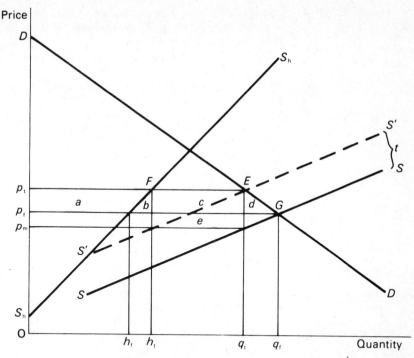

Figure 8.1 Simple tariff analysis

price p_t and, total quantity q_t, comprising h_t domestic supplies and $(q_t - h_t)$ of imports. Imports fall because both total consumption has fallen and local output has increased. Consumers pay p_t for every unit bought – but, whereas for domestic sales all this accrues to the producer, for imported sales only p_m accrues to the producer while t accrues to the government. The import price is lower than under free trade, because, with a rising supply curve for imports, the reduced quantity of imports can be called forth at a lower price.

Welfare analysis

The welfare effects of the tariff may be calculated by means of consumer and producer surplus.

Consumer surplus represents the utility that consumers get from consuming a good over and above what they surrendered to get it. If the marginal utility of money is constant, both can be measured in money terms – hence our earlier assumption that X is too insignificant to affect the purchasing power of money. Consider the demand curve in Figure 8.1. For the first unit a buyer is willing to pay just £D, hence £D is the utility he gains from it. For the next unit someone is willing to pay slightly below £D; hence the value of two units is this amount plus £D. We can similarly calculate the total value of n units by adding up the prices at which each would be the marginal unit sold. This amounts to calculating the area under the demand curve between the axis and the last unit. Thus the utility derived from the consumption of q_t units of X is the area DEq_tO in Figure 8.1. The consumer surplus of selling q_t, at the unit price of p_t is therefore area DEp_t – i.e. total utility less total expenditure, which is price × quantity, or area Op_tEq_t.

Producer surplus is similar: roughly speaking, it represents profits. For a competitive industry, the supply curve shows what each successive unit costs

91

(supply price = marginal cost) and producer surplus is the difference between this and total revenue. Thus, for domestic sales of h_t, producer surplus is area $p_t F S_h$ ($= Op_t F h_t$ less $OS_h F h_t$).

We now consider moving from the free-trade equilibrium G to the tariff equilibrium E. Consumption falls to q_t, consumers' surplus falls by area $a + b + c + d$ ($Dp_f G - Dp_t E$). Production on the other hand rises to h_t, increasing producer surplus by a. Government revenue also increases, because the remaining $(q_t - h_t)$ of imports pay $(p_t - p_m)$ in tariffs, generating revenue $c + e$. Hence the total loss of welfare at E relative to G is $a + b + c + d - a - (c + e) = b + d - e$. This could be either positive or negative. Area b represents a producer loss, area d a consumer loss and area e the gain from the reduction in the price of imports. The areas a and c are consumer surpluses redistributed towards producers and government respectively.

The small country

In this simple model, any gain from tariffs arises from the fall in the price of imports. This occurs because falling demand for imports cuts the supply price. If our country is very small, however, such market power will not exist. If any unit not sold to us can be sold elsewhere in the world for p_f, the price we face will never fall below p_f. Figure 8.2 illustrates this special case using the previous notation. The foreign supply curve is horizontal at p_f and is raised to p_t ($= p_f + t$) by the tariff.

Clearly the tariff is now harmful, because b and d remain while e has disappeared. In fact, the free-trade point G is the welfare-maximising point. Consumers consume X until the marginal utility of the last unit (the height of the demand curve) just equals the marginal cost of producing it (the height of

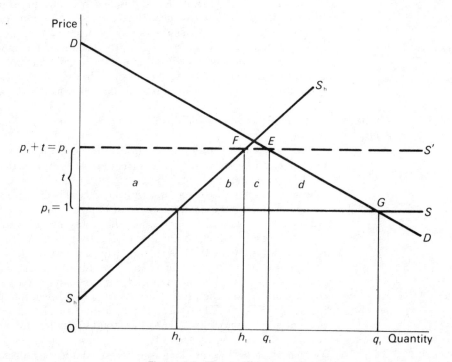

Figure 8.2 The tariff in a small country

the supply, or marginal cost curve). Any further units would involve costs above marginal utility, while any fewer units would involve losing the excess of utility over costs at consumption below q_f. The two sources of X – home production and imports – both have the same marginal costs. Hence no rearrangement of sources could reduce the overall cost of consuming q_f of X.

Measuring the welfare effects

Figure 8.2 illustrates an approximate method of measuring the loss of welfare from the tariff. The area of triangle b is measured by $\frac{1}{2}t\,(h_t - h_f)$ and the area of d by $\frac{1}{2}t\,(q_f - q_t)$. Hence welfare loss ($\Delta W$) is

$$\Delta W = \tfrac{1}{2}t\,(h_t - h_f) + \tfrac{1}{2}t\,(q_f - q_t) = \tfrac{1}{2}t\,\Delta m \tag{8.1}$$

where Δm is the change in imports (m), which is $(q_f - h_f) - (q_t - h_t)$. Now, if we measure X in units such that its free-trade price (p_f) is 1, the change in imports equals $m \cdot \epsilon_m \cdot t$, where ϵ_m is the price elasticity of demand for imports and t, the tariff, represents the proportionate price change between free trade and tariffs. Hence

$$\Delta W = \tfrac{1}{2}m \cdot \epsilon_m \cdot t^2 \tag{8.2}$$

This formula, which is due to Meade (1951), is quite widely applied. Strictly it is applicable only to small markets and in the absence of other tariff changes, in order to be sure that the supply and demand curves do not shift with the imposition of the tariff, and that the marginal utility of money is constant. Moreover, the derivation assumes linear supply and demand schedules; to the extent that this is violated, (8.2) will be a poor approximation to the welfare loss. However, some economists believe that it is possible to correct for these difficulties even for large markets, and (8.2) has been applied to total imports.

General equilibrium

The assumption above that our industry was small allowed us to ignore any effects that protection of X had on any other industry. We now correct that by examining tariffs in a two-good general equilibrium model, assuming for convenience that we are still dealing with a small country.

Figure 8.3 summarises the analysis. *FF* is the transformation frontier and slope *TT* is the world terms of trade (exogenous to our country). By previous analysis, production takes place at *P*, maximising the value of domestic output, and consumption at *C*, maximising welfare along the consumption possibility locus *TT*. Trade is shown by triangle *PHC* – exporting *PH* of Y and importing *HC* of X. Suppose a tariff is levied on imports of X. The world price is unaffected, but residents now have to surrender more Y per unit X than previously. Suppose the tariff converts the world price ratio *TT* into an internal price ratio *II*. Producers now maximise the value of output at those prices (setting *MRT* = slope *II*) and choose point *P'*. Given *P'* and world prices *TT*, the consumption locus is *T'T'*; consumers also face internal prices *II*, and so choose the point along *T' T'* where *MRS* = slope *II*; that is, point *C'*. Tariff-ridden trade involves exchanging *P'H'* of Y for *H'C'* of X, although, of the latter, only *H'D'* goes directly to local residents, *D'C'* being tariff revenue.

Note how domestic *MRT* and *MRS* are equal, but, because of the tariff, they do not equal the rate at which goods can be transformed through trade (slope *TT*). Observe also how, given the full optimality of free trade, the tariff equilibrium must be sub-optimal. As before the difference comprises a production and a consumption component. The former is the loss in the value

93

Figure 8.3 Tariff in a small country: general equilibrium

of national output at world prices between P and P'. (World prices represent the 'true worth' of goods, since X and Y can always be converted at that rate through trade.) The latter arises because the social indifference curve at C' is not the highest possible, even given consumption locus $T'T'$.

An implicit assumption in all this is that the government spends its revenue just as the private sector would. This is necessary in order that we have the same community indifference map before and after the tariff change, and it is usually excused by assuming that the revenue is returned to consumers by means of non-distortionary lump-sum transfers. It does not, in fact, matter whether the tariff is paid in good X or Y, so long as the revenue is returned in this manner. Perhaps more remarkable, however, is that neither does it matter whether exports or imports are subject to the tariff. It is the act of trading that is taxed, in effect; any effort to convert surplus Y into X through trade results in the loss of some goods, which means that less X is available to the private transactor per unit Y than is offered by foreigners. This equivalence between export and import taxes is known as *Lerner's symmetry theorem* (Lerner, 1936). Looked at alternatively, given fixed world prices, an import tax on X raises the internal relative price of X, while an export tax on Y reduces the internal relative price of Y; these two changes are equivalent.

8.2 TAXES AND SUBSIDIES

We digress from tariffs briefly to note the effects of taxes and subsidies on production and consumption. Return to Figure 8.2 and suppose that producers are offered a subsidy of t. The domestic price is still determined by the import price p_f (no one will pay more if X is available from abroad at p_f), so consumption remains at q_f, but producers are now paid $(p_f + t) = p_t$ per unit. Hence domestic output rises from h_f to h_t, and imports falls by $(h_t - h_f)$.

The government loses area $a + b$ in terms of net revenue, but producers' surplus rises by a. A net loss of b is recorded. The subsidy has the same effect on producers as the tariff, but has no consumption effect.

Now imagine free trade but with a consumption tax of t. Again imports still occur, so producers cannot charge above p_f, but the consumers' price on both domestic and imported units is $(p_f + t) = p_t$. Consumption falls to q_t, production remains at h_f, and imports make up the difference. Area $a + b + c + d$ is lost to consumers' surplus but $a + b + c$ accrues to the government as tax revenue. The net cost is thus d. The consumption tax affects consumers just as the tariff does, but does not influence producers. Thus, the tariff is equivalent in all respects to the simultaneous application of an identical consumption tax and production subsidy.

A similar analysis can be made for Figure 8.3, the general equilibrium case. A production subsidy for X shifts the producers' price ratio to II, and production to P', but consumers, still facing world prices $TT(= T' T')$, consume where MRS = slope TT, i.e. at C''. The subsidy involves production costs, as with the tariff, but no consumption costs. A consumption tax, on the other hand, involves no production loss, so production remains at P, but along the consumption locus TT consumers choose the point where MRS = slope II (the tax-ridden price ratio). This is C''', which may be better or worse than C''. Both, however, are dominated by C and dominate C'.

For both tariffs and taxes and for subsidies it is relative prices that are important, as is obvious from the general equilibrium model. Hence *relative* not absolute protection matters: a tax of 100 per cent on X is equivalent to a 50 per cent tax on X plus a 25 per cent subsidy on Y:

$$\frac{2.0 p_x}{p_Y} = \frac{1.5 p_x}{0.75 p_Y}$$

where p_X and p_Y are the pre-tax prices of X and Y respectively. Clearly, both policies double the relative price of X. Note that, in contrast to the analysis of Lerner's symmetry theorem, we are talking here about production and consumption taxes, not trade taxes.

8.3 EFFECTIVE PROTECTION

So far we have assumed that industries are completely vertically integrated: they take primary factors of production and transform them into goods for final consumption, without any intervening market transactions. This is plainly untrue – intermediate goods obviously exist, and, more important, are obviously traded internationally (e.g. car engines). The theory of effective protection – 'discovered' by economists in the 1960s, but well known by every Victorian businessman – attempts to allow for this. Crudely, if tariffs or taxes are levied on an industry's inputs, profits are likely to fall – the industry is 'dis-protected' – and factors will tend to move out of it.

A definition   If an industry can buy any amount of intermediate goods and services at fixed prices on the world market, its output is determined by its supply of primary factors of production. This in turn is determined largely by the rewards that those factors receive. Hence to relate an industry's output to its protection we must find the effect of protection on factor rewards. The sum of all factor rewards in an industry is known as its *value-added*. An industry takes physical inputs worth, say, £x, adds value from primary factors worth £V, to produce gross output of £$z = £(x + V)$. Value-added equals the value of gross output less the value of physical inputs. An industry's effective protection (g) is the extent to which taxes and tariffs raise its value-added. Denote valued-added under free trade by V and with protection by V', then for industry i

$$g_i = \frac{V_i' - V_i}{V_i}. \tag{8.3}$$

Effective protection depends not only on an industry's own tariff, but also on those on all its inputs.

Measurement   Imagine starting from free trade and imposing tariffs, at differing rates, on all the various goods (final and intermediate) that are traded. One would expect this to affect industries' values-added in a very complex fashion: demand would change if relative prices did, cheaper inputs would be substituted for dearer ones, and the amount (or even direction) of foreign trade may be changed, thus altering the terms of trade. This would make measuring effective protection very difficult. Economists have, therefore, sought to restrict their measurements to much simpler circumstances, hoping that, although their assumptions may not be literally true, they will be sufficiently robust for the measurements still to have some value.

In the simplest case five assumptions are made:

(i)   the country is small, i.e. world prices are fixed;
(ii)   every good traded without tariffs remains traded with tariffs;
(iii)   the inputs required for producing a unit of each output are rigidly fixed in physical terms;
(iv)   there are no non-traded inputs other than primary factors;
(v)   there are no other taxes or distortions in the system.

Value-added per unit of output is the price of a unit less the value of intermediate inputs. Under free trade,

$$V_i = p_i - \sum_j a_{ij} p_j, \tag{8.4}$$

where V_i is value-added per unit of i, p_i is the (world) price of i, and a_{ij} are the inputs of j required per unit of output of i. Assumptions (i) and (ii) ensure that the post-tariff price of every good, p_i', is given by

$$p_i' = (1 + t_i) p_i. \tag{8.5}$$

Hence post-tax value-added is

$$\begin{aligned} V_i' &= p_i' - \sum_j a_{ij} p_j' \\ &= (1 + t_i) p_i - \sum_j a_{ij}(1 + t_j) p_j. \end{aligned} \tag{8.6}$$

Now, measuring all goods in units such that $p_i = 1$ and substituting (8.5) and (8.6) into (8.3) yields:

$$g_i = \frac{t_i - \sum_j a_{ij} t_j}{1 - \sum_j a_{ij}} \qquad (8.7)$$

The last step depends crucially on (8.5) and (8.6) having the same a_{ij}, i.e. on protection not altering input–output coefficients (assumption (iii)). This assumption also ensures that g_i reflects factor rewards, because, if factor values rise without factor quantities changing, rewards must have risen.

For students who find it useful, a numerical example of effective protection is given in the Appendix to this chapter.

It may seem surprising that demand figures nowhere in this formula. This is because assumptions (i) and (ii) divorce supply from demand. Any difference (positive and negative) between local supply and demand can always be made up at the ruling world price. Local producers produce until marginal cost equals price; hence, since demand does not affect price (which is the world price plus the tariff), neither can it affect local output. It may also appear surprising that, while tariffs on inputs are important, tariffs on inputs into inputs are not. The reason again is the small country assumption. This fixes the local price of inputs quite independently of their local costs of production, provided, of course, that they remain traded (assumption (ii)). Thus, it is of no interest to car producers whether steel producers pay taxes on their coal, so long as steel is always available at a fixed price.

If i's tariff is low but its inputs' tariffs are high, g_i could be negative, meaning that the tariff structure discourages production. If all tariffs are equal $t_i = t_j = t$, g_i also equals t for every industry. If, however, tariff structures are escalating – i.e. they increase with the degree of processing – outputs will tend to be higher rated than inputs and g_i will exceed t_i: effective protection will exceed nominal protection.

Some refinements

Various refinements are possible to the basic formula.

First, *other taxes and subsidies* can be incorporated: taxes raise internal prices like tariffs; subsidies reduce them. Hence, for example, a coal tax will reduce value-added in the iron and steel industry.

Second, *non-tradable inputs* can be handled in two possible ways. If they are supplied at constant cost, they can be treated just like traded goods but with zero tariffs. If, alternatively, they are wholly fixed in supply, they can be treated as factors of production. Then g_i measures the change in the sum of value-added plus expenditure on non-traded inputs; but, of course, its implications for the industry are then less clear, because it is not known whether factors or non-traded industries will collect any additional rewards. Between these extremes, and also if they have traded inputs themselves, non-traded inputs are difficult to incorporate into effective protection calculations.

Third, some *factors* may not have the rigidly fixed supply generally assumed in trade theory. If a factor has perfectly elastic supply (e.g. capital if it may be imported, or labour if there is a reserve army of unemployed), then its reward (price) will not change, and all the extra value-added will accrue to the other factors, with proportionately larger effects.

Fourth, some *substitution* between physical inputs can be handled, although substitution between physical inputs and primary factors is much more complex.

Fifth, the tariff structure may unbalance trade; assuming this is corrected by an *exchange rate* change, this too must be incorporated into the formula. An *x* per cent depreciation is equivalent to an *x* per cent import tariff and export subsidy. It raises the prices of all traded goods by *x* per cent, and hence affects protective levels. This stresses the relativeness of protection. At the old exchange rate it is possible for all tradable industries to have positive effective protection. This, however, will generate a balance of payments surplus, which will appreciate the exchange rate and so dis-protect tradable relative to non-tradable industries. The net result will be that some tradables will be protected and others dis-protected relative to non-tradables. Non-tradables may or may not gain relative to their former position.

In practice, only the first two of these refinements are regularly made. The remainder are more complex and are more usually handled by means of an econometric model. Rather than solve the model analytically as in equation (8.7), this approach involves solving a model of the economy numerically, once with tariffs and once without. Value-added in each industry is then compared between solutions. Such models can be generalised in many other ways, but of course their requirements in terms of information and computing resources frequently exceed those available to researchers – especially for developing countries. Hence the imperfect measures introduced here are still commonly used.

Rates of effective protection give information about the impact of protection on production. (Consumers react to the level of prices, not value-added, and hence are affected by nominal protection.) For example, an industry with a 50 per cent effective rate of protection can afford to be 50 per cent less efficient (use 50 per cent more labour and capital) than its foreign rivals, and still maintains its domestic sales. Thus, to break into an industrial country market where the local industry has high effective rates of protection, a developing country must really be very efficient indeed (or highly subsidised). Effective protection studies of developing countries' own protection frequently reveal huge production distortions – effective rates of 200 per cent and above – and occasionally even negative value-added at world prices. (This arises when domestic taxes and subsidies conceal the fact that the physical inputs alone cost more than the value of the final output.) Although the effective rate calculations have been subject to many reservations above, very high rates of protection certainly indicate major distortions requiring some policy response.

8.4   TARIFFS AND IMPERFECT COMPETITION

So far we have assumed that both import supply and import-competing supply are perfectly competitive. As we saw in Chapter 5, however, imperfect competition and economies of scale can affect trade patterns quite dramatically and so we must allow for them in our analysis of tariffs. The simplest observation is that protection often allows production of a good to become fragmented internationally. Markets that should be supplied by imports are supplied domestically and, if the firms concerned still have unexploited economies of scale, then fragmentation will have raised costs. This certainly applies at home where consumers are obliged to consume local output, but whether it applies abroad depends on whether the number of firms can adjust. If foreign firms leave industry as the result of losing their share of the home market, firm size stays at its cost-minimising optimum, and thus costs are unchanged. If, on the other hand, the number of firms is unchanged, lost sales mean smaller firms and higher costs. The costs in this example are not those of the misallocation of production (although they too might be present), but those of fragmentation, independent of comparative advantage.

In the extreme, protection could conceivably cause foreign firms to quit the market entirely, leaving it open to domestic firms, which would then reap the economies of scale of the entire world market. Thus the tariff would have reversed the pattern of trade and, incidently, rendered itself redundant. The welfare implications of this switch are not clear for either party, for economies of scale can foster specialisation in the wrong direction (see section 5.2 above). Moreover, if the original exporting country retaliated in kind, we would be back at an inefficient fragmented outcome.

The analysis of fragmentation has implicitly concerned *external* economies of scale, in which extra output reduces industry costs but in which no individual firm can reduce its own costs by expanding output. (This assumption is necessary to reconcile the presence of economies of scale with the existence of many producers.) If, on the other hand, unexploited economies of scale are internal to the firm, we must have imperfect competition, for the existing firms can always undercut new rivals by virtue of their higher output.

Figure 8.4 considers tariffs and monopoly in the presence of declining marginal costs, an extreme case of economies of scale. As drawn, the world price, p_w, is too low for the domestic producer to survive, for it does not cover marginal costs, let alone average costs, which will lie above marginal costs when the latter are falling and there are fixed costs. At some level of tariff, however, average costs and revenues for the domestic monopolist will be equal, and domestic production will commence, capturing the whole market. The monopolist prefers the normal profits available where $AR = AC$ to the zero profit available when he produces nothing. Let the required tariff be t_s. It

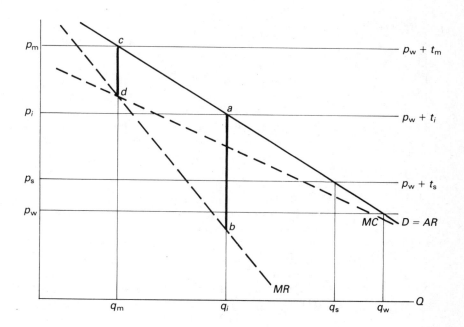

Figure 8.4 Tariffs and monopoly

99

clearly entails social losses because at q_s imports cost p_w while domestic supplies cost $p_s = (p_w + t_s)$, even ignoring lost consumer surplus from cutting consumption.

As the tariff is increased above t_s – say to t_i – the monopolist cuts production! With tariff t_i his effective marginal revenue curve is given by p_i: imports prevent him from selling at prices above $(p_w + t_i)$, thus up to q_i each extra unit generates $(p_w + t_i)$ of revenue. To sell the q_ith unit, however, he has to reduce prices on all previous units, so the marginal revenue of this unit plummets to the usual marginal revenue curve, which could even be negative at this point. Thus the profit-maximising condition $MC = MR$ dictates output q_i for a wide range of levels of marginal costs. The higher tariff reduces domestic output in this case because it allows the monopolist more scope to exploit his domestic monopoly power. In the absence of the threat of international trade the monopolist would choose to produce q_m and sell at p_m. A tariff of t_m would also produce this outcome (the effective MR curve becomes $p_m cdMR$) and further increases will have no effect.

The decline in marginal costs is not a crucial part of this analysis. Even with perfectly ordinary cost curves, tariffs beyond a certain level will encourage monopoly exploitation. Thus international trade has an important role in disciplining domestic producers, a result which also generalises to situations of oligopoly. This is referred to as the *pro-competitive effects of trade*, and can be quantitatively very important. Conversely, tariffs can be doubly harmful if, in addition to raising production costs, they reduce competitive pressures on domestic firms and allow them to increase their profit margins unjustifiably.

8.5 TARIFFS IN FACT

Measurement Before we can discuss real-world tariffs we need a measure of them. For precisely defined goods this is easy, but for aggregates substantial difficulties emerge. How does one aggregate high tariffs on apples with low ones on bananas to get a single figure for fruit? If we take a simple unweighted mean, tariffs on minor items of trade figure too strongly. If, on the other hand, we weight tariffs by the share of total imports they cover, high tariffs are under-represented, for high tariffs, *ceteris paribus*, reduce imports. Popular among the latter style of measure is dividing total tariff revenue by total import value – this generates a Paasche (current weighted) index of tariffs. Possibly more convincing is to weight tariffs together by local consumption or production (which respectively under- and over-represent high tariffs – check that you see why) or by hypothesised free-trade levels of trade. These, however, are all much more difficult to apply, and consequently the simple averages are used more frequently. However, one should always ask the nature of the tariff measure before making use of it.

History Tariffs are as old as international trade itself, and, however we measure them, there have been considerable fluctuations in their levels over time. For example, the mid-nineteenth century is usually thought of as a period of relatively free trade, whereas the latter part was relatively protectionist. Similarly Britain has been mainly a free trader since 1850, whereas America has a more protectionist tradition. However, as Capie (1983) has shown, these generalities can be overstated. In the 1870s, for example, 'free-trade' Britain had average tariffs (duties ÷ imports) of 5 per cent, while allegedly protectionist France and Germany had averages of 7 per cent and 8 per cent respectively. America and Russia, however, were more protectionist, with average tariff rates of about 30 per cent over most of the period 1850–1910.

By the First World War, British tariffs were fairly low; furthermore they were balanced by excise taxes on competing domestic goods and hence offered virtually no protection to British industry. In 1915, the McKenna Duties changed this, imposing $33\frac{1}{3}$ per cent duties on cars, instruments and time-pieces. The next large increase came in 1921 with a more widespread tariff of 30 per cent. These and the McKenna tariffs were renewed and gradually extended until the Import Duties Act of 1932 instituted a general tariff of at least 10 per cent, from which only Commonwealth and Empire countries were exempt, under the Imperial Preference system. This protectionist stance persisted until the Second World War.

After the Second World War there was widespread agreement that protection should be reduced, and the General Agreement on Tariffs and Trade (GATT) was established in 1947 to stimulate and codify the process. A series of rounds of negotiations have occurred since then, the most recent of which is the Uruguay Round (1986–90), which have reduced industrial countries' tariffs on most goods to very low levels (see Table 8.1). In addition, most industrial countries offer tariff concessions to certain trading partners, further reducing the impact of tariffs. Such preferences and the GATT are described in more detail in Chapter 12 below.

British tariffs A recent study of British tariffs is Ennew, Greenway and Reed (1990), some of whose results are reported in Table 8.2. These refer to 1986 and thus, so far as tariffs are concerned, are merely the rates required by the EC's Common External Tariff, which all EC member countries are obliged to use. They show

Table 8.1 Tariffs and the Tokyo Round

		Pre-Tokyo	Tariff averages Post-Tokyo	Rate of reduction %
(A) *By product*:				
Total industrial products	W[a]	7.2	4.9	33
	S[a]	10.6	6.5	38
Raw materials	W	0.8	0.4	52
	S	2.6	1.7	36
Semi-manufactures	W	5.8	4.1	30
	S	9.7	6.2	36
Finished manufactures	W	10.3	6.9	33
	S	12.2	7.4	39
(B) *By country*:				
United States	W	6.2	4.4	30
	S	12.1	7.0	42
EC[b]	W	6.6	4.8	27
	S	8.1	5.6	31
Japan	W	5.2	2.6	49
	S	10.2	6.0	41

Notes:
[a] W denotes weighted average (by imports), S simple average.
[b] Separate UK figures are unavailable because all EC countries negotiated together.
Sources: (A) General Agreement on Tariffs and Trade (1979); (B) Corbet (1979).

Table 8.2 UK tariffs and protection, 1986 (%)

	Tariffs		Total protection	
	Nominal[a]	Effective[a]	Nominal	Effective
(A) *By group*:				
Primary activities	0.1	−0.2	—	—
Agriculture, food				
and beverages	3.9	8.9	—	—
Intermediate goods I[b]	0.5	0.7	—	—
Intermediate goods II[b]	1.4	2.4	—	—
Machinery and transport				
equipment	1.8	3.0	—	—
Finished goods	2.4	4.6	—	—
Services and distribution	0.0	−0.5	—	—
(B) *Selected industries*:				
Man-made fibres	0.8	1.2	10.8	50.9
Motor vehicles	0.1	1.3	11.0	33.4
Cotton etc. spinning				
and weaving	2.1	3.0	12.1	29.1
Hosiery and knitted goods	5.4	12.3	15.4	35.4
Textile finishing	0.0	−1.1	10.0	20.7
Footwear	3.6	6.1	17.6	41.5
Clothing and fur	5.8	11.6	20.8	46.2
Household textiles	4.9	13.6	14.9	39.4

Notes:
[a] Weighted averages for group results.
[b] Intermediate goods II are more highly processed than intermediate goods I.
— not available.
Source: Ennew, Greenaway and Reed (1990).

the low levels to which tariff protection has fallen. A small degree of escalation causes effective rates to exceed nominal rates, but neither nominal nor effective tariffs are high: among Ennew *et al.*'s sectors, agriculture records the highest effective tariff (21.8 per cent) and telecommunications equipment the highest nominal tariffs (6.7 per cent). The situation is different, however, when total protection – which includes the effects of some non-tariff barriers – is considered. Then the most heavily protected manufacturing sectors record nominal rates of up to 20 per cent and effective rates of around 50 per cent. (See Chapter 9 for further details of non-tariff barriers.)

The effects of tariffs

Many attempts have been made to calculate the effects of tariff structures on production, trade and welfare. The major empirical problem is estimating the relevant price elasticities of demand – the slopes of the supply and demand schedules in the figures we drew above. This is discussed in Chapter 19 below, where we conclude that, although figures are estimable, they are subject to considerable margins of error. Once the elasticity is 'known' (or assumed), formula (8.2) can be simply applied. It merely remains to decide whether or not its assumptions are sufficiently well satisfied for us to believe the result.

An excellent early study, which carefully lays out the underlying analysis and data, is Magee (1972) on the US economy in 1971. For imports not subject to quotas but where local substitutes existed, Magee assumed price elasticities of demand and supply of −0.75 and −1.50 respectively. The average tariff was 7.9 per cent and, with local production of $45 b. (= h_t in Figure 8.2) and consumption of $57 b. ($q_t$), Magee calculated a producers' surplus loss (area *b*) of $177 m. and consumers' surplus loss of $114 m. Thus, tariffs imposed a loss equivalent to 2.4 per cent of such imports. For non-competitive imports (where US supply was very small), tariffs cost about $202 m. or 0.8 per cent of imports. Import quotas, on the other hand, were significantly more costly: welfare costs amounted to $3.6 b. or 40 per cent of imports, of which about $2.4 b. were losses equivalent to the tariff losses and $1.2 b. resulted from quotas' inability to raise revenue. (This is discussed in Chapter 9.) Magee also considered US exports, concluding that foreign tariffs did not greatly affect US welfare from manufacturing, but that on agricultural exports they cost up to $5 b. p.a.

The overall estimate is that in 1971 import restrictions cost the US economy $3–5 b. in lost welfare – about 0.3–0.5 per cent of national income – mostly arising from quotas. This is based on the small country assumption and would be reduced if we relaxed it to allow the terms of trade to change. Moreover, if trade restrictions were abolished, considerable adjustment costs would arise in the short term. Against this we should recognise that, as the economy grows, so do these costs, and that protection might reduce efficiency and/or the rate of economic growth in a way that these simple static calculations cannot capture.

A much more sophisticated, model-based, estimate of welfare effects comes from Deardorff and Stern (1983b). They roughly repeated Magee's exercise but allowed for terms of trade effects, exchange rate adjustment, changes in consumption and production, and substitution between factors of production. They considered the changes negotiated in the Tokyo Round of tariff negotiations under the GATT – including certain minor non-tariff agreements – and their results appear in Table 8.3.

Table 8.3 The effects of the Tokyo Round on trade and welfare[a]

	Exports $b.	Changes in Imports $b.	Welfare % of GDP
All countries[a]	13.2	13.7	0.10
Industrialised countries	13.4	14.1	0.11
UK	1.2	1.2	0.18
France	1.5	1.5	0.05
Sweden	0.4	0.8	0.98
Japan	0.4	0.6	0.08
USA	3.3	2.3	0.03
Developing countries	− 0.2	− 0.3	0.00

Notes:
[a] Based on economies as in 1976 – i.e. applying the changes to 1976 economies.
[b] The changes in total exports and imports are not equal because certain countries are omitted from the analysis.
Source: Deardorff and Stern (1983b).

The negotiations brought the developing countries negligible or negative gains. This is probably because general reductions in tariffs reduce the advantages they reap from their tariff concessions (see Chapter 12), while the non-tariff barriers they face are not being altered. Among the industrialised countries, the gains from the Tokyo Round do not appear to be evenly shared. Sweden is a strong beneficiary, whereas larger countries like the USA appear to gain less. These results are clearly no better than the model they derive from. They should be treated with caution, and the interested reader should consult the original source for details. They are also subject to the caveats listed above. Nevertheless, both this and the Magee analysis leave a strong impression that tariffs do not matter much so far as static efficiency is concerned. This is not to deny that protection might affect economic growth or X-efficiency, but just to note that the static analysis of tariffs in this chapter, although a useful benchmark, is not quantitatively very significant at present.

More recent work on the effect of tariffs has suggested rather greater effects than the studies mentioned above – largely by exploring the pro-competitive effects of trade liberalisation. Harris and Cox (1984), for example, suggest that protection reduces Canadian GDP by up to 9 per cent, by encouraging the proliferation of small and inefficient firms. For a number of technical reasons these estimates are probably rather too high, but current opinion certainly holds tariffs to be more harmful than Magee suggests; see also the industry studies described in case-studies 9.1 and 9.2 below.

FURTHER READING

The basic model of tariff protection is provided by *Corden* (1974), and exploited by *Magee* (1972) and *Baldwin* (1976) to measure US protection levels. Effective protection stems from *Corden* (1966) and is most thoroughly explained in *Corden* (1971). *Little, Scitovsky and Scott* (1970) and *Balassa* (1971) provide data on developing countries, as does The World Bank's *World Development Report 1987. Preeg* (1970) and *Cline et al.* (1978) discuss tariff averages and *Greenaway* (1983) supplements the treatment in the text. The model of tariffs and imperfect competition may be supplemented by *Helpman and Krugman* (1989), chapter 3.

KEY CONCEPTS

tariff averages   consumer surplus
producer surplus   equivalence of tariffs, subsidies and taxes
Lerner's symmetry theorem   small country assumption
effective protection   value-added
protection and monopoly

QUESTIONS FOR REVIEW

8.1   Analyse the output effects of a tariff under different market structures.
8.2   Show that in a two-good general equilibrium model a 50% tariff on X is equivalent to $33\frac{1}{3}$% export subsidy on Y. Spell out the assumption you need to make.
8.3   What are the virtues of the various restrictive assumptions made in the model of effective protection? Do they outweigh the costs?
8.4   What are the problems inherent in applying the model of section 8.1 to total imports? Should we therefore mistrust Magee's results?

APPENDIX: EFFECTIVE PROTECTION – AN EXAMPLE

Imagine a very simple pig iron industry, which produces pig iron from iron ore and coal. The first three columns of Table 8.A.1 summarise its technology and the world price it faces. Thus, 1 ton of pig iron requires 2 tons of ore and 1 of coal. At world prices the iron ore costs £200 and the coal £300, and so, with pig iron worth £1,000 per ton, value-added amounts to £500. Now suppose we impose tariffs of

Table 8.A.1

	Parameters		Free trade value (£)	Tariff (%) (t_i)	Tariff-ridden internal price per ton (£) (p_i)	Value (£)
	Quantities (tons)	World price per ton (£) (p_i)				
Iron ore	2	100	200	25	125	250
Coal	1	300	300	16⅔	350	350
Value-added[a]	—	—	(500)	—	—	(700)
Pig iron	1	1,000	1,000	30	1,300	1,300

Note:
[a] Derived from the other rows.

25 per cent, 16.67 per cent and 30 per cent on ore, coal and pig iron, respectively (column 4). The internal price structure changes (column 5) and, given fixed physical input–output coefficients, the relative values of the inputs and outputs change (column 6). Thus, for 1 ton of output, ore input now costs £250 and coal input £350, but, with the output now worth £1,300, value-added has risen to £700. This is an increase of 40 per cent over free-trade value-added, so the rate of effective protection on pig iron production is 40 per cent.

Now recast the exercise in terms of the formulae in the text. First, all physical units are re-defined so that free-trade prices are unity. Thus, column 2 of Table 8.A.2 contains only ones. In column 1 we show how many new units of iron ore (one hundredth of a ton) are required to make one new unit of pig iron (one thousandth of a ton); if 2 tons of ore go into 1 ton of pig iron, then 0.2 one hundredths of ore enter 1 thousandth of pig iron. The coal coefficient is calculated similarly. This column defines the input–output coefficients a_{ij}. Column 3 now shows the free-trade value of inputs required for £1 worth of output; £0.5 of the input is value-added, which equals $1 - \Sigma a_{ij}$. Column 4 expresses the tariffs as proportions, column 5 defines the new, tariff-ridden, prices and column 6 gives the same physical inputs and outputs valued at the new prices. Value-added is now 0.7, which is $p_i' - \Sigma_j a_{ij} p_j'$, in the terms of equation (8.6). Clearly, effective protection is again calculated as $(0.7 - 0.5)/0.5$ expressed as a percentage, and this can immediately be verified as the result of formula (8.7).

Table 8.A.2

	Parameters		Free trade value (£)	Tariff (t_i)	Tariff-ridden internal price (p_i')	Value (£)
	Quantities (a_{ij})	World price (p_i)				
Iron ore	0.2	1	0.2	0.25	1.25	0.25
Coal	0.3	1	0.3	0.1667	1.1667	0.35
Value-added[a]	—	—	(0.5)	—	—	(0.7)
Pig iron	1	1	1.0	0.30	1.3	1.3

Note:
[a] Derived from the other rows.

9 Methods of Protection: (B) Non-Tariff Barriers

Trade can be restricted by a large range of measures other than tariffs, ranging from import prohibition to the vague wording of customs instructions. These are called non-tariff barriers (NTBs). This chapter starts with the simplest NTB – a simple import quota, examining its effects and comparing them with those of the tariff. We then consider a recent variant – the voluntary export restraint, whereby exporters 'voluntarily' restrict their exports. The next section introduces NTBs in all their variety, and attempts a formal definition. Finally, section 9.3 considers the effects of non-tariff barriers and tries to gauge their economic costs.

Quantitative restrictions on trade become prevalent during the First World War, and although they were reduced at the Armistice they never entirely disappeared. The late 1920s and 1930s saw their re-emergence – especially in the planned economy of Germany – as a supplement to tariff protection. The Second World War exacerbated the position, as did the post-war dollar shortage and huge structural readjustment required in Europe. Between about 1960 and 1975 the European countries sought to reduce their barriers in most areas of trade – agricultural support policies and textile industries being the main exceptions. Since then, however, there seems to have been some drift back towards increased protection.

Between 1950 and 1990 the GATT sponsored a substantial reduction in tariffs. In some cases these were immediately replaced by NTBs, but, even if they were not, NTBs became relatively more important and, of course, visible. The Tokyo Round explicitly considered the problem and made modest progress in the codification and limitation of NTBs on developed countries' mutual trade. Simultaneously, however, barriers were being raised on 'sensitive' manufactures, where developing countries – especially those of South-East Asia – and Japan were competing effectively, and on agricultural goods.

9.1 QUANTITATIVE RESTRICTIONS

The archetypal NTB is the import quota. This fixes a maximum level (quantity or value) for imports, allowing free access up to the quota but complete prohibition beyond it. Quotas seem attractive to both governments and domestic industry by virtue of their certainty. The effect of a tariff on local output or on expenditure on imports can be 'undermined' by reductions in the supply price of imports. With a quota, however, maximum import penetration or expenditure are fixed. Of course, consumers have different interests: with a tariff they can benefit from import price reductions; with a quota they cannot.

The effects of a quota

Figure 9.1 illustrates the effect of a quota in the simplest case: a small country facing competitive supplies and with a competitive local industry. Under free trade at the world price p_w, consumption of X would be q_f and domestic supply, according to supply curve SS, h_f; imports would be $(q_f - h_f)$. Now

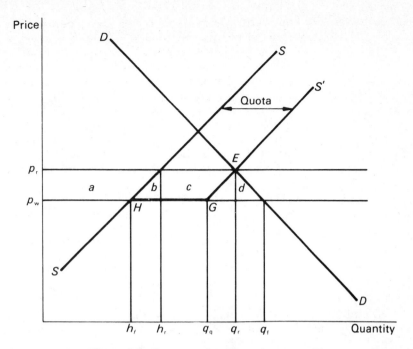

Figure 9.1 Quotas and tariffs under competition

suppose imports are restricted by a physical quota to $(q_q - h_f)$. The overall supply schedule of X to the home market is now $SHGS'$: at prices below p_w, only domestic supplies are available, at p_w imports up to $(q_q - h_f)$ are available, but beyond quantity q_q marginal units are available only from domestic sources, so the supply curve slopes upward again. With this supply curve and the original demand curve, equilibrium obtains at E, with price p_r, consumption q_r, output h_r and imports $(q_r - h_r) = (q_q - h_f)$.

The welfare effects may be calculated in the way used for tariffs in Chapter 8. Area a is transferred from consumers to producers, rectangle c from consumers to importers (who buy abroad at p_w and sell at home at p_r), and triangles b and d from consumers to nobody. These last represent the deadweight loss of the quota. Area c represents the rents accruing on the artificially scarce imports – often referred to as the 'quota rents'.

The equivalence of tariffs and quotas

Comparing Figures 8.2 and 9.1 reveals that, if the government could gain area c to compensate for the revenue it took under tariffs, tariffs and quotas would be precisely equivalent. (Imagine imposing a tariff of $(p_r - p_w)$ in Figure 9.1.) Equivalence means that the explicit tariff required to reduce imports to $(q_r - h_r)$ equals the 'implicit tariff' – i.e. the difference between local and world prices – that results from a quota of $(q_r - h_r)$. In these circumstances, the effects of quotas can be fitted into our earlier analyses by converting them into their tariff equivalents and proceeding as before.

Unfortunately this equivalence is not a robust result. It generalises to the case of a large country (where the foreign supply curve slopes unwards), but not any further. Bhagwati (1969a, ch. 9) showed that any one of monopoly in domestic production, monopoly in foreign supply or monopoly among quota holders is sufficient to destroy the equivalence, and later research has shown that it also breaks down in the presence of uncertainty (Pelcovits, 1976) and under retaliation (Rodriguez, 1974).

The intuition of the first case is quite straightforward. Imagine a domestic monopolist protected by a tariff: a rise in his price would both cut demand and increase imports, cutting his sales by two routes. Now imagine exactly the same starting point, but brought about by a quota: the same rise in price would cut demand but *not* increase imports. Thus raising prices under a quota carries less penalty than under a tariff. In other words, because imports do not respond to internal price changes under quotas, quotas grant the local monopolist more monopoly power than he has under tariffs. Hence, for a given level of imports, the implicit tariff under quotas exceeds the explicit tariff.

The case of a monopoly importer is also straightforward. Under the quota nothing can increase the importer's supply of goods, whereas under a tariff a higher price generates higher supplies. Clearly, then, the importer is likely to behave differently under the two systems. Perhaps more important, however, is that quotas often *create* importing monopolies. Whereas under tariffs anyone may import, under quotas only quota holders may, and great care must be taken in distributing quotas if this is not to induce monopoly.

Distributing quotas

Several methods are available for distributing quotas, and they have rather different economic effects. Alternatives include:

- *First come first served*. This entails allowing imports from 1 January until the quota is exhausted and then just closing the border. It imposes huge uncertainty on buyers and exporters, and grants the quota rents to people with storage facilities.

- *Auction*. The government sells quotas to the highest bidders. This grants the quota rent to the government, but may involve creating monopoly if the highest bidder is willing to take on the whole quota. If buyers are limited to, say, 10 per cent of the total quota, monopoly is avoided, but possibly at the expense of some rent and at the cost of enforcing laws against trading quotas.

- *Administrative allocation*. This may avoid monopoly, but quota holders get the rent. It may also involve inefficiency, because quotas may not be issued to those who can make most use of them.

- *Non-price bidding*. Quotas may be allocated by some non-price, resource-using method, e.g. physically queuing for them, or, for industrial inputs, on the basis of the using firms' levels of capacity. These methods tie up real resources in bidding for quotas, and in the limit, firms will be prepared to spend up to £c to get the rights to quota rents of £c. In other words, rather than worry about the distribution of area c, it is merely wasted by resource-using bidding. This is probably the least efficient allocation method. Krueger (1974) estimated that quota rents accounted for 7.3 per cent of Indian GDP in 1964 and 15 per cent of Turkish GDP in 1968. If equivalent amounts were wasted in competition for these rents, the losses are staggering. This rent-seeking behaviour that Krueger describes is an example of *directly unproductive profit-seeking* activity, which is analysed more thoroughly in Chapter 12 below.

Quotas are generally held to be less efficient than tariffs. They preclude an importer benefiting from technical progress abroad, thus increasing instability abroad and reducing foreigners' incentives to innovate. They also become increasingly restrictive as the importing economy grows, because imports cannot grow with income, whereas under tariffs they would. For these reasons international institutions have been rather strict about quotas. The GATT allows emergency quotas, but they are subject to international surveillance, cannot be discriminatory and possibly involve retaliation and paying compensation. Countries have, therefore, been hesitant about introducing them, and recently they have been displaced by voluntary export restraints (VERs).

Under a VER, the importing country 'persuades' an exporter or group of exporters 'voluntarily' to restrain their exports. It is usually signed in the face of threatened action by the importer, being accepted by the exporter as the lesser of two evils. A VER is basically a quota administered by the exporter. It differs from import quotas in that the quota rent definitely accrues to the exporters (rather than to importing agencies), because, being exporter specific, the restriction necessarily grants the exporting country monopoly power over its permitted level of trade. Hence exporters will generally raise export prices until demand is just cut back to the permitted level. Moreover, relative to quotas, VERs may be more sympathetically (and laxly?) administered, and, because they have to be negotiated periodically, may have a higher political profile than quotas, and thus be less long-lived or restrictive.[1]

The attractions of VERs to importers are less obvious. By granting the rents to the exporters, VERs worsen the terms of trade, and, by forgoing the administration, the government loses some control over its details. Furthermore, the need to allocate the permitted trade over suppliers may cartelise a previously competitive foreign supply, thus worsening the importer's terms of trade even more. Against this, VERs fall outside the GATT system, bind exporters into complicity in controlling trade and can be applied discriminatorily. In short, VERs appear to trade political gains against economic losses.

A formalisation of the possible political advantages of VERs is due to Melvin (1986). Imagine a two-country world in which both trade flows face tariffs. Suppose that the final outcome leaves the terms of trade p_X/p_Y at their free-trade value, but has reduced A's imports to $\bar{X}$ of X and B's to $\bar{Y}$ of Y. Can import quotas support the same equilibrium? Probably not. If both countries replaced their tariffs by import quotas at levels $\bar{X}$ and $\bar{Y}$ the equilibrium might persist, but it would be unstable. If a random shock raised the price of X slightly, residents in A would still demand the $\bar{X}$ units that their government permitted them (ideally they would like more), but the residents of B, who export X, would supply less. They are not allowed more than $\bar{Y}$, and so when the price of X rises they need to sell less X to obtain it. Hence an increase in p_X has generated excess demand for X which exacerbates the price increase, and so on. Only when p_X has risen so far that A's import quota at $\bar{X}$ no longer binds will the process stop. In this case it is B's import quota of $\bar{Y}$ that binds and B secures large terms-of-trade advantages; A is certainly worse off than under free trade. Had the initial shock been to raise p_Y, however, the whole situation would have been reversed.

Melvin observes that with import quotas only one restriction can be binding, and that the terms of trade will necessarily deviate strongly from their free-trade levels. That is, trade intervention conducted with import quotas will not be able to replicate most tariff-ridden equilibria, and will be highly divisive. Contrast this with VERs, whereby A restricts its exports to $\bar{Y}$ and B its to $\bar{X}$. Starting from the same point as before, a small rise in p_X is now self-correcting. B's residents will still export $\bar{X}$ (they would prefer to export more), but A's residents find that the $\bar{Y}$ they can export no longer purchases $\bar{X}$ units, but rather less. Hence there is excess supply of X, which drives the price back to its starting point. Hence VERs can replicate tariff equilibria and thus are consistent with a wider range of resulting terms of trade. If governments are intent on managing trade, Melvin argues, VERs are a much less contentious way of doing so than are import quotas. While we believe that Melvin overstates his case for VERs, it is true that VERs do ease trade diplomacy by improving the restricted exporters' terms of trade.

9.2 OTHER NON-TARIFF BARRIERS

A definition   Non-tariff barriers to international trade (NTBs) strictly comprise any measures, other than tariffs, that affect trade. Such a definition is too broad to be practically useful, however, because it could include policies ranging from the restriction of textile imports – which we would wish to include – to the provision of public fire services – which we presumably would not. The distinction between the two examples is one of *intent*: the former policy is clearly intended to affect trade, whereas any consequences of the latter for trade are coincidental. With this in mind, UNCTAD (the United Nations Conference on Trade and Development) has proposed a three-fold classification of NTBs. Within each class of NTB, they distinguish Group A measures, which operate primarily through quantitative restrictions on trade, from Group B measures, which operate through prices and costs. The three classes are:

- *Type I*: commercial policies designed primarily to protect import-competing sectors or to promote exporting sectors; e.g.

  Group A (quantitative measures): import quotas, restrictions of public purchases to domestic goods, export restraints.
  Group B (price–cost measures): variable levies, production subsidies, income tax concessions on export profits, advanced deposit schemes for imports, different exchange rates for different transactions (multiple exchange rates).

- *Type II*: measures not primarily associated with commercial policy, but that have occasionally been used for protective purposes; e.g.

  Group A: excess trade documentation, delays in customs procedures, advertising restrictions.
  Group B: customs valuation procedures, health requirements, labelling requirements, sales and excise taxes, selective employment taxes.

- *Type III*: measures applied with no intent of protection, but that may have spill-over effects on trade; e.g.

  Group A: government spending plans,[2] restrictions on toxic materials.
  Group B: regional subsidies, monopoly policy, variations in national insurance provisions, national weights and measures.

The limit on class IIIB is rather contentious. Even factors such as the public provision of education and roads could affect the prices of tradable goods, and hence could arguably be included. We feel, however, that to include such measures among NTBs is to raise the free market on to too high a pedestal. Their inclusion would imply that any deviation from the free market is a 'barrier' or 'distortion' from the 'proper' state of affairs, whereas in fact economists have long recognised that governments have a legitimate role in the provision of certain goods and services. For example, defence and judicial services must be publicly provided because they are collectively consumed (they are 'public goods' in the technical sense – see Winch, 1971); water and electricity must be publicly controlled as natural monopolies; roads are most efficiently provided publicly because of the huge transactions costs of a wholly private system; and education and health may be more efficiently and equitably supplied centrally. (Equity is a legitimate political objective of government; economics is concerned only with the *means* of achieving it, e.g. whether or not the provision of services or income supplements is a more efficient way to achieve equity, not with the *end* itself.) Such items as these should be excluded from the realms of NTBs because they correct, rather than introduce, deficiencies in the free market.

A similar argument affects some of the measures in other lists. For example, not all health regulations should be regarded as potential NTBs. The illegality of the non-medical use of heroin in Britain must affect heroin growers abroad, but it is hardly an NTB, and similarly for the Saudi Arabian ban on alcohol. More difficult to judge are circumstances where, say, milk has to be of a particular standard before being sold in Britain. Basic health requirements such as being free from tuberculosis seem uncontentious; if potential exporters cannot meet that standard it is just unfortunate for them. On the other hand, the British government's decision in early 1983 that UHT milk, sold all over France and subject to rigorous French health regulations, might be dangerous for Britons was, *prima facie*, an NTB.[3]

A further possible consideration in defining NTBs is *differential incidence*. To be classed as an NTB, a measure should affect domestic and foreign suppliers or buyers differently. Measures do not have to be explicitly discriminatory to have differential incidence, however. For example, a banana tax in Britain might notionally be levied on both British and foreign banana supplies, but the non-existence of British supplies would render the tax *de facto* differential.

The definition of NTBs has important political implications. By so categorising a measure one is implying that it constitutes a legitimate area of international concern over national economic policy, and, indeed, that ultimately it should be removed. The definition should include both intent and differential incidence as criteria: wheras Type I and II measures are clearly NTBs, the case for including Type III measures is weaker. Only where the declared objective of a Type III measure could be achieved more efficiently in some less trade-distorting way, or where it is trivial relative to the trade distortions it causes, would we recommend calling the measure an NTB. This does not remove such measures from economists' scrutiny, because spill-over effects can be very important, but it does limit the extent to which international views on health, safety, distribution, etc., can implicitly be forced on an independent country.

The definition of the NTBs has recently taken concrete form in the USA's Omnibus Trade Act of 1988. This Act defines certain practices as either NTBs or implicit export subsidies – for example, the absence of some worker rights and export targeting (coordinated efforts to sell in certain markets). It also

111

requires periodic identification of 'priority' countries where policies are held to be particularly harmful to US interests, and with which the US has a large trade deficit. It then authorises, and for priority cases obliges, the US government to seek the revocation of the allegedly offensive practices. In the discussions with Japan that were initiated under the procedure, the US demanded reductions in the working week and reforms in Japan's quaint distribution system. Faced with sanctions Japan agreed to address these issues, and suggested in reply that Americans be restricted to one credit card each (to curb spending) and that the US undertake educational reforms (to boost competitiveness)! It is difficult to defend either set of requests as the legitimate sphere of trade negotiation between independent countries, and the potential for conflict is very high.

The level of NTBs

Non-tariff barriers present even greater problems of meaurement than do tariffs. One approach is to try to estimate the extent to which they raise the prices of the restricted goods, as, for example, in Ennew, Greenaway and Reed's (1990) data shown in Table 8.2(B). For quantitative measures (Group A, above), however, we know that this will not always represent the true tariff equivalent of the NTB, and it might also be very difficult to calculate. Moreover, in a sense it amounts to putting the cart before the horse, because frequently one is interested in measuring an NTB in order to estimate its economic effects, which are, of course, primarily felt through its effects on price.

An alternative approach involves counting NTBs or the amount of the trade that they affect. The resulting measures reflect the extent, rather than the restrictiveness, of the NTBs, but that is sufficient for many purposes. The *frequency ratio* shows the proportion of headings in a trade classification which are subject to a particular type or set of NTBs. The *coverage ratio* calculates the proportion of total trade falling in the affected headings. Frequency ratios tend to overstate the extent of NTBs because they give equal weight to each NTB and trade classifications tend to become more finely subdivided the more sensitive (i.e. the more likely to be restricted) an area of trade becomes. Coverage ratios, on the other hand, tend to understate extent, because NTBs reduce the levels of trade in the headings they affect. In the limit, an import prohibition receives zero weight in the coverage ratio, just as would an unrestricted trade heading! This bias can sometimes be reduced by using trade from a previous year or a different country from the NTB data, but this reduces the ratio's accuracy and the bias remains if, as is usual, NTB patterns are similar across countries and through time.

Both frequency and coverage ratios will be more accurate the finer the disaggregation of the trade and NTB data and, naturally, the more accurate are the original sources. The imprecision of the definition of NTBs and the fact that many of them are ostensibly between private parties – e.g. the definition of some standards, and VERs between producer organisations in exporting and importing countries – mean that even official inventories are incomplete. The best available data – collected by UNCTAD and analysed by them and the World Bank – are plausibly complete only for governmental commodity-specific, border measures and voluntary export restraints – and even these are subject to considerable error and frequent revision. They were most comprehensively analysed by Nogues, Olechowski and Winters (1986), some of whose results are reported in Table 9.1.

Table 9.1 prompts several observations. First, in most cases the 'own trade'

Table 9.1 The extent of industrial countries' non-tariff barriers to imports, 1983 (%)

| | Coverage ratios (1981 imports) | | Frequency ratios |
	Own trade	World trade[a]	
All imports	27.1	21.8	12.8
(A) *By products*:			
Fuels	43.0	31.0	23.9
Agriculture	36.1	40.4	29.5
Manufactures	16.1	14.9	10.8
Textiles	44.8	37.8	38.1
Iron and steel	35.4	35.8	18.3
Electrical machinery	10.0	10.8	5.4
Vehicles	30.4	25.9	7.4
(B) *By measure*:			
Quantitative restrictions[b]	8.6	9.5	5.0
VERs[c]	3.0	1.4	3.4
Monitoring, etc.[d]	14.8	9.8	4.6
(C) *By country*:			
USA[e]	43.0	34.3	7.0
Japan	11.9	9.0	9.3
EC (10)	22.3	18.9	13.8
France	57.1	44.2	24.0
Germany	12.4	14.7	12.5
UK	14.3	13.9	13.8

Notes:
[a] Coverage ratio using industrial countries' trade.
[b] Quotas, prohibitions, licensing.
[c] Including the Multifibre Arrangement.
[d] Import surveillance, anti-dumping and countervailing duties and investigations.
[e] These figures are strongly influenced by import quotas on oil, which were not binding in 1983 and were removed in 1984. Without oil the row would read: 17.3, 12.3, 6.6.
Source: Nogues, Olechowski and Winters (1986).

coverage ratio exceeds the 'world trade' coverage ratio, which in turn exceeds the frequency ratio; this implies that countries typically restrict their larger trade flows. Second, agriculture suffers more restriction than manufacturing, although in the latter there are several hot-spots. Much agricultural protection is in the form of variable levies (see below) which figure in the totals but are not separately recorded in part (B) of the table. Third, the sum of entries in part (B), plus similar entries for the NTBs not explicitly reported, exceeds the totals at the top of the table because many import flows are subject to several NTBs. Fourth, the inclusion of monitoring measures as NTBs is legitimate: merely investigating a claim of dumping or imposing import surveillance (a heightened degree of statistical recording of imports) tends to curtail imports, and is probably pursued by importing governments partly with that intent. Fifth, despite a strong folklore to the contrary, Japan is less, not more, restrictive than the USA and the EC. Finally, although many measures are omitted from Table 9.1, NTBs still cover a large volume of industrial countries' trade.

Non-tariff protection has shown a distinct tendency to increase since about 1970. Detailed data are not available for the whole of this period but, using a broad definition of NTBs and fairly crude trade data, Laird and Yeats (1988) show that the coverage ratio of industrial countries' total trade increased from 25 per cent in 1966 to 48 per cent in 1986, with the frequency ratio increasing from 17 per cent to 54 per cent. Agriculture and food showed the largest increases, but manufactures also recorded large rises: frequency up from 5 per cent to 51 per cent and coverage up from 19 per cent to 58 per cent. The latter increases are largest for textiles, iron and steel and electric machinery.

A further important element of non-tariff protection is subsidies. Outside agriculture, export subsidies are rare (they are banned by the GATT) but production subsidies are not. Yet again there are conceptual and practical difficulties of measurement, but even on conservative definitions the Commission of the European Communities (1989) suggests that subsidy payments amounted to significant proportions of manufactured value-added in the early 1980s: for example, 16 per cent in Italy, 12 per cent in Ireland and 3 per cent in the UK. These include subsidies for research and development, as well as support through the official underwriting of losses and subsidised capital restructuring. The main recipients include iron and steel and vehicles, which are both also supported by border measures. (Observe how the same sectors receive support through several channels.) Subsidies are even greater in primary sectors – e.g. agriculture and coal – and for transportation – e.g. railways.

9.3 THE EFFECTS OF NTBs

Measurement   When we estimate the economic effects of a tariff we know immediately the wedge that it causes between domestic and world prices. If we also know the elasticities of supply and demand we can calculate the effects of the wedge on prices and quantities and hence, using equation (8.2), calculate the change in economic welfare between the tariff-ridden and hypothetical free-trade situations. Moreover, even if we do not know the elasticities, we may be able to estimate them, for, although a tariff affects the price of imports, it does not affect their responsiveness to changes in prices. NTBs are more complex. We have direct observations on neither their effect on the quantities traded nor the wedge between world and domestic prices, and neither can we easily estimate elasticities because NTBs frequently prevent quantities from responding to prices. The latter problem is largely intractable; the former means that we need indirect approaches to prices and quantities. Several alternatives exist.

Most Group B NTBs can be treated like tariffs. For example, an import deposit scheme is basically a tariff on imports. Before receiving customs clearance, importers have to deposit at the central bank some fraction or multiple of the value of their imports. This deposit receives no interest, so the importer is making an interest-free loan to the authorities, and the interest forgone represents the implicit tariff. Similarly, requiring excessive health and safety tests on imports raises their prices like a tariff, although here resources may be wasted in the protection, and any revenue generated may accrue to private firms if they undertake the tests on behalf of the government.

In other cases it is necessary to estimate what the import price would have been in the absence of the NTB. The most direct way is to compare domestic prices with world prices. Under a small country assumption, the latter reflects the hypothetical import price directly, but even for a large country the estimated wedge can be combined with elasticity information to estimate the free-trade outcome. The problem with this approach is that, for any but the simplest products, it is impossible to be sure that the domestic and world price observations are for identical goods at the same stage of production, or to know how much to allow for transport costs. As a result this approach is most commonly used for agricultural products.

Other approaches to estimating free-trade prices include comparing price

114

changes in restricted and unrestricted markets over the period when the NTB is imposed and/or removed; using cost data; and extrapolating the trends in pre-NTB prices into the NTB period. It is also occasionally possible to estimate the rents accruing to exporters or import agents as a result of the NTB. When quotas or VERs are in operation, the right to sell in the restricted market is valuable – it allows one to charge p_r in Figure 9.1 for goods which one would supply for p_w. In theory one would be prepared to pay a quota premium of very nearly $(p_r - p_w)$ for that right, and so if there were a market for quota rights one might expect it to reflect the wedge between the restricted price and minimum supply price directly. The problem is that markets only occasionally exist and even then are thin or illegal. Moreover, complex allocation rules can distort the size of the quota premium; for example, if next year's allocation of quota depends on this year's sales it may be worth paying over the odds this year in order to increase your sales (profits) next year.

A final approach to NTBs is to estimate the change in the quantity of imports they induce. This may be evident from changes in a time series of quantities when the NTB is imposed.

The costs of QRs Table 9.2 reports some estimates of the costs of quantitative restrictions (QRs). They use the various approaches to estimating the price and quantity effects discussed above and from them calculate the equivalents of areas a, b, c and d in Figure 9.1. Since QRs are mostly exporter specific, areas c, the quota-rents, are mostly transferred to the exporters; they are usually the largest component of costs.

Table 9.2 The costs of quantitative restrictions: some examples

Product	Year	Restricted countries	Consumer cost	Total cost	Source
(A) *United Kingdom*:					
Video cassette recorders	1983	Japan	£80 m.	£80 m.	Greenaway and Hindley (1985)
Cars	1983	Japan	£180 m.	n.a.	Greenaway and Hindley (1985)
Footwear	1979	Korea Taiwan Poland	£79 m.	£57 m.	Takacs and Winters (1990)
(B) *United States*:					
Cars	1983–4	Japan	$2.3 b.	n.a.	Feenstra (1988a)
Footwear (non-rubber)	1981	Korea Taiwan	$700 m.	$236 m.	Hufbauer, Berliner and Elliott (1986)
Colour TVs	1982	Japan Korea Taiwan	$420 m.	$147 m.	Hufbauer, Berliner and Elliott (1986)
Sugar	1983	Many	$735 m.	$252 m.	Tarr and Morkre (1984)

Upgrading Import quotas and VERs often impose a single limit on a broadly defined aggregate of goods – for example, cars or non-rubber footwear. This can cause the mix of varieties of good within the aggregate to change. Imagine an exporter deciding which variety to supply against his last unit of quota: he will choose the one offering the highest profit per unit. Generalising, exporters will

115

allocate their quotas across varieties until the last unit of each variety yields the same absolute profit. If unit profits are higher on better-quality varieties – say, because percentage mark-ups are equal across varieties – restricted exporters will bias their export bundles towards better-quality goods. By the same token, consumers may well bias their demand towards better varieties. Under free trade the marginal unit of each variety supplied earns zero profit; under a VER it earns a common amount k. Hence from the consumer's viewpoint the VER is like a flat-rate tax at rate k; such a tax increases the prices of lower-priced varieties proportionally more than those of higher-priced varieties and hence may shift demand.

Upgrading is not inevitable even in theory, as Bark and de Melo (1987) show, so in the end the issue is an empirical one. Apart from causal observation, two approaches have been adopted. The first expresses each variety in terms of several characteristics, e.g. for cars, size, horsepower, seating capacity, etc. Then by regressing the prices of the various cars on sale prior to the imposition of the VER on their characteristics, the implicit value of each characteristic may be calculated. That is, the price of car i, π_i, can be expressed in terms of its set characteristics c_{ij}, where j counts across characteristics, and $\hat{p}_j$ is the (estimated) value of characteristic j:

$$\pi_i^0 = \sum_j c_{ij}^0 \hat{p}_j^0, \tag{9.1}$$

where superscript ^{0} denotes the original, free-trade, situation.

Turning to the VER-ridden position, which we denote by superscript ^{1}, three things can occur. First, the price of a given car can rise, i.e.

$$\pi_i^1 > \sum_j c_{ij}^0 \hat{p}_j^0; \tag{9.2}$$

this is just the rent transfer we noted above. Second, certain cars might be adapted to embody more or better characteristics; since the $\hat{p}_j$ reflect the value of each characteristic, we can detect this if for any i

$$\sum_j c_{ij}^1 \hat{p}_j^0 > \sum_j c_{ij}^0 \hat{p}_j^0. \tag{9.3}$$

Third, the composition of the total bundle of cars imported might swing towards better cars. Writing s_i for the share of type i in total car imports, this occurs if

$$\sum_i s_i^1 \left(\sum_j c_{ij}^0 \hat{p}_j^0 \right) > \sum_i s_i^0 \left(\sum_j c_{ij}^0 \hat{p}_j^0 \right) \tag{9.4}$$

This approach is feasible only where the characteristics of goods are easily identifiable and measurable. Hence it has largely been restricted to motor vehicles, and is closely associated with Feenstra (1988a). Feenstra calculated that the USA's VER on Japanese car exports over the period 1981–4 led to a pure price increase (9.2) of over $1,000 per car; quality upgrading (9.3) of 25 per cent; and a composition shift (9.4) raising average quality by 6 per cent. Moreover, repeating the exercise on US imports of Japanese trucks, which were restricted by an *ad valorem* tariff rather than a VER, he found no serious evidence of upgrading. (Rework the theoretical discussion above to see why none would be predicted.)

The second approach to quality upgrading is cruder, but is feasible when characteristics cannot be measured. Using (9.1), (9.4) may be written as

$$\sum_i s_i^1 \pi_i^0 > \sum_i s_i^0 \pi_i^0; \tag{9.5}$$

hence if we find that a VER induces a shift towards varieties which originally had higher prices we might conclude that average quality has increased. This approach has been adopted most commonly for footwear, although using more complex index numbers than (9.5) implies. Both Aw and Roberts (1986) and de Melo and Winters (1989) found evidence that the USA's restriction on footwear imports from Korea and Taiwan over the period 1977–81 raised prices. The former, using US import data, found evidence of upgrading, especially for Taiwan, while the latter, using Korean export data, found none. The issue remains open.

Finally, the costs of NTBs in agriculture and in textiles and clothing are illustrated in case-studies 9.1 and 9.2, which pull together some of the theories of this and the previous chapter.

CASE-STUDY 9.1: AGRICULTURE IN INDUSTRIAL COUNTRIES

Agriculture is the most protected and distorted sector in most industrial economies. International trade is variously subject to variable import levies, export subsidies, tariffs, import quotas, VERs, and restrictive sanitary and quality regulations. Domestic production receives subsidies, high guaranteed prices, transport subsidies, capital improvement grants, production quotas and input quotas. These policies interact in such complex ways that it is virtually impossible to model their effects directly. Most general studies of agricultural protection, therefore, summarise their effects in one of two measures – the nominal protection coefficient, which is the percentage excess of domestic over world prices, or the producer subsidy equivalent, the subsidy which farmers would have to receive to maintain their current income levels at current production levels, if all support policies were abolished. Both measures indicate huge support, as Table 9.3 shows. The most protectionist of OECD countries are Japan and members of EFTA followed by the EC, but even the USA and Canada support agriculture heavily.

Table 9.3 Agricultural protection in industrial countries (%)

	Nominal protection coefficients 1980–2	Producer subsidy equivalents 1986[a]
Wheat	25	61
Rice	150	91
Ruminant meat	50	50
Sugar	50	72
Dairy products	90	78

Note:
[a] As % of the value of output under free trade.
Sources: NPC – Tyers and Anderson (1988); PSE – OECD (1989).

117

With such large price wedges, agricultural support is very costly in terms of welfare – equation (8.2) shows that deadweight losses are proportional to the square of the price wedge; consumer surplus is reduced (perhaps as much as $800 per household in the EC and $1,120 in Japan), taxpayers frequently have to pay out for subsidies, and resources are wasted as factors are pulled out of industry and into agriculture. The principal beneficiaries of agricultural support are land-owners. Land is necessary to growing crops to sell at subsidised prices; since it is in almost wholly inelastic supply, when people bid for agricultural resources they bid up the price of land until it absorbs all the excess profit offered via the subsidies. Other agricultural inputs are elastic in supply – the bidding increases their quantities strongly but their prices relatively little. This is particularly true of labour: subsidies hardly increase farmers' incomes from farming as opposed to land-owning at all. The principal domestic casualties of agricultural support are consumers; moreover, since the poor spend a higher share of their incomes on food they suffer disproportionately from food price increases. Agricultural support is thus highly regressive.

OECD agricultural support also hits food producers world-wide. By increasing world supplies it reduces world prices and turns the terms of trade against efficient producers. The principal casualties are countries such as Australia, New Zealand, Argentina and Thailand. On the other hand, it must be noted that food-importing developing countries such as Bangladesh gain from the world price reductions induced by farm policy.

There have been many studies of the costs of agricultural support (see Winters, 1987a). For example, Tyers and Anderson (1988) estimated that support for grains, livestock and sugar in 1980–2 cost EC consumers $55 b., with a net economy-wide cost of $9 b.; corresponding figures for EFTA are $12 b. and $3 b., for Japan $36 b. and $9 b., and for the USA $18 b. and $3 b. The net cost of all industrial country support after allowing for the interactions between policies was $20 b. By now all these figures would be substantially larger.

The most recent estimates concern the effects of liberalising agricultural policy in the main OECD economies in 1986–8 (Martin *et al.*, 1990). Table 9.4 reports some of the principal results. Abolishing agricultural support in the six areas treated would boost their real income by $72 b. – nearly 1 per cent. In most economies it would allow factors of production to move out of food and agriculture and into other sectors where they would be more productive; Australia and New Zealand would experience the reverse movement. The

Table 9.4 The economy-wide effects of agricultural liberalisation, 1986–8

	Australia	Canada	EC	Japan	New Zealand	USA	Average
Percentage change in:							
Household income	0.8	1.3	1.4	1.1	2.7	0.3	0.9
Output:							
Agriculture	4.4	− 16.7	− 18.7	− 24.2	7.9	− 7.0	− 13.6
Food processing	14.4	1.0	− 21.3	− 13.9	18.9	− 2.8	− 11.9
Other	− 0.7	0.9	2.1	1.2	− 2.4	0.4	1.1
Land rents	− 4.4	− 53.0	− 40.3	− 44.3	38.7	− 41.2	− 39.6
Cost per job in agriculture ($'000, 1988)	—	99	20	13	—	20	—

Source: Martin *et al.* (1990).

abolition of support would reduce land rents by an average of 40 per cent. Finally, the last row reports the net deadweight cost per job preserved in agriculture by current policies. This figure excludes the transfers made to farmers and ignores the fact that jobs saved in agriculture are jobs lost elsewhere; nevertheless, the costs are huge.

**Variable
import levies**

The principal instrument of agricultural protection in the EC and certain EFTA countries is the variable levy. Crudely, a domestic (EC) price is fixed for each good – the reference price at Duisberg in Germany – and imports have to pay the tariff that just makes their net price equal the reference price allowing for transport to Duisberg. The European price is thus entirely fixed; consumers can never gain from, nor producers be threatened by, foreign efficiency.

The levy is re-calculated every day to bring the lowest available import offer price up to the reference price; provided that there is competition between exporters, this ensures that they cannot capture the levy by raising their prices. The levy means that European production and consumption are independent of world prices. Hence any fluctuations in foreign supply or demand fall disproportionately more heavily on other markets: fixing the European price makes prices elsewhere in the world more variable. Tyers and Anderson (1988) estimated that liberalising the EC's Common Agricultural Policy would reduce world price instability by one-half for dairy products, and one-quarter for wheat.

CASE-STUDY 9.2: TEXTILES AND CLOTHING

Among manufacturers, textiles and clothing have the longest and deepest traditions of protection. They mostly entail standardised labour-intensive processes applied to widely available raw materials, and hence are ideally suited to developing countries' early stages of industrialisation. Unfortunately they also still comprise a substantial part of developed countries' industrial output, frequently employing relatively elderly workers and being highly concentrated geographically. They have thus become a battleground for trade diplomacy and a hunting ground for trade economists seeking evidence.

The market for textiles has grown less rapidly than the markets for other goods since at least 1900. In the early twentieth century, established producers were already being squeezed between new suppliers and a static demand; by the 1930s the USA had negotiated a 'gentleman's agreement' with Japan and the UK had arranged preferential treatment of her textiles throughout the Empire. In the early GATT rounds, textiles received special treatment, but this could not reverse the decline of traditional producers in the face of expansion by developing countries and Japan, and in the late 1950s Britain concluded VERs with Hong Kong, Japan and India.

Britain was not alone in feeling the pinch. In 1961, multilateral controls were introduced under the auspices of the GATT. Designed to avoid 'serious damage' to developed country producers, these provisions were contrary to several GATT principles (unilateral and discriminatory quotas being forbidden). In allowing them, the GATT was just recognising, and seeking to

119

contain, their grave threat to the emerging liberal trading order. The restrictions initially formed a 'Short-Term Arrangement on Cotton Textiles', but within a year were encompassed by a stronger 'Long-Term Arrangement Regarding International Trade in Cotton Textiles' (LTA). The LTA applied for five years at first, but was then extended until 1970 and then 1973. It covered twenty-nine countries and provided for only a limited growth in quotas over the period (5 per cent per annum). This permitted European output to expand rather than contract in an orderly way (although employment fell), which suggests that its intent was protectionist rather than merely to smooth adjustment.

The LTA was superseded by the MFA (the Multi-Fibre Arrangement), which covered more textile fibres and more countries. Its provisions were originally somewhat more liberal over the nature and extent of quotas, but its renewals and re-negotiation in 1979, 1982 and 1986 have produced ever fiercer controls. MFA IV, which continues until 1991, covers thirty-nine developing country exporters, twelve industrial importing countries (counting the EC as one), and many fabrics and types of clothes. All told there are over 3,000 bilateral restraints on trade!

Behind these international controls, Britain has sought to stimulate some adjustment in the textile industry. Incentives have been offered to rationalise the industry – replacing old plant with new, and moving into new lines. Indeed, the improvement in productivity has outweighed import pentration as the immediate cause of job losses. Output and employment are nevertheless still much higher than can be justified by any notion of comparative advantage.

The net effect of the MFA has been to raise textile and clothing prices in industrial countries by 5–10 per cent (this is the 'quota effect', in addition to that of tariffs) and to induce exporters to diversify into non-protected and higher-quality lines of produce. In the longer run, this has exacerbated the pressure on domestic producers and has probably stimulated the development of the South-East Asian producers from simple to sophisticated goods and processes. It has also led to trade diversion whereby restricted exporters lose market shares to unrestricted ones – partly to new developing country suppliers (who are promptly brought within the MFA) and partly to (unrestrained) industrial suppliers.

A recent study of the UK (Silberston, 1989) suggested that, on average, clothing cost 5 per cent more and textiles 2 per cent as a result of the MFA in 1988. This imposed consumer losses of around £1 b., amounting perhaps to £30,000 per clothing job preserved. Earlier, Greenaway and Hindley (1985) had found quota premia of 15 per cent added to tariffs of 17 per cent on three types of clothing in 1982. These amounts suggest consumer losses of £170 m. and net economic losses of £68 m. The principal sources of loss are tariff revenue (the UK loses 17 per cent for every unit kept out by quota) and transfers, not only the rents earned by the restrained exporters, but also the higher prices paid to other suppliers as a result of trade diversion.

For developing countries the MFA has two effects. First, it diverts purchases from restrained to unrestrained suppliers; this has helped some unrestrained suppliers to grow, but, in general, trade diversion to developing suppliers has not been very great. Second, it increases developing countries' rents. It is sometimes argued that these transfers outweigh the welfare losses from the reduction in trade, but in fact this seems only rarely to be the case. Trela and Whalley (1990) estimate that the abolition of the MFA and its

120

associated tariffs in 1986 would have raised welfare in developing countries by $7.75 b. Korea, Taiwan and mainland China would have been the major beneficiaries, reflecting their ability to expand their sales; only Macao and Hong Kong would have shown net losses. These authors also calculate that industrial countries would have gained from liberalisation by $7.25 b., making the global benefit of abolition $15 b.

FURTHER READING

The theoretical analysis of quotas is best accomplished by *Bhagwati* (1969a, ch. 9), who covers the basic case and the (non-) equivalence with tariffs. *Corden* (1971) also provides useful insight, and *Krueger* (1974) is the classic reference on rent-seeking. Voluntary export restraints are introduced by *Takacs* (1978) and *Hamilton* (1986). *Baldwin* (1970) provides a thorough and classic early survey of non-tariff barriers in general, while later work is to be found in *Nogues, Olechowski and Winters* (1986) and *Laird and Yeats* (1988, 1990). *Tarr and Morkre* (1984), *Greenaway and Hindley* (1985), and *Hufbauer, Berliner and Elliott* (1986) offer straightforward quantifications of the welfare effects of NTBs. General works on protectionism include *Yeats* (1979), *Greenaway* (1983), *Corden* (1984), the World Bank's *World Development Report 1987*, and *Kelly et al.* (1988). *Grinols* (1989) discusses the US 1988 Trade Act. Upgrading is analysed by *Hamilton* (1986) and *Bark and de Melo* (1987; note that the captions of figures 2 and 3 have been reversed), as well as by the empirical references in the text. Agricultural protection is covered accessibly by the World Bank's *World Development Report, 1986* and *Winters* (1987a). On textiles and clothing *Hamilton* (1990) is excellent, while *Keesing and Wolf* (1980), *Hamilton* (1981), *Goto* (1989), *Silberston* (1989), and *National Consumer Council* (1990) are also useful. *Dore* (1982) considers sociological aspects of textiles decline.

KEY CONCEPTS

import quota	VER
quota allocation	rent-seeking
coverage ratio	frequency ratio
upgrading	rent transfer
trade diversion	producer subsidy equivalents
variable levies	

QUESTIONS FOR REVIEW

9.1 Draw diagrams to show the non-equivalence of tariffs and quotas under demand uncertainty. (Hint: consider just the market for imports, with a linear demand schedule and a fixed world price; assume that demand is either 'high' or 'low' with equal probability and set the tariff and quota so that they have equal effects at the average level of demand. Consider the welfare effects.)

9.2 What are the principal differences between import quotas and VERs?

9.3 Discuss the merits of different measures of the extent of NTBs.

9.4 Suppose a VER increases the average price of Japanese TVs by £50. How could you decompose this into price and quality effects? How would the decomposition affect your estimate of the welfare effects of the VER?

9.5 In what ways are variable import levies and import quotas similar? (Consider changes in demand and supply.)

NOTES

1 VERs and quotas also differ in circumstances of monopoly and where they are applied discriminatorily – see Takacs (1978).

2 For example, a non-nuclear electricity generating programme limits other countries' exports of reactors.

3 Among the evidence produced in the House of Commons was that the Secretary of State for Trade and Industry's dog would not drink UHT milk! Wisely the British government rapidly rescinded the ban. See *The Times* of 9 February and 18 March 1983 for further details.

10 Static Arguments for Protection

This chapter and the next examine the arguments for protection and also the form that protection should take. Intervention may be justified economically when the conditions for the optimality of free trade are violated, but different violations entail different solutions. This chapter considers static arguments – conditions that would entail protection forever – while the next considers dynamic and 'strategic' arguments. Frequently the case for protection is ostensibly non-economic: e.g. the desire for a domestic steel industry in case of war. These are perfectly legitimate objectives, but the political gains should be weighed against the economic losses that they entail. These vary with the form that protection takes.

Before commencing, let us dispose of one entirely spurious argument for protection: that free trade exposes our producers to 'unfair' competition from cheaper factors of production abroad. This implies that all cheap imports from abroad should be discouraged, which clearly undermines the whole of international trade based on comparative advantage. Closely related is the view that by importing the products of under-paid 'sweated labour' elsewhere in the world we are conniving at these peoples' exploitation. To substantiate this we should need to show that, when 'sweated labourers' are offered the choice of producing for export or not at all, they mistake their own interests in choosing the former. This is possible, but it is not an easy proposition to uphold. On a more practical level, even if it were the case, we should still need to be sure that a trade embargo would improve their lot.

10.1 DOMESTIC DISTORTIONS

Conditions for optimality   We have seen above (section 7.1) that a necessary condition for the maximisation of welfare in an open economy is

$$MRTT_S = MRT_S = MRS_S \qquad (10.1)$$

where $MRTT$ is the marginal rate of transformation through trade, MRT is the marginal rate of transformation (through production), and MRS is the marginal rate of substitution (in consumption). All refer to social and not private marginal rates, and are thus subscripted S. The equality of the two marginal rates of transformation ensures that no increase in output is achievable by switching between domestic production and trade as a means of transformation. The equality of the marginal rate of substitution and the (common) marginal rate of transformation ensures that no increase in welfare is achievable by altering the bundle of goods made available by production and trade.

This section considers an economy where (10.1) does not apply, and asks (i) how the equalities can be achieved, i.e. how optimality can be brought about, and (ii) whether, failing that, some second-best improvement may be made. At the same time, it considers the opposite question: if we have an economy satisfying (10.1), but wish for some *apparently non-economic* reason to

123

alter the resulting equilibrium, what is the least-cost method of doing so? The answers are intimately related.

It does not matter whether (10.1) is brought about by prices or by planning, but we shall concentrate on the price mechanism. Under the latter, agents set their marginal rates equal to prices, which they take as given. The economics links in that process are shown in Figure 10.1. In the absence of any distortions, the consumer price ratio (P_C) determines the private marginal rate of substitution (MRS_P), which in turn determines the social rate (MRS_S); similarly for the production and trade sectors. In the perfect economy, all links are characterised by equality.

TRADE

$MRTT_S$

$MRTT_P$

P_F

CONSUMPTION P_D PRODUCTION

P_C P_T

MRS_P MRT_P

MRS_S MRT_S

P_C, P_T and P_F are consumers', producers' and world relative prices, respectively.
P_D is domestic tax-exclusive prices.
MRS is the marginal rate of substitution (in consumption).
MRT is the marginal rate of transformation (in production).
$MRTT$ is the marginal rate of transformation through trade.
Subscript S denotes social values and subscript P denotes private values.

Figure 10.1 Price signals in the market economy

Distortions   Two basic sets of distortions can corrupt (10.1): (a) market imperfections, which cause private and social marginal rates to differ, and (b) taxes, which cause the prices that agents face to differ from domestic tax-exclusive prices. (We include in the concept 'taxes' subsidies, which are merely negative taxes.) Group (a) distortions are autonomous, but group (b) are policy variables.

Suppose we have an economy with perfect markets everywhere except in consumption, where an autonomous externality causes private and social rates of transformation to diverge. Assume

$$MRS_P = Z . MRS_S \qquad (10.2)$$

where $Z \neq 1$. Overall we have

124

$$MRTT_S = MRT_S = P_D = P_C = MRS_P \neq MRS_S. \qquad (10.3)$$

To restore full optimality we could manipulate $MRTT$ and MRT, but a simpler procedure would be to operate directly on consumption. We require a policy such that when private consumers set $MRS_P = P_C$ they also produce $MRS_S = P_D$. An obvious candidate is a consumption tax that sets

$$P_C = Z \cdot P_D, \qquad (10.4)$$

which produces the required equality

$$MRTT_S = MRT_S = P_D = P_C/Z = MRS_P/Z = MRS_S. \qquad (10.5)$$

This illustrates the following general rule: if there is a distortion in any sector of the economy, it is optimality met by a countervailing distortion *in the same sector*.

We shall look at some detailed examples later, but we now consider the related question. Suppose we have an undistorted economy but that for security reasons we wish to stimulate the output of steel. This means that, relative to the market equilibrium, we wish to allow a rise in the MRT of steel, because if output is to rise, so too, in increasing costs industries, must marginal costs. Again Figure 10.1 suggests that, if we use a production subsidy that raises P_T relative to P_D we can avoid disturbing the equalities elsewhere in the system. In general, to impose some non-economic change on a sector of the economy, the optimal policy is applied only in that sector.

These rules define first-best policies, but even among other, second-best, alternatives some ranking is usually possible.

Production Our first example concerns a production externality in an otherwise perfect small trading economy. To maximise welfare, the general rules suggest that a production tax is the first-best response. Second best is a tariff because, although the tariff introduces distortions to the consumption sector, it does at least have some effect on production. Third best is free trade, and last a consumption tax (which merely introduces further distortions without touching the original one).

Figure 10.2(A) summarises the argument. The transformation curve FF reflects the true (social) opportunity costs of Y in terms of X, MRT_S. Private producers, on the other hand, who do not recognise the externality, perceive a different trade-off, MRT_P. Because factor markets are not distorted by a production externality the economy will still operate on FF, but the point chosen will equate MRT_P, rather than MRT_S, to P_T. Figure 10.2(A) is drawn so that the social opportunity cost of Y exceeds the private cost – that is, as in the top right-hand corner, the social cost ratio is flatter than the private one, the difference in slope representing the externality. Under free trade, and assuming a small economy, the terms of trade (TT) define the domestic price ratio, P_D, which defines the producer price ratio, P_T; this is equated with MRT_P, which happens to imply production point P. (At P the social opportunity cost ratio which allows for the externality, MRT_S, is given by II.) The problem arises because, at P, $MRTT_S = P_F = P_D = P_T = MRT_P \neq MRT_S$, so that P does not maximise the value of production at world prices. *Given production*, however, consumption is undistorted, so that $MRS_S = P_C = P_D = P_F = MRTT_S$ ensures the selection of the optimal bundle, C, conditional on output P.

Now suppose we subsidise X to just offset the externality. At the prevailing prices – defined by slope TT – producers' returns on X rise; they thus switch

(A) *A production externality*

(B) *A production objective*

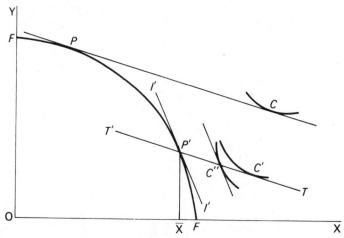

Figure 10.2 Trade policy and distortions. (A) A production externality. (B) A production objective

from Y to X, moving round the transformation frontier to P'. Internal prices (P_D) still equal slope TT, but private producer prices (P_T) equal slope $J'J'$ (steeper, because X is subsidised); private MRT_P is set to P_T, and, accounting for the externality, this just ensures that $MRT_S = P_D$. Thus at prices $P_D = P_F$, P' maximises the social value of output. Given P', undistorted trade and consumption allow consumption to settle at C', which is plainly the optimum. Thus a production subsidy is first best.

The figure also illustrates the consequences of imposing a tariff on X at a rate below that of the optimum production subsidy. This moves production from

126

P to P'', not so far round as P' because the tariff does not fully off-set the externality. The tariff-ridden private costs are shown by $J''J''$ both at P'' and also at C'', the consumption point. The consumption distortion inherent in the tariff means that the improved production allocation is now partly off-set by a new consumption misallocation. However, it may be shown that a tariff can always be found to improve on *laissez-faire*. Thus, in the presence of a production externality, a production tax/subsidy is optimal, but a tariff is second best. The second-best tariff will be at a rate below the first-best production subsidy.

The related question is how best to shift production away from the free-trade point if that is what is desired. This is illustrated in Figure 10.2(B). Free trade produces equilibrium P and C, but suppose society requires at least $\bar{X}$ of X for security reasons. This implies that production must shift to P', at which point producers must face prices of slope $I'I'$. If a production subsidy is used, consumption is undistorted and can be at C', but if a tariff is used $MRS = MRT = P_D \neq P_F$, and consumption settles at C'', which is clearly inferior. The tariff introduces an additional distortion (on consumption) relative to the production tax.

Consumption

The analysis of consumption externalities and external objectives is very similar to that just carried out. To cure a consumption distortion, or to change the consumption basket for non-economic reasons, consumption taxes are first best, tariffs are second best, free trade is next, and production taxes are last.

Factor market distortions

So far we have assumed that factor markets are perfect, so that industries can purchase factors at their true opportunity cost, and production always takes place on the transformation frontier. Unfortunately, factor markets are as frequently distorted as other markets. For example, industries tend to pay different wages to their labour. If this reflects differences in levels of skill or in the non-pecuniary elements of the job, this is not distortionary, but if it arises from the industries' different monopsony power, or from any monopoly powers of the trades unions, or from social legislation, it is distortionary and imposes economic costs. Similarly, differential labour taxes or differential institutional hindrances on borrowing capital also constitute distortions.

The effects of factor market distortions are, first, to shrink the transformation frontier inwards and, second, to distort relative costs so that, even along the shrunken-in frontier, private and social costs differ. The latter is equivalent to the production externality just analysed and may be treated accordingly. However, although a production tax would find the optimal point along the ruling transformation frontier, it does nothing about the frontier itself. The first-best solution is to cure the factor market distortion, which both pushes the transformation frontier out to its maximum and ensures a tangency solution along it. This cure could involve countervailing factor taxes or institutional changes. Either way the moral is the same: policy should be directed at the distorted sector – in this case the factor markets. The general rule also carries through to the reverse question: to stimulate factor use (employment, say) factors taxes are first best, followed by production taxes and then tariffs. Bhagwati and Srinivasan (1969) showed that to maintain employment in a particular sector a wage subsidy is optimal: a production subsidy pulls both factors of production out of the rest of the economy, reducing its output strongly relative to free trade, whereas a wage subsidy pulls only labour across and hence involves smaller output distortions.

127

Conclusion   This analysis is a fine example of the theory of second best. It shows that, in the presence of one distortion, applying the optimality conditions to the other sectors (i.e. free trade) is not optimal. It also shows, however, that this does not leave us powerless; we can still make rather strong orderings among the remaining second-best policies.

The practical conclusion of the analysis is that incurable distortions should be treated in the sector in which they occur, and not by more general policies. Thus, while domestic distortions constitute a valid case for protection via taxes or subsidies, they do not constitute a case for tariffs or quotas. The empirical application of the results of this section is unusual, for governments do not usually justify protection in terms of static distortions within their own economies. None the less, the prevalence of domestic distortions suggests that there is considerable scope for application. An interesting example of the use – or strictly, abuse – of the non-economic objectives argument is the case of agricultural protection. Every industrial country appeals to ostensibly non-economic objectives as a reason for agricultural protection. These include keeping the countryside beautiful, the maintenance of rural societies, food security in the face of war or embargo, and environmental objectives. Winters (1989b) makes two sets of points about these so-called non-economic objectives (SNOs). First, they are basically economic: they are generally quantifiable in monetary terms (Pigou's definition of economic), e.g. via the premia that rural houses command, and even when they are not so measurable they clearly involve trade-offs of the sort that economics is concerned with. For example, a more beautiful countryside may require sacrifices in the level of output. Second, existing agricultural policy, which comprises production subsidies and protection, is a very inefficient way of achieving SNOs. For instance, high output prices encourage the immediate utilisation of every scrap of land, reducing its long-term fertility and destroying various amenity features such as hedgerows, coppices and pure water supplies. Indeed, Winters argues, the dissonance between ends and means is so great that one has to question whether SNOs really are the reason for agricultural support. Case-study 10.1 considers one SNO – national security – in greater detail.

Even acceping that output policies are justified for agriculture, there is room for greater efficiency. Prior to acceding to the EC, Britain used a system of deficiency payments – income subsidies – but on accession she adopted the less efficient approach of tariff protection. The result was a large rise in British food prices, because, whereas under the former system consumers faced world prices, under the latter they faced the same (distorted) prices as farmers received. The loss of consumers' surplus was considerable. Miller (1971) quoted *predicted* welfare losses from the switch in protective methods as £200–500 m. per annum at 1969 prices. This is about 3–8 per cent of food consumption or about 0.5–1.25 per cent of national income in 1969.

Johnson (1967a), following Snape (1963), explored this issue more fully in the case of the sugar market. Most Western nations protect their domestic sugar-beet producers from competition from tropical cane producers, but use tariffs rather than deficiency payments. He suggested that using the inappropriate policy to support output cost the protecting nations about $200 m. in lost welfare and the efficient world producers about another $200 m. in lost producer surpluses. These figures refer to 1959 (before the EC was effective) and together accounted for approaching 50 per cent of the value of world sugar trade! The situation has not improved.

128

CASE-STUDY 10.1: AGRICULTURE AND NATIONAL SECURITY

Agricultural support is frequently justified by appealing to the security advantages of self-sufficiency in food, and it is often implied that such considerations are above economic analysis. Winters (1990), in a case-study of the UK, argues the contrary. National security is economic in that, first, the amount of security desired must depend on its cost in terms of other things forgone, and, second, choices must be made between more and less efficient means of achieving a given level of security. Moreover, while national security is a legitimate objective for a society, an economic approach to the problem shows both that the threat to Britain's food supplies is exaggerated and that current agricultural policies do nothing to address it.

There are five strands of argument. First, in preparing for an embargo of imports, official intervention is required in the pre-embargo situation only if two conditions are met. First, there must be an identifiable market failure that makes the private sector incapable of preparing adequately for an embargo – for example, private sector ignorance of the threats, or a fear that in a crisis the government will prevent private agents from charging the full value of their output. Second, there must be an intertemporal link between production in the pre- and post-embargo situations, for otherwise there would be no virtue in government intervention until the embargo actually occurred. This is relevant if, say, agricultural capacity can be expanded only at a finite speed.

The second issue is the costs of a food embargo. There is considerable flexibility in food demands with respect to both the composition and the total amount of food required in a crisis. Disruptions in food supplies that fall short of causing starvation may be inconvenient, but no more so than disruptions in other goods. They offer no case for the special treatment of food and agriculture. Starvation, on the other hand, is different, and would entail almost infinite costs, but in fact is most unlikely to occur. UK agricultural production currently far exceeds the population's minimal dietary requirements, once 'food-efficient' consumption patterns are adopted.

Next consider the probability of an effective embargo. Food is produced by many countries and is easy to trade and transport; consequently food embargoes are extremely hard to enforce. Even under almost universal condemnation over its invasion of Afghanistan, the USSR was able to maintain reasonable food imports in 1980. Similar ineffectiveness has characterised nearly all other food embargoes. Besides, the main perpetrator of food embargoes has been the USA, Britain's principal ally. Oil and chemicals, on the other hand, are essential inputs to modern agriculture, and, given their countries of origin, appear to be more likely than food to be cut off. The UK's own fuel supplies would offer some security against an oil embargo, but in the case of active hostilities they would be very vulnerable. It is difficult to envisage circumstances in which food was entirely cut off but oil was available in sufficient quantities both to fight a hot war *and* run an energy-intensive agricultural sector. Finally, if hostilities did entail total embargo, the nuclear threat would be prominent; then growing one's own food seems a monumental irrelevance.

But suppose there were a general embargo including oil and chemicals. Current agricultural policy is counter-productive: in the absence of the necessary material inputs, current agricultural output would be unsustainable and output would be lower than would be possible if pre-embargo farming had been less intensive. Artificial fertilisers have to be replenished every year and leave the land exhausted and unproductive if they are withdrawn. Newly ploughed grass and clover ley, on the other hand, is highly productive for a few years, even in the total absence of fertilisers; even two or three years of ley offer significant increases in fertility. Moreover, a total embargo would mean no exports as well as no imports, and so would release a lot of labour from commercial tasks; hence cultivating new land would not need to be very energy or capital intensive. Thus a sensible security policy would be to preserve fertility so that agricultural output could expand rapidly when necessary.

Finally, stock-piling offers an efficient approach to strategic security. Stocks sufficient to cover two years of total embargo might cost around £400–500 m. per year to maintain, much less than the costs of current agricultural policy. And, if longer-term threats are feared, not only should food be stored, but so too should agricultural inputs such as fertilisers, natural fertility and breeding stock, so that in the event of a long crisis output could be expanded effectively.

Current price-raising and output-enhancing agricultural policy cannot be defended by appealing to national security. Indeed it is not clear that policy contributes to security at all. Thus on national security grounds as well as income-maximising ones, agricultural reform is long overdue.

10.2 THE OPTIMUM TARIFF

A general analysis

Figure 10.1 suggests that there is scope for the private and social marginal rates of transformation through trade to differ. Furthermore, the general rules suggest that, if this is so, it should be met by a counterprevailing policy distortion in the trade sector; one such is a tariff.

The cause of any discrepancy between private and social MRTT is market power in international trade. Suppose Britain were the only market for tea, and that tea were produced abroad under conditions of increasing costs. A reduction in Britain's demand for tea would thus cut the world price and improve Britain's terms of trade. However, to exploit this market power Britons must act in concert. Each individual takes the price of tea as given: his own influence on the price is negligible and hence the cost of his marginal unit is just the ruling world price. In general equilibrium notation, $MRTT_P = P_F$. For Britain as a whole, however, the marginal cost exceeds the price, because purchasing an extra unit not only costs the ruling price but also drives up the price on all previous units. The latter element is ignored by individuals because it is borne by other people (it is a sort of externality), but socially it should be taken into account. Hence socially we have, say,

$$MRTT_S = Z \cdot P_F = Z \cdot MRTT_P, \qquad (10.6)$$

with $Z > 1$. Overall the situation is

$$MRTT_S \neq MRTT_P = P_F = P_D = MRS_S = MRT_S. \qquad (10.7)$$

Our general rule suggests meeting this with a tariff that drives a wedge between P_F and P_D such that $P_D = Z \cdot P_F$. This implies:

$$MRTT_S = Z \cdot MRTT_P = Z \cdot P_F = P_D = MRS_S = MRT_S. \qquad (10.8)$$

This tariff, which maximises welfare, is known as the optimum tariff.

We saw in section 8.2 that a tariff is equivalent to a production subsidy plus a consumption tax. Figure 10.1 confirms this. A production subsidy such that $P_T = Z \cdot P_D$ and a consumption tax such that $P_C = Z \cdot P_D$ would have the following effects:

$$MRTT_S = Z \cdot MRTT_P = Z \cdot P_F = Z \cdot P_D = P_C = MRS_S$$
$$= P_T = MRT_S \qquad (10.9)$$

Equation (10.9) shows that neither a production tax nor a consumption tax alone could produce optimality; however, it may be shown that either (at the right rate) is superior to free trade. For non-economic objectives a tariff is first best only if the objective is defined in terms of trade rather than output or consumption.

A partial equilibrium illustration

The optimum tariff has a long history in international economics – Mill and Marshall were quite aware of the argument – and so we now analyse it more explicitly. The essence of the case for the tariff is that, acting individually, residents fail to take account of their collective market power, and hence fail to reap the benefits that it would accord. A single monopsonist would realise that each unit bought forced up the price on all units and would exploit this to maximise his welfare (profits) from importing. The tariff works by inducing the many individuals acting separately to behave as if they were a single monopsonist.

The position of the profit-maximising monopsonist is illustrated in Figure 10.3. He buys imports until the marginal cost (MC) just equals the price at which he can resell them domestically, as shown by the demand curve. Thus he chooses equilibrium B. The individuals, on the other hand, do not recognise (or care about) the effect that they have on each other's prices, and thus buy for as long as their demand price exceeds the supply price (as shown by the supply curve). Thus they choose equilibrium A. The tariff essentially taxes them for the extent to which they harm each other. Thus an *ad valorem*

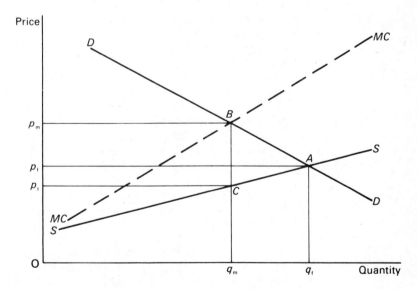

Figure 10.3 The optimum tariff: partial equilibrium

131.

tariff of t would raise the import supply curve *to residents* up to MC in the figure: q_m costs p_t per unit paid to the exporter and $t \cdot p_t$ to the government. The new competitive equilibrium becomes B. The supply curve to the country as a whole, however, is unchanged, and the fall in the price paid abroad $(p_f - p_t)$ represents the terms of trade gain.

The size of the optimum tariff is easily calculable in this case. Write the import supply curve as $p = p(q)$, where p, the price necessary to call forth supply q, is a function of q. Then the total cost of q is $p \cdot q$ and marginal cost is

$$MC = p + \frac{dp}{dq} \cdot q \tag{10.10}$$

$$= \left(1 + \frac{1}{\epsilon}\right) p$$

where ϵ is the price elasticity of supply of imports $(dq/dp)(p/q)$. Hence the tariff necessary to shift the private supply price up to (social) marginal cost at any given quantity is given by $(1 + t)p = MC$. Thus

$$t = MC/p - 1$$
$$t = 1/\epsilon \tag{10.11}$$

The optimum tariff is just the reciprocal of the elasticity of supply. Observe how if supply is perfectly elastic $(\epsilon = \infty)$ the optimum tariff is zero, which is just the small country case.

General equilibrium

We now consider the general equilibrium analysis of the optimum tariff in Figure 10.4. Part (A) of the figure displays the foreign offer curve facing a country with some market power (GG): it shows all the combinations of X and Y that the rest of the world is prepared to trade with us. Our imports are shown with a $+$ and exports with a $-$. GG's curvature indicates that more imports are available only at the cost of raising their price in terms of X. The terms of trade (price) are indicated by the slope of the line from the origin to the trade point (e.g. OC), while the $MRTT$ is given by the offer curve's slope at the trade point.

Figure 10.4 (B) shows the free-trade equilibrium. FF is the transformation frontier. Given any production point, P, the consumption possibilities are defined by the foreign offer curve with its origin positioned at P; the consumption point must lie on such a locus. Under free trade, producers set $MRT_P = P_T = P_F$ and consumers $MRS_P = P_C = P_F$. Hence at equilibrium the terms of trade line CP is tangent to FF at the production point P, and tangent to the social indifference curve at the consumption point C. C is clearly sub-optimal, because even with production fixed at P we could reach a higher indifference curve along GG, and once we let production shift we can do even better.

In Figure 10.4(C) we have constructed the so-called 'Baldwin-envelope', the broken line BF. This represents the consumption possibility locus allowing both production and the amount of foreign trade to change. It is constructed by drawing in the consumption locus for each production point in turn (that is, sketching in the foreign offer curve with its origin at every point along FF in turn), and then joining up the outermost points of these loci. The resulting curve envelopes all the consumption possibilities – hence its name. The envelope has one very special property: at any point, the envelope's slope, the

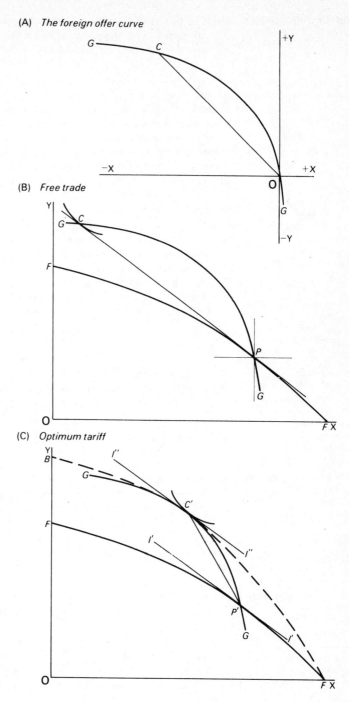

(A) *The foreign offer curve*

(B) *Free trade*

(C) *Optimum tariff*

Figure 10.4 The optimum tariff: general equilibrium

slope of GG at that point and the slope of FF at the relevant production point are all equal. The tangency of GG and BF is obvious; if it were not so, GG would cross BF, and BF would not be the outer locus. The result with FF may be seen as follows: suppose GG and FF had different slopes at the relevant points, say $2X:1Y$ and $3X:1Y$ respectively; if we produced one unit less Y we would gain 3X, and trading these gain $1\frac{1}{2}Y$ – a net gain of $\frac{1}{2}Y$; hence if the slopes differ, a net gain in consumption is possible, which shows that consumption was not being maximised at such a position.

Since the Baldwin envelope shows the maximal consumption possibilities, the welfare maximum must be where it is tangent to a social indifference curve – that is, point C' in the figure. Tracing back along the foreign offer curve tangent at C' defines production point P', and the terms of trade – slope $P'C'$. To achieve P', producers must set their MRT to slope $I'I'$ and with terms of trade $P'C'$ this involves a production subsidy on Y. Similarly, given P', if consumers are to achieve C', they must pay a tax on Y to convert trade prices $P'C'$ into internal prices $I''I''$, which equal MRS at C'. Now, by the envelope theorem, we know that the slopes of BF and GG at C' and of FF at P' are equal. Hence consumers' and producers' price ratios are equal, but not equal to the terms of trade; i.e. $P_C = P_T \neq P_F$. This, of course, is the hallmark of a tariff. Hence a tariff enables us to reach the maximum welfare point C'. Finally, the envelope theorem immediately provides our optimality conditions.

$$MRTT_S = MRS_S = MRT_S$$

$$\text{(slope } GG) \quad \text{(slope } BF) \quad \text{(slope } FF)$$

(10.12)

All this analysis can be combined with the domestic distortions cases to examine distortions in large countries. It is rather messy, but the basic result is that two policies are required: the optimum tariff to maximise the benefit from changing the terms of trade, and a domestic policy to counteract the other distortion.

Export taxes

In general equilibrium, export and import taxes are equivalent (see section 10.1 above), so all the previous analysis could be applied to export taxes: by surcharging exports the final price asked of foreigners is driven up, provided of course that the price elasticity of demand is not infinite. In fact there is probably more scope for export taxes than for optimal tariffs, because exports are usually more specialised than imports and hence are more likely to permit market power.

Retaliation

The optimum tariff improves the tariff-imposing country's welfare, but only at the expense of the rest of the world, which suffers a deterioration in its terms of trade as well as the inefficiencies associated with reduced specialisation. This has led economists to ask what happens if the rest of the world retaliates. Johnson (1953) analysed this case, assuming that two countries take it in turns to impose the optimum tariff against each other on the (mistaken) assumption that the other country will not retaliate. His conclusions were:

(i)   Several 'rounds' will be required, because by imposing a tariff a country alters its own offer curve. Hence, retaliation would shift GG in our Figure 10.4, making our previously optimum tariff no longer optimal.

(ii) Equilibrium would, however, eventually be achieved before trade was entirely eliminated. This is because the gain from the optimum tariff arises solely from changes in the terms of trade; thus no trade implies no gain, but merely the loss of specialisation. Hence each party has an interest in stopping short of eliminating trade.

(iii) One or other country *could* remain better off after the tariff war than under free trade, but since free trade is Pareto optimal it is not possible for both to gain from a trade war.

As we saw in Chapter 9, import quotas cannot reproduce two-country tariff equilibria, while VERs can. These results apply *a fortiori* to trade policy with retaliation.

Applications

The optimum tariff is a wholly selfish piece of economic policy: it raises A's welfare at the expense of B's. Thus governments do not readily admit to using it. None the less it may be empirically important. Nearly all developed countries appear to have some market power over their exports, at least in the short run, as witnessed by the non-infinite price elasticities of demand that they face (see Chapter 19). Thus there may be scope for optimum tariffs. The benefits claimed by advocates of protectionism frequently stem largely from the terms of trade effects – e.g. Cambridge Economic Policy Group (*Cambridge Economic Policy Review*, 1979), where import controls raise the terms of trade by about 20 per cent, which accounts for around half the perceived benefits of protection. Terms of trade effects also figure prominently in general assessments of trade policy – e.g. Whalley (1985) – indeed, probably more prominently than they should for the long run.

10.3 THE REVENUE TARIFF

All the previous analysis assumes that governments can raise or distribute revenues costlessly and without distortion. Hence the most obvious difference between tariffs and subsidies – that one earns and the other absorbs revenue – is quite irrelevant. Once we recognise the falsity of this premise, however, we have another element of second best to consider. The preference for subsidies for stimulating output, for example, may be entirely outweighed by the distortions entailed, and the resources absorbed, in raising the cash to fund them.

This problem is particularly acute for developing countries, where the information necessary for levying taxes on incomes or domestic transactions frequently does not exist, at least not without a huge expenditure of resources. Foreign trade, on the other hand, is eminently taxable: it is always monetised (unlike many domestic transactions); it is conducted by sophisticated agents; it is extensively documented; it is geographically concentrated at the main ports; and it is frequently concentrated in terms of products and traders. For these countries, then, the major considerations in favour of tariffs are their efficient revenue-raising effects and their ease of administration. Greenaway and Sapsford (1987) showed that trade taxes are particularly important for middle-income developing countries.

10.4 FULL EMPLOYMENT ARGUMENTS

The basic argument

Another common argument for tariffs is to boost employment. Generalising (incorrectly) from partial equilibrium analysis, people argue that, since tariffs increase the demand for domestic output, they will surely draw resources out of the pool of unemployed. This presupposes that the pool has the right skills and location, and even then tariffs are only second best.

At a subtler level, however, we should note that, in the simple first-best market economy normally assumed by trade theorists, unemployment is impossible. Some sort of market failure is necessary to generate it, and rigidities in prices and wages are the most usual candidates. If wages do not adjust to changes in the demand for labour, recession is met by laying off labour rather than by reducing its wage. (This is not necessarily irrational – see section 20.3.) This is essentially the Keynesian world, in which any increase in demand leads to increased output and income rather than to rising prices.

Let us assume we are in such a world, and that nothing can be done about money wages. Assume also that we have a fixed exchange rate. Any attempt to expand the domestic economy by monetary or fiscal means is likely to cause a balance of payments crisis by dragging in imports. To cure this, we require an expenditure-switching policy, to switch demand from foreign to domestic goods. (This is explained in detail in Chapter 20 below.) Compare two such policies: a devaluation of the exchange rate and a tariff. The former raises import prices at home and lowers export prices abroad, stimulating the demand for domestic goods in both markets; the latter only raises import prices at home, putting all the strain on that side of the market, and stimulating import-competing industries relative to export industries. This sacrifices the benefits of specialisation and may involve considerable welfare loss. (It has also been argued that tariffs are likely to entail retaliation by trading partners, thus further penalising export industries, whereas devaluations will not. This is not empirically well supported, however; competitive devaluations are not at all unknown.)

The assumption of the fixed exchange rate is necessary for tariffs to have much effect at all. Suppose the exchange rate were flexible and we imposed a tariff from a position of equilibrium. This would induce a tendency towards balance of payments surplus, which would be offset by an appreciation of the exchange rate. The net result would be virtually no change in the net demand for domestic output, and hence no employment benefit, but a continuing distortion towards import-competing industries.

Thus, any case for tariffs to stimulate employment rests on the need to permit domestic expansion without balance of payments crises and the rigidity of both money wages and the exchange rate.

Keynes and the tariff

An excellent exposition of this argument is Keynes (1931). Accepting the impossibility of devaluing sterling in the early 1930s Keynes suggested a uniform tariff on imports and, if possible, an equal subsidy on exports. This, he argued, would be equivalent to a devaluation and could provide a screen behind which expansionary domestic policies could be pursued. Retaliation would not follow because the level of imports would not be reduced by the tariff; it was just that a given level of imports would be consistent with a higher level of national income. Indeed, he said, if partners were more liberal or expansionary, and hence bought more British exports, the British tariff would not be necessary at all! The second-best nature of the argument was fully recognised by Keynes, and when sterling was eventually devalued he immediately repudiated his protectionist stance.

Cambridge and the tariff

More recently, similar arguments have been advanced in the UK by the Cambridge Economic Policy Group (*Cambridge Economic Policy Review*, especially 1978). They advocate tariffs on imports of manufactures and semi-manufactures high enough to offset the increase in imports arising from a domestic expansion necessary to remove unemployment. This would involve tariffs of around 50–100 per cent. They argue that any distortions these tariffs would entail would be of secondary welfare significance relative to the increase in output that the extra employment would permit. They also dismiss as unimportant any consumer losses arising from having to consume British variants of goods rather than the foreign varieties that consumers manifestly prefer.

The novel part of their argument is to say that devaluation, even though possible today, will not work. Their reason is that devaluation raises import prices and, by thus cutting real wages and raising the cost of imported materials, stimulates domestic inflation to such an extent that the devaluation is offset and British goods end up relatively no cheaper. Tariffs, on the other hand, do not stimulate inflation: first, because, although they raise import prices, this can be offset by redistributing the tariff revenue to the workers and thus maintaining real wages; and, second, because provided only finished manufactures are taxed the prices of industrial materials do not rise. This, they say, will allow the domestic expansion to proceed and, by increasing output, actually raise wages. The difference between devaluation and tariffs derives from two crucial assumptions: first, that real wages are rigid (and thus that labour bids up money wages to compensate for any real income loss due to inflation), and, second, that domestic prices are fixed as a constant mark-up over costs. The former means that devaluation is inflated away, while the latter prevents inflation in response to tariffs.

There are several strong objections to the Cambridge argument. First, wages are protected at the expense of profits, and one must fear for the future of investment. Second, there is no evidence that protection will not worsen Britain's productivity record by removing the pressure from manufacturers. Third, the loss of desired foreign varieties of goods represents a real income loss as surely as do rising prices. Hence wage pressure could occur under tariffs. Fourth, there is no evidence that, despite tariffs of over 50 per cent and huge rises in demand, domestic manufacturers will not raise their prices! The evidence adduced by CEPG themselves is quite inappropriate. Fifth, there is very little evidence that real wages would not be somewhat reduced by devaluation.

Liberalisation and employment

The fact that tariffs are not a good policy for ensuring long-run employment does not mean that, in the short run, tariffs should be abolished. The success of trade liberalisation depends on resources being able to move between industries according to comparative advantage, and this requires both mobility and wage flexibility. If these are missing in the short run, the resources released by the contraction of formerly protected industries will not all be re-absorbed elsewhere, and unemployment will result. There is therefore a reasonable case to be made for not exacerbating short-term cyclical unemployment by cutting tariffs or subsidies during a slump. This does not weaken the long-run case for freer trade, nor does it apply if the unemployment is long run or structural; it merely recognises that adjustment costs can be high and that choosing the 'right' time for adjustment can be beneficial. Adjustment should not be postponed forever on these grounds, however.

The balance of payments tariff

A corollary of the 'employment tariff' is the balance of payments tariff. The former is introduced to permit domestic expansion without balance of payments crises, whereas the latter is introduced during the crisis to avoid the need for dometic contraction or devaluation. It is subject to all the above objections, but balance of payments crises are none the less accepted by the GATT as a legitimate reason for (temporary) protection. Among protective devices, however, the tariff is the best, because, unlike the full employment case, the objective here is clearly defined in terms of foreign trade rather than employment. Examples of crisis protection are the UK import surcharge of 15 per cent introduced in 1964 and the USA's 10 per cent surcharge introduced in August 1971.

FURTHER READING

Much of this chapter is based on *Corden*'s excellent article (1957). Domestic distortions are discussed in *Haberler* (1950), *Bhagwati and Ramaswami* (1963) and *Johnson* (1965a); *Bhagwati, Ramaswami and Srinivasan* (1969) provide a simple mathematical summary, while *Bhagwati* (1971) offers a general theory of distortions, economic growth and welfare. Greater detail on factor market distortions may be found in *Magee* (1973a), while *Johnson* (1971) also covers some useful ground. The Cambridge arguments are presented in the *Cambridge Economic Policy Review* (1978) to which *Hindley* (1983) provides the antidote.

    Bhagwati (1968a) and *Corden* (1974) cover all the issues in this chapter as well as broader questions of commercial policy. The latter contains much detail but works almost entirely in a partial equilibrium framework. *Bhagwati* (1981, part IV) covers several related topics, although not all the essays are easy. Many of Bhagwati's essays may also be found in *Bhagwati* (1983a).

KEY CONCEPTS

distortions	first-order (marginal) conditions
so-called non-economic objectives	externalities
optimum tariff	Baldwin envelope
retaliation	revenue tariffs
employment effects of protection	

QUESTIONS FOR REVIEW

10.1   Give four examples of distortions that require policy intervention. Give four examples of wage differences between industries that do not.

10.2   Analyse three policies which might be used to stimulate agricultural employment. Rank them.

10.3 What distortion might give scope for an 'employment tariff'? Discuss carefully what alternative policies may offer a better solution to unemployment.

10.4 Is the USA likely to have a non-zero optimal export tax on wheat? Why? How would you sell such a policy to farmers?

10.5 Construct a diagrammatic illustration of the superiority of consumption taxes over trade taxes in addressing (a) a consumption externality and (b) a consumption objective.

11 Dynamic and Strategic Arguments for Protection

This chapter presents a further set of arguments about protection in which the passage of real time and strategic behaviour are important. The former group – the cases of dumping, infant industries and uncertainty – all rely on something changing through time. The latter refers to strategic behaviour in the sense of actions taken to influence another agent's response; the 1980s saw great strides in this area of theory based on the interactions between firms in imperfectly competitive markets, as was analysed in Chapter 5 above.

11.1 DUMPING

According to Article VI of the GATT, dumping occurs when countries sell products abroad 'at less than the normal value'. 'Normal value' is usually defined as the price of home sales. Dumping is not proscribed *per se*, but if it causes injury to producers in the importing country, their government may impose anti-dumping duties (ADDs) to counteract its effects. Nearly all governments have translated the relatively imprecise GATT provision into detailed domestic law which specifies the circumstances in which anti-dumping duty may be requested and how it is to be calculated and administered. National provisions vary, but over the late-1980s the EC led the world in the restrictiveness and frequency of application of anti-dumping law.

The economics of dumping

Why should firms wish to supply goods at below normal value, and, if they do, why should recipient countries object? The only case in which dumping is both plausible and socially costly is *predatory dumping*, where the intention is to force import-competing firms out of business, and it is this for which the whole anti-dumping edifice exists. If cheap imports were guaranteed to eternity, that would be fine, but the worry is that once the dumping firm has eliminated its domestic competitors it will exploit its new-found monopoly position to the detriment of the importing consumers. Since it is costly to re-establish industries once they have closed down, it might pay to support domestic producers even though, *pro tem*, imports undercut local prices. Thus the crux of the argument lies in the prospect of dumping being stopped at some time in the future, and in the costs of closing down and starting up industries as the import price varies.

There are several points to be made about this argument. First, predation is far from obviously the best strategy for an exporting firm. Before it can reap monopoly rents it must destroy every significant rival – not only in the importing country, but also elsewhere in the world and even in its own country. This is a tall order; it suggests that effective predation will need to be global, and hence may not even show up in the price differentials between markets that are normally used to identify dumping in practice. Second, if an exporting firm has rivals it would probably be more profitable to seek an accommodation with them (e.g. implicit market sharing) than to engage in all-out war. Third, if predation is the problem there is no need for separate ADD law – domestic competition law already defines criteria for identifying it and proposes remedies. Fourth, if policy is called for, it is not a tariff but a production subsidy. Finally, and hardly surprisingly, there are almost no recorded instances of predatory dumping wars between existing firms.[1]

Two other sets of circumstances might also give rise to dumping as defined by the GATT. The first set is simple *price discrimination*, whereby a firm exports at the world price but exploits its monopoly power at home to raise domestic prices. In this case any harm done is entirely borne by the exporter's domestic economy and dumping constitutes no case at all for protection by the importer. Rather, it should just accept the goods gratefully.

The second set is *counter-cyclical dumping*, which hinges around what set of costs should be subsumed under 'normal value'. For example, should we consider short-run marginal cost (SRMC) or long-run average costs, which allow for the costs of capacity? During a slump, when spare capacity exists, SRMC is often very low in capital-intensive industries and economic theory suggests that any sales at prices above that level should be sought. Import-competing producers facing such competition, however, argue that long-run costs are relevant and that such exports constitute dumping. The steel industry is often held to be prone to such 'counter-cyclical' dumping, but Tarr (1979), in a detailed study, could not detect it.

An alternative cause of counter-cyclical dumping arises from labour markets. If labour cannot be laid off during a slump it will pay firms to sell their output at below apparent marginal cost on the grounds that some sales are better than none if costs are predetermined. Observe again, however, that such behaviour has no necessary implication for price differentials between markets.

The arguments for ADDs have little credibility *per se*, but some economists argue that none the less anti-dumping law is important. Producers are said to be more willing to allow general tariff reductions if they know that they have a counter to the most pressing foreign competition (Bhagwati, 1988). Such political economy issues are discussed in the next chapter.

EC anti-dumping law

The EC imposes anti-dumping duties after investigations of (i) the *dumping margin* – the difference between the export price to the EC and 'normal value' – and (ii) the *injury margin* – the difference between the actual export price and that which implies no injury to EC producers. The ADD is the smaller of the two margins.[2] Despite official claims to the contrary, EC practice is protectionist both in effect and in intent. Its attractions to the EC as a means of protection are that it is under EC rather than national (member state) control; it discriminates between exporters, whereas all GATT-permitted import restrictions must operate multilaterally; and it is politically safe because it ostensibly rights a wrong – unfair trade (see Chapter 12 for more on these motives).

Among the most obvious biases of anti-dumping law are, first, that investigations of dumping are initiated by a complaint from a local producer and are judged mainly by the criterion of injury to that (and other) producers. Consumer and user interests are not formally considered. Second, most of the costs of investigation, except those of defence against the accusation, are borne by the authorities. Hence ADD suits are a cheap form of harassment against foreign rivals.

Third, the definition of normal value is biased. 'Normal value' is generally defined by the price of sales in the exporter's home market adjusted for sales expenses and transport costs, but if that is unavailable it may be related to costs of production (allowing for 'normal' profit margins), to the price of sales in third markets, or even to costs of production in third countries. The last route is used particularly for exporters from state trading countries, whose own costs and prices are held to be so distorted as to be entirely uninformative. If anti-dumping duties are to be imposed, the authorities must find high normal values; hence, for example, they treat selling expenses differently for home sales and exports, they assume high profit margins for exports, they use high-cost countries to define costs of production, and they define as normal the prices of exports to restricted and high-price markets.

Fourth, having defined a normal value, the EC measures the *dumping margin* not relative to the average import price but relative to the average price of all imports with prices *below* normal value; it may then apply a duty equal to that margin to all imports. For example, suppose an importer makes ten shipments: nine at £100 per unit and one at £80; suppose their normal value is declared to be £90. The EC calculates the dumping margin as £10 (£90–80), even though the average import price is £98!

Fifth, once an ADD has been imposed, the EC counts it as a production cost and hence adds it to 'normal value'. Thus if an exporter is to avoid paying the duty he must raise his price by the EC's calculated dumping margin *plus* the ADD! This provides a strong incentive for exporters not to allow ADD cases to come to fruition, but to raise their prices or agree to a VER as soon as a complaint is made. Even then the EC need not, and for Far Eastern exporters frequently does not, accept these undertakings and proceeds with the (biased) investigation. The disincentive to exporting to the EC is obvious.

The biases of EC anti-dumping law are documented by Norall (1986) and Hindley (1988, 1990); their effects are analysed by Messerlin (1989, 1990). Among the latter's results are:

- ADDs, and the VERs and price understandings that substitute for them, are, on average, equivalent to tariffs of over 20 per cent;
- nearly 40 per cent of all ADD investigations end with undertakings on prices or quantities (VERs) rather than duties, but only 6 per cent of those on Japan and 10 per cent of those on the Asian NICs do;
- a positive dumping finding typically leads to a decline in imports of over 50 per cent of five years;
- even in cases where no dumping is found, imports decline by 10 per cent immediately, and possibly by 30 per cent eventually;
- ADDs and their substitutes lead to significant trade diversion, to increased import prices, and to strong rises in intra-EC prices;
- there is a correlation between ADDs and the need for subsequent action against EC firms for anti-competitive practices.

11.2 INFANT INDUSTRY PROTECTION

The basic argument

The infant industry argument is perhaps the most widely quoted justification for protection. Suppose that country A has a potential comparative advantage in an industry, but that because of an earlier start country B has established that industry to such an extent that A's producers cannot compete in the short run. If the infant industry were protected over this vital stage, eventually the world would be better off from the more appropriate exploitation of comparative advantage in the long run.

This argument is not as persuasive as it first seems, but let us accept its basic case for now. As with several other arguments, however, it is more a case for a subsidy than for a tariff. The objective concerns production – and thus the consumption restriction stemming from the tariff is an unwanted distortion. Indeed, curtailing domestic consumption of a good whose output is being stimulated but which cannot be exported seems particularly perverse.

If the current costs of protection are to be adequately repaid, the industry will have to earn above-normal profits in its later years. In technical terms, protection will be justified only if the discounted value of all future profits exceeds the discounted value of all the costs incurred. By itself, however, this is not sufficient to justify protection, because, if private profits cover private costs, the industry should be established without any public intervention at all. Every private investment involves forgoing current consumption (i.e. making 'losses') in return for higher future consumption. Thus, in order to justify protection we have also to show either that the private sector is unable to undertake some (privately) profitable investment, or that a privately unprofitable industry is none the less socially desirable, i.e. that there is an externality.

We now consider the circumstances that may lead to a new industry suffering short-term losses despite being potentially profitable in the long run. First, with imports still entering, the domestic industry may be unable to achieve sufficient economies of scale. Second, the industry may be subject to 'learning by doing': either labour or management may reach maximum productivity only after a prolonged period of experience with production, so the early (learning) units will be relatively costly.

These two factors, however, do not separate private and social costs; to justify protection they need to be supplemented by reasons for the failure of the private sector to undertake the required investment. First the private sector may have worse *information* than the government: although the government may not have superior knowledge about particular cost structures or market prospects, it may well be better informed about future macro-economic conditions, infrastructure investment, education, factor market conditions and so on. Thus what seems privately unprofitable may actually be profitable on the government's information. Of course, the first-best solution to this situation is to stimulate the information flow, but given governments' credibility problems this may not be easy.

The second private market failure concerns *capital market imperfections*: it may be that private capital markets are unwilling to finance the infant industry even though it is expected to yield at least market rates of return. This may be because of an unwillingness to

- finance investment in 'human capital' (the learned skills of the workers), because they offer no saleable collateral if the loan is not repaid;
- make very large loans – this is particularly relevant to the economies of scale case;
- finance new (unknown) entrepreneurs and products; or
- make long illiquid investments – that is particularly relevant to the learning by doing case.

The last three stem partly from a difference in private and social attitudes to risk. Private risk exceeds social risk because, if a loan is repudiated or has to be liquidated quickly at a low price, there is private loss but no social loss since the lender's loss is balanced by someone else's gain. This difference is likely to be greatest for long, large and inherently risky loans, especially in developing countries where capital markets are thin.

Capital markets imperfections have considerable relevance, even in developed countries so far as research and development based industries are concerned. However, yet again the first-best solution is to overcome the imperfection rather than restrict international trade. For example, the government might issue its own debt and re-lend to new industries at 'correct' rates – 'development banks', both national and international, essentially do this.

Externalities

A third cause of infant industries' falling costs through time concerns the *training of labour*. If labour must be trained to undertake manufacturing tasks, someone must bear the cost. If the first firm or industry in the field does so, however, the workers, once trained, can leave to work for other firms, which, because they do not bear the training costs, can pay higher wages. In other words, an individual firm cannot always appropriate the benefits of its training programme, and this discourages it from starting such a programme. Thus industry never gets off the ground. This is a classic externality – in the factor markets – and should accordingly be met by subsidies to industrial training or the provision of free technical education. Again, tariffs are only third best.

Another externality that reduces social costs for an established industry concerns *external economies of scale*. As it grows, an industry may stimulate facilities that benefit other industries, e.g. research institutions, infrastructure and specialist suppliers. The economy-wide benefits that these institutions confer should be set against the original industry's costs. Yet again, however, first best would be for the government to support these institutions directly rather than offer tariff protection. More difficult to subsidise directly, however, is any change in the atmosphere or attitude towards industrialisation that the growth of a new industry engenders; such externalities are best met by production subsidies.

A final externality concerns *reputation*. If it is difficult to assess a good's quality when it is bought, consumers rely on firms' reputations in making their choices, and, if they steer clear of unknown sellers, a new entrant may have to sell at very low prices for a period to establish a reputation. This is a market failure, but not one that is addressable by tariffs or output subsidies. Subsidies cannot discriminate between 'good' and 'bad' suppliers and hence will neither stimulate 'good' firms nor be of direct use to consumers in making their choices. Moreover, subsidies will enable firms with worse products to survive for longer before their private capital is exhausted, which will lower the average quality of domestic output and be socially wasteful. As Grossman and Horn (1988) observe, it is not that the market solves the problems prefectly, but that protection does not help.

Practical difficulties

Even if the arguments above apply in theory, there still remains the question of whether protection will actually allow the benefits to be reaped. Young protected industries are frequently rather concentrated and this often hinders efficiency. For example, several authors have found profits to be abnormally high in industries that are both protected *and* concentrated (e.g. Lyons, 1981).

Others have found that costs are not minimised in such cases – e.g. Leibenstein's (1966) X-inefficiency, Bloch's (1974) finding that costs rise with protection, or Caves *et al.*'s (1980) finding that economies of scale are *not* properly exploited behind tariff barriers.

The question must also be faced of how and when to remove infant protection. The industry can frequently claim that a few more years will 'do the trick', and no government likes to admit defeat by abandoning an industry formerly favoured in the 'national interest'.

The infant industry argument was first stated by Alexander Hamilton (1790), advocating protection in the newly formed USA, and it has figured strongly in American commercial policy ever since. List (1841) also developed it in the German context, although his approach is more infant country than infant industry – see section 15.5 below.

A recent empirical examination of infant industry protection is Krueger and Tuncer (1982). This examined the *necessary (but not sufficient)* condition for successful infant protection that costs in the protected industry should fall through time. Judging what would have happened without protection by cost changes elsewhere in the economy, Krueger and Tuncer interpreted this to mean that protected infants' costs should fall faster than costs elsewhere. Using data on Turkish industry, they found that neither industry nor firm improvements in productivity bore any relationship to the amount of protection offered to an industry. Hence, they argued, the infant industry case is lost because one of the necessary conditions for its success is violated. This is slightly overstated because the analysis ignores external effects outside the protected industry and, of course, it refers to only one country, but it is certainly salutary.

Conclusion

We have seen that the infant industry case for protection rests on two tenets: first, that *through time* the social costs of production will fall, and, second, that some of the benefits of this are not appropriated by the private sector, either because they are external to the firm (industry) or because the private sector is unable to exploit the opportunities offered. Although the infant industry case is frequently cited to justify tariffs, we have seen that tariffs are not first best even under the postulated conditions. Tariffs can really only be justified on administrative or revenue-raising grounds. Furthermore, there are some reasons to doubt the empirical success of infant industry protection, although further research is necessary to be sure.

The senescent industry

Closely related to the infant industry case is an argument for protecting senescent (senile) industries. This is frequently advanced in the UK context (e.g. Trades Union Congress, 1983): British industry is old and has suffered years of neglect and mismanagement, runs the argument, but behind a temporary tariff wall it could re-equip and emerge lean and competitive. This argument is subject to all the caveats stated above plus the additional question of whether such an industry could actually be saved given that its initial comparative advantage has clearly been eroded. One should also ask what will be changed so dramatically that an industry, whose management and labour have let it decline so far already, could be regenerated. Only in very specific cases, e.g. of dramatically new technology or new lines of production, does success seem plausible.

11.3 UNCERTAINTY

In section 7.1 we noted that opening up international trade could be Pareto harmful in the presence of uncertainty because it caused a goods market that was coincidentally offering perfect insurance no longer to do so. This might look like an argument for protection. At a more prosaic level, trade policy is sometimes justified as a response to uncertainty in the absence of insurance markets in the following terms. No one knows which industries will retain their comparative advantage twenty years from now. Hence society should be prepared to maintain those people who, through no fault of their own, choose the wrong set of skills or location, by guaranteeing that industries will not be allowed to fail, or at least not to collapse very suddenly. This trades off the small costs of protection to the many against the avoidance of very large costs to the few, and many people find it acceptable on the grounds of 'but for the grace of God, there go I'.

Persuasive as the argument of the previous paragraph sounds, it is flawed, as Dixit (1990) has shown. First, if our concern is with income distribution, there are better ways of addressing it. Second, insurance markets – including contingent contracts, such as crop-sharing and issuing equity in firms – exist to cope with uncertainty efficiently. It is true that such markets are frequently absent, but then one must ask what causes their absence, and allow for those same causes to operate in the presence of trade policy. Dixit states that three sets of factors can lead to the non-existence of contingent markets: unobservable outcomes, unobservable behaviour (moral hazard) and unobservable characteristics (adverse selection). All make trade policy more complex. For example, suppose that farmers cannot insure against low output levels because insurance firms cannot detect whether their output really is low or not. A tariff or production subsidy does not address the fundamental issue – paying farmers when their incomes are low and charging them when incomes are high, but there is a second-best tax policy. It is to tax *sales* (not output) of agricultural output and redistribute the revenue equally to all farmers: farmers with good crops have more to sell and hence pay more tax than those with poor crops, so a measure of redistribution is achieved. If agriculture is traded internationally and only border measures are feasible, this prescription calls for import subsidies to keep agricultural prices down and boost real incomes generally – the very opposite of farmers' calls for protection.

Similar issues surround moral hazard – the danger that when insurance is available people will be careless or lazy because they are protected from the consequences of such behaviour – and adverse selection – the fact that 'good risks' may not take up insurance if they have to pay a high enough premium to support the 'bad risks'. Any governmental substitute for insurance will induce the same sort of behaviour as made private insurance unprofitable – for example, moral hazard is essentially the cause of poor productivity on the collective farms of the Soviet Union – why work hard if your income does not depend on it? Altering the conditions of international trade will generally impose distortions on other parts of the economy without addressing the fundamental market failures.

146

The inclusion of economies of scale and imperfect competition has given rise to a number of new models of trade policy. These are known generically as models of 'strategic trade policy', because they mostly entail taking firms' reactions into account in the formulation of economic policy. This is a new and rapidly advancing area of theory, and is held by its advocates to offer explanations, and even justifications, for the sorts of policies that governments often pursue, such as export subsidies, R&D subsidies and import restrictions. The main ideas are simply illustrated using the model of duopoly developed in section 5.2 above. More thorough surveys are available in Krugman (1987b) and, more analytically, Helpman and Krugman (1989).

Export subsidies

We start with a duopoly in which two firms (A and B) from different countries (countries A and B) compete for sales in the rest of the world. By assuming away any domestic consumption in the producing countries we can temporarily avoid considering consumer welfare in these countries. We assume that the duopoly sector accounts for only a small proportion of the economies' output, so that we can use partial equilibrium analysis. The basic situation is illustrated in Figure 11.1. At first we will assume Cournot behaviour in which firms treat outputs as their decision variables and optimise their own outputs taking as given the level of their rival's output: A's reaction curve (R_A) reports A's preferred – i.e. profit-maximising – output for each level of B's output (see Appendix). R_B is analogous. The Cournot equilibrium is given by C, at which, we assume, each firm earns positive profits.

Imperfect competition means that, at C, price exceeds marginal cost, but the firms do not expand their sales because the benefits of greater sales are balanced by the decline in price necessary to bring the increase about. But if A could induce B to reduce its output, A could increase its own sales with less of

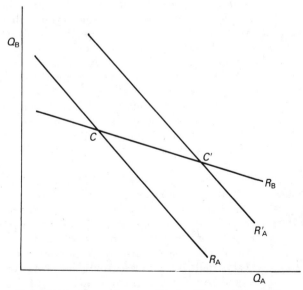

Figure 11.1 Cournot competition with export subsidies

H

an effect on price; this would shift some of the profits available in the market from B to A, so the case is often referred to as *profit shifting* or *profit snatching*. Like the optimum tariff case, it clearly entails one country gaining at the expense of the other.

The problem is how to induce B to reduce its output. A could just threaten to increase its output unilaterally, but, assuming full information, B will recognise this as an empty threat: the Cournot equilibrium is an equilibrium *precisely* because, given Q_B, Q_A is the optimum response for A. Thus while there may be a short-term price war, B can be fairly confident of withstanding the onslaught because A will be damaging itself as well as B. But suppose A's government offered a production or export subsidy (they are the same in the absence of domestic sales). It would now be profitable for A to maintain a higher output for any given level of output by B. Along R_A, marginal cost equals perceived marginal revenue (marginal revenue given the Cournot assumption); if a subsidy reduces A's marginal cost, it can operate with a lower marginal revenue, and for any Q_B this entails a higher Q_A; that is, A's reaction curve will shift out to R'_A. At the new equilibrium, C', Q_A has risen, Q_B has fallen (by less) and profits have shifted. Country A is better off and firm A's profits have risen by more than the subsidy it received. B's reduction in output is the strategic component: the subsidy made A's threat of expanding output credible in a way that it was not without government backing, and so reducing output in order to prevent the market price from falling too far was the rational response for B. It is also worth noting that in this case consumers in the rest of the world have benefited because their supplies of the good concerned have increased and its price correspondingly decreased. The reason is that at C the duopoly was constraining supply in order to keep prices up and the subsidy partially overcame that distortion. In fact, in this simple case the world as a whole benefits from the subsidy because *de facto* it reduces the level of monopoly power.

This argument can be generalised to situations with domestic consumption. If the policy under consideration is a production subsidy, country A can still expect to gain from intervention: the production effects are the same as previously but now some of the consumer benefits also accrue at home as well. Moreover, even country B might gain if its consumer benefits outweigh its profit losses. Country A will be doing the world a favour by (partially) breaking down the monopoly power of the industry.

When we come to consider export subsidies, however, the effects are less clear. An export subsidy to firm A will encourage it to divert output from domestic to foreign markets; this will increase monopoly exploitation at home, possibly by enough to offset the profit snatched from B. Thus now A and/or B could lose from the policy, and, while consumers in the rest of the world would benefit, there may or may not be gains overall.

Import protection as export promotion

The existence of a home market raises the possibility of a third kind of policy – import protection as export promotion (Krugman, 1984). Imagine that, as well as selling in third markets, both A and B supplied part of each other's markets for widgets, and that both had unexploited economies of scale in the form of declining marginal costs. A Cournot equilibrium is still possible between the two firms, with prices exceeding marginal costs. Since average costs would also exceed marginal costs, we cannot be sure that each firm would be making positive profits, but all that matters for the argument is that additional sales would contribute positively to profits. Now suppose that government A excluded all imports of widgets. B would lose sales and hence experience increasing costs per unit, while A would experience the opposite. The price of widgets in country A would almost certainly rise given the new monopoly, but A's new-found competitive edge would also allow it credibly to increase its sales in world markets. Profits would have been shifted from B to A; A-consumers would almost certainly lose, as would B-consumers because their main supplier, B, would have higher costs. Thus for neither country, nor for foreign consumers nor for the world as a whole can unambiguous welfare conclusions be drawn. However, the attraction of the policy for firm A is obvious enough, and one frequently hears industries protesting how effective they could be abroad if only their home market were secure.

A particular case of this argument concerns technically sophisticated industries subject to 'learning by doing'. This entails the improvement of firms' production skills as their experience increases – i.e. as their cumulative volume of output increases. Learning by doing is held to be very important for aircraft manufacture (the industry for which Arrow, 1962, developed the concept) and for silicon chips (semi-conductors) which are produced on almost a trial and error basis. Where learning by doing is significant, any policy which increases a firm's rate of output reduces its costs and could establish it in a dominant position almost permanently.

A further wrinkle to this argument comes from Brander and Spencer (1981), the original contribution to the strategic trade policy literature. Imagine that firm A does not exist and that B, aware of the danger of encouraging its creation, sets its price at just that level which would prevent a new firm from making profits. (This is the so-called limit price; see, for example, Scherer, 1980, although more recent work, e.g. Dixit, 1979, has suggested severe short-comings of the limit pricing concept.) If government A imposes a tariff, B will not raise the price it charges in A for fear of encouragiing firm A to start up, so country A will just collect some of B's rent. In the end, however, the tariff could be raised so high that entry deterrence was no longer worthwhile and firm A will enter and capture some of the home market. If A is efficient once it has arrived, it may earn rents abroad and hence country A could be the gainer from the policy as higher domestic prices are offset by profit shifting. Again the strategic element is important: A's threat of entry, which looked hollow on commercial grounds, suddenly becomes effective given a protected market. This argument appears uniquely applicable to the subsidies paid by EC governments to Airbus to help it challenge Boeing in the market for large airliners (see Dixit and Kyle, 1985).

Entry and exit

So far we have taken industrial structure as given so that improved profitability is reflected in extra profits to identifiable firms. There is, however, another alternative. In industries with free exit and entry, shifts in profitability induce changes in the number of firms until profits are returned to their normal level. Thus the surpluses that were under contention in the previous analysis no longer exist. Nevertheless, if domestic sales occur, trade policy can still be attractive in theory provided that one crucial assumption is satisfied: that the home and foreign markets are segmented – i.e. that they can have different prices without arbitrage occurring.

Venables (1985) built on the reciprocal dumping model to describe a simple case of two countries, each with free entry to its industry; each firm, of which there are several, has constant marginal costs but large fixed costs, so that average costs are always falling. Starting from equilibrium, let country A

149

impose a tariff. This switches demand from B's to A's goods: as A's firms expand, their costs fall, while the opposite happens to B's firms. Now, provided that A-firms have the larger share of A's market (e.g. because of transport costs), average consumer prices fall in A, but rise in B. This benefits A's consumers; A also gains overall because, in addition to consumer gains, the government collects some tariff revenue, while profits are maintained constant at normal levels by entry or exit. By similar reasoning, B loses overall. The argument for the export subsidy is similar. Higher exports by A-firms reduce prices in A and thus increase consumer welfare.

The segmented market assumption is very important to this result. If sales in A and B had to occur at identical prices it would not be possible for the higher prices in B to subsidise the lower prices in A that benefit A-consumers. Any policy-induced increase in profitability would be dissipated by excessive entry, which would increase total expenditure on fixed costs.

The degree of market segmentation in the real world almost certainly lies between the extremes assumed in the models above – some price discrepancies are clearly possible, but they are circumscribed by the possibilities of arbitrage trade. Horstmann and Markusen (1986), who analysed the integrated market case, argued that theirs is the relevant one; particularly in smaller industrial economies such as Canada and Australia, protection has been accompanied by a proliferation of companies of below minimum efficient scale. This tendency was first noted by Eastman and Stykolt (1960) but more recent evidence comes from Baldwin and Gorecki (1983) who documented the following responses by manufacturing industry to Canadian trade liberalisation over the period 1970–9:

- 16 per cent of sales in 1979 were by post-1970 entrants;
- 30 per cent of sales in 1970 were by firms which had exited by 1979; and
- plant size and length of run increased significantly over 1970–9, especially in industries with high initial tariffs and large minimum efficient sizes.

Quantification of those effects is provided in a study of Canadian liberalisation by Harris and Cox (1984). The benefits of free trade are greatly increased once these pro-competitive effects are allowed for.

Strategic trade policy: a critique

Strategic trade policy results have been prominent in the recent development of the theory of commercial policy. They are held by many economists to offer an important step towards reality, in that they offer some explanation of – or even justification for – the constant calls for protection and subsidy that characterise the real world. In particular, businessmen frequently claim that if only they had a secure home market they could export more effectively, while politicians often appear to believe that higher market shares are a key indicator of economic welfare. Traditional theory finds it hard to give these arguments any intellectual basis, for the optimal tariff is the only watertight case for protection in the neo-classical tradition. Strategic trade policy, on the other hand, can accommodate such views and can thus, it is argued, provide a framework within which economists and 'practical men' can debate the need for policy.

Providing a framework for thinking about protection is, indeed, a useful contribution, but there are other explanations for protection (see Chapter 12), and the strategic trade policy results are very sensitive to the assumptions of the models from which they stem. Thus small changes in the assumptions can completely reverse the policy prescription. We have already seen, for example, how crucial the integration/segmentation of markets is in the free entry case; other important dimensions include general equilibrium repercussions and the nature of competition.

General equilibrium

The analysis so far has considered only a single industry, and has assumed that it is small enough to face fixed factor prices. Dixit and Grossman (1986) offer an important generalisation to the case of many industries. The necessary conditions for strategic trade policy gains are that industries have increasing returns to scale and be imperfectly competitive. The high-technology sector is frequently believed to exhibit these features because R&D is a fixed cost and successful innovation confers temporary competitive advantage. R&D and innovation arise from the application of highly skilled labour – scientists, in a convenient shorthand. If a country has a finite stock of scientists, which is always fully employed, using them in industry X necessarily precludes using them in industry Y. Thus the policy issue is no longer whether protecting/ subsidising hi-tech industry X would increase welfare in the X-market, but whether it will do so to the extent necessary to offset the corresponding losses as scientists are withdrawn from industry Y. Even if all hi-tech industries could potentially snatch rents, optimality requires that the subsidies be targeted to those which offer the greatest opportunities. If industries all display equal abilities to snatch rents, or if governments have insufficient information to identify the best candidates, then the policy prescription reverts to the traditional one of no intervention. To do otherwise would just increase scientists' wages (as industries used the subsidies to compete for them) and drag other factors into the hi-tech sector to a greater extent than desirable.

If the Dixit and Grossman argument holds, countries may be able to gain by increasing their supply of scientists. This has obvious implications for education policy, but it also suggests that the international mobility of scientists – the so-called brain drain – is important. Winters (1988) analyses a case where subsidising the whole of the hi-tech sector begins to look more attractive again, if by so doing a country can attract additional scientists from the rest of the world. The problem here, however, is the obvious scope for retaliation which, Winters shows, could lead to protracted and wholly damaging subsidy wars.

The nature of competition

All the analysis so far has assumed that firms compete by choosing their optimal quantity *given* the quantitative supplied by other firms – so-called Cournot competition. A polar alternative, however, is Bertrand competition, whereby firms fix their prices *given* the prices charged by all other firms. This is often characterised as being fiercer than Cournot competition, for it typically generates outcomes closer to perfect competition. In simple cases the switch from Cournot to Bertrand competition completely reverses the Brander and Spencer policy prescription: exports should be taxed!

Imagine again the duopoly model with no home sales. Starting from a Bertrand equilibrium, the firms (and exporting countries) will benefit if they can *raise* prices. In Figure 11.2, firms' reaction curves in price space slope up and, we assume, intersect only once. (This figure requires that the firms produce different varieties in order that the curves have the shape shown. Recall that A's reaction curve R_A gives the best p_A for any given p_B.) An attempt by A to raise its price, say to p'_A, would induce either no move by B, in which case A would revert to p_A by definition of its reaction curve, or an increase in p_B to p'_B, which would then set off a series of adjustments converging back at E. If, however, A's reaction curve could be shifted out to R'_A, then its price rise would be credible and it would pay B to react constructively by raising its prices too; the equilibrium would be E'. But what would cause A to raise its preferred price for any given p_B? Not a subsidy, but an export tax!

Figure 11.2 Bertrand competition

A further aspect of the assumption about the nature of competition is that the case for intervention relies wholly on firms having inconsistent conjectures; that is, on firms mistaking in some way the nature of the game they are playing. Intervention is then desirable to correct the errors that arise – it assumes that governments know better. (The parallel with the optimum tariff case is perfect: there governments step in to get firms to exercise the market power they possess but do not perceive.) The simplest form of consistent conjectures is the Stackelberg assumption, and a useful way of thinking about the simple strategic trade policies analysed here is as a way of moving the local firm from the position of a Cournot competitor to that of a Stackelberg leader. (See Appendix for a discussion of the Stackelberg point.)

The importance of these results is not that Bertrand or Stackelberg competition is more common than Cournot competition. It is that the Brander-Spencer results depends on the type of oligopolistic competition that rules, and that economists have virtually no idea which of Cournot, Bertrand or many other alternatives actually applies in any particular market. Thus the basis on which intervention (either tax or subsidy) can be recommended is extremely fragile.

152

Number of domestic firms

If there are two or more firms from country A, competition between them will tend to keep output up and prices down, possibly below the level optimal for country A as a whole. If so, an export tax is called for, just as in the optimal tariff/tax argument above. Precisely when one switches from requiring a subsidy to requiring a tax as the number of A-firms increases depends on many factors, but it could be as low as two.

Identifying rent to shift

Profits are high in many hi-tech industries, but this does not necessarily indicate the existence of rent to snatch. Suppose that, as is frequently the case, imperfect competition reflects technological superiority, possibly bolstered by patents. For every successful producer there are likely to be others which have devoted resources to R&D but have lost the race. Thus in the long run the returns from successful innovation must be high enough to cover the unsuccessful attempts as well; they should be judged excessive (i.e. to include rents) only if the expected return (i.e. the return if successful multiplied by the probability of success) exceeds normal profit. Thus high *ex post* profits are not sufficient to prove the existence of rents if the volume of future R&D and innovation is endogenous.

This line of reasoning introduces two further complications. First, if the government offers export subsidies to successful innovators, and this is anticipated, the subsidy is likely to encourage more firms to undertake R&D. With higher returns to success (because of the subsidy), firms will be prepared to invest in R&D even if their probability of success falls. But ultimately only one firm can succeed; it may earn high profits, but society need not do so because of the resources used by all the unsuccessful firms. This is just a particular case of inefficient entry that we analysed above. The second complication concerns the imitability of innovation. If an innovation is easily imitated, it cannot generate much rent. A wise firm and a wise government, far from wishing to stimulate R&D, would hold back and try to cash in on other firms' research when it has borne fruit. In these circumstances, subsidies are quite inappropriate at the national level.

Another dimension of rent identification, however, suggests that traditional measures of profit could understate the case of activist policy. Dixit (1988) emphasised that if factor markets are imperfect, rent could be included in factor rewards rather than in measured surplus. For example, trades unions may be able to bid surpluses away from company owners, as is often held to have occurred in the US and UK vehicles and steel sectors during the 1970s. Thus, even if profits are normal, there may be rents enough to render trade policy desirable and provide a second-best case for trade policy to stimulate output and employment. First-best policy, however, would require the removal of the factor market distortion.

Are tariffs and subsidies best?

The models described so far have asked whether subsidies and tariffs are effective, not whether they are the best policies available. That is, they pose the 'second-best' question, not, as economists ideally should, the 'first-best' one. Collie and de Meza (1986) show that imposing a maximum import price would be a more effective and cheaper means of disciplining foreign firms than would domestic subsidies. Consider the subsidies paid to Airbus to allow it to rival Boeing in the market for large airliners. Not only is de Meza's prescription relevant, but one might also ask whether it would not have been cheaper for European governments to have subsidised Lockheed or McDonnell-Douglas as the rivals, for they at least were already established in the field. That this alternative was not chosen suggests that something else was behind European policy.

Retaliation

So far we have considered only one government; but surely the others could respond in kind. This raises the possibility that the final outcome would be worse for both parties than non-intervention, even though neither party finds it desirable to cease intervention unilaterally.[3] In these circumstances simple, robust and enforceable rules of behaviour, such as no intervention, can save a lot of hardship even though they may occasionally require countries to pass up the chances of economic benefits in a few particular cases.

The empirical implementation

The empirical problems of using the strategic trade policy models are formidable. Actual oligopoly is much more complex than Bertrand's or Cournot's representations of it and firms' perceptions and expectations of their rivals are likely to change frequently, not least in response to changes in government policy. The parameters of demand are difficult to measure, especially those affecting the desire for variety. Even production costs are not straightforward: how is R&D to be allocated over projects, and at what rate does efficiency improve with experience (learning by doing)? Such questions are doubly difficult to answer prior to full-scale production, which is, after all, the stage at which policy decisions must be taken. It can also be difficult to detect the true price at which hi-tech goods are sold and also whether they are subject to other policy distortions.

This list of difficulties has spurred the economics profession to considerable efforts, but empirical work to date has involved assuming the basic model to be correct and trying to deduce its parameters. This process has come to be known as *calibration*. Having written down the model, including an assumption about the type of competition, economists borrow estimates of some parameters from other studies and then determine the remainder so that the model will reproduce the data for one particular year. Once calibrated, the model is solved under a number of different policy scenarios and the results compared to isolate the effects of policy. No doubt this is the best that can be done at present, but it involves much less empirical information than many other exercises in applied economics and is a slender reed on which to hang radical economic policies such as protection. Case-study 11.1 describes a calibration exercise which illustrates the difficulties involved.

The results of the calibration studies extant show considerable variation, but, given the sensitivity of the theory to industry-specific factors such as the type of competition and the number of firms, it is not surprising. Dixit (1988), for example, found trade policy unimportant for the US auto sector unless one assumes that there are large rents included in workers' wages; he also found that the estimated returns to subsidies are sensitive to changes in the parameters of the model, and are largely offset by the likely distortion costs of raising revenue to finance them. Daltung, Eskeland and Norman (1988) also found great sensitivity in their study of the Caribbean cruiseliner business: if the main US firm in the business was irrevocably committed to buying a new ship, Norway had nothing to gain from subsidising her own firms, but if the US firm could be scared off, then the subsidy would be beneficial. The authors

CASE-STUDY 11.1: COMMUTER AIRCRAFT – A CASE FOR POLICY?

The market for modern commuter aircraft is tailormade for strategic trade policy. Three firms produce such aircraft (30–40 seaters): Embraer of Brazil, de Havilland of Canada and Saab of Sweden. They compete for world markets, probably – according to Baldwin and Flam (1989) – with the help of their governments. Producing aircraft is a complex and capital-intensive business and, having once chosen their capacities, firms are largely committed to the quantities they can produce. Thus competition in their market is basically Cournot at the time when capacities are chosen (early 1980s). Aircraft are durable goods, which introduces complications about discounting and the scheduling of purchases, but we ignore these below and express everything in terms of discounted net present values.

Airlines demand aircraft until their marginal revenue just equals their price. Given data or assumptions about the form of the marginal revenue equation, the elasticity of demand and the price of aircraft, the demand curve can be defined. This is stage 1 of the calibration. Stage 2 concerns the production process. R&D costs are heavy (assumed to be $220 m. per firm), and labour inputs decline with production experience (learning by doing, with a decrease of 20 per cent per aircraft). Non-labour costs are assumed to be equal between firms because they comprise mostly imported materials. Given these assumptions, and again assuming a simple functional form for the cost curve, Baldwin and Flam fix the level of each firms' initial costs to replicate actual market shares in 1987. They use the relationship

$$MC_i = p[1 + (s_i/\epsilon)],$$

which we derived in Chapter 5 above, and which allows more efficient firms to have larger market shares.

Inspection of market shares and discussion with industrialists lead Baldwin and Flam to postulate that (a) Brazil offers a production subsidy (she appears very competitive) and (b) Canada has market access restrictions (de Havilland is the only supplier to Canada). They solve their model assuming the abolition of either or both of these policies, comparing the outcome with their stylised version of reality to calculate the policy effects.

The effects of these two policies are reported in Table 11.1. Both policies increase the sales and profits of the firms affected by the policies and penalise the Swedish firm, as theory predicts. More interestingly, however, they appear to increase world welfare! This is because both policies increase output and lower world prices, by increasing competition and economies of scale. In the case of the market access restriction, Canadian output increases by nearly 50 per cent with dramatic effects on costs and on Canadian prices; the decreases in output by the other producers are smaller and do not offset the former effect. Note that these benefits are reaped without any transfers or government expenditure – a big attraction for governments. The Brazilian export subsidy, on the other hand, has smaller effects on domestic net profit, but offers large returns to world consumers because it boosts output by a relatively efficient producer.

Baldwin and Flam show that these results are robust with respect to changes in the elasticity of demand and the elasticity of learning. On the other hand, many factors of the model are very particular, e.g. the shapes of the

155

Table 11.1 Changes in welfare and sales due to trade policies for commuter aircraft

	Canadian market access restriction	Brazilian export subsidy of 10%
Profits ($m.):		
Brazil	− 39	152[a]
Canada	82	− 53
Sweden	− 69	− 65
Consumer surplus ($m.):		
Canada	20	18
Rest of the world	9	103
Sales (number):		
Brazil	− 53	117
Canada	133	− 45
Sweden	− 68	− 19
Total	12	53

Note:
[a] $30 m. exclusive of subsidies.
Source: Baldwin and Flam (1989).

demand and cost curves, so it would be premature to conclude that policy is desirable in this, let alone any other, market.

speculated on how the Norwegian government could possibly get such information as this on which to base policy. Finally Baldwin and Krugman (1988), in an elegant piece on silicon chips (16k RAMs), found that a supposed restriction on US sales in Japan was necessary to establish the Japanese industry and, *a fortiori*, to its winning a considerable share of world markets. However, the costs of such market shares – higher prices at home, higher fixed costs, etc. – outweighed the benefits, and Japan was the loser overall from her restrictions.

There is a danger in all this work. Much of the information required to assess the worth of strategic trade policy can come only from the businesses seeking protection themselves. Their incentives in this regard are clear, and so at the minimum we must display some caution over the information offered.[4] Chapter 12 discusses some of the pressures that businesses put on governments to provide protection, and it would be naive to believe that the apparent legitimacy offered by strategic trade policy arguments will remain unexploited. This perhaps increases the value of a simple policy rule such as no intervention, since while some opportunities for gain may go begging, it precludes many more opportunities for bias and overall loss. Even some governments and economists, however, find political attractions in strategic trade policy. For governments it can legitimise policies that they wish to pursue anyway (possibly because they cannot resist particular interest groups). For economists it offers a wider menu of 'respectable' policies, and so can give them a larger role in policy-making than does simple non-intervention.

These pressures, and the radical nature of the policies they promote, make it doubly important that strategic trade policy be subjected to proper empirical test rather than just calibration. That is, economists should ask not only what are the correct strategic policies in various cases, but whether strategic policy is a useful way of thinking about the world in a positive sense. De Meza (1986) has offered one such test. He showed that Brander and Spencer's (1985) export subsidy model suggests that subsidies will be larger the *more* efficient is an industry. Casual comparison of support levels both between industries in one country and between countries for one industry suggests the opposite: subsidies tend to offset inefficiency. This suggests that strategic trade policy is not a good explanation of modern protectionism.

FURTHER READING

Dumping is discussed accessibly by *Yarrow* (1987) and *Davenport* (1990) and at a more advanced level by *Ethier* (1982) and *Dixit* (1988). *Hindley* (1988, 1990) and *Messerlin* (1989, 1990) are excellent on the EC details. *Johnson* (1965a) and especially *Baldwin* (1969) are good on the infant industry case, as is *Dixit* (1990) on the uncertainty case. As before, *Corden* (1974) offers good general coverage.

  The literature on strategic trade policy is huge and unwieldy. The thoeretical work started with *Brander and Spencer* (1981) and these authors have produced several further articles, e.g. (1985). Other important contributions include *Krugman* (1984), *Dixit* (1984), *Venables* (1985), *Horstmann and Markusen* (1986), *Eaton and Grossman* (1986) and *Dixit and Grossman* (1986). The major empirical studies have been noted in the text, to which should be added *Smith and Venables* (1986, 1988), who consider the benefits of product variety more formally – see case-study 14.1. Several non-technical surveys exist: *Krugman* (1987a) offers a summary while *Krugman* (1987b) contains many useful chapters – especially those of Brander and Grossman. More technical surveys include chapters in *Stern* (1987), *Markusen and Venables* (1988), *Rodrik* (1988), *Deardorff* (1989) and *Helpman and Krugman* (1989).

KEY CONCEPTS

predatory dumping	price discrimination
normal value	market failure
cost reductions in new industries	missing contingent markets
rent shifting	import protection as export promotion
free entry	economic rents
calibration	Cournot vs. Bertrand competition

QUESTIONS FOR REVIEW

11.1 What criteria would you apply in deciding whether EC anti-dumping law is protectionist? Is it?

11.2 Should dumping be prevented? If so, how?

11.3 What market failures can lead to a country having an inappropriate set of industries? What should the government do about this, if anything?

11.4 Consider the argument that the EC should subscribe to the MFA because textile workers have suffered a large and unforeseeable shock which society as a whole should bear.

11.5 What are the main elements of the strategic argument for protection? Describe carefully the importance of the nature of competition in this argument.

11.6 Is the strategic trade policy argument a sufficient intellectual basis on which to recommend protection?

Consider the model of duopoly described in the text, and plot out the combinations of Q_A and Q_B which grant firm A particular levels of profit π_A^0, π_A^1, etc. These are shown in Figure 11.A.1 by the broken lines. They are best understood by considering how profits change as Q_A increases for a given level of Q_B. Moving horizontally from the vertical axis, profits rise at first (we move from π_A^0 to π_A^1, etc.) because A is selling more units. Eventually, however, the effect of the extra units on price outweighs the quantity effect and profits start to fall again. An implication of this pattern is that for every Q_B there is a unique profit-maximising level of Q_A. We can link up these optima to create R_A, A's *reaction curve*, which tells us A's optimum response to B's output. Note that A's profits increase as we move down R_A to M, at which point it earns monopoly profits, and that the iso-profit lines are horizontal where R_A cuts them. Obviously we can carry out the same procedure for B to create R_B.

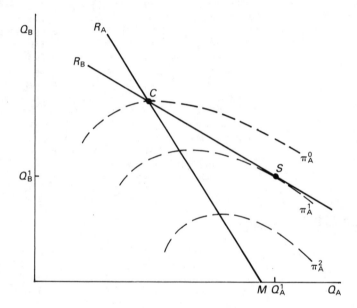

Figure 11.A.1 Cournot competition

If each firm takes the other's output as given and optimises its own response, the equilibrium must lie on both R_A and R_B – i.e. at C, the Cournot point. However, suppose that A knew that B would always take Q_A as given and choose a point on R_B; if A had the first move it could exploit this information to choose its preferred point along R_B. That is, it could declare its output as Q_A^1, B would choose Q_B^1 and A would earn π_A^1. This equilibrium, S, is the Stackelberg equilibrium with A leading, and an interpretation of strategic trade policy is that, by imposing policy, A's government gives A a first-mover advantage.

NOTES

1 It may, however, be true that, where learning by doing is important, dumping enhances a firm's long-run efficiency and hence precludes the establishment of rivals – see section 11.4 below.

2 The EC also has a so-called 'screwdriver plant' provision, whereby ADDs applied to imports can be applied to identical goods assembled in the EC by the allegedly dumping firms. In 1990 the GATT ruled that this was not legal. At the time of writing neither the EC response to the GATT ruling nor the likelihood of further complaints against EC practice is clear, but a moderation of EC practices may result.

3 This is the so-called Prisoners' Dilemma case; see, for example, Bacharach (1976).

4 Dixit (1987) quotes G. H. Hardy on the value of information: 'If the Archbishop of Canterbury says he believes in God, that's all in the way of business, but if he says he doesn't, one may take it that he means what he says.'

12 The Political Economy of Protection

We have now encountered the main arguments for protection in general and for tariffs in particular. The only first-best case for tariffs is the optimum tariff or terms of trade argument, which was seen to be definitely anti-social. Among second-best arguments perhaps the most persuasive is the revenue argument – that, among protective policies, tariffs are the least distortionary in terms of their collection, and that this might outweigh any allocative disadvantages they have. The arguments for protection in general – and thus for tariffs if these fiscal considerations apply – include domestic distortions (including the infant industry case), employment objectives, industrialisation policy and anti-dumping policy. For most countries, the first is probably the most relevant.

It is important to note that these arguments for protection are very specific, both in the circumstances to which they apply and in the remedies they recommend. It is not legitimate to observe that the economy is full of imperfections and thus that protection is justified. Rather, the economist must be sure which distortion he is trying to cure, that his policies will address it efficiently, that there are no untoward spill-over effects, and that the existence or even the possibility of protection will not set up incentives to behave strategically.

In fact, tariffs are rarely, if ever, justified directly in terms of distortions, and the evidence suggests that neither are they determined by such criteria. Although governments may decide their general attitude towards protection on the basis of a broad economic philosophy, the details of protection under either relatively liberal or relatively protectionist regimes owe as much to politics as to economics. This chapter considers this interaction. It starts by considering the implications of directly unproductive profit-seeking activities – lobbying – for the theory of protection. It then sketches some of the political-economy aspects of protection in the real world. The last two sections consider the General Agreement on Tariffs and Trade (GATT), the principal international trade agreement governing trade policy.

12.1 DIRECTLY UNPRODUCTIVE PROFIT-SEEKING ACTIVITY

Directly unproductive profit-seeking activities (DUPs – said 'dupes') are activities which, while privately profitable, generate no increase in social product. They are concerned with the distribution of national product rather than its creation. Two polar forms should be distinguished. First, *policy-exogenous* DUPs take policy as given and seek to redistribute the revenues or rents that it creates. Examples include Krueger's (1974) rent seeking (see p. 108 above), revenue seeking (whereby groups try to pre-empt the revenue of particular taxes or tariffs) and smuggling. They are economically costly to the extent that they use resources, which have to be withdrawn from productive uses, and that governments have to find less efficient ways of managing the economy. Particularly in the latter regard, however, DUPs can also be constructive – as, for example, if smuggling undermines a highly distortionary system of import quotas. Second, *policy-endogenous* DUPs seek to influence policy via lobbying or by strategic behaviour. They are costly both in their use of resources and to the extent that they introduce new economic distortions.

The incentives for DUPs are obvious, but, at least within Western societies, a number of factors help to keep them within limits: social conventions discourage the most blatant self-serving lobbying or revenue-seeking, and political processes provide fora in which issues can be settled and impose limits on the arbitrary use of power. The discipline of 'repeated games' is also important. If two parties know that they will have to meet over more issues in future, their behaviour is likely to be far more cooperative (social) than in one-off negotiations. None the less, DUPs are undoubtedly an important part of the trade policy system.

Revenue seeking

To illustrate the effects of a policy-exogenous DUP we consider competition for the revenue of a tariff. Assume a standard small country 2×2 model and add a third non-traded DUP sector which competes with the goods sectors for factors of production. We assume that DUP activities are competitively supplied and demanded and that all of them absorb resources as opposed to merely being transfers (such as bribes). We also assume that revenue seekers are risk-neutral – they maximise their expected gain regardless of its variance. These assumptions ensure that for every £1 of revenue available for seeking, £1 of resources will be absorbed. Roughly speaking, each of n bidders has a $1/n$ chance of getting the £1 revenue and so will spend up to £$(1/n)$. This one-for-one assumption almost certainly overstates the costs of DUPs (see Varian, 1989), but it provides an upper limit for their costs.

In Figure 12.1, *FF* is the production possibility frontier between X and Y in the absence of DUPs. Assume that a tariff drives a wedge between world prices, *TT*, and internal prices, *II*: this would generate production and consumption points P_t and C_t. Now introduce the DUP. The small-country assumption fixes goods prices which, in turn, fix factor prices and factor proportions throughout the economy. Hence we know in what proportions the DUP withdraws factors from X and Y, and hence how it would shrink *FF* inwards. Also, given *II*, we know what points on the shrunken transformation frontier producers would choose. Joining up these points we obtain RP_t – the Rybczynski line, so called because it plots out the effects on output of changing factor supplies to the productive economy. The final production point must lie on the Rybczynski line.

The consumption point is found as follows. With fixed factor supplies and fixed factor rewards, total income is constant in terms of domestic prices regardless of how much DUP occurs. With no DUP, total income is given by the value of P_t, hence, even with DUPs, consumers may choose any point along *II*. Only one point on *II*, however, has a marginal rate of substitution equal to the internal price ratio; that is, C_r. To reconcile consumption at C_r with production along the Rybczynski line, international trade is required. It can occur only at terms of trade *TT* and so the production point must lie at the intersection of RP_t and $C_r T'$, the foreign offer curve through C_r. The output of DUP and the value of the tariff revenue are given by the difference between P_r and $P_t - AI$ in terms of X.

Figure 12.1 shows revenue seeking reducing output of both goods and being welfare worsening. It is easy to see, however, that the net effect of a tariff and revenue seeking could be to reduce the output of the protected good (Y in our

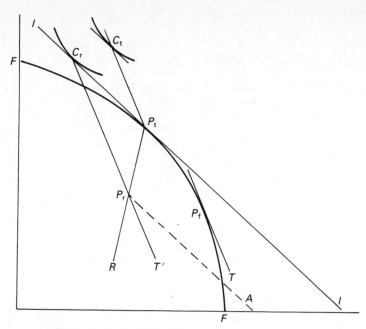

Figure 12.1 Tariff equilibrium with revenue seeking

case) below free-trade levels – P_r lying south of P_t. Revenue seeking could also increase output of the unprotected good relative to the no revenue seeking case. If the DUP was intensive in the factor used intensively in Y, the Rybczynski could go south-east from P_t. Indeed, if this effect were strong, and if not all the revenue were wasted in revenue seeking (i.e. less than one-for-one diversion), it is possible that revenue seeking would reduce the costs of the tariff. The tariff distorts the economy by expanding Y output and reducing X output. If revenue seeking undoes some of this effect, and if just some of the benefit of undoing it remains for consumption rather than being wasted in the DUP, the net effect can be beneficial. Of course, revenue seeking can never restore the full benefits of free trade.

It is also clear that import quotas and tariffs lose their equivalence under revenue or rent seeking. With an import quota on Y, the changes in domestic supplies of X and Y induced by the DUP change internal prices, and hence the DUP's factor-intensity ratio. This in turn shifts the Rybczynski line and hence the final equilibrium. The original contributor to this field, Krueger (1974), did not pursue this non-equivalence; she implicitly compared quotas plus rent seeking with tariffs plus *no* revenue seeking. Not surprisingly, she found tariffs preferable. Bhagwati and Brecher (1987) showed that import quotas and VERs are also non-equivalent in the presence of DUPs. Since the rents accrue in different countries, so does the lobbying. Indeed, one might argue that a particularly pernicious effect of VERs on exporting countries is to establish incentives for lobbying and corruption where none previously existed.

Tariff seeking We turn now to policy-endogenous DUPs and again restrict ourselves to the simple case of lobbying to obtain a tariff. The analysis is less powerful than

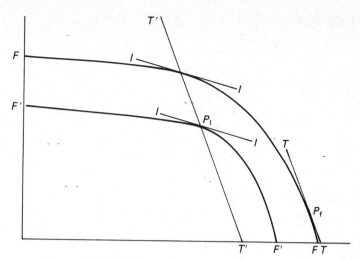

Figure 12.2 Tariff equilibrium with endogenous tariffs

the previous case but is at least illustrative. Consider Figure 12.2, where FF is again the DUP-free production possibility frontier and TT the small country's terms of trade. Suppose now that Y-producers lobby for a tariff and that in the final equilibrium they have absorbed resources sufficient to shrink FF inwards to $F'F'$ and to obtain internal price ratio II. The new production point is P_1, and the new consumption locus $T'T$. The consumption point, C_1 (not shown), will lie on $T'T$ where a community indifference curve has MRS equal to slope II.

Clearly C_1 is dominated by free-trade consumption, for all the usual reasons. However, it may or may not be preferable to the consumption point available with the same tariff applied exogenously. In the latter case, the production point would be where FF had slope II. In our figure the two outcomes are equally bad, but it is obvious that, if FF were slightly different, the result could go either way. There is, however, a conceptual problem in this comparison. If society is organised in such a way that policy is endogenous, the policy-exogenous outcome is not very relevant. Indeed, in some sense $F'F'$ and P_1 is the best we can hope to achieve. On the other hand, to take political pressure as given and to gear all economic advice to 'political realities' is merely to be an apologist for existing power structures. Economists should do better than that, and at least point out to their policy-making masters that, if political structures were changed to preclude or alter lobbying behaviour, then much better economic outcomes may be possible.

It is policy-endogenous DUPs more than any other single reason that persuade this author to advocate a strong commitment – perhaps a constitutional rule – to free trade. As we have seen in previous chapters, such a rule would surely miss a few opportunities for gain through trade policy, but, as we also saw, it would avoid many self-inflicted costs; the next section shows that, if policy is permitted, the odds are heavily stacked in favour of its imposing costs.

12.2 TARIFF SETTING IN INDUSTRIAL COUNTRIES

Even if we accept all the second-best arguments for intervening in trade – those where intervention is beneficial but not optimal – there are far more tariffs and quotas in the world than our theory would lead us to expect. This means that some – possibly most – are economically harmful, at least by the criteria we have applied so far. This may, of course, be mere ignorance on the part of policy-makers: they may be either unable to observe the consequences of tariffs or unable to interpret their observations. More likely, however, is that protection is actually determined in ways other than to maximise national income in the way we have assumed.

Costs and benefits

Before examining the evidence on tariff structure we should perhaps emphasise two effects that have been largely ignored in our previous analysis of protection and national welfare. In practice they are among the most important influences on private perceptions of the case for protection.

Distribution: We implicitly ignored this by assuming that the benefits of trade or of optimal protective policies could always be redistributed so that everybody benefited. In the usual situation of no redistribution, however, some people may lose when society gains and vice versa. For the interested parties, distributive factors frequently outweigh their share of any communal costs or benefits.

Adjustment costs: Most of our theory was of a comparative static nature – comparing equilibria with and without protection. It did not explore how the shift from one to another was made. If the *transition costs* of such a shift are high, it may not be worth making the change, even though doing so eventually yields higher welfare. This is particularly so if society has a strong preference for current over future consumption (a characteristic of poor people), because the transition costs are immediate whereas the benefits may be distant. Empirical studies suggest, however, that adjustment costs are frequently overestimated by the affected parties and only very rarely get close to offsetting the benefits of removing distortions.

Voting for protection

Trade policy is not determined by popular vote, but it is useful to consider briefly what would happen if it were. Suppose a referendum were held on whether to have a tariff on car imports. Imagine that all factors of production were sector specific, and that all producers of cars would benefit from the tariff by £g per year while all consumers would lose by £l. Since the number of consumers will outweigh the number of producers, we would expect the tariff to be rejected. Now, however, assume that it costs each voter £c to vote – say in lost time. If, plausibly, $g > c > l$, the vote will now accept protection, for no anti-votes will be cast. This is so even though total producer gains may fall well short of total consumer losses.

Even this simple example illustrates some important points. First, while possibly not very relevant to voting, it is readily applicable to any process of making one's views known. Who would protest in the rain or even write to their Member of Parliament over costs of, say, 25p per year? Hence any British policy imposing say £10 million of social cost might get a free run through Parliament. Second, even if there are some non-specific factors of production, the larger gains to specific factors could easily dominate the general, Stolper–Samuelson, effects. Third, however, if every voter had identical factor endowments and consumption patterns, all would face losses in excess of their gains and the tariff would be rejected. That is, it is the uneven distribution of factors of production that generates calls for protection. Fourth, since the costs of protection increase with the height of the tariff, l may eventually outweigh c, and at some level the tariff would be rejected. Note in this regard the power of the 'gate-keeper' or agenda-setter, who decides what should be voted upon: a tariff of t_1 may be passed while one of $t_2 > t_1$, may be rejected.

Finally, however, the voting model overlooks one vital issue – *free-riding*. In the original model why would any producer incur costs of £c to vote? After all, he knows that consumers won't vote and that since other producers will gain they will have a sufficient incentive to vote for the measure; hence can't he save his £c without affecting the outcome? The difficulty is obvious, and can be resolved only by appealing to external pressures to vote or make one's opinions known – to which we turn below.

Politicians

Once we recognise that voting on protection is indirect, via politicians, and that it is often tied in with other issues, the situation becomes much more complex. Voting in legislatures – Parliament or Congress – is often subject to *log-rolling* or voting coalitions whereby A and B agree to vote for each other's pet schemes at the expense of C. This will be efficient if A's and B's projects (i) generate social benefits and (ii) could not otherwise be passed because in isolation each would be lost by two votes to one. It could also be very inefficient, however, as A and B might impose high costs on C in return for relatively little gain themselves. The passage of the infamous Smoot–Hawley tariff through the US Congress in 1930 illustrates this danger. The bill started with tariff increases mainly for agriculture, but to pass it allies were necessary. Urban congressmen gradually fell in behind the measure in return for high tariffs on the goods produced in their constituencies. The result was a hike in nearly all tariffs, vigorous retaliation by other countries, collapsing world trade, the exacerbation of the world slump, and, in 1934, new legislation which removed the power to make commercial policy from Congress to the Presidency. In the UK, party discipline is a means of log-rolling, while in the USA the process is helped by the use of Omnibus Bills into which nearly anything can be written. Shepsle and Weingast (1981) show how the political incentive system encourages such practices.

Linking protection to other issues can also be important: it facilitates log-rolling across issues; it increases the leverage of groups' financial contributions to or publicly articulated support for a politician, because the politician can use support on one issue to pursue other issues in which he is interested; and it can introduce random shocks. Political systems function on complex trade-offs, and having received favours on one issue politicians feel obliged to offer concessions on another. The public choice school of theorists holds that politicians make these trade-offs with the sole objective of re-election. This view may provide a useful approximation for analytical purposes, but it is exaggerated: concern for the disadvantaged, perception of the public interest and even principle also play a role. The first can be particularly important in trade policy, for industries coming under import pressure in the industrial country democracies typically have rather poor and unskilled workers. It is also true that politicians are usually anxious to avoid causing absolute declines in the real incomes of identifiable groups. This is Corden's (1974) *conservative social welfare function* (CSWF), which places a high value on *status quo*. The CSWF's prevalence in policy-making is indisputable, but whether it stems from principle or pragmatism is not, because in adopting it politicians may equally well be reflecting popular sentiment as expressing their own views. On the other hand, for the purposes of assessing its effects, its origins hardly matter.

Bureaucrats

Politicians are not the only group which can dispense protection to petitioners – bureaucrats can also do so. Indeed in Europe, bureaucrats are typically in post longer than politicians and are frequently better informed and more powerful. Building on Niskanen's (1971) general theory of bureaucracy, Messerlin (1983) considered the implication of these facts for protection. He noted first that senior bureaucrats become closely identified with the sectors they manage – their skills are rather specific, their prestige and status depend on how their sectors perform, and they often develop close relationships with managers in those sectors. He also observed that bureaux compete with each other for influence and that they resist external interference from politicians and particularly from other bureaucrats in 'general' ministries such as Finance or Foreign Affairs.

One implication of these observations is that bureaucrats tend to offer more protection than politicians. Imagine that a political institution can generate profits by granting its clients protection. These might include money payments but more likely comprise goodwill and general support. Politicians can benefit from some of these profits and will favour profit-maximising levels of protection, but bureaucrats cannot, and hence, being interested mainly in the size of their administrative units, will favour output-maximising or revenue-maximising tariffs, both of which exceed profit-maximising ones. Bureaucrats will also favour more complex means of protection: these both generate jobs and reduce external interference and monitoring because no one else can understand how the system works. It is difficult to test such conjectures, but the case of agricultural protection suggests their plausibility. Agricultural bureaucracies grew very large during the Second World War, and have since maintained immensely restrictive and complex systems of protection relying on quality and quantity controls. Attempts at reform have certainly been frustrated by civil servants in Japan and probably elsewhere as well.

Bureaucratic protection can also escalate because of *limited competence* – the fact that one bureau controls only a subset of available policy instruments. For example, protection is relative: protection for one sector means disprotection for the rest. Hence the Ministries of Agriculture and Industry might compete with each other to stimulate their own sector by protection, escalating tariffs beyond the levels they would choose if they cooperated. Similarly, the Ministry of Agriculture might accept that reducing agricultural protection would be Pareto improving if simultaneously the Treasury increased income transfers to farmers. But because it cannot control the latter issue, the ministry dare not recommend the former. It is only at higher levels of government that combinations of policies can be guaranteed, which is one reason why higher levels are typically more liberal in their approach to foreign trade than are lower levels. Another is that the top levels of government are responsible for both the benefits and the costs of protection. Hence to stimulate trade liberalisation it is usually more effective to deal with the Ministries of Finance and Foreign Affairs, to which the domestic and foreign costs of protection matter, than with the sectoral ministries such as Agricultue, Industry or Energy.[1]

Interest groups

Interest groups lobby for protection. They are present in all capital cities and work through a variety of means depending on the country concerned. They are important to politicians for things such as campaign contributions and public statements of support, and to bureaucrats as sources of information and for easing the administration of policy. For example, the British National Farmers' Union is regularly consulted by the Ministry of Agriculture. In return the NFU rarely condemns policy publicly and even administers certain policies for the ministry, such as disaster relief.

Many public decisions may be seen as the outcome of lobbying and counter-lobbying by interested parties (Becker, 1983), so it is important to ask what determines the effectiveness of a lobby. The first issue is *free-riding*. The results of lobbying are usually public goods – i.e. tariffs for the whole industry. Hence each potential member of the lobby would prefer others to bear its costs while he does not. Free-riding is much easier to prevent in small groups where culprits may be easily identified. It also appears to be easier to convert organisations that exist for non-lobbying purposes into lobbies than to start from scratch, and that lobbies which provide some private services (e.g. special insurance or concessionary sales) have less difficulty in extracting members' dues to cover their public good activities. Lobbies are also likely to be more effective the more homogeneous are their members' interests and the greater the threat they face. It is easier to mobilise to defend the *status quo* than to improve it: the objective is clear, there is less uncertainty about the extent to which it can be achieved, people apparently weight actual declines in income more heavily than lost opportunities for gain, and there is less danger of new entrants to a sector diluting the gains from lobbying. These factors help to explain why defensive lobbies are more successful (and get more public sympathy), and why radical change can usually occur only when the *status quo* is widely recognised as unviable; that is, in a crisis when 'something must be done'.

The previous paragraph suggests several reasons why producer lobbies are more effective than consumer lobbies. Indeed, regrettably, the latter hardly figure at all in the debate about protectionism. A more effective counter to protectionist producer lobbies comes from other industries – user-industries or exporting industries whose markets are threatened by retaliation (see Destler and Odell, 1987). Both case-studies (e.g. Petit, 1985) and econometric evidence (e.g. Chappell, 1982, and Esty and Caves, 1983) attest to the effects of lobbying on congressional voting patterns and hence on policy.

Empirical evidence

There have been many studies of protectionism designed to test and quantify the various hypotheses discussed above on cross-sections of US industries. Their results are rather mixed, but there is support for several of the factors identified. Baldwin (1984, 1985) and Lavergne (1983) summarised the literature and then added their own conclusions. Lavergne distinguished five sets of explanatory variables in his study of the levels and changes in US tariffs:[2]

- *Pressure group variables.* The following appear *not* to be useful in explaining protection: the industry concentration ratio, geographical concentration, skill levels or the presence or strength of trades unions. On the other

167

hand, an industry's size and the sizes of the states in which it is prominent do seem to enhance its level of protection.

- *Adjustment costs.* Adjustment to imports seems likely to be more difficult the poorer an industry's workers, the less prosperous the regions it is in, and the slower its total demand is growing. In fact, these were not generally good explanatory variables of tariff levels, although fast-growing industries did seem to receive fewer non-tariff barriers and rural industries got somewhat higher protection.

The relative failure of thse first two sets of variables led Lavergne to suggest that pressure groups are not dominant in the protectionism game. On the other hand, other researchers have found stronger evidence of their importance, so they should not be discounted entirely.

- *Comparative disadvantage* can influence protection if governments seek to counter its effects. Measured by variables such as import penetration, industry wage rates and capital intensity, it appears to have a significant role in the explanation of tariff levels. The protection offered to textiles, iron and steel and agriculture supports this view, although it must be recognised that it is virtually impossible to disentangle the effects of comparative disadvantage from those of adjustment costs discussed above.
- *Historical continuity*: The best single explanation of tariff levels in 1964, 1972 and 1980 was tariffs in 1930. Once established, protection is generally difficult to remove, because people feel that they have acquired a 'right' to it. Once an industry has responded to protection by investing, it is difficult for governments deliberately and consciously to undermine it by explicitly withdrawing that protection. The importance of explicitness in this process is corroborated by Lavergne's finding that, while *ad valorem* tariffs have tended to persist, governments have been prepared to let the value of *specific* duties be eroded by inflation.
- *Negotiation*: The principal means of reducing tariffs has been rounds of international negotiation (see below). Lavergne found the US tariff structure biased in favour of Canada, a strong and regular negotiator with the US, and against the Japanese and the developing countries, which are relatively weak members of the GATT.

Administered protection

We have written as if each item of protection were consciously debated and decided upon by politicians and bureaucrats after weighing up its political costs and benefits. This may be true of the broad thrust of trade policy and also of major items such as the VERs on cars. The bulk of new protection, however, arises from another process: administered protection – protection which is granted after an administrative procedure has investigated whether it is warranted under some existing legislation. The best examples are anti-dumping and countervailing duties (countervailing duties are imposed to offset – countervail – export subsidies). An industry has merely to prove that it has been injured by unfair (less-than-fair-value, LFV) trade and, subject to minor exceptions, protection is granted. The proof takes place not in the political arena, although a good deal of publicity often accompanies the investigation, but in front of specially appointed commissioners or officials. The process is essentially a legal one, and hinges around how well a particular case fits the relevant legislation or precedent.

A second branch of administered protection is the 'escape clause'. This allows countries to impose temporary restrictions on imports if they are causing severe difficulties for local producers. The criteria of injury are tougher than in LFV cases and the process is more discretionary and political, but the basic procedures are still administrative.

It would seem at first that no process of considering protection could be fairer than a legal one – after all, all our actions are governed by the law. But this is not so, for, as we saw in section 11.1, the process itself is biased. First, there are no penalties for the plaintiffs of failed actions; hence bringing LFV cases is a cheap way of harassing foreign competitors. Second, the criterion for protection is injury to producers: consumers may stress that the national interest is best served by over-ruling the 'right' of injured producers to protection, but the right to cheap imports and competitive supplies is not recognised in law. Third, the expense of presenting evidence and proving precedent favours well-organised lobbies – namely, producers.

These biases make administered protection attractive to an industry seeking support, but they are also attractive to politicians and even bureaucrats. Although the net welfare losses from protection are substantial, they are usually small relative to the gross transfers involved. That is, protection's most obvious feature is taxing Peter to pay Paul. Western political systems are poorly equipped to make such redistributive decisions, and administrative protection is a way of insulating the authorities from them – i.e. of taking the political sting out of redistribution. Finger (1981) argued that while the commissions and boards of experts are ostensibly designed to collect and process information, their real purpose is to slow down, obfuscate and confuse the situation. In that way, if protection emerges at the conclusion, the public will not blame the politicians but will accept that, if the law says protection is necessary, it must be.

Administered protection has become far more common over the last twenty years, and, within it, the more technical LFV procedures have come to dominate the more political escape clause one (see Finger, Hall and Nelson, 1982). Firms have come to realise that there is no need to confront the political system if they can largely bypass it. Only the large and politically active sectors – e.g. agriculture, iron and steel and vehicles – pursue the political route, and even they sometimes use LFV action as their opening move. As we saw in section 11.1, dumping actions frequently result in quantitative restrictions rather than duties and the same is true of other LFV and escape clause actions. Moreover, changes in legal procedures over the last decade have, particularly in the USA (Grinols, 1989), made it easier to obtain administered protection. Hence a safety valve which was intended to cover a few extreme cases and to authorise the temporary use of tariffs has, in fact, led to the widespread control of international trade. The lobbies have got progressively better at manipulating the trading rules, and have now captured and exploited a small exception to free trade to such an extent that the whole system looks threatened. This raises the issue again of whether the best approach is just a simple 'no intervention' rule, even though this would leave one exposed to occasional dumping and subsidised exports.

12.3 THE GENERAL AGREEMENT ON TARIFFS AND TRADE (GATT)

The origins of the GATT

During the Second World War the allies put considerable effort into planning the post-war economic order. It was universally agreed that the trade

169

restrictions and competitive devaluations of the 1930s had been counter-productive and plans were made to create an International Trade Organisation (ITO) and an International Monetary Fund (IMF) to administer a better system.[3] The ITO was to have had extensive powers over trade and the real economies of its members, but in the end these issues proved so contentious that the ITO was not ratified. While negotiations were going on, however, twenty-three countries wanted to get on with liberalising trade, and, having agreed a set of mutual tariff reductions, signed a treaty outlining them and the conditions surrounding them. This was the GATT, which became effective in 1948. It was a temporary measure designed merely to codify and sustain tariff reductions that were desired in their own right. It has grown, however, into the world's main trade agreement and now has ninety members, known as the Contracting Parties.

The preamble to the GATT states that the Contracting Parties (members) should '[enter] into reciprocal and mutually advantageous arrangements directed to the substantial reduction of tariffs and other barriers to trade and to the elimination of discriminatory treatment in international commerce.' The Treaty is vague about precisely how these objectives should be achieved and has only the very weakest of enforcement mechanisms, but it does specify two important precepts for a liberal trading order:

- *non-discrimination*: the 'most favoured nation' (MFN) clause requires that every trading partner be treated as well as the most favoured partner – i.e. that all are treated equally; and
- *national treatment*: imports should receive equal treatment with national goods once they have crossed the border.

The bulk of the Treaty then enumerates the circumstance under which these precepts may be violated. For example, customs unions may grant mutual tariff preferences, less-than-fair-value trade may be taxed, and export subsidies may be granted for agricultural products. The treaty also constrains governments' ability to withdraw or undermine tariff concessions previously offered under the GATT. Once a tariff has been *bound* – fixed – under the GATT it may be raised again only after an arduous negotiating procedure and if compensation is offered to trading partners. Similarly, emergency protection (the escape clause) must be temporary and non-discriminatory, import quotas are generally prohibited and customs procedures must satisfy elementary concepts of fairness.

GATT negotiations

The procedure adopted by GATT has entailed a series of rounds of trade negotiations in which tariff reductions are agreed and bound. At first these rounds were relatively short and informal affairs, and negotiations were conducted bilaterally, with their results being extended to other partners via the MFN clause. Bilateralism was a way of overcoming industry's and hence governments' fears about liberalisation. While they may possibly have accepted the case for universal free trade, they certainly did not accept that for unilateral free trade. Thus, before reducing their tariffs – 'making a concession' – governments believed that they should receive a compensating reciprocal concession from their trading partners.

The main theoretical argument for demanding a reciprocal reduction is that it will improve the terms of trade, which implies that the partner (or partners together) constitute a large country whose tariff initially worsened the terms of trade. If the partner is small, the benefits of its liberalisation must be sought in terms of the extra exports generating infant industry and full employment effects. In practice, one suspects, just as governments tend to overemphasise the adjustment costs of contracting existing import-competing industries, they also overemphasise the benefits of expanding existing export industries.

Such bilateral negotiations can lead to substantial biases in the pattern of trade liberalisation. For instance, when Britain seeks tariff reductions by her partners, she will aim to negotiate about an industry in which she believes she has a comparative advantage, in order that when the reduction is extended to competing exporters by the MFN clause she will be able to capture much of the newly opened market. She will also negotiate with other industrial countries, because their markets, being larger, offer greater returns to liberalisation. These countries in turn will seek reciprocal concessions from Britain in areas of their comparative advantage. They will also offer concessions in Britain's area of comparative advantage in order that, of their extra imports, the greatest share possible comes from Britain, thus encouraging her to make greater reciprocal concessions. For example, Britain and France might find considerable mutual benefits in swapping tariff reductions on beer and claret – much of the French concession on beer would benefit Britain, while Britain's claret concession would benefit France. They would find little gain, however, from negotiating reductions on tea and coffee because all the extra trade would accrue to other producers.

Thus, under this old system, tariff reductions became heavily concentrated on goods of interest to the industrial markets. The developing countries, having little to offer by way of markets, could gain no reductions in their areas of interest. This was exacerbated by the fact that, as we saw in Chapter 5, expanding intra-industry trade is probably less painful than expanding inter-industry trade, since it involves lower adjustment costs and less likelihood of any factor actually suffering from liberalisation. There was therefore an additional incentive towards freeing intra-industrial country trade rather than industrial–developing trade, since the former is mainly intra-industry and the latter inter-industry.

By 1963, however, the 'easy' reductions had been exhausted and a much more comprehensive approach was adopted. The Kennedy Round (1963–7) and the Tokyo Round (1973–9) adopted tariff-cutting rules but with exceptions for specific products. The exceptions, however, were widespread and served largely to prevent or curtail reductions in sensitive areas. Hence, sectors such as textiles and agriculture escaped 'lightly'. None the less, both rounds cut average tariffs by about one-third; this compared well with the first (1948) round and was much better than had been achieved in those of the late 1950s and early 1960s. The Uruguay Round (1986–90) never agreed on a tariff-cutting formula.

The Kennedy and Tokyo Rounds were also innovative in trying to address a wider range of issues than mere tariff cutting. These initiatives resulted in agreements such as the Subsidies Code and the Public Procurement Code which extended GATT control into these areas. Both also tackled non-tariff barriers to imports, but with a few exceptions were not notably successful.

The Uruguay Round

The Uruguay Round is the latest and most extensive GATT round. It has taken serious steps to address trade in agriculture and services as well as to consider the strengthening of the GATT procedures. In particular, in the face of the abuse of LFV actions, the increasing use of NTBs and an increasing tendency (especially by the USA) to act unilaterally in trade matters, medium-sized countries have sought to improve GATT disciplines by first speeding up rulings on complaints and then making them more enforceable. This has led to talk of reviving something like the ITO.

It is too early to predict the outcome of the Uruguay Round, but talk of its being critical for GATT and the world trading system is probably not exaggerated. Over recent years little progress has been made on issues such as agriculture, NTBs and LFV cases. Many countries are feeling frustrated, and the large ones (USA and EC) are increasingly breaking the spirit if not the letter of GATT law. A major failure would only exacerbate this decline.

The political economy of the GATT

The GATT is no free-traders' charter. It does not oblige countries to liberalise their trade, but rather seeks to constrain such restrictions as they have to relatively less harmful forms. It stresses the rights of other countries, even though the principal harm of protectionism is to the protecting country itself. It considers the difficulties that trade creates for industry rather than asserts the economic pre-eminence of consumer interests. None the less, and despite its currently fragile form, it has been highly successful in fostering the openness and growth of the world economy. In practical terms three factors have been important.

First, reciprocity turns business's wish for markets into a liberalising force. Import-competing producers will resist liberalisation – and are well placed to do, as we saw above – but if their resistance means that exporters lose overseas markets there is immediately a counterweight. For so long as all, or even a wide selection of, tariff concessions are linked into one package, intersectoral trade-offs can be very effective. They are much less potent when negotiations are organised along sectoral lines, however – as, for example, with the agricultural talks in the Uruguay Round – for then almost all interested producer groups in a country are on the same side of the protectionist debate.

Second, while governments will act illegally, they do not like to. Hence they go to great lengths to show that they are being GATT-consistent in their trade restrictions and mostly acknowledge GATT rulings even though the rulings have no enforcement mechanism. Legality represents a strong counter-argument to domestic lobbies seeking protection, and in many respects the most important function of GATT is to bolster governments against their own lobbies.

Third, by offering some escape from crushing competition the GATT has allowed industry to experiment with liberalisation. The concept of rounds of GATT talks arose because at first negotiators made only temporary commitments and agreed to meet again in two years in case things were so bad that back-tracking was required. In the event it was not, and they just kept going forward. Such pragmatism is probably more effective than trying to get binding agreements from the start.

12.4 DEVELOPING COUNTRIES AND THE GATT

Developing countries have not faced particularly well under the GATT. As we saw above, bilateral negotiation is biased against them and they have been particular victims of GATT derogations over textiles (the MFA) and agriculture (in which their exports are curtailed). In part these problems reflect their lack of economic and political power, but in part they are due to the developing countries' unwillingness to be active within the GATT. Finger (1979) showed that those developing countries that played a full role in the Kennedy Round – i.e. offered their own concessions – did very much better in terms of obtaining (MFN) concessions on products of interest to them than other developing countries: 77 per cent of the USA's concessions to these developing countries were for products in which they were the USA's principal (i.e. largest) supplier. Similarly Winters (1987b) showed that industrial and developing countries have plenty of quantitative restrictions on each others' goods which could be negotiated away in the Uruguay Round.

The difficulty is that the developing countries have clung almost religiously to the special and differential treatment that the GATT accords them, despite the fact that it does them virtually no good. The GATT permits developing countries to maintain trade restrictions for developmental and balance of payments reasons, and explicitly removes their obligation to make reciprocal concessions during the negotiating rounds. Even in the Uruguay Round, which the developing countries were prominent in launching, special and differential treatment figures large. From the theory of the preceding chapters and also Chapter 15 below it should be clear that this amounts to a licence to developing countries to score economic own goals.

The Generalised System of Preferences

Developing countries also receive special and differential treatment on their exports. Disenchantment over the tariff negotiations and the alleged secular decline in the relative price of primary exports led to the formation of the United Nations Conference on Trade and Development (UNCTAD) in 1964. UNCTAD has functioned in parallel with the GATT and has witnessed many of the most bitter North–South arguments. One of its early apparent successes was the Generalised System of Preferences (GSP), which allowed OECD ('donor') countries to reduce tariff levels on developing country manufactured exports below their MFN rates. The European countries and Japan introduced GSP schemes in 1971–2, and renewed and reformulated them in 1981. Canada and the USA introduced their schemes in 1974 and 1976 respectively.

The benefits of the GSP were seen primarily in terms of the infant industry case: the additional demand for exports would stimulate economies of scale and externalities such that eventually world income would rise. Additionally, even if the quantities traded did not change (because donors' internal prices did not change), the existing developing country exporters would earn higher revenue, for they would receive themselves what was formerly paid in MFN tariffs. This was seen as an acceptable redistribution. There was some possibility of trade diversion whereby the donor's demand for imports was diverted from efficient OECD suppliers paying the full tariff to developing country suppliers whose real costs exceeded OECD's but who could undercut the latter because they were paying only reduced tariffs. This would be a real cost to the world, but was expected to be relatively small and easily outweighed by the benefits from stimulating trade.

In fact, the GSP has been disappointing for a number of reasons. First, nearly all the included products are subject to quotas on preferential imports; beyond the quota, MFN tariffs are payable. Second, many goods are excluded entirely or subject to very restrictive quotas; these are the usual set of labour-intensive low-technology goods that developing countries can produce effectively – textiles, leather, clothing, and processed agricultural goods. Third, the GSP contains escape clauses, allowing concessions to be withdrawn if 'market disruption' occurs. All these factors discourage developing countries from investing in extra capacity in response to the GSP, because they make preferential treatment uncertain. Indeed, they make its removal certain if the developing countries are too successful!

The actual benefits rely, therefore, mainly on the revenue effects to existing exporters. However, developing country manufactured exports are relatively small and, more importantly, are concentrated among a few relatively advanced 'newly industrialising countries' (NICs), which could probably manage well enough without preferences. Furthermore, MFN tariffs are mostly low anyway, so preferences offer little revenue or competitive advantage, especially since the Tokyo Round. Finally, the EC offers greater preferences to its 'associated states' than under the GSP (see section 14.1), so the little preference that exists is 'undercut' as well.

Murray (1977) quantified these factors starkly. In 1976, GSP 'donors' imported goods worth nearly $36 b. from GSP beneficiaries: of these, 58 per cent faced zero MFN tariffs; 15 per cent were agricultural goods excluded from the GSP; 14 per cent were industrial goods excluded from the GSP to protect domestic producers; and just 13 per cent fell under the GSP! Furthermore, among the $3.6 b. of industrialised imports that did receive concessions, 47 per cent came from four countries – Taiwan (15 per cent), Mexico (12 per cent), Yugoslavia (11 per cent) and South Korea (9 per cent).

Murray estimated that the net increase in trade due to the GSP was about $0.4 b. (at 1970 prices) and that the scheme could have displaced up to 25,000 jobs in donor countries. This is clearly very small. MacBean and Snowden (1981), on the other hand, argued that the GSP had been more beneficial than these figures suggest, first because significant dynamic and external effects would eventually emerge in the major beneficiaries, and second because the GSP encouraged developing countries to maintain outward- rather than inward-looking strategies. Appealing to the evidence to be presented in Chapter 15, they argued that this represents a useful contribution.

The EC's new GSP attempts to meet some of the criticisms voiced above. In particular, certain NICs receive little or no preference, and quotas on preferential imports are now country-specific. This gives poorer countries a chance to benefit and offers them some certainty over how much they will be able to sell. In addition, imports from the world's poorest nations are guaranteed duty-free access in any event.

FURTHER READING

DUPs are analysed thoroughly by *Bhagwati* (1980, 1982a) and *Bhagwati and Srinivasan* (1980, 1982). *Bhagwati and Brecher* (1987) is also useful and *Varian* (1989) is interesting on the costs of rent seeking. The political economy of trade policy is a large and fascinating subject. Finger is the most insightful commentator – see the text references – and early work such as *Cheh* (1974), *Pincus* (1975) and *Helleiner* (1977) is stimulating. *Baldwin* (1984, 1985, 1989) is excellent and *Magee, Brock and Young* (1990) the most comprehensive theoretically. *Becker* (1983) offers a simple model of pressure group competition, *Olsen* (1965) is the classic on their functioning, and *Niskanen* (1971) the classic on bureaucracy. *Shepsle and Weingast* (1981) and *Peltzman* (1985) offer congressional voting models and *Mayer* (1984) a model of direct democracy. *Petit* (1985) and *Winters* (1987c) consider agriculture as a special case and stress the role of chance in the politics of protection.

The mechanics of bilateral tariff negotiation are discussed by *Johnson* (1965b, 1967a). The GSP is briefly discussed by *Morton and Tulloch* (1977) and *MacBean and Snowden* (1981). Greater detail is to be found in *Murray* (1977), *Weston* (1981) and United Nations Conference on Trade and Development, *General Report on the Implementation of the Generalized System of Preferences*. *Baldwin and Murray* (1977), *Ahmed* (1978) and *Langhammer and Sapir* (1987) present empirical estimates of the effects of the GSP. The GATT has stimulated many books – e.g. *Dam* (1970), *Preeg* (1970), *Winham* (1986) and *Hudec* (1987). *Winters* (1990b) offers a brief summary. On the Uruguay Round, *Finger and Olechowski* (1987) is a must, and *Whalley et al.* (1989) is useful.

KEY CONCEPTS

policy-exogenous DUPs	Rybczynski line
voting costs	log-rolling
bureaucratic protection	limited competence
free-riding	administered protection
reciprocity	most favoured nation clause
negotiating rounds	special and differential treatment

QUESTIONS FOR REVIEW

12.1 Is the one-for-one assumption of revenue seeking realistic? What factors suggest that it should be relaxed? What are the consequences of such a relaxation?

12.2 What are the consequences of the conservative social welfare function for trade policy?

12.3 Compare carefully the types and levels of protection likely to be delivered by bureaucrats and politicians.

12.4 What factors might explain the high level of agricultural protection?

12.5 'Developing countries should become full active members of the GATT.' Discuss.

NOTES

1 The scripts of the TV comedy programme 'Yes Minister' (Lynn and Jay, 1981) offer an enjoyable and insightful view of bureaucrats and their political masters.

2 Lavergne considered non-tariff barriers, but his treatment is sketchy.

3 The IMF and the International Bank for Reconstruction and Development (IBRD – the World Bank) are discussed in chapter 28 below.

13 Customs Unions

International trade is still subject to many restrictions. In this chapter, therefore, we examine attempts by groups of countries to integrate their economies to a greater extent than ordinary trade permits, by arranging some sort of preferential trading system. Perhaps the most visible of such attempts is the European Communities (EC) formed by twelve West European states.[1] This is described in the next chapter. The present chapter deals with the theory of international economic integration.

Degrees of integration

International economic integration takes many forms. In order of increasing strength of preference and commitment the main types are:

Preference areas, whereby certain countries agree to levy reduced, or preferential, tariffs on their mutual trade. These are outlawed under the GATT except for those already in existence when the GATT was signed in 1947. Most prominent among the latter were Britain's Commonwealth Preference System, and similar arrangements between France and Belgium and their overseas possessions, which have been perpetuated by means of the EC's Association Convention. The GSP (see Chapter 12) is also a form of non-reciprocal preference area.

Free trade areas, whereby partners abolish tariffs on mutual trade, but each partner determines its own tariff on extra-area trade. A potential problem here is that traders will try to import into the partner with the lowest external tariff and then re-export to the others tariff-free from there. To avoid this, complex rules of origin tend to govern intra-area trade to ensure that free trade refers only to partners' produce and not their imports. EFTA and LAFTA (respectively the European and Latin American Free Trade Associations) are examples.

Customs unions involve intra-union free trade but also a common external tariff.

Common markets are customs unions with additional provisions to encourage trade through the free mobility of factors of production and the harmonisation of trading standards and practices.

Economic union adds further harmonisation in the areas of general economic, legal and social policies, and the development of union-wide policies. This is an expressed goal of the EC. Economic union may be supplemented by *monetary union*, which would greatly ease the process of coordination (see Chapter 26).

Political union is the ultimate form of economic integration. It involves the submersion of all separate national institutions. Even within this category, however, several degrees of integration exist. For example, in the USA the states have substantial powers of taxation, whereas in the UK local government has few such powers.

Despite the GATT's code of non-discrimination, it does permit free trade areas and fuller schemes of integration, provided that they (i) cover nearly all partners' mutual trade, (ii) have a definite timetable for the elimination of intra-area tariffs, and (iii) do not increase the average restrictiveness of the partners' external tariffs.

13.1   TRADE CREATION AND TRADE DIVERSION

In this section we examine the simple analysis of preferential tariff reductions. We assume that tariffs are abolished on imports from some subset of exporters (the 'partners') but not on those from others; we examine both the positive and normative consequences of this situation.

Second best

Before 1950, economists tended to assume that, since free trade was preferable to restricted trade, partially free trade would also be preferable since it represented a step in the right direction. As we saw in Chapter 7, however, this is fallacious as a general rule: the general theory of second best states that, unless all the conditions necessary for optimality can be achieved, it may not be desirable to achieve just some of them. Hence, unless every country's exports to Britain enter free from restriction, it may not be desirable to allow exports from France to do so. This was first formally demonstrated for customs unions by Viner (1950).

Trade creation and trade diversion

Viner coined the phrases 'trade creation' and 'trade diversion' to cover the two *production* effects of a customs union. Consider country A's welfare when it forms a customs union with B; let C represent the rest of the world. Consider only a single good and assume that A, B and C can supply it at prices (opportunity costs) of £5, £4 and £3 respectively. That is, C is the cheapest source. Before union, both B and C face the same tariff; after union B faces no tariffs, but C, we shall assume, faces the same rate as before.

If the initial tariff were 100 per cent, A would undercut both B and C (with tariff-inclusive prices of £8 and £6 respectively) and hence supply its own market. Forming a customs union would lead to *trade creation*, because B's post-union price would fall to £4 and so it would capture A's market. Imports would replace home sales and A would gain because supplies would now be available from a lower-cost source than previously.

Alternatively, assume the initial tariff were only 50 per cent. Now the pre-union position would entail A's importing from C, for C's net price would be only £4.50. The post-union position, however, would be as before, with imports from B at price £4. This is *trade diversion* (existing imports are diverted to new partner sources) and it involves a social loss, because imports previously costing £3 (with the government collecting the remaining £1.50) are displaced by those costing £4.

A slightly more complex case is illustrated in Figure 13.1. Here A's domestic supply curve (SS) exhibits increasing costs, and we also introduce a demand curve (DD). We persist with partial equilibrium and with fixed prices for B and C, however. (Both these assumptions may be easily relaxed.) The case illustrated involves elements of both diversion and creation. The pre-union equilibrium involves imports from C, since $p_C(1+t) < p_B(1+t)$, domestic output h_t, and consumption q_t. The tariff revenue on the imports is given by area $c+e$. The post-union equilibrium has imports from B, since $p_B < p_C(1+t)$, domestic output h_u and consumption q_u. Trade creation has occurred, in that imports have displaced home output by $(h_t - h_u)$, and trade diversion in that the imports have switched from C to B. There is also an increase in consumption as the internal (tariff-inclusive) price falls, which Viner did not take into account but which is also really trade creation.

The welfare effects are easily calculated. Consumer surplus rises by $a+b+c+d$ as consumption expands from q_t to q_u. Of this, a is gained from

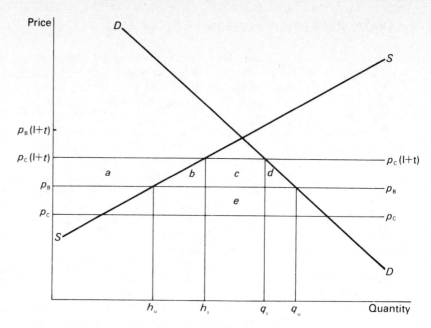

Figure 13.1 A customs union for one country

producers, whose surplus falls with their output, and *c* is gained from the government, since the latter has lost its tariff revenue. Areas *b* and *d* are pure gain: *d* from the better allocation of consumption expenditures and *b* from the resources released as the (inefficient) domestic industry contracts. This represents the gain from trade creation. There is one further component, however: area *e*. This was initially part of tariff revenue (imports cost society only p_C) but, post-union, it is lost to B's producers. This represents the loss due to trade diversion. The net effect of the customs union is, therefore, $b + d - e$, which may take either sign. Note, in particular, that even with no trade creation ($b = 0$) the customs union could still be beneficial if the consumption effects (*d*) outweighed the diversion effects (*e*). This result, contrary to Viner's view, is due to Lipsey (1960).

Desirable unions

It is possible to generalise these results somewhat to cover more complex cost conditions, general equilibrium and many goods, but the analysis is messy and the results increasingly ambiguous. Nevertheless, trade creation is generally found to be preferable to trade diversion, and on this basis economists have attempted to identify the conditions under which a given union is likely to be beneficial. A customs union will tend to be more beneficial:

- the larger the union, because then there is more chance of including the least-cost producer; in the limit, the world is the optimal customs union;
- the higher pre-union tariffs, because the pre-union position then involves greater production and consumption distortions;
- the lower post-union external tariffs, because this reduces the scope for diversion;
- the greater the overlap between partners' production bundles, because no overlap would entail no scope for trade creation on the production side; and

178

● given the degree of overlap, the greater the cost difference between partners, in order to increase the benefits of specialisation.

So far we have considered only the country granting the preferences. The benefits its partners receive may be in the terms of trade (see section 13.2), through infant industry or export promotion considerations, or from easing their balance of payments constraints (assuming that for some reason they cannot cure their deficits any other way). For example, in Figure 13.1, area e was lost to country A but, to the extent that B's producers earned producers' surplus on their extra output, it would not be lost to the union as a whole. Thus, even if one member of a union loses, the union as a whole may gain. Indeed, as with so many trade policies, it is likely that the benefits will not be evenly spread, and that some redistribution will be necessary to persuade certain countries to join. Newlyn (1965) argued that, among developing countries, distributional issues are the most important and that failure to solve them led, for example, to the demise of the East African Common Market. Even within the EC, there is constant debate over distribution.

Once we admit the possibility of costless redistribution between partners, however, we can elegantly prove that customs unions need never harm any country. Suppose the world is in full (tariff-ridden) equilibrium before union. After union, a particular common external tariff structure could be found that made the union's net trade with C precisely equal the sum of A's and B's pre-union net trade with C. This would leave C quite unaffected by the union. Now consider A and B. Their original consumption bundles would still be available, because their combined production possibilities and net trade with C would be unchanged. Hence, at worst the union need have no effect on them and in all probability production and consumption could be rearranged to make both A and B better off.

This argument (due to Kemp and Wan, 1976) is, of course, unrealistic, but it does serve an analytic purpose. It shows that any harmful effects of customs unions stem from the absence of optimal policy and redistribution, features whose presence is frequently assumed in other areas of trade theory (e.g. the benefits of free trade, and the literature on domestic distortions). It also shows that, under the assumptions, it is possible to shift the world economy from tariff-ridden trade to free trade in a series of Pareto-improving customs unions, which lends some support to the pre-Vinerian view that customs unions are a step in the right direction.

An alternative view of the desirability of customs unions comes from Ethier and Horn (1984). They showed that full customs union with no internal tariffs is necessarily worse than partial union with non-zero internal tariffs. Start from full union in which a good is supplied (at the same net price) by home, partner and foreign firms and raise the internal tariff slightly. This reduces both trade creation and trade diversion slightly. The marginal unit of creation contributes almost no welfare, for it substitutes partner goods for home goods, which *on the margin* have the same real cost ($p_A = p_B$). The marginal unit of diversion, on the other hand, is costly because in full customs union the partner price p_B exceeds the world price p_C by the amount of the tariff. Hence losing a unit each of creation and diversion is, on balance, beneficial. This result does not imply that customs unions are necessarily costly relative to MFN trade or that all internal trade frictions are beneficial, but it does highlight the difficulties of discriminatory trade policy.

Ethier and Horn also introduced the notion of *trade modification*. For example,

179

if a customs union affects the quantity of cars demanded it will also affect the quantity of petrol imported.

The rest of the world

In our simple model, trade diversion reduced the rest of the world's sales in country A. This could have negative effects along infant industry or balance of payments lines, or by reducing specialisation. It could also worsen the terms of trade, if C's supply curve sloped upwards, because lower sales would then entail lower prices. Hence, despite Kemp and Wan's conclusion that it need not happen, a customs union will probably harm the rest of the world. It was partly in fear of such adverse effects from the formation of the EC that the USA initiated the Kennedy Round of tariff negotiations in 1963, aiming to reduce the degree of members' preference by reducing MFN tariffs.

Occasionally, a customs union may generate 'external trade creation' whereby trade with the rest of the world is increased. This occurs if C's goods are complementary to goods whose internal consumption is increased by the union. There is some evidence that British and American exports of capital goods rose after the formation of the EC in response to the investment boom that the latter produced in member countries.

13.2 THE MOTIVES FOR CUSTOMS UNIONS

The previous section asked the question 'if, starting from tariff-ridden trade, we were to form a particular customs union, what would be the effects?' This begs the question of why trade was tariff-ridden in the first place when we know that free trade is (Pareto) optimal. It compares customs unions with a non-optimal starting point, rather than with the outcome of optimal economic policy.

This is illustrated by treating customs union formation as the result of two separate steps: first, the reduction of tariffs on all imports, to generate the post-union internal price (p_B in Figure 13.1) but with imports still coming from C; and, second, the subsequent switching of imports from C to B. The first step is unambiguously beneficial – generating all the trade creation we found above – while the second – whose sole effect is to give away customs revenue – is unambiguously harmful. Thus, the real question is why countries choose to implement both steps when just one would yield higher welfare: why prefer customs unions to unilateral trade liberalisation?

This is another aspect of the reciprocity question. Above we suggested that counties seek reciprocal tariff concessions instead of unilateral free trade for terms of trade reasons, infant industry and country reasons, domestic political reasons and, occasionally (and usually misguidedly) balance of payments reasons. The same factors are at play with customs unions.

Transport costs

Most international trade theory ignores transport costs. This is not usually a serious omission, but it does obscure one motive for forming customs unions. Wonnacott and Wonnacott (1981) observed that most unions are between neighbours, and postulated that this is because they are trying to avoid transactions costs – transport costs or tariffs – on their trade with the rest of the world. Imagine that the rest of the world is large and would trade in either direction at price ratio $(p_X/p_Y) = p$. A and B, both small countries, would not be able to agree to trade mutually at any price other than p. Now suppose, however, that C will buy X for Y at p_L and Y for X at $p_H > p_L$, the wedge being accounted for by transport or tariffs. Suppose that, if they traded together, A and B would settle at price p, $p_L < p < p_H$. Then both would experience a terms of trade gain from mutual trade compared with global trade. Since, within the price range p_L to p_H, C is out of the picture so far as A and B's trading opportunities are concerned, the usual free trade prescription will lead to mutual tariff reductions between A and B, i.e. a customs union. More remarkable, the Wonnacotts showed that, even if prior to the union A and B traded with C, a trade-diverting customs union could be beneficial. Suppose that before union (i.e. with MFN tariffs) A/B trade would yield price $p_0 < p_L$. That would be unattractive to whichever country exported X, so that country would choose to trade with C and the other country would be forced to follow suit. However, if mutual trade with tariff preferences produced price p_1, $p_L < p_1 < p_H$, the union could still be beneficial. The country whose terms of trade worsened as a result of the union could be sufficiently compensated by the increase in trade to think union worthwhile.

The terms of trade

If the partners in a customs union have some market power, the union may provide a means of exploiting it better. Mundell (1964) explored the terms of trade consequences of A's preferential tariff reduction in favour of B. He examined the changes in the value of trade that would result if prices were constant, and then asked how prices would have to change to restore equilibrium. We would expect A's discrimination to raise the demand for B's goods and reduce that for the rest of the world's (C's). Hence, we would expect B's terms of trade to improve (B's prices rise) while C's worsen. A's terms of trade may go either way depending on whether it trades more heavily with B or C, and on the extent of the trade creation. Symmetrically, B's discrimination in favour of A will generally improve A's terms of trade and worsen C's. Combining these to consider mutual preferences between A and B – i.e. a customs union – we see that C's terms of trade will worsen, while those of A and B are indeterminate. However, the union as a whole experiences an improvement because the rest of the world suffers; thus at least one of A or B must gain, and it is always possible to arrange things so that both do.

It is the partner's discrimination that yields a country's welfare gains, and in general such discrimination is not in the partner's best interests. Thus the role of the customs union is the trading of discrimination, which, at the expense of the rest of the world, can benefit both partners relative to free trade. There are two attractions to achieving these terms of trade gains through customs union rather than by A and B individually imposing (non-discriminatory) optimum tariffs. First, the trade diversion deriving from the preferential tariff cuts improves the union's terms of trade by cutting trade with C. Second, to maximise A and B's joint welfare, each has to impose tariffs beyond the level that would maximise its own welfare given the tariff imposed by the other. Thus, without the strict institutional control of a customs union, neither country can be entirely confident that its partner would fully cooperate in restricting trade.

Infant industry considerations

If for some strategic or infant industry reason countries wish to have more industry than free trade would permit, a customs union can achieve this at a lower cost than can non-discriminatory tariff reductions. Thus, provided that the initial decision to sponsor industry was well founded, the customs union represents an improvement over free trade. The gains are analogous to those of opening trade in our simple models above – namely, increased specialisation and economies of scale.

Suppose A and B are concerned only about having industry in general, and not about the particular manufactured products that are produced. Before integration each may, for example, have sufficient protection to ensure that it has both a hat and a coat industry. The customs union permits the mutual penetration of partners' markets, and so, for example, after integration A could supply all the union's hats and B all its coats. This would be beneficial either if A had comparative advantage in hats and B in coats or if the industries had economies of scale such that concentrating production reduced costs regardless of location. It seems that much of this sort of readjustment followed from the formation of the EC; specialisation took place at a very specific level of product design, and resulted in increased intra-industry rather than inter-industry trade.

Economies of scale

So far we have assumed constant or increasing costs. However, much of the political discussion of economic integration hinges around creating a larger 'home' market in which to reap economies of scale, and so we now briefly consider the case of decreasing costs.

If decreasing costs are internal to the firm we will have imperfect competition and economic integration will almost certainly have pro-competitive effects. In the extreme, monopolies in each member state might suddenly find themselves playing an n-firm oligopoly game for the enlarged market. Further details of this effect are given in case-study 14.1 below. Here we deal with the more prosaic case where, following Corden (1972a), there is no change in market structure.

Imagine we have two small countries forming a union. In each country industry X has falling average costs and sets price equal to average costs; that is, for some (exogenous) reason there is no exploitation of market power. Figure 13.2 illustrates several possibilities. It assumes that the public authorities offer firms made-to-measure tariffs and that country B is the more efficient. (Note, however, that neither cost curve gets as low as the world price, p_W. If if did, output would be expanded to achieve that level of costs by exporting.) The demand curve D_{AB} is the sum of the separate demand curves D_A and D_B. Suppose, first, that both countries maintain production prior to union. This requires tariffs of $(p_A - p_W)$ and $(p_B - p_W)$ and generates outputs of X_A and X_B respectively. Post-union, all production will relocate to B, giving costs of p_U, consumption $\bar{X}_A$ and $\bar{X}_B$, and requiring a common tariff of $(p_U - p_W)$. A experiences trade creation as above, but B also benefits from the union via *cost reduction*.

If, pre-union, production had occurred only in B, with A importing from the rest of the world, A would have suffered trade diversion from the union. Alternatively if only A had had pre-union production, A would have benefited from trade creation but B would have experienced *trade suppression* – the displacement of imports by local output, which in this model is harmful.

While this simple model has illustrated two new and useful concepts, it should not be taken too seriously. Its conclusions rest on special assumptions – made-to-measure tariffs, average cost pricing, and no monopoly exploitation – and arise because governments choose a lower common tariff than either had individually before union. It does, however, help to nail one fallacy: for simple homogeneous goods models such as this, no amount of integration makes the union efficient enough to become an exporter. If that were feasible it would already have happened pre-union.

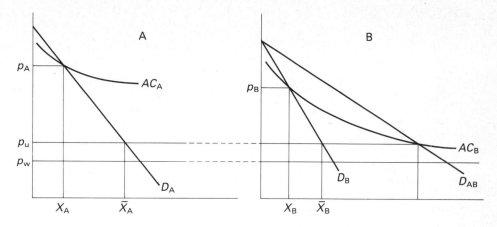

Figure 13.2 Economies of scale in a customs union

There are two alternative approaches to customs unions with economies of scale. First, if the tariff is exogenous rather than made to measure, the internal price is fixed and any benefits from reduced costs accrue to producers. Consumers are affected only to the extent that pre- and post-union tariffs differ. Second, if goods are heterogeneous, economies of scale will induce imperfect competition and a customs union may have strong pro-competitive effects as previously segmented markets are brought together. This analysed further in case-study 14.1.

Dynamic effects

In discussing Britain's entry to the EC much was made of possibly 'dynamic' effects. These were essentially the infant industry benefits that we discussed above: larger markets would generate economies of scale, external benefits, reinvestment in modern plant, and so on. There was also talk about the benefits of the 'cold winds of competition' increasing efficiency – the X-efficiency argument of section 7.1 above. These benefits would probably have been available from an export-oriented non-discriminatory policy; but it is possible that, because of political factors, they could stem only from EC markets. By joining the EC, British exporters received a firm commitment of duty-free access to EC markets, much firmer than could ever have been given (or believed) for markets where no political link existed. Thus the political dimension of the EC increased exporters' confidence (certainty) and may consequently have led to stronger investment and external effects than free trade.

Political factors

Many commentators view customs unions as the first step towards political cooperation and unification betwen nations. Certainly the EC was seen by some as a way of ensuring that France and Germany never had the means to fight each other again. Also, political arguments were prominent in Britain's desire to join the EC: it was felt that she would have more influence as a leading member of a powerful bloc than as a medium-sized individual nation. Such objectives are perfectly legitimate and all that economists can do is to note that political aims sometimes have economic costs.

FURTHER READING

The best introductions to the theory and measurement of customs unions are *Robson* (1987) and *Pomfret* (1987), while *Robson* (1971) presents an interesting selection of essays.

Early theoretical developments are surveyed by *Lipsey* (1960) and more recently by *Krause* (1972) and *Lloyd* (1982), although the latter is rather hard work. The arguments for the formation of customs unions were initiated by *Mundell* (1964), *Cooper and Massell* (1965a,b), *Johnson* (1965b) and *Corden* (1972a). *Ethier and Horn* (1984) is good, but technical.

KEY CONCEPTS

customs union	trade creation
trade diversion	Kemp–Wan theorem
trade suppression	unilateral vs. reciprocal tariff reductions
political commitment	dynamic effects of union

QUESTIONS FOR REVIEW

13.1 Show that a trade-diverting customs union can be welfare improving. Does this make the concept of trade diversion irrelevant?

13.2 The GATT bans preferential trading arrangements unless they cover nearly all goods and impose no tariffs on internal trade. Should it?

13.3 Kemp and Wan show that from any starting point a welfare-improving customs union can always be found. Ethier and Horn show that every customs union can be improved by small internal tariffs. Reconcile these views.

13.4 Draw a diagram showing trade diversion and creation when all supply curves are upward sloping. Hint: this is best done with three sets of axes – one for A, one for B and one showing the horizontal sums of A's and B's demand and supply curves.

NOTE

1 The European Communities (EC) comprise the European Coal and Steel Community (ECSC), the European Economic Community (EEC) and the European Atomic Energy Community (Euratom). We use EC as the generic term.

14 The European Communities

To most readers of this book, the best-known example of international economic integration will be the European Communities (EC). It would be inappropriate in a book such as this to devote much space to its institutional structure and detailed history, but we stop briefly to consider these matters.

Section 14.1 outlines the history of Western European integration and describes the EC as presently constituted. Section 14.2 then deals with empirical attempts to assess the effects of such integration. Finally section 14.3 considers the intended completion of the European internal market in 1992.

14.1 ECONOMIC INTEGRATION IN WESTERN EUROPE

Modern economic integration in Western Europe began in 1948 with the formation of Benelux – a customs union comprising Belgium and Luxembourg (which already had some links) and the Netherlands. This took several years to become fully operational because, although internal tariffs were abolished, NTBs persisted into the 1950s. The Netherlands in particular had to undertake substantial adjustment as it reduced the extent to which trade and internal economic activity were controlled. Nevertheless, the union became well established and the economies are now very highly integrated.

The European Coal and Steel Community

The European Coal and Steel Community (ECSC) represented the first major step towards the EC. Its origins were as much political as economic, its purpose being to stimulate the recovery of heavy industries in (West) Germany while making it impossible for their output ever to be used to wage war again. The proposal – due to Jean Monnet and Robert Schuman – was that, by establishing a truly common European market in coal, iron and steel, countries would become so interdependent that war would be not only 'unthinkable, but materially impossible'. The customs union was to be supplemented by a 'High Authority', which had the power to dictate national output quotas, establish maximum and minimum prices, and enforce the laws of free competition (which outlawed subsidies, etc.). The High Authority was an administrative body, controlled in policy but not day-to-day matters by a Council of the Community on which the separate governments were represented, and also by a European Parliament. A Court of Justice was also established to oversee the legal aspects of the Community.

The ECSC was born in 1951 by the Treaty of Paris. The members were 'the Six' – Belgium, France, West Germany, Italy, Luxembourg and the Netherlands. The UK was invited to join but declined – ostensibly fearing to grant power over vital industries to a non-elected extra-parliamentary body like the High Authority. In fact, Britain resisted any measures of integration that contained elements of federalism, parliamentary or otherwise. The ECSC was a qualified success. The coordination of investment improved and tariffs were abolished, but frequently national NTBs were permitted, such as subsidies to Belgian coal producers.

185

<table>
<tr><td>

The European
Economic
Community

</td><td>

Subsequent to the ECSC, attempts were made to establish further supra-national European organisations. A defence community (the EDC) and a political community (the EPC) were negotiated between 'the Six' but foundered mainly on the rocks of French politics. Then in 1955 plans were made for the formation of a general common market (the European Economic Community, EEC), and an atomic energy community (Euratom). These came to fruition in the Treaties of Rome in 1957, after a period of intense negotiation. Again, although taking part in the early negotiations, Britain remained aloof from the final agreements. At first, the EEC and Euratom existed separately but parallel to the ECSC, but in 1967 the three bodies were merged, with one Commission (successor to the High Authority – the 'European executive'), one Council, one Parliament and one Court. Together they constitute the European Communities (EC).

</td></tr>
</table>

The EC provided a general common market among 'the Six'. The customs union covered trade in all goods; internal tariffs were reduced in stages so that by 1968 all intra-EC trade was duty free. Eventually, it was hoped, legal and administrative harmonisation would allow the abolition of internal customs posts, but this has yet to occur. The common external tariff was set at the average of the rates in the partner countries. This involved tariff increases for West Germany and Benelux and decreases for France and Italy.

For most goods the EC promoted competition and the free market, but for agriculture considerable intervention was envisaged. In all members, agriculture provided a substantial part of income and employment, and in all it was strongly protected. Among the initial administrative and political successes of the EC was the establishment of a Common Agricultural Policy (CAP), which treated all community farms equally. As we saw above, this involves high and guaranteed domestic prices, variable import levies and considerable surpluses of certain goods; it is a costly and inefficient policy. Moreover, it now no longer guarantees equal prices throughout the community, because agricultural trade is conducted at bogus exchange rates – so-called 'green' exchange rates – and is subject to levies or subsidies – so-called monetary compensation amounts (MCAs). Nevertheless, the CAP was probably an essential part of the politics of integration – the French wanted access to German markets and the Germans wanted high prices – and until recently was a symbol of Europeanism. Criticism of the CAP was viewed as an attack on the EC itself.

The Treaty of Rome envisaged common policies in many other areas too: for example, transport, fiscal structure, general macro-economic policy, competition policy, standards and measures and social policy. These have been achieved with varying degrees of success. For example, Commission rulings on aspects of competition are frequent and powerful, whereas virtually nothing has happened in the transport sector. It was also intended that both labour and capital should be freely mobile within the EC, and this has now largely been achieved.

<table>
<tr><td>

Britain and
European
integration

</td><td>

Britain did nothing to hinder integration among 'the Six', but she was shy of joining anything smacking of supra-nationality or federalism. She felt herself different from the other European countries, with stronger ties with America and the rest of the world and also with a much smaller and more efficient agricultural sector. (Recall that Britain supported farmers by deficiency payments – essentially income supplements – which kept food prices low and avoided surpluses, unlike 'the Six's' tariff-based policies.) Hence, although

</td></tr>
</table>

Britain favoured intra-European free trade, she resisted the administrative and political structures of the EC. The Scandinavian countries held similar suspicions, while the Swiss constitution explicitly forbade any international political associations. Thus, these countries excluded themselves from the EC and, fearful that they would suffer as the EC stimulated 'the Six's' economic growth, formed a looser association in 1960 – the European Free Trade Association (EFTA). The members were Austria, Denmark, Norway, Portugal, Sweden, Switzerland and the UK, of which the last was entirely dominant.

EFTA provided for mutual free trade in manufactured goods and some primaries between members. It made no effort to establish common external tariffs, however, or to coordinate any other aspect of economic life. The absence of a common external tariff meant that elaborate rules of origin were necessary to prevent non-EFTA goods from entering via the lowest tariff country and then moving freely from there. This required a secretariat, but beyond that EFTA had no administrative structure.

Very soon after EFTA was initiated, the UK changed her mind and sought full membership of the EC. She sought many concessions from the Treaty of Rome, however, especially over agricultural protection and the rights to continue some form of Commonwealth Preference; consequently in 1962 negotiations closed without reaching a conclusion. A further, and less combative, application was made in 1967, but this too failed, largely because of French fears of the political consequences of expanding the Community. Finally in late 1968 the issue was revived again, and agreement was reached in 1971 for accessions on 1 January 1973. Ireland, Denmark and Norway reached similar agreements, although at the last moment Norway withdrew her application after she had voted to stay out in a referendum.

The terms reached for British accession were very complex, but broadly speaking they were not very favourable to the new member. The CAP was hardly changed at all, and Britain assumed a substantial part of its financing costs – she was expected to provide about 19 per cent of the EC's total budget. The provisions for Commonwealth sugar and New Zealand dairy products and meat were not generous to the suppliers, although long transitional periods were allowed to permit them to diversify away from the British market. The transitional period for industrial tariffs and the agricultural system was set at five years. A number of problems, such as the role of sterling, were left entirely undecided.

The Labour Party (in opposition in 1971) argued that these terms were not acceptable and promised to re-negotiate them and put the result to the people in a referendum. Re-negotiation during 1974 led to some improvements – Britain's long-run budget share was reduced and the rate of increase of agricultural prices slowed – and on the (Labour) government's recommendation the new terms were accepted in the referendum of 1976. Political opposition to membership still smouldered on, however, with the Labour Party fighting (and losing) the 1983 general election on a secessionist ticket. The issues dominating the negotiations also still persist. Every year sees an argument over agricultural prices between Britain, favouring lower prices, and most other members, favouring higher prices, at least for their surplus products. Similarly, frequent attempts to reform the CAP have largely failed in the face of French, Irish and Danish opposition; and the allocation of fishery rights brought gunboats into the North Sea in 1983. The early 1980s also produced acrimonious debates as Britain sought to draw back some of her 'excessive' budget contributions.

The Community today

The EC currently comprises twelve European states: 'the Six' (Belgium, France, Germany, Italy, Luxembourg and the Netherlands), Britain, Denmark and Ireland (who acceded in 1973), Greece (who acceded in 1980) and Spain and Portugal (who acceded in 1986). Free trade agreements for manufactures exist with Austria, Finland, Iceland, Norway, Sweden and Switzerland – the rump of EFTA. Thus the EC offers its members a large and affluent market, unimpeded by tariffs. In 1984, the EC(12) accounted for about 29 per cent of market economies' total GDP – ECU 3,008b. compared with the USA's ECU 5,172b. and Japan's ECU 1,593b. – while GDP per head was ECU 9,360 compared with ECU 19,880 and ECU 13,280 respectively. Of members' total international trade, around half is conducted with other members – rather more for the small continental countries and rather less for Britain. If we include such intra-EC trade as 'foreign trade', the EC accounts for 34 per cent of industrial countries' exports (USA 11 per cent), whereas if we treat it as internal trade the EC's world share is 18.5 per cent (USA's 13.5 per cent).

Although the countries of the EC form a single large bloc, they are not entirely alike. Incomes vary from ECU 2,418 per capita for Portugal to ECU 12,812 for West Germany (1984, at purchasing power parities). The sources of income also vary. For example, Greece derives 19 per cent of GDP from agriculture, whereas West Germany and the UK derive only 1.9 per cent and 1.7 per cent respectively from that source.

Related to per capita incomes and agricultural shares are the costs and benefits of the Community budget. Almost 70 per cent of expenditure is devoted to agriculture (65 per cent on supporting prices), while a substantial portion of income comes from the levies on agricultural imports. Thus, countries with large agricultural sectors tend to benefit relative to those with smaller output and greater imports.

The disproportionate share of agriculture in the budget reflects both the political power of farmers and the importance of the Common Agricultural Policy as the most 'European' of policies. It also, however, reflects the very small size of the EC budget, which accounts for well under 1.5 per cent of GDP, compared with federal budgets elsewhere in the world of over 20 per cent. (The Brussels bureaucracy numbers fewer than 10,000 – about one-quarter of that of Kent County Council!) It is intended that in future agriculture will surrender some of its share of the budget to the Regional and Social Funds, which support isolated and declining regions of the EC, and it must be expected that, as the EC becomes more integrated, its central budget will grow.

The associated states

The EC has special relations with two other broad groups of countries. First, the African, Caribbean and Pacific (ACP) States: these sixty-eight developing countries receive tariff-free access to EC markets for nearly all their exports, as well as significant aid flows and an export earnings guarantee scheme that offers grants from the EC if export earnings decline seriously. In return, they offer EC members certain concessions in their own markets, but stop short of tariff-free access.

The association is governed by the Lomé Convention of 1975, the most recent edition of which was signed in 1990. Its origins lay in France's insistence that her overseas territories be included within the EC structure, since they were formally considered as part of France herself. Full membership was not appropriate, so associateship was developed, which had the added

188

attraction to the French that other members bore some of the costs of aid and support. Certain other countries were brought into the association – defined at first by the Yaoundé Convention – including former possessions of other members.

When Britain acceded she wished her developing partners in the Commonwealth and Empire to be granted association. This was allowed except for the Asian states, which, the French argued, were qualitatively different from existing associates. Although separate, but less favourable, agreements have been negotiated with most of the excluded states, in general British accession required a considerable reorientation of their trade. Winters (1984b) has shown, for example, that India and Sri Lanka's share of Britain's tea imports fell from 57 per cent to 35 per cent between 1971 and 1979.

On the other hand, even full Lomé concessions did little to sustain ACP trade over the 1970s and 1980s. *The World Development Report, 1987* (Box 9.2) shows ACP non-oil exports to the EC falling as a share of both total ACP non-oil exports and EC non-oil imports from developing countries.

The second type of association is with certain Mediterranean countries. These associates receive tariff-free access for industrial goods and certain concessions, subject to quota, on agricultural goods; in return they have to grant almost full reciprocity. They also receive some aid flows and technical cooperation. As this book is being written, the EC is trying to define its relations with the newly liberalised economies of Eastern Europe. These will probably entail some form of association.

The main institutions

The Commission comprises seventeen commissioners appointed by member states for four-year terms: two from each of the larger members and one from the others. It initiates Community policy and executes it, but it cannot actually make policy – that falls to the *Council*. The Commission is explicitly supra-national, and represents the EC as a body in world negotiations, such as at the GATT.

The Council formally comprises the heads of government from all member states, although most business is, of course, conducted by deputies – either the ministers concerned with specific issues (e.g. agriculture ministers discuss the CAP, and finance ministers the budget), or, for day-to-day matters, permanent officials. The Council shares executive power with the Commission. It may adopt the latter's policy proposals, in which case they become law, but it may not generally amend them. Decisions are theoretically taken by majority vote, but a country's right of veto on important issues of national interest is recognised. In practice, most decisions are reached by trading compromises on (often unrelated) issues to obtain a unanimously acceptable package.

The Court of Justice interprets Community law. Its findings are binding even on member governments. The judges are appointed by member states, but they are required to be quite independent of national interests and cannot be removed by member governments.

The European Parliament has a small but growing role in the Community. It must be consulted by the Commission and the Council before they decide many issues, and it has some power over the Community budget. Its greatest power is to dismiss the Commission *en masse*, although this is such an unwieldy weapon that it is of little practical use.

The Single European Act   The period 1978–82 represented a low point in EC relations. Preoccupied with their own economic problems (oil price rises, inflation and recession), the members turned inwards, integration stopped or even reversed, and the EC fell further behind the USA and Japan in income per head and technological advance. The early 1980s saw a worldwide renaissance of liberal (market) economics, and almost in desperation the EC authorities embraced it as a means of reviving the lagging European economies. They agreed an extensive programme to 'complete the internal market' by the end of 1992. This entailed removing *all* barriers to intra-EC trade and mobility, harmonising regulatory standards (mostly through relaxation), and centralising a certain amount of policy making. This process was governed by the Single European Act, which reaffirmed the objective of unity and instituted more effective decision-making procedures in the Community. The result has been a surge of Europeanism in excess of almost all predictions, and at least some improvement in economic performance. The economic aspects of '1992' are discussed in section 14.3 below.

14.2   THE EVIDENCE ON CUSTOMS UNIONS

Considerable effort has been devoted to estimating the effects of international economic integration both *ex ante* (before the event) and *ex post* (afterwards). Some studies have concentrated merely on trade flows, while other have made welfare comparisons. This section samples the literature on European integration – especially Britain's position – starting with simple trade effects.

Integration and international trade   To measure the effect of integration on international trade flows we need estimates of trade both with and without integration. In the simplest case – an *ex post* study – the former is directly observable, but trade under identical conditions except for integration has to be hypothesised. This hypothesis has come to be known as the *anti-monde*, and its construction is clearly the critical task in assessing integration effects. Economists generally assume that, in the absence of integration, trade patterns between partners would either have followed pre-integration trends (a time-series approach) or have been determined by the same factors as determine trade between non-partners (a cross-section approach). The former presupposes constancy of behaviour through time, but not across countries, whereas the latter assumes the opposite.

'The Six' and EFTA   Table 14.1 presents some impression of the potency of integration in Europe. Intra-bloc trade – i.e. trade between members – grew substantially as a share of total trade in the early years of the EC and EFTA, and after the realignment of 1973 the new EC members switched away from their former EFTA partners towards their new EC partners. (The EC–EFTA trade share fell between 1973 and 1975, but this is not reported in the table.)

Of the many studies of European integration in the 1960s we shall consider just two. Truman (1975) examined nineteen goods in ten European markets. For each he looked at the shares of partner countries, of non-partner countries and of domestic suppliers in total absorption of the good. He compared observed shares under integration with *anti-monde* shares evolving along their pre-integration trends, interpreting differences as in column 3 of Table 14.2.

Table 14.1 Intra-bloc trade in Europe, 1960–81

	Intra-bloc exports as percentage of total exports			
	1960	1970	1975	1981
'The Six'	34.6	48.9	—	—
'The Nine'[a]	—	—	49.4	51.5
EFTA	15.7	21.8	—	—
'Residual EFTA'[bd]	—	—	16.1	12.2
'The Nine' and 'residual EFTA'[cd]	—	—	12.9	12.6

Notes:
[a] Excludes Greece.
[b] EFTA less countries acceding to the EEC in 1973.
[c] Inter-bloc trade covered by free trade agreement.
[d] Manufactures only.
Source: United Nations Conference on Trade and Development, *Handbook of International Trade and Development Statistics* (1983).

Table 14.2 Trade creation and diversion in Europe

Share	Movement	Interpretation	Estimates ($b.) 1968	
			EEC	EFTA
Domestic share	lower	trade creation	7.2	0.9
	higher	trade suppression	0.4	0.8
Partner share	higher	trade creation plus diversion	8.2	1.2
Non-partner share	lower	trade diversion	1.0	0.3
	higher	external trade creation	2.4	3.0

Source: Truman (1975), Table 1.4.

Over half his cases exhibit internal and external trade creation, and in half the cases where non-partners suffer it is partly as a result of rising domestic shares. This might reflect integration-induced economies of scale or, for the EC, that the common external tariff exceeded the pre-integration national tariff. The magnitudes of the effects are also shown in Table 14.2. Total trade creation amounts to 8.6 per cent of the change in demand between the pre- and post-integration years – a relatively modest amount. Obviously, the welfare effects will fall short of the gross trade effects, but some gains are likely given the excess of creation over diversion.

A second study of European integration is Aitken (1973). Aitken considered only the origin of imports and so could not separate creation and diversion. He explained trade flows between European countries in terms of their GNPs, populations and locations. Prior to integration, all countries' trade flows appear to derive from the same explanation, whereas after integration intra-EC and intra-EFTA trade became relatively more important than trade between unrelated countries. He suggested that in 1967 integration increased intra-EC trade by $9–11b. and intra-EFTA trade by between $1.3–2.4b. Exports from EFTA to EC fell by other $0.6b. and those from EC to EFTA by $0.2b. The latter figures represent only part of the diversion induced by integration, of course, since they cover only a subset of non-partner countries.

In a similar study, Aitken and Obutelewicz (1976) examined the impact that association has had on trade between the EC and the original associated states. The results are startling, suggesting that up to 95 per cent of the relevant trade flows can be explained by the institutional links! This is probably overestimated, but it cannot be denied that association has significant effects.

191

UK accession to the EC was the subject of many *ex ante* studies during the 1960s. Methodologies varied greatly, as did the results, but the basic conclusion was that in *static* terms accession would impose a small cost on the economy, worsening both the balance of payments and economic welfare. The losses were predicted to arise primarily from food imports and budget transfers. The effects on net manufactured trade (exports minus imports) were expected to be small, but several economists expected significant increases in both exports and imports.

Much more contentious were estimates of the dynamic effects of entry. Dynamic benefits were forecast to arise from greater specialisation (and hence economies of scale); re-equipping with modern plant to exploit new markets; inflows of foreign investment from EC partners and from US firms using Britain as a platform for serving Europe; and gains in efficiency induced by the 'cold winds of competition'. Professor Nicholas Kaldor, on the other hand, predicted dynamic losses as weak British industries collapsed under fierce European competition.

Despite fifteen years' experience, these predictions have not yet been properly tested – not least because none of them allowed for the economic turmoil of the 1970s. Thus, disentangling integration effects from those of the oil price rise, high inflation and floating exchange rates has proved very complex.

Some simple figures are reported in Table 14.3. They show how, over the 1960s, Britain's international trade – both exports and imports – was slowly gravitating towards EC countries – not least because they were among the most dynamic in the developed world. A stronger shift towards EFTA is also evident, doubtless stimulated by the free-trade arrangements. After accession to the EC, however, a dramatic realignment is evident. Britain's trade with 'the Six' increased its share at the expense of both 'other developed countries' and her former partners in EFTA. On the export side, this corresponded to an increase in Britain's share of EC imports, reversing many years of decline and despite continuing decline in Britain's share of other markets (see Winters, 1983b, 1984b, 1985). Mere trade shares do not prove causation, but it is difficult to avoid the conclusion that integration has had a substantial effect.

Table 14.3 Shares in the UK's visible trade, 1962–86 (%)

	The EC(6)[a]	EFTA and Irish Republic	Other developed countries	Developing countries
Exports:				
1962	19.8	15.7	34.4	30.1
1970–2	21.8	18.6	32.8	26.8
1979–81	34.0	17.9	22.5	25.6
1986	37.7	14.9	28.8	18.0
1987	38.9	14.7	28.6	17.2
Imports:				
1962	15.8	13.4	36.0	34.8
1970–2	22.3	18.8	32.3	26.6
1979–81	36.6	17.1	25.4	20.9
1986	42.8	18.4	26.0	12.2
1987	43.5	18.3	26.0	11.7

Note:
[a] The original six members of the EEC.
Sources: Department of Trade and Industry (1983), Central Statistical Office, *Annual Abstract of Statistics*, various issues.

There are also a few formal *ex post* studies of Britain's accession. For
example, Bacon, Godley and McFarquhar (1978) estimated that in 1977
British food imports cost £300m. more than they need have done, while Bale
and Lutz (1981) suggested welfare losses of around £50m. stemming from
CAP protection in just five commodities in 1976. Winters (1984b) presented
the most sophisticated estimates for UK manufactured imports: by 1979, he
suggested, trade creation could have been as great as £12b. (£10b. internal
and £2b. external), and certainly exceeded £6b. Total sales of manufacturing
were around £104b. in 1979, so these figures indicate a significant shift in the
sourcing of UK consumption of manufactures. Winters (1985) applied similar
methodology to UK manufactured exports. He found evidence of increased
exports to partner countries – around £4.5b. – but decreased exports to other
industrial countries – around £1.7b. All these figures are subject to broad
bounds of error, but they certainly suggest that as a result of EC accession the
UK increased its consumption of manufactures relative to production;
although this means that the manufactured trade balance deteriorated, it is
still a source of improved welfare.

14.3 COMPLETING THE EUROPEAN INTERNAL MARKET

The notion of completing the EC's internal market was born in the early 1980s
as a response to the EC's increasingly obvious economic failure. It had long
been recognised that the actual integration of the EC economies fell short of the
aspirations of the Treaty of Rome, and there were signs that it was reversing.
Recalling the stimulus that the initial creation of the EEC had induced, and
following the prevailing trend towards economic liberalisation, the European
Commission pressed the case for a bold step towards complete integration.
The Single European Act provided the political framework, while the
economic and legislative programme were defined in the White Paper
introduced by Commissioner Lord Cockfield in 1985 (Commission of the
European Communities, *Completing the Internal Market*, Com (85), 310).

The political skill with which the fractious and self-absorbed member
governments were led to subscribe to such dramatic economic reform was of
the highest order. The process of completion clearly involves some loss of
national sovereignty to EC institutions, and yet it has achieved sufficient
momentum to carry along even the most doubtful of governments.[1] This is
mainly due to the Commission which, standing to gain considerable power
from the process, is naturally a strong advocate of completion. It is now plain
that not all the items in Cockfield's list will be achieved by the end of 1992,
but other issues have been added and the overall outcome will be a significant
increase in integration relative to the 1980s. The remainder of this section
sketches some of the economics of completion.

Internal barriers Completing the European internal market entails four freedoms of movement
within the EC – goods, services, capital and persons. Free trade encourages
efficiency in consumption and production, and, to the extent that some goods
and services cannot be traded, the movement of capital, labour and
technology can substitute. The movement of people is clearly related to the
other movements, as well as being a *sine qua non* of an integrated society.

Broadly, the current barriers to movement (and hence the '1992' programme's agenda of reforms) comprise: restrictions on *market access* – through, for instance, customs formalities, different national technical standards and foreign exchange controls; distortions of *competitive conditions* – for instance, state aids (subsidies), biased public purchasing, merger regulations, and the airline cartel; and different national approaches to *market functioning* – as in, for example, trade marks, company law, the prudential regulation of banks and professional qualifications. The first two sets of barriers are to be treated by the elimination of the offending practices. The third entails the *harmonisation* of national regulations, although it currently looks as if in the majority of cases this will also entail liberalisation – i.e. harmonisation to a less restrictive or interventionary level. It mostly involves the mutual recognition by member states of each other's regulations, rather than the imposition of common regulations by Brussels.

The Cockfield White Paper gives primacy to the question of market access. There are, after all, traditions of negotiating trade restrictions (e.g. in the GATT), and there is much greater agreement that trade restrictions are harmful than that domestic policy should be subject to international control. Moreover, once free market access is assured, it becomes much more difficult and expensive for governments to pursue other distortionary policies because they can be undermined by international trade.

A survey of 20,000 businesses (Commission of the European Communities, CEC, 1988) ranked the existing barriers to intra-EC trade in the following descending order of importance):

> technical standards and regulations
> administrative barriers
> frontier formalities
> freight transport regulations
> value added tax differences
> capital market controls
> government procurement restrictions
> implementation of community law.

Although the Commission was too delicate to ask in this particular survey, which was restricted to the 'real' side of the economy, exchange rate changes and interest rate differences also figure strongly in most businesses's views of the difficulties of intra-EC commerce.

The costs of non-Europe

Well after the '1992' programme was agreed and under way, the EC conducted a detailed assessment of its economic implications, *The Costs of Non-Europe*.[2] It was a massive undertaking, with sixteen volumes of reports and papers, a full economic report (CEC, 1988) and a popular edition (Cecchini, 1988), referred to as the Cecchini report. The work has come under severe attack from some quarters since 1988, but its conclusion that the 1992 programme will raise EC GNP by around 5 per cent still commands fairly wide acceptance.

Cecchini identified four broad areas of economic loss from the fragmentation of the EC market (see Table 14.4). Within the two sets of barriers there are both cost-increasing and revenue-generating barriers. The former impose excess real costs on market access or production and so essentially waste what would, for tariffs or taxes, be revenue. Prominent in this class are border formalities, estimated to cost approaching 2 per cent of the value of intra-EC

Table 14.4 The costs of non-Europe

	ECU billion 1985 prices	% of GDP
VARIANT I[a]		
1 Cost of barriers to trade	9	0.3
2 Cost of barriers affecting all production	71	2.4
3 Economies of scale arising from restructuring and increased production	61	2.1
4 Competitive effects on X-inefficiency and monopoly rents	46	1.6
Total	187	6.4
VARIANT II[a]		
Alternative measure of competition and economies of scale (3 plus 4)	62	2.1
Alternative total	142	4.8

Note:
[a] The difference between variants I and II is explained in case-study 14.1.
Source: CEC (1988).

trade, and disparate technical standards between members, which impose extra design and testing costs on producers. Closer to traditional trade instruments are public procurement biases (buying locally). These distortions generate rents for local firms, but their deadweight losses are still estimated to exceed ECU 20b. per year. They are particularly heavy in pharmaceuticals, heavy engineering and telecommunications, where governments tend to support local producers with huge implicit tariffs.

Cecchini's third set of costs arise from the sub-optimal scale of production. The fragmentation of the market allows small and inefficient firms to survive. Integration eliminates the least efficient and allows the more efficient to expand and so reduce their costs. The final set of costs arises from X-inefficiency and monopoly profits: their elimination is the pro-competitive effect of trade. They are analysed more fully in case-study 14.1, where we also explain how the two variants in Table 14.4 differ.

CASE-STUDY 14.1: THE PRO-COMPETITIVE EFFECTS OF '1992'

Imagine that internal barriers keep the twelve EC markets for good X entirely segmented, and that each country has just one domestic supplier. (This is almost true for railway engines.) Each firm exploits its monopoly power, and consumers suffer. Now remove the barriers and allow the twelve firms to play a Cournot game for the whole EC market. As equation (5.2) shows, the mark-up over marginal costs is roughly proportional to market shares, and so, on average, will fall by a factor of twelve. Of course, if there are economies of scale, so that $AC > MC$, some firms may be unprofitable at the new lower prices and hence will go out of business. This will both reduce the costs and raise the mark-up of the remaining firms.

This is the essence of Smith and Venables' (1988) model of '1992'. They calibrate and simulate reciprocal dumping models with heterogeneous goods for ten EC industries. Their model assumes that

195

- consumer demand for a broadly defined good depends on its price averaged over the available varieties (Smith and Venables' equation 4);
- consumers desire variety as well as quantity (equation 1), and from their utility function the weights for the average price index (equation 2) and the demand for each individual variety (equation 5) are derivable;
- firms maximise profits (equation 6) by setting perceived $MR = MC$ (equations 7 and 14), where perceived MR depends on the demand curve for each variety and firms' conjectures about how their rivals will behave (equation 8);
- the number of varieties per firm is endogenous (equation 10); and
- in some exercises free entry forces firms' profits to zero.

The authors consider two interpretations of '1992': (S) '1992' reduces the costs of intra-EC trade by 2.5 per cent of its gross value, but allows the continuation of market *segmentation*; and (I) '1992' reduces trade costs *and* imposes full market *integration* such that prices net of remaining trade costs are equalised across the EC. In addition, Smith and Venables explore Cournot vs. Bertrand competition and fixed (F) vs. variable (V) numbers of firms. Their results are very sensitive to the assumptions made, and indicate in particular that I induces far greater effects than S. That is, it is the pro-competitive effects of '1992' that really matter. Table 14.5 gives some representative results.

Table 14.5 Estimates of the welfare effects of '1992'

		Welfare effects as % of total consumption of the good concerned		
		Electric motors	Electrical household appliances	Synthetic fibres
Direct effects[a]	D	0.22	0.49	0.91
Direct plus indirect effects:				
Segmented: fixed number of firms	SF	0.29	0.64	0.99
variable number of firms	SV	0.29	0.70	1.17
Integrated: fixed number of firms	IF	0.52	1.79	4.14
variable number of firms	IV	0.40	2.28	5.57

Note:
[a] Calculated as 2.5% of total trade flows.
Source: Smith and Venables (1988).

The Cecchini report is based heavily on Smith and Venables (see CEC, 1988). For each of their ten illustrative industries, CEC calculates the ratio of total welfare effects to the 'direct' (i.e. the traditional static) effects of '1992' (D); it then uses these ratios to gross up the estimates of direct welfare effects for all industries that are similar in terms of economies of scale and current levels of concentration. For example, for highly concentrated industries with large economies of scale, pro-competitive effects are important, and the ratio of total to direct effects is six; where concentration and economies of scale are already low, on the other hand, it is one, e.g. footwear.

CEC calculates two sets of ratios: the first – variant II in Table 14.4 – calculates the restructuring, economies of scale and the competitive effects of integration from Smith and Venables; it is based on the ratio IV/D. The second – CEC's variant I – uses Smith and Venables to calculate only the competitive effect and adds this to a different estimate of the economies of scale effect. The competitive effect is estimated as the difference between Smith and Venables' segmented estimate (SF or SV) and the full one (IV). Hence the multiplier of total to direct effects is based on (IV − SV)/D. Since SF and SV hardly exceed D, CEC's variation I captures nearly all Smith and Venables' welfare effects of '1992', and adds to them the substantial benefits of economies of scale from a conceptually quite different model.

Extending Cecchini

It is worth making a few observations about the Cecchini report. First, the sector exhibiting the largest direct losses from existing barriers is financial services. Trade in financial services is highly restricted, and different EC members regulate their financial sectors quite differently: in Germany, for example, heavy costs are entailed in the very conservative reserve and liquidity requirements, while in Spain ownership regulations allow considerable fragmentation of the banking sector. Cecchini's consultants estimated the costs of these regulations by making price comparisons. They sampled only sixteen products and for only one year. They then assumed that '1992' would induce a degree of convergence towards the lowest observed prices and reported the consumer gains from the resulting price reductions as the economic effect of '1992'. They made no allowance for lost producer surpluses or for any price increases as efficient producers in one member diverted output to (newly opened) export markets. Coupled with their rather unrepresentative data, these facts suggest a serious possibility of the overestimation of the benefits of '1992'.

Second, economies of scale figure very large in Cecchini and even larger in the popular discussion of '1992'. Most of the information on economies of scale came from engineering studies of plant-level economies, and much referred to the 1960s, well before recent developments in computer-aided design and manufacture removed the need for long production runs in many sectors. Moreover, the evidence that EC firms are too small is actually rather weak (Geroski and Jacquemin, 1986). We have already seen that, except where oligopolistic interactions are very strong, economies of scale worth, say, x per cent on costs will be frustrated only by barriers exceeding x per cent. Hence, if barriers are generally rather low, so too will be any remaining unexploited economies of scale. The largest effective barriers are probably the public procurement biases. For other sectors, e.g. chemicals, in which EC firms are already world-size, economies of scale may have been overestimated. Finally, as case-study 14.1 shows, Cecchini obtained the greatest possible estimates from his model of oligopolistic interactions.

Third, Baldwin (1989) argued – rather contentiously – that Cecchini had ignored important dynamic benefits of increased integration. Two issues are potentially important. First, as industries grow, they generate positive spill-overs for other industries: they may, for example, permit a finer division of labour in supplying firms, learn to produce better inputs for other firms, or train more labour. Cecchini's industry-by-industry approach missed these effects. Second, a richer economy offers higher returns to innovation, so the rate of technical progress may increase, permanently increasing the EC growth trade. In fact the EC has sought to stimulate European R&D directly, which would compound the latter effect. It is difficult to quantify these dynamic gains – Baldwin thought they could even double Cecchini's figures, and it is worth noting that the growth stimulated by the original integration of

197

'the Six' far outshone any predictions.

Finally, the benefits of integration mostly stem from increased competition. To reap them the EC needs a strong competition policy, first to prevent governments from frustrating necessary adjustment and second to prevent collusion among large firms. An important component of the latter policy will be open trade with the rest of the world. Jacquemin and Sapir (1991) found that intra-EC imports do little to constrain EC domestic firms' profit margins, whereas extra-EC imports do a lot.

'1992' and international trade

'1992' will affect EC international trade in a number of ways. First, by reducing internal transactions costs it will cause some trade diversion. However, many of the reductions – for example, harmonising standards and improving internal transport – will help imports as well as intra-EC trade, so this effect may not be very large. Second, greater competition and economies of scale will make EC goods more competitive abroad as well as in the EC. In markets with heterogeneous goods this will boost EC market shares, and could even drive other producers out of business analogously to strategic trade policy. Third, on the other hand, a richer EC means a bigger market – external trade creation. This could easily offset the two previous effects on partners' trade, leaving them net gainers. Fourth, the definition of EC standards may implicitly discriminate against other producers. Fifth, the EC, with its power and confidence restored by '1992', may pursue a more aggressive trade policy, for example on anti-dumping. These two issues worry the Americans considerably, but they are not logically part of the '1992' programme.

Finally, EC members currently maintain a number of national import quotas or VERs, e.g. on clothing (the MFA), cars and footwear. These will be quite impossible to operate if all the restrictions on the internal movement of goods are abolished, because goods will enter an unrestricted country and flow to the restricted one internally. The replacement of national quotas by a single EC quota set for the same aggregate level will affect economic welfare. Consider Figure 14.1.[3] Country A has an import quota $\bar{M}_H$ which, given demand curve D_A, implies price p_H, while B has a quota $\bar{M}_L$ and price p_L. Now let A and B integrate and impose a single quota $\bar{M} = \bar{M}_L + \bar{M}_H$. Integration implies a common price, p, and new levels of imports M'_A and M'_B. The changes in economic welfare for A and B are as follows:

consumer surplus	$(a+b)$	$-(e+f)$
rent	$(c+d)-(a+c)$	$(e+g)-(g+h)$
sum	$(b+d)$	$-(f+h)$

These results indicate a conflict of interest. The previously restricted country, A, gains from the relaxation of its quota, but B loses, as some of its import supplies are diverted to A. Overall, however, there is a net economic gain from integration; $(b+d) > (f+h)$, because they have the same base (the change in trade), while the maximum height of $(f+h)$ equals the minimum height of $(b+d)$. If A and B were able to collect the rents both before and after integration, then, with some redistribution, integration would be Pareto improving. If, on the other hand, we were dealing with VERs or bilateral quotas, from which exporters collected the rent, the union could lose and the exporters gain from integration, as in the diagram. Question 14.5 invites you

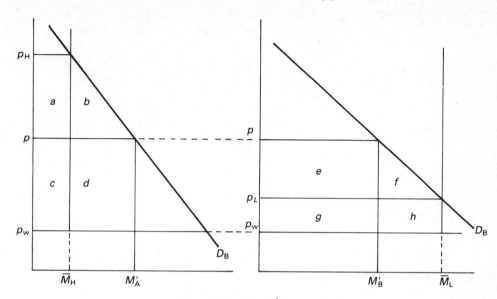

Figure 14.1 Market integration

to draw an example with the opposite outcome.

Winters' (1988) illustrative calculations suggest that, if the market for jeans had been integrated in this fashion in 1982, the UK would have gained about ECU 24m. per year, while Germany would have lost ECU 14m. Smith (1989), in a sophisticated model of the car market, considered the oligopolistic interactions between firms based in Europe. He showed that either free trade or the conversion of national quotas into a single EC quota would induce major losses of profits for firms in France and Italy and gains for Japanese exporters. Free trade implies EC net welfare gains of about 3 per cent of total car sales. The single quota, on the other hand, leaves overall welfare broadly constant but has strong redistributive effects. The Japanese producers divert their given volume of sales towards the formerly restricted markets (France and Italy), hitting producers and benefiting consumers, to give net welfare gains of ECU 0.25b. and ECU 0.75b. respectively; elsewhere (e.g. the UK and Germany), Japanese prices rise by up to 20 per cent, reducing consumer welfare but giving some gains to the producers with large shares of those markets, e.g. Rover, but with overall welfare losses of ECU 0.25b. (UK) and approaching ECU 1b. (Germany). (These national welfare calculations are very rough because the precise locations of production and equity returns are unknown for these multinational firms.)

FURTHER READING

The best single introduction to the European Economic Community is *Swann* (1988). Brief introductions to empirical work are given by *Mayes* (1978), *Robson* (1987) and *Winters* (1982, 1987d). The references in the text might be supplemented by *Williamson and Bottrill* (1969) and *Balassa* (1975) for estimates concerning 'the Six' and EFTA, and by *Miller* (1971), *National Institute* (1971), *Williamson* (1971) and *Miller and Spencer* (1977)

199

on predictions of the UK's accession (the last with an elegant equilibrium welfare model). *Grinols* (1984) offers an innovative assessment of UK accession, while *Jacquemin and Sapir* (1989) reprint a wide range of studies. *Fukuda* (1973) is good on the Third World effects of UK accession; the Overseas Development Institute's series *The EEC and the Third World – A Survey* covers issues such as Lomé and the MFA, while *Pomfret* (1987) surveys the literature on non-EC integration.

Completing the internal market has a large but unwieldy literature, much of it of indifferent quality. *Pelkmans and Winters* (1988) offers a good introduction and CEC (1988) offers a lot of fascinating detail. The *European Economic Review*, vol. 32, no. 7 (1988) contains useful papers – especially by Smith and Venables – as does *Economic Policy*, no. 9 (1989) – Baldwin and Norman (who is very good on third-country effects) – and no. 10 (1990) – Neven (on gainers and losers). *Winters* (1988) and *Sapir* (1990) consider EC trade policy.

KEY CONCEPTS

Associated States	Treaty of Rome
Single European Act	*anti-monde*
barriers to intra-EC trade	costs of non-Europe
market integration	economies of scale

QUESTIONS FOR REVIEW

14.1 Discuss the argument that UK accession to the EC was harmful because it worsened her manufacturing trade balance.

14.2 How does the EC measure up to the criteria for a 'desirable' customs union noted in Chapter 13?

14.3 'Completing the internal market will give the EC such a boost in efficiency that it should pursue an entirely open policy vis-à-vis the rest of the world.' Discuss both the premise and the conclusion of this statement.

14.4 To what extent are economies of scale fundamental to the analysis of the expected benefits of '1992'? Is their anticipated role reasonable?

14.5 Redraw Figure 14.1 to show both the union and the exporters gaining from integration. Redraw it to show only the union gaining. What factors determine which case rules?

NOTES

1 As Prime Minister, Mrs Thatcher was a strong advocate of free and unfettered trade, but a most reluctant European so far as sovereignty is concerned.

2 The ordering is not accidental. In the short run, politics is much easier if economists are not busy identifying winners and, more particularly, losers.

3 This is a correct version of the figure given in Winters (1988).

15 International Trade and Economic Growth

The ultimate purpose of economics is to increase economic welfare. So far we have concentrated almost entirely on the optimal allocation of a given bundle of resources, but it is obvious that welfare may also be improved either by increasing the quantity of resources available or by learning to do more with a given bundle. Both of these possibilities represent economic growth – the first through factor augmentation and the second through technical progress. Some economists feel that conventional measures of economic growth based on the output of goods and services (gross national product) do not satisfactorily reflect economic welfare, arguing that they ignore factors such as pollution and the negative externalities from congestion (see Mishan, 1967, and a reply by Beckerman, 1974). We shall ignore this controversy here, however, and assume that increased productive capabilities represent improved opportunities for economic welfare. We shall, however, encounter one instance where growth may be harmful – in section 15.2.

In many respects, then, the subject of this chapter is among the most important treated in the whole book. Unfortunately, it is also among the least satisfactory. We have seen already how international trade theory possesses its share of ambiguities and conundrums, and growth theory is just as bad. In combination they conspire to make economic theorising a most frustrating activity.

15.1 THE RYBCZYNSKI THEOREM

The Heckscher–Ohlin case

We start by recapitulating one of the fundamental components of the Heckscher–Ohlin theorem trade model: the Rybczynski theorem. This comparative static theorem states that comparing two small open economies, identical in every respect except their factor endowments, the economy better endowed with capital will produce *absolutely* more of the capital-intensive good and *absolutely* less of the labour-intensive good than the other economy. Ignoring the dynamics of transition from one equilibrium to another, this translates into the following theorem of growth: *if a small trading country's endowment of one factor increases, its output of the good using that factor intensity will rise and output of the other good fall.*

A proof of the Rybczynski theorem was presented in Chapter 3, but we will briefly repeat it here. Adopting all the Heckscher–Ohlin assumptions plus non-specialisation and the small country assumption, let us assume that our country has attained a full trading equilibrium. Now assume that it receives a grant of real capital from abroad. How is the extra capital to be used? With fixed good and factor prices (deriving from the small country assumption and factor price equalisation), factor proportions in each industry will be fixed. Thus the only way of absorbing capital is to increase output in the capital-intensive sector (say, X) and reduce it in the other (Y). As Y-output is reduced, factors are related in ratio $K_Y : L_Y$; if X takes on all the labour released, it will require more than K_Y of capital, by virtue of its being the capital intensive sector, and this extra capital can be obtained only from the capital grant. The only limit to this process is if specialisation occurs before the capital is fully absorbed. In this case, the remaining capital is absorbed by X (as its price falls), but, of course, Y-output cannot fall any further.

Notice that nothing has been said about imports or exports. The increased endowment may entail higher output of either importables or exportables; excepting extreme demand conditions, the former change will reduce international trade while the latter will increase it. Notice also that the theorem referred to a small country. A large country would experience similar pressures but its changes in output would affect world prices and the results would no longer be unambiguous.

The specific factors case

A development of the standard Heckscher–Ohlin model is the specific factors case. Suppose now a small country receives an increment of one sector-specific capital – say, K_X. This raises output in industry X by two mechanisms: first because capital has a positive marginal product, holding labour input constant; and second because by raising the capital/labour ratio, it increases labour's marginal revenue product in X, which raises wages and bids labour away from Y. With no increment in its own capital, therefore, industry Y loses output as it loses labour. Thus, in this respect factor growth has similar effects to those in the Heckscher–Ohlin model: one industry increases output absolutely while the other reduces it absolutely.

The specific factors model differs from Heckscher–Ohlin, however, in one important respect. Heckscher–Ohlin maintained constant factor prices, at least in the absence of specialisation, but with specific factors they vary. We saw in the previous paragraph how industry X's capital/labour ratio rose, and how by bidding labour from Y it caused Y's to do likewise. Thus labour's marginal revenue product (given prices) rose in both industries, raising wages, while capital's fell in both, reducing capital rentals. Thus, an increment of one sort of capital reduced returns not only to existing holders of that capital, but also to holders of the other capital.

Long-run growth

We have treated changes in factor supplies as exogenously given data, but this is not realistic. Both population growth and the capital stock are affected by economic growth. We shall not consider the former, but two observations may be made on the latter. First, the capital stock is incremented by investment, and, since, in the long run, investment equals saving, the ultimate determinant of the supply of capital is the propensity to save. Countries more willing to save will generally increase their relative capital abundance.

Second, the process of economic growth tends to generate changes in factor endowments. Poor countries are less able than richer countries to generate surplus income to save, and are thus most unlikely to be relatively capital-abundant. Similarly, at the top end of the income scale there appears to be a tendency for endowments to shift from physical to human capital abundance as growth occurs. Thus we expect to find dynamic countries changing their patterns of trade relatively rapidly: Japan, a prime example, moved rapidly from exporting labour-intensive goods (e.g. textiles and toys), through physical–capital-intensive goods (e.g. ships and steel) into skill- and technology-intensive sectors (e.g. electronics). A more recent instance is South Korea, which seems to be entering the human capital stage now, often displacing Japan from her former markets.

Observe that these stages of comparative advantage may allow us to make predictions about unusually dynamic or stagnant economies, but not about

changes in the general pattern of trade in response to general economic
growth. This is because trade is determined by *relative* factor abundance and, if
all countries evolve roughly together, relativities are not easily predictable.

Technical progress

The previous analysis referred to factor accumulation, but technological
advance is probably a more important source of economic growth. Frequently,
however, we can treat the latter as being factor augmenting, and thus apply
the earlier analysis anyway. For example, progress may have the result of
increasing the productivity of all units of capital by x per cent; we can then
analyse the economy as if it were applying x per cent more capital to a given
technology, rather than an unchanged capital stock to a new technology.

If this 'dodge' does not work – because, for example, technical progress is
restricted to one industry – matters become much more complex. In general,
we would expect output of the good experiencing technical progress to rise, since
its costs fall below the given world price at unchanged output. This may or
may not reduce output of the other good, however, depending on how many
(and which) factors the advancing technology releases or absorbs.

15.2 IMMISERISING GROWTH

Growth and trade

The previous section considered the consequences of economic growth on
production and on factor rewards, but not on the direction of trade. The
reason is that trade results from differences between countries, and growth in
any country might either increase or decrease these. Thus, for example, a
country experiencing capital augmentation will switch production from
labour- to capital-intensive goods; this will increase trade if the country
previously exported capital-intensive goods or reduce it if it exported labour-
intensive goods. Similarly, technical progress may boost either export or
import-competing sectors and so increase or decrease trade.

A further complication arises from demand. If demand is not homothetic –
i.e. if goods have different income elasticities – economic growth changes the
pattern of demand. Thus a country suddenly becoming very rich may increase
its demand for Rolls-Royces disproportionately, and this will be reflected in its
international trade. Such demand factors will be experienced even if growth
leaves the pattern of production quite unchanged.

If our country is small, it is not of great consequence whether growth
stimulates or reduces world trade, because a small country can conduct any
amount (or direction) of trade at fixed world prices. This allows us to assert
that economic growth should always be beneficial. By definition, economic
growth will allow a country to produce its pre-growth bundle of goods plus
some output in addition. The country can thus reach its pre-growth
consumption bundle (trading as before), and then have some further
consumption as it trades or consumes the additional output. Of course, it may
not actually choose to detemine its consumption along these lines: it may, for
example, consume less X after growth than before. Nevertheless, provided
that all the price signals are correct – i.e. that they maintain the marginal
equalities $MRS = MRT = MRTT$ – we know that the chosen position is
preferred to the one with consumption of more of both goods and that this, in
turn, is preferred to the pre-growth position.

**The terms
of trade**

Now consider a large country, whose terms of trade vary with the amount of trade. If economic growth increases the supply of exports, and the world's demand for those exports is inelastic, it is possible that the export price falls so far that the country is actually worse off for growing! This possibility, known as *immiserising growth*, is illustrated in Figure 15.1. The pre-growth position has transformation frontier *FF*, production at *P*, consumption at *C*, and terms of trade *TT*. Both *P* and *C* lie on the foreign offer curve, which is not drawn, but which would be curved to reflect the dependence of prices on the amounts traded. (Figure 10.4(B) illustrates equilibrium for a large country in this type of diagram.) After growth, the transformation frontier shifts out to *F'F'* and, although nothing else changes, a completely new equilibrium arises, with consumption at *C'*. The foreign offer curve linking *P'* and *C'* is the same as that linking *P* and *C*, but with its origin shifted from *P* to *P'*. Its curvature means that the country is unable to convert its additional output into consumption at so favourable a rate. Thus, the extra supply of exports of X (up from *JP* to *J'P'*) brings forth virtually no extra Y from the rest of the world.

Figure 15.1 Immiserising growth for a large country

Certain primary commodity producers may find themselves with something approaching immiserising growth. The price elasticities of demand for food and raw materials are low, at least in the short run, and so bumper harvests are met by falling world prices. This leads certain major producers to curtail output with a view to supporting the price. For example, the USA pays farmers not to produce wheat, Saudi Arabia controls oil production and Brazil controls coffee sales. All this suggests that economic growth based on these sectors may not be viewed as a blessing.

204

The difficulty faced by the large country is that, as it pushes out the transformation frontier, economic growth also, in some sense, exacerbates the (large country) distortion of the marginal conditions. Thus, the additional utility obtainable from the former is outweighed by the additional loss from the latter. This suggests a cure: the optimal tariff. The optimal tariff corrects the marginal trade distortion and ensures that consumption occurs at the optimal point on the consumption possibility locus (the Baldwin envelope). The post-growth transformation frontier lies everywhere outside (strictly speaking: not inside) the pre-growth one; hence, with an unchanged foreign offer curve, the post-growth consumption possibility locus also lies everywhere outside its pre-growth equivalent. Thus, if, by means of optimal tariffs, the optimum points are chosen both before and after growth, welfare will certainly be increased by growth, since, for any point on the pre-growth consumption possibility locus, some point on the post-growth locus allows more of both goods.

Growth and domestic distortions

A similar analysis in fact applies to all distortions. Growth in the presence of any distortion might not be beneficial, because it both pushes out the transformation frontier and alters (possibly increasing) the degree of distortion. Thus, even for small countries, growth could be immiserising in the presence of a tariff, a production externality, consumption taxes, etc. The first mentioned is illustrated in Figure 15.2. World prices are given by the slope of PC or P'C', and with a fixed tariff they imply internal prices of slope II. Post-growth consumption at C' is below pre-growth consumption at C. The problem is that growth enlarges the tariff's production distortionary effect. As drawn, free trade would entail specialisation in X both before and after growth, and P' is further from that position than is P.

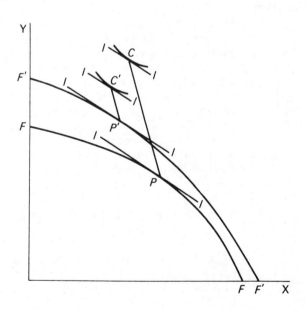

Figure 15.2 Immiserising growth with a tariff

205

These results generalise to multi-commodity and multi-factor settings, and given the prevalence of distortions one might expect them to have a wide applicability. To our knowledge, no empirical study exists that considers whether economic growth has actually been harmful by virtue of increasing distortions. Returning to the large country case, multi-dimensionality introduces the possibility of a fate worse than immiserising growth. If a country has the same trade pattern as a growing economy but without the growth, it suffers the terms of trade deterioration without any counteracting quantity effects.

15.3   THE TRANSFER PROBLEM

The previous section considered the consequences of one country's economic growth on world equilibrium. We noted that in extreme cases growth could actually be harmful because it exacerbated an existing market distortion. We now examine the related issue of one country giving or transferring income to another, and ask a similar set of questions. History has produced several instances of such pure transfers – most notably German reparations paid to the Allies after World War I and the USA's grants of Marshall Aid to Europe after World War II. Currently, the analysis applies to donations of foreign aid and also, if we ignore the subsequent repayments, to flows of international investment.

The issue we shall address is whether a transfer affects the terms of trade between the two countries, and if so, how. In particular, we ask whether it is possible for the donor to gain more through terms of trade changes than it loses through the initial transfer, and, correspondingly, whether the recipient could suffer a net loss.

The terms of trade We start with a simple two-country model, assuming that the transfer shifts purchasing power from A to B but does not affect the distribution of productive resources at all. We ask how the demand for each good would be affected at unchanged world prices (terms of trade), and from this deduce how prices must change in order to re-establish equilibrium. Notice that we are dealing here with the large country case again.

Suppose that, starting from full equilibrium, the transfer from A to B is of $£T$. Of this additional income, B will spend $m^B T$ on imports, where m^B is B's marginal propensity to import, and the remainder, $(1 - m^B)T$, on B's exportable good.[1] Correspondingly, A will allocate her income change of $-£T$ as $-m^A T$ on imports and $-(1 - m^A)T$ on exportables. Now, B's imports and A's exportable are the same good; hence, at unchanged terms of trade, world demand for that good changes by

$$\Delta D = m^B T - (1 - m^A)T = (m^A + m^B - 1)T. \tag{15.1}$$

Thus, the transfer increases demand for A's exportable good if

$$m^A + m^B > 1. \tag{15.2}$$

If this is so, A's term of trade would have to improve (i.e. her export price rise) in order to bring post-transfer demands back into line with unchanged supplies. (Exactly the same conclusion would arise if we examined demand for B's exportable.)

Thus we see that the donor's terms of trade will improve if, on average, countries' marginal consumption is biased towards foreign goods – i.e. towards each other's goods. Given the existence of transport costs and non-tradable services, this seems unlikely, although Jones (1975) argued to the contrary.

Changes in the terms of trade affect real incomes in the two countries on top of the direct effects of the transfer. These effects are known as the 'secondary burden' or 'secondary gain', according to sign. The question then arises whether the donor's secondary gain could offset its primary loss from the initial transfer. The answer is generally 'no' – at least provided markets are stable. Suppose for a moment that the primary and secondary changes just balance – i.e. that the terms of trade changed by just enough to leave both donor and recipient at their pre-transfer levels of income. Could this represent a final equilibrium? With incomes unchanged, only prices differ between the pre- and post-transfer equilibria. However, provided markets are stable, the higher prices of A's exportable will boost supply and cut demand for it; thus, at the assumed terms of trade, there would be an excess supply of A's exportable, which would serve to reduce its price. Hence, a completely offsetting terms of trade change could not be an equilibrium; that could only exist with a lower price for A's export, i.e. with a smaller terms of trade change.

As might be guessed from previous sections, these results are not particularly robust to changes in assumptions. Immiserising transfers are possible for large countries in a multi-country world, and in the presence of domestic distortions. Unlike the immiserising growth case, however, the circumstances necessary to produce immiserising transfers are sufficiently strict and unlikely for us to ignore such transfers as a practical possibility.

An early debate on the transfer problem was between Keynes (1929) and Ohlin (1929). Keynes argued that post-war reparations would greatly reduce Germany's export prices as she sought to earn a sufficient export surplus to pay the transfer to the Allies. This assumed that the price mechanism had to bear all the burden of adjustment. Ohlin, on the other hand, pointed out that, since transfers affected incomes, income effects could generate Germany's required surplus, with the richer Allies importing more and the poorer Germans importing less, thus entailing a much smaller terms of trade change than Keynes allowed. It is clear that modern treatments run much closer to Ohlin's view than to Keynes'.

15.4 EXPORTS AND GROWTH

We turn now very briefly from pure theory to an empirical approach to the question of international trade and growth. Both through history and across countries, economic growth appears to be correlated with higher levels of international trade. This is far from inevitable from the preceding analysis, however. One explanation might be that countries are actually rather specialised – in particular varieties of goods, if not in particular goods (see Chapter 5). If so, domestic growth increases the supply of rather few of the items consumed, and so, almost inevitably, it must be accompanied by additional trade to convert its fruits into a consumable bundle of goods. Coupled with this is the fact that, as incomes rise, consumers are likely to increase their demand for foreign varieties of goods (they are more able to pay the additional costs that importing involves, see p. 67 above). Thus growth is likely to increase trade from the import side as well. This effect will be supplemented if countries that are growing fast also tend to reduce their trade barriers more rapidly.

Export-led growth

An entirely different approach is to argue that, if exports grew for some exogenous reason, this actually stimulates growth. Several possible analyses of this exist. First, there is the straightforward Keynesian notion that exports are injections into the circular flow of income and that they boost income and output via the multiplier. (This is explained further in Chapter 18.) This is fine as far as it goes, but, if injections are all that is required, would not increasing government expenditure do as well?

Part of the answer to this comes from the second analysis of export-led growth. By increasing foreign exchange receipts, exports permit a higher level of imports. This could stimulate growth if these imports comprise essential raw materials or capital equipment – an argument relevant to development economics. It may also *allow* more domestically generated growth if this has been constrained by the need to keep import demand below a certain level. Growth is curtailed in order that import payments do not exceed export revenues – thus more exports allow more imports and thus more growth. This approach was expounded by Thirlwall (1980). It has some truth in it, but it is more an 'import' or 'foreign exchange' theory of growth than an 'export' theory, because anything that raises imports (e.g. an export price rise or a transfer) stimulates growth.

A third view is that exposure to international competition helps to remove allocative inefficiencies that may build up in relatively closed economies. Thus an increasing rate of exporting does not cause a country's transformation frontier to shift outwards any faster, but it does allow the actual production point to approach any given frontier more closely. During the transitional stage, as misallocations are removed, the economy will thus grow faster than usual, since both 'natural growth' and 'reallocative growth' will be combined. In the long run, however, when maximum allocative efficiency has been achieved, growth rates will slip back to normal rates, although, of course, at a higher *level* of income than would have been achieved without the external stimulus.

Part of this argument is that resources have higher productivity in export industries than elsewhere. Thus, shifting them into export processes raises output independent of any dynamic considerations. Gains may arise from any of the following. Greater capacity utilisation and economies of scale may be possible because industries are no longer constrained by the domestic economy. Rent-seeking in the import-competing sector may fall as resources leave for the export sector; i.e. there is less competition for import-related rents as the attractions of exporting increase. Similarly, other misallocations associated with too much concentration on the home market may evaporate: e.g. excessive capital intensity. New technologies may be available from foreign rivals, or have emerged locally in response to greater competition in exporting. Management may be better for similar reasons.

Closely related but logically different are two further factors. First, the export sector may be more dynamic than the rest of the economy for similar reasons to those outlined above. Thus, increasing its size will raise overall growth rates without any change in individual sectors' growth rates. Second, as the export sector grows it may create even more positive externalities for

208

the rest of the economy, thereby raising the latter's levels or growth rates of productivity. Among the relevant externalities may be training labour and management, spin-offs from research, and new investment opportunities (see Chapter 11).

Empirical results

Many studies exist of the exports–growth relationship. They are hindered by the simultaneous causation that inevitably exists: exports may stimulate growth, but growth also stimulates exports by increasing supply. Furthermore, since exports comprise part of GDP, export and GDP growth must inevitably be somewhat related. Thus, finding a positive correlation between export and GDP growth does not constitute a thorough test of the export-led growth hypothesis. However, little other evidence exists.

Among the most convincing of such studies is Feder (1983). Feder decomposed the export effect into a part due to differences in productivity between export and non-export sectors and a part due to positive externalities between sectors. He found, in a cross-section of thirty-one LDCs' growth over 1964–73, that a 1 per cent increase in export growth was associated with a 0.08 per cent per annum increase in GDP growth via productivity differences, and a 0.13 per cent increase via externalities. Decomposing actual growth over the decade into its causes, he found that, of mean growth of 6.5 per cent per annum, investment explained 2.5 per cent per annum, labour-force growth 1.6 per cent per annum, productivity differences between exports and other sectors 0.7 per cent per annum, externalities 1.1 per cent per annum, and other trends 0.6 per cent per annum.

15.5 TRADE AND DEVELOPMENT

If export-led growth is feasible one would expect it to be of particular interest to developing countries, especially if they see it as a means of establishing a modern industrial economy. This section considers three strands of this argument. First, the possible drawbacks of depending on primary commodity exports: second, the extent to which developing country exports – and hence growth – are dependent on industrial country growth; and third, the relative merits of approaching industrialisation via inward- or outward-looking policies.

Commodity price trends

It is widely believed that the real prices of primary commodities (i.e. their prices relative to those of manufactures) fall through time, and that, as a consequence, there is little future in exporting them. This view is overly simple: the tendency for prices to fall is not beyond dispute, and many countries are highly successful despite depending heavily on primaries – for example, Saudi Arabia (oil is a primary commodity), New Zealand, Canada and the USA. On the other hand, many of the world's poorest countries obtain very high proportions of their export revenue from primaries, often from only one or two products, so there is potentially a real problem.

Several theoretical reasons have been advanced for commodity prices to fall relative to those of manufactures in the long run. The income elasticity of demand for primaries may be lower. Technical progress appears to allow ever-decreasing amounts of primary inputs per unit of manufactured output. Synthetic materials sometimes displace primaries. The markets for primary commodities and the labour producing them are competitive, whereas those for manufactures allow market power. Hence technical progress in the primary sector is passed on to consumers in lower prices, while that in manufactures is absorbed by labour into wages that cannot easily be reduced; as a result the prices of manufactures rarely fall and so are ratcheted upwards in relative terms. Finally, the supply of most primaries has expanded, with improved crop yields and technologies of extraction. With relatively low price elasticities of demand, this too has driven prices down.

A major problem in primaries research is establishing the facts, let alone considering causation, because it is very difficult to measure prices consistently over periods of a century or more. The commodities themselves change (e.g. in their degrees of purity), but more so do the weights relevant to any index number and the quality of manufactures. If, as seems reasonable, the growth in the prices of manufactures is associated with improvements in quality, the price per unit of service from manufactures will rise less rapidly than the price per unit.

A recent study by the World Bank (Grilli and Yang, 1988) offers probably the best data on primary prices – an index of the prices of twenty-four commodities weighted together by their share of world trade in 1977–79. Grilli and Yang found real commodity prices declining by about 0.5 per cent per year over their sample in the period 1900–86. The fall is not uniform over commodities – see Table 15.1 – but it does seem to be fairly steady. Only for metals is the change in trend significant: since 1942, the multinational mining firms seem to have been able to control output enough to raise real metal prices, although since 1970 the tendency has been weaker than previously.

Table 15.1 The trend rate of growth of real commodity prices, 1900–86[a]

Commodity	Annual growth rate (%)
Food	− 0.36
Tropical beverages	0.63
Non-beverage foods	− 0.54
Cereals	− 0.68
Non-food agricultural	− 0.82
Metals	− 0.84
All non-fuel commodities	− 0.57
All commodities	− 0.52

Note:
[a] Primary prices relative to the price of manufactured imports in US dollars.
Source: Grilli and Yang (1988).

The terms of trade The ratio of the prices of a country's export and imports is known as its *net barter terms of trade* (NBTT). For commodity exporters the NBTT will be closely related to the relevant commodity prices, but for developing countries as a whole the NBTT is only loosely related to real commodity prices. This is because these countries export significant amounts of manufactures and import some primaries, even non-fuel primaries. The NBTTs of most of the world's poorest countries have declined since about 1960, as have those of most developing countries since 1980, but the trends in NBTT are much less marked than those for real commodity prices.

A decline in the terms of trade (NBTT) is welfare-worsening *ceteris paribus*, but, as we saw above, it may stem from an increase in the supply of exports, which could offset its effect through time. Hence a better welfare measure may be the *income terms of trade* – the value of a country's exports divided by the price of its imports – which measures the volume of imports that may be bought by exporting. For developing countries as a whole and for each major sub-set of them, the income terms of trade have improved strongly since the 1950s. Thus, even if the prices they received have fallen, international trade has allowed developing countries to command increasing volumes of industrial countries' output.

Commodity price fluctuations

A further difficulty of commodity export dependence is the fluctuations in export prices and revenue. MacBean and Nguyen (1987) showed that the prices of primary exports are considerably more variable than those of manufactured exports: while most manufactured goods show root mean squared deviations about their trends $(RMSD)^2$ of below 10 per cent, most commodities have values exceeding 15 per cent and many exceeding 30 per cent. Among the possible reasons for these differences are the low price elasticities of supply and demand, which translate small quantity shocks into large price shocks, the restrictions on international trade in foods, the fact that commodities are storable and hence have an asset dimension to their prices (see Chapter 22 below), and the different natures of manufactures and primary markets described above.

As before, the relative instability of primary prices need not necessarily translate into the relative instability of developing countries' export prices or earnings, but, in fact, it does. On MacBean and Nguyen's data, developing country earnings have an average RMSD of 11 per cent (greater for low-income countries) compared with 6 per cent for industrial countries.

While the evidence that the instability of export earnings harms economic growth is rather tenuous (see MacBean, 1966, and Lim, 1976), there is no doubt that it causes considerable problems for both private agents and the public authorities. Consequently there have been many attempts to stabilise prices – international commodity agreements – and earnings – compensatory finance (see Chapter 28); none has been very successful. Developing countries, therefore, have sought to diversify into new commodities and manufactures.

Trade as the engine of growth

Several economists have argued that trade is the most important engine of economic growth for developing countries – namely, that selling in the industrial world generates the resources with which to buy improved capital equipment. Conjoining this with the observations that primary exports face declining terms of trade and considerable instability, that the demand for them is rigidly linked to the level of demand in industrial countries, and that that demand is erratic and possibly subject to a long-run upper limit, has led to calls to decouple the developing countries from the industrial world (Nurkse's, 1959, sponsorship of inward-looking development) or to sponsor intra-developing country trade as an alternative to trade with industrial countries (Lewis, 1980).

Two excellent pieces of applied economics have challenged this analysis. Kravis (1970) considered the link between exports and growth in the nineteenth century. He showed first that exports played relatively little role in successful growth during that century. For example, in the USA they accounted for a constant share of GDP, their movement lagged those in GDP, they were mostly in agriculture, and foreign investment accounted for only

211

about 5 per cent of net capital formation over the century. Second, he showed conversely that some countries had strong export records but poor growth performances – for example, Latin America, India and Ceylon (Sri Lanka). Kravis's conclusion, supported by further evidence on developing countries in the twentieth century, was that growth is essentially a result of internal factors to which external demand is just a welcome addition. He argued, in fact, that developing countries' trade problems reflect the inadequacy of supply rather than of demand.

Riedel (1984) emphasised a different stand of the argument. If developing countries exported only tropical products with no temperate or synthetic substitutes, one would expect there to be a tight link between industrial country growth and developing country exports. But they don't and there isn't. Developing countries also export temperate products, products with substitutes, services (tourism, shipping) and, above all, manufactures. In these cases the link to industrial country aggregate demand is much weaker because price competition allows exporters to increase their sales even if demand is sluggish.

Riedel showed that most developing countries are switching rapidly towards manufactured exports – even those countries which started with virtually no such exports. Manufactures generally have higher income elasticities of demand than primaries, and thus offer a more favourable link between exports and industrial country growth. But Riedel's point was that the act of switching export composition dissolves the link between exports and industrial country growth. By breaking into new markets, developing countries get export growth even if total demand is stagnant. Moreover, the developing countries currently have sufficiently small shares of industrial markets that such market growth as there is can easily accommodate developing country export growth,[3] and developing countries can chisel shares from other suppliers with little threat of retaliation. Riedel observed that the boom in developing country manufactured exports occurred over a period of depression in industrial countries and so cannot be linked to their growth. Thus, he argued, while OECD growth clearly affects developing countries, the link is complex and depends to a large extent on developing countries' ability to supply manufactures and to compete through prices.

Riedel's conclusions have entirely different policy implications from the traditional engine-of-growth model. Rather than seek insulation or alternative markets, developing countries should embrace vigorously the opportunities they have in OECD markets.

The case for industrialisation

As well as avoiding the adverse trends and fluctuations associated with primary exporting, industrialisation is frequently held to offer a number of other benefits. First, manufacturing may offer more scope for improvements in productivity than does agriculture. For example, technology advances faster, economies of scale are more common and external benefits are greater. Second, marginal productivity in manufacturing may exceed that in agriculture – especially subsistence agriculture – and hence transferring labour into manufacturing will increase total output. Some economists, e.g. Lewis (1954), have argued that the marginal product of agricultural workers can be zero or negative. This seems rather exaggerated, but productivity is probably lower in agriculture than elsewhere in developing economies. Third, employment in industry affects attitudes in matters such as punctuality, the precision of work, and so on, and this has general economic benefits. Fourth, in the very long run, the world as a whole will probably become more industrialised because, as per capita incomes grow, the demand for manufactures tends to grow faster than that for primaries. Thus industrialisation appears desirable in a dynamic sense.

Against all these arguments we should observe that, if every country switched into manufacturing, the relative price of manufactures would fall, negating the purpose of switching. Most economists feel that developing economies would do better to improve their agriculture rather than switch out of it entirely. Others have observed that industry tends to accumulate in the towns and its growth is associated with high urban unemployment. People migrate to the towns hoping to obtain industrial jobs (which are relatively well paid), but are frustrated. This is harmful both socially and economically – at least if the marginal product of agricultural workers exceeds zero. To some extent it may be alleviated, however, by encouraging small-scale 'intermediate technology' rural industry.

Overall there is probably some case for industrialisation by developing countries, although it is far from the universal panacea that is sometimes assumed. We therefore now consider how industrialisation may be fostered.

Import substitution vs. export promotion

The policy of industrialisation behind protective barriers is known as import substitution (IS). Essentially the government seeks gradually to replace imported manufactures by indigenous output; this is contrasted with a policy of export promotion (EP), which seeks to boost manufactured exports or, at least, not to hinder them. The terms *inward-* and *outward-oriented* policies have become more popular than IS and EP recently because they convey better the notion that exactly the same set of issues arise over primaries and services as over manufactures, even if the desire to develop these sectors is weaker. In the 1950s and 1960s IS was the generally preferred route to development, but more recently there has been a strong switch towards EP.

The factors that might encourage IS relative to EP are:

- *The terms of trade effects*: if the country is large in any of its markets, EP would worsen its terms of trade, whereas IS would improve them. This is just the optimum tariff argument and is logically separate from IS or EP: the country should impose the optimum tariff and then decide whether to pursue EP or IS *from there*.
- *Information*: EP requires knowledge of world markets, whereas for IS the government need look only at actual imports to gauge demand.
- *Certainty*: the major problem with EP is that if it is successful the importing countries tend to get resentful. For example, the huge export successes of the East Asian countries – e.g. Japan, Taiwan, Korea – have been met by increasing restrictions in the West. Even ignoring this, EP involves greater specialisation and hence greater risks if market conditions change.
- *Insulation*: if the rest of the world economy is unstable, EP is likely to involve greater domestic shocks than IS. It is also often felt that EP increases economic dependency, which can be harmful both politically and economically (e.g. in bargaining situations.)

In favour of EP over IS are:

- *Comparative advantage*: EP allows one to exploit comparative advantage rather than frustrate it.

213

- *Specialisation*: exports are generally more concentrated than imports, so concentrating on them involves greater specialisation, which lowers costs via economies of scale and comparative advantage.
- *Transparency*: to the extent that EP requires subsidies, the costs are obvious and this probably leads to regular policy assessments. To the extent that IS relief on tariffs and quotas, its costs are largely hidden.
- *Administration*: EP is as often pursued by fixing a realistic exchange rate as by explicit subsidies. This is very cheap to administer compared with the quotas and production subsidies of IS.
- *Long-run structure*: if the belief is that eventually policy will not be necessary – i.e. that IS and EP are temporary phases – the ultimate shape of the economy must be considered. More often than not this will involve significant export industries, hence EP is moving in the right direction.
- *Rent-seeking*: IS gives scope for rent-seeking, and although a highly targeted EP policy also does so, most EP policies rely on relatively broad policies and so are more robust in this respect.
- *Flexibility*: the need to take regard of market signals makes economies more flexible. This allows them to adapt better and more quickly to exogenous shocks and opportunities. Despite suffering more severe oil shocks as a result of their openness, outward-oriented economies appeared to cope much better than inward-oriented ones over the mid-1970s (Balassa, 1981).
- *Resource allocation*: If EP really only involves not penalising exports and imports – i.e. neutral trade incentives – it is efficient for all reasons we have encountered above.

Experiences with IS and EP

Over the 1950s and 1960s IS was tried extensively both in Latin America and in newly independent countries around the world. Studies of these episodes are in general rather discouraging. Partly this reflects poorly designed IS policies: the strength of protection rarely seemed to reflect the externalities stemming from industries, barriers tended to proliferate, bureaucracies grew, and new industries were discouraged (protection tending to go to existing ones). Partly, however, the problems of IS are inherent: industries are limited to small scale; exports fall as they are starved of resources; foreign exchange shortages emerge that curtail imports of essential raw materials and capital goods; and income is redistributed towards scarce factors – e.g. capital.

IS regimes tend to follow a fairly regular pattern. The early stages appear to be quite successful in reducing imports and foreign exchange outgoings as imported consumer goods are displaced. This is an 'easy' stage, for such goods are usually well suited to developing countries' productive abilities. Such growth, however, eventually runs out, because in such countries the consumer market is relatively small. Then follows a more difficult stage as intermediate and capital goods fall under the controls. This tends to generate bureaucracy, as the controls are fashioned to allow essential imports and exclude others. Increasingly the private sector has to devote resources to dealing with the bureaucrats and winning the right to import – the rent-seeking behaviour discussed in section 12.1. Thus ultimately IS is usually disappointing.

The alternative of EP appears generally more successful. For example, Krueger (1983a) examined twenty policy episodes, covering ten developing countries, since 1953. In the EP episodes, the average rate of GDP growth was 8.5 per cent, whereas in four moderate IS cases growth averaged 7.75 per cent and in ten full IS cases 4.25 per cent. Similarly the prodigious growth of

Table 15.2 Macro-economic performance and trade orientation, 1973–85

Indicator	Averages over groups of countries (%)		
	Strongly outward oriented	Intermediate[a]	Strongly inward oriented
Growth of real GDP	7.7	4.5	2.5
Growth of real GDP per head	5.9	1.8	− 0.1
Growth of exports of goods	11.2	7.1	− 1.4
Gross domestic savings rate	31.4	22.4	17.9
Incremental capital/output ratio	4.5	5.6	8.7

Note:
[a] Average of moderately outward- and moderately inward-oriented groups.
Source: Greenaway and Nam (1988).

countries such as Korea, Taiwan and Hong Kong testifies to the success of their export-oriented policies. Of course, GDP growth is not an end in itself, but such growth rates must ultimately boost consumption. We should note, however, that there may be an element of reverse causation in these figures: rapidly expanding economies may feel more able to dismantle protection than stagnant ones. Also they refer to EP only over a period of trade liberalisation; recent Western protectionism may dull its gloss. At present, however, the evidence seems to indicate that outward- rather than inward-looking industrialisation policies are to be preferred in the long run.

Greenaway and Nam (1988) examined a sample of forty-one developing countries and classified them into strongly and moderately inward and outward looking. Such classification is necessarily a little arbitrary, but the extreme groups are fairly well defined. Greenaway and Nam found strong evidence that openness boosts macro-economic performance (see Table 15.2). Outward orientation appears to enhance growth by stimulating exports and savings, and by allowing a more efficient use of capital. (The incremental capital/output ratio shows the investment requirement per unit growth in output.) Moreover, although Greenaway and Nam's later period was one of rising protectionism, the outward-oriented strategy still proved successful. Neither the tendency of industrial countries to close their markets to developing country products, nor the fact that the more developing countries that export the fiercer will be world competition, eliminates the advantages of outward orientation, which stem as much from the discipline of the market on internal behaviour as from the extra demand available abroad.

FURTHER READING

The standard results on the Rybczynski theorem may be pursued in the references given for Chapter 3. *Smallwood* (1975) approaches the subject by adding international trade to standard growth theory (rather than vice versa) and generates some interesting insights. *Balassa* (1979) explores the changing stages of economic development with respect to trade patterns. On immiserising growth, *Bhagwati* (1971) provides the most useful reference, integrating the subject with the theory of distortions. For multi-dimensional generalisations, see *Eaton and Panagariya* (1982) and *Smith* (1982).

Classic references on the transfer problem are *Samuelson* (1952, 1954) and *Mundell*

(1960), while *Brecher and Bhagwati* (1981, 1982) analyse immiserising transfers under various conditions.

Export-led growth is considered by *Cornwall* (1977) and *Thirlwall* (1980), for developed countries, and by *Balassa* (1979) and *Tyler* (1981), among others, for developing countries.

Trade and development issues are explored well in *Greenaway* (1988) – especially the chapters by Riedel, Sapsford and Milner; in addition, the references in the text should be consulted, along with *The World Development Report, 1987* and *Bhagwati* (1986).

KEY CONCEPTS

stages of comparative advantage	Rybczynski theorem
immiserising growth and distortions	transfer problem
secondary burden	externalities of growth
net barter terms of trade	income terms of trade
engine of growth	outward orientation

QUESTIONS FOR REVIEW

15.1 How would the discovery of oil reserves affect a country's production pattern, trade pattern and factor rewards? Could the discovery be economically harmful?

15.2 Construct a diagram to show how technical progress in agriculture could be harmful if there are production subsidies for agriculture. What would be the situation if there were free trade?

15.3 What is the theory behind the notion of export-led growth? Is the theory convincing empirically?

15.4 If you were advising a developing country on its growth strategy would you recommend outward-orientation? Why? Would your view be different if the country's only current export were coffee?

15.5 Plot the data on export growth against GDP growth for eighteen developing countries – six Latin American, six African and six East Asian. What patterns do you observe? Can you offer any explanation for them?

NOTES

1 The marginal propensity to import records the proportion of an additional unit of income that is spent on imports.

2 RMSD is defined as

$$\frac{1}{n} \sum_{i=1}^{n} [(x_i - \hat{x}_i)/\hat{x}_i]^2,$$

where x is the series concerned, $\hat{x}$ is the predicted (trend) value, and $i = 1 \ldots n$ counts over periods.

3 If all of a market's 1 per cent growth goes to an exporter with a market share of 1 per cent, that exporter doubles his sales.

16 Capital Movements and the Multinationals

Everybody has heard of the multinationals, and nearly everybody has a view about them. This chapter looks beyond the rhetoric and asks, first, why multinationals have come about and, second, in precisely what ways they affect economic welfare. We discover that the predominant feature of multinationality is market failure. The chapter starts by considering the mobility of factors of production in general and introducing some data on the extent of multinational activity. It concludes by seeing how far multinationality affects the theory of the preceding chapters.

16.1 INTRODUCTION

Factor prices and factor mobility

We saw above (Chapters 3 and 7) that, if the value of world output is to be maximised, each factor of production must be distributed among industries and countries such that its marginal social product is identical in all uses. If this were not the case, output could be raised by shifting factors from low to high marginal product activities. Thus international factor mobility is required to maximise world output if, without it, marginal products would differ between countries. If, on the other hand, marginal products were equalised across the world, no such mobility would be necessary.

Let us take the argument one step further. If we assume perfect competition, full information, costless adjustment and no externalities or economies of scale, factors' rewards (prices) will equal their marginal social products (see Chapter 7). Under these circumstances, differing factor prices across countries will signal the need for factor mobility, and, equally important, any international migration that equalised factor prices would maximise world output. In general, factor migration will tend to equalise rewards: as, say, labour leaves low-wage areas for high-wage areas the supply of labour falls in the former, raising wages, and rises in the latter, reducing them. Thus, just as international trade, which shifts goods from areas of low prices to areas of high prices, is beneficial, so too is international migration, which shifts factors from areas of low rewards to areas of high rewards.

Of course, in comparing factor rewards over countries, care must be taken to compare like with like. Differences between average wages in, say, Britain and Burundi would not prescribe mobility if they arose from Britons' greater skills or compensated for the non-pecuniary disadvantages of living in an industrial country. They would, however, indicate gains to mobility if they stemmed from the greater amounts of physical capital or better technology available to *any* worker, either Briton or Burundian, working in Britain.

Factor price differences

The Heckscher–Ohlin model predicts that goods trade alone is sufficient for factor price equalisation (FPE), but in the real world, even allowing for measurement problems, it is plain that factor prices differ. Before considering the specific issues surrounding capital mobility it is worth exploring the reasons for these differences in the abstract.

We saw above how *complete specialisation* and *factor-intensity reversals* can upset

217

the equalisation result. The latter is probably not of great significance practically (see p. 48 above), but the former may be. Clearly some countries do not produce some goods and this may lead to differences in rewards and to migration. For example, computer engineers tend to migrate from poor to rich countries, presumably because they are unable to earn sufficient at home where computers are not produced.

A further case of factor price differences is trade impediments, which preclude the complete equality of goods prices across the world. *Transport costs* affect all trade while *tariffs* and *non-tariff barriers* affect most. Together they raise the relative price of a country's importable good and thus raise its intensive factor's reward relative to Samuelson's no impediment case. Tariffs mean that, for so long as any trade exists, the goods price ratios in the two countries must differ by the amount of the tariff. Thus trade *prevents* FPE and will eventually be displaced by factor mobility: if mobility is possible, even the smallest tariff eventually becomes prohibitive of international trade!

The phenomenon probably responsible for most of the observed differences in factor rewards is the technology assumptions. Different countries appear to have *'differences in atmosphere'* that affect the productivity of their industries independently of factor inputs. For example, Pratten (1976) reported that German firms commonly obtain 25 per cent per worker more than British firms from identical machines. Similarly, part of the higher productivity of American managers over most others probably stems as much from the social conventions militating towards working hard and succeeding as from other factor inputs. Whatever their cause, and whether they affect particular industries or factors, or whole economies, differences in atmosphere will generally prevent FPE and will make migration necessary if world output is to be maximised.

A further technological cause of factor price differences may be *economies of scale*. If different countries are reaping differing economies of scale, they may have identical prices (average costs) but different marginal productivities and thence different factor prices. An interesting feature of this case is that even if factor prices are equal there may be gains to migration, because concentrating production geographically may reduce costs below free-trade levels.

Portfolio vs. direct investment

We turn now specifically to capital mobility. Two forms exist. *Portfolio investment* overseas is investment in the bonds or securities or organisations in one country by residents of another. It confers no special rights on the investor; in particular he has no more control over the borrowing firm than any other shareholder does. Firms and individuals undertake portfolio investment for financial reasons: for example, foreign firms may offer particularly high or secure rates of return, or variations in their returns may tend to cancel out variations in domestic returns, if foreign and domestic returns are negatively correlated.

Foreign direct investment (FDI), on the other hand, is the purchase *and control* of an entity in one country by residents of another. A transaction falls into this class if it grants the lender 'significant influence' over the foreign entity or increases his stake in any such entity (Central Statistical Office, *United Kingdom Balance of Payments*). The important distinction between direct and portfolio investment lies in control, and explanations of FDI must reflect this.

The result of FDI is a multinational, or transnational, enterprise (MNE) – a company that owns or controls significant activities in at least two countries. Each MNE has a parent company or head office situated in its 'home' country, and subsidiaries situated abroad in 'host' countries. The precise relationship between parent and subsidiaries varies between companies, but we shall not investigate this. We merely assume that the parent exercises significant control over each subsidiary.

Some history

Foreign investment was prominent in the nineteenth century, but it mainly involved portfolio lending to developing countries for railway or municipal development. Britain was the major creditor and London the predominant centre; however, except indirectly through her political power, Britain exercised no control over the borrowers of funds. This lending reached its zenith around 1913. Between the wars, foreign investment declined: direct investment grew to about one-quarter of the total and the USA became a principal creditor. Although the Second World War caused very substantial losses of foreign assets, the climate that followed it – especially after 1958 – proved highly conducive to foreign investment. Post-war investment, however, has been primarily direct rather than portfolio.

The growth of FDI owed much to the improvements in transport and communications since 1945, which made it feasible to exercise control from a distance. It also stemmed from the economic need for the USA to export capital to the rest of the world – both to stimulate recovery and to keep the international financial system functioning (see Chapter 28) – and from the US tax laws, which favoured FDI. By the 1960s these factors were weakening, and resistance emerged around the world to US control of local industry. The US outflow eased and other countries started FDI in the USA. The 1970s generally saw less FDI than the 1960s, although for Britain the oil surpluses and the removal of foreign currency controls in 1979 generated a large outflow.

During the 1980s, two major changes occurred. First, the USA became a net recipient of FDI, reflecting both her need to borrow abroad (see Chapter 25) and her restrictive trade policy. Second, Japan became a major supplier of FDI, although in a limited range of sectors. It has been most prominent in the service sectors, but has also grown strongly in the transport equipment and electrical machinery sectors. This sectoral concentration reflects the difficulties of supplying markets for these things by means of exports because of regulations and trade policy. In the industrial world, the USA was the principal recipient of Japanese investment, but by 1988 EC manufacturing had over $4.6b. of Japanese FDI supporting some 116,000 jobs. Investment was also strong in East Asia as Japanese firms sought to keep labour costs down by relocating to developing countries.

MNEs today

Past investment has bequeathed us a very substantial amount of multi-nationality. In 1983, the developed economies owned an outstanding stock of FDI of about $515b. – equivalent to 5.5 per cent of world GDP excluding the centrally planned economies. Of this, 44 per cent was American owned, with the UK (17 per cent) and West Germany (8 per cent) coming next (Organization for Economic Co-operation and Development, 1987b). The USA was host to the largest proportion of this (16 per cent), followed by Canada (10 per cent) and the UK (10 per cent); developing countries received 27 per cent in all. While the location of FDI is more dispersed than the ownership, MNE subsidiaries still account for formidable proportions of their hosts' economic activity. For example, in the late 1970s they provided over half of Canadian manufacturing output, with corresponding figures of 21 per

219

L

cent for the UK, 29 per cent for Australia, 28 per cent for France and 22 per cent for West Germany. Japan, however, pursued an anti-FDI policy and had only 4 per cent of manufacturing due to MNEs (United Nations, 1978).

Not all MNEs are large, but they are larger than domestic firms on average and some are truly immense. The turnover of the largest exceeds the GNP of certain OECD and most developing countries. In 1973, 12 per cent of total OECD employment was due to just 260 MNEs. Nearly half of MNEs have interests in only one country other than their base country, but 11 per cent have interests in ten or more countries. Recent years have seen considerable increases in geographical diversification.

MNE activity is not spread evenly over industries. Indeed, it is differences between industries that offer most opportunities for identifying the causes of FDI. MNEs tend to predominate in technological sectors – (e.g. chemicals and electrical engineering), but also to be strong where brand images are important (e.g. food and tobacco) and where economies of scale require huge levels of output (e.g. petrol refining and motor vehicles). For example, in Britain in 1968 MNE subsidiaries accounted for 0 per cent of the output of metal furniture and 1 per cent of industrial fans, but 48 per cent of pharmaceuticals, 69 per cent of office machinery, 74 per cent of tractors, and 82 per cent of soups (Business Statistics Office, *Report on the Census of Production*, 1968, vol. 158).

Theoretically more interesting are the data in Table 16.1, which show the breakdown between FDI and exports as a means of serving foreign markets. Column 3 shows that technological industries tend to be more open than others (as we would expect from Chapter 15); but, within that, FDI and exporting appear to be substitutes. Office equipment, chemicals, rubber, vehicles and tobacco stress FDI, whereas aerospace, shipbuilding, metals and textiles favour exporting. The next section seeks explanations of these differences.

16.2 THE CAUSES OF FOREIGN DIRECT INVESTMENT

In asking why FDI takes place we are essentially asking the following two questions. First, if there is a demand for good X in country A, why is it not met either by (a) local firms in A, or (b) exports from country B. Second, suppose a firm in country B wishes to expand; why does it not do so by (a) producing more X in B and exporting, (b) expanding into some other line within B, (c) buying shares (portfolio investment) in A, or (d) licensing some firm in A to use its technology to produce X? The answers, of course, are, first, that a B-owned subsidiary in A can out-compete other potential suppliers, and, second, that the profits from FDI appear to exceed those from the alternative means of expansion. But why?

We shall answer these questions using Dunning's (1979, 1988) *eclectic theory* of FDI. This incorporates a wide range of possible causes without being too precise about how they interrelate. Other theorists have been more definite but, as yet, simpler more powerful theories have not proved universally successful.

The eclectic theory of FDI

Dunning distinguished three groups of 'advantages' that determine the propensity of a firm, industry or country to be a net recipient or exporter of FDI:

Table 16.1 Foreign involvement of 866 largest industrial firms, 1977[a]

Industry	Foreign involvement[b]			
	Overseas production ratio	Parent export ratio	Overseas sales ratio	Overseas market sourcing ratio
	$\dfrac{F}{P+F}$	$\dfrac{X}{P}$	$\dfrac{F+X}{P+F}$	$\dfrac{F}{F+X}$
High research intensity:				
Aerospace	7.5	33.8	38.7	19.3
Office equipment (incl. computers)	41.5	8.2	46.3	89.6
Petroleum	42.7	17.9	53.0	80.6
Measurement, scientific and photographic equipment	33.1	19.3	46.0	72.0
Electronics and electrical appliances	20.5	22.8	38.6	53.2
Chemicals and pharmaceuticals (incl. soap and cosmetics)	29.0	20.3	43.4	66.8
Total	33.5	20.2	47.0	71.3
Medium research intensity:				
Industrial and farm equipment	22.9	28.3	44.7	51.2
Shipbuilding, railroad and transportation equipment	8.8	32.2	38.2	23.1
Rubber	34.2	7.0	38.8	88.1
Motor vehicles (incl. components)	20.6	20.7	37.0	55.7
Metal manufacturing and products	13.5	23.2	33.5	40.3
Total	18.4	22.7	36.9	49.8
Low research intensity:				
Bulding materials	27.9	8.3	33.9	82.3
Tobacco	40.8	5.9	44.3	92.1
Beverages	17.4	3.8	20.5	84.7
Food	28.8	5.1	32.5	88.8
Paper and wood products	18.1	15.9	31.1	58.1
Textiles, apparel, leather goods	15.5	15.1	28.3	54.8
Publishing and printing	9.2	2.7	11.6	78.9
Total	25.0	8.3	31.2	80.2
Other manufacturing	5.8	14.8	19.7	29.6
TOTAL	26.6	18.8	40.4	65.9

Notes:
[a] Although the data refer only to the largest firms they are probably not unrepresentative of all firms.
[b] In symbols, F is sales by subsidiaries outside parent's home country; P is parent's total sales; and X is parent's exports.
Source: Dunning and Pearce (1981), Table 6.6.

- *Ownership advantages* – factors that enable a particular firm to expand at all, e.g. rights to particular technologies or supplies of factors.
- *Internalisation advantages* – whether expansion is best accomplished within the firm, or by selling the rights to the means of expansion to other firms.
- *Locational advantages* – whether expansion is best achieved at home or abroad (regardless of who undertakes it). This is essentially a question of comparative advantage.

We shall examine the determinants of these advantages later, but first we see how they fit together to influence FDI, as a form of foreign involvement.

Suppose there is a foreign demand for X and that a particular domestic firm has an ownership advantage in X. Table 16.2 relates this firm's approach to expansion to its other advantages. If there is no internalisation gain, the firm may as well license its ownership advantage to another firm; this is especially so if locational factors indicate expansion abroad, because foreign firms will normally be better attuned to local conditions and hence better able to manage such expansion than our own firm. If, on the other hand, there are internalisation gains, our firm should undertake the expansion itself; if locational factors favour home expansion it expands at home and exports, whereas if they favour foreign expansion FDI occurs and an MNE is born. Observe how all three advantages are necessary to induce multinational activity.

Table 16.2 The foreign involvement decision

| | Locational advantage | |
	Abroad	Home
Internalisation advantage		
Yes	MNE	export
No	license, abroad	license, home

An alternative formalisation of the export/FDI decision is due to Hirsch (1976). Again assume demand exists in country A, and that a firm in country B is deciding its policy. It considers four groups of costs:

P_A, P_B production costs in A and B respectively – the *locational variables*;

K the cost to *other firms* of matching our firms' knowledge and intangible assets; i.e. our firm's *ownership advantages*;

M the additional cost of exporting to A rather than selling local produce (e.g. transport, tariffs, etc.); and

C the additional cost of controlling a plant abroad rather than at home.

M and C are elements of the *internalisation advantages*.

These costs identify three alternatives for serving A:

(i) a local firm sets up in A, with costs $(P_A + K)$, i.e. it has to overcome our ownership advantages;

(ii) our firm exports, with costs $(P_B + M)$; and

(iii) our firm establishes a foreign plant, with costs $(P_A + C)$.

Assuming that the good produced is identical under all three outcomes, and that there are no further complications such as dynamic or strategic factors to consider, the least-cost choice will be made.

If the foreign firm's costs $(P_A + K)$ are least, there is perhaps also scope for licensing to occur: if A is going to erode B's ownership advantages anyway, B may as well benefit from that by selling them to A at slightly under K.

This example is grossly over-simplified, because many different considerations enter the simple costs K, M and C (as we shall see below), but it does provide a framework on which to hang a more realistic analysis. It also stresses that it is relative, not absolute, advantages that are important in determining FDI.

Ownership advantages Ownership advantages are advantages specific to the expanding firm relative to its competitors overseas. They are a necessary condition for FDI and stem from various market imperfections. (Under perfect competition firms are identical.) They may already exist within a firm, or alternatively arise only through the act of FDI. We consider the former category first.

Technology. The expanding firm may have superior products, processes, management techniques or marketing skills. Ignoring the costs of technology transfer, such factors are *public goods* within the firm, because their use in one area does not reduce the amount usable elsewhere. They therefore provide an ideal base for expansion. Such advantages are frequently embodied within an existing skilled labour force.

Industrial organisation and size. Large and diversified firms may be better equipped for innovation and certainly have more resources to fight price wars or legal suits over patents. Monopolies have excess profits and less concern over technology leaking out to rivals. Large firms are more likely to have reaped firm-level economies of scale, for instance in marketing, research and finance.

Access. Access to raw materials may be embodied in property rights, while access to markets may arise from government action. Companies backed by large and powerful governments may derive advantages in other markets through their governments' political influence.

Finance. Large and diverse firms are frequently able to raise money more cheaply than others, largely because their profits show less variability. This may apply to a firm with several interests in a single country, but is more likely to apply once a firm has become multinational. Operating and selling in several countries stabilises profits because problems in one country are normally offset by success in another. Since investors desire stability they are willing to buy MNE shares at relatively high prices. This argument is frequently rejected by arguing that, rather than buy equity in a single firm operating in many countries, investors could get equal stability but more flexibility by buying equity in separate firms in each country. This, however, ignores the transaction costs, exchange restrictions and imperfect knowledge that would blight such an alternative. MNEs therefore offer investors a cheap and simple method of geographical diversification.

Ownership advantages also arise directly from multinationality itself via MNEs' access to many capital markets, their ability to deal freely in many currencies, the ease with which they can shift activity in response to changing factor endowments and governments policy, and their freedom from dependence on a single government.

Internalisation advantages Many economists feel that internalisation is the key condition for FDI. Internalisation gains arise if market imperfections prevent the effective sale of ownership advantages to other firms, thus making their exploitation by their original owner the only possibility. The role of internalisation was first identified in a classic article by Coase (1937). Coase asked why the market ruled for transactions *between* firms, but not for transactions *within* firms. The reason is that in the latter case transactions costs outweigh any efficiency gains that the market may have over administrative allocation. He further suggested that any transactions subject to such market costs would eventually be internalised – that is, brought under one administrative head to eliminate the market.

The nature of the market failures giving rise to FDI clearly depend on the ownership advantage whose sale is impeded, but we give here some examples.

Costs of negotiation. If legal charges or stamp duty are very high for example contract-making may be discouraged. Closely related is the impossibility of transferring some things to other firms – e.g. the ingenuity of a particular personnel manager.

Opportunism. Suppose I have a simple idea for making £1m. How can I persuade you to pay £0.5m. for it without revealing so much that you discover it for nothing? Conversely, unless you see it first, how can you know it is worth anything? This problem blights technological and managerial innovations, especially where patent control is weak. Related to this is

Uncertainty. Suppose we can fix the sale somehow; neither of us can be sure it will work until afterwards, and this uncertainty is likely to reduce your offer price.

Control over the use of the advantage. For example, if the advantage resides in brand loyalty, the production of poor goods under a brand-mark damages all users of that mark, not just the offending licensee. Alternatively, selling your latest technology to rivals increases the probability that they will improve on it and overtake you in future.

Unexploited economies of scale. These are frequently argued to apply to under-utilised managerial capacity: a firm cannot generally hire out 20 per cent of its management capacity, and so to use it the firm must expand itself. Relatedly, the acquisition of *monopoly power* through expansion is also a (private) internalisation gain, as is any *financial benefit* from foreign diversification.

Taxes and tariffs. By manipulating the prices of *intra-firm* sales of parts or services, a firm may be able to reduce the taxes or tariffs that would hit market transactions. This is known as *transfer pricing*. Although it is illegal in nearly all countries, it is probably widespread because it is almost impossible for the authorities to know what the 'correct' price should be. This is especially so for transfers of technical or managerial services from HQ to subsidiaries. Kopits (1976) suggested that MNE subsidiaries in the UK probably pay 30–50 per cent more than they should for such services.

Internalisation advantages all arise from market imperfections. Their precise nature depends on the ownership advantage whose transfer is blocked: some give rise to huge internalisation gains (e.g. management capacity), others very few (e.g. mining rights, which can easily be let).

Locational advantages

Locational advantages provide the international element of multinationality. They derive from the mainstream of international economics, essentially reflecting comparative advantage or distortions of it. Obvious contributors are: the *relative transportation costs* of raw materials and finished goods; the *locations* of materials and markets; the *cultural similarities* between an MNE's home and potential host countries; *unexploited economies of scale* at plant level; *factor endowments*; government *tax concessions, tariff rates, investment grants, etc.*, and *risks* of expropriation.

Under this heading we should perhaps note a fact that apparently does not explain FDI: relative rates of return. If different countries have different rates of return on capital, simple theory would lead us to expect a migration of capital towards the higher returns. While this explains some of the American outflow of investment since 1950, it cannot explain the preference for direct over portfolio investment, or why the outflow of FDI was partly balanced by a portfolio inflow.

There is much descriptive empirical work on MNEs, but less formal hypothesis testing; this is because of the formidable difficulties of measuring the various effects just described – especially those pertaining to internalisation. As with intra-industry trade – to which FDI research is often linked – conclusions tend to vary according to which proxies are used for immeasurable effects.

Caves (1974a) considered the shares of US subsidaries in the output of cross-sections of UK and Canadian industries, relating them to 'intangible assets', the propensity to multi-plant production at home, entrepreneurial capacity and locations factors. 'Intangibles' included research effort, advertising intensity, size and economies of scale. These all represent ownership advantages, and they proved, especially the first two, significant explanations for both Canadian and UK samples. Multi-plant activity basically reflects internalisation: the MNE is, after all, just a special form of multi-plant operation. It proved important for the US share of Canadian industry, but not for the UK. The entrepreneurial hypotheses (either ownership or internalisation) received no support, while locational factors (relative wages) helped explain US penetration of UK industry.

Caves found little role for firm size in explaining FDI. Horst (1972) replicated this result in an industry cross-section of US investment in Canada, finding only the extent of the Canadian market and the level of protection signficant; however *within* an industry he concluded that *only* size distinguishes MNEs from single-country firms. That is, size captures all the firm-specific ownership and internalisation advantages such as innovativeness, bargaining power and spreading fixed costs.

Further evidence on size comes from Wolf (1977). He compared three modes of expansion – diversification at home, exporting and FDI – and related them, across US industries, to average firm size and technological level (the proportion of scientists and engineers in total employment). He found domestic diversification more closely related to size, and foreign involvement (exports plus FDI) more closely related to technology. Within the latter, however, industries with large firms showed more bias towards FDI than others. Hence, while technological leadership helps foreign involvement (ownership advantages), large firm sizes appear to relate to multi-plant expansion at home and abroad.

A refinement of the eclectic theory investigated by Lall (1980) concerns the transferability of ownership advantages. We have so far implicitly considered them costlessly transferable public goods within the MNE, but this is too simple. Lall examined various ownership advantages and argued that those most easily transferable geographically will give rise to most FDI. American MNEs' advantages will be non-transferable if they are tied either to the firms' HQs or to the US economy. He argued that new technology falls into the former class (cf. the product cycle), whereas plant economies of scale and skilled manual labour fall into the latter. All these variables stimulate exports relative to FDI, although technology and plant economies do affect FDI positively to some extent. Among transferable ownership advantages, which boost FDI as a share of foreign involvement, are product differentiation (advertising) and managerial inputs.

FDI is related to three groups of 'advantages': ownership, internalisation and location. Internalisation has proved difficult to pin down empirically, although theoretically it is crucial. The other two have received empirical support. The most important ownership advantages for FDI appear to be technological sophistication, advertising intensity and economies of scale on an industry level, and size at a firm level. The role of technology is plainly visible from column 1 of Table 16.1. Case-study 16.1, on the international hotel industry, illustrates how the three effects interact in a real example.

CASE-STUDY 16.1: MULTINATIONAL HOTEL CHAINS

The Hilton, the Sheraton, Holiday Inn, Hyatt International: no city is complete without its crop of international hotels. Why do business customers use these soulless giants rather than characterful local hotels? Dunning's eclectic theory (Dunning and McQueen, 1981, and Dunning, 1988) offers some insight.

The eclectic theory explains multinational investment in terms of location, ownership and internalisation advantages. In the hotel business, *location* is fairly much determined – hotels need to be where people want to go – although international conference facilities are somewhat foot-loose, and choice may be possible close to international borders. If so, the usual factors such as the supply of staff, taxation and investment grants will be influential.

Ownership advantages are most important. The prime one is reputation. Hotels are 'experience' goods – inspection before purchase is usually impossible, so the best guide to the quality and nature of service is previous experience of a chain. This explains the alleged characterlessness of international chains; they are attractive precisely because they are uniform and hence largely riskless for the customer. Chains also have advantages in terms of production experience. The intangible and logistical skills of providing hotel services are transferable within the chain; having solved the problems in Memphis it is easier to establish in Mombasa. The high expenditure on internal staff training and the mobility of senior management within the chains indicate these advantages. Similar advantages may be evident in central purchasing and in the design of the packages of services that customers want.

Further ownership advantages accrue through reservation systems. Centralised reservation facilities and onward-booking between hotels in the same chain help chains out-compete local firms for international custom, and connections with airlines and tour operators are also important. These are ownership rather than internalisation issues, because they reduce the customers', not the MNE's, transactions costs. Reservation facilities could be established between independent groups for little difference in cost.

Genuine *internalisation advantages* arise from control. The joint control of hotels within a chain is necessary not so much to prevent undue competition as to ensure the quality and efficiency required to preserve the chain's brand image. The means and criteria for this are fairly easy to codify and hence may be embodied in contracts, with the result that the ownership and management of hotels may be separated. Franchising is not common in high-quality chains, but the long-term delegation of the management of the whole chain to a separate firm is. (Long-term contracts are necessary to ensure the management's continued interest in the chain's reputation.) Managing hotel chains is quite different from the multi-currency financing and property development skills that are entailed in hotel ownership; hence in the hotel trade the division of ownership and (active) control is quite feasible. Ownership has a strong element of portfolio investment, while it is management that encourages direct multinationality.

16.3   MULTINATIONALS AND WELFARE

Multinationals affect the welfare of both their home and host countries. This section concentrates mainly on the latter, but some comments are passed on the former. MNEs maximise profits on a world scale – shifting resources to areas where their returns are highest and buying inputs where their prices are lowest. Such efficiency would seem sure to increase world welfare; however, because MNEs exist primarily because of market imperfections, this is not necessarily so. As we saw above, unless all markets are perfect, growth in one sector need not be beneficial: improved resource allocation has to be traded against (possible) increases in market imperfections.

Pure capital flows   We start by considering a pure capital flow between countries, devoid of any of the special advantages listed above. Assume two countries, a single good and a fixed world stock of capital. In Figure 16.1, MPK_A represents the marginal product of capital in country A, which, assuming perfect markets and constant returns to scale, equals capital's return (rent) in A. More capital involves lower rents by diminishing marginal returns. MPK_B is the corresponding schedule for B, but measured from origin O_B rather than O_A. In the absence of capital mobility, let A have $O_A K$ of capital and B, $O_B K$. Assuming no factor price equalisation, rentals are r_A and r_B respectively.

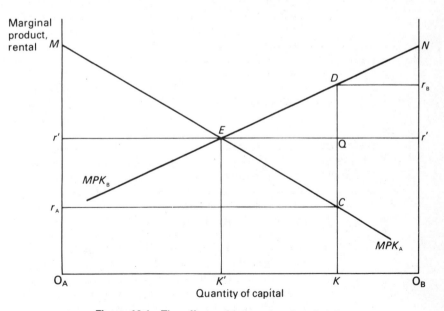

Figure 16.1   The effects of international capital flow

If capital were now allowed to move (costlessly), it would flow from A to B in search of higher rewards. Rentals in A would rise and those in B fall, until ultimately both would equal r' and the world stock of capital would be allocated $O_A K'$ and $O_B K'$. This involves a gain in world output. When the first unit of capital is shifted, country A's output falls by $KC (= MPK_A)$ but B's rises by $KD (= MPK_B)$. Repeating this analysis for every unit, world output increases by area CED.

The flow also has implications for the distribution of income. Without mobility, capitalists in A earn area $O_A KCr_A$, i.e. capital stock multiplied by rental. The remainder of A's output, MCr_A, accrues to labour. (A's output is the area under MPK_A: the first unit of capital produces $O_A M$, the second slightly less, until the last produces KC; the total is the sum of these amounts, namely area $O_A MCK$). After the switch, labour's returns fall to MEr'. Labour in B, on the other hand, increases its earnings from NDr_B to NEr' because it has more capital to work with. A's capitalists gain from the change (assuming they still own the capital switched to B), because their returns rise with no change in quantity owned, while B's capitalists suffer. Taking countries as a whole, capital mobility means that income and output now differ. For example, after the switch, A produces $O_A MEK'$, but earns $(MEr' + O_A KQr')$; B produces $O_B NEK'$, but earns $(NEr' + O_B KQr')$. Note that, although A loses output by exporting capital, it gains income (by amount EQC). B gains both output and income.

Thus we see that pure capital mobility with perfect markets raises both countries' incomes – and hence world income. Even in this simple case, however, complex distributional changes occur. In particular, if no redistribution occurs, labour in the exporting country and capitalists in the importing country lose from capital mobility.

Generalising, now, to several goods we can develop some further results. For example, the Rybczynski theorem (or its specific factor analogue) states that, for a small country, a capital inflow absolutely reduces output (specific factor rewards) in the labour-intensive industry. Similarly, for a large country, immiserising growth is possible if FDI substantially reduces the relative price of an inelastically demanded export. In both these cases, the costs to local residents are greater than in the standard cases because the returns to the 'new' capital accrue abroad.

We now look at MNEs in a less rigorous but more realistic fashion. Following Hood and Young (1979) we consider their effects under three headings: resource transfer effects, balance of payments effects, and sovereignty.

Resource transfer effects

MNEs transfer to their hosts bundles of resources comprising different proportions of technology, management, sales ability and capital. If capital alone is required, it is much more cheaply available through other borrowing, so FDI should not be viewed simply as a source of capital. Furthermore, MNEs often raise local funds and, if through their market power they can do so cheaply, their presence could crowd out other socially desirable activities.

Technology is the most significant component of the package – at least to developing countries which have no alternative sources for it. Any problems arise from the terms on which it is bought. MNEs are very skilled negotiators (see below) and in a bilateral negotiation with the government of a poor country are likely to be able to strike a very favourable bargain. This is particularly so over technology where the buyer has so little information. Hence royalties are often high, and licences to use technology restricted in terms of servicing, the provision of parts, the extent of development permitted, etc. There is also complaint about the appropriateness of technology. MNEs frequently pass old techniques from the developed countries on to developing countries without any adaptation. These can be too capital-intensive for the local economy, resulting in a 'dualistic' structure: a small advanced industrial sector linked to the outside world surrounded by a large, capital-starved poor sector. For developed hosts, however, the opposite complaint is often heard: MNEs' technology is too unsophisticated, and local R&D is reduced in favour of R&D at head office.

The effect of the management component on economic welfare is two-edged. MNEs may train local management who then move into local business to its benefit. Britain is also thought to have benefited from such a flow from US subsidiaries, and also from local managers emulating their MNE colleagues. Alternatively, by paying relatively well and conferring great status, MNEs may absorb entrepreneurial talents from local enterprise.

Overall, MNEs probably raise their hosts' efficiency. They tend to improve allocation by (a) concentrating on a country's comparative advantage goods (the locational advantage), (b) stimulating competition, (c) demonstrating better techniques, and (d) introducing technology. Caves (1974b), for example, reported that in Australian industries the share of MNEs in output is positively related to productivity and negatively to profits. It is not clear, however, either that this is always the case, or that, even when efficiency does improve, most or even any of the gains accrue locally. The cases where efficiency does not improve arise where the MNEs introduce more distortions into the economy.

Balance of payments effects

MNEs are often blamed for their balance of payments effects: the capital-exporting country faces a large sudden deficit when the FDI occurs, while the host faces a small perpetual deficit as profits are repatriated. The corresponding benefits are usually forgotten. The exporter's deficit can be troublesome if it pushes the balance of payments into crisis, stimulating harsh corrective measures. In theory, if the investment is sound, the country should be able to borrow abroad to finance it, for a sound investment will generate the wherewithal to service the debt (and more). In practice, however, this is not always the case because, unless the investing company undertakes the borrowing itself (which it might not wish to do, if, say, it had large domestic cash balances), the potential lenders may not know about the direct investment or be able to assess its viability. To them, it may merely look like capital flight, which will not encourage them to lend.

The host country's perpetual deficit will also be problematic if the investment is unsound, because then it will not generate the income for its own service. A sound investment should not produce such difficulties, although it may imply a change in the relative price of tradable and non-tradable goods if the FDI is in a non-tradable sector, since profit repatriation must eventually be paid for in tradable goods. This may involve some costly restructuring elsewhere in the economy and/or make economic policy more difficult to conduct; however, it seems unlikely to make a sound investment harmful absolutely.

Hence the basic problem seems to be one of unsound investment; as we saw before, only market imperfections can make socially unsound projects privately profitable. A related, but conceptually different, problem concerning uncertainty should also be mentioned here. A change in the environment could render an initially sound project unprofitable, both socially and

229

privately. FDI clearly affects the exposure of the economy to different exogenous shocks, but this observation justifies intervention only if the government has better information than private agents about future shocks (or if shocks have different private and social impacts).

Concern has also been expressed over the effects of MNEs on trade flows. MNEs are often thought to be more trade-intensive than other companies, but this reflects the industries they inhabit more than their own behaviour. In Britain, for example, Solomon and Ingham (1977) suggested that MNEs export less than home firms in engineering industries, while Panić and Joyce (1980) suggested that their exports were stagnant relative to other firms' over the 1970s. On the other hand, there is evidence that subsidiaries tend to import parts and capital equipment from the home country, and also finished goods for models not made locally. For example, Ford (UK) claims to be both the largest exporter and the largest importer of vehicles in Britain. The use of imported components absorbs foreign exchange and reduces MNEs' stimulus to the local economy. In the end, however, unless there are identifiable market failures – e.g. MNE monopsony in factor markets or disequilibrium exchange rates – there is no case for intervention to change MNE trade behaviour.

Sovereignty

Sovereignty lies at the heart of many of the concerns voiced so far. MNEs are less dependent on their host countries, or countries of origin, than domestic companies, and are consequently more difficult to control. This is particularly the case for subsidiaries in developing countries, which are often implicitly protected by the political power of their home country. It is not at all unknown for MNEs to pursue covert political objectives in their host countries – for example, ITT's resistance to Allende's regime in Chile in the early 1970s.

By means of their internationality, MNEs are frequently able to circumvent local economic policies, for example by frustrating credit squeezes or avoiding exchange restrictions by transferring money from abroad. They are also, by means of their political and economic power, more able to confront local policy directly. For example, when Ford (UK) broke the British government's pay policy in 1978 the government proved quite powerless.

Possibly even more disturbing, MNEs are able to influence government policy, especially when they are selecting a site for expansion. This can lead to distortions and loss. Host governments are keen to attract investment, and MNEs, with their large resources and experience, are able to dominate local governments in negotiations. In particular, host governments lack the information needed to assess what incentives have to be offered to secure the investment. The result is that MNEs are often able to obtain investment grants, tax holidays, protection, etc., in excess of their needs and sometimes in excess of the benefits they bring to the host nation. The countries of the Andean Pact (in northern Latin America) have sought quite successfully to overcome this by pooling information on MNEs (Vaitsos, 1976), and similar efforts have been made in the EC. Nevertheless, when in the late 1970s Ford planned to build a new engine plant in Europe they played one country against another (notably Spain, Belgium and the UK), to the extent of persuading the UK, the final choice, to pay nearly half the capital costs of the project.

Less dramatically, the restrictions that MNEs impose on their subsidiaries frequently prevent the subsidiaries from behaving optimally. For example, Hood and Young (1979) reported that 75 per cent of subsidiaries in Scotland carried out no R&D at all, and that 81 per cent of Andean subsidiaries were subject to restrictions on their exports; Steuer (1973) reported that 30 per cent of UK subsidiaries had their exports controlled by their head office. These restrictions can clearly be harmful to the host nation.

Conclusion

It is difficult to generalise about MNEs because their behaviour and circumstances are so varied. Their success at becoming multinational suggests some degree of efficiency, and their movement of resources to areas of highest return suggests that they improve resource allocation. The competition of hosts for their presence also suggests that they are felt to be beneficial, because they boost output, offer employment, pay taxes and stimulate competition. Against this we must note that their *raison d'être* is market imperfections and that their existence and growth may strengthen such distortions in the ways we have just discussed. In summary, MNEs probably increase world income, but given their distributional effects their growth may not be Pareto improving. The cases where they are not beneficial arise from economic distortions; if the distortions are of the MNEs' making, there is a case for corrective action against them but, if they are merely exploiting existing distortions (e.g. existing investment grants, etc.), it is the distortions that are at fault. Indeed MNEs may even be beneficial in undermining local distortions or bad policy.

The capital exporter

We have already sketched some welfare and balance of payments effects on the capital exporter and we now consider them slightly more thoroughly. The important question for the exporter is: what is the alternative to FDI? Three possibilities exist: (i) no investment occurs, (ii) the investing country invests at home, or (iii) some foreign firm makes the (foreign) investment. Presumably the firm will not undertake FDI unless it thinks it privately profitable, so our question is whether the investment is *socially* desirable.

Under alternatives (i) and (iii) – i.e. when there is no alternative home investment – the main wedge between private and social gains concerns the balance of payments. If the investment would cause a balance of payments crisis, maybe it should be financed from abroad. However, as we noted above, if the investment is sound it is not obvious why it should cause a crisis. Under (i) one might also consider that FDI raises the world capital stock in the industry concerned and hence reduces the rate of return. If much of the existing stock is owned by our nationals, this reduction in their earnings must be balanced against the increase in the earnings of the investing company.

Alternative (ii) assumes an equivalent home investment is feasible. This introduces several other possible private–social wedges. First, *taxation*: the private company looks at profits net of tax, caring not to whom the tax is paid. Socially, however, we would prefer taxes to be paid to us rather than to foreigners. Second, *default risk*: investors make allowance for the default or confiscation of their investment. If default occurs abroad, both private and social losses occur, but, if it occurs at home, the same private loss occurs but no social loss, because the investment remains with our nationals. Third, *externalities*: if the domestic economy suffers unemployment, domestic investment will reduce it via the multiplier. Similarly Balogh and Streeten (1960) argued that the economy is in perpetual disequilibrium, so that one investment creates scope for another: e.g. a shoe factor generates opportunities for a new tannery, which generates demand for hides, etc. With domestic investment, most of this dynamic linkage occurs at home; with foreign investment, abroad.

231

All these arguments suggest that, if there is a genuine choice between equivalent domestic and overseas investments, private criteria will over-emphasise the latter. Much of the agitation against FDI presupposes this choice exists, but we suspect that this is not so. Domestic investment may be available, but only for lower social returns than FDI. Hence this sub-section suggests reasons for being careful over FDI, not for automatically restricting it.

16.4 MULTINATIONALS AND INTERNATIONAL TRADE THEORY

The gap between the analysis of this chapter, relying on imperfect competition, and the bulk of international trade theory, relying on perfect competition, is obvious. The Ricardian theory of trade can incorporate capital flows but not direct investment. With Heckscher–Ohlin, trade and factor movements are entirely substitutable: trade equalises factor prices, eliminating any need for factor mobility, whereas, if factor mobility equalised factor prices, commodity prices would be equalised, thus eliminating trade. Only the modern theories of Chapter 5 are compatible with FDI, and they relate trade and investment to the same stimuli. This, and the extent to which MNEs shift components and finished goods between branches (intra-firm trade), suggest that trade and FDI may well be complementary.

Trade theory is not well developed for imperfect competition, so that aspects of FDI presents considerable analytical difficulties. If, however, we ignore this, the foreign ownership aspect presents few problems. MNEs respond to comparative advantage (their locational decisions), and, given their lack of dependence on any one country, are possibly more sensitive to changes in comparative advantage than are national firms. We saw above how trade and growth theory could handle capital flows once we allow for production in one country to be income in another. Finally, although MNEs might influence the pattern of commercial policy, or reduce its effectiveness, they do not affect the fundamental analysis. Thus, while MNEs are an important topic for further research, their existence does not demolish international trade theory, as has sometimes been claimed.

FURTHER READING

Mundell (1957) is the classic on factor mobility, while more recent work includes the essays in *Bhagwati* (1983b) and the *Journal of International Economics*, vol. 14, no. 3/4 (1983). MNEs have a complete literature of their own. Among textbooks *Grubel* (1981) and *Lindert and Kindleberger* (1982) offer some detail on this topic, but the best introductions are two book-length surveys: *Hood and Young* (1979) and *Caves* (1982). Two useful collections of essays are *Dunning* (1972, 1974); see especially *Horst* and *Streeten* in the latter. On the causes of FDI, *Caves* (1974a), *Dunning* (1979) and *Lall* (1980) are important, while *Hymer* (1979) is a classic reference. *Dunning* (1988) is useful on the eclectic theory. *Lipsey and Weiss* (1981) examine exports and FDI empirically, while *Reddaway* (1968) provides a wealth of data on balance of payments effects. *Lall* (1973) examines transfer pricing in detail. For the role of MNEs in developing countries, *Lall and Streeten* (1977) is an excellent study of both theory and empirical evidence, and *Vaitsos* (1974, 1976) provides a strong critique. *Helleiner* (1973) provides evidence on the question of trade. *Helpman and Krugman* (1985) integrates MNEs into the theory of trade under imperfect competition.

KEY CONCEPTS

factor price equalisation
and world welfare
portfolio investment vs. FDI
licensing
ownership advantages

imperfect competition
locational advantages
internalisation
externalities
marginal product of capital

QUESTIONS FOR REVIEW

16.1 In what circumstances are trade in goods and factor mobility equivalent? What are the transactions costs involved in each?

16.2 Why do firms not always license their brands to foreign companies?

16.3 When countries close their borders to Japanese goods, the Japanese sometimes invest behind the restrictions. Should this be encouraged or not?

16.4 What industry characteristics are likely to lead to a high incidence of FDI?

Part II

17 The Balance of Payments

Part I of this book dealt with the causes of effects of international trade in a barter economy. Every transaction involved the exchange of one good for another. We now add an element of realism by introducing money. In the real world, virtually every transaction involves swapping goods (or assets) for money. This, of course, is much more efficient than barter: it removes the need for the double coincidence of wants and it allows one to sell in one period and buy in another. However, it also introduces additional analytical problems: we have to consider the causes and consequences of imbalance between sales and purchases, we have to recognise that money and financial assets may cross international borders, and we have to handle additional relative prices – in particular the price of one country's money in terms of another's. Adding money also allows us more easily to aggregate trade flows in the many different goods that exist, and takes us naturally into the macro-economics of the international economy.

Part II of this book tackles these problems. It considers the determinants of the level of exports and imports – prices, incomes and various non-price factors – and examines the interaction of international trade and national income. It looks at the foreign exchange market and seeks explanations of the movements in exchange rates. It considers how exchange rates affect the macro-economic control of an economy and its insulation from economic shocks abroad, and it also discusses the pros and cons of the floating exchange rates. Finally, combining all this analysis it considers the impact of the oil price rises of the 1970s, the discovery of North Sea oil and the US deficits of the 1980s.

This chapter sets the scene for these analyses by introducing two important concepts. Before we can discuss international transactions meaningfully, we must measure them. This is done in section 17.1, where the balance of payments accounts are described. Section 17.2 offers a very brief description of the main British international transactions. Section 17.3 then introduces the exchange rate, defining various concepts and briefly surveying recent experience. Finally, section 17.4 summarises the remaining chapters of Part II.

17.1 BALANCE OF PAYMENTS CONCEPTS

The principles   The balance of payments accounts record all economic transactions between a country's residents and the rest of the world. These include not only buying and selling goods and assets, but also, for example, gifts, and transfers within companies when no money changes hands. Residents include individuals who live permanently within the country, government agencies and companies, although not their overseas subsidiaries.

In theory, the accounts are drawn up by double-entry bookkeeping methods, by which every transaction appears twice, once as a credit and once as a debit; that is, broadly speaking, once as the object bought or sold is transferred, and once as payment is made for it. We define a credit (recorded with a + sign) as any transaction notionally giving rise to an inflow of cash,

237

and a debit (−) as any transaction notionally causing an outflow of cash. Consider the following simple examples, which are recorded in Table 17.1.

(i) An export worth £5 bartered for an import worth £5. We record + £5 for the export (notional cash inflow) and − £5 for imports (cash outflow).

(ii) An export worth £10 paid for by the (foreign) importer running down his bank balance in London. We record + £10 for the export and − £10 for the reduction in foreign holdings of sterling.

(iii) An export worth £10 paid for in foreign currency. We record + £10 for the export and − £10 for the increase in domestic holdings of foreign cash. (Holding foreign cash amounts to making a deposit in a foreign central bank, and this requires an outflow of cash.)

(iv) The purchase, for £100, of a foreign subsidiary by a British firm, financed by borrowing abroad. We record − £100 for the purchase, and + £100 for the increase in foreign holdings of sterling.

(v) The repayment of the debt incurred in (iv) from the subsidiary's earnings. We record + £100 for the inflow of profits and − £100 for the reduction in foreign claims.

Table 17.1 A specimen balance of payments account

Credits (+)			Debits (−)		
Exports	£25	(i + ii + iii)	Imports	£5	(i)
Profits from abroad	£100	(v)			
			Investment abroad	£100	(iv)
			Reduction in foreign holdings of £	£10	(ii)
			Increase in holdings of foreign currency	£10	(iii)
Increase in claims by foreigners	£100	(iv)	Reduction in claims by foreigners	£100	(v)

Observe that, although we define our signs by reference to notional cash flow, no flow need actually occur. For example, transaction (i) involved no cash at all, and transactions (iv) and (v) could be effected entirely abroad, with no money crossing the British border. In Table 17.1 we recorded separately both an increase and a decrease in claims by foreigners; in all actual accounts, however, these are combined to yield a single figure for changes in net liabilities, rises in which are recorded as a credit.

Two transactions do not fall happily into this system. First, gifts. A gift of sterling to a foreigner is recorded as a debit under transfers, and the corresponding credit is, say, the increase in claims by foreigners as the recipient banks his gift in London. Gifts of goods are recorded as exports of goods with the debit item recorded as a transfer, just as if we made a gift of money that was immediately spent on British exports. The second difficulty concerns the foreign exchange reserves. The government holds a stock of foreign currency, and when this is reduced it is recorded in the balance of payments accounts as a credit (+). Think of the reserves as comprising stocks of gold (as they used to), which can only be sold abroad. A reduction in the stock involves exporting and hence receives a + sign.

Balance of payments disequilibrium

Since every transaction enters the balance of payments account twice (with opposite signs), the sum of the account must be zero. What, then, constitutes balance of payments disequilibrium? Disequilibrium is when some crucial subset of the accounts fails to sum to zero. What is crucial depends on the question being asked, and we shall discover below that there are several subsets, or balances, of interest. Economists refer to the selection of the 'crucial' subset as 'drawing the line'. If we imagine all transactions listed in a column, we put the ones of interest 'above the line' and the rest 'below the line'. Clearly, if the whole column sums to zero, the sum (balance) above the line must be equal and opposite to the sum below the line. Equilibrium requires that both be zero.

Normally we are interested in having balance over *autonomous transactions*. These are transactions that occur regardless of the size of other items in the balance of payments – i.e. transactions undertaken in their own right. The remaining transactions, called *accommodating transactions*, occur only to complete some other foreign transaction. For example, exporting goods is autonomous, but the resulting increase in balances of foreign currencies is accommodating. It is obviously impossible to discover the motive of every transactor, or to classify all motives unambiguously as either autonomous or accommodating. We therefore adopt various conventions of classification, and different conventions give rise to different balance of payments concepts.

The UK balance of payments accounts

We now illustrate the principles of balance of payments accounting by looking at the layout of the UK accounts. These are summarised in Table 17.2.

The current account

The main element of the current account is visible trade – imports and exports of tangible, or visible, goods, the net balance of which is referred to as the *visible balance*. The remainder are invisibles, which comprise: trade in services –

Table 17.2 The UK balance of payments, 1988[a]

Current Account	£m.	
Visible balance	− 20,826	
+ services	+ 4,165	
= *Trade balance*		− 16,661
+ Interest, profits and dividends	+ 5,619	
+ Transfers	− 3,575	
= *Current balance*		− 14,617
Long-Term Capital		
+ Direct investments	− 7,873	
+ Portfolio investments	− 5,079	
+ Official long-term capital	− 190	
= *Basic balance*		− 13,142
Short-Term Capital		
+ UK banks' dealings	+ 14,595	
+ UK corporate dealings	+ 3,441	
+ UK government dealings	+ 200	
+ Balancing item	+ 12,283	
= *Balance for official financing*		2,761
Official financing		
+ Changes in official reserves	− 2,761	
+ Other official finance	0	
= *Sum*		0

Note:
[a] All figures are net – i.e. credits less debits.
Source: Central Statistical Office, *United Kingdom Balance of Payments* (1989), Tables 1.1, 1.4, 8.4, 8.5, 8.6.

239

such as earnings from providing sea and air transport to foreigners and commissions on insurance deals; interest, profits and dividends earned and paid abroad; and transfers. Service trade is conceptually identical to visible trade: the items traded have to be produced and enter the production side of the national accounts. The balances on service and visible trade comprise the *trade balance*, which shows the net claim on the country's resources that international trade imposes. Earnings from abroad record Britain's earnings from foreign production, while earnings paid abroad show the part of the incomes derived from British production that accrues to foreigners. Net earnings from abroad reflect the difference between domestic product (output produced in Britain) and national product (output owned by Britons). Finally, transfers have no direct effect on production. They merely reflect one use that income is put to, and their net value is recorded in the national accounts as an item of expenditure.

The sum of all current transactions is the *current balance*. It measures the difference between national income and national expenditure.

Let Y be national income (output plus income from abroad),
A be national expenditure,
N be sales by residents to residents,
X be sales abroad plus income earned abroad (i.e. total credits), and
M be purchases from and income paid abroad.

Now, expenditure not spend abroad must go on local goods, and similarly income not earned abroad must come from local sales. Hence:

$$Y - X = N = A - M \qquad (17.1)$$

from which

$$\text{current balance} = X - M = Y - A. \qquad (17.2)$$

We shall return to this fundamental equation of balance of payments theory below. Now we move down the accounts to look at capital transactions.

The capital accounts

Apart from occasional capital transfers, the first component of the capital account is investment, which includes direct investment, portfolio investment and certain long-term official flows. Direct investment abroad occurs when a British resident acquires direct ownership of real assets abroad, while an inflow of direct investment represents the purchase of British assets by foreigners. Portfolio investment, on the other hand, arises from dealings in long-term financial instruments such as shares and government stock. Clearly there are arbitrary elements in these definitions: for instance, how many shares in a foreign company must a resident buy before acquiring control; what constitutes a long-term instrument? You should, therefore, check your national definitions before using published figures.

The sum of the current and long-term capital balances constitutes the *basic balance*. This was once considered very important – indeed, it was identified as '*the*' balance of payments – because, with strong controls on short-term capital flows, it was felt possible to define 'basic' transactions as autonomous and all the rest as accommodating. This is no longer so, but basic balance is still significant for a country's liquidity (the amount of immediately accessible funds it has). 'Basic' deficits require financing from stocks of short-term liquid assets; and if these are scarce, the basic balance is important.

240

The remainder of the capital account considers short-term capital flows. These range from trade credits, through private loans and bank lending, to changes in foreign central banks' holdings of sterling and government stocks. Monetary transactions such as these are carried out mainly by telephone and computer links, and huge amounts of money can flow backwards and forwards during an hour. Hence, unlike the transactions above, it is impossible to record gross flows. Rather, statisticians record net flows over a period of time (e.g. a day) by comparing the stocks of assets at the beginning and end of the period. Thus, despite the relatively modest net figures, massive gross flows can occur on particular occasions.

Official financing

The final major element of the accounts is official financing. This records only accommodating transactions undertaken by official institutions. The main elements are transactions between monetary authorities (loans to or from the International Monetary Fund, or other central banks), government borrowing on foreign money markets, and changes in the UK foreign exchange reserves.

These transactions form the basis of another attempt to separate autonomous from accommodating transactions, captured in the *balance for official financing*. All private transactions and all government transactions except those explicitly aimed at managing the exchange rate are treated as autonomous. This balance therefore reflects the extent to which the monetary authorities have to intervene in the market to take up the imbalance in total private and government non-monetary transactions. It is of interest in that it summarises the pressure on the foreign exchange reserves and also the extent to which foreign transactions inject money into, or withdraw it from, the domestic economy.

By including the whole of the current and capital balances, the official financing balance clearly defines too much as autonomous – for example, many changes in private bank balances are accommodating. However, with the current high degree of international capital mobility, it is probably a more relevant summary than the basic balance, which includes too little.

The balancing item

One final component remains in Table 17.2: the balancing item. If accounting methods were perfect, double-entry accounts would always sum to zero because every transaction would appear twice – once positively and once negatively. In practice, however, we cannot simultaneously observe both sides of every transaction. We may observe you importing £100 worth of goods, but we cannot at that precise time observe whether you pay be borrowing abroad or by running down your balance of foreign exchange. All we can do is to look, at the end of the day, at how overall borrowing and cash positions have changed. Hence, for most transactions the two sides are measured independently, and, since different components of the accounts are measured with different degrees of accuracy and with slightly different timing conventions, it is no longer guaranteed that they will sum to zero. The balancing item is introduced as an extra item to ensure that, in the end, they do so. The government may be assumed to know its own transactions perfectly, so the balancing item is best thought of as a component of the current and capital balances, introduced to ensure that their sum is equal and opposite to the official financing balance.

The balancing item can be very significant in particular years, but, over the course of several years, positive and negative entries tend to cancel out, leaving a very small unexplained residual. The same is not true of balancing items summed over countries, however – as case-study 17.1 shows.

The current account again

We have seen that the current account measures the difference between national income and expenditure. We can now see that this involves net investment abroad. Drawing the line below the current account means that (ignoring the balancing item) the current balance must be equal and opposite to the sum of the capital and official financing balances. These explicitly involve dealings in foreign assets, with net acquisitions appearing with a negative sign because they involve an outflow of cash. Now suppose that we have a current surplus; the other accounts must be equally in deficit. Thus, we acquire net foreign assets, i.e. increase our wealth, by the extent of the current surplus. This is so whether the surplus is spent redeeming foreign debts, adding to the reserves or buying new foreign assets. This is, of course, precisely analogous to our personal finances. If you have a grant of £1,500 and spend only £1,400 over the year, your current assets (wealth) rise by £100.

To summarise, the current balance measures the excess of our receipts from abroad over our expenditure abroad. By definition this equals, *ex post*, the difference between national income and expenditure, and also the national net acquisition of foreign assets.

CASE-STUDY 17.1: THE CURRENT ACCOUNT DISCREPANCY

Since every transaction is a credit for one person and a debit for another, the whole world's current account balance should sum to zero. Deficits and surpluses should cancel out, but they don't. Since 1979 the sum of all countries' current accounts has been large and negative (see Table 17.3), which implies that some deficits are being overstated and/or some surpluses understated. This is potentially a serious problem because balance of payments difficulties influence economic policy. Incomplete statistics may generate inappropriate policy and, with the red ink on the world current account exceeding $100b. in 1982, the potential for unduly contractionary policies being adopted was acute.

Three components of the current account accounted for over 85 per cent of apparent world deficit in 1983–4: investment income, shipping and transportation, and official unrequited transfers.

Table 17.3 Reported world current account balances, 1978 84 ($USb.)

	1978	1981	1984
Trade balance	18.1	24.9	11.0
Service balance			
of which transportation + travel	– 26.2	– 40.1	– 30.1
investment income	– 4.1	– 22.6	– 47.5
Transfers	– 13.0	– 14.2	– 10.5
of which official	– 17.5	– 18.9	– 14.2
Current account	– 19.7	– 69.0	– 95.8

Source: International Monetary Fund (1987).

Investment income was the most serious problem, not only because it was the largest single discrepancy but also because it was persistently rising. Since 1979 when the controls regulating capital flows began to be loosened, a large stock of cross-border assets has grown up. Debits in this stock are more easily recognised than credits because the private non-bank sector reduces its tax bill by revealing its liabilities but not its assets. The authorities cannot recognise this asymmetry through national flow of funds' statistics because offshore financial centres and financial instruments take many transactions beyond their view. Thus, if a UK firm reports a sterling debt in the Cayman Islands, the UK government has no means of corroborating its existence.

The reason for the shipping discrepancy is that several economies with large maritime sectors (e.g. Greece, Hong Kong and Eastern Europe) do not report the freight earnings of their fleets. There is also poor reporting of port expenditure by fleets, which are debits for the 'shipping' country but credits for the 'port' country.

17.2 UK FOREIGN TRANSACTIONS

We now turn from the form to the content of the balance of payments accounts, and consider briefly the nature and size of the UK's various foreign transactions. These are described in figures and tables that you should look at carefully. The text outlines only the most obvious features. We do not consider the measurement of the various series. For anyone wishing to use these data, this essential question should be pursued in the official literature – e.g. Central Statistical Office, *United Kingdom Balance of Payments* (annual) and *Economic Trends* (monthly); Department of Trade and Industry, *British Business* (weekly).

Visible trade
Visibles account for the bulk of Britain's current transactions. Their pattern in 1987 is summarised in Figure 17.1 (lower part) and Table 17.4. Table 17.4 shows the huge extent to which British trade has become concentrated on the EC. It also clearly shows that EC links have primarily displaced links with the Commonwealth countries – Britain's traditional markets. North Sea oil is evident in the recent switch from deficit to surplus with oil-exporting countries.

Possibly the most striking feature of the commodity composition of visible trade is the similarity of exports and imports in the major groups. It is no longer true that the UK exports manufactures to pay for food and raw materials. Figure 17.1 shows a strong deficit in manufactured trade in 1987. The growth of manufactured imports has occurred fairly steadily, from 18 per cent of total imports in 1950, to 33 per cent in 1960, 53 per cent in 1970, 63 per cent in 1980 and 80 per cent by 1987, but there has been strong recent growth in finished manufactures, with shares of 4 per cent, 11 per cent, 24 per cent, 36 per cent and 51 per cent respectively. Coupled with relatively stagnant home demand, this expansion has considerably increased the import penetration of UK markets. For instance, the share of imports in home demand rose from 17 per cent in 1968 to 25 per cent in 1980 for manufacturing as a whole, with particularly strong growth in clothing and footwear (12 per cent to 30 per cent), motor vehicles (5 per cent to 46 per cent), instrument engineering (30 per cent to 61 per cent) and electrical

Government transfers
Private transfers
Direct investment earnings
Portfolio investment earnings
Other interest, profits and dividends
Government services
Sea transport
Civil aviation
Travel
Other services
Food, drink, tobacco
Basic materials
Mineral fuels
Chemicals
Other semi-manufactures
Machinery
Other finished manufactures
Other visibles

5   10   20   30   34   £ billion

Notes:
[a] Credits (exports) unshaded; debits (imports) shaded.
[b] Profits accruing to oil companies appear under 'direct investment earnings' for debits, but under 'other interest, profits and dividends' for credits.
Sources: Central Statistical Office, *United Kingdom Balance of Payments* (1988).

Figure 17.1   UK balance of payments, 1987

Table 17.4   The geographical composition of UK visible trade, 1950–87 (%)

	Exports[a]						Imports[a]					
	1950	1960	1970	1980	1987 (A)	1987 (B)	1950	1960	1970	1980	1987 (A)	1987 (B)
European Community[b]	19	22	29	45	45	49	19	20	27	45	49	53
Rest of West Europe	12	12	17	12	14	10	8	11	14	13	18	14
North America	11	16	15	11	16	16	15	20	21	15	11	11
Other developed countries	21	15	12	6	5	5	16	12	9	6	8	8
Oil-exporting countries	6	7	6	10	7	7	9	11	9	8	2	2
Other developing countries	29	25	17	12	11	11	30	22	15	11	10	10
Centrally planned economies	2	3	4	3	2	2	3	4	4	2	2	2
Total	100	100	100	100	100	100	100	100	100	100	100	100
of which Commonwealth	38	34	20	12	10	10	40	31	23	11	6	6

Notes:
[a] Overseas Trade Statistics Basis; figures may not sum to 100 because of rounding.
[b] Belgium, Denmark, France, West Germany, Ireland, Italy, Luxembourg and the Netherlands, plus Greece, Portugal and Spain in 1987 column (B).
Sources: Mansell (1980); Central Statistical Office, *Monthly Digest of Statistics* (July 1988).

engineering (14 per cent to 37 per cent) (Wells and Imber, 1977; Business Statistics Office, *Business Monitor*). Exports also rose as a proportion of sales, but not to the same extent. Note, however, that the overall openness and penetration of the UK market are not high by historical standards. During much of the nineteenth century, total credits and debits were both around one-third of GNP – above their share today.

Figure 17.2 shows shares in industrial countries' exports of manufactures since 1899. The obvious message is the gradual, and natural, displacement of the UK as the prime exporter of manufactures over the twentieth century (in fact, the process started well before 1899). It also shows the effects of the world wars. The first hit the European nations very hard, and, following the second, West Germany and Japan had to rebuild their trade from very low bases. At least part of the post-war decline in Britain's share has arisen because of its artificial inflation in 1950. This decline was arrested during the 1970s, but has now resumed its progress.

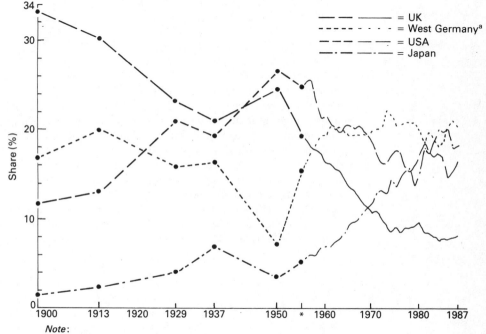

Note:
[a] West Germany estimated until 1937.
Sources: Maizels (1965); Mansell (1980); *National Institute Economic Review* (December 1988).
* denotes change to annual data.

Figure 17.2 Shares of manufactured exports, 1900–87

Britain has almost always had a visible trade deficit, financing it through an invisible surplus. Since 1825, only six years have shown visible surpluses – in each case associated with a severe squeeze of the domestic economy: 1956, 1958, 1971, 1980, 1981 and 1982.

Invisible trade

Invisible or service trade is described in the middle part of Figure 17.1. The amounts are quite significant – invisible exports amount to one-third of visible exports – but it should never be believed that they could in any sense replace visible exports. Among the various headings, shipping, civil aviation and tourism are roughly in balance. Years ago, Britain was a net exporter of shipping services; however, with the growth of other fleets, the decline of Commonwealth links and the increasing insistence by nations that they carry their own trade, she is now usually in deficit. Civil aviation has similarly slipped from regular surplus into deficit during the 1980s.

Travel expenditure comprises about 20 per cent business travel and the remainder leisure travel or tourism. The former records a modest surplus every year and is relatively insensitive to economic conditions. The latter is volatile, responding to prices and incomes as well as to non-economic factors such as the Olympic Games. The mid-1970s saw strong surpluses, probably due to the relative cheapness of Britain following the depreciations of sterling in 1972/3 and 1976, with the peak surplus coinciding with the Royal Jubilee in 1977. Since 1979, appreciation has cut receipts and boosted debits, resulting in deficits in every year but one since 1981. The principal source of travel receipts is the EC, followed by North America (reversing their positions in 1970), while debits accrue mostly to the EC and the rest of Western Europe.

The government service account has always shown a substantial deficit. About half the credits (£27m. in 1987) accrue through military expenditure – e.g. the US hiring of military bases in the UK – and a further fifth comprise receipts for services provided to EC institutions. Of the debits, 12 per cent is diplomatic and administrative expenditure abroad and the rest (£1,792m.) is military expenditure, 60 per cent of which is in West Germany. The final element of the account is 'other services', which is in substantial surplus. These include commissions on foreign trade, consultancy fees, royalties, telecommunications and postal fees, and expenditure by foreign students and journalists in the UK. The main credit item, however, is the earnings of financial institutions, such as banks and insurance companies, which account for £5,472m. in all. This is one of the most buoyant elements of British trade – both credits and debits increased five-fold over the 1970s and trebled over the 1980s. Nevertheless, it is still small relative to manufacturing: to balance a 1 per cent fall in manufacturing exports, other services would have to raise their exports by 4.5 per cent, or financial services raise theirs by 11 per cent.

Invisible earnings

The other elements of the invisible balance are interest, profits and dividends and transfers. These are shown in the top section of Figure 17.1 for 1987: total credits of these items were £52b. and there was an overall surplus of £2b. The principal contributor to this deficit was government transfers abroad, totalling £3,228m., of which net contributions to EC institutions of £1,795m. and foreign aid (excluding military) of £1,012m. were the main identifiable components. The earnings on portfolio investments were small and roughly balanced, while direct investment earnings showed a surplus and other interest profits and dividends a small deficit. The main component of 'other interest, profits and dividends' is interest accruing on various short-term loans, mostly channelled through the financial institutions of the City. Combining this with their fees, it is estimated that City institutions earned around £8,698m. in 1980 – about 14 per cent of manufacturing's earnings.

Interest, profits and dividends have recorded surpluses in every year except one (1980) since the Napoleonic wars. Data are obviously not perfect but, over the nineteenth century, net invisible earnings appear to have grown steadily until, in 1910–13, they alone paid for 25 per cent of visible imports. The slump of the 1930s reduced earnings substantially but, since import prices also fell,

246

earnings still financed about 20 per cent of imports. The Second World War substantially reduced Britain's overseas assets: many were sold and many destroyed or neglected. By 1946–8 net earnings covered only 10 per cent of visible imports. This improved over 1949–52 – probably because of the boom in primary commodity prices – but thereafter gradually declined to the deficit of 1980. This decline partly reflected Britain's loss of political and industrial power: foreign assets were not maintained, further investment was increasingly restricted, and the government took on increasing amounts of debt to support the value of sterling. It also reflected growing investment in Britain by American multinational companies; this grew rapidly in the 1970s as the North Sea was developed. Over the early and mid 1980s, Britain ran current account surpluses, and investing these at the high nominal rates of interest available turned interest, profits and dividends back into surplus.

Investment transactions

Investment flows show much greater volatility than trade flows; hence our discussion ranges more widely than the single year's figures given in Table 17.2. Over the 1970s there was a fairly steady inflow of direct investment – especially from the oil companies – and periods of strong portfolio investment coinciding with high rates of interest. Outflows were fairly modest at first, but grew as economic growth seemed less secure in Britain and, after 1979, as exchange controls on investment were removed. Recently, massive outflows of both direct and portfolio investment have occurred. The largest single source of direct investment abroad is the unremitted profits of foreign subsidiaries. These profits are treated as if they were paid to the British parent company – showing up as invisible earnings – and then reinvested – showing up as direct investment. In fact, of course, no explicit transfer occurs. The main inflows of portfolio investment are purchases of government stock. There is no information on the assets purchased by outgoing portfolio investment, but it is known that over half of such investment is undertaken by pensions funds, investment trusts and insurance companies.

There is nothing new in these flows of international investment. Britain's high invisible earnings of the nineteenth century reflected earlier investment, mostly in mines and plantations and in social investment in developing areas. The former constituted direct investment, but the latter should be classed as portfolio investment, as British residents took up the stock of foreign governments. Post Second World War investment has been concentrated in manufacturing, and, until the 1970s, conducted principally with the USA. During the 1970s, investment was of more general origin and the phenomenon of 'cross-hauling' – two countries investing in each other – has grown. In 1980, however, over 60 per cent of UK inward and outward direct investment was still with North America.

Turning to short-term capital movements, there are four main elements to consider. First, trade credit, which is basically an accommodating flow lubricating the machinery of international trade in goods. Second, UK banks' overseas transactions, which were legally restricted until 1979 but have since expanded rapidly. Third, 'exchange reserves in sterling', which are other countries' official holdings of sterling – sometimes known as the 'sterling balances'. Fourth, 'other external liabilities', which are short-term sterling debts held privately abroad. The last two elements are the main components of 'hot money', movements of which are generally large and volatile. Unfortunately, data are no longer presented according to this classification, but it should be obvious in which reported category each falls.

247

Table 17.5 Balance sheet of UK foreign assets and liabilities (£b.)

	1981 Assets	1981 Liabilities	1988 Assets	1988 Liabilities
Direct investment	44.9	30.0	101.5	66.2
Portfolio investment	25.8	12.7	147.5	58.0
UK banks	219.1	232.3	448.1	511.7
UK non-bank private sector	23.5	19.5	36.0	34.8
Government	5.1	3.5	9.3	6.3
Official reserves	12.0	—	28.7	—
Total	329.9	298.1	771.0	677.0

Source: Central Statistical Office, *United Kingdom Balance of Payments* (1989).

The final element of capital flows is official financing. This mainly comprises changes in foreign exchange reserves, but also includes government borrowing from the IMF, other governments and private banks and individuals.

Foreign assets and liabilities

So far we have considered the flows of investment; we now turn to the stocks of assets and liabilities – i.e. to Britain's net worth in foreign assets. Table 17.5 summarises the position (although we should note that data are very imprecise in this area). Direct investment accounts for about 12 per cent of the UK's gross assets abroad, and these considerably outweigh foreign-owned assets in the UK. Portfolio investment has grown over the 1980s and, with assets approximately twice the level of liabilities, has contributed substantial net wealth. Liabilities exceed assets in UK banks' dealings; these are mainly composed of very short-term borrowing and lending and illustrate well the scope for periodic liquidity crises (sterling crises). In 1988, the ample surplus of official reserves offered some protection from flights of short-term capital, but Britain was still, and is, a net borrower of short-term funds.

To put these figures in perspective we note that in 1988 net worth would finance visible and invisible imports for only six months, while gross assets would last about four years. Also, the total worth of the domestic capital stock in 1987 was about £1,750b. About 6 per cent of this was foreign-owned, while UK assets abroad added about 12 per cent to the domestic stock.

17.3 THE FOREIGN EXCHANGE RATE

One of the most obvious features of most international trade is that the partners wish to work in different currencies. A British manufacturer buys most of his inputs and consumes his profits in Britain – paying in terms of sterling. If he sells his wares in France, however, his purchasers will normally have only francs to offer. Some exchange is therefore necessary between sterling and francs, and this defines the rate of exchange or exchange rate. Quite simply, the exchange rate is the price of one money in terms of another, and, like other prices, it is determined by supply and demand in the market. We shall examine the determinants of these in Chapters 22 and 23 below; here we need merely note that they may arise from current or capital transactions and from private or official sources.

Some terminology

The exchange rate may be expressed in two ways: $2.00 per £1.00 or, equivalently, £0.50 per $1.00. The former – the foreign currency price of one unit of domestic currency – is the UK's convention, and will be used throughout this book. Most countries, and many journal articles, however, use the latter – the local currency price of one unit of foreign currency.

Changes in the exchange rate are known as *appreciations* and *depreciations*, or, if they occur under a fixed exchange rate regime (see below), as *revaluations* and *devaluations*. An appreciation (revaluation) indicates an increase in value: e.g. for sterling, a rise from $2.00:£1.00 to $2.50:£1.00, or, in the other convention, a fall from £0.50:$1.00 to £0.40:$1.00. (Observe, it is beneficial to hold an appreciating currency.) Obviously, if the pound appreciates relative to the dollar, the dollar depreciates relative to the pound – not, however, by the same percentage! A move from $2.00 to $2.50 represents a 25 per cent appreciation of sterling, but only a 20 per cent depreciation of the dollar, £0.50 to £0.40. The $ per £ rate is multiplied by 5/4, while the £ per $ rate is divided by 5/4.

With many currencies in the world, there must be many exchange rates, e.g. $:£, $:DM, DM:£, etc. We refer to each individual rate as a *nominal exchange rate*. Often, however, it is useful to have a summary measure of, say, the value of sterling relative to the value of all other currencies. This is particularly so when exchange rates are flexible, because sterling may appreciate relative to some and depreciate relative to others. This summary measure is known as the *effective exchange rate*. It is really no more than an index number, and the only problem about it is the weights with which to combine the rates against each currency. If we were interested in imports, we might use weights based on the value of imports denominated in each currency. Obviously depreciation relative to the US dollar (supplying at least 10 per cent of UK imports) is more important than depreciation relative to the Swedish krona (3 per cent of imports), so the dollar gets more weight.

Generally, however, we are interested in both exports and imports and the weights are based on both. They take account not only of bilateral trade, i.e. trade flowing directly between two countries, but also of the extent to which the countries compete in third markets. For example, Japan and Italy have very little mutual trade, but, because they sell in the same third markets, a change in the yen exchange rate impinges on Italian trade, and hence affects the lira effective exchange rate. The weight of the yen in the lira effective rate shows the amount that the lira would have to depreciate (relative to all currencies) to just offset the balance of trade effects on Italy of a 1 per cent depreciation of the yen (relative to all currencies), taking account of world trade patterns and the responsiveness to trade flows to relative prices.

Economists have recently started referring to the '*real exchange rate*'. This measures not the price of two monies, but the relative prices of two nations' bundles of output. It is no use being able to buy more dollars per pound if each dollar now buys fewer goods. If we express things relative to some base date, and if the nominal $:£ exchange rate is r and the USA and UK price indices p_s and p_k respectively, the 'real sterling exchange rate' is rp_k/p_s. A 'real' appreciation occurs either through a nominal appreciation (rising r), or through a relative rise in UK local currency prices (a rise in p_k/p_s). The 'real exchange rate' is no more than the ratio of UK to USA prices measured in dollars – the sterling value of p_k is converted to dollars by means of r – and hence it reflects relative UK:US competitiveness. Clearly, by simultaneously considering many exchange rates and price levels, one could construct real effective exchange rates.

249

The exchange rate – the price of foreign currency – is determined by supply and demand. The demand for foreign currency arises from debit items on the balance of payments, i.e. from spending abroad; the supply arises from credit items. Any tendency towards surplus on the balance of payments creates an excess supply of foreign currency, driving down its price in terms of domestic currency or driving up (appreciating) the value of domestic currency in terms of foreign currency. Hence if, at any given exchange rate, credits exceed debits, the exchange rate is forced above that level. Equilibrium can occur only where excess supply is zero, i.e. where credits equal debits, and the exchange rate must move to bring this about.

There are two polar ways of bringing about this equality. First, under a system of *perfectly flexible exchange rates* (or *'clean floating'*), the monetary authorities keep out of the foreign exchange market entirely. Official finance is thus set to zero, and the balance of the remaining accounts must also be zero, since total credit and debits are equalised. For such a market to be useful it must be stable: the excess supply of foreign currency must be eliminated by the appreciation of the home currency that it induces. In the long run this occurs through items in the basic balance. An appreciation of sterling raises the dollar price of goods and assets priced in sterling (a good worth £1.00 sells for $2.00 before appreciation and for $2.50 afterwards). Hence British goods and assets lose competitiveness abroad and net credits fall, so reducing the excess supply of foreign currency. These processes take time, however, and so, in the short run, stability depends on the short-term capital account. The main mechanism assumed is as follows: if people have some expected level of the exchange rate in mind, rises above that level are expected to be followed by falls. To hold sterling while expecting a fall is to expect losses, so, once the rate has risen above your expected level, it pays to sell and move your capital into foreign currency. If everyone does so, however, the excess supply of foreign currency disappears (because demand for it has risen), and the rise in sterling stops or reverses itself. These processes are explored in Chapters 19–23 below.

The second polar approach to equalising total credits and debits is a system of *fixed exchange rates*. Here the authorities are committed to maintaining a particular exchange rate – or rather a narrow band of exchange rates, e.g. from $2.38 to $2.42 per £1.00. They do this by being always prepared to buy pounds for dollars at $2.38 and sell them at $2.42. Their purchases and sales show up as official finance. Disequilibrium now appears as movements in the reserves rather than as changes in the exchange rate. In other words, whereas previously price bore the adjustment in the exchange market, here quantity does. The only limits to this process are the extent of the official finance available, and the ability of the economy to balance the current and capital accounts in the long run without exchange rate changes. This is explored below in Chapter 18, 20 and 21.

Between these polar cases lie a number of exchange rate regimes that try to combine the advantages of both systems. Under the *adjustable-peg* system – or *Bretton Woods* system (named after the international conference at which it was devised) – countries generally maintain fixed rates, but at times of 'fundamental disequilibrium' the parity, or peg rate, may be altered. This system was used from 1945 to 1971. Although it was basically successful, it broke down because countries were reluctant to make parity changes and because, since all countries pegged their currencies to the dollar, there was nothing the USA could do about its exchange rate. This is discussed in Chapter 28 below.

A variant of the adjustable-peg is the *crawling-peg*. The problem of the former is that parity changes are traumatic events that give rise to huge volumes of speculation because the direction of the impending change is obvious to everyone. The crawling-peg replaces one large change with a continuous series of changes small enough to make speculation not worthwhile. It has been adopted by several inflation-prone middle-income countries, but has not proved popular in the developed world.

At the other extreme, perfect flexibility was felt to encourage volatility when it was tried briefly in late 1973. It was therefore adapted into *managed floating*. This permits some official activity, but in a basically floating exchange rate market. Least interventionist is *leaning-against-the-wind* – aimed at smoothing out day-to-day fluctuations in the exchange rate without trying to influence its longer-run trends. More interventionist is the so-called '*dirty' float*, which involves the government pursuing some unspecified exchange rate target. The essence is in the 'unspecified' part, because by keeping their intentions secret the authorities hope to avoid giving speculators information on which to act. This may curb speculation, but it may also merely give rise to large volumes of uninformed and highly volatile speculation. The role of speculation is discussed in sections 22.2 and 26.1. Managed floating – with different amounts of management – has been the predominant regime since 1973. Governments mostly protest that they are merely leaning against the wind, but the persistence, in both extent and direction, of much official financing suggests more than that. (A persistent official surplus must reflect a persistent current and capital deficit; since under pure floating this would be impossible, it is hard to believe it actually arises purely from day-to-day smoothing.)

Some data Figure 17.3 shows the recent history of sterling. The nominal exchange rate series shows clearly the periods of fixity, the crises of 1976, and the subsequent rise and fall of sterling. The effective exchange rate differs from this series by

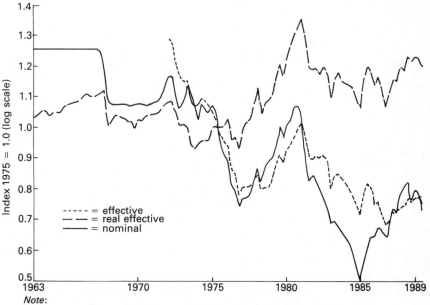

Note:
[a] All rates are measured in dollars per pound and as index numbers (1975 = 1.0).
Sources: International Monetary Fund, *International Financial Statistics* for nominal; Central Statistical Office, *Economic Trends*, for effective.

Figure 17.3 The UK exchange rate – different concepts, 1963–89

the extent to which the dollar moved against other currencies; it tells much the same story. The 'real' effective exchange rate series used here refers to UK export prices for manufactures relative to competing exporters' prices, and uses total manufactured exports as weights, but other 'real' exchange rates would tell roughly the same story. Over 1960–72, Britain suffered greater inflation than her competitors, and, although the 1967 devaluation improved competitiveness, it did not cure the basic problem: with fixed exchange rates, higher inflation eventually results in uncompetitiveness. The float downwards over 1972–3 greatly improved competitiveness – i.e. reduced the 'real' exchange rate – but over 1974–6 the real and nominal rates bore little relation to each other. The nominal depreciation just balanced higher inflation. This coincided with a period of great monetary expansion. Once the monetary position began to be brought under control, however, the real and nominal exchange rates linked up again, and the subsequent appreciation of sterling made British industry hugely uncompetitive. From the peaks of 1980–1, the real exchange rate of sterling has fallen in a series of steps. It is now well below the levels experienced over the 1970s, probably reflecting the relatively poor quality of British goods – they are saleable only at relatively low prices.

17.4   A SUMMARY OF PART II

This chapter has introduced the balance of payments and the exchange rate. The rest of Part II analyses them – their behaviour under particular circumstances, their causes and their effects. We start in Chapter 18 with the simplest, but empirically most important, determinant of the level of international trade – national income. We show how income and trade interact and also how incomes in different countries are connected through international trade. We next consider how prices affect trade in Chapter 19, taking the principal determinant of relative prices to be the exchange rate. A section is devoted to measuring price elasticities in international trade, and another to elements of non-price competitiveness such as design and quality.

Chapter 20 broadens the discussion to examine how trade fits into the macro-economic balance of an economy. In particular we observe that any change in trade performance must have concomitant change somewhere else in the economy. Only by recognising these changes can satisfactory policy be devised for controlling the current account. This chapter considers the 'small, open economy' – an economy that has no influence over the prices at which it trades with the rest of the world – and also the importance of wage rigidity in balance of payments theory.

Chapter 21 introduces a further macro-economic approach to the balance of payments – the monetary approach, comparing it with the results and models of the previous chapters. We then leave the fixed exchange rate world and consider the determination of exchange rates under a flexible system in Chapters 22 and 23. After examining various transactions in foreign exchange, we consider the simple purchasing power parity theory of exchange rates and find it deficient. Next we examine recent work on exchange rates and financial assets – viewing the exchange rates as a means of equating the supply of and demand for world stocks of various assets. The chapters conclude with a discussion of recent exchange rate behaviour.

The exchange rate regime – fixed or floating – turns out to be an important influence on the effectiveness of macro-economic policy. After a brief discussion of the theory of economic policy in general. Chapter 24 considers this issue. It starts with a simple analysis due to Mundell and Fleming, and develops it in several directions. It concludes with some evidence on the degree of financial integration in the world economy. This discussion is extended into a general discussion of the pros and cons of floating exchange rates in Chapter 26. Particular attention is paid to the ability of flexible rates to insulate an economy from external shocks and to the form and role of speculation. Finally there are brief discussions of international policy coordination and optimum currency areas, during which the European Monetary System is described.

The intervening chapter (Chapter 25) is devoted to the analysis of the oil shocks of the 1970s and fiscal shocks of the 1980s. We start with the effects of the oil price rise – falling income but increased manufactured output in the West – and then consider the effects of an oil discovery such as in the North Sea – which involves some de-industrialisation, but none the less raises national income. The two shocks are combined in a study of the UK economy over the 1970s. Last we considerr the effects on the world economy of the USA's massive public sector deficits during the late 1980s.

FURTHER READING

The conceptual problems of the balance of payments are explored in *Meade* (1951) and *Machlup* (1966). *Cohen* (1969) gives a useful alternative textbook treatment, and the introduction of Central Statistics Office, *United Kingdom Balance of Payments* (annual) provides a useful official summary. The latter also, of course, provides data on the UK position and also detailed explanatory notes. The US accounts appear in *Department of Commerce, Survey of Current Business* (monthly) and are discussed by *Stern et al.* (1977). For the history of the UK balance of payments, see *Thirlwall* (1980), ch. 7, *Mansell* (1980), *Imlah* (1958) – on the nineteenth century – and *Dornbusch and Fischer* (1980) – on the 1970s. Effective exchange rates were introduced in *Artus and Rhomberg* (1978) and recent UK practice is described in Central Statistical Office, *Economic Trends* (March 1981).

18 National Income and The Trade Balance

We start our explanation of the macro-economics of the open economy with the simplest of aggregate models. For this chapter we shall assume fixed exchange rates and fixed prices throughout the world economy and, ignoring all assets and income from abroad, focus solely on the trade balance. The first two assumptions place us in a Keynesian world where income can settle, at least temporarily, at a level insufficient to generate full employment. Below full employment, income is determined by the level of demand because, with fixed prices and spare resources, supply can expand to meet any rise in demand, whereas, if demand fell further, supply would fall with it as there would be no virtue in producing goods that could not be sold. In this world there is no guarantee that the balance of trade will be in equilibrium either. As we shall discover, there is a relationship between the balance of trade and income (via the demand for domestic output), but in the absence of price flexibility and/or changes in stocks of assets this is not sufficient to ensure balance.

We would not wish to pretend that this model provides a complete or realistic view of the economy. We introduce these simplifications to enable us to concentrate on the relationship between trade and the national income. On the other hand, plenty of econometric evidence suggests that over the short run, when prices *are* sticky and asset stocks *are* fairly constant, income is a major determinant of trade movements and vice versa. Hence even the simple analysis provided here gives us considerable insight into the real world.

The chapter starts by modifying the well-known closed-economy multiplier to take account of imports. It then goes on to a two-country model in which one country's imports are recognised as the other's exports. This further modifies the multiplier, and also illustrates the interdependence of the world economy. Section 18.3 introduces two econometric models of the international multiplier, while the last section presents some evidence on the relationship between incomes and international trade in the real world.

18.1 FOREIGN TRADE AND THE MULTIPLIER

The concept of the multiplier is familiar to any student of economics. (If it is not, consult an elementary book on macro-economics, such as Brooman, 1970.) Briefly, the multiplier records the extent to which national income rises in response to the injection of one unit of extra expenditure. It is derived from the circular flow of income by noting that if income is to be in equilibrium (i.e. at the same level at every point in the circular flow) total injections must equal total withdrawals. In a simple closed-economy model with no government, the multiplier takes the value of $1/s$, where s is the marginal propensity to save.

We now generalise the multiplier to take account of international trade. We start with an economy small enough that its actions have no perceptible effect on incomes in the rest of the world. International trade introduces a new injection to the circular flow – namely exports, which provide demand for our output independent of our level of income – and a new withdrawal – imports.

254

Like savings, imports absorb expenditure without generating any corresponding demand for local goods. Continuing with the assumption of no government, and adopting the simplest linear equations, we describe this situation algebraically as follows:

$$S = a + sY, \tag{18.1}$$

where savings (S) are a function of income (Y), s the marginal propensity to save and a a constant amount of savings independent of income.

$$M = b + mY, \tag{18.2}$$

where imports (M) are also related to income, with m being the marginal propensity to import.

$$I + X = S + M, \tag{18.3}$$

where total injections (investment, I, plus exports, X) equal total withdrawals, which is the equilibrium condition. Substituting (18.1) and (18.2) into (18.3) and regrouping yields

$$Y = \frac{-(a + b)}{(s + m)} + \frac{1}{(s + m)}(I + X). \tag{18.4}$$

Hence the multiplier, the increment in Y per unit increment in I, is $1/(s + m)$. Mathematically:

$$\frac{\mathrm{d}Y}{\mathrm{d}I} = \frac{1}{s + m}. \tag{18.5}$$

Since m is positive – imports rise with income – the open-economy multiplier $1/(s + m)$ is less than the closed-economy multiplier $1/s$. In other words, the more open the economy, in the sense of the higher the *marginal* propensity to import, the less sensitive is national income to changes in injections, because more of the effect seeps away overseas.

The multiplier applies to increases in exports as well as in investment. Starting from equilibrium, suppose exports rise by a small increment ΔX. Equation (18.4) shows that income rises by $\Delta Y = \Delta X/(s + m)$ and substituting this into (18.1) shows that imports rise by $\Delta M = m\Delta X/(s + m)$. Now, if there were no domestic savings, $s = 0$, $\Delta M = \Delta X$, so the trade balance would be unaffected by the increase in exports. However, if $s > 0$, the fraction $m/(s + m)$ is less than 1, and so $\Delta M < \Delta X$; that is, imports rise but not sufficiently to offset the rise in exports. Hence, even when we allow for the multiplier, an increase in exports improves the balance of trade.

$$\Delta B = \Delta X - \Delta M = \Delta X - \frac{m}{s + m}\Delta X = \frac{s}{s + m}\Delta X. \tag{18.6}$$

The extent of the improvement depends crucially on the marginal propensity to save. If this is small, although rising exports may boost income and output substantially, they do little for the balance of payments because imports rise almost in line.

18.2   REPERCUSSION EFFECTS

We now relax the small country assumption. Assume that our economy is large enough to affect incomes abroad. For instance, if our imports account for 10 per cent of the demand for the rest of world's goods, a 20 per cent increase in our imports will immediately raise the demand for their goods by 2 per cent. This, of course, raises their incomes, increasing their demand for goods, some of which is met by exports from our country. Hence in this case not all expenditure on imports is lost to an economy. By boosting incomes abroad, some of it finds its way back via increased exports.

We examine this situation in a model of a world comprising two countries, each satisfying all but the small country assumptions used in the previous section. We denote all foreign variables by an asterisk (*). Individually, both countries will satisfy equations (18.1)–(18.4), but now, instead of exports being an exogenous variable, we recognise that our exports are their imports, i.e. $X = M^*$, and vice versa, $M = X^*$. We now have two equilibrium conditions:

$$I + X = S + M$$

and
$$I^* + X^* = S^* + M^*. \tag{18.7}$$

Substituting from (18.1) and (18.2) for S, M and X ($\equiv M^*$) and similar equations for S^*, M^* and X^* yields:

$$I + b^* + m^* Y^* = a + sY + b + mY$$

and
$$I^* + b + mY = a^* + s^* Y^* + b^* + m^* Y^*. \tag{18.8}$$

With I and I^* still exogenous, these two equations in two unknowns (Y and Y^*) may be solved simultaneously to yield:

$$\frac{dY}{dI} = \frac{1}{s + m \left(\dfrac{s^*}{s^* + m^*} \right)} \tag{18.9}$$

$$\frac{dY}{dI^*} = \frac{m^*}{(s^* + m^*)} \frac{1}{\left[s + m \dfrac{s^*}{s^* + m^*} \right]} \tag{18.10}$$

Equation (18.9) defines the multiplier effect of our own exogenous expenditure (investment) changes. It is plainly greater than the simple open-economy multiplier of the previous section, because the denominator of the fraction is reduced: $s^*/(s^* + m^*) < 1$. This makes sense intuitively because previously we assumed exports to be fixed, whereas here we assume them to be positively related to our income via our imports and foreign income. There are also, however, multiplier effects from foreign investment, as shown by (18.10). This is the product of two effects: first, the increase in their imports (our exports), ignoring any repercussion effects (see ΔM in (18.6)), and, second, the standard (repercussion) foreign trade multiplier effect on exogenous increases in demand (see 18.9)). Hence, once we allow for repercussion effects, the two economies become interconnected. Each economy is affected by both exogenous changes and the parameters of economic behaviour in the other.

Several modifications to this model are possible. First, we can generalise the results to many countries (Metzler, 1950, 1951). This should be clear

256

intuitively – breaking up the rest of the world into many separate countries changes nothing fundamental – but it is slightly complex mathematically. It may be shown that, as above, the closed-economy multiplier is the largest, the small open-economy multiplier smallest and the (repercussion) foreign trade multiplier in between.

Second, it would be possible – and more realistic – to relate imports not to national income but to national expenditure. This alters the various multipliers in detail and, while possibly significant in some practical applications, is not of great significance theoretically (Meade, 1951; Thirlwall, 1980).

Third, we could use very much more realistic functions for the variables than we have done. It is easy to introduce a government sector with exogenous expenditure and tax revenue a function of income, and it is also simple to allow either investment or exports to vary with income. Further, if one is prepared to solve the model numerically (by computer) rather than analytically (as above), it is possible to break free of the simple linear forms, and to introduce additional explanatory variables into the functions.

18.3 THE TRANSMISSIONS OF ECONOMIC DISTURBANCES

We have just seen how an economic shock in one country affects other countries' economies via the mechanism of international trade. Hence a government no longer has sole control over its own economy; the economy is affected by other governments, and so economic policy-making exhibits some interdependence. Crudely, the more open an economy, the more it responds to external shocks and hence the greater its dependence on policy-making elsewhere. All of this raises the possibility that a country may raise its own level of income and employment more effectively by persuading other countries to expand than by trying to expand, say by fiscal stimulus, itself. This lies at the heart of many economic summit meetings at which the weaker economies try to persuade their stronger and larger neighbours to pursue more expansionary policies for the 'common good'.

During the latter half of the 1970s, the theory of expansion by selected countries pulling the rest of the world economies out of the slump was graced with the name 'the locomotive theory'. The idea was that, if the United States, West Germany and Japan expanded and therefore imported more, they would increase the demand for goods from other developed countries. This would create income and employment in these countries, and improve their balances of trade. The latter would then allow them to expand their economies in turn reinforcing their earlier growth and returning some of it to the 'locomotive' economies. To some extent this happened – over 1977 the USA expanded strongly – but overall the policy was not a great success. The extent of the expansion required in the locomotive countries was too great; besides, they had internal reasons – mostly to do with inflation – for not wishing to expand.

The 'locomotive theory' was briefly superseded by the 'convoy theory'. This held that, although it might not be feasible for a few countries to expand sufficiently to pull the remainder along, if all OECD countries expanded together, all would experience rising exports as well as rising imports and hence at least most would avoid balance of payments difficulties. This would allow weaker economies to undertake expansion of an order that they could not contemplate alone. This idea also foundered – again largely because the

257

strong fully employed economies had little interest in expansion whether initiated by themselves or others.

Case-study 18.1 looks at the feasibility of these policies and the extent of international interdependence, using a simple econometric model designed by the Organisation for Economic Co-operation and Development (OECD) for this very purpose.

CASE-STUDY 18.1: LOCOMOTIVES AND CONVOYS: OECD'S INTERLINK MODEL

OECD (1979) describes a simple multi-country model of the world economy based almost entirely on the theory of this chapter. For each of twenty-three OECD countries, it has an equation relating income to exogenous injections via the multiplier (like (18.4) above), and an import function (like (18.2)). It also has a world trade segment, which converts imports by OECD and non-OECD countries into exports by the OECD countries. In a multi-country setting, of course, we cannot just equate M^* and X as we did above; we have to build up country j's exports, X_j, as the sum of imports into each market times j's share of that market, i.e. $X_j = \sum 1_i \alpha_{ij} M_i$.

The market shares α_{ij}, determine the direction of the transmission of economic shocks. For example, suppose West Germany reflates her economy by a fiscal expansion. The resulting imports are then shared out via the α_{ij}s among Germany's trading partners, where, as exports, they set off further multiplier processes. Countries trading very little with Germany (e.g. Portugal) gain little direct benefit from her expansion, whereas those trading a lot (e.g. Austria) gain substantially. Once Germany's partners start to expand, of course, this passes through to their partners, including Germany, in a second round of expansion, and so on.

Table 18.1 reports some results from the OECD model for 1978. The first three rows give various background statistics: GNP, to indicate the size of each economy, and estimates of the multiplier and the marginal propensity to import. Each column shows the effect of an increase in government expenditure, equal to 1 per cent of total domestic demand, carried out by the country named at the top of the column. We report in part (A) the percentage increase in each country's GNP over the year of the stimulus, and in part (B) the effect on each country's balance of trade over that year.

Consider, for example, an expansion of government expenditure in the USA by 1 per cent of total demand (this is a large stimulus – around $20b.). In the year after the injection, GNP is 1.47 per cent higher in the USA, 0.38 per cent higher in Ireland and 0.15 per cent higher in France. Similarly, the USA trade balance worsens by $3.35b., while those of her partners improve. For OECD overall, the expansion amounts to 0.74 per cent of total GNP and the balance of payments deterioration to $0.72b.

There are several points to be noted from these results. First, the effects of each country's stimulus on its own GNP, given along the diagonal of part (A) of Table 18.1, show how more open economies benefit less from their own stimuli.(The multiplier of below unity for Ireland stems from the implausible marginal propensity to import of above unity.) Second, the effects on other countries depend partly on the size of the economy undertaking expansion and partly on its openness. For example, the West German economy is 33 per cent smaller than the Japanese economy, but its greater openness makes it a more effective 'locomotive'. (The German influence on

Table 18.1 Results from the OECD linkage model

	USA	Japan	W. Germany	France	UK	Ireland	All OECD
GNP[a] ($USb.)	2,156	963	643	476	316	12	6,775
Multiplier[b]	1.40	1.43	1.19	1.16	1.11	0.91	—
Marginal propensity to import[c]	0.19	0.15	0.48	0.48	0.64	1.01	—
(A) Effects on growth rate of 1% stimulus of country in heading							
USA	1.47	0.04	0.05	0.04	0.04	0.00	1.81
Japan	0.25	1.26	0.06	0.05	0.05	0.00	1.84
W. Germany	0.23	0.05	1.25	0.21	0.11	0.01	2.38
France	0.15	0.04	0.19	1.21	0.09	0.00	2.03
UK	0.28	0.06	0.16	0.14	1.17	0.03	2.32
Ireland	0.38	0.06	0.22	0.17	0.73	0.98	3.07
All OECD	0.74	0.21	0.23	0.18	0.13	0.01	2.04
(B) Effects on balance of trade ($USb.) of 1% stimulus of country in heading							
USA	− 3.35	0.44	0.49	0.41	0.40	0.02	− 1.13
Japan	0.93	− 1.20	0.27	0.23	0.23	0.01	0.68
W. Germany	0.35	0.10	− 2.43	0.37	0.22	0.01	− 0.08
France	0.19	0.05	0.26	− 2.15	0.14	0.01	− 0.81
UK	0.13	0.04	0.09	0.08	− 1.91	0.02	− 0.55
Ireland	0.00	0.00	0.00	0.00	0.01	− 0.12	0.01
All OECD	− 0.72	− 0.31	− 0.42	− 0.39	− 0.33	− 0.02	− 1.70

Notes:
[a] 1978 at current prices. *Source*: International Monetary Fund, *International Financial Statistics*, Yearbook, 1981.
[b] Multiplier on exports and government expenditure: average for the year after the stimulus occurs. *Source*: OECD (1979), Table 2, column 1 × [column 2 + column 3]/2.
[c] OECD present income elasticities for imports (ϵ_M). But $\epsilon_M = (dM/dY) . (Y/M)$, hence marginal propensity is $\epsilon_M (M/Y)$. *Source*: ϵ_M from OECD (1979), Table 3, Y from row 1, and M from International Monetary Fund, *Annual Reports*.
Source: (A) and (B) – Organization for Economic Co-operation and Development (1979).

total OECD income exceeds that of Japan, 0.23 per cent compared with 0.21 per cent.) Indeed, the pressure on the Japanese over the 1970s and 1980s was as much to open their economy as to expand it. Third, we can see the importance of the direction of trade. For instance, the USA is the most effective stimulator of the world economy, being both large and, on the margin, fairly open; yet France is more reliant on Germany, which takes 17 per cent of her exports and Ireland on the UK, which takes 46 per cent of hers.

A fourth feature is the strong expansionary effect of 'the convoy'. If all OECD countries expand together (see the last column), total GNP rises by twice the stimulus, even over the first year. Allowing for subsequent effects, the long-run multiplier is around 3. The benefits are not perfectly equally divided, but it is clear that most countries gain significantly from the 'convoy'. In part (B) of the table we see the balance of trade effects of overall expansion. Most countries in the OECD conduct over 60 per cent of their trade with other OECD countries, hence expansion in concert involves less strain on their balances of payments than does expansion alone. For example, expanding alone worsens the UK deficit by $1.9b., whereas in a convoy the decline is only $0.55b. In fact some countries, notably Japan, actually improve their trade balances in the convoy. This reflects Japan's low marginal propensity to import and high *marginal* share of other OECD markets. The net worsening of the OECD's trade balance from concerted expansion is only $1.70b. This reflects the extra imports from outside the group, and is surprisingly small.

It is well known from Keynes that, if income is transferred from people who spend it to people who do not, aggregate demand drops and a multiple contraction can occur. The presence of a banking system helps to avoid this possibility by receiving deposits from people who have spare cash and transferring them, temporarily, to those who are short and who are therefore likely to spend it. The world is just a single large economy, and we can view it too in this way. Any country earning more than it spends is withdrawing demand from the world economy – i.e. it is hoarding – and, unless its surplus spending power is transferred elsewhere by lending, total demand is reduced.

The multiplier model assumes that nearly all of any injection of income is passed on as extra demand for goods; that is, that marginal propensities to save are fairly low, and hence multipliers fairly high. But suppose we had a country that did not wish to increase its demand and merely neutralised any injection from increased exports by increasing savings or taxes. Then there would be no multiplier effect and the whole expansionary impulse would cease. Two sets of countries come immediately to mind as candidates for this sort of behaviour: countries that are already satiated with goods and services, and countries that have reached full employment.

At least in the short run, the oil producers found themselves in the former group after the large oil price rises. They received huge transfers of spending power, but were initially just unable to make use of it. This was a major reason for the mid-1970s depression. In order to pay for their oil, Western nations had to improve their balances of trade in manufactures. Most attempted this by deflating and reducing imports, but, of course, just as expansion gets shared out among the OECD nations so does contraction. Each country found its exports falling as a result of its partners' contraction, and so had to reduce imports further, and so on. The result was a deep slump. Just as a concerted expansion worsens the total OECD trade balance with non-OECD relatively little, so the large surplus required to pay the higher oil prices required a large contraction.

Definitions of full employment differ, but there are certainly times when countries do not welcome extra demand. Frequently in that position over the last thirty years has been West Germany, which, having suffered two hyper-inflations, has been sensitive to any degree of economic overheating. Japan, on the other hand, has had a more pragmatic view of externally generated demand, but seems to have been unable to return much of it to the rest of the world by raising imports. Hence among developed nations, Germany and Japan have been the nearest to being hoarders.

We shall discuss international finance in detail later, but here we should note that, if OPEC and the developed surplus countries like West Germany and Japan lent out their surpluses, world expansion could still proceed, but only within limits. The countries that borrow are running balance of payments deficits and, if their deficits are persistent, questions must eventually arise about their credit-worthiness. Gradually, then, loans will be made only conditionally – usually on condition that the recipient cure its deficit, which usually entails deflation. Hence we could find a world divided into two classes of country: those that could expand but will not, and those that would expand but cannot.

This is the view adopted by the Cambridge Economic Policy Group (CEPG) in a series of reports (*Cambridge Economic Policy Review*, April 1979, December 1980 and December 1981). They distinguish countries constrained from expansion by their balances of payments from those that are unconstrained. The former have some maximum deficit that they can finance, and determine their GNP so as to bring this about. Given a level of exports determined by other countries' behaviour, they know how many imports they can afford; the import function then indicates what level of income this implies and fiscal policy is used to bring it about. The import function (18.2) is being used 'backwards'. These countries welcome any boost to exports because, by relaxing their payments constraint, it permits further growth. Hence, constrained countries pass on their expansionary stimuli and permit the international multiplier to work.

The unconstrained countries, on the other hand, can choose their level of GNP independently of their balance of payments and with regard to other criteria – usually domestic employment and inflation. Assuming these countries have already settled at their desired income level, they will not permit any extra exports to expand the economy. Hence, an increase in their exports generates no feedback effects for other countries' exports. Consequently, they represent a block in the multiplier process.

The CEPG use this framework to draw a radical solution. They argue that imports from unconstrained countries are basically wasted, because they increase income in neither the supplying (unconstrained) country nor any other. Hence, if an expansionary stimulus is not to run rapidly into the sand, care must be taken to avoid buying *extra* goods from such countries. For oil this is impossible except to the extent that alternative energy sources are available, but for manufacturers they suggest that import controls should be used to direct incremental trade to flow only between constrained countries. By these means, they argue, the multiplier can be kept high and its effects concentrated on those countries that desire growth.

Within the confines of the simple, fixed-price, single-good model these conclusions are correct. When we consider the complexities of the real world, however, they are not very robust. We have already seen that trade controls reduce welfare, and we shall see later that a devaluation by the constrained countries relative to the unconstrained countries should redirect trade in the desired fashions without incurring these losses. There would also clearly be difficulties as countries shifted between being constrained and not. In 1990, the UK was certainly balance of payments constrained (economic policy was heavily focused on the external sector), but in 1985 she was clearly unconstrained (with a substantial current surplus). Hence, in 1990 her partners were to discriminate in Britain's favour, whereas five years earlier they were to have discriminated against her. Pity the diplomats who had to negotiate that!

We have dwelt long on this simple Keynesian model for two reasons. First, it illustrates simply the interdependencies that occur in international economics. International transmission and policy-making encompass much more than simple fiscal stimuli, but the basic notion that countries affect each other is just the same as in our simple model. It is taken up further in Chapter 26 below. Second, despite its strong assumptions, this model has actually much to teach us. In the short run (six–nine months) the assumptions of the model are fairly well met, and the simple Keynesian transmission process is dominant. Even in the longer run, with flexible prices and important changes in stocks of assets, the basic income effects still operate, even if we observe them rather less closely.

18.4 INCOME EFFECTS – THE EMPIRICAL EVIDENCE

So far, we have looked at the relationships between income and international trade from a purely theoretical viewpoint. We *assumed* that the import function took the form (18.2) and in the case-study we plugged some *a priori* numbers into it. We now have to complete the picture by asking what evidence there is of a relationship and also what its nature is. We shall ignore the effect of prices and exchange rates by, as above, assuming them constant. This is done in econometrics by estimating multiple regressions relating imports to both prices and incomes (and possibly other effects). We then interpret the regression coefficient on income as showing the effects on imports of a unit change in income holding prices constant.

Imports and income

Imagine an economy in equilibrium; then let us give it an injection of income from abroad holding everything else – prices, output, tastes, etc. – constant. Unless any of the goods it consumes are inferior, consumption of every good will increase. With constant domestic output, this will certainly increase imports. Unfortunately, however, in nearly all circumstances, income increases not in isolation, but in conjunction with output, and this causes complications, because the additional domestic output is likely to displace imports. Hence the net effect of an *income and output* expansion is not certain *a priori*, being comprised of both positive and negative effects. (This, of course, is precisely what we saw in Chapter 15; economic growth may be pro- or anti-import biased.) When economists talk of 'income elasticities of demand for imports' or 'the marginal propensity to import', they are almost invariably referring to this combined effect rather than to that of income alone.

These ideas can be formalised as follows. Assuming for now that we have a single good and that imported and domestically supplied units are perfect substitutes, we can write:

$$M = D - S. \tag{18.11}$$

That is, imports equal the difference between demand and supply. Then, differentiating with respect to income and output (Y), and multiplying by (Y/M) yields

$$\frac{dM}{dY} \cdot \frac{Y}{M} = \frac{dD}{dY} \cdot \frac{Y}{M} - \frac{dS}{dY} \cdot \frac{Y}{M}.$$

If we multiply the first term on the right by (D/D) and the second by (S/S) and substitute for the elasticity terms, we get

$$\epsilon_M = \epsilon_D \cdot \frac{D}{M} - \epsilon_S \cdot \frac{S}{M}. \tag{18.12}$$

That is, the income elasticity of imports depends positively on the demand elasticity and negatively on the supply elasticity. In general we expect both to be positive, and, although for imports $D > S$ (so that ϵ_D receives greater weight), it would be possible for the import elasticity to be negative if ϵ_S were large. This could easily be the case for those goods where the extra output was concentrated.

Equation (18.12) illustrates two other features. *If* domestic and foreign goods are perfectly substitutable, the import elasticity is merely a derived parameter arising from the basic supply and demand relationships. There is no reason to believe it constant or to use it in economic policy-making (Pearce, 1970). If, on the other hand, goods are strongly differentiated, as Barker (1977) and Krugman (1989a) believe, and we are looking at an imported variety, local supply will be zero (or very small), and hence ϵ_M will closely approximate ϵ_D, aand will be positive.

Let us now look at some results. The level of imports relative to income (the average propensity to consume) is determined by factors like the size of a country and the extent of specialisation, but by far the most important factor in explaining *changes* in imports, even over fairly long periods, is current changes in income.

A representative set of income elasticities is given in Table 18.2. These are taken from Panić (1975) and come from regressions of imports on income, the extent of capacity working (see below), and prices over the period 1957–72. They therefore reflect the effect of income, holding the other two variables constant. They are reported in elasticity form so they show the percentage change in imports for a 1 per cent change in income. To obtain the marginal propensity to import, we multiply the elasticity by the average propensity.

Table 18.2 Income elasticities of demand for imports

	UK	W. Germany	France
Food, beverages and tobacco	0.35	0.86	0.84
Basic materials	0.66	1.22	0.70
Fuels	2.47	2.66	1.26
Manufactured goods	3.09	2.14	2.19
semi-manufactures	2.37	2.06	n.a.
finished products	4.30	3.52	n.a.
Total imports	1.82	1.31	1.63

Note:
n.a. = not available.
Source: Panić (1975).

There are marked differences between the UK and the other two economies. The UK's imports of food and basic materials have lower income elasticities than the others' because of her high level of imports. More serious is the greater sensitivity of the UK's manufactured imports, especially finished manufactures. The latter have always exhibited higher income elasticities than other imports, partly because they include luxury and durable goods, and partly because, with greater scope for product differentiation, variety considerations have more play. In the 1950s, this hardly mattered, because in 1957 finished manufactures accounted for only 8 per cent of total imports, but by 1988 this had risen to 51 per cent; in 1988, on Panić's figures, if they still applied, for every £1.00 increment of national income, £0.47 would be spent on imports of finished manufactures!

Panić's results may be criticised on a number of grounds. For instance, they ignore tariffs (which fell substantially over his sample period) and his data are now rather dated and are too aggregated. All these points are true but there is little reason to suppose that they substantially change the story. For example, Barker (1977) and Thirlwall (1980) both reported high elasticities from disaggregated data, while Taplin (1973) and Marquez (1988) both show the UK and USA to have the highest elasticities for total manufactures among samples of twenty-six and seven countries respectively.

Panić's variable on capacity working was intended to capture the possibility

263

that, as British industry approached full capacity, it would be less able to expand – i.e. ϵ_S in (18.12) would fall. Under these circumstances, ϵ_M would reflect ϵ_D more closely and would consequently be greater. In fact, he found no such effect. A more successful separation of the roles ϵ_S and ϵ_D is found in Khan and Ross (1975). They argued that in the long run there will be an equilibrium relationship between imports and income that reflects the adjustment of both domestic supply and demand, and that will be manifest in the relation of trend imports to trend income. In addition, there will be short-run effects that reflect only the demand side of domestic behaviour (because supply is assumed fixed in the short run), which will be reflected in a relationship between the deviations of actual imports from trend and actual income from trend. Combining these components, Khan and Ross estimated cyclical (short-run, demand) elasticities and secular (long-run, equilibrium) elasticities for a sample of fourteen industrial countries' visible imports. The former are all positive, but the latter have mixed signs. The more dynamic economies tend to have negative secular income elasticities (e.g. − 0.71 for Japan, − 0.21 for West Germany), showing that local output can reduce imports in the long run, but the less successful ones have positive elasticities (e.g. 1.91 for the USA, 0.89 for the UK, 0.50 for Belgium); see Table 18.3.

Table 18.3 Income elasticities for various OECD countries' trade

	Total visible imports Khan–Ross (1958–72)		Total visible exports Goldstein–Khan (1955–70)		Manufactures Krugman (1971–86)	
	Current[a]	Potential	Current[b]	Secular	Imports	Exports
Belgium	1.58	0.50	0.98	1.90	1.99	1.24
France	3.56	− 1.71	1.40	1.70	—	—
W. Germany	2.23	− 0.21	0.40	2.07	2.83	2.15
Italy	2.13	− 0.47	0.95	2.21	3.65	2.41
Japan	1.94	0.71	1.21	3.64	0.80	1.65
Netherlands	1.40	0.44	1.02	1.92	2.66	3.86
United States	0.55	1.91	0.60	1.01	1.31	1.70
United Kingdom	0.94	0.89	0.90	0.90	—	—

Notes:
[a] Current half-year.
[b] Current quarter.
Sources: Khan and Ross (1975); Goldstein and Khan (1976); Krugman (1989a).

A ratchet effect

These results suggest that rapid increases in demand generate more imports than the same increase spread over a longer period. They also imply, however, that rapid declines cut imports correspondingly quickly. In fact we have little experience of falling imports, so the latter implications is rather weak. It has been challenged by Brechling and Wolfe (1965), who argued that there is a ratchet effect whereby imports sucked in during a boom are not pushed out over the next slump. Hence import penetration rises in a series of steps, each step coinciding with a boom.

The basic idea is that capturing new markets is expensive. Hence, once foreign producers have a share of the British market, they try to maintain it even though it may not be very profitable during a slump. However, if, when the slump ends, they can increase their supplies faster than British producers (perhaps by switching goods from other markets), they can reap the benefits in terms of rapidly rising sales. The evidence for this is weak, but it is an idea worthy of consideration, especially if a government is contemplating a dash for growth.

The conclusion must be that, especially for manufactures, but also for imports as a whole, income elasticities exceed 1, often quite substantially. This explains why, as economies have grown over the last thirty years, the average propensity to import (imports/income) has risen, for every 1 per cent in income causes a larger than 1 per cent rise in imports. There is also plenty of evidence that in the UK import elasticities are rather higher than elsewhere in OECD. Of course, as economists we should not stop here; we must ask why the elasticities take these values, but that issue is held over until the end of the next chapter.

Exports and income

Exports from one country are merely the imports for another. Thus, all that we have said above about imports carries over to exports except that exports are determined by foreign rather than domestic incomes. There are, however, two additional factors that warrant consideration. First, the possibility of importers switching their demand between competing exporters and, second, the possibility that exports are affected by domestic as well as foreign incomes.

Above we argued that rising incomes in, say, France would normally stimulate French imports. That raises other countries' exports in total, but it does not necessarily raise British exports, because France need not buy any extra goods from Britain. Thus if we are concerned with British exports we need to consider not only our partners' marginal propensities to import but also how they allocate their imports over competing suppliers. If one supplier is relatively unpopular, or is unable to meet all its demands, imports from that supplier may not keep pace with imports from other sources. This appears to be Britain's position. Even ignoring relative prices, it seems that, as countries' incomes increase, their imports from Britain increase less rapidly than total imports. Considering all importers at once, this means that as world income grows it appears that Britain's share of world trade declines.

We say 'appears' because it is not unambiguously clear that the cause of Britain's declining share of world trade is rising incomes abroad. Over time, Britain's share of world trade has fallen dramatically, and world incomes have risen dramatically, but this does not necessarily add up to a causal relationship. An equally good empirical explanation is that the income elasticity of demand for British exports is the same as for other countries' exports (which would imply a constant share of world trade), but that there is some additional factor that causes Britain's exports to be displaced by others'. It is true that economists have not yet identified that additional factor – it is usually captured as a strong declining trend term in econometric work on exports – but it is well to be aware that it is not yet proven beyond doubt that British exports suffer from an unusually low income elasticity. Functions explaining British exports exhibit either a low income elasticity and no trend, or a normal elasticity and a strong negative trend. There is as yet no way of telling them apart and these two different descriptions must at the moment be taken to be referring to the same phenomenon.

To illustrate the orders of magnitude involved, we consider the work of Goldstein and Khan (1976). These authors estimated both supply and demand functions for total exports for a sample of nine OECD countries over the years 1955–70 (see Table 18.3). Their demand curves contained relative prices and world income and allowed for the effects of these variables to take several quarters to affect exports fully. The long-run income elasticities ranged from 3.64 for Japan and 2.07 for West Germany to 1.01 for the USA and 0.90 for the UK. The elasticity of total world trade with respect to world income is approximately 1.4, so these figures reflect Japan's and Germany's rising shares of world trade and the USA's and the UK's falling shares. Note that no trend or additional factor was included in the demand equations.

A disaggregated study of UK exports from 1955 to 1973 by Winters (1981) showed that considerable variations occur in income effects over destinations and commodities. For British visible exports as a whole Winters found an income elasticity of 1.35 counteracted by a decline of 3.4 per cent per annum due to unspecified trend factors; at a disaggregated level, income elasticities ranged from 0.66 (textiles) to 1.76 (scientific instruments) and trend factors from − 12.6 per cent per annum (textile fibres) to + 2.7 per cent per annum (drink). Consumer goods and metal-based intermediate goods showed the greatest sensitivity to income, and non-metallic intermediates the least.

This low income elasticity or negative trend result is one of the most interesting and crucial of the questions surrounding British trade performance. We shall return to it in section 19.3 below.

The 45° rule

The last two columns of Table 18.3 refer to more recent estimates of the income elasticities for trade in manufactures, which are based solely on the demand for variety. Using the model of monopolistic competition described in section 5.2, Krugman (1989a) argued that the larger a country's output, the more varieties of good it will be able to produce at minimum efficient scale, and hence the larger its sales will be both at home and abroad. In terms of growth, the faster a country grows the more rapidly its sales will grow, and, given the rate of foreign growth, the higher will be its apparent income elasticity for exports and the lower its apparent income elasticity for imports. Indeed, in the simplest model, the ratio of the export to import income elasticities will equal the ratio of the growth rates at home and abroad. (Hence if the two ratios are plotted, they will describe a 45° line.) Krugman found his prediction vindicated in several data-sets and found, additionally, that, whereas in a sample covering 1955–65 Japan had an exceptionally high ratio of export to import elasticities and the USA an exceptionally low one, in 1971–86 both had reverted towards more typical values. This precisely mirrors their growth experience.

Exports and the pressure of demand

The second factor specific to exports is the so-called pressure of demand hypothesis. This suggests that, as the British economy expands, British firms find it easier to sell at home than to export. This is usually supposed to occur through either the physical curtailment of the supply of exports or the worsening of non-price competitiveness. The latter includes factors such as delivery times, after-sales service, design of goods and the willingness to adapt goods to foreign requirements. Some of these factors are fixed in the short run, for instance design, but some, especially delivery delays, are amenable to short-run manipulation.

Before considering the evidence on this hypothesis, we should note that it presumes a different mode of behaviour of exporting firms from that normally assumed. In the simple profit-maximising model of the exporting firm, firms ration exports by price, so in order to justify the pressure of demand hypothesis we need to find some reason why prices are not flexible. This is normally explained in terms of oligopolistic behaviour, where price rigidities tend to be observed. We also, incidentally, need a good explanation of why the

266

home market should be preferred to the export market. This is an issue that is not often confronted in the literature, but the usual reasoning is that export markets are more costly and risky to service and therefore less profitable.

Among empirical studies, Artus (1970) found significant pressure of demand effects on UK exports of motor vehicles and chemicals, while Winters (1974) confirmed that the strength of the effect depended on the relative profitability of home and export markets: the relatively more profitable the export market, the smaller the effect of the pressure of demand on exports. The magnitude of the effects of the pressure of demand is not very large: Winters (1974) found that on average a 1 per cent increase in the pressure of demand reduced manufactured exports by around 0.2 per cent, while in Winters (1981) the corresponding figure for total exports was 0.36 per cent. Looking more directly at one quantifiable dimension of non-price competitiveness, Lund and Miner (1973) found that a 10 per cent increase in waiting times reduced export orders by about 2 per cent, while Artus (1973) estimated that a 10 per cent rise in domestic demand increased the waiting time for machine-tools export orders by around 3 per cent. None of this is very precise, but overall there is a strong impression that exports do suffer somewhat in the face of strong domestic demand.

FURTHER READING

The classic references on international multipliers are *Machlup* (1943), *Meade* (1951) and *Metzler* (1950, 1951). Alternative textbook explanations are *Thirlwall* (1980), *Lindert and Kindleberger* (1982) for a geometric approach, and *Dornbusch* (1980b) for more algebra.

Organization of Economic Co-operation and Development (1979) describes both the OECD model and its use in policy-making, while *OECD Economic Outlook* – especially December 1976 and 1977 – and *Feinstein and Reddaway* (1978) describe economic policy discussions during the 1970s. *Komiya* (1980) discusses interdependence generally, as does section 26.2 below.

For evidence on income effects see *Panić* (1975) and *Khan and Ross* (1975), which are straightforward. More complex are *Barker* (1977) and *Magee* (1975). On the pressure of demand effect for imports see *Hughes and Thirlwall* (1977), *Barker* (1979) and *Whitley and Wilson* (1979). For export income elasticities *Goldstein and Khan* (1978) and *Winters* (1981) are accessible if you ignore the technical material. Exports and the pressure of demand are discussed by *Steuer, Ball and Eaton* (1966). *Artus* (1970), *Winters* (1974) and *Greene* (1975), and by *Henry* (1970), who adopts a different approach.

Recent studies of elasticities include, for example, *National Institute Economic Review*, various issues, *Yang* (1987), *Marquez* (1988), and the references given in the next chapter. While the precise results differ, the basic messages and modes of analysis are the same as those in the classic references used in the text. For developing countries, see, for example, *Bond* (1987), *Moran* (1988), and *Winters and Yu* (1988).

KEY CONCEPTS

foreign trade multiplier	repercussion effects
'locomotive' theory	'convoy' theory
payments-constrained countries	blocked transmission
output and demand elasticities	capacity and the pressure of demand
secular and cyclical elasticities	45° rule

QUESTIONS FOR REVIEW

18.1 Distinguish between the closed-economy, open-economy and repercussion multipliers.

18.2 What problems would a 'growth convoy' face?

18.3 What are the main practical and conceptual problems of estimating income elasticities of demand for international trade flows?

18.4 Using data from *International Financial Statistics* and elasticity estimates from Spencer (1984, tables 7 and 9), examine the 45° rule.

19 Prices, Competitiveness and the Current Account

Having considered the way that incomes affect international trade, we now turn to the major economic variable: prices, including the price of foreign money – the exchange rate. Just as before we sought to isolate the income effects, here we shall try to isolate the price effects. It is not quite as straightforward as before, however, because price changes affect real incomes by changing the relationship between money expenditure and the quantities bought. However, provided we are careful, this complication should not cause too much trouble. We shall assume that the government's fiscal stance is fixed, so that income changes, if at all, only in response to price changes. We shall also for convenience assume that foreign incomes are unchanged. This is the same 'small country' assumption that we used in Chapter 18, and it does not imply that the home economy is necessarily a price-taker. We shall consider only the current account of the balance of payments, and indeed we shall concentrate mainly on the trade balance.

The price we consider in most detail is the exchange rate. We shall not yet ask what determines the exchange rate; rather we shall investigate the effects of its shifting from one exogenous value to another.

The chapter starts with an early analysis of devaluation that concentrates exclusively on price effects – the elasticities approach. This involves deriving the demand curve for imports and the supply curve for exports and then examining the equilibria in these two markets. The results of exchange rate changes depend on the elasticities of demand and supply, hence the name. The approach is subject to some limitations, however, and these are spelt out at the end of section 19.1. Section 19.2 examines the empirical evidence on price elasticities. Most of it refers to visible trade, but price and income elasticities for invisible trade are also reported. As well as reporting numbers, this section also introduces certain methodological points. The final part of the chapter digresses slightly to deal with non-price competitiveness. After offering a definition it discusses various aspects of this phenomenon: supply rigidities, research and development, design, marketing effort and the link between the quality of exports and the exchange rate.

19.1 DEVALUATION: THE ELASTICITIES ANALYSIS

The elasticities approach to devaluation concentrates on the price elasticities of demand and supply for exports and imports. It has a long pedigree, culminating with Robinson (1937), but it is no longer considered a sufficient analysis by itself. We study it in detail partly because price responses are the essence of contemporary economics, but mainly because it analyses the impact effects of devaluation from which all the later developments are born.

The import demand curve
We start with the market for a single implemented good – say, oranges. We assume that the UK – the importer – produces some oranges, identical to the imported ones; hence her demand for imports is the difference between local demand in total and local supply. As the price changes, import demand will

reflect the changes in both local supply and demand, and, since those are normally in opposite directions, we would expect imports to be relatively sensitive to prices.

We can see this diagrammatically in Figure 19.1. On the left we have the UK's demand (D) and supply (S) schedules for oranges. For any price, we can calculate the residual, which is imports, and transfer this horizontally to the right of the diagram to plot imports against prices. The import demand curve is flatter (more elastic) than either of the two basic relationships. If price exceeds p_0, the supply exceeds demand, and we observe exports rather than imports; our procedure would then yield a supply curve for exports.

Figure 19.1 The home market and the demand for imports

The import market

We now combine our demand curve for imported oranges with a corresponding supply curve of imported oranges, to explore the market equilibrium. Assuming that the rest of the world conducts all its transactions in dollars, foreign exporters will be interested in their returns in terms of dollars rather than pounds. Hence, in order to plot the demand and supply curves on one diagram, we need to convert the two prices to the same currency. We choose to work in terms of sterling, so we divide the dollar prices in the foreign supply schedule by the exchange rate to get their sterling equivalent. The final outcome is shown in Figure 19.2(A) where we plot the demand for (D) and supply of (S) imported oranges in the UK against the sterling price.

Now suppose the exchange rate is devalued from, say \$2.50:£1.00 to \$2.00:£1.00. Assuming other prices and incomes are unchanged, the demand curve does not shift at all. The supply curve, on the other hand, rises by one quarter to S', because the sterling that orange sellers earn is now worth fewer dollars than before: in order to supply the same quantity of oranges they require more pounds. To be specific, suppose the marginal kilo of oranges is worth \$1.00 to the foreign producers (that is, the price they can earn by selling elsewhere). Before devaluation they require £0.40 to cover this (= \$1 ÷ 2.5), but afterwards they require £0.50 (\$1 ÷ 2). With unchanged demand but a

270

Figure 19.2 Devaluation in import and export markets. (A) Imports of oranges. (B) Exports of whisky

higher supply schedule, the market equilibrium moves to give a lower quantity but a higher price. The exact movements in price and quantity depend on both schedules, but the direction of the change in total expenditure on imports depends only on the elasticity of demand. If demand is elastic, the percentage fall in quantity exceeds the percentage rise in price and expenditure falls.

We now repeat the exercise for exports – of whisky, say. An export supply curve (S) – derived from Britain's underlying demand and supply relationships – and the foreign demand curve (D) are shown in Figure 19.2(B). As before, the figure is fundamentally in terms of dollar prices but has been converted into sterling. Suppose we now devalue; this time the supply curve remains unaffected (assuming incomes and all other prices including factor prices in the UK are unchanged), but the demand curve shifts. A bottle of whisky costing £10.00 originally sold abroad for $25.00, but now it sells for a mere $20.00. Hence, without harming sales, the whisky producers could charge £12.50 a bottle; this is reflected in a rise of the demand curve by one quarter to D'. As before, this produces a new equilibrium, but this time both price and quantity rise, so we know immediately that revenue rises.

The net result of devaluation is that export earnings from whisky certainly rise, while import expenditure on oranges could have risen or fallen. Overall, the balance of these changes could be positive or negative, depending on the elasticities of demand and supply in the two markets.

Some special cases   It is instructive at this point to consider a few particular values of these elasticities. First, suppose that demand in neither market were sensitive to price (because, say, of import quotas). Both demand curves would be vertical. Devaluation would affect neither quantity, but by raising import prices and not changing export prices it would necessarily worsen the trade balance. If supply were completely fixed, on the other hand, unchanged quantities but rising export prices would improve the trade balance. (Draw your own

271

diagrams to confirm this.)

Second, consider a small country proper that faces fixed world prices in dollars for both its exports and imports. At these prices it is assumed to be able to sell and buy unlimited quantities. Hence at any particular exchange rate the supply curve of imports and the demand curve for exports are horizontal – that is, the elasticities of supply of imports and of demand for exports are infinite. The price in Britain is just the sterling equivalent of the fixed world price. A devaluation acts much as before, raising the supply curve of imports by 25 per cent along its length and the demand curve for exports similarly, as is shown in Figure 19.3(A) and (B). Obviously the improvement in the trade balance will be greater the more elastic are import demand (reducing imports) and export supply (expanding exports). Furthermore, we can show that, if devaluation occurs from a point of balanced trade, the trade balance cannot deteriorate. Export and import prices rise equally, hence, even with no quantity changes, trade would remain balanced because the values of exports and imports would be equally affected. But any quantity effects that do exist will improve the balance – hence the result.

(A) *Imports – small country* ($\epsilon_M^S = \infty$)

(B) *Exports – small country* ($\epsilon_X^D = \infty$)

(C) *Exports – Keynesian supply* ($\epsilon_X^S = \infty$)

Figure 19.3 Some special cases. (A) Imports – small country. (B) Exports – small country. (C) Exports – Keynesian supply

Finally consider the Keynesian case where the prices of both exports and imports are fixed in the seller's currency and there is, at least around the market equilibrium, unlimited supply at those prices – i.e. infinite supply elasticities. The import market is still as in Figure 19.3(A), but the export market is transformed. Instead of a horizontal demand curve, we have a horizontal supply curve, and we revert to the downward sloping demand curve. Devaluation raises this proportionately – as before – with the result shown in Figure 19.3(C). The extent of the revenue increase depends entirely on how much is sold abroad. Given a fixed sterling price, the devaluation reduces the dollar price of whisky by the full extent (i.e. from $25.00 to $20.00 a bottle), so the quantity change depends solely on the foreign elasticity of demand for whisky.

We can formalise this case quite simply. Consider a 1 per cent devaluation. From Figure 19.3(A) we know that import prices rise by 1 per cent and import quantities by ϵ_M^D per cent, where ϵ_M^D is the import demand elasticity ($\epsilon_M^D < 0$). Hence import expenditure rises by $(1 + \epsilon_M^D)$ per cent. From Figure 19.3(C) we also know that (sterling) export prices remain unchanged, but that quantity, and therefore revenue, rise $-\epsilon_X^D$ per cent, where ϵ_X^D is the (negative) foreign elasticity of demand for our exports. Now, if the value of exports and imports are equal, these percentage changes apply to the same base, and so the trade balance will improve if the percentage change in exports exceeds that in imports – that is, if

$$-\epsilon_X^D > (1 + \epsilon_M^D) \tag{19.1}$$

or if

$$\epsilon_X^D + \epsilon_M^D < -1. \tag{19.2}$$

In words, a small devaluation will improve the trade balance in the presence of infinite supply elasticities if the sum of the elasticities of demand is less than -1 (i.e. is absolutely greater than 1). This is known as the *Marshall–Lerner* condition and it has figured prominently in the history of international economics. Note its restrictive assumptions: infinite elasticities of supply at home and abroad, and initially balanced trade. The latter is easily relaxed, an initial trade deficit making improvement less likely, but the introduction of supply elasticities is messy. The basic result is that devaluation is more likely to be successful if high demand elasticities are matched by high supply elasticities and low demand elasticities by low supply elasticities. This may be seen by experimenting with Figure 19.2, but for formal details see Stern (1973) or Lindert and Kindleberger (1982).

We have conducted all our analysis in terms of sterling. This makes sense if we are primarily interested in the effects of trade on the internal UK economy. If, on the other hand, we are interested in the effect of devaluation on the foreign exchange reserves, it would be better to work in terms of foreign currency (dollars). To check your understanding, you should work out some examples for this case also. The results are the same except where trade is initially unbalanced, when minor differences occur.

The elasticities approach and its problems

So far we have spoken only of the markets for (imported) oranges and (exported) whisky. We have assumed that, when the exchange rate changes, only the price of the good we are analysing is affected, leaving all other prices and incomes unchanged. In analysing oranges, we implicitly assumed the price of whisky to be constant and vice versa, even though when we added the two markets to calculate the trade balance we knew that this must be false. The elasticities approach to the balance of payments proceeds by treating total imports as we have treated oranges, and total exports as we have treated whisky. And it is precisely these *ceteris paribus* (other things being equal) assumptions that prove its main weakness, for devaluation affects the whole of the economy, not just small sections in isolation.

The elasticities approach deals only with two goods – imports and exports – but it plainly cannot claim to be derived from a two-good model. With only two goods it would be impossible for 'other prices' to remain constant while we considered exports, for 'other' would imply 'import' and we know that import prices change. Similarly, even if we assume that sterling export prices are constant while we consider imports, the extra demand for exports must affect incomes and the factor markets and so affect the production of importable goods. Hence behind the elasticities model there must lie at least one more market – a market for non-traded goods. It is possible that changes in the output of this sector could compensate for changes in the output of the tradable goods, and so allow the latter to move up and down their supply curves without affecting incomes and factor prices. Even then, however, there are complications, because devaluation may disturb the price of non-tradables (see section 20.2). In fact, it requires very restrictive assumptions to justify the elasticities approach in a full economic model (see Dornbusch, 1975a).

Why study such an unrealistic model? Partly to introduce tools that will be useful later on, but also because the elasticities approach offers a reasonable approximation in certain circumstances. The horizontal supply schedules may be realistic if there is unemployment, as may be the fixed non-traded price if domestic markets are oligopolistic. In the short run, therefore, elasticity results may apply. Also, of course, although everything may change in response to devaluation, the impact of devaluation operates through the channels we have just discussed. Thus, while income will be affected ultimately, the stimulus is felt only through the effects analysed in the elasticities approach. Hence this section quantifies the initial impact of devaluation and provides the first step to the analysis of its final incidence.

19.2 PRICE ELASTICITIES IN PRACTICE

Before going on to more complete models of devaluation, we evaluate some of the elasticities that have proved crucial so far. For considerable periods of the past it was felt that international trade elasticities were so low that the Marshall–Lerner conditions would be violated, a view known as elasticity pessimism. This is relatively rare now, mainly because of an influential study by Orcutt (1950), which catalogued several reasons why existing econometric estimates tended to be understatements, and a subsequent series of estimates based on new data and more careful methodology. That said, however, current estimates must still be treated with great caution, and are even now not very high.

Estimating import price elasticities — Given our derivation of the import demand curve as the residual of total domestic demand and domestic supply, the obvious way to calculate the import elasticity would be to estimate the domestic parameters and calculate it from those. In fact this is rarely pursued – especially for manufactures – because it is rare that the perfect substitutability of domestic and foreign supplies actually applies. Most investigators, therefore, work directly on the import market, relating import quantities to import prices. The vast majority also simplify the process further by assuming that the supply elasticity of imports is infinite. This fixes the import price quite independently of the quantity that our country demands. Can we therefore expect that regressing total imports on their average price will give a fair estimate of the elasticity of demand for imports? The answer, following Orcutt (1950), is generally 'no', for the following reasons.

Identification. Suppose the elasticity of supply is not infinite. Then the price and quantity of imports are determined simultaneously by both demand and supply factors, and the observed values reflect both sets of effects. The elasticity that arises from the regression of such data will be a mixture of the (negative) demand elasticity and the (positive) supply elasticity.

Aggregation. If elasticities of supply are not infinite, the effect of supply shifts on prices depends on the elasticity of demand: the lower the elasticity, the greater the price change and the lower the quantity change. When we add many imports together into total imports, the changes in the average price will be dominated by the inelastic goods, and since these will be associated with small quantity changes the overall estimate of the elasticity will be too low. This problem is significant for total imports, but, where basic raw materials and manufactures are separated, it is probably less so.

The quantum effect. Orcutt suggested that small changes in prices (as occur in the absence of exchange rate changes) will have less effect than large (devaluation-induced) changes. In fact, the evidence for this is very weak (Goldstein and Khan, 1976).

Errors of measurement. If the price series are measured with error – that is, if they appear to reflect price changes that did not occur and that therefore have no associated quantity change – then the average response to price changes will be biased towards zero. This is probably rather significant, not least because econometricians are usually forced to use unit value series instead of price indices. Official trade statistics record the value of transactions of a particular sort and also the quantity, but not the price. The only price indicator available is the value divided by the quantity, which is known as the unit value. If the headings under which trade is recorded are homogeneous – e.g. coffee of a particular standard – then the unit value closely approximates the price. But, if the heading is very heterogeneous – e.g. tractors of engine power 25–37 kW – there is room for trouble.

Suppose there are two types of tractor, A and B, which sell for £10,000 and £20,000 respectively. Suppose initially that 100 of each are imported. The unit value of tractor imports is £15,000. Now suppose that sales shift, so that only 50 of A are bought and 150 of B. The quantity is unchanged but the value has increased, hence the unit value has increased despite the fact that no price has changed.

There is only one way to avoid this problem – better data. Some genuine price indices are available for international trade and, in general, using these increases the size of the estimated elasticities (e.g. Kravis and Lipsey, 1971, 1982).

Lags. Orcutt argued that relating the current year's imports to the current year's prices would omit any effect that took longer than a year to appear. This is undoubtedly important. There are five possible reasons why lags may exist: information lags – it takes time to discover that prices have changed, although not in the case of devaluation; technical lags – it is necessary to sell old stock before buying new; adjustment costs – drawing up new contracts and liquidating old ones takes time; order–delivery lags – for most goods there is a significant lag between placing an order and receiving the goods; and expectations – if a price change is believed to be transitory, people will not react until it has proved itself otherwise. Fortunately, given its pervasiveness, this problem is easily overcome: one includes lagged prices in the regression as well as current ones, and this is now almost universal practice.

Some representative estimates of price elasticities of demand for total visible imports appear in Table 19.1. The first set is taken from Khan and Ross (1975). In view of their aggregation and their omission of lagged prices, they

275

are probably biased positively; in particular, the three positive values should not be taken seriously. Probably more reliable are Taplin's (1973) in the second column. These stem from annual data and allow for lags of up to one year on prices. Taplin found negative price elasticities for total imports into twenty-four of the twenty-five countries he studied. He also calculated elasticities for broad groups of goods, finding manufactured imports generally more elastic than basic materials and food.

Table 19.1 Price elasticities for various OECD countries' trade

	Total visible imports		Total visible exports Goldstein–Khan (1955–70)		
	Khan–Ross (1958–72)[a]	Taplin (1954–70)	Demand		Supply
			Short-run[b]	Long-run	Long-run
Belgium	− 0.22	− 0.65	− 0.04	− 0.07	1.6
France	− 0.30	− 0.39	− 1.10	− 1.34	1.3
W. Germany	− 0.53	− 0.61	− 0.25	− 1.32	1.2
Italy	− 1.67	− 1.03	− 1.02	− 2.36	2.0
Japan	0.15	− 0.81	0.07	0.20	− 0.1
Netherlands	0.38	− 0.02	− 1.26	− 2.39	2.3
USA	− 1.00	− 1.05	− 1.26	− 2.12	3.9
UK	0.40	− 0.22	− 1.17	− 1.18	− 0.8

Notes:
[a] Current half-year only.
[b] Current quarter.
Sources: Khan and Ross (1975); Taplin (1973); Goldstein and Khan (1976).

These results suggest that British imports are relatively insensitive to prices. Disaggregated studies dispute this, however; prominent among them is Barker (1970). Barker examined UK imports disaggregated into eighty-four commodity groups. Using specially constructed unit value series to approximate prices, he searched carefully for price effects. His results are summarised in Table 19.2. As hinted above, elasticities appear to increase with the degree of processing. These results are rather dated now, but subsequent research, although slightly less detailed, suggests that time has not changed the basic conclusions.

Table 19.2 UK import price elasticities[a]

Food, drink and tobacco	− 0.31
Raw materials	− 0.06
Fuels	− 0.56
Semi-manufactures	− 1.22
Finished manufactures	− 1.62
Total visible imports	0.65

Note:
[a] Estimated 1955–66; elasticities refer to 1966.
Source: Barker (1970).

Estimating export price elasticities

The formalities of estimating export price elasticities are the same as those for import price elasticities, but some of the practicalities are rather different. First, neither demand nor supply elasticities are infinite, which makes the identification problem more significant. This means that supply and demand factors have to be estimated simultaneously either as two separate equations (Goldstein and Khan, 1978) or combined into a single quantity function derived from the theory of oligopolistic markets (e.g. Winters, 1981).

The second difference concerns the nature of competition in export markets. As we saw above, exports are affected not only by the rate at which partner countries import but also by the extent to which they switch their given level of imports among competing suppliers. If the switching is more price sensitive than the import decision, exports could be substantially more price elastic than imports. Looked at differently, this says that British exports to France compete partly with local French goods (the import dimension) and partly with German and Italian exports to France (the switching dimension). Hence, export equations should include two foreign price terms.

The third practical difference concerns lags. Possibly because of the switching dimension, exports seem to take longer to react than imports. Hence lags of up to five years are not rare in export equations.

Table 19.1 above presents Goldstein and Khan's estimates of elasticities for total visible exports in both the long and short runs. Their results are highly aggregated, and, although they allow for lags, they require both price and income responses to show the same pattern through time. In Chapter 18 we argued that incomes are the main determinant of export behaviour and that they are not subject to long lags; thus Table 19.1 probably overstates the export price elasticity in the short run and understates it in the long run. On the basis of this table, the Marshall–Lerner conditions are satisfied for every country except Japan and Belgium. The Japanese results for both exports and imports are very strange, however, and should not be taken seriously. Both exports and imports for the UK appear to be relatively insensitive to prices.

We have mentioned the Marshall–Lerner condition, but the last column of Table 19.1 shows quite clearly that its assumptions are not satisfied. The elasticities of supply reported there are nowhere near infinity. The UK appears to be relatively insensitive to prices in this respect also, and it is tempting to try to explain her poor trade performance by reference to this feature; however, so far there is no firm evidence to relate the two phenomena. Nevertheless the pervasiveness of relatively low price elasticities for the UK does suggest some degree of inflexibility.

More detailed work is harder to find for exports than for imports, but Winters (1981) provided some evidence for the UK. Disaggregating visible exports by sixteen commodities and ten areas of destination, Winters explained UK exports with reference to three price terms: UK prices (in dollars) relative to competing exporters' prices (the switching dimension); UK prices relative to importers' domestic prices (the importing dimension); and UK export prices (in sterling) relative to UK domestic prices (a supply side variable). The extent and time pattern of responses differ substantially between both areas and commodities. For example, in Table 19.3 the most price-sensitive goods are seen to be either (a) not highly differentiated (e.g. textiles and petroleum products), or (b) finished manufactures (e.g. metal manufactures and other manufactures).

In general, the longest response lags are on the competitors' prices and the shortest on the importers' own domestic prices. Winters hypothesised that this is due to informational problems: foreign importers of UK goods discover local price trends substantially sooner than they discover price changes in potential alternative suppliers.

The 'J-curve'

These results suggest that, while in the long run elasticities may be sufficient to make devaluation successful, the short-run response may be perverse. This

Table 19.3 UK export price elasticities with respect to different prices[a]

Commodity	Price[b]		
	$\bar{p}^{UK}/p^C$	$\bar{p}^{UK}/p^L$	p^{UK}/p^H
Food	0.0	− 0.88	2.23
Drink	− 0.93	− 0.44	0.69
Textile fibres	0.0	− 0.83	0.13
Petroleum products	− 2.19	− 1.75	0.21
Other non-manufactures	− 0.68	− 0.29	0.10
Chemicals	− 0.31	− 0.42	0.57
Textiles	− 1.83	− 0.34	0.68
Iron and steel	0.0	0.0	0.16
Non-ferrous metals	0.0	− 0.62	0.12
Metal manufactures	− 2.72	− 0.27	0.95
Mechanical engineering	− 1.50	0.0	0.15
Electrical engineering	− 1.55	− 0.30	0.14
Transport equipment	− 1.36	− 0.33	0.0
Scientific instruments, etc.	− 0.71	− 0.34	0.14
Clothing, footwear, travel goods	− 1.37	− 1.03	0.17
Other manufacturing	− 1.76	− 0.33	0.61
Total	− 1.18	− 0.35	0.36

Notes:
[a] Annual data 1958–73.
[b] $\bar{p}^{UK}$ is the UK price in dollars
p^{UK} is the UK price in sterling
p^C is competitors' prices in dollars
p^L is the importers' local prices in dollars
p^H is the UK domestic price in sterling.
Source: Winters (1981).

would produce a sort of J-shape in a graph of the balance of trade through time, with the balance worsening before it improved in response to devaluation. A particular factor in the short-run responses is the currency in which trade is invoiced. Most trade in the few months after a devaluation will have been arranged before it. If prices were fixed then in terms of sterling, British traders will receive or pay what they expected regardless of devaluation; if they were fixed in dollars, however, devaluation will raise the sterling value of the transaction. Hence importers of dollar-priced goods will pay out more and exporters receive more than anticipated. Unfortunately, most manufactured trade is invoiced in the exporter's currency – hence devaluation will usually cause an immediate worsening of the trade balance. The duration of this effect depends on the longevity of pre-devaluation contracts; Carse, Williamson and Wood (1980) estimated that a 10 per cent devaluation worsens the British trade balance by about 3 per cent of export value for six months, gradually reducing to 0.5 per cent after two years. Once old contracts have been worked off, the extent of the J-curve depends on how rapidly prices are adjusted to the new exchange rate and how quickly quantities respond to the new prices. Thirlwall (1980) quoted the worsening as lasting about nine months for the 1967 devaluation.

Hysteresis The hypothesis of *hysteresis* allows for the possibility that large price changes can have irreversible effects. If firms face fixed costs – for instance, in designing new goods or in creating marketing organisations – or if consumers cannot easily switch between suppliers, the average and variable costs of trading differ. For example, an appreciation of sterling will make imports more competitive and may allow importers to cover the fixed costs of creating a new distribution chain in Britain in order to increase their market share. A subsequent depreciation of sterling to its original exchange rate may not, however, reverse the process and drive those imports out of Britain, for importers may still earn enough to cover their variable costs of supply even if they no longer earn a contribution towards the sunk costs of establishing the distribution chain. Such circumstances suggest that exchange rate changes may have permanent, asymmetrical or quantum effects on trade, according to whether or not they cause jumps in firms' trading capacities. The consequences for econometric estimation are unfortunate; those for the actual economy may be deleterious. Baldwin (1988) found evidence consistent with hysteresis in US import patterns over the 1980s, while Bean (1987) found hints of it in British export data over the twentieth century.

Invisibles

Invisibles account for around one-third of British current credits, but nothing like that proportion of the econometric effort devoted to trade. In principle, invisible trade is no different from visible trade, but in practice it has proved hard to estimate its parameters. Since most invisibles are intermediate services – i.e. sold to businesses rather than to final consumers – we often relate sales to the level of activity in the purchasing sector than to income. Table 19.4 presents some estimates of income and price elasticities of demand for the UK. The price elasticities are in a form that reports the change in sterling receipts with respect to exchange rate changes. This highlights the role of the currency in which flows are denominated in determining the effect of the exchange rate on the balance of payments. We comment briefly on each type of invisible trade.

Table 19.4 Some parameters of UK invisible trade[a]

| | Exchange rate effects | | | Activity effects | |
	Debits	Credits	Variable	Short-run elasticity Debits	Credits
Freight transport	0.6	− 1.0[b]	UK and world trade	0.68	1.14
Passenger transport and travel	− 0.56	− 3.25	Permanent income	1.03	0.66[c]
Other services	− 1.0[b]	− 0.55	GNP	0.30	0.35[c]
Direct investment earnings	0.0[d]	− 1.0[b]	Actual output ÷ potential output	− 1.02	3.63
Other earnings	0.0[d]	− 1.0[b]	None	—	—
Private transfers	0.0[d]	− 1.0[b]	GNP	1.73	4.13

Notes:
[a] Sample period 1961–74. All relationships contain effects additional to those listed.
[b] Small country assumption: Britain adopts world price fixed in dollars. Hence sterling payments rise by the proportion of devaluation.
[c] Elasticity of British exports with respect to total world exports of the service concerned.
[d] Flows are insensitive to the exchange rate and are denominated in sterling.
Source: Bond (1979).

Freight transport is related to the amount of international trade carried out both by Britain and on routes not passing through Britain but for which Britain provides much shipping. The market for shipping is competitive; prices are set in dollars, and Britain is a small country. With the world demand for shipping fixed, Britain's receipts from shipping increase as the exchange rate falls. Sterling expenditure per unit of imported shipping rises similarly, but the higher cost of shipping relative to domestic services leads to some economies in its use, so total expenditure rises by only 0.6 per cent per 1 per cent depreciation in sterling.

Passenger transport and travel are complementary goods and are best considered together. There are two components – business travel, which is inelastic, and personal travel, which is highly elastic with respect to both prices and incomes. The exchange rate elasticities reflect both a substitution effect, as Britain becomes relatively more expensive or cheaper, and, for credits, a valuation effect that foreigners' dollar expenditure is worth more sterling as the exchange rate falls. The high elasticity for credits reflects the ability of cheap countries to capture tourists from dear ones. Not shown here, but also important, are special events like the Olympics.

Imports of *other services* are surprisingly income inelastic and Britain is losing her share of the world market very rapidly: every 1 per cent growth of world exports generates only 0.35 per cent growth in UK exports. The debit exchange rate elasticity of -1.0 again reflects world prices fixed in terms of dollars, coupled with quantities quite insensitive to prices.

Investment earnings depend mainly on the stocks of assets held and their rates of return, neither of which is given in the table; however, there is some cyclical fluctuation in profits on direct investments, which explains the activity elasticities given. The exchange rate effects reflect the fact that flows are denominated in the debtor's currency. Hence devaluation raises the sterling value of dollar-denominated earnings from abroad but does not affect sterling-denominated outflows (debits). If, on the other hand, Britain were obliged to make outflows denominated in dollars, we would record -1.0 under debits, which would indicate that devaluation increased the outflow proportionately. In these circumstances, a country that was a net debtor would find that devaluation increased the net outflow of income abroad thus deflating the economy. Cooper (1971) has argued that this is a problem for many developing countries.

Finally, *private transfers* are very income sensitive and are generally denominated in the donor's currency.

19.3   TRADE PERFORMANCE AND NON-PRICE COMPETITIVENESS

An overriding feature of post-war British economic history has been her apparently poor trade performance: we have just examined the price elasticities for British trade and have found them rather low. In the previous chapter we considered income elasticities and found British imports very sensitive to incomes and British exports either insensitive or subject to strong negative trends. Both intellectually and from the point of view of economic policy, these income elasticities or trends present one of the most crucial and challenging question in this area of economics. Moreover, it is now clear that the USA has begun to demonstrate exactly the same tendencies: nearly all the arguments of this section apply equally to the USA as to the UK. This section asks whether economics has anything to contribute to explaining the trend declines in US and UK shares of their markets. First, however, it asks whether the declines matter.

Trade performance: does it matter?

The short answer to this question is 'yes, it does matter'. High imports do not matter *per se* – they just show that one is exploiting the gains from specialisation. Neither does a falling share of world trade necessarily matter.

Britain's share of world exports of manufactures has fallen from around 33 per cent in 1899 to 30 per cent by 1913, 26 per cent in 1950 and 9.5 per cent in 1980. Britain was the predominant manufacturing nation in the nineteenth century and it would be absurd to hope that, as others emerged, she should still undertake a third or more of world trade. Similarly, as Germany and Japan emerged from the devastation of the Second World War, it was plain that they must take up their shares of world commerce.

The problem is that the UK's trade performance has constrained her economic growth. Low export growth means relatively stagnant injections, while a high marginal propensity to import means a low multiplier. Furthermore, for most of the post-war period the divergent growth of exports and imports resulted in a balance of payments constraint: the government wished to expand the economy, but was prevented from doing so because the trade accounts would become unbalanced. During the 1950s and 1960s this was manifest in large balance of payments deficits on official settlements. As autonomous expenditure rose above autonomous receipts, there was an excess supply of sterling. Committed to maintaining the exchange rate, the authorities had to spend the foreign exchange reserves to buy up the surplus sterling; when the reserves ran out, economic growth had to stop. During this period the succession of fiscal expansions followed by balance of payments induced contractions became known as 'stop–go'.

After 1972, sterling was floated: the government was no longer committed to maintaining the exchange rate. For a while it believed that this cut it free of the foreign constraint and would permit an almost unlimited 'go'; thus it embarked on the Heath–Barber boom of 1972–3. It rapidly became plain, however, that a poor trade performance was still a constraint – it was just manifest differently. Since floating, 'go's have resulted in rapid inflation coupled with the rapid depreciation of the exchange rate. We shall explore these phenomena in detail later. Here it suffices to say that no amount of floating can break the identity that the value of exports must roughly equal the value of imports; and, if you have some immutable relationship between imports and income, then trade performance largely determines growth.

Even during the 1980s British growth was constrained by her trade performance. Exports were buoyed up by the huge injection of revenue from North Sea oil, but the very high marginal propensity to import still left a low multiplier. Autonomous injections – either from increased investment or from fiscal policy – rapidly leaked out of the economy into extra imports, leaving little to boost domestic employment, and causing rising imports to eat into the oil revenues. That the fundamental problem remained became obvious over 1986–9, as a balanced current account was transformed into a deficit of around £19b. by GDP growth of around 4 per cent per year for three years.

Let us now consider the main question: why is Britain's trade performance so weak? There is a short answer here, too: we just do not know. There are many theories, and there are also some strong indications about what does *not* cause the problems, but as yet there is no generally accepted explanation.

Among the factors that do not explain Britain's trade performance are the following. It is not solely due to prices: Britain lost her share of world trade even over quite long periods when price competitiveness was improving. It is not due to Britain's trade being concentrated on the wrong markets or in the wrong types of goods: demand for the types of good that Britain produces has grown more rapidly than average (Panić and Rajan, 1971). It is not due to weaknesses in particular sectors: there is hardly a single good in which Britain

281

has increased her share of world trade. It is not just due to the loss of her Commonwealth links: it is true that former colonies have moved away from British goods faster than other markets, but again Britain has lost out in all markets.

The answer appears to be, therefore, in non-price competitiveness.

Non-price competitiveness is a nebulous concept. It covers all aspects of competitiveness excluding price; it therefore helps determine the position of the demand curve in price–quantity space. An improvement in non-price competitiveness shifts the demand curve out – more can be sold at the same price. Actually there is a conceptual difficulty here, which we can mention although not solve. Imagine that there were only two sorts of car: Rolls-Royces, which sell for £50,000 and Mini-Metros that sell for £5,000. Suppose now that British Leyland raised the price of the Metro to £50,000; not many would sell! But would this be because Metros were uncompetitive in the price sense (i.e. just too expensive), or in the non-price sense (not as good as the alternatives)? The answer is either or both. The moral is that almost any degree of non-price uncompetitiveness could be overcome by charging a low enough price. This has led Armington (1977) to argue that non-price competitiveness is an unnecessary and meaningless concept.

In this sub-section we shall assume that there is some meaning to the term non-price competitiveness, and we shall assume that for some reason relative prices cannot be changed very much.

Supply problems

There are three main groups of reasons that have been advanced for Britain's poor trade performance. The first is just straightforward supply inelasticity. Strictly speaking this is not a dimension of non-price competitiveness, but in practice it is difficult to distinguish the two problems. First, if supply cannot expand to keep pace with demand, it may appear that the demand for British goods is growing more slowly than other countries' demand even if it is not. Second, a persistent inability to satisfy demand will eventually lead to its curtailment. In the traditional theory of the firm this occurs through rising prices, but in oligopolistic markets it is likely to occur through non-price rationing, e.g. lengthening delivery lags, reduced sales efforts, etc. Hence, supply difficulties will eventually lead to shifting demand curves anyway.

Goldstein and Khan (1978) found Britain's export price elasticity of supply rather low, which is perhaps indicative of supply problems, but they found nothing exceptional about her elasticity of supply with respect to the level of productive capacity. Of course, we should also ask what determines capacity and this is more contentious. In the 1970s 'supply-side' economists held that economic conditions in Britain were not conducive to investment, especially of a risky nature, because of high personal tax rates and the antipathy between management and labour. The objective indicators of labour relations, such as days lost to strikes, did not support the latter view: Britain had many strike-free industries and was overall around the average for OECD (*Department of Employment Gazette*, November 1980). However, a general mistrust of labour could easily lead to lower investment in Britain (especially among multi-national companies), quite independent of such indicators. (Indeed, the infrequency of strikes could just indicate that management always gives in to labour!) Similarly, the evidence was far from obvious that Britain's tax system imposed higher burdens on entrepreneurs than that in most other countries (e.g. Central Statistical Office, *Economic Trends*, December issues, especially 1979).

The proof of the pudding, however, was in the eating. A dominant theme of Mrs Thatcher's early administrations was supply-side economics, with substantially lower taxes on high incomes, stable or increased taxes on poorer workers, the privatisation of state industries, the erosion of (some) restrictive practices and a determined attempt to redress the power of trades unions vis-à-vis management.[1] At first manufactured exports were stagnant, despite mild economic growth abroad, but in the mid-1980s they briefly boomed. Landesmann and Snell (1989) suggested that this pattern reflected changes in the income elasticity of demand for UK exports: downward at first, as UK manufacturing capacity shrank, but then climbing, to allow Britain to maintain a constant share of world trade. The difficulty, however, is in knowing whether the observed pattern was due to the income elasticity or to changes in UK competitiveness, which fell and recovered over the same period, and whether the postulated effects were permanent.

Profitability

We must also ask some questions about profitability. In the long run, we expect the supply of exports to be related to the difference between export prices and costs. Most empirical work, on the other hand, relates it to the difference between export and home price indices. This gives us some hint that increasing true profitability would help exports, but it is far from certain. Neither is the direct evidence very convincing. For example, Gribbin (1971) found that UK exports were on average less profitable than home sales, but neither he nor Oppenheimer *et al.* (1978) found strong evidence that this seriously harmed exports.

Productivity

Probably more important is Britain's poor productivity record. This does not necessarily show up in lower profitability if wages are sufficiently low or if investment projects that would have been profitable with higher productivity are in fact ignored. That productivity is low in Britain is beyond doubts. For example, Pratten (1976) found that, on average, UK branches of multinational companies were 50 per cent less efficient than North American branches and around 20 per cent less efficient than European branches, while the Central Policy Review Staff (CPRS, 1975) found productivity in Britain 30 per cent or more below that in West Germany on identical plant in the vehicles industry. Possible explanations are many: low investment, short production runs, restrictive practices and labour unrest, too much 'down-time' on assembly lines, inadequate stocks of spare parts for machinery, poorly qualified and insufficient skilled workers, and so on.

Corresponding to the mid-1980s' export boom was an apparent 'productivity miracle' as output recovered more quickly from the recession than did employment. This period was also one of uncharacteristic industrial peace, and improving supply-side factors. The importance of the supply side was further underlined by the late-1980s, in which the UK boomed, productivity growth slowed, and labour relations deteriorated, while imports boomed and exports stagnated. This latter experience suggests that, for permanent effect, supply-side policies must address long-term issues such as research and development and education and training levels, in both of which Britain lags lamentably behind her major competitors – see, for example, OECD (1987a),

Prais and Wagner (1988) and Crafts (1991). We return to research and development below.

Further evidence of the role of productivity comes from Krugman's 45° rule (see section 18.4). Productivity is the proximate determinant of the growth of output in industrial economies, and Krugman showed how relatively high growth permits high income elasticities of demand for a country's exports and low income elasticities for its imports.

Design and sales effort

The other two sets of explanations for poor trade performance take us into non-price competitiveness proper. The first concerns product design – including factors like technical specification, reliability, servicing arrangements, and aesthetics – and the second concerns the process of selling – including the number and type of outlets, the size and quality of the sales staff, and the extent of advertising. Many of these factors are very difficult to quantify, and as a result much of our evidence is impressionistic; nevertheless, there are good reasons for believing that both elements are important.

Several surveys have asked traders to rank by importance various factors affecting their behaviour. All suggest that non-price factors are at least as important as prices, especially in engineering-based industries. For example, the National Economic Development Council (NEDC, 1965) asked UK investors the main cause of their buying foreign machine-tools: price was mentioned by 5 per cent, but it was dominated by technical superiority (30 per cent), the absence of a British alternative (21 per cent), better delivery terms (20 per cent), and a willingness to meet special requirements (8 per cent). Similarly, in a sample of twenty-six large successful US exporters, 28 per cent attributed their success to prices, 25 per cent to technical factors, 12 per cent to after-sales service and 10 per cent to unique product design (Kravis and Lipsey, 1971). Finally, the Mechanical Engineering Economic Development Committee (MEDC, 1968), surveying over 200 UK engineering firms, found that marketing techniques were a more important explanation of changes in exports (28 per cent of the reasons offered) than product specification (14 per cent) or any other reason. Among marketing techniques were mentioned the quality of marketing staff, the frequency of customer visits, attendance at trade fairs, and advertising. Interestingly, both large and successful exporters found it better to administer their export sales themselves than to entrust them to agents, although for small and new exporters the latter is probably unavoidable.

The problem with survey material is the doubt about whether respondents are being truthful or whether indeed they actually understand the process they are describing. However, we also have some evidence on non-price competitiveness from other sources. For example, a detailed study of the British motorcar industry (CPRS, 1975) attributed the stagnant exports and rapidly rising import penetration in Britain to a lack of economies of scale, inefficiency, poor quality, inappropriate product ranges, poor delivery times and reliability, and inadequate distribution networks. These results are largely confirmed in an econometric study by Leach and Cubbin (1978).

Research and development

An important determinant of technical design is research and development effort. We have seen in Chapter 5 how this affects the composition of international trade. Can it, then, explain Britain's poor trade performance?

The UK's research and development effort is now proportionately well below that of many countries, but during the 1950s and 1960s, when her trade performance was already strongly in decline, Britain was second only to the USA. However, in a sense that was the very problem. The sectoral break-down of UK research and development was almost identical to that of the USA, whereas her competitors, especially West Germany and Japan, had a completely different structure (Freeman, 1979). While the latter concentrated on 'commercial' sectors, by far the largest expenditure in the Anglo-Saxon countries was on aircraft, much of it military (see Table 19.5). Hence Britain failed in certain sectors almost by default. But neither did she get very far in her favoured field. Research and development is like the Cup Final – coming second is not much use. The USA with its huge resources captured most of the advances, and reaped great economies of scale from its large domestic market. Furthermore, UK research and development tended to be concentrated on a few very large projects – for instance, Concorde and the advanced gas-cooled nuclear reactor – which bore little or no commercial return (see Henderson, 1977).

Table 19.5 The industrial structure of R&D in 1962–3 (% of total)

	UK (1962)	USA (1962)	W. Germany (1963)	Japan (1963)
Aircraft	35.4	36.3	—	—
Vehicles and machinery	10.3	15.6	19.2	12.7
Electrical machinery and instruments	24.0	25.5	33.8	28.0
Chemicals	11.6	12.6	32.9	28.3
Metals	4.1	2.6	6.6	9.7

Sources: Freeman and Young (1965), quoted in Freeman (1979).

It has even been argued that, because of its pattern, UK research and development has had a perverse effect on trade performance. By creaming off the best brains to these esoteric enterprises, research and development has denuded the production aspects of industry of qualified manpower. Hence, while nearly all West German managers hold engineering qualifications, few British managers do: Ray (1979) quoted the percentages of qualified engineers in the metal working industries in 1974 – Sweden 6.6, Germany 5.7, France 5.3 and Britain 1.8.

Quality

The previous sub-section treated R&D as if it were entirely exogenous, but in fact it arises from the trade-off between the quality of goods provided and their costs of production. This is a complex area, which we cannot tackle fully here, but we do consider one aspect of it.

First, however, in order to investigate hypotheses about quality we need a measure of it. One possible candidate is the unit value of trade. Above we interpreted unit values as proxying prices: a rise in Britain's unit value relative to competitors' was bad for competitiveness. Now, however, we turn this on its head and argue that price might reflect quality. If the composition of trade within a trade heading shifts towards more expensive varieties of the good, the unit value rises and, if the higher-priced varieties are also better, we have an indicator of quality. Hence rising unit values indicate improving (non-price) competitiveness. Without detailed studies we cannot arbitrate between these

285

two interpretations of the unit value series, but let us for now accept the quality interpretation.

On this interpretation, the evidence is convincing that Britain has been gradually moving 'down market' relative to her competitors. For example, the National Economic Development Office (NEDO, 1977) considered thirty-five industrial sectors and it found that, over 1970–4, West Germany increased her share of world trade in thirty-one of them and Britain in only three, despite the fact that the German unit values exceeded the British ones in twenty-nine cases. Similarly, it found that, for Britain, the unit value of imports exceeded that of exports in twenty-five sectors while the same was true for only nine German sectors. Connell (1979) considered time-series of unit values for exports of non-electrical machinery (20 per cent of UK exports), and found a declining UK world share along with a declining unit value relative to France and Germany.

Since more sophisticated and better-quality goods are likely to be purchased by the affluent, the UK's drift down market could easily be manifest in apparently low income elasticities of demand. Brech and Stout (1981) found evidence of such a link in an interesting study of the British engineering industry. They constructed a unit value based index of export quality over the 1970s, and related it to the exchange rate, world income and time. They found that UK product quality rises with world income (richer people buy better goods), declines through time, and is positively related to the exchange rate.

This last result implies that depreciation reduces product quality. It is argued to occur because depreciation tends to reduce export prices in foreign currency and/or raise them in local currency. With no change in the quality of goods, this allows exporters to sell more units abroad and/or earn higher profits per unit of exports. In other words, it reduces the pressure on them, allowing them to sell the same old designs for a little longer. An appreciation, on the other hand, worsens price competitiveness and reduces profitability, forcing exporters to innovate if they are to stay in business. Hence, runs the argument, appreciation enhances quality and this eventually boosts export performance.

Two assumptions underlie this hypothesis. First, it assumes that firms are satisficers not maximisers. If opportunities exist to raise profits by quality change, maximisers will take them even at lower exchange rates; only satisficers must be forced into it by appreciation. Second, it presupposes that 'poor' goods compete on price, while 'superior' goods compete on quality. In other words, at the bottom of the range, quality is not necessary to sell your goods provided their price is low enough, whereas, at the top, high prices are not a deterrent to selling quality goods.

Provocative though Brech and Stout's results are, we cannot immediately jump to the policy conclusion that appreciation is good for exports. Brech and Stout's sample contained only about six quarters of appreciation, so the improvements they observe may be only short-run effects. In the long run, even exporters in the top end of the range may feel that the low profits engendered by the high exchange rates make exporting not worthwhile. Also Brech and Stout were looking at the average quality of exports. The average can rise either by increasing the number of high-quality exports or by decreasing the number of low-quality exports. Their results might just show that appreciation drives out low-quality exporters without stimulating any high-quality ones.

Conclusion

Non-price comptetitiveness encompasses a wide range of effects that might plausibly affect trade performances. They range from delivery lags (which we examined in Chapter 18) to product design and sales effort. Since we cannot explain Britain's poor trade performance with prices or incomes, we must conclude that non-price competitiveness is important, but so far measurement problems have precluded our identifying precisely which aspects are dominant. The causal chains from these non-price variables to export performance are usually rather vague, and furthermore many of the apparently significant variables are not amenable to policy-induced improvements. Hence we should beware of trying to draw too firm a set of policy conclusions from this chapter. Rather, we should learn the negative lessons that certain economic policies, desirable from other standpoints, may have untoward trade effects via their influence on non-price competitiveness.

On the intellectual front, the interesting feature of non-price competitiveness is the doubt it must cast on our simple economic models. The manipulation of price with a view to profit maximisation looks excessively simple-minded when confronted with the evidence of sales effort, research and development, and exchange rate induced quality change. This is not to dismiss such models, merely to caution the reader against their seductive elegance and simplicity. Prices are important, but if this subsection teaches us anything it is that they are but one aspect of economic performance in the real world.

FURTHER READING

The elasticities approach is surveyed in *Lindert and Kindleberger* (1982) and *Stern* (1973), and an interesting early reference is *Haberler* (1949). *McKinnon* (1981) also offers some useful insight. The empirical literature is huge, but is more suited to the specialist than to the average student: *Magee* (1975) and *Thirlwall* (1980) survey the field, while *Stern, Francis and Schumacher* (1976) list many results. More details may be found in the text references. On currencies of invoice see *Magee* (1973a) and *Page* (1977).

In addition to *Thirlwall*, probably the best introduction to non-price competitiveness is *Ray* (1966). For a more recent analysis, as well as a survey of price and non-price effects, see National Economic Development Office (1977) and *Armington*'s (1977) review of it. On export unit values and marketing, *Connell* (1979) is excellent, while on research and development and technical manpower see *Freeman* (1979), *Ray* (1979), *Greenhalgh* (1990) and the references in the text, especially *Crafts* (1991). An insightful early analysis of both price and non-price influences on British exports is *Wells* (1964). *Kravis and Lispey* (1971) is a seminal study of trade, especially price aspects, but it is too long for any but the keenest students.

KEY CONCEPTS

import demand/export supply curve
price effects of devaluation
disaggregation and price elasticities
J-curve
non-price competitiveness
sales effort

Marshall–Lerner condition
identification of price elasticities
hysteresis
supply-side problems
unit values – price or quality?
R&D and competitiveness

QUESTIONS FOR REVIEW

19.1 Distinguish between the effects of devaluation for (a) a small country and (b) a country with 'Keynesian' pricing.

19.2 What are the problems of the elasticities approach to devaluation?

19.3 What factors might give rise to a J-curve. How important are they empirically?

19.4 Why does trade performance matter? (There is more to this question than the view that exports are a 'good thing'!)

19.5 How would you (i) define and (ii) measure non-price competitiveness?

19.6 What factors explain Britain's declining share of world manufacturing trade until 1980? What caused the decline to halt in the mid-1980s and what factors will determine whether it will continue into the 1990s?

NOTE

1 J. K. Galbraith has characterised 'supply-side' policy as stemming from the belief that the rich do not work because they are paid too little, while the poor do not work because they are paid too much (*Observer*, 5 September 1982).

20 Macro-economics and the Current Account

This chapter continues our discussion of devaluation by looking at macro-economic models of the balance of payments. These approaches see the foreign account as just one more element of the macro-economic balance of an economy and they show how the current account is intimately connected with developments in other sectors.

We start with the 'absorption approach', which expresses the trade balance as the difference between national output and expenditure. This illustrates that, unless these macro-variables are affected, no balance of payments policy can be effective. The next section specialises this model to look at a small, open economy, in which the prices of traded goods are entirely determined by world prices, but in which non-traded goods are explicitly considered. We then consider the role of wage rigidities in balance of payments policy and the effect of devaluation on local prices: these sections involve some empirical evidence. Finally we consider certain alternative policies to devaluation – in particular tariffs.

This chapter still assumes a fixed exchange rate regime and concentrates exclusively on the current balance. However, because of its macro-economic orientation, it attends more closely to income changes than did the previous chapter. Indeed, here we begin to see the interaction between price and income effects.

20.1 DEVALUATION: THE ABSORPTION APPROACH

To meet the criticism of the elasticities approach's partial equilibrium nature we now consider a simple but more general model. It is not a complete general equilibrium model because it largely ignores assets and inter-temporal questions, but at least it covers all goods markets. This approach takes us back to the links between income and foreign trade and to the accounting identities of section 17.1.

The fundamental equation

National income (Y) is defined as the sum of all final demands less the part of them that is met from imports (M). If we define total domestic final expenditure (consumption, investment and government expenditure) as A (for absorption) we have

$$Y = A + X - M, \tag{20.1}$$

where X is final demand stemming from abroad, namely exports. From this we can derive the fundamental equation of balance of payments theory

$$B = Y - A, \tag{20.2}$$

where B is the balance of payments on current account. This equation states that the current balance is merely the difference between total income (output) and total absorption (expenditure). It is easiest to think of (20.2) in real (constant price) terms, although occasionally this causes difficulties if the relative prices of exports and imports change. Such occasions will be noted below.

Actually (20.2) may be viewed in two ways. Interpreted *ex ante*, that is, in terms of intended values, it specifies an equilibrium condition: if you intend to spend more than you earn you must be prepared to run a deficit. On the other hand, interpreted *ex post*, it is an accounting identity: given the way we construct the national accounts, it *must* apply in terms of actual outcomes to any economy. The strength of identities in economic analysis is that they cannot be violated – they constrain the set of feasible solutions, helping to limit the cases that need to be considered. Their great weakness is that alone they cannot tell us anything about causation. Hence, if we observe a deficit, i.e. $B < 0$, we know that income falls short of spending, i.e. $Y < A$, but we do not know why. Without further input we do not know whether economic policy should be directed at Y or A or both.

For balance of payments policy, (20.2) has one simple message. If you wish to manipulate B, your policy must affect either income or expenditure. Thus, the elasticities approach, which concentrates solely on the left-hand side of the equation, is deficient in that it says nothing about whether devaluation will raise Y or cut A.

On this basis we can divide balance of payments policies into *expenditure-reducing* and *expenditure-switching* policies. The former, fairly obviously, aim to change A, leaving Y unchanged in the first instance. The latter act initially on Y, leaving A unchanged. (The term 'switching' arises because you can raise Y for a given level of A only by switching some of A from foreign goods to your own goods.) Most actual policies have direct impacts on both elements of the account, and obviously all do so eventually because income and expenditure are linked through the circular flow of income.

The effect of these types of policy on the current balance may be easily seen. In terms of changes, (20.2) may be written

$$dB = dY - dA. \tag{20.3}$$

However, the change in absorption will comprise a direct part (dA_D) and also an indirect part stemming from changes in income (dA_I). If we let the marginal propensity to absorb be α, the latter component will be

$$dA_I = \alpha dY \tag{20.4}$$

so that

$$dB = (1 - \alpha)dY - dA_D. \tag{20.5}$$

We now examine the three elements of this equation.

The marginal propensity to absorb (α)

The marginal propensity to absorb is the sum of the marginal propensities to consume, invest and undertake government expenditure. In general, we would expect it to be below unity, but it is possible that an investment boom could raise it above temporarily. For example, the growth of output could generate accelerator effects, or devaluation make investment by multinationals very attractive. (A multinational seeking to expand, and financing its expansion with foreign currency, gets more for its money after devaluation. Its investment will be the greater if it believes that the devaluation is temporary, because then, while the exchange rate is low, it is buying local resources at what it believes to be an unsustainably low price – McKinnon, 1980.)

The direct income effects of devaluation (dY)

Devaluation can have any of three main direct effects on income. First, the idle resources effect: the price effects of devaluation will stimulate the production of importables and exportables; if there are spare resources, this expansion will not be entirely at the expensive of non-traded goods, and so income may rise directly. Second, there is the terms of trade effect. The terms of trade report the rate at which we can transform a unit of exports into a unit of imports – thus they determine how favourably national product can be converted into national income; given production, a deterioration in the terms of trade directly reduces income. The third effect is a real resources effect. If the exchange rate has been overvalued prior to devaluation this may have distorted the production sector of the economy – in particular reducing the output of tradables relative to non-tradables. By correcting this distortion, devaluation raises real output.

There is one special case to note here. If the economy is at full employment, income cannot rise; that is $dY = 0$. Hence, to be successful, devaluation must either reduce absorption directly or be accompanied by other expenditure-reducing policies. We turn now to the first of these possibilities.

The direct absorption effects of devaluation (dA_D)

We have seen that devaluation tends to raise the domestic currency prices of tradables and that non-tradables' prices might also rise. This may reduce absorption directly through any of several mechanisms.

Money illusion may cause people to reduce real expenditure when prices rise, even though their incomes have risen in line; this may reflect mistakes, or lags between price and income changes, or a reaction to the uncertainty that price and income changes engender.

Income distribution may also be affected by devaluation. First, devaluation raises prices, and so, if wages do not rise, there is a redistribution towards profits. If profit earners save more than wage earners, this may reduce overall absorption. Second, income may be redistributed between sectors. A common case is where a primary goods sector exports at a fixed world price, while manufacturing industry, with specialist output, faces a steep demand curve. In local currency terms, the former increases its prices proportionately to devaluation while the latter increases them by less. The result is redistribution towards the primary sector, which, especially if rurally situated, is likely to have a lower marginal propensity to absorb. Lindert and Kindleberger (1982) suggested that these factors accompanied the Argentinian devaluation of the peso in 1958. Third, most direct tax systems are progressive, but in terms of nominal not real incomes. Hence, inflation tends to push people into higher tax brackets and so reduce post-tax real income. Devaluation could obviously initiate this process, which is known as fiscal drag. Finally, on the other hand, if wages increase more than certain prices, real incomes will rise. This may particularly apply to rents, which are frequently fixed by law. In these cases, wage earners (spenders) gain income at the expense of rentiers (savers).

If we introduce assets, there are further direct absorption effects. If people hold stocks of money, rising prices reduce the real value of these cash balances. This so-called *real balance* effect argues that, given real income, society has some optimal level of real balances. If these balances are reduced through the price rises associated with devaluation, people will replenish them by saving additional amounts. While this is going on, absorption will be reduced although, once real balances have regained their desired level, absorption too will return to its original rate. Finally, if we also introduce bonds, there may well be *interest rate* effects from devaluation. These could go

291

either way, however, and we shall leave them to be examined later.

There is one further point to be mentioned here concerning the valuation of imports and exports. It is not easily incorporated into our formal analysis but the intuition is quite straightforward. Imagine a small country that devalues: in local currency, both imports and export prices rise in proportion to the devaluation. Suppose further that there are no quantity effects, so that export revenue and import expenditure both rise by the extent of the devaluation. If trade was initially balanced, the two rises cancel out, but if, as is usual with devaluations, import expenditure exceeds export revenue, the burden of higher import prices outweighs the benefit of higher export prices. The net result is that real absorption must be reduced in order to balance income and expenditure. The effect is like a terms of trade effect, but it arises not because relative import and export prices change but because the price of a good that the country is a net buyer of (tradables) has risen, hence reducing real income relative to real demand.

Expansion vs. contraction

The conventional wisdom is that devaluation is expansionary. If there are idle resources this shows up as rising incomes and employment, while if the economy is at full employment it appears as rising prices. (Traded goods producers, trying to obtain the extra factors with which to expand, bid up factor prices, and non-traded producers facing excess demand raise their output prices.) We have tended towards that position too, but it is not inevitable: the direct contraction of absorption could reduce output further than the direct income effects raise it. Krugman and Taylor (1978) argued that the valuation problem of the previous paragraph and the redistribution of income from wages to profits and from private to government hands tend to make devaluation contractionary in many developing countries.

Monetary aspects of the absorption approach

The real balance effect is not the only monetary aspect of the absorption approach. Just as, if an individual spends more than he earns during a period, he has to dip into his stocks of money, so too does a country. If Britain is buying more from abroad than she is earning and she has to pay in foreign cash, this must involve running down the foreign exchange reserves (we are still ignoring the capital accounts). Hence the deficit can persist only while the authorities have the exchange with which to finance it. Once this is exhausted, the exchange rate can no longer be supported, and it will fall, presumably far enough to balance future payments.

There is also a domestic dimension to this. The difference between UK income and expenditure is just the sum of the differences between income and expenditure for each of its residents. Hence a national deficit implies private deficits among its residents, and so private cash balances must also be declining. Unless these balances are replenished, the deficit must eventually stop, because the balances will eventually reach some minimum acceptable level. The only constraint on this automatic process is whether the government has sufficient foreign exchange to finance the deficit while it works. However, the fact that letting real balances fall works, does not make it optimal. Even if a deficit could be financed for long enough, this may be a very painful and inefficient way of curing it. Similarly, just because the deficit involves running down cash balances it does not mean that excessive liquidity was the cause of the deficit. However, more of this when we look at the monetary approach to the balance of payments.

The monetary aspects of the absorption analysis also illustrate the distinction between stock and flow disequilibria (Johnson, 1958a). A stock disequilibrium arises if residents wish to alter their stocks of assets. For example, if the rate of inflation is expected to rise, holding money becomes less desirable, and if people run down their cash balances by increasing absorption there will be a current account deficit. Alternatively, as an economy is about to expand, manufacturers often wish to build up their stocks of raw materials. This too leads to a temporary deficit. The important feature of the stock disequilibrium is that it is temporary: once stocks have adjusted, the disequilibrium disappears. The only problem it presents is a financing one.

Contrast this with a flow deficit. If in the inflation example in the previous paragraph the government kept replenishing residents' cash balances, the deficit would persist. In this case, given government behaviour, there would be no natural end to the disequilibrium and some economic policy changes would be required. The obvious candidate might be to stop increasing the supply of domestic cash, but other expenditure-reducing policies might also suffice.

We seem to have reached the conclusion that flow deficits are the fundamental disequilibria and that stock deficits are merely temporary storms that have to be weathered. That is true in a sense, but it is worth remarking that economic crises are almost all of the stock variety.

Take, for example, the floating of sterling in June 1972. The UK current account was in record surplus during 1971, and although, by 1972, it was declining, it was still healthy by historical standards: £214m. surplus over the first half of the year. Furthermore, the foreign exchange reserves were also strong: over $8b. at the end of 1971. Nevertheless, the aggressive expansion of the economy, coupled with the threat of a dock strike and a comment by the Shadow Chancellor of the Exchequer that he expected a devaluation soon, led to a huge loss of confidence. Anyone who could, changed his stocks of sterling into other currencies. The result was that over three days nearly one-third of the exchange reserves was spent supporting the pound! This was a 'mere' stock deficit – temporarily sterling looked unattractive so people moved out of it – but the result was a strong bout of expenditure-switching. The pound was cut free and within a year had depreciated by over 20 per cent.

This episode also illustrates another aspect of the absorption approach to the balance of payments. The depreciation of sterling might have been expected to improve the trade balance, but in fact the opposite happened: 1973 showed a record visible trade deficit. This was partly because of the lags in the responses of trade to depreciation, but largely because the government accompanied it with no expenditure-reducing policies. The British government believed that by floating the exchange rate it could free domestic growth from foreign constraints, because any incipient deficit would be corrected by further depreciation. Hence, until mid-1973 it encouraged absorption to rise even though the economy was rapidly running out of capacity. The result of ignoring the simple accounting identity $B = Y - A$ was a huge deficit, accelerating inflation and, at the end of 1973, a viciously deflationary emergency budget.

The application of the absorption approach

The elasticities analysis was criticised because the relevant (total) elasticities were virtually impossible to measure. Unfortunately, the absorption approach is as bad, because the marginal propensity to absorb and the various direct effects are all likely to vary substantially between different episodes. Hence, as a predictive tool, equation (20.5) is not much use alone. Its importance, however, is that it leads us to ask the right questions and that it highlights the necessary concomitant changes to any shift in the balance of trade. It shows that high elasticities are not sufficient for devaluation to improve the current account, and that any policy that achieves that end must raise income or reduce absorption. Except for the terms of trade and resource reallocation effects, that amounts to saying that we cannot improve the balance of trade without someone producing more and/or consuming less. That is a fundamental insight into the balance of payments and it captures immediately the basic problem of balance of payments policy.

20.2 NON-TRADED GOODS – THE SMALL, OPEN ECONOMY

Non-traded goods have slipped into our analysis in several places already: in Chapter 19 they provided a buffer between the traded goods output and domestic incomes, while in Chapter 18 and section 20.1 they have comprised that section of consumption that was not imported. We now take a detailed look at their role in current account adjustment.

The small, open economy

For simplicity, we consider a small country proper, with no influence over its terms of trade. These are fixed by world prices, which we assume constant. This allows us to combine all importables and exportables into a single aggregate called tradables. The bundle of tradables produced will contain more exportables than the bundle consumed (the difference being exports), but we ignore this for now: international trade consists solely of swapping one tradable for another.

We are now back in a two-good model, but instead of exports and imports we have tradables and non-tradables. We can represent this economy diagrammatically in a manner very similar to that used in Part I of this book. In Figure 20.1, FF represents the production possibility frontier – assuming, as before, full employment, flexible wages, mobile capital, etc. – and the curves marked S represent social indifference curves. The position E represents a complete equilibrium: consumption and production of non-tradables (which must be equal) are OA, while production and consumption of tradables are AE. The equilibrium price ratio is given by the slope of $T_0 T_0$, and the perceived consumption frontier (the maximum consumption combinations that appear to be allowed by production at E coupled with unlimited trade at the given price ratio) is given by the line $T_0 T_0$.[1]

Now suppose that for some reason the economy actually had a relatively lower price for tradables – $T_1 T_1$, say. This would entail disequilibrium, because, at those prices, producers produce more non-tradables and fewer tradables by moving to P, while consumers, moving along the new consumption frontier, do the opposite by moving to C. Hence there is an excess supply of non-tradables (DP) and an excess demand for tradables (DC). The latter can be met by a trade deficit – we merely import more than we export – but the former will be reflected in growing stocks of non-tradables if production stays at P or unemployment if non-tradables cut back to D. (In this case we assume that the government maintains the consumption frontier at $T_1 T_1$ by some sort of income supplement.)

The excess supply of non-tradables results in pressure to reduce their prices, but suppose that for some reason this is impossible. Similarly, while the government maintains the exchange rate, tradable prices cannot be raised,

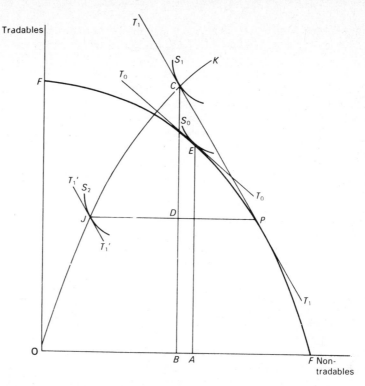

Figure 20.1 Devaluation in a small country

because world prices are fixed. What then becomes of the disequilibrium? Since we have ruled out the automatic adjustment mechanisms, we have to appeal to economic policy.

**The policy
solution**

The first alternative is expenditure reduction – i.e. deflation – maintaining the disequilibrium terms of trade. As expenditure is reduced, by say taxation, the consumption frontier shrinks inwards parallel to $T_1 T_1$. The income expansion line (or Engel curve) for that terms of trade is OK; it shows the consumption points chosen at prices $T_1 T_1$ for each level of expenditure. Clearly, if expenditure reduction is to balance the foreign account it must reduce absorption until the consumption frontier becomes $T_1' T_1'$, at which point (J) the demand for and supply of tradables are equal. However, this is at the price of even greater excess supply of non-tradables (JP) and presumably greater unemployment.

The second policy alternative is devaluation to restore the equilibrium price ratio $T_0 T_0$. (Devaluation raises tradable prices, boosting production and cutting consumption.) This is an expenditure-switching policy and in this instance it alone is sufficient to restore both balance of payments equilibrium and domestic full employment. It does not require support from expenditure-reducing policies because it is implemented in the presence of unemployment and also because the correction of the price distortion permits the movement of production from inside the transformation curve to a point on it.

295

Over-absorption A similar analysis can be pursued where the cause of the current account deficit is over-absorption rather than incorrect relative prices. In this case the temporary consumption frontier is parallel to T_0T_0 but further out, and the deficit is accompanied by excess demand for non-tradables, as well as for tradables. Clearly, then, the policy solution is expenditure reduction, dragging the economy back to E.

It is possible, however, that the excess demand for non-tradables would bid up their price, so that in time the economy would be characterised by both excess absorption and incorrect relative prices. This is the most common predicament for deficit countries, and our analysis shows that, in these circumstances, attaining equilibrium requires both expenditure switching and expenditure reduction.

This model, as well as illustrating some of the points made in the previous section, shows how devaluation works without affecting the terms of trade – namely by altering the relative prices of tradables and non-tradables. Many economists feel that this is a far more important channel of effect than the terms of trade, and it underlies much modern theory. Even if the extreme assumptions of the model are not satisfied, the insight that it gives us into the role of non-traded goods in the adjustment process is very important.

Price flexibility Before leaving this section we should reiterate the important assumptions that we made about prices. If non-tradable prices were perfectly flexible, it would be impossible to deviate from E, because the disequilibrium forces would always return relative prices to the level T_0T_0. For example, suppose we revalue from E, trying to attain prices T_1T_1. Tradable prices fall and this leads to an excess demand for tradables and excess supply of non-tradables. The latter would drive down the price of non-tradables until the excess supply was eliminated – i.e. until the economy returned to E. Hence the perfectly flexible economy does not need devaluation at all, and indeed, except for brief transitional periods while prices are adjusting, does not even suffer balance of payments difficulties. Left to itself such an economy will always settle at E.

In a simple barter model like ours, this automatic adjustment would be quite painless: the net result of any revaluation would be a lower price level but no real changes at all. In the real world, however, there may well be problems, because falling prices destroy confidence, increase the real value of nominal debt, and affect the distribution of income. For this reason, even if prices were flexible in the long run, an economy finding itself producing at P and consuming at C may prefer to devalue, hence raising tradables prices to attain T_0T_0, rather than let the market reduce non-tradables prices. The only difference in the long run would be in the final price level, which would be higher with devaluation. The case for devaluation (or any other form of intervention), then, depends largely on the adjustment costs of policy compared with those of the free market. There is not yet much evidence on this matter, and disagreements about such costs lie at the heart of the controversy between what might loosely be described at the 'Keynesian' and 'monetarist' schools of economic policy.

20.3 DEVALUATION AND WAGE RIDIGITY

So far we have not paid much attention to wages – we have assumed that they adjust passively to validate our conclusions. However, even the slightest acquaintance with the real world will convince the reader that wage formation is one of the most contentious parts of economic life; it is necessary to ask, therefore, what the consequences of less than passive adjustment are. First, however, we should ask how devaluation will affect wages.

Devaluation and income distribution

The precise effects of devaluation on income distribution depend critically on the assumptions made about the productive side of the economy. We shall not pursue this matter in detail but rather try to draw some broad conclusions.

The fundamental equation (20.2) suggests that to cure a deficit someone has either to work harder for the same consumption or to consume less for the same output.[2] The latter certainly suggests a decline in real post-tax incomes and the former also suggests some decline in welfare unless all the extra output stems from people who were previously involuntarily unemployed. Furthermore, since in Britain wages and salaries account for around 70 per cent of income before tax, and 60 per cent after direct taxes, any cut in real incomes seems very likely to impinge on wages.

This may also be seen from the model of the previous section. Assuming that non-tradables are relatively labour-intensive – they contain most services – the Stolper–Samuelson result of Chapter 3 states that a reduction in the relative price of non-tradables will reduce real wages. This is so whether the reduction occurs through falling money prices or through devaluation.

Finally, and perhaps most directly, devaluation raises tradables' prices and also possibly non-tradables' prices. If money wages are sticky, this will reduce real wages. Hence, there are several grounds for believing that, at least temporarily, devaluation will cut real wages.

Real wage rigidity

Now suppose that labour is able to resist the pressure on real wages. Imagine that at some historically determined level of wages and profits, the economy finds itself at a point like C in Figure 20.1, with tradables relatively under-priced and consumption at unsustainably high levels.

If the government now attempts a devaluation to achieve equilibrium, we may observe the following sequence of events. First, devaluation raises tradables' prices, but, we assume, does not affect non-tradables prices. At the original money wage this increases real profits in tradables, reduces them in non-tradables, and reduces real wages everywhere. However, if labour can resist the real wage cut by raising money wages, profits will fall in both industries relative to the first stage.

Now, if it were possible to cut profits to these levels without reducing output – i.e. if the money wage rise induced no further price rises – it would be possible to reach full equilibrium, because devaluation would have produced the correct price ratio, and profits in tradables would have risen relative to those in non-tradables, encouraging the shift in resources towards tradables. In this way, real wages would have been maintained in the face of devaluation at the expense of profits, particularly in the non-traded sector.

Much more likely, however, is that rising money wages drive up prices in the non-tradable sector (tradable prices cannot rise further because they are constrained by world prices.) This could occur because profits were already at a minimum through competition, or because firms set prices as a straight mark-up over costs. Either way the rise in non-tradable prices reduces the real wage further, and, when this is matched by further money wage increases, non-tradable prices have to rise again, and so on. If neither profit margins nor real wages can be squeezed at all, we can attain equilibrium only after non-tradable prices have risen in line with tradable prices. But of course this new equilibrium has precisely the same relative prices as we started with. In other words, wage and profit rigidity frustrate any real effects of devaluation, merely converting an x per cent devaluation into an x per cent general price rise. Thus, eventually income and output must be contracted to balance the foreign account, resulting in a point like J in Figure 20.1.

The money supply

There is, in fact, one feature that may prevent us from getting back to precisely the same position as we started from – the money supply. If the total value of spending were related to the money supply and if the money supply were held fixed even though prices had risen, the real value of spending would fall after a devaluation. This, of course, is just the real balance effect mentioned above, but, with the stronger inflation entailed by rigid wages and profits, it would be stronger in this case.

Expectations

A further complication is the formation of price expectations. In this model, devaluation causes an equi-proportionate rise in the price level. This is not inflation proper because, once the new price level is achieved, price rises stop. However, it is possible that observing these price changes will lead people to expect further price increases in later years. This will lead to even greater money wage demands, validating the expectations and possibly leading to an even worse real squeeze. This could be an important consideration in avoiding, or at least postponing, a devaluation in the real world.

Money wage rigidity

Money wage rigidity is not normally such a problem in economic policy-making, because the real wage can still be reduced by price rises. It would, however, be equivalent to real wage rigidity in circumstances where one was wanting prices to fall – e.g. after a revaluation, or in section 20.2, where devaluation would be preferred to solve the economic problem in Figure 20.1 rather than allowing the excess supply of non-tradables to drive down their price.

The costs of wage rigidity

Real wage rigidity makes economic management very difficult. In our simple model, it is impossible to alter real wages, and therefore impossible to alter the relative prices of tradables and non-tradables, the economy will eventually have to settle at J, with social welfare at level S_2. Since with flexibility we could achieve S_0, the cost of rigidity must be $(S_0 - S_2)$ – although of course this is quite unmeasurable.

Why, then, does such rigidity persist? There are many reasons, but most ultimately come down to distribution. First, if I resist my cut in real wages while everybody else accepts his, the economy will be in equilibrium (because one individual is infinitesimal compared with the whole economy), and yet I shall be consuming my higher, disequilibrium, amounts. Hence the problem is partly one of coordination: each waits to see others making sacrifices before he makes his own, and as a result nothing happens. Second, the bulk of any sacrifice is borne by a relatively small group of people – the unemployed. Since these are often the weakest members of society and are concentrated geographically (usually away from the country's capital city), it is very difficult for them to alter the rigidity that harms them. They have little political muscle and more often than not they are concentrated in the wrong areas and wrong trades to be able to take work at below the prevailing wage rate. Mobility is hindered by the vagaries of the housing market, by its considerable cost, and by the uncertainty of finding work anywhere if unemployment is widespread. Besides, even when the unemployed are prepared to undercut existing workers, employers valuing a quiet life and their own investments in their current workforce are often unwilling to take them on (Okun, 1981). In short, wage rigidities are not necessarily irrational for the individual, or even for individual employers, and eliminating them would require wide-ranging social and political measures that no government has yet shown the will to take.

**Some
estimates**

It is obviously critical to our view of devaluation – or, indeed, of any economic policy – whether or not real wages are rigid. Unfortunately this has proved difficult to assess, because no one has yet discovered an econometrically satisfactory equation to explain wages. Equations that seem fine on one sample period are quite hopeless on another. Among the best references on this subject is Henry, Sawyer and Smith (1976). They examined several models of wage formation and found Sargan's the most satisfactory: this related the rate of wage increase in the UK to the rate of inflation, unemployment and real post-tax earnings. Over 1948–74, unemployment had little effect, but wages made up 60 per cent of the previous year's inflation, and were raised by 1 per cent for every 10 per cent reduction in real post-tax earnings. The latter suggests some degree of rigidity – past frustration in real pay result in large claims to catch up. However, neither this nor the inflation effect amounts to full rigidity: together they imply that a 1 per cent rise in last year's prices will raise this year's wages by about 0.7 per cent.

Similar results stem from estimates of the other popular form of wage equation – the expectations-augmented Phillips curve – which relates wages to unemployment and expected prices. In general, inflation (past or anticipated) is not entirely made up in wage claims, while the coefficient on unemployment is small enough that a devaluation would have to be hugely expansionary before it would produce an equivalent wage rise through this mechanism – see, for example, Levačić and Rebmann (1982). Gordon (1982) found evidence of wage flexibility in the UK and Japan during the 1970s. Finally, the experience of the 1980s suggests considerable wage flexibility in the USA: the mid-to-late-1980s recovery saw rapidly increasing employment and static or even falling real wages. In the UK, on the other hand, real wages continued to rise steadily despite high levels of unemployment.

To summarise, wages do react to price rises, and also probably to excess demand, but they are not so sensitive as to prevent the reduction of real wages.

20.4 PRICES AND DEVALUATION

It is clear that the behaviour of internal prices in the face of devaluation is an important issue, and we take a little time off now to consider some evidence on this issue. We shall see that, in a relatively large country like the UK, devaluation raises prices by raising costs and by cutting import competition. However, for all but the most open sectors, prices rise by less than the percentage of devaluation.

Material costs

Devaluation will raise the cost of imported material inputs for British industry. The importance of this varies over industries, depending on the share of such inputs in total costs (both directly and indirectly via inputs bought from other industries). For example, Barker (1968) estimated that in 1967 the sterling devaluation of 16.7 per cent raised British costs by 2.7 per cent on average (3.3 per cent in manufacturing), ranging from 13.1 per cent in petrol refining to 0.6 per cent in miscellaneous services.

The Law of One Price (LOOP)

The theory and evidence that the internal prices of tradable goods depend on world prices and the exchange rate are overwhelming. The issue is whether or not they depend on anything else. At one extreme, local prices might just be equal to world prices converted into local currency. This is the so-called LOOP; it implies that an x per cent change in the exchange rate will induce an x per cent change in local tradables' prices, and is the assumption used in section 20.2. At the other extreme, the existence of imperfectly competitive product markets or the possibility that unit costs depend on the level of outut may make prices sensitive to demand and hence mitigate the effects of exchange rate changes on tradables' prices.

The LOOP asserts that, apart from known and exogenous factors like tariffs, British prices must equal the world prices for identical goods. The LOOP does not specify any particular chain of causation – for instance, equality could arise from competition in perfect markets, or because British costs adjust to bring cost-determined prices into line with world prices – it merely asserts that the equality holds.

To the extent that identical goods can be observed emanating from different countries (and if they cannot the theory is entirely vacuous), all the best evidence refutes the LOOP. Although a little support can be found at the level of aggregate price indices, if we are to accept the LOOP as something other than mere coincidence, the same sort of equality must hold for individual goods. While there are goods that roughly satisfy the equality (e.g. plywood, paper products), the majority do not. For example, Isard (1977), comparing West German export prices and USA domestic prices over the early 1970s, found massive divergences that were systematically related to exchange rate changes. In Figure 20.2. the LOOP would imply that the broken lines – the ratios of German to US prices in dollars – should fluctuate about a constant level, regardless of what happened to the exchange rate (the continuous line). In fact, they move almost identically with the latter, indicating that goods prices are fixed in local currency and that competitiveness (the ratio of prices in common currency) is mainly determined by the exchange rate. As time proceeds, the relative price of paper begins to fall back to its original level, suggesting a tendency for local currency prices to adjust as indicated by the LOOP, but even after four years the adjustment is incomplete. The apparel price relatively shows no tendency at all to compensate for the exchange rate shock.

The two goods illustrated are fairly typical, as may be seen by consulting the original article. Further evidence – possibly more damning for the LOOP because it refers to small countries – may be found in Richardson (1978) and Marsden and Hollander (1983). The former found no case out of twenty-eight examined where Canadian prices precisely followed American prices, while the latter found evidence of large and long-lived divergences between Australian and world prices. Finally, recent detailed work on Japan, Germany and the USA has refuted the LOOP for precisely defined manufactured goods (e.g. Giovannini, 1988, and Knetter, 1989). These papers, along with Dornbusch (1987) and Krugman (1987c), develop theoretical models stressing

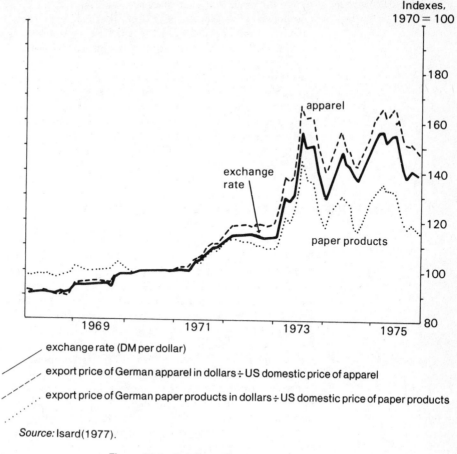

Indexes,
1970 = 100

Figure 20.2 Relative prices and the exchange rate

the role of imperfect competition in the break-down of the LOOP.

All this evidence suggests that, at least in the medium term, the exchange rate affects relative prices; this means that it has real effects and is potentially a useful tool of economic policy.

The causes and consequences of refuting the LOOP

The LOOP fails because of market imperfections. A perfectly homogeneous good sold by many suppliers in a single market – e.g. foreign exchange – can have only one price. In world trade, however, different markets are isolated (e.g. through transport costs, tariffs, culture and linguistic barriers); some goods effectively have few suppliers (e.g. refined oil, large aeroplanes); and most goods are differentiated. The upshot is that sellers have much discretion over their prices, and although market forces may generate some tendency towards one price the process is rarely completed. Hence, we observe throughout international trade substantial and sustained differences in the prices of similar goods from different countries.

Much of our theory depends on the LOOP (the small country assumption), however, so we must ask where its failure leaves us. For some issues the failure has serious implications: for example, the failure of the LOOP implies that the demand curves for British exports are not horizontal, and hence that price competitiveness matters and that the exchange rate is an important tool of macro-economic policy. On the other hand, in many circumstances the LOOP is adopted as a simplifying rather than a critical assumption, and in these cases its loss complicates the analysis without invalidating the main insights. Examples include the analyses of non-traded goods above and that of effective protection (Chapter 8). Even in these cases, however, losing the LOOP invalidates the simple bold conclusions that so often seduce economists. For instance, with the LOOP, an x per cent monetary expansion in the small economy model merely raises prices by x per cent, but, without it, prices do not necessarily rise uniformly by x per cent, and so we can no longer rule out real effects.

20.5   TRADE POLICY AND THE BALANCE OF PAYMENTS

An alternative to devaluation for switching expenditure may be tariffs and related policies. In fact, an x per cent subsidy to all exports and an x per cent tariff on all imports is equivalent to an x per cent devaluation: just as devaluation raises the local price of imports by x per cent, so would tariffs, and similarly both devaluation and subsidy lower foreign currency export prices. Hence, if devaluation were impossible, a uniform tariff-cum-subsidy would do just as well. We saw in Chapter 10 how Keynes (1931) recommended it as an alternative to devaluation, and how the Cambridge Economic Policy Group (*Cambridge Economic Policy Review*, 1978) recommended tariffs in circumstances where, they felt, devaluation would not work.

Import quotas and other non-tariff barriers will also have balance of payments consequences, although they will probably have different fiscal implications from tariffs. Financial disincentives to importing may be imposed, such as requiring importers to deposit funds at the central bank for six months to cover their imports; this amounts to a tariff equal to the interest forgone on these funds. Dual or split exchange rates may exist, whereby traders in one sort of good face a different exchange rate from traders in another. Most common is to have a fixed exchange rate for visible trade and services and a floating rate for other transactions. If we view the latter as 'the true exchange rate' (not necessarily a reasonable assumption, because only a small proportion of transactions may pass through it), then this amounts to the tariff–subsidy solution, with imports being taxed if the 'trade' rate is below the 'true' rate and subsidised if it is above.

Compared with these alternative policies, devaluation will almost invariably be the most efficient expenditure-switching policy, because it introduces no additional distortions within the tradables sector. Moreover, although all the switching policies differ in detail, we should never forget that none of them can break the identity $B = Y - A$. In other words, no policy can be effective unless it raises output, given absorption, or reduces absorption, given output.

FURTHER READING

The absorption approach was initiated in *Alexander* (1952); the other classic reference is *Johnson* (1958a). *Thirlwall* (1980) gives a more thorough analysis than ours, and is particularly good on the history of the UK balance of payments; this is also surveyed in

Dornbusch and Fischer (1980) from a more monetarist viewpoint. Both this reference and *McKinnon* (1980), who uses the absorption approach interestingly, will be more accessible after you have read the next chapter. *Cooper* (1971) offers a sensible analysis of devaluation in developing countries, along with some evidence of its effectiveness, while *Krueger* (1983b) offers a concise summary of the whole field.

Corden (1977) is a straightforward reference on the small open economy and on wage rigidities. The former model was introduced by *Salter* (1959), while *Corden and Jones* (1976) were among the theoretical pioneers on the latter problem. *Dornbusch* (1975b) extends the tradables/non-tradables distinction to large countries and provides interesting insight on devaluation, as does *Dornbusch* (1980, part 2). *Pearce* (1961, 1970) integrates non-tradables into the standard model.

For the empirical work on wage and price formation, consult the references in the text, although some are econometrically difficult. *Brown, Enoch and Mortimer-Lee* (1980) summarise recent UK results. On the law of one price the *Journal of International Economics* (1978, no. 2) provides a useful symposium, while *Kreinin and Officer* (1978) offer a brief survey. *Winters* (1983a) uses the theory of this chapter to examine the case for a sterling depreciation in 1982. The recent work on the LOOP ties in closely with the references on hysteresis (Chapter 19) and the US trade deficit (Chapter 25).

Finally, much of the ground in this chapter was covered by *Meade* (1951) forty years ago!

KEY CONCEPTS

marginal propensity to absorb	expenditure-reducing policies
expenditure-switching policies	real-balance effect
small open economy (SOE)	over-absorption
wage rigidity	the LOOP

QUESTIONS FOR REVIEW

20.1 What will happen if a large economy with full employment devalues?

20.2 What determines the marginal propensity to absorb? What role does that marginal propensity play in the theory of devaluation?

20.3 Use the small open economy model to show how real wage rigidity can lead to unemployment.

20.4 Discuss the ways in which devaluation might affect the relative prices of different tradable goods. (This question will require revision of material in Chapter 5.)

20.5 How might devaluation affect the real incomes of various sections of society? Do these effects shed light on governments' reluctance to devalue their currencies?

NOTES

1 Of course, because consumption of non-tradables cannot exceed production, the economy could not move right of E, but this is not evident to any of the price-taking agents in the economy.

2 The immediate cut in absorption may occur in investment or government expenditure as well as directly in consumption, but ultimately these feed back into falling consumption.

21 Money and the Balance of Payments

Money has led a shadowy existence over the last few chapters. It certainly existed, for we spoke extensively of the price of different monies (the exchange rate), nominal wages and even real balance effects. However, it received little attention directly, and now we rectify this. The monetary approach to the balance of payments, which emphasises money above all else, takes us from a Keynesian world of fixed prices to a neo-classical one of perfectly flexible prices and wages, and consequently full employment.

The second part of this chapter reviews the various balance of payments theories within the same accounting framework. This shows their differences and similarities as well as giving the student a chance to review her understanding of each.

21.1 THE SIMPLE MONETARY THEORY OF THE BALANCE OF PAYMENTS

We start with a very stark and simple model of the balance of payments that not only concentrates on money, but does so to the exclusion of everything else of interest. It requires a fierce set of assumptions and bears little relationship to the real world; it nevertheless illustrates the monetarists' insights very well.

Frenkel and Johnson (1976) stated that the balance of payments is a monetary phenomenon. They were referring to the official settlements balance, which is monetary in the sense that it can be non-zero only if residents (including the government, but excluding the central bank) are either accumulating or decumulating money. Let the official settlements balance be denoted B, and let R_f be total receipts from abroad (from all transactions) and P_f be total payments abroad. As we saw in Chapter 17,

$$B = R_f - P_f. \qquad (21.1)$$

Now define R_d as total receipts of residents from residents, which obviously equals P_d, total payments by residents to residents, and we see that

$$B = R_f + R_d - P_f - P_d = R - P, \qquad (21.2)$$

where $R = R_f + R_d$ and $P = P_f + P_d$. The difference between total receipts and payments is net accumulation of money and (21.2) shows this to equal the official settlements balance.

Viewed backwards, (21.2) shows that official settlements surpluses and deficits must be reflected in hoarding and dishoarding respectively. Hence a surplus serves to increase the stock of money held in the economy, i.e. raise the supply of money, while a deficit serves to reduce it. (The mechanism is that the excess of foreign currency earned over that spent is sold to the foreign exchange reserves in return for sterling, which is then held by residents.) In this way, residents can vary the stock of money in the economy regardless of what the central bank does, because any money created that they do not wish to hold can be disposed of by spending it abroad – i.e. running a deficit. The only constraint on this is that money spent abroad has to be converted into foreign exchange and so the process requires sufficient reserves to finance the desired outflow. For surpluses, there is no constraint as long as the authorities are willing to accumulate reserves indefinitely.

This process is the basis of the monetary approach to the balance of payments. To isolate it, however, and to obtain concrete results many other assumptions are necessary. We shall list these, then discuss the mechanism in more detail, and finally return to assess the roles of the assumptions again.

The assumptions

(i) The demand for money is a stable function of a few known exogenous variables – usually incomes, interest rates and prices, demand being proportional to prices. Residents hold only local currency.

(ii) The exchange rate is fixed.

(iii) The country is small; it is therefore a price-taker on world markets (including capital markets), so prices and interest rates are fixed exogenously. Its money supply is small relative to the world's.

(iv) Wages are perfectly flexible and are determined competitively – hence there is full employment.

(v) Product and asset markets are competitive and have perfect information.

(vi) Changes in reserves are not sterilised. This means that the central bank does not try to prevent changes in reserves from affecting the money supply by adopting offsetting open market operations. Hence the money supply is endogenous.

These assumptions – especially (iv) and (v) – guarantee the independence of the real economy from all monetary phenomena. The composition of output, factor rewards, relative prices and asset portfolios are determined as in standard general equilibrium models without money, by reference to marginal utilities, marginal productivities and so on. Given its composition, the level of output is fixed by the fact that full employment rules. In fact, the real economy is taken to be in long-run equilibrium at all times, so that, for instance, all unemployment is voluntary. This is precisely the economy described at the end of section 20.2, where economic policy is unnecessary because nothing ever goes wrong.

The mechanism

This dichotomy between real and monetary effects is well known in closed economy monetarist models, where the money supply determines the price level but nothing else. In our model, however, domestic prices are fixed by world prices, and monetary policy is isolated from the real economy by another mechanism. Imagine an economy, of the type described, in full equilibrium and in a perfectly static world. Equilibrium would cover both flows, such as income equalling expenditure, and stocks, so that all assets were willingly held at the prevailing prices. In particular, the demand for money would equal the supply. Now suppose that the central bank injected some extra money. With no change in income, prices or interest rates, people would not wish to hold this cash and so would seek to dispose of it by spending it on goods or assets. To the extent that residents buy from one another, the excess cash is shuffled around, always remaining surplus to national demand. If, however, it is spent abroad it disappears from the domestic economy and, in view of our country's smallness, is painlessly absorbed elsewhere. Hence the balance of payments provides a drain through which any excess money can be poured, subject always to there being sufficient reserves to effect the transfer.

During the process of adjustment the country runs a deficit, but, once the excess money has been drained off, the deficit ceases and the economy regains its former equilibrium. The cumulated deficit and hence the overall loss of reserves just equal the initial cash injection. Thus the only lasting effect of the injection is to change the composition of the (unchanged) money stock: the amount backed by domestic instruments rises, while the amount backed by foreign assets (the reserves) falls correspondingly. The whole process is like a huge national stock adjustment, switching from foreign to national assets, and the deficit is a stock deficit.

The only way that this model could generate anything like a flow deficit would be if the authorities persistently tried to supply too much money. This might occur if, for example, they constantly printed money to finance a budget deficit. Even this, however, is best thought of as a series of stock deficits, and a little thought will convince you that it is hardly surprising that a model in which economic behaviour is primarily defined in terms of stocks (as in the money demand equation) can generate only stock deficits.

Equation (21.2) is really just an accounting identity (think how it was derived), so it does not tell us that every deficit is *caused* by excessive money creation, but merely that each is *accompanied* by dishoarding. Deficits may arise as residents tide themselves over a bad harvest, say, or because misinformation leads people not to associate their consumption with declining cash balances elsewhere. The theory tells us that such deficits *could* be cured by cutting the money supply to match demand, or, if time and reserves permit, merely letting it fall to this level. This simple model also suggests that such a course would be optimal, but this most certainly does not generalise to the real world with all its rigidities and imperfections. One need only observe Britain in the early 1980s to see the agonies of cutting the rate of growth of the money supply, let alone the money supply itself.

Devaluation

Devaluation is not necessary in this model, but suppose it occurs. For a small country, an x per cent devaluation raises all tradable prices by x per cent; furthermore, since relative prices are determined by (unchanged) real factors, all other prices must also rise by x per cent. The uniform rise in prices increases the demand for money by x per cent, and, since supply is not affected initially, this demand can only be met from abroad. As residents cut expenditure in an effort to reconstitute their cash balances the country runs an official settlements surplus and cash flows in. This can only be temporary, however: once cash balances have reached the desired level the old equilibrium is restored. The only long-run difference that devaluation makes, therefore, is to raise all prices and the money supply equi-proportionately, and to raise the reserves by the amount of the extra money supply.

Assumptions again

These bold and simple results require that the *only* way money demand and supply can be equated is via the balance of payments; and this is where the bulk of the assumptions fit in. The stock demand for money depends on prices, interest rates and income; if these are constant then so too is money demand. If, on the other hand, increasing the money supply raised prices or incomes or lowered the rate of interest, then some of the additional cash would be held by residents and the payments deficit would not equal the money injection. Hence assumptions (iii)–(v) – namely, the independence of the real economy and the exogeneity of prices – are merely ways of blocking up alternative escape routes for the excess money. The remaining two assumptions define the stock behaviour that drives the model: excluding sterilisation ensures that the money stock is endogenous only through the balance of payments, while the demand for money function, which is the behavioural cornerstone of the theory, is assumed stable just because theories cannot cope with arbitrary changes in behaviour.

The basic insights of the monetary approach are two: first, it brings out the real balance effect more strongly than other approaches; second, it emphasises that we must take account of the monetary (or rather asset-stock) implications of balance of payments disequilibria. Although these should be important factors in any theorising or empirical application, they will be the predominant influences only under a relatively special set of circumstances. Building a general theory around them is usually justified in terms of strategic simplification: 'by ignoring other (realistic) complications', runs the argument, 'we get a simple and accurate explanation of an important phenomenon.' There are several counter-arguments to this, however.

First, it is not clear that the monetary approach is an accurate explanation. The basic relationship is an accounting identity – any consistent set of data satisfies it – so it cannot separate one hypothesis from another. We therefore have to test the theory indirectly. There are considerable technical difficulties in this, which we cannot explore here, but overall the results are mixed. One approach is to test whether monetary expansions or contractions are completely offset by balance of payments flows – in general they are not. An alternative is to consider the balance of payments implications of economic growth: the Keynesian theories predict a deficit (via rising absorption and imports) whereas monetary theory predicts a surplus (via rising demand for money). Here the monetary theory is probably better supported than the Keynesian, but this is not conclusive because (a) both could be true, since they refer to different balances of payments, and (b) in the most striking cases of high growth and positive trade balances (Japan, West Germany) the causation could run from trade performance to growth and not vice versa as payments theory assumes. A third test concerns the permanence of the balance of payments improvements induced by devaluation. Miles (1979), considering fourteen devaluations, suggested strongly that the gains were only temporary, which supports the monetary view. However, his model of the monetary and fiscal policy accompanying devaluation is very simple, and his results are at variance with detailed studies in the Keynesian mould, such as Artus (1975), who found the British current account £1.3b. stronger in 1971 as a result of the 1967 'devaluation package'. In short, empirical evidence has not yet permitted the rejection of one of the rival approaches in favour of the other.

Second, the level of the official settlements balance is not often a crucial economic question. It is if reserve exhaustion is the problem, but for most questions of economic policy – including that of how to *avoid* reserve exhaustion – it is necessary to have more detail of where the deficit arises. The monetary approach requires supplementing for these questions. For example, it does not determine whether a deficit arises from excessive absorption or from residents increasing their stocks of foreign bonds. (Indeed it ignores the fact that desired stocks of bonds might be subject to economic forces just as the desired stock of money is.) Similarly, in its simple form, it assumes away the problems of unemployment and terms of trade changes, which are clearly issues of great importance. Thus its simplicity and directness are bought at a high price in terms of relevance.

Third, there are problems of the internal consistency. Assumptions (iii)–(v) guarantee that a real equilibrium that exists at one money supply would also be available if the money supply were twice as large. They do not, however, guarantee that actually doubling the money supply will not disturb the real economy, because economists have yet to prove either the uniqueness or the stability of such equilibria. In other words, the process of adjusting to money supply changes may cause the economy to settle at a new, different, real equilibrium. This is especially likely if we recognise the existence of physical capital that is not instantly and costlessly transferable between uses. Furthermore, periods long enough to allow the real economy to attain equilibrium after a shock may well be too long for the supposed stability of the demand for money.

Fourth, there may be difficulties over the money demand equation. The equation relating demand to income implies a transaction demand for money – money to spend – but the emphasis in the analysis on money balances implies an asset demand – money to hold. During the course of a year people might both demand more money to hold, but then actually spend it, which, in the statistics, would disturb the assumed mutual exclusiveness of holding money and spending on goods. This is essentially saying that, if people are not in equilibrium, the attempt to build up cash balances does not necessarily imply a willingness to forgo goods.

Summary The model presented here is the simplest of the monetary models, and few professional economists, even among those sympathetic to monetarist analysis, would claim much for its realism. Current research stresses the uncertain and variable lags in the adjustment of the economy to monetary shocks, and the role of real changes over this transitional period. This has its costs in terms of the simplicity and certitude of the policy prescriptions, but regrettably one still encounters the stark conclusions of the simple model in public debate, despite its theoretical shortcomings and the uncertainty over the time-scale to which it applies. It is wrong to believe that every deficit is caused by monetary disturbances just because each is accompanied by them. Similarly, just because a monetary contraction would eventually cure any deficit, it does not follow that contraction would be the optimum policy in all, or even any, circumstances. Therefore it is not desirable to work with models that admit only monetary solutions.

The importance of the monetary theory lies not in its identifying the fundamental determinants of the balance of payments – it has not – but in its reminding economists that any theory must satisfy certain monetary identities. Just as any current account policy must affect income or absorption, so any balance of payments policy must bring the demand and supply of money into balance.

21.2 THE BALANCE OF PAYMENTS THEORIES COMPARED

We have presented three balance of payments theories. Our explanations have implied various similarities and differences but these have not been emphasised. We therefore complete our discussion of this area by bringing the theories together under one framework in order to compare and constrast them.

Let us aggregate the economy into three sectors: a private sector – all firms and individuals; an official sector – the government and the central bank; and a foreign sector – to record all transactions with foreigners. Let us also distinguish three markets: goods and services; bonds – which includes all financial instruments; and money. We can then draw up a social accounting matrix that records each sector's net transactions in each market. This is shown in Table 21.1. Now, since all bonds sold must be bought, the three net acquisitions of bonds must sum to zero, and likewise for goods and money. Similarly, because the acquisition of goods must be matched by the surrender of something else (the means of payments), so each sector's net acquisitions sum to zero.

Table 21.1 Social accounting matrix

Net acquisition of:	Private		Sector Official		Foreign		Total
Goods	$(I-S)$	+	$(G-T)$	+	$(X-M)$	=	0
	+		+		+		
Bonds	ΔD	+	ΔB	+	ΔF	=	0
	+		+		+		
Money	ΔM	+	ΔC	+	$-\Delta R$	=	0
	‖		‖		‖		
Total	0		0		0		

The matrix is quite easy to interpret. Consider the first row: private net acquisition of goods is expenditure (consumption, C, plus investment, I) minus income (consumption plus savings, S), which is just $(C + I) - (C + S) = I - S$; official net acquisitions are government expenditures (G) less those goods and services granted to it via taxation (T); and foreign net acquisition of goods is just exports (X) less imports (M). In the second row, D, B and F are net holdings of bonds by the private, official and foreign sectors, respectively, and the Δs denote changes. For example, ΔB represents the change in official net holdings of bonds; if, as is usual, the public sector issues more of its own bonds than it buys from other sectors, ΔB is negative. In the last row, ΔM represents private accumulations of money, ΔC official accumulations – usually negative because the central bank issues cash – and ΔR accumulations by the foreign sector. (To effect a cash transfer abroad our residents have to convert local currency into foreign currency, which runs down our foreign exchange reserves, R; hence the negative sign.) From this it is obvious that the last column measures the balance of payments: the current account, the capital account and the compensating reserve movements. For example, a deficit in the current account, $X - M < 0$, must be reflected either in borrowing from abroad (increasing foreign bond holdings, $\Delta F > 0$) or by running down the reserves, $\Delta R < 0$, so $-\Delta R > 0$.

The relationships between the entries in the matrix may be viewed either as *ex post* accounting identities, which must hold in any consistent set of data, or as *ex ante* equilibrium conditions. Either way they do not define causation – that is the job of economic theory – and we now turn to see how the various theories move from their postulates about behaviour in one part of the economy through to the balance of payments.

The elasticities approach looks at the current account, dealing with X and M directly. The matrix shows, however, that it must assume compensating changes elsewhere in the goods market if it is to explain the balance of payments.

The absorption approach also deals with the current account, and is just a rewritten version of the top row. The absorption equation is

$$B = Y - A, \tag{21.3}$$

and if we break up income by its various uses – consumption (C), savings (S) and taxes (T) – and absorption into its various components – consumption, investment (I) and government expenditure (G) – we have

$$B = X - M = (S - I) + (T - G). \tag{21.4}$$

Hence any improvement in the trade balance must involve a smaller net acquisition of goods by the private sector (reducing $I - S$) or the government sector (reducing $G - T$).

The matrix also illustrates a special case of the absorption approach pioneered by certain Cambridge economists – Cripps, Godley and Fetherston (1974). They assumed that the private net acquisition of financial assets (NAFA) is fixed exogenously, i.e. that $\Delta D + \Delta M$ cannot change. The second and third rows of the matrix then tell us that changes in official NAFA $(\Delta B + \Delta C)$ must be balanced by changes in foreign NAFA $(\Delta F - \Delta R)$. But the second and third columns show that changes in official NAFA must be balanced by changes in the government budget deficit $(G - T)$ and changes in foreign NAFA by changes in the current account $(X - M)$. Hence, Cambridge concluded, the main determinant of changes in the current account is the government's budgetary stance. But this of course follows immediately from equation (21.4) once we realise that fixing $\Delta D + \Delta M$ also fixes $I - S$. Hence, with $\Delta(I - S) = 0$, $\Delta(G - T) = - \Delta(X - M)$.

The Cambridge view is interesting partly because it makes the special assumption that the marginal propensity to absorb is unity (with $I - S$ fixed, any extra income must be spent), but mainly because it shows how asset portfolio behaviour can drive absorption-type theories. Recent evidence has belied their simple portfolio assumption, however, so their approach represents more a mode of thought than a predictive tool.

The monetary approach is similar to the Cambridge view, but it combines the first two rows of the matrix instead of the last two. The monetarists claim that M (and therefore ΔM) is determined by incomes, etc., and that ΔC is determined by policy. Any discrepancy between ΔM and ΔC shows up as ΔR and this, via the last column, has implications for the official settlements balance $(X - M + \Delta F)$.

Each theory discussed comprises behavioural assumptions about one cell (or groups of cells) of the matrix (e.g. the monetarists claim to know ΔM) and 'convenience' assumptions (constancy or accommodating changes) about others. A theory will be better, the more predictable are the former and the more plausible are the latter. In fact, it is not necessary to limit theory to a single behavioural cell. It is possible to have independent behaviour for any two cells out of each row and column without violating the consistency of the matrix. Hence, for example, Stern (1973) examined models with independent behaviour in the goods and money markets and in the goods and bonds market. The drawback of this, of course, is the complexity: the models are difficult to analyse and rarely produce the clear-cut results that we have found. Nevertheless, professional economists must, at times, recognise that the world is a complex place and be less willing than they usually are to purchase elegance and simplicity at the expense of realism and accuracy.

FURTHER READING

The principal references for the monetary theory are *Frenkel and Johnson* (1976), and *Whitman* (1975). *Batchelor and Horne* (1979) is also useful. Critical commentaries are *Thirlwall* (1980), and *Hahn* (1977), which is difficult but worthwhile. The empirical literature is summarised in *Kreinin and Officer* (1978) and discussed in *Magee* (1976); the references to *Miles* (1979) and *Artus* (1975) are also useful.

Section 21.2 is based on *Winters* (1978), which offers some further simple analysis.

KEY CONCEPTS

hoarding and dishoarding
stable demand for money function
multiple equilibria
net acquisition of financial assets

money–real dichotomy
accounting identity
social accounting matrix
balance on official settlements

QUESTIONS FOR REVIEW

21.1 How might one test the monetary theory of the balance of payments?
21.2 Discuss the role of 'strategic simplification' in economic theorising with regard to the monetary theory of the balance of payments. Is the trade-off worthwhile?
21.3 Compare the absorption, 'new Cambridge', and monetary approaches to the balance of payments.

22 The Foreign Exchange Rate

We now move from a world of fixed but movable exchange rates to one of perfectly flexible rates. This has consequences for economic policy that we shall examine in Chapter 24, but for the present we concentrate just on the factors determining the exchange rate. Fortunately we do not have to rework all the analysis of the previous four chapters because there is a very simple relationship between the balance of payments and the exchange rate. Under a perfectly flexible exchange rate the central bank does not intervene in the foreign exchange market at all. Hence any tendency towards deficit is met not by disbursements from the reserves but by a decline in the exchange rate. A deficit shows that more dollars are demanded for purchases abroad than are supplied by sales abroad. Under fixed rates the reserves make up the difference, whereas under flexible rates the price of dollars is allowed to rise; that is, the value of sterling falls. Hence any factor that at a fixed exchange rate would worsen the balance of payments tends, under flexible rates, to depreciate the currency.

Of course the exchange rate responds to any excess supply or demand for foreign exchange, so the relevant balance of payments concept is the balance on official settlements. In the absence of official intervention this must constantly be zero, and the exchange rate will adjust to bring this about. Hence we must look at the capital account as well as the current account, especially in the short run during which short-term capital flows can swamp any development on the basic balance. One result of the absence of intervention, and the consequent absence of reserve movements, is that the domestic money supply is perfectly insulated from the foreign sector.

This chapter starts by considering the structure and participants of the foreign exchange market. In section 22.2 it pays particular attention to speculation and asks whether foreign exchange markets are efficient in the sense of using all the information that is available to them about the determinants of exchange rates. This section includes a discussion of so-called rational expectations and the impact of news on the markets. Finally it considers the purchasing power parity theory of exchange rates. This is the oldest and most intuitive view of exchange rate determination, but is found seriously wanting in today's circumstances. Chapter 23 continues the theme of exchange rate determination by introducing the demand for financial assets. It shows how wealth affects exchange rates and presents several models of exchange rate over-shooting. Finally it considers the empirical evidence on exchange rate determination.

22.1 THE FOREIGN EXCHANGE MARKET

This section describes the foreign exchange market and the types of transaction that occur within it.

The foreign exchange market

The foreign exchange market is not a physical institution where traders meet; transactions are made by telephone and computer rather than face-to-face. Although anyone in Britain can now hold foreign currency, the London foreign exchange market itself is still the preserve of specialised dealers. These firms, with their accumulated skills and world-wide communications, conduct wholesale transactions between themselves and with their foreign counterparts. 'Retail' foreign exchange transactions – such as buying currency to pay for a foreign holiday – all have to be effected ultimately through these main dealers.

Trading in the exchange market is extremely rapid and involves huge sums: the turnover of a large dealer can amount to several billion pounds per day, although by the end of the day its net purchases of foreign currency may be very small. Profits are made by constantly buying and selling on small margins as the price fluctuates hour by hour. Of course, only a small fraction of exchange deals give rise to physical transfers of cash. In the main, traders are merely swapping the ownership of deposits of cash in some bank. The turnover of the London market – the world's largest – averaged $187b. per day in April 1989 (*Financial Times*, 14 September 1989). Most of this represents movements of very short-term capital: estimates vary, but certainly no more than 10 per cent of turn-over is linked directly to trade or long-term investment transactions.

During the week, foreign exchange can be traded twenty-four hours a day because, when London is closed, Tokyo or Singapore is trading, and so on. Furthermore, it is possible to trade in almost any currency in the big financial centres. It is not necessary, for instance, to go to Paris to trade francs – banks, the world over, are willing to deal in them. Rates are equalised in the various centres by so-called *triangular arbitrage*. If Frankfurt were offering $2.00 per £1.00 and London $1.90 per £1.00, it would be profitable to buy pounds in London for sale in Frankfurt, which would rapidly bring rates into line. Arbitrage also ensures that the many different rates of exchange are consistent. For example, if $1 US will buy $1 Australian and $1 Canadian, $1 Australian must also buy $1 Canadian; if not, profit opportunities exist. (Imagine $1.5 A = $1 C, how would you make money?)

Although you can buy most currencies in London, you cannot effect direct swaps between any arbitrary pair of currencies. To convert Greek drachmas into Colombian pesos, for instance, you would trade drachma for dollars and dollars for pesos. Just as trading shoes for mutton is smoothed by the existence of money, which removes the need for the double coincidence of wants, so trading drachmas for pesos is smoothed by the existence of an international money like the dollar. Without it, dealers would have either to have matched requirements or to hold stocks of every single currency. With a common *vehicle currency* in which to trade, however, these balances can be replaced by a single dollar balance and a knowledge of where each other currency can be swapped for dollars in the rare event of it showing up (the issuing central bank). Even so, the costs of trading in small currencies can be relatively high, so trade between small countries is often conducted entirely in terms of one of the vehicle currencies.

Spot and forward exchange rates

When we talk of 'the exchange rate' we almost always mean the price of dollars, say, if we bought *and received* them now. This is the *spot rate* and it corresponds to most other prices in the economy. It is not necessary, however, to complete the deal now. It would be possible, as say when reserving a hotel room, to agree now that we will buy so many dollars at a particular price at some specified time in the future. This would be a forward transaction, and its price the *forward exchange rate*. The price and the maturity are set now, but both sides of the transaction are effected in the future. The possible advantages of this will become apparent soon.

The forward exchange rate is determined by supply and demand in the foreign exchange market, just as is the spot rate. There are, however, large markets only for certain standard maturities: thirty and ninety days, six months, a year, and, for the main currencies, two years. Other time-spans are possible but tend to involve high transactions costs. Obviously the spot and forward rates can differ: we refer to the percentage excess of the latter over the former as the *forward premium*. Sterling is at a forward premium if it takes more dollars to buy one pound forward than spot. A negative premium is known as a *discount*.

With its relatively large number of dealers, nearly perfect communication and nearly costless transactions, the foreign exchange market is as perfect a market as exists. The price of foreign exchange is merely the price that equates the sum of all demands to the sum of all supplies. We now turn to these demands and supplies by looking at the various types of transaction in the market.

Trade The most obvious transaction in foreign exchange is the purchase of foreign currency for spending on imports or the sale of currency arising from exports. The extent of these demands and supplies depends on the value of international trade, which, in part, depends on the exchange rate itself. A rise in the exchange rate (measured in dollars per pound) will tend to increase the supply of sterling and the demand for dollars. Typically traders deal in the spot market, and this mechanism relates the exchange rate to the current account.

Hedging The lag between ordering and paying for an import involves one or other of the parties in exchange risk. Suppose a British exporter is interested only in his receipts in sterling terms, but that he prices his goods in dollars. Between agreeing a price and receiving payment he bears exchange risk, because a change in the exchange rate will alter his sterling returns from a given dollar sale. He might find this uncertainty inconvenient or unpleasant, and hence seek to avoid it by hedging. The most obvious way to do this is to sell the dollars forward. He knows how many dollars he will receive in, say, three months, and the forward market allows him *now* to fix the price at which they will convert into sterling. This mechanism, designed solely to avoid risk, relates the forward rate to trading behaviour.

Arbitrage Arbitrage is the process of buying in one place (or time) and selling in another with a view to making profits. If there are several markets selling the same commodity, arbitrageurs are likely to equalise the prices, for they will buy cheap and sell dear. The important thing about arbitrage is that it involves no risks: both buying and selling prices are known before the transactions take place.

As well as equalising exchange rates across different markets, arbitrage also links the spot and forward rates. Suppose I have £1 to invest for a year. I could invest it in London at interest rate i, and receive $£(1 + i_k)$ after a year. Alternatively, I could convert it into $\$S$ at spot rate S, invest it in New York at

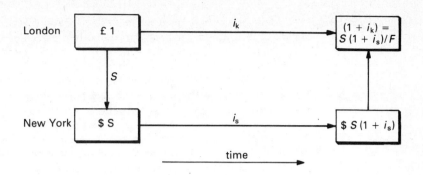

Figure 22.1 Interest arbitrage

interest rate i_s to receive $\$S(1 + i_s)$ after a year, and agree *now* to sell the dollars forward at rate F, finally collecting $£[S(1 + i_s)/F]$. Both chains involve only information that is available *now*, so neither involves uncertainty. Hence, provided plenty of funds exist to exploit any arbitrage opportunities, the two rates of return should be equalised. That is

$$(1 + i_k) = S(1 + i_s)/F \tag{22.1}$$

which is known as the *covered interest arbitrage condition*. Figure 22.1 illustrates the two ways of investing the pound: one either goes straight across and earns $(1 + i_k)$ or one goes the long way round, earning $S(1 + i_s)/F$.

Suppose that, given the two interest rates, the spot rate were too high relative to the forward rate for (22.1) to hold. Arbitrageurs would immediately sell pounds spot and buy them forward: this would reduce S (the spot price of pounds) and raise F, thus restoring the equality. Also, since no one would be investing in London, i_k would probably also rise and this would further help re-establish (22.1). In fact, the only thing that can prevent the interest arbitrage condition from holding is transactions costs (including legal contraints) and default risks. For large stable countries, therefore, where default is almost inconceivable, (22.1) holds almost exactly (see, in particular, Taylor, 1987).

The interest arbitrage condition can also be written in terms of the forward premium (p), the proportionate difference between forward and spot rates:

$$p = \frac{F - S}{S} = \frac{i_s - i_k}{1 + i_k}, \tag{22.2}$$

which, when i_k is small (e.g. for short loans), may be approximated by

$$p = i_s - i_k, \tag{22.3}$$

Note that interest arbitrage alone is not a theory of the exchange rate; it is more an equlibrium condition that any other theory must satisfy. This is because any or all of the four variables it relates could adjust to bring it about.

The authorities The transactions just described are undertaken, often simultaneously, by a variety of market participants. However, our last class of transaction is defined by its executor – namely, official transactions.

Under a fixed exchange rate regime the Bank of England fixes a parity rate, say $2.40. It then sells pounds to prevent the rate moving above, say, $2.42,

315

Q

and buys them to prevent it falling below \$2.38, but between these limits keeps out of the market. At the other extreme, under a perfectly flexible exchange rate regime, the central bank would never intervene in the market, although of course it may conduct commercial activities on behalf of the government or other customers. In between lies the 'dirty float', where the Bank intervenes but not around any pre-announced target. It may aim just to smooth out day-to-day fluctuations or to influence the rate significantly. Intervention may occur in the forward market as well as the spot market, although exchange rate targets and commitments invariably refer to the latter. We shall consider different intervention regimes later; for the rest of this chapter we imagine a clean float, or perfectly flexible rate.

22.2 SPECULATION, EXPECTATIONS AND EFFICIENCY

This section considers speculation, the formation of expectations and the notion of market efficiency. It asks whether exchange markets use information efficiently and also whether speculators can push the exchange rate to the 'wrong' level.

Speculation

The transactions considered so far have sought to avoid the uncertainty of changing exchange rates. Speculators, on the other hand, seek it and aim to benefit from it. Speculation consists of taking an 'open position' in something – namely, having unequal assets and liabilities in it. Hence a speculator, expecting the dollar to appreciate next week, will seek to hold more claims on dollars then than he has liabilities. If he achieves this, and is right in his prediction, he will become wealthier, because something of which he is a net holder will have risen in value.

The essence of speculation is expectations – in the present circumstances, expectations about the future exchange rate. In the simplest case, suppose one expects the spot rate in a year to be below the present forward rate for that maturity. One would sell pounds forward now and plan to buy them back at the then ruling spot rate, expecting to make $\$(F - \hat{S}_1)$ on each pound, where $\hat{S}_1$ is the expected spot rate one year hence. Obviously the actual unit profit will be $\$(F - S_1)$, where S_1 is the actual spot rate in one year, which could be positive or negative. Notice that this transaction involves no commitment of cash until the settlement date: any profit arises solely from the speculator's willingness to take risks.

The obvious effects of speculation is to bring today's forward rate towards the expected future spot rate, and if there is widespread agreement about that future rate this effect can be very strong. It also, of course, affects the current spot rate, because that is linked to the forward rate by interest arbitrage.

Speculation could also occur directly in the spot market. Indeed, available evidence (e.g. Goodhart, 1988) suggests that it mostly does. If one expected a fall in sterling ($\hat{S}_1 < S$), it would pay to sell sterling now and buy it back later. If one also took interest rates into account one would compare £1 invested in London, to yield $(1 + i_k)$, with £1 converted spot, invested in New York and converted back *at the expected rate* in one year; i.e. with $S(1 + i_s)/\hat{S}_1$. One would sell sterling now if the latter dominated. Such speculation through the spot market gives rise to *uncovered interest arbitrage*. Compared with holding sterling for a year and earning i_k, traders could hold dollars and earn i_s less the extent to which the dollar depreciated relative to sterling over the year.

Writing $\hat{s}$ for the expected proportionate rate of dollar depreciation (sterling appreciation), $\hat{s} = (\hat{S}_1 - S)/S$; this gives us

$$i_k = i_s - \hat{s}, \tag{22.4}$$

which is clearly very similar to (22.3). Uncovered interest arbitrage implies that investors are indifferent about the currency in which their assets are denominated provided that they earn the same rate of return.

Speculation might appear to tie the forward rate rigidly to the expected future spot rate, but this is not necessarily true. Speculation involves risk and this must be compensated by higher returns. Speculators will operate only if F and $\hat{S}_1$ diverge by enough to pay transactions costs and reward risk. Furthermore, if they are not certain of their estimate of $\hat{S}_1$, they may be unwilling to bet heavily on it, hence there may be insufficient speculation to force F all the way to $\hat{S}_1$.

Speculation is often thought to be anti-social. It is true that speculative flows can be very disruptive of the real economy – e.g. Britain in 1972, see p. 293 above – but in general they merely speed up an inevitable change in the exchange rate. Without any speculation, exchange markets would be very inefficient, because if no one were willing to take open positions in foreign currency every trader selling pounds would have to find another who wished to buy them. This would be more difficult than the present requirement of finding someone who is willing to hold pounds temporarily. Indeed it would be impossible unless trade were balanced! Looked at alternatively, if no one were willing to bear uncertainty, only riskless transactions could be effected, and this is surely a very small subset of what we actually observe today.

Expectations

Expectations are the key to speculative behaviour, and so it is natural to ask how they are formed. There are two main approaches in economic theory. First, there are autoregressive expectations – basically those formed from previous and current values of the variable concerned. These may be simple – for instance that tomorrow's exchange rate will be the same as today's – or much more complex, involving the extrapolation of rates of change, or even the rate of change of rates of change. The difficulty with this approach is that it uses very little information: it is easy to construct examples where expectations are always wrong, and also where expectations feed back onto themselves in an explosive manner. The main advantage of the approach is its simplicity.

The second expectational mechanism is so-called *rational expectations*. These were first introduced by Muth (1961), but have become fashionable in macro-economics only since about the mid-1970s. Expectations are said to be rational if the value of a variable that an agent expects is the same as the mathematical expectation of that variable given the avaiable information.[1] The basic idea is that *all* existing information is used optimally to make forecasts. In particular it is assumed that agents in the market know all that economists know, so that if *we* know the true mechanism of the exchange rate determination so does the market. Hence models have an element of self-reference in them that makes testing them very difficult: one is looking for a process which, *if* it explained expectations, could also explain reality, and there is rarely an assurance that only one such process exists.

An implication of rational expectations (embedded in the right model, of course) is that expectations are unbiased: that is, they are not consistently in error in any particular fashion. If that were not the case, they could not be rational because they would be ignoring the information embodied in the consistency of the errors. The corollary of this is that future actual rates are unbiased estimates of the expectations, so that in applications it is sometimes possible to substitute actual outcomes for forecasts. If we then ignore the random errors – as is often done – rational expectations take us back to perfect foresight, dissolving the need for expectations mechanisms anyway!

The strengths of rational expectations are, first, that they reflect the fact that forecasts are made using diverse sources of information and an analytical frame-work, and, second, that they have an internal consistency, in that the model cannot be correct if expectations are consistently falsified. Against these must be set their empirical difficulties and their assumption of an implausible degree of sophistication on the part of most operators. They have proved theoretically fruitful over the last decade, but, as yet, their empirical relevance is not established: as we shall see below, there are no entirely successful models of exchange rates, whether with rational expectations or not.

Market efficiency

In a previous paragraph we used the term 'efficient' to describe the foreign exchange market in a loose and everyday fashion. However, market efficiency also has a precise technical meaning and there is considerable debate whether foreign exchange markets satisfy its conditions. An asset market is said to be efficient if the current asset price reflects fully all relevant information and there are no remaining *ex ante* opportunities for making profits through speculation. The full reflection of all relevant information is just the rational expectation again, but market efficiency adds the requirement that, as well as knowing on average where the price is going, agents force it there immediately. Let us denote the expected foreign exchange rate as $E(S_{t+1}|I_t)$: this is the value of the spot exchange rate (S) at time $(t+1)$ that is expected given the information set at time t (I_t). The notation $E(\ )$ refers to the mathematical expectation of S_{t+1}.

Efficiency occurs if the deviation of the actual outcome of S_{t+1} from its expectation in period t, $E(S_{t+1}|I_t)$, is uncorrelated with I_t and with past values of itself. If neither past values of S nor anything in I_t explains $[S_{t+1} - E(S_{t+1}|I_t)]$ we may conclude that all the information in I_t has been incorporated into $E(S_{t+1}|I_t)$ and that the forecast errors of S_{t+1} are random and entirely unpredictable. Note that we are not saying that S_{t+1}, nor even changes in $S(\Delta S \equiv S_{t+1} - S_t)$, should be random and uncorrelated, just that the *deviations* of S_{t+1} from $E(S_{t+1}|I_t)$ should be. *Weak-form efficiency* is said to occur if I_t, the relevant information set, contains only past and present values of S_t, *semi-strong efficiency* if I_t also contains all information publicly available at time t (e.g. money supply and current account data), and *strong-form efficiency* if I_t contains all public and private information. In general only the first two are of practical interest.

Consider now the efficiency of the forward market for foreign exchange. If traders – hedgers, arbitrageurs and speculators – have ample funds, may trade free of restrictions and at zero cost, and are risk neutral (that is, they consider only the expected value of their profits not their dispersion), then they will buy and sell forward until

$$F_t^{t+1} = E(S_{t+1}|I_t), \qquad (22.5)$$

where F_t^{t+1} is the forward rate at time t for foreign exchange delivered at time $(t+1)$. This gives us a test of foreign exchange market efficiency, for we can check $(S_{t+1} - F_t^{t+1})$ for the required independence from I_t and randomness.

318

The test is best conducted in logarithms and often involves estimating
equations of the form

$$s_t = a + bf_{t-1}^t + v_t, \qquad (22.6)$$

where $s \equiv \log S$, $f \equiv \log F$, and v_t is a random error reflecting unforeseen factors.

If $a = 0$, $b = 1$ and v_t is genuinely random, then $E(s_t) = f_{t-1}^t$, and the
hypothesis of market efficiency cannot be rejected – that is, markets may be
considered efficient. Unfortunately, however, estimates of (22.6) and similar
equations frequently reject these conditions, most commonly because v_t
appears to be related to data that were observable at time t.

We cannot automatically conclude from this, however, that traders are
inefficient or irrational in their behaviour. Even if the statistical tests
undertaken were appropriate – which some commentators doubt – they
necessarily cover, in addition to market efficiency, several auxiliary hypotheses,
any one of which could be the cause of the failure. For example, if the rules for
government intervention change frequently, traders may not have time to
discover them and incorporate them into f_{t-1}^t even if they use information
efficiently. Ignorance of other variables – e.g. recent money supply statistics –
could similarly cause apparent inefficiency. Transactions costs may prevent
complete trading, or traders may be risk averse rather than risk neutral. A
risk-averse trader considers both the expected value *and* the degree of the
uncertainty of his returns to speculation, and finds speculation less attractive
the greater the uncertainty. This point appears to be particularly relevant to
recent exchange rate experience, and the difficulties it causes for testing
market efficiency are compounded by the fact that risk premia – the
compensation necessary to get traders to bear uncertainty – change through
time.

Similar difficulties best any other test of the efficiency of an expected
exchange rate in an efficient market. Suppose we hypothesised that the
expected exchange rate was a function of a set of variables X_t – say $g(X_t)$. If we
substituted $g(X_t)$ for f_{t-1}^t in equation (22.6) and found the hypothesis $a = 0$,
$b = 1$ and v_t genuinely random rejected, we would not know whether $g(X_t)$ was
an inappropriate expectation or whether transactions costs or risk aversion
were at fault. All this makes testing exchange rate models with market
efficiency very difficult, for in a rational expectations model the expression for
expectations, $g(X_t)$ above, is the model itself. Moreover, this is not a merely
hypothetical problem. We will see in the next chapter that models of the
exchange rate generally predict very badly, but we really just do not know
why.

The difficulties of the previous paragraphs have led economists to adopt two
more direct approaches to testing the statistical implications of market
efficiency and rational expectations. First, they have sought trading rules or
traders who have persistently made profits from foreign exchange dealings. It
is quite easy to devise statistical rules which would have made profits over any
particular sample period, but in general they break down as soon as they have
to make genuine out-of-sample forecasts. The records of professional exchange
rate forecasters are pretty poor – see, for example, Blake, Beenstock and
Brasse (1986). Likewise, while it is possible to find plenty of people who claim
to make money out of foreign exchange dealing, it is not clear that they make
it by exploiting *changes* in the exchange rate (i.e. speculation) rather than just
from the margins between buying and selling rates (i.e. dealing) (Goodhart,
1988).

319

The second more direct approach to testing expectations has entailed collecting data directly on market participants' expectations. Most of this research has found significant risk aversion among agents and suggests that the risk premium varies through time. MacDonald and Torrance (1988) argue additionally that expectations are formed extrapolatively (i.e. that past changes are expected to continue) rather than rationally. While there are clearly problems in getting good evidence on expectations, this alternative approach does look very fruitful.

News An implication of market efficiency is that, apart from interest rate differentials, only unforeseen shocks, i.e. news, can cause changes in exchange rates; anything that is foreseen has, by the definition of efficiency, been taken into account already. Not only does this observation justify the statement above that forecast errors should be purely random, but it also helps to explain the large impact that news can have on the exchange rate. Suppose that the exchange rate is determined by some factor z, such that

$$s_{t+1} = \gamma z_{t+1} + \epsilon_{t+1}, \tag{22.7}$$

where ϵ_t are random errors with zero expectation. (22.7) clearly implies that $E(s_{t+1}) = \gamma E(z_{t+1})$, and substituting this into the uncovered interest arbitrage relationship gives[2]

$$s_t = \gamma E(z_{t+1}) + (i_d - i_f)_t, \tag{22.8}$$

where i_d is the domestic interest rate (previously i_k) and i_f the foreign interest rate.

Anything that causes large changes in the expectation of z_{t+1} – e.g. a policy announcement or a change of government – but that does not much affect the interest differential will greatly affect the current exchange rate.

Substracting (22.8) from (22.7) shows that

$$\Delta s_t = s_{t+1} - s_t = \gamma[z_{t+1} - E(z_{t+1})] - (i_d - i_f)_t + \epsilon_{t+1}; \tag{22.9}$$

i.e. that changes in the exchange rate reflect news about z, the interest differential and random factors.

Equation (22.9) embodies two important features of exchange rate determination. First, the efficiency of markets and, second, a model of the systematic determinants of the exchange rate in the form of γz_{t+1} – i.e. the things about which news matters. If we assume efficiency and allow for interest differentials, actual exchange rate changes will reflect the systematic part of (22.9) and allow us to estimate it. Before examining such tests, however, we must consider the theory of what might enter z_{t+1}. This is done in section 22.3 and Chapter 23.

Rational bubbles In this sub-section we ask whether speculators could 'capture' the foreign exchange rate and force it away from the 'correct' rate. Bubbles occur when speculation pushes an asset price – for us, the exchange rate – far from its fundamental equilibrium for significant periods of time. Implicit in the notion is that the process is self-reinforcing but that eventually the bubble will burst. Until it does, however, speculators are in some sense determining the exchange rate and influencing the real economy.

Dornbusch (1986) offered a very simple example of a rational bubble. Assume that we have uncovered interest arbitrage so that

$$E(s_{t+1}) - s_t = i_f - i_d, \tag{22.10}$$

where, as before, s_t is the logarithm of the exchange rate, and i_f and i_d the foreign and domestic interest rates.

Now let there be a probability α that by time $(t+1)$ the exchange rate will have crashed to $\bar{s}$ – its fundamental level – and a probability $(1 - \alpha)$ that the bubble will continue to the next period with the exchange rate attaining level s_{t+1}^b. Rational expectations require that the expectation $E(s_{t+1})$ correctly reflect these values and probabilities. Thus

$$E(s_{t+1}) = \alpha \bar{s} + (1 - \alpha) s_{t+1}^b. \tag{22.11}$$

Substituting (22.11) into (22.10) and subtracting s_t from both sides, we get

$$s_{t+1}^b - s_t = \frac{1}{1 - \alpha} \left[(i_f - i_d) + \alpha (s_t - \bar{s}) \right]. \tag{22.12}$$

This expresses the rate of appreciation (if the bubble continues) as a function of the interest differential and the *existing* rate of overvaluation – note that $(s_t - \bar{s})$ is the logarithm of the ratio of the current rate to its equilibrium value.

Temporarily ignoring the interest differential, equation (22.12) shows two elements of self-reinforcing instability. The 'bubble rate' increases by more the *greater* the probability of a crash (α) and the *greater* the existing overvaluation. If the bubble is to continue – i.e. if people are to continue holding the currency – a faster rate of appreciation is necessary to compensate for the more unfavourable objective circumstances. The process of acceleration in the wrong direction will end only with a crash.

Equation (22.12) may also be used to explain a constant rate of overvaluation. Setting $(s_{t+1}^b - s_t)$ equal to zero gives

$$s_t - \bar{s} = \frac{i_d - i_f}{\alpha}. \tag{22.13}$$

Thus, for example, an interest differential of 5 per cent coupled with a crash probability of 0.2 – perfectly plausible magnitudes – could support persistent overvaluation of 25 per cent.

Goodhart (1988) described another, quite separate, model in which speculation can 'capture' the exchange rate. Suppose that foreign exchange dealers have two sorts of advisers, those who adhere to the market efficiency view, and hence whose best forecast for next period is always 'no change', and those who model fundamentals. Suppose also that dealers form their expectations of next period's rate by taking a weighted average of the two groups' forecasts, and that the weights used are modified each period to increase the influence of the group which got nearest to the actual outcome in the last period. Imagine that the exchange rate is overvalued, so that the fundamentalists predict a fall; the weighted average will also indicate a fall. But suppose that in fact there is a positive random shock which causes the rate to rise. In the next period dealers will give more weight to the efficiency view (which was less wrong) and hence may well predict a smaller fall than they did for the previous period. With a smaller expected depreciation, the local currency will have a higher expected rate of return and so dealers will be prepared to hold more of it. If supplies are fixed, this will drive up its prices – i.e. appreciate the exchange rate further – and cause the whole cycle to be renewed. This process could continue until the fundamentalists received no weight at all, at which point the exchange rate would stabilise with the 'efficiency-men' predicting and getting no change. Only when there was a negative random shock would the fundamentalists regain any influence and the exchange rate start a cumulative descent to its fundamental level.

22.3 PURCHASING POWER PARITY

Purchasing power parity is the oldest and simplest of theories about the exchange rate. It is implicit in the work of certain nineteenth-century economists, and was formalised by Cassel around 1920. In one form it involves only the market for goods and services, but at a more sophisticated level it also takes account of the money market.

The exchange rate and the goods market

At its simplest, purchasing power parity (PPP) is really the same as the law of one price, which we have already met. If there were no imperfections in world markets and all goods were traded, the price of any good would be the same regardless of its origin. Imagine some typical basket of American goods valued at $100. If the value of an identical basket originating in Britain were £50, the only equilibrium exchange rate possible would be $2.00 : £1.00, equating the price of the basket in the two countries. If, for example, the rate were $1.90 : £1.00, everyone would buy from Britain: starting with $100, one could buy £52.63 on the exchange market and hence get the basket of goods plus £2.63 by buying British. The resultant increased demand for pounds would drive up their price towards $2.00. This *absolute* version of PPP may easily be as formalised follows.

Imagine that the LOOP holds for every good (i) such that in a common currency US and UK prices are identical

$$p_i^{US} \ (\$) = S(\$/£) \ p_i^{UK} \ (£), \tag{22.14}$$

where the currencies of denomination are given in brackets. Since (22.14) holds for all i, it will hold for a weighted sum across i, with weights w_i, and since S is invariant with respect to i we can take it outside the summation sign. Thus

$$\sum_{i=1}^{n} w_i p_i^{US} = S \sum_{i=1}^{n} w_i p_i^{UK},$$

from which

$$S = \sum_{i=1}^{n} w_i p_i^{US} / \sum_{i=1}^{n} w_i p_i^{UK},$$

or

$$S = P^{US}/P^{UK}, \tag{22.15}$$

where P^j are price index numbers $j = $ US, UK.

Various restrictions to trade such as transport costs and tariffs and the existence of non-tradable goods combine to frustrate absolute PPP, and this has led to a more sophisticated version of the theory – relative PPP. Suppose that our typical American basket were, in fact, worth $110 in America and £50 in Britain, but that because of these imperfections the exchange rate of $2.00 : £1.00 were an equilibrium. Relative PPP asserts that, if British prices doubled, the exchange rate would halve: in other words, the original price

322

relativity between British and American goods would be preserved; despite the inflationary shock, American goods would still be 10 per cent more expensive than British goods. The justification for this is the dichotomy between the real and nominal economies that we encountered in section 21.1 above. The relative price of American and British goods is a real phenomenon so, provided no real changes accompanied the assumed inflation, it would be unaffected.

Formally, relative PPP assumes that goods market frictions mean that

$$P_i^{US} = S . t . P_i^{UK}, \tag{22.16}$$

where t is the 'real price wedge' due, perhaps, to tariffs. Repeating the analysis leading to (22.15) gives

$$S = (1/t)(P^{US}/P^{UK}), \tag{22.17}$$

which shows that, for so long as t is constant, S is proportional to relative prices.

A monetary approach

So far we have considered only the goods market, but many economists argue that PPP also has a monetary dimension. To explore this we return to the monetary model of Chapter 21, repeating all the assumptions but assuming a perfectly flexible rather than a perfectly fixed exchange rate. Previously the domestic money supply varied with the foreign exchange reserves; any excess money created flowed out of the economy via an official settlements deficit. Now, however, the money cannot escape, because by not intervening in the exchange market the central bank prevents any movements in the reserves. Since it also controls domestic credit, the bank now has complete control of the money supply under flexible exchange rates.

What then happens to excess money? By assumption, nothing real can change, so as people attempt to rid themselves of excess cash they bid up local currency prices. Previously this had been prevented by fixed world prices and a fixed exchange rate, but under floating rates domestic inflation is consistent with given world prices provided that the exchange rate falls equi-proportionately.

In the simple monetarist model starting from equilibrium, a 1 per cent increase in the money supply raises prices by 1 per cent; to preserve PPP (or the LOOP) the exchange rate must fall by 1 per cent (strictly by 100/101 per cent), leaving the real economy entirely unaffected. In terms of PPP, the monetarists add to the theory by offering an explanation of the price level, which had previously just been assumed.

Some difficulties with PPP

Before PPP can be of practical use in explaining or predicting the exchange rate, it must be implemented empirically. This raises a number of difficulties, which we examine before passing on to the empirical evidence.

The price index. Which basket of goods should PPP refer to, or more practically which price index numbers are to be used?

First, if one believes that goods arbitrage (the LOOP) drives the PPP result the same price index weights should be used in both (all) countries. For example, suppose that wheat prices double, while still satisfying the LOOP at the initial exchange rate. If wheat figures heavily in the US price index but lightly in the UK's, the change in P^{US} would exceed that in P^{UK} and PPP would predict a rise in S. But since all goods markets are in equilibrium at the initial S, that prediction would be wrong.

Second, if the (identical) price index used is dominated by tradable primary goods (e.g. wheat, metals) we may appear to have PPP, but in fact have reverse causation. Homogeneous goods like these tend to satisfy the LOOP, hence whatever the exchange rate local currency prices adjust to ensure equality with world prices in a common currency. This does not invalidate PPP, but it does preclude its being a theory of the exchange rate. For that, we require exogenous prices with the exchange rate adjusting. Consequently economists prefer to test PPP on indices containing more manufactures and non-traded goods. Of course, if one holds the monetarist interpretation of PPP, the index should be the one that appears in the money demand equation, because it is the latter that drives that model. Both these arguments lead us to prefer consumer price indices or GDP deflators to the more commonly used wholesale price indices, although, in a monetarist model with monetary shocks, all prices would move identically so that any price index would indicate the same overall rate of inflation.

Ultimately the exchange rate adjusts to clear the foreign exchange market. The special assumptions of PPP are made in order that the exchange market respond only to the aggregate price level. This might be disturbed in real life, however, in a number of ways.

Capital flows. Either short-run flows seeking interest rate advantages (see Chapter 23) or long-run direct investment could be important. Imbalances in the latter can be very long-lived – for example, the USA ran a capital account surplus for about sixty consecutive years during the nineteenth century.

Income changes. The monetarists believe that growth will stimulate a foreign surplus, appreciating the exchange rate, whereas Keynesians hold that it will generate a deficit and depreciation via imports. Also world growth could be significant if different countries' exports face different income elasticities. If Britain's exports have low income elasticities, we would expect a gradual depreciation of sterling to offset the deleterious income effects.

Non-traded goods. Suppose the LOOP applies to all traded goods. In rich, high-productivity countries, these world prices can support high wages, but in low-productivity countries they can support only low wages. Now suppose that there is also a non-traded sector, in which productivity is the same in all countries (e.g. haircuts). In rich countries, with high wages, these goods and services will be expensive, but in poor, low-wage economies they will be cheap. When we combine traded and non-traded sectors, therefore, average prices will be higher in rich than in poor countries. Hence if the exchange rate is really determined by tradables but we apply the general indices, PPP will appear to be violated: rich countries will appear to have overvalued exchange rates (see Balassa, 1964). Case-study 22.1 gives an example of Balassa's productivity bias.

Structural change. Change of a more random nature, for example the discovery of oil, can also affect exchange rates.

Impediments to trade. Changes in transport costs, tariffs or trading institutions could upset PPP by making balance of payments equilibrium possible at different price levels.

Empirical evidence We have seen how PPP's close cousin the LOOP fails to stand up to the evidence on individual prices. We now briefly confront PPP with the evidence of aggregate price indices. As virtually no data exist on absolute prices (price indices report price changes since a base year), all of these tests refer to the relative version of PPP.

Continued on page 326

CASE-STUDY 22.1: THE PRODUCTIVITY BIAS IN PPP

PPP calculations can be seriously distorted if the countries compared are at different levels of development. Imagine that all tradable goods satisfy the LOOP and that the exchange rate is determined by the need to balance the trade account. Let the exchange rate between India and the USA be, say, 20

Table 22.1 PPP: a hypothetical example

	Prices		Men per unit of output		Wages	
	USA $	India R	USA	India	USA $	India R
Tradables	100	2,000	1	10	100	200
Non-tradables	100	200	1	1	100	200
Total price index	100	1,100				

rupees to the dollar. A unit of tradables would then cost, say, $100 in the USA or R2,000 in India (items 1 and 2 of row 1 of Table 22.1).

Suppose now that US factors of production are ten times as productive as Indian factors in tradables production: it would take, say, one man to produce a unit of tradables in the USA and he earns $100, whereas it takes ten men to do the job in India, so each earns only R200 (see the remainder of row 1). If wages are equalised across sectors in each country, non-tradables producers face wages of $100 and R200 respectively, and, if there are no differences in productivity in non-tradables between countries (say, one man per unit output), the prices of non-tradables are $100 and R200 respectively. This sequence is shown from right to left in row 2 of the table.

Now suppose that a (misguided) economist estimated the PPP exchange rate using total rather than just tradables price indices. If the price index used gave weights of one-half to each of tradables and non-tradables, he would put the exchange rate at 11 rupees per dollar rather than 20. The problem is that he would be using the wrong index number – including non-tradables when they had no direct effect on the exchange rate.

The productivity bias is not a serious problem for short- or medium-term exchange rate predictions using *relative* PPP: productivity differences do not change rapidly and can easily be incorporated into the constant (t) of the relative PPP equation. It is important, however, for long-term comparisons of growing economies; Marston (1986), for example, found that the dollar:yen exchange rate had appreciated since 1960 despite rising relative price indices in Japan.

The productivity bias is also vitally important to comparisons of living standards between countries. A visitor to the USA from India finds life very expensive. To buy half a unit each of tradables and non-tradables at home requires R11,000, but converted to dollars at the actual exchange rate (20 in this example) this cash buys only just over half that amount in the USA. In terms of buying a general basket of goods, therefore, the PPP exchange rate provides a better guide to the relative values of money than does the actual exchange rate, precisely because it is based on a general basket rather than merely a basket of tradables. At actual exchange rates the average Indian appeared to be fifty times poorer than an average American in 1975, but at PPP rates he was 'only' sixteen times poorer (Kravis, Heston and Summers, 1982).

The story behind PPP is essentially a monetary one and so one would expect PPP to perform best for extreme monetary shocks. The German hyper-inflation of 1921–3 is an excellent example of this. The Reichbank largely financed reparations to the allies by printing money. Between August 1922 and November 1923, the money supply and prices rose by 10,000 million times! Frenkel (1976) related the spot exchange rate to various price indices. His equations explained over 99 per cent of the variation in exchange rates and showed a close proportionality between prices and the exchange rate, although there was still some evidence of other systematic factors at work.

Under more normal circumstances, when real factors are relatively more significant, PPP fares worse. For each of eleven industrial countries over the period 1950–70, Kravis and Lipsey (1978) compared changes in the GDP deflator in dollars with changes in the US GDP deflator. If PPP held, the two would be identical, but actually strong deviations emerge. Even over short periods like two years, changes in the national deflators differed from those in the US deflator by more than 5 per cent in 26 per cent of the cases observed. For changes over ten years, 86 per cent of the differences exceeded 5 per cent.

These results refer to a period of fixed but adjustable exchange rates, but PPP does not fare any better on more recent floating rate data. For example, Genberg (1978) found that floating increased both the extent and the duration of deviations from PPP, the average quarterly deviation after 1973 being 4.1 per cent and the average duration more than three years. Frenkel (1981) examined the USA, France, West Germany and the UK over 1973–9. He found PPP rejected for all exchange rates except the pound–DM rate, arguing that only the last rate is not disturbed by real changes in one or other of the economies. This is supported by Branson (1981), who identified a strong downward trend in the USA's equilibrium exchange rate relative to PPP after the early 1970s.

PPP asserts that the real exchange rate (SP^{UK}/P^{US}) is constant, and the results above reject it because actual rates deviate from constancy by enough, and for long enough, to render PPP a poor guide to the future exchange rate. A new stream of work suggests an even more alarming prospect, namely that there is not even a long-run tendency for actual rates to revert to PPP values after a shock. Thus if the actual real rate gets above the PPP constant, instead of tending to fall back towards it, it just fluctuates randomly around the new level. This is the so-called random-walk model of the real exchange rate. It received some empirical support over the 1980s (e.g. Baillie and Selover, 1987), but it is probably true to say that the time periods tested have been too short to provide a sound basis for rejecting all reversionary tendencies in the real exchange rate.

PPP – a summary

Purchasing power parity is a simple and bold theory of the exchange rate. Such theories are easy to knock down because they make such uncompromising predictions, and this has been the fate of PPP. However, while it is quite inadequate in itself – except under very rare circumstances – the author's view is that it clearly has some role in exchange rate theory. One could no more claim that exchange rates were independent of prices than that they were completely dependent on them. A satisfactory exchange rate theory must take account of real as well as monetary factors. Many of the real determinants of exchange rates have been encountered above under our balance of payments theory. To these must be added asset considerations and expectations, to which we turn next. It is hardly surprising that a single variable – relative prices – is insufficient to represent such a wide range of causes.

FURTHER READING

The anatomy of the exchange market is presented well in *Yeager* (1976), *Cohen* (1969) and *McKinnon* (1979). Purchasing power parity has an enormous literature: *Officer* (1976a) and *Katseli-Papaefstratiou* (1979) provide useful surveys and the *Journal of International Economics* (1978, no. 2) covers empirical applications. *Frenkel* (1981) extends the evidence to the late 1970s, and *Branson* (1981) offers an excellent alternative analysis of his evidence. The monetary theory is surveyed in *Kreinin and Officer* (1978), *Frenkel and Johnson* (1978) and *Laidler* (1981). Recent general surveys include *MacDonald* (1988) and *Baillie and McMahon* (1989), both of which include many references on testing market efficiency.

KEY CONCEPTS

forward exchange rate	arbitrage
covered interest arbitrage	uncovered interest arbitrage
rational expectations	market efficiency (three forms)
risk aversion	news
rational bubbles	relative purchasing power parity
productivity bias	real shocks

QUESTIONS FOR REVIEW

22.1 What is the difference between covered and uncovered interest arbitrage?

22.2 What are the problems of testing rational expectations models of the exchange rate (a) indirectly by looking at actual exchange rates, (b) directly?

22.3 Why can the exchange rate rise for considerable periods even though no one expects it to?

22.4 What price index should one use for testing PPP?

NOTES

1 Any elementary statistics book will define the expectation. It is the sum of the products of each possible value of a variable multiplied by its probability of occurring. For example, the expected value of a throw of a die is $3\frac{1}{2}$: each face has a one-sixth chance of occurring, thus $E(\text{die}) = (1 \times \frac{1}{6}) + (2 \times \frac{1}{6}) + \ldots + (6 \times \frac{1}{6}) = 3\frac{1}{2}$.

2 Because s is measured logarithms, $\hat{s} \equiv E(s_{t+1}) - s_t$.

23 Assets and Exchange Rates

The purchasing power parity theory of exchange rates effectively considers only the prices of goods. Even to the extent that money is mentioned it is for transactions, not money to hold. We now relax this restriction and introduce assets into exchange rate determination. The huge range of assets in the real world is far too complex to model, but by simplifying drastically we can explore some of the main issues and generate some concrete results. We consider below the so-called sticky price monetary model, a currency substitution model and a general portfolio model. First, however, we introduce some of the conceptual tools of asset analysis: portfolio equilibrium, the role of wealth in adjustment, and overshooting.

23.1 BASIC CONCEPTS FOR EXCHANGE RATE ANALYSIS

The introduction of assets into exchange rate models raises the issue of wealth – its level and its composition. To keep the analysis tractable we shall assume in all that follows that wealth can be held in, at most, only four forms: domestic and foreign money and domestic and foreign short-term bills. This does not do justice to the menu of financial assets actually available, but it suffices for our purposes. (We use short-term bills as our non-monetary asset in order to avoid the difficulty that the capital values of long-run instruments vary with the interest rate.)

Portfolio equilibrium

How do people allocate their wealth over these assets? Two factors are important: the rate of return on each asset and the extent of risk. We shall not say much about the latter, save to note that risk can normally be reduced by diversification. In a diversified portfolio the assets that are doing badly are at least partly compensated for by those that are doing well; in a concentrated one you may do very well, but you may do very badly if you choose wrongly. Hence, if people are risk averse, they will hold assets with returns lower than the maximum available, just in order to be more secure. That is, they will trade off returns against security. If the risk properties of an asset change, people may well rearrange their portfolio because the terms of this trade-off will have altered.

The rate of return on an asset has several dimensions. Most obvious is the rate of interest. Just as important, however, is any capital gain it makes, and against both must be set the transactions costs of liquidating it. The ease and certainty with which money can be converted into other things is one of its major attractions as an asset. We shall assume that this is sufficient to ensure a demand for money no matter how high the rate of interest. Capital gains enter our discussion via the exchange rate, changes in which affect the relative worth of domestic and foreign assets. Specifically, we shall define the rate of return on foreign bills as the rate of interest less the proportionate change in the exchange rate over the holding period $(i_f - \dot{r})$; an appreciation of the pound, i.e. a depreciation of the dollar, reduces the worth of Britain's dollar assets.

Risk and the rate of return determine how a given stock of wealth is allocated over assets, but changes in wealth are also important. First, some assets may be 'luxury assets' whose share of a portfolio grows with wealth, while others may do the opposite. Second, if wealth is growing we have something like a flow demand for assets, because 'new' wealth must be allocated across assets. Under these circumstances, a rise in the attractiveness of an asset raises its share not only in present wealth but also in future increments, and hence leads to a permanently increasing demand for it. Third, wealth can get revalued; a depreciation immediately raises the domestic value of foreign assets. This could unbalance the relationship between wealth and income or the division of the portfolio between home and foreign assets. Fourth, if wealth is redistributed from one country to another (e.g. from OECD to OPEC during the 1970s), and if these countries have different asset demands, the overall demand for different assets will change.

Equilibrium and adjustment with asset markets

Given total wealth, and the rates of return and risks on all the various assets, residents have some preferred portfolio: they know in what proportions they wish to hold the alternative assets. Hence the demand for assets is known. It is, however, a *stock demand*: we know how many of each asset people are willing to hold, not immediately how many they will buy in any period. Since the supply of assets is also a stock phenomenon (namely, how many bonds exist), equilibrium in asset markets is a *stock equilibrium*. We define it as being when all existing assets are willingly held.

The exchange rate is involved in these stock processes in two basic ways. First, the adjustment of asset portfolios may require current account changes, and these are normally achieved by exchange rate changes. For example, we know that foreign investment – a current account surplus – is one way of accumulating extra wealth; if we exclude real capital and if the government will not issue any more bonds, it is the only way. If rising income increases desired wealth or stimulates the demand for foreign assets, this could be met by depreciating the exchange rate and running a current surplus. On the other hand, a higher stock of foreign assets means more income from abroad. Hence, once the accumulation has occurred, we will then require a small surplus from trade to achieve current balance, which means that the exchange rate could eventually appreciate.

Second, anticipated changes in the exchange rate influence relative rates of return, and thus impinge on the asset markets. Conversely, therefore, asset equilibrium could influence the current exchange rate, given expectations. This occurs through the stock adjustments associated with interest arbitrage and speculation. It is most easily seen in speculation. If domestic and foreign bills are perfect substitutes, if speculators are risk neutral (do not require compensating for bearing risk) and if there are no transactions costs, then the returns on all bills are equal, so $i_d = i_f - \dot{r}$. This is the uncovered interest arbitrage condition (22.4) in a more general notation. Now, if the expected exchange rate at the maturity of these bills is $\hat{S}_1$, the expected change in the rate ($\dot{r}$), is $(\hat{S}_1 - S)/S$, and if i_d, i_f and $\hat{S}_1$ are fixed, only one value of S can ensure equilibrium. Once we relax the assumptions, the uniqueness goes, but the principle remains. For example, if speculators require higher returns to compensate for risk, holders of sterling will require $i_f - \dot{r} > i_d$ before speculating, while dollar speculators will require $i_d + \dot{r} > i_f$. Hence, there will exist some feasible band for S given the other variables.

Arbitrage and speculation do not actually have to occur to bring these relationships about. Merely the threat of them is sufficient: no one will offer to trade at prices that do not roughly reflect covered interest arbitrage because he would be overwhelmed. Hence prices are constrained even though no actual trade may occur. An important corollary of this is that exchange rates can jump from one value to another. Changed conditions can be reflected immediately in a discrete change in the exchange rate. This is in stark contrast to variables such as the stock of bills that can evolve only gradually.

Equilibrium and overshooting

The equilibrium exchange rate is one that is under no pressure to change. The equality between the stock demand and supply of assets implies that portfolios are not changing, which in turn implies that the equilibrium exchange rate must produce balance on official settlements. During the short run, this implies that deficits on basic balance must be matched by short-term capital surpluses, and vice versa. Over the longer run, however, short-term flows must roughly balance out, so the long-run equilibrium exchange rate is determined by the basic balance, of which the predominant element is generally the current account.

Overshooting occurs if a variable has to adjust in the long run, but actually adjusts by more than the required amount in the short run. The idea is unique to neither exchange rate theory nor the last twenty years. The easiest example is Marshall's 'market period', during which quantities are quite inflexible. Imagine a fish market that, from equilibrium, experiences an unforeseen jump in demand. While supplies are rigid, price shoots up, but if, after a day, supply is able to increase, the final price will be higher than originally but lower than immediately after the demand surge.[1] This overshooting is caused by the different speeds of adjustment of different parts of the market, and the same applies to some exchange rate overshooting. However, the latter can also occur without differential speeds of adjustment if there are fixed nominal magnitudes in the economy, such as the supply of money. Either way the basic cause is that, in the short run, only part of the economy adjusts. As Friedman (1953, p. 183) wrote, introducing the idea of exchange rate overshooting.

> It is clear that the initial change in exchange rates will be greater than the ultimate change required, for, to begin with, all the adjustment will have to be borne in those directions in which prompt adjustment is possible and relatively easy. As time passes, the slower-moving adjustments will take over part of the burden, permitting exchange rates to rebound toward a final position which is between the position prior to the external change and the position shortly thereafter. This is, of course, a highly oversimplified picture: the actual path of adjustment may involve repeated overshooting and undershooting of the final position . . .

Interest in exchange rate overshooting revived in the 1970s because flexible exchange rates proved much more volatile than had been predicted. This could of course have been due to the volatility of events exogenous to exchange rate determination, but it raised the question of whether the volatility might not be inherent. For example, during 1973 the dollar first fell by around 20 per cent against the DM and then recovered to end nearly 20 per cent above its original level. Similarly, sterling covered a range of around 40 per cent over 1976 and 1977. Batchelor (1979) found that the mean monthly deviation of sterling about its trend over 1973–8 was nearly 7 per cent, while the figures for DM and francs were around 5 per cent. Finally, it is quite common to find daily changes of 2 per cent in a currency's value and 4 per cent is not unknown. It is at least plausible to ask whether such variability reflects over-

reaction in the exchange market rather than variability in the real economic
environment.

23.2   THE STICKY PRICE MONETARY MODEL

The first, and now classic, formal analysis of exchange rate overshooting was
by Dornbusch (1976), who adapted the simple monetary model that we have
already examined. Residents have stock demands for money and the exchange
rate adjusts to bring these into line with the exogenous supply of money.
Above we assumed that all the adjustment had to be borne directly by goods
prices and the exchange rate, but now, with bills in the picture, we can be
more sophisticated.

Imagine that, in the long run, PPP holds perfectly. In the short run,
however, we assume that nothing can change in the goods market, but that
asset markets are perfectly flexible, and hence bear all immediate adjustment.
Suppose that equilibrium is disturbed by an x per cent increase in the money
supply. Goods prices cannot adjust, but domestic interest rates (i_d) fall
immediately. This reduces the attractiveness of domestic assets, and so a
capital outflow threatens to depreciate the exchange rate. How far will it fall?
Our long-run assumptions suggest x per cent, and with rational expectations
people know this. But in the short run this is not far enough, because at this
long-run exchange rate no further change is anticipated; hence the return on
foreign bills (i_f) still exceeds the reduced i_d, and a depreciation of x per cent is
insufficient to stem the capital outflow. That can be done only when the net
returns on foreign and domestic bills are equalised, i.e. when the lower
domestic interest rate is supplemented by an anticipated appreciation. This
requires the exchange rate to fall below its equilibrium level, so that its return
to that level gives the required appreciation.

The formal analysis   This story is simple to formalise, which at least partly explains its popularity.
Measuring all variables except interest rates in logarithms and taking very
small units of time, there are three basic behavioural relationships driving the
exchange rate: (a) uncovered interest arbitrage

$$i_d = i_f - \dot{r};\tag{23.1}$$

(b) the demand for real money balances (nominal balances, m, divided by
prices, p) as a function of income (y) and interest rates

$$m - p = \phi y - \lambda i_d; \quad \phi, \ \lambda > 0;\tag{23.2}$$

and (c) an exchange rate adjustment equation in which in each period the
exchange rate takes up a given fraction ($\theta; \ 0 < \theta < 1$) of the difference
between its current value (r) and its long-run equilibrium ($\bar{r}$)

$$\dot{r} = \theta(\bar{r} - r).\tag{23.3}$$

Substituting (23.1) for i_d in (23.2), and (23.3) for $\dot{r}$ in the resulting equation
we get

$$m - p = \phi y - \lambda i_f + \lambda \theta(\bar{r} - r).\tag{23.4}$$

Now if we take the long-run value of (23.4) and remember that, following
the monetarists, y never deviates from full employment,

331

$$\bar{p} = m - \theta y + \lambda i. \tag{23.5}$$

Subtracting this from (23.4) and re-arranging

$$\dot{r} = \bar{r} + \frac{1}{\lambda \theta} (p - \bar{p}), \tag{23.6}$$

which states that for so long as prices differ from their equilibrium value so too will the exchange rate.

Suppose now that the money supply increases by dm holding world prices and interest rates constant.[2] Remembering that everything is measured in logarithms and that PPP applies in the long run, d$\bar{p}$ = − d$\bar{r}$ = dm. In the short run, however, goods prices are fixed, dp = 0, so that from (23.6) the initial change in the exchange rate must be

$$- dr = \left(1 + \frac{1}{\lambda \theta} \right) dm. \tag{23.7}$$

Since $\lambda \theta > 0$, $- dr > - d\bar{r}$, that is, the exchange rate falls by more than its long-run depreciation − it overshoots.

Figure 23.1 illustrates the result. It plots p, the logarithm of prices, against r, the logarithm of the exchange rate. The 45° line, PP, represents PPP: $\bar{p} + \bar{r}$ = constant, i.e. the (log of the) real exchange rate is constant; the line QQ shows the short-term asset-determined relationship between r and p, given by equation (23.6). It is positively sloped because if, given the money supply, prices rise, the resulting increase in the domestic interest rate must be offset by an expected depreciation, which can only be induced by raising the current level of the exchange rate. The initial equilibrium is at A. When the money supply is increased, the long-run equilibrium remains on PP but the short-run locus shifts up to $Q'Q'$: at fixed prices the exchange rate must be lower in order to promise the subsequent appreciation necessary to get residents to

Figure 23.1 The sticky price monetary model

hold the additional money. Because equation (23.6) reflects instantaneous asset market behaviour, the economy must always be on the prevailing asset locus. With fixed prices this is possible only if the exchange rate jumps from A to B, i.e. if it overshoots its long-run equilibrium at C. The shift from A to B is instantaneous, but the move from B to C occurs through real time as the extra foreign demand induced by the excess depreciation bids up domestic prices. (We have not modelled this process above, but it is in Dornbusch, 1976.)

An assessment

Dornbusch's model is elegant and powerful – it shows that overshooting can occur even if everyone knows the final equilibrium level of the exchange rate. It is, however, subject to a number of criticisms. First, it is very short run: it admits no changes in output or wealth, despite implying a non-zero current account during the adjustment period. Second, it presumes, implicitly, that a change in the domestic interest rate produces a continuous outflow of capital rather than a once-and-for-all stock adjustment. Third, it prevents domestic residents from holding foreign money. This is crucial to the results because, if residents could substitute between currencies, they would do so in response to anticipated exchange rate changes and in consequence make those changes instantaneous (see section 23.3). As it is, residents hold domestic currency whether it appreciates or depreciates – they have no choice. Fourth, residents continue to hold domestic currency even though it is devalued by inflation. During the move from B to C, real cash balances are eroded, and rational agents might be expected to try to hold goods rather than money over that period; the attempt to do so, of course, would increase p instantaneously rather than gradually. This criticism arises from Dornbusch's assumed relative speeds of adjustment; but, in fact, goods markets can adjust very quickly (e.g. commodity markets) and asset markets can take time (e.g. housing). Fifth, the assumption of perfect asset substitutability – i.e. that uncovered interest arbitrage holds – is implausible. Frenkel and Rodriguez (1982) showed elegantly that, with lower levels of capital mobility, undershooting rather than overshooting occurs. Finally, the sticky price model has received only mixed empirical support. On the one hand, assuming it to be true, Frankel (1979) estimated that an unanticipated 1 per cent increase in the US money supply induced a 1.23 per cent depreciation of the \$:DM exchange rate, and thus offered some support for the model. More direct tests of the model, however, have been less favourable (see section 23.4 below) and, as Goodhart (1988) observed, if Dornbusch had been correct, we would have expected to see far *more* exchange rate volatility than we have. Exchange rates may move quite quickly, but they certainly do not jump in a Dornbuschian fashion.

23.3 PORTFOLIO MODELS

Portfolio models of the exchange rate include any model with more than one asset. They are potentially very complex because they must determine the exchange rate, interest rates, total wealth and possibly various real variables in order to balance the demands for assets with their exogenous supplies. A general introduction is given in Branson (1983), but here we discuss three specialisations of the general model: the currency substitution model, in which domestic and foreign monies are the only assets; a short-term model with an exogenous real sector but four assets – two monies plus foreign and domestic bills; and a longer-run model, in which wealth effects predominate.

333

Currency substitution occurs when residents hold more than one currency and switch between them in response to changes in expected rates of return. If one adds it to the sticky price monetary model one gets immediate and full exchange rate adjustment, but in more sophisticated models it too can lead to overshooting. In this section we sketch a model by Calvo and Rodriguez (1977) in which prices are perfectly flexible and expectations rational and yet in which overshooting occurs. Residents may hold their wealth only as domestic or foreign money, and, although there are no explicit rates of interest, holding money still entails a potential loss of return.

We consider a small country facing fixed world prices. Our country may be inflating at x per cent per annum, i.e. increasing its money supply and local prices at x per cent, but in dynamic equilibrium this will be offset by x per cent per annum depreciation, thus maintaining PPP. The stocks of foreign ($\$$) and domestic (£) money that residents wish to hold will be determined by these rates of inflation, bearing in mind the shares of their budgets that residents spend on tradable goods (which, given the LOOP and PPP, are effectively priced in $\$$) and non-tradables (which are necessarily priced in £). If suddenly the rate of increase in the money supply rose to y per cent ($y > x$), holding £ would be less attractive than previously and residents would try to switch into $\$$. If, and this is crucial, they can earn extra $\$$ only by running a current account surplus, the real £:$\$$ exchange rate will have to depreciate to facilitate this. In the long run, however, when the portfolio shift has been achieved, equilibrium requires no change in the real exchange rate, so we have witnessed a form of overshooting.

The formal analysis

This presentation of the currency substitution model comes from Frenkel and Rodriguez (1982); it is simplified, but not simple. The model has two crucial variables: total assets measured in foreign currency terms (a) and the real exchange rate (s). The former is the sum of domestic money (M) times the exchange rate (r) plus holdings of foreign money (F)

$$a = rM + F. \tag{23.8}$$

The real exchange rate reflects the relative prices of tradable and non-tradable goods. If tradables satisfy the LOOP and world prices are arbitrarily fixed to unity,

$$s = P_N/(P_T^*/r) = rP_N, \tag{23.9}$$

where P_N is the £ price of non-tradables and P_T^* the world price of tradables ($= 1$). Either an appreciation or a rise in the price of non-tradables raises the real exchange rate, making our country less competitive.

In this simple model the production (Q) of tradables and non-tradables is assumed to depend only on their relative prices (i.e. on s), while consumption (C) depends on that and total wealth (assets). Thus we can write market balance equations for non-tradables (N) and tradables (T) as

$$C_N(s,a) + Q_N(s) = 0 \tag{23.10}$$

and

$$C_T(s,a) + Q_T(s) = \dot{F}, \tag{23.11}$$

where $\dot{F}$ is the change in foreign money holdings per unit of time.

Equation (23.10) shows that the domestic market for non-tradables must clear, and from it we can calculate the value of s necessary to clear the market given any value of a:

$$s = s(a). \qquad (23.12)$$

Equation (23.11) shows the current account. If we further assume that the rest of the world is not interested in holding our country's money, any deficit or surplus must be reflected in residents' holdings of foreign money. Substituting (23.12) into (23.11) tells us that in full equilibrium the current account depends only on total assets

$$\dot{F} = f(a). \qquad (23.13)$$

To complete the model we need to find what effect $\dot{F}$ has on total assets (a). First observe that the relative shares of rM and F in a depend on their expected relative rates of return, that is, on changes in the nominal exchange rate. Reversing the argument, if rM and F are held in particular proportions, that can be consistent with only one expected percentage change in r: writing this as $\hat{r}$,

$$\hat{r} = l\left(\frac{rM}{F}\right) = l\left(\frac{a-F}{F}\right), \qquad (23.14)$$

where $l(\ )$ is a general function.

If we take the change through time of (23.8) we get[3]

$$\dot{a} = (a-F)\left[\hat{M} + l\left(\frac{a-F}{F}\right)\right] + f(a), \qquad (23.15)$$

where $\hat{M}$ is the proportionate rate of increase of the domestic money supply.

Equations (23.13) and (23.15) define a dynamic system in assets and foreign money from which, by (23.12), we can derive the exchange rate. Observe first that if $\dot{F} = 0$, i.e. there is current account equilibrium, and if $\dot{a} = 0$, i.e. total assets are stable, then $\hat{M} + \hat{r} = 0$, i.e. PPP is maintained and the real exchange rate is constant. This represents an outcome of full equilibrium.

Now let us plot the dynamics in Figure 23.2 by finding values of a and F for which there is no change in either variable. From (23.13) only one value of a is consistent with current account balance, $\dot{F} = 0$. If actual a exceeds this level, consumption will be too high, there will be a deficit and so F will fall. The horizontal arrows in the right-hand quadrant of Figure 23.2 show the directions of change in F above and below the locus $\dot{F} = 0$. The line $\dot{a} = 0$ plots combinations of a and F setting (23.15) to zero. It could have either positive or negative slope, but the latter is more likely; if the economy is above the locus, a will fall and if it is below it, a will rise. This explains the vertical arrows in the right-hand quadrant. These two sets of arrows show the directions in which a and F will evolve in each sector of the figure; they suggest that at points like B we move towards equilibrium (at point C), whereas at points like D we move away. In fact it may be shown that under certain conditions there will be only one path of evolution which leads to equilibrium – this is known as the saddle-path and is marked in the diagram as SP. If the economy is stable, it is argued, then it must always be on the saddle-path leading to its ruling long-run equilibrium. (While the conditions for a unique stable path and equilibrium are very frequently assumed, they are far from innocuous; see Oxley and George, 1989.)

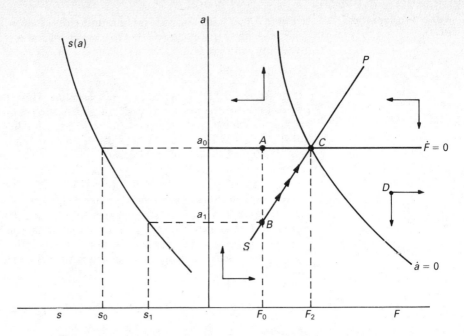

Figure 23.2 Overshooting with flexible prices – Calvo and Rodriguez

We can now analyse a monetary shock. Suppose that initially we are in equilibrium at A, on the $\dot{a} = 0$, $\dot{F} = 0$, and saddle-path loci relevant to the given rate of monetary increase. Now let $\hat{M}$ rise. From (23.13) the $\dot{F} = 0$ locus does not shift. (23.15), however, tells us that the $\dot{a} = 0$ locus will shift rightwards, implying higher F for any given a, because, with higher $\hat{M}$, even in steady state the exchange rate will be depreciating faster. The new equilibrium will be at C and the saddle-path will shift accordingly. But getting from A to C involves accumulating foreign assets, which cannot occur instantaneously. Given the fixed initial level of F, the only point via which the economy can get to C is B on the new saddle-path. It can jump from A to B by reducing total assets, a, which it does by a step depreciation of r and, consequently, s, the real exchange rate. Then, as the current account surplus allows F to rise, s starts to climb back to its former level. This pattern is illustrated in the left-hand panel of Figure 23.2, which plots the relationship (23.12) between total assets and the real exchange rate. The exchange rate overshoots in the sense that, after the shock, the nominal rate depreciates by more than $\hat{M}$ in order to reduce the real rate temporarily.

An assessment

The currency substitution model is no more realistic than the sticky price model, but it does illustrate different factors. The overshooting arises because of the nominal rigidity of foreign money holdings and the fact that they can be changed only via the current account. The depreciation is necessary to generate the required surplus. The rise in the rate of increase of the money supply makes domestic money less desirable; given fixed foreign prices, the shift to foreign money is equivalent to a shift into foreign goods and acts as a hedge against inflation. If residents could accumulate future claims on domestic goods as an alternative hedge, there would be no overshooting.

There is no empirical work dealing directly with this form of the currency substitution model, and work on other versions is not particularly convincing because so many other factors could account for the relatively small effects identified. Hence it is rather difficult to assess the relevance of Calvo and Rodriguez's work, but one might argue that it sheds some light on the UK disinflation of the early 1980s. A sharp and apparently long-lasting decline in the rate of money supply growth occurred with the Medium Term Financial Strategy of 1980 and was followed by a sharp appreciation of the pound. As we noted in the last section, this was not, strictly speaking, a jump, but it is quite possible that it reflected a reassessment of sterling's asset properties in the manner of the currency substitution model.

Imperfect asset substitutability

An important feature of Dornbusch's sticky price model was the perfect substitutability between assets which, in turn, implied uncovered interest arbitrage. The currency substitution model rectified this, but in a very restricted way. We now consider a more general model with four assets based on Niehans (1980), but in order to solve it we have to ignore the real side of the economy.

Abandoning perfect substitutability means that the domestic interest rate is determined jointly with the exchange rate. Let the four assets be domestic and foreign money and domestic and foreign bills. Freezing the foreign interest rate and the long-run equilibrium exchange rate, we relate the demand for domestic bills and money to the domestic interest rate (i_d) and the exchange rate (r). Figure 23.3 plots combinations of i_d and r that maintain equilibrium in the money market (MM) and the bill market (BB) Consider the money market: the money supply is fixed, so any rise in the interest rate, which cuts money demand, must be offset by a fall in the exchange rate, which, by promising an appreciation, increases demand. Hence MM slopes downwards. Note also that an increase in the exogenous money supply shifts MM inwards,

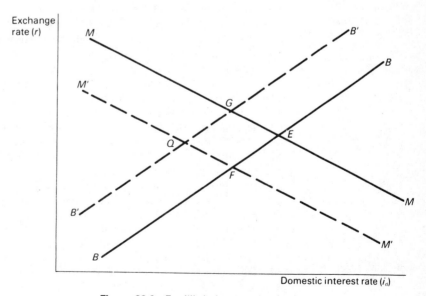

Figure 23.3 Equilibria in asset markets

because more money will be held only at lower interest rates. The bill market reacts in the opposite fashion. Higher interest rates, which raise demand, must be offset by a higher exchange rate promising a capital loss: an increased supply of bills shifts BB to the right since it will be held only at higher rates of interest.

We now use Figure 23.3 to explore various shocks to the asset markets. First, increasing the foreign exchange reserves – that is, official purchases of foreign money. This does not appear explicitly in the figure, but the issue of domestic money to effect the purchase shifts MM inwards, moving equilibrium from E to F, and reducing both r and i_d. Second, a reduction in the supply of domestic bills. This shifts BB leftwards and produces a new equilibrium at G, raising r and lowering i_d. Finally, an open market operation buying bills; this shifts MM in and BB up. The net result is equilibrium at Q, where i_d has fallen but r could have risen or fallen. Obviously the effect on r depends on the asset demand behaviour, which determines the relative shifts in MM and BB.

The longer run

In the longer run, expectational mechanisms are gradually displaced by real and asset-accumulation effects on the exchange rate. For example, a money supply increase produces a depreciation, as we have just seen, which will be worsened by any J-cure effect from the real economy. In time, however, the depreciation will generate a current surplus, and if this outweighs the J-curve (which is likely) it will cause the net accumulation of wealth in terms of foreign assets. This will affect interest receipts and consumption behaviour, and possibly also the accumulation of real capital.

Higher interest receipts from abroad (or reduced payments) mean that the equilibrium trade balance is lower than before the shock, and thus that the exchange rate can be higher. The higher consumption, on the other hand, will worsen the trade balance and may thus require a lower equilibrium exchange rate. If the temporary depreciation stimulates real capital accumulation, it may have very long-lived effects on prices and costs, through its effects on technological progress. In this way it could lead to a nearly permanent strengthening of the trade balance.

Similar effects may be felt if firms face fixed costs to capturing market share. The depreciation may make it worthwhile for exporters to invest in increasing their sales abroad, e.g. by setting up sales networks, etc.; when the exchange rate subsequently increases, the profitability of these sales will decline (appreciation reduces local currency tradables prices), but maybe not enough to make exporters withdraw from the markets they have already captured. That is, they may still be able to cover the variable costs of selling abroad after the appreciation. In this way temporary depreciation may permanently boost exports and thus allow a permanently higher equilibrium exchange rate. This argument is unlikely to apply to simple tradable goods where price competition is fierce, for they do not typically have high market set-up costs; it may, however, be relevant to a significant proportion of the trade of industrial countries. Certainly this sort of argument has been advanced to explain the difficulties of US and UK manufacturers following the large overvaluations of the dollar and sterling in the early 1980s – see, for example, Bean (1987) and Baldwin (1988), and the discussion of hysteresis in Chapter 19 above.

The arguments sketched above make very clear the huge difficulty of modelling exchange rates over the long run. The real–nominal dichotomy of the monetary theory is a useful rule of thumb when extreme monetary disturbances are considered, but in the ordinary course of events the two sides of the economy are intertwined, and in no place is this more evident than in exchange rate determination.

23.4 EMPIRICAL RESULTS

This final section takes a brief look at the burgeoning empirical literature on asset models of exchange rate determination. The monetary theory assumes PPP, so one might take the rejection of the latter to imply the rejection of the former. Nevertheless there have been many direct tests of it. Writing the demand for money as a function of real income, prices and interest rates, the exchange rate between two countries' currencies can be written as a function of their relative incomes, interest rates and money supplies. Estimating such equations has proved adequate for the hyper-inflations of the 1920s (Frenkel, 1978), but thoroughly unsuccesssful for the 1970s: exchange rates have deviated from PPP by up to 30 per cent, and frequently the current exchange rate seems quite independent of the money supplies. There is now overwhelming evidence that the flexible-price monetary theory alone is not sufficient.

Turning to the asset theories, much less empirical evidence exists, not least because the theories are much less precise. A useful general exploration is by Hacche and Townend (1981a), who examined the effective exchange rates of eight major currencies over 1972–80. They calculated only the simplest of summary statistics and reached the following conclusions. PPP had almost nothing to contribute, even over long periods. Interest rates affected exchange rates but sometimes positively (as above) and sometimes negatively if interest rate rises were interpreted as indicating an attempt by the central bank to support the exchange rate above its equilibrium level. Portfolio diversification was significant over the late 1970s: world wealth moved towards OPEC, which caused a substitution of other currencies for the dollar. There was a marked positive relationship between current balances and exchange rates: in part this may reflect the J-curve (falling exchange rates reduce the current surplus temporarily), but mainly it reflects the influence of current balances on exchange rate expectations. Countries with current deficits seem likely to have to depreciate sometime.

The relevance of the current balance was also explored by Dornbusch (1980a). Combining the portfolio approach with the efficiency of the foreign exchange markets, Dornbusch related unanticipated exchange rate changes to 'news' about the current account, output and interest rates. Unanticipated exchange rate changes were defined as actual exchange rate changes less the interest rate differential, which, assuming perfect asset substitutability, measures expected changes (remember $i_d = i_f - \dot{r}$, p. 329 above). 'News' was defined as the difference between the actual current balance and output and the values predicted six months earlier by OECD, and for the interest rates as the actual rate minus that predicted by an estimating equation. The results suggested strongly that unforeseen US current surpluses induced dollar appreciation; for example, a surplus of \$1b. over six months induced a 0.25–0.5 per cent appreciation in the effective exchange rate. Interest rate shocks also had a role – rises usually inducing depreciation – as did output shocks – an unforeseen expansion in GDP of 1 per cent inducing a 1–2 per cent depreciation. These results reinforce the view that expectations are important.

339

While Dornbusch's results offer some support for the portfolio approach to exchange rates there are several problems: for example, markets may not be efficient (see section 22.2 above), or his definition of news may not be appropriate, first with respect to the identification of expected values and second in ignoring the role of risk aversion which places value on having even perfect predictions confirmed as such. Finally, even if the model is correct in its estimates of the mean value of exchange rates, the residual errors may be so large that it is of little practical use.

Perhaps the crowning ignominy for exchange rate modelling is the work of Meese and Rogoff (1983, 1988). They tested the predictions of four simple exchange rate models over the late 1970s: the monetary model, the Dornbusch (1976) model, an asset model adding current account factors to the Dornbusch model, and a market-efficiency model stating that the exchange rate follows a random walk, i.e. that next period's exchange rate will equal this period's save for a random element. The economic models are represented by the following equation

$$r = a_0 + a_1(m_d - m_f) + a_2(y_d - y_f) + a_3(i_d - i_f)$$
$$+ a_4(\hat{\pi}_d - \hat{\pi}_f) + a_5 B_d + a_6 B_f + \epsilon, \tag{23.16}$$

where, measured in logarithms, r is the exchange rate, m the money supply, y real income, i the short-term interest rate, $\hat{\pi}$ expected inflation, B the (unlogged) cumulative trade balance, and ϵ a random disturbance; the a_i are coefficients to be estimated and the subscripts d and f refer to domestic and foreign variables respectively. Note that all the economic variables except for the wealth effects (B) enter as symmetrical ratios (differences in logarithms). The monetary model allows only the first three effects to matter – i.e. it sets $a_4 = a_5 = a_6 = 0$; the Dornbusch sticky price model allows additionally for inflation differentials while the economy works its way back to equilibrium and thus sets only $a_5 = a_6 = 0$; finally, the portfolio model allows wealth and portfolio effects to influence the exchange rate. The latter are represented by the accumulation or decumulation of assets through the trade balance.

The coefficient estimates in Meese and Rogoff (1988) suggest a plausible role for real interest rate differentials $[(i_d - i_f) - (\hat{\pi}_d - \hat{\pi}_f)]$ in explaining exchange rates: higher interest rates induce appreciation. But the relationship is wildly unstable through time and no sense can be made out of the trade balance effects. When it comes to prediction, the situation is even worse. For the dollar's various bilateral rates, the prediction errors of the best-performing model averaged 3.5 per cent for one-month forecasts and a massive 13 per cent for twelve-month forecasts. These figures indicate considerable ignorance about exchange rate determination, and this is confirmed when we discover that the best-performing model is the random walk, which states that the best predictor of next period's exchange rate is this period's! In other words, for general forecasting purposes (i.e. in the absence of identifiable special economic factors), economic theories appear to add nothing to our understanding of exchange rate behaviour.

One suspects that at least part of the failure of the economic models is due to the difficulties of their empirical implementation – for example, errors of measurement, finding the relevant periods over which to measure things, and the interactions between markets. It is, after all, difficult to believe that monetary factors, wealth and speeds of adjustment have no influence in exchange rates. However, the models incorporate many auxiliary hypotheses, such as the rationality of expectations, any of which could be wrong and which should now be examined explicitly. The models also exclude many factors which may turn out to be more important than has previously been assumed. Meese and Rogoff (1988) themselves suggested that we should consider real factors (e.g. productivity shocks and fiscal variables) and also the possibility of speculative bubbles. Until this is done it is impossible to tell why our models are failing, let alone set about rectifying them. In the meantime, if ever there was a subject for economists to be modest about, this is it!

FURTHER READING

The sticky price monetary model should be read in the original – *Dornbusch* (1976) – and also as extended by *Frenkel and Rodriguez* (1982). The latter also offers a good exposition of the currency substitution model. More general studies of exchange rates include *Isard* (1978), *Niehans* (1980) and *Hacche and Townend* (1981a), all of which are excellent. *Dornbusch* (1980a) provides an interesting excursion from the monetary theory to the portfolio theories, complemented by an interesting comment by *Branson* (1980), and *Dornbusch* (1986, Part I) brings it somewhat more up to date. A clear (though mathematical) exposition of the simple portfolio model is given by *Branson* (1977, 1983) and *Branson, Halttunen and Masson* (1977). These references spend considerable time on a version of the model with static expectations which is intimately related to the Mundell–Fleming model described in the next chapter. An extension and application of that model appears in *Buiter and Miller* (1981b). *Meese and Rogoff* (1983, 1988) are important for their empirical results, *Dornbusch* (1980b) offers an advanced analysis of many of the problems of this chapter, and *MacDonald* (1988) and *Baillie and McMahon* (1989) give thorough expositions of exchange rate theory and empirics in general. For the sterling exchange rate *Batchelor* (1977) and *Hacche and Townend* (1981b) are useful, and on overshooting see *Schadler* (1977).

KEY CONCEPTS

portfolio stock equilibrium	overshooting
sticky price monetary model	jump variables
currency substitution	hedging in goods markets
saddle-path	wealth accumulation through trade
hysteresis	random walk model

QUESTIONS FOR REVIEW

23.1 Asset equilibrium is a stock concept. Explain what this entails, and discuss how none the less one might observe pseudo-flow phenomena in response to portfolio shocks.

23.2 Discuss how Dornbusch's assumptions contribute to his overshooting result.

23.3 Why are stabilisation programmes involving a cut in the rate of increase of money supply often accompanied by exchange rate appreciations?

23.4 Is it worthwhile trying to explain exchange rates empirically?

NOTES

1 In the accompanying figure, when demand increases from D to D', price at first rises from p_e to p_m, while supplies are fixed at q_e, and then falls part-way back (to p_a) as supplies expand.

2 The notation dm denotes a small change in m.

3 This derivation relies on the following substitutions: $(\dot{rM}) = rM(\hat{rM})$ ($\cdot$ denotes changes per time period, $\hat{\ }$ denotes proportionate changes per time period); $(\hat{rM}) = \hat{r} + \hat{M}$; $rM = a - F$ ((23.13) and (23.14)).

24 Macro-economic Policy in the Open Economy

So far we have considered what determines the balance of payments and the exchange rate, but have not explicitly asked whether such factors can be used for the purposes of economic policy. Neither have we asked how the openness of the economy affects the use of other instruments of policy to achieve other targets, e.g. full employment. This chapter extends our discussion in these directions. We first consider the achievement of internal and external balance in the open economy, and then consider the ways in which the exchange rate regime and the degree of capital mobility influence the effectiveness of monetary and fiscal policies as instruments for internal balance. Finally we briefly examine empirical work on the degree of capital mobility and financial integration.

24.1 POLICIES FOR INTERNAL AND EXTERNAL BALANCE

Targets and instruments

The purpose of economics, at least as a prescriptive science, it to increase (economic) welfare. This is too vague a target for policy purposes, however, so economists set themselves various intermediate goals. In the long run, these include items such as raising economic growth and improving the distribution of income; over the shorter run, however, the most prominent has been *internal balance*. This broadly means the achievement of full employment and price stability. The two elements are linked together because, although each may have some independent existence, there are strong grounds for treating them as opposite ends of the same measure: high unemployment is likely to reduce price inflation, while over-full employment will exacerbate it. We shall assume that internal balance has just one dimension, but the interested student will be able to see how to generalise the principles, if not the practice, to the broader case.

The other principal target is *external balance*; for this, read balance of payments equilibrium. Unlike internal balance, external balance has no direct implications for welfare; it is, rather, a constraint that any feasible economic policy package must satisfy, because one cannot run deficits or surpluses indefinitely. Hence, for short-term macro-economic policy we assume that governments are simultaneously trying to achieve full employment and payments equilibrium.

Before considering specific policies, there is an important principle to note: to achieve n independent targets require at least n independent policy instruments (Tinbergen, 1952). Imagine driving a car about an airfield. To reach any particular spot of longitude and latitude you need two controls – a forward–back control and a left–right control. Now imagine flying an aeroplane to any particular location: the target is defined by three dimensions, longitude, latitude and height, and in general you will require three controls. Similarly, if we are to achieve the two independent economic goals of internal and external equilibrium, we shall require at least two independent policy instruments. If there are fewer, the complete attainment of both targets will be

343

precluded, and the policy-maker will have to trade off one objective against the other. Such a trade-off may also be necessary when there are constraints or costs on the use of certain instruments. For example, you cannot change the standard rate of income tax every week, so it may prove impossible to achieve joint internal and external balance at all points of time. Our formal analysis ignores both this latter problem and the difficulties arising from uncertainty over how the policies affect the targets. Both of these considerations are important in practice, and both make it advantageous to have more instruments than targets.

Policy in a Keynesian economy

To illustrate these principles of economic policy we return to a very simple model of the open economy. We assume a Keynesian world, with fixed local currency prices and a fixed, but adjustable, exchange rate. The government has available both expenditure-switching and expenditure-reducing policies – say, the exchange rate and government expenditure. How can it then achieve internal and external balance? The first step is to discover – from economic theory – how each policy affects each target. An increase in government expenditure raises income and employment, but, through that, worsens the balance of payments; a devaluation improves the balance of payments, and through that raises income and employment. We can show these results diagrammatically in Figure 24.1. The line YY plots those combinations of government expenditure (G) and the exchange rate (r) that produce internal equilibrium. Starting from point A on YY, suppose G is increased; this increases employment and, to bring it back to equilibrium along YY, a rise in the exchange rate is necessary; hence YY slopes upward. Conversely, BB, the locus of points ensuring balance of payments equilibrium, slopes downwards.

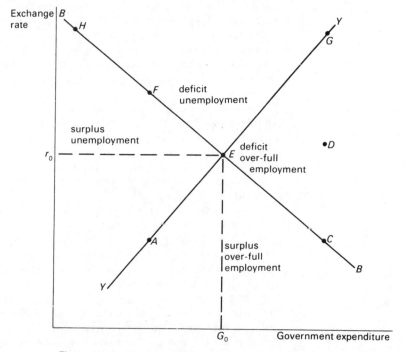

Figure 24.1 Policies for internal and external balance

Starting from C, an increase in G produces a deficit and this must be counteracted by a depreciation to restore balance.

It is plain from Figure 24.1 that, if YY gives all combinations of G and r for internal equilibrium, and BB gives those for external equilibrium, the only policy combination that ensures both is (G_0, r_0), i.e. point E. This is the heart of the policy problem. Provided the government knows the locations of BB and YY – that is, provided it knows both the nature and the parameters of economic behaviour – it can calculate their intersection, impose (G_0, r_0), and all is well.

Unfortunately, life is not so simple, not least because the government does not know the precise locations of BB and YY. Even so, it can make some progress as follows. The loci BB and YY divide the graph into what Swan (1955), the originator of this analysis, called four zones of 'economic unhappiness'. Any point above and to the right of BB involves a balance of payments deficit (starting on BB, either an appreciation or a rise in government spending will cause a deficit), while any point below or left of it involves a surplus. Similarly, any point above or left of YY involves unemployment (consider government contraction from a point on YY), while any point below or right involves over-full employment. There are, thus, four possible zones, which are marked in the diagram; merely by observing the state of the economy, the government knows which applies. Furthermore, in each zone the direction of change for one policy instrument is known: for instance, whenever we have a deficit and unemployment we know the exchange rate should fall. We do not know by how much, nor do we know what to do about government expenditure, so there is still a role for econometricians in establishing the positions of the loci. Nevertheless, even without full information, some qualitative guidance is available.

The assignment problem

Another approach to our ignorance of the precise locations of BB and YY would be trial and error. Just jumping about the graph randomly would not be very helpful, especially if there were costs to changing policies; but some economists have suggested allocating each policy to a separate target, and then changing each in turn. For example, suppose the economy started at point D in Figure 24.1 and that the exchange rate had been allocated external balance and government expenditure internal balance. From D, observing the deficit, we would devalue by sufficient to induce external balance; on the diagram, we fall vertically from D to the BB line, arriving at C. We would then alter government spending to achieve internal balance, moving horizontally to the YY line at A. From there the exchange rate would be altered to reach the BB line at F, and so on until we gradually converged in a cobweb to the joint equilibrium point E.

There are several objections to such an approach. First, it requires the correct assignment of instruments to target. Suppose the opposite assignment had been chosen. Starting from D, the iterations would have taken us outwards along the cobweb to G and H, rather than inwards to C and so on. Hence the assignment would have been divergent. Roughly speaking, to get convergence, the instruments must be assigned to the target on which they have relatively greatest influence; thus some information is required in order to make the assignment. Second, even if we have a convergent path, it involves considerable variability of both instruments and targets. This is expensive in terms of transition costs and in introducing greater uncertainty into the economy. Much of the variability could be avoided by using the policies in conjunction. Third, unless we know the locations of *BB* and *YY* it is impossible to know by how much to move the policy instruments, so there is further variability and time loss as this is discovered experimentally.

Hence, 'one-to-one' assignment does not reduce the need for information; it merely shows that independently controlled instruments *could* be assigned objectives such that the final outcome was acceptable. However, except where institutional factors entirely preclude cooperation between the controllers of the two policy instruments, a much better solution is likely to be the joint use of both instruments for both targets.

The prime conclusion of all this is that, although each instrument affects each target, achieving *n* targets requires *n* independent instruments. We also showed that an essential ingredient of successful policy-making is knowledge of how the economy works. The simple model used here has been subject to many refinements in earlier chapters, but the same rule applies to all models. If we wish to control *n* endogenous variables, we need both *n* policy instruments and a knowledge of how the system works.

Internal and external balance with a fixed exchange rate

If the exchange rate were no longer available to us, how could we then achieve external and internal balance? Mundell (1962) suggested a short-run solution involving monetary and fiscal policy and recognising the role of capital flows. Consider expanding national income by *x* per cent, using either fiscal or monetary policy. Although each policy worsens the current account by the same amount (dependent on *x*), each has different implications for the capital account. Both policies raise the demand for money by raising income, but, whereas this is met by an increasing supply of money with monetary policy, it is not accommodated in the case of fiscal policy. As a result, fiscal expansion entails a higher interest rate than monetary expansion, and hence attracts an inflow of capital to offset the current account deficit. (The inflow may exceed or fall short of the current deficit.) Overall, therefore, for a given income effect, fiscal policy has less impact on the total balance of payments than monetary policy.

Monetary and fiscal policy could, therefore, be used to improve the external balance without altering the level of income: a monetary contraction would lower income and produce an external surplus, while a fiscal expansion would return income to its previous level and, although worsening the balance of payments, would not entirely offset the beneficial effect of the monetary policy. This policy combination was pursued by the USA over the early 1960s and also by Britain during the stop–go policy of the 1950s and 1960s. High interest rates were used to defend the balance of payments from the consequences of fiscal (vote-catching) expansion. It is, however, only a short-term palliative rather than a solution of the policy problem: high interest rates may have harmful domestic effects; nothing occurs to cure the current account deficit – the capital inflow merely finances it; one cannot borrow for ever because eventually lenders' confidence collapses; and high interest payments abroad reduce the level of domestic consumption supported by any given level of output.

A similar situation arose in the early 1980s in the USA. Tight monetary policy (designed to cure inflation), coupled with an expansionary fiscal stance (a huge budget deficit), generated very high interest rates and strong upward pressure on the dollar.

24.2 DOMESTIC POLICY AND THE EXCHANGE RATE

We now turn to the second of the questions raised in the introduction: how does the openness of the economy influence the effectiveness of domestic economic policy? In particular we examine the influence of international capital mobility and exchange rate flexibility on the operation of monetary and fiscal policies. Throughout, we shall take national income as the variable to be controlled.

The *IS–LM* model   As a preliminary we introduce a slightly different method of analysing the economy. Much closed-economy macro-economic analysis uses the *IS–LM* framework, and we now adapt this to the open economy. The present exposition is very cryptic and the student is advised to seek further information in standard macro textbooks for the basic model, and in Stern (1973) or Argy (1981) on the open-economy variant.

The *IS–LM* model analyses a fixed price Keynesian economy with goods, bonds and money markets. It is best explored by means of a diagram with the interest rate (i) and national income (Y) on the axes (see Figure 24.2). The *IS* curve connects combinations of i and Y that ensure the equality of the supply and demand for goods and services; that is

$$Y = C + I + G + X - M, \qquad (24.1)$$

where Y is income, C consumption, I investment, G government expenditure, X exports and M imports. The *IS* curve slopes downwards because lower interest rates stimulate higher investment and hence require higher income/output to equate supply and demand. If the exchange rate falls, exports rise and/or imports fall; hence, with constant interest rates, demand rises and the *IS* curve moves outwards. Similarly, expansionary fiscal policy shifts *IS* outwards.

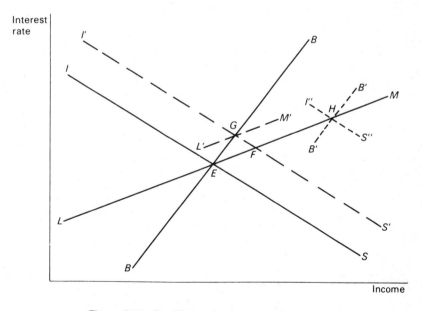

Figure 24.2 Equilibrium in the open IS-LM model

The *LM* curve plots combinations of i and Y that ensure equilibrium in the money market. The supply of money is assumed exogenous in nominal terms, but the demand depends on both interest rates and income. Income affects demand positively through the transactions demand: the more income you have, the more cash you require for spending. Interest rates have a negative effect by affecting the costs of holding cash: the higher the interest rate, the more the interest forgone by holding money instead of bonds. Hence a higher income must be offset by a higher rate of interest if demand is to equal a given supply, and so *LM* slopes up. (We ignore any horizontal segment of *LM* arising from the liquidity trap.) Money demand also depends on prices. Income and interest rates determine the real demand for cash, and this must be multiplied by the price level to find the nominal demand to be equated with the nominal supply. When prices rise, *LM* shifts up and to the left because, with given nominal supply, real demand must fall if equality is to continue.

The third locus in Figure 24.2 is *BB*, which plots levels of interest rates and incomes consistent with external balance, recognising both capital and current accounts. Higher income worsens the current account and so must be offset along *BB* by a rise in interest rates. The slope of *BB* depends on the degree of capital mobility, which in turn depends on the degree of substitutability between foreign and domestic assets in desired portfolios, and on the extent of transaction costs. If assets are entirely non-substitutable, or if transactions costs are prohibitively high, *BB* is vertical – that is, external equilibrium depends only on the current account, and thus, given income, is quite independent of the rate of interest. If, on the other hand, substitutability is perfect and transactions costs minimal, *BB* is horizontal – any deviation between world and domestic interest rates generates an infinite inflow or outflow of capital. A fall in the exchange rate shifts *BB* to the right: the improved competitiveness must be offset by higher incomes, given the interest rate, if balance is to be maintained.

The intersection of *LM* and *IS* defines internal equilibrium, but we can have full equilibrium only if all three curves intersect at one point. If not, we assume that domestic equilibrium is maintained (that is, *LM* and *IS* determine income and the interest rate) and that there is balance of payments disequilibrium. Above and left of *BB* there is a surplus, and below and right a deficit. (Check that you understand why.) Such disequilibria are, at least eventually, self-correcting, because they involve constant accumulation or decumulation of assets. For example, suppose that, in Figure 24.2, *IS* were shifted by fiscal expansion to *I'S'*. Point *F* defines the temporary internal equilibrium, which implies a payments deficit. Under a fixed exchange rate, and assuming that the central bank does not try to sterilise the outflow, this contracts the domestic money supply (see Chapter 21), and thus shifts *LM* leftwards. This process occurs until *LM* has shrunk back to *I'M'* and full equilibrium is restored at *G*. Under flexible exchange rates, on the other hand, the deficit at *F* would cause depreciation and this would push both *I'S'* and *BB* to the right. Assuming, for now, that prices are fixed in local currency terms, *LM* would be unaffected, and the final equilibrium would be given by a point such as *H*.

Do not be deceived by the simplicity of this analysis. There are many assumptions underlying the basic model; and the shapes of the curves, which depend on the various parameters of economic behaviour, could be very complex. Nevertheless, this approach is very popular among macro-economists and your should explore some more examples to ensure that you are familiar with it. (Try, in particular, the case where *LM* is steeper than *BB*.) We now use the model to develop some further results on economic policy.

An influential piece of analysis from the early 1960s – Fleming (1962) and Mundell (1963) – considered the effectiveness of monetary and fiscal policy as controllers of income. Making the crucial assumption that international capital flows were perfectly mobile, Mundell and Fleming concluded that monetary policy was effective only under flexible exchange rates, and that fiscal policy was effective only under fixed rates. Their model was a neo-Keynesian one, and the nature of their results is simply explored in the *IS–LM* framework. Perfect capital mobility makes the *BB* curve horizontal at the ruling world rate of interest. Any other interest rate would lead to an infinite inflow or outflow of capital, preventing equilibrium.

We consider first the fixed exchange rate case, shown in Figure 24.3. Starting from complete equilibrium at *E*, imagine a fiscal expansion, shifting *IS* to *I'S'*. The potential domestic equilibrium would be at *F*, with a higher interest rate and income. The higher interest rate would not, however, be sustainable, because it would immediately cause a huge capital inflow (balance of payments surplus), which would expand the money supply and push out the *LM* curve. Only when *LM* had reached *L'M'* would equilibrium be re-established in all three markets. At the new equilibrium, income would have risen and the balance of payments would show a current account deficit balanced by a capital account surplus. (Higher income generates higher imports, and these are paid for by borrowing at the world rate of interest.)

Now consider a monetary expansion. *LM* shifts out to *L'M'*, implying domestic equilibrium *G*. This entails a large foreign deficit (capital flowing out because of the fall in interest rates), and this serves to drag *L'M'* back. Only

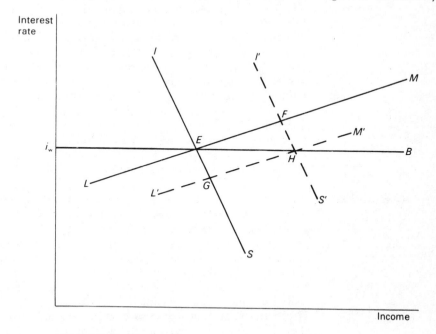

Figure 24.3 Monetary and fiscal policy with capital mobility

International Economics

when it has reached *LM* again does the process stop. This is just the result of Chapter 21: with fixed exchange rates, governments cannot control their money supplies, hence monetary policy is useless.

Turning to flexible exchange rates, we again start from *E*, and let fiscal policy shift *IS* to *I'S'*. Again we have a potential domestic equilibrium at *F*, but now the capital inflow appreciates the currency and brings *I'S'* back towards *IS* as exports fall and imports rise. Ultimately, equilibrium re-emerges at *E*, where a balance of payments current deficit is balanced by a capital surplus. This is a case of complete 'crowding-out': raising government expenditure merely results in an equivalent worsening of the trade balance. Monetary policy, on the other hand, would be highly effective – and for essentially the same reason. Expanding the money supply to shift *LM* to *L'M'* produces a payments deficit and thereby a depreciation. This shifts *IS* out to *I'S'* and produces equilibrium at *H*, where income has risen and a current surplus is balanced by a capital deficit. Hence, shifting from fixed to flexible exchange rates completely reverses the comparative advantages of monetary and fiscal policy.

These are stark results and they do not accord entirely with reality. Under fixed rates governments certainly did exercise some monetary policy, and under flexible rates we still find some use of fiscal policy. What then is wrong with the model? An obvious candidate is the assumption of perfect capital mobility, but from Figure 24.3 it is plain that a slight relaxation of this (a slight tilting of *BB*) does not change the relative rankings of the two policies. We shall look at the drastic alteration of this assumption below, but first we examine certain other refinements of the *IS-LM* model. They are introduced in the Mundell–Fleming framework, but are perfectly applicable to the general model with imperfect capital mobility.

Price effects

The basic Keynesian model assumes that prices are fixed in the producer's local currency and are unaffected by depreciation. If, however, as we found in Chapter 20, depreciation raises local prices, there will be two additional effects in the flexible exchange rate case. First, *IS* will move less in response to exchange rate changes, because competitiveness will alter by less. Second, depreciation will shift the *LM* curve leftwards because, by raising prices, it reduces the real money supply. Consider, for example, an expansionary fiscal policy. The potential equilibrium at *F* induces an appreciation; this reduces internal prices, hence *LM* shifts right while *I'S'* does not shrink completely back to its original position. The resulting equilibrium lies somewhere to the right of *E*. In other words, fiscal policy now works. By similar analysis we can see that monetary policy is less effective.

Wealth effects

As specified, the *BB* line refers to the overall balance of payments, being indifferent to whether a current deficit is balanced by a capital surplus or vice versa. This may be acceptable in the short run, but not in the longer run. A persistent current account deficit, financed by borrowing, reduces the country's net wealth, and ultimately this will affect behaviour. Specifically, as net worth falls, the *IS* curve falls back, as savings rise to try to reconstitute wealth holdings, and the *LM* curve shifts out because, as the demand for money declines, higher income is required to absorb the given money supply. Hence the final points described above are not long-run equilibria because they involve the accumulation or decumulation of assets. Full equilibrium is possible only where the current account is in balance. In terms of the *IS–LM* model, the locus of current balance equilibrium is a vertical line, since the current balance is independent of the domestic interest rate. It will shift to the right with depreciation, and to the left as the *accumulated* value of foreign debt rises, because higher debt involves higher interest payments abroad. For full equilibrium, the other loci must all intersect on this vertical line.

We illustrate these features for fiscal policy under fixed exchange rates. At H in Figure 24.3, the point previously called an equilibrium, there is a current deficit; hence over time, $I'S'$ falls back and $L'M'$ tries to move right. This, however, produces downward pressure on the interest rate causing a capital outflow and an immediate drawing back of $L'M'$. Indeed, the capital mobility assumption ensures that the money supply is always fixed at just the level that causes LM to intersect IS along BB. Hence, as $I'S'$ moves back, $L'M'$ comes with it. Suppose both curves contract back to their original positions – does this now restore complete equilibrium? The answer is 'no', because the accumulated current account deficit during the adjustment period has reduced net interest receipts from abroad, thus lowering the level of income consistent with current account balance. The contraction, therefore, has to continue further, ending somewhere to the left of E. Indeed, it may not stop there, but proceed even further left, to a position of temporary current surplus, so that net wealth can be recouped. If asset behaviour is entirely unaffected by these disequilibria, the accumulated surpluses will balance the previously accumulated deficits, eventually making E re-attainable as a full equilibrium. In such an economy, policy may have temporary effects, but long-run control is impossible.

Under flexible rates there is a third wealth effect to consider. To the extent that prices are determined in local currency, and domestic wealth holders intend to spend their wealth locally, the exchange rate affects total real wealth, because a depreciation will raise the value of assets denominated in foreign currency. If domestic residents are net holders of foreign assets, this will raise domestic wealth, raising money demand and pulling the LM curve back to the left, whereas if residents are net debtors the opposite happens. This is an immediate effect, and initially it will dominate the LM shift arising from changing stocks of assets.

Imagine a fiscal stimulus under flexible exchange rates. The Mundell–Fleming analysis of the temporary equilibrium implies no change in income but a current account deficit brought about by an appreciation. Assuming that residents are neither net borrowers nor lenders of foreign assets, we can ignore valuation effects on foreign assets and assert that, from the 'Mundell–Fleming' point E, IS will shift left and LM shift right. This implies downward pressure on the exchange rate, which tends to reverse the shift in IS and raise the level of income consistent with current balance. If we ignore the price effects of depreciation on the LM curve, there is nothing to reverse its gradual outward drift, hence the final equilibrium (if there is one) must be to the right of E; that is, fiscal policy recovers some effect on income. Similar reasoning suggests that wealth effects reduce the effectiveness of monetary policy under flexible rates.

The wealth effects reverse the exchange rate implications of the original policy measures. For example, with monetary policy the temporary equilibrium involves a lower exchange rate and a current surplus, but from there the exchange rate gradually appreciates to its long-run position. This is a form of overshooting. In the short term the level of wealth is fixed, so all adjustment is borne by the exchange rate, but gradually wealth does adjust, thus relaxing the pressure on the exchange rate.

351

Expectations   Implicit in the Mundell–Fleming analysis is the assumption that people never
expect any change in the exchange rate from its present position. Under a
firmly controlled fixed-rate system this may be reasonable, but not under
flexible rates. We therefore now introduce expectations into the model,
assuming, for simplicity, rational expectations. Coupled with the assumed
absence of uncertainty, this amounts to assuming perfect foresight.

Anticipated changes in the exchange rate alter the relationship between the
domestic and the foreign rates of interest. Capital mobility equates the net
return on bills, but the return on home bills bought by foreigners is the home
rate of interest plus any appreciation. Thus, if appreciation is expected
(known to be coming), the domestic interest rate will have to fall below the
world rate if capital flows are to be avoided (see Chapter 23).

We now add expectations to a model that already includes wealth and price
effects. Under flexible exchange rates, but without expectations, monetary
policy shifts the economy from E to H in Figure 24.4. (Unlike in Figure 24.3,
we assume that H involves some allowance for price changes.) At H the
exchange rate has depreciated and there is a current account surplus. This
will, in time, appreciate the exchange rate, leading to a new equilibrium as
described above. Now suppose this appreciation is foreseen: to gain from it,
people will start buying domestic currency, so H cannot be considered even a
temporary equilibrium. Indeed, even before the economy had reached H,
people would have started buying in anticipation, with the result that, under
rational expectations, the exchange rate will not fall as far as without
expectations. Hence our 'expectations-ridden' IS curve lies to the left of one
through H and the LM curve to the right of its position through H – say, $I''S''$
and $L''M''$ respectively.

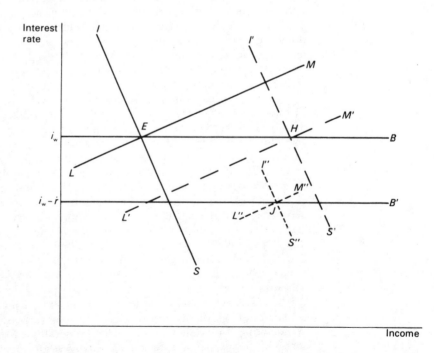

Figure 24.4 Monetary policy with flexible rates and rational expectations

The anticipated appreciation (call it $\dot{r}$) also has another effect. By raising the return on domestic bonds it reduces the domestic rate of interest consistent with capital equilibrium from i_w to $(i_w - \dot{r})$; i.e. it lowers the external balance line B to B'. For equilibrium under rational expectations, $I''S''$ and $L''M''$ must intersect at this lower rate of interest – at J, say. Without further information we cannot locate J precisely; it depends on the extent and the speed of the expected appreciation ($\dot{r}$ is measured as percentage change *per year*, to be compatible with i_w), which, in turn, depends on how strongly expectations mitigate the original decline. As before, the wealth effects will gradually shift the economy back from J, and as the appreciation occurs there will be less to expect, so B' will gradually return to B.

A similar analysis can be conducted for fiscal policy under floating rates. The current deficit that would apply at the temporary equilibrium without expectations would cause a depreciation. The anticipation of this mitigates the original appreciation, and prevents IS from shrinking right back to its original position. It also means that the domestic interest rate must rise to equate the net return on domestic bills with the world rate of interest.

Capital immobility

This analysis can all be repeated with the opposite assumption to Mundell and Fleming's – namely, complete capital immobility. This renders the balance of payments locus vertical, because only the current account would exist, and that would depend only on income. It quite transforms the results – at least in the simplest cases.

Consider a regime of fixed exchange rates. In Figure 24.5(A), fiscal policy would shift IS out to $I'S'$. In temporary equilibrium there is a current deficit, for nothing has happened to shift BB, and this will continue until either the deficit has depleted the money stock sufficiently to shift LM back to $L'M'$, or the government has run out of reserves and reversed its fiscal stance. In the former case, the new equilibrium would be G, and in the latter it would revert back to E; in neither case, however, would any increase in income be possible. This is because the need for current account equilibrium dictates the level of income, and no policy available can change that relationship. Note that, unlike the mobile capital case, the progress to the new equilibrium takes a finite time because $L'M'$ can shrink back only at the rate of the current deficit.

The case of monetary policy is similarly simple. An expansion of LM to $L''M''$ leads to a deficit (at H) and, again, either to the gradual run-down of the money supply, re-establishing LM, or to a policy reversal. Hence again income cannot be manipulated because of the external constraint.

Under flexible rates the current account/income relationship is no longer rigidly fixed: a depreciation will shift BB to the right. Consider monetary policy – illustrated in Figure 24.5(B). LM is shifted to $L'M'$, leading temporarily to F, at which there is a deficit. The resulting depreciation shifts both IS and BB outwards, producing a new equilibrium at G. Hence monetary policy is effective under flexible rates even without capital mobility. Fiscal policy, on the other hand, is dramatically dependent on the degree of mobility: with capital mobility it is impotent, whereas with immobility it is very powerful. A fiscal expansion taking IS to $I'S'$ generates a payments deficit and a consequent depreciation. This shifts BB rightwards and also enhances the shift in IS out to $I'S'$. The final equilibrium is given by a point such as H.

These cases are also subject to the qualifications about price and wealth effects discussed above, but the details are left to the student, as is the case

(A) *With fixed exchange rates*

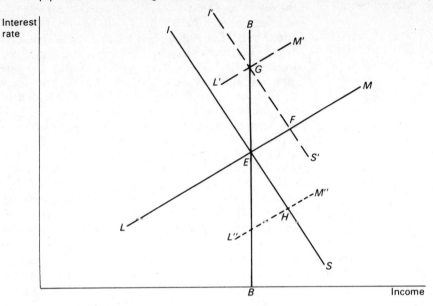

(B) *With flexible exchange rates*

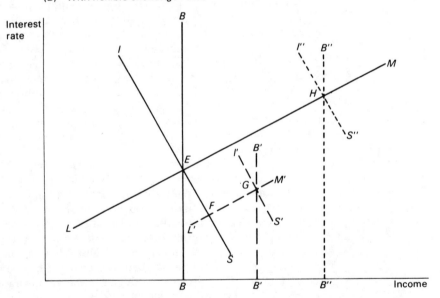

Figure 24.5 Economic policy with capital immobile. (A) With fixed exchange rates. (B) With flexible exchange rates

where imperfect capital mobility makes *BB* upward-sloping. Of course, with no capital flows, exchange rate expectations are of hardly any interest.

Summary and qualification

The models examined in this section are very definite in their conclusions. These are summarised in Table 24.1 in terms of 'weak' or 'strong'. Although in the simple Mundell–Fleming model, the 'weak' outcomes amount to complete ineffectiveness, we have listed above several factors that moderate this extreme. These moderating influences could, in fact, reverse the original rankings of policies, but, in the absence of evidence that they do, we report the more likely outcome that they do not.

Table 24.1 The effects of fiscal and monetary policy[a]

	Exchange rate regime	
Capital assumption	Fixed	Flexible
Mobile	strong	weak
	weak	*strong*
Immobile	weak	very strong
	weak	*strong*

Note:
[a] Fiscal policy is described in roman print, monetary policy in italics.
Source: text.

The table speaks for itself, but before adopting it as fact we should review certain qualifications to the exercise from which it was derived. First, we compared rigidly fixed exchange rates with perfectly flexible ones, whereas nearly every country in the world has some sort of intermediate regime. In particular, we normally view fixed rates as being occasionally movable. This would have entirely changed the analysis of fixed rates under capital immobility because, with a devaluation, it would have been possible to shift *BB* to the right. Obviously, the exchange rate could not be moved with every change in fiscal or monetary policy, but occasional change could avoid the worst limitations on policy.

Second, there are difficulties over the timing of the responses we have reported. Capital flows adjust rapidly, but the adjustment of money demand, and particularly of real demand, takes some time. Hence strictly we should not assume that the economy jumps easily from, say, *E* to *H* in Figure 24.3. However, as soon as we acknowledge that transition takes time, there is a need for compensatory capital flows, and expectations become involved. One particular case occurs if depreciation initially worsens the balance of trade (the J-curve). Now, an initial trade deficit, instead of being self-correcting through depreciation, is self-exacerbating, so that payments equilibrium is possible only if the exchange rate falls sufficiently to generate a counter-balancing capital inflow on the strength of an anticipated appreciation. This is another case of overshooting, and it seems unfortunately realistic.

Third, one may question the Keynesian framework. We admitted above that depreciation may affect prices, but if it does so proportionately, thus allowing no control over the degree of competitiveness, all the flexible exchange rate results change. If, furthermore, we adopt the other monetarist assumption of full employment, there is no role for policy and the whole exercise is futile!

Fourth, we could argue that any degree of policy effectiveness is sufficient to control the economy, provided we are willing to pull the levers on the less effective policies sufficiently hard. This is logically correct, but it ignores the costs of large policy changes, such as the increased variability in interest rates and profits, and the increased transition costs borne privately as people adjust.

Fifth, even in the regimes described, the fluctuations required for effective policy may be too great. Specifically, monetary policy under flexible rates works through exchange rate changes, and over the 1970s and 1980s there was obvious conflict between maintaining monetary policy and choosing the exchange rate. Once we recognise the possibility of exchange rate overshooting in response to policy changes, governments may prefer some loss of monetary independence to the devastation of the real economy that an incorrect, or sharply fluctuating exchange rate could cause. In other words, although under flexible rates monetary policy is an effective macro-economic policy, it may be that its detailed effects are too severe to permit governments to exploit that effectiveness. Similarly, if capital is less than perfectly mobile, the maintenance of a fixed exchange rate may involve very sharp swings in interest rates which could disrupt investment and growth.

Sixth, many economists question whether the assumed degree of capital mobility is desirable. Some international capital flows are obviously useful in smoothing out the day-to-day fluctuations in the current account, although this could as well be achieved by official intervention in the exchange market. However, the mass migration of funds in search of capital gains – and the consequent shifts in interest rates they produce – serves little social purpose, especially if expectations are poorly formed. There may thus be a case for limiting the mobility of short-term capital. While this would involve administrative costs and some loss of speculators' profits, it may well enhance the control and the stability of the economy, by preventing excessive exchange rate fluctuations and permitting greater freedom in the choice of interest rates. The counterweights to such a view are that it may be difficult to control short-term capital flows without disrupting trade credit and long-term flows, both of which are important, and that speculative pressures often serve to discipline governments from pursuing policies that place short-term expediency before long-term viability.

24.3 THE EVIDENCE ON FINANCIAL INTEGRATION

The degree of capital mobility – or rather the extent of international financial integration – is clearly an important consideration in the choice of economic policy tools and exchange rate regime. It also intimately affects the behaviour of the exchange rate and foreign exchange reserves, as we have seen in earlier chapters. This section, therefore, examines the empirical evidence on financial integration.

Some difficulties   Before looking at the econometric results, we should consider certain empirical and theoretical difficulties. In the former group fall problems of measurement and of causation. It is almost impossible to measure gross capital flows because they change direction so rapidly, but some data on net positions are possible. More serious is our inability to measure net wealth satisfactorily or expectations at all. The more dramatic shifts in international capital occur because of expectations, but more often than not such episodes are omitted from empirical work because no measure is available for 'speculative sentiment'.

The problems over causation are even greater. First, it is rarely clear whether the authorities are pursuing their monetary policy despite, or because of, the movements in capital flows, interest rates and exchange rates. Second, although the interest parity relationship is known to hold well, we do not know which variable adjusts to bring it about (see section 22.1). These problems can cause bias in econometric estimates (simultaneity bias) and considerably reduce the confidence we can place in them.

The major theoretical difficulty concerns the practical definition of financial integration. Complete integration would involve the loss of all national control over the interest rate and either the money supply (under fixed rates) or the exchange rate (under flexible rates). It could occur, however, without our actually observing any capital flows at all – the mere threat of huge inflows or outflows would prevent the domestic interest rate from deviating from the world rate. We should, therefore, concentrate on the interest rate rather than on capital flows themselves. We then have to decide whether to examine the 'covered' or 'uncovered' interest differential between countries. The uncovered differential is just the difference between rates in, say, London and Paris, whereas the covered differential adjusts the crude difference for the expected change in the pound–franc exchange rate (see section 22.1). For assessing international capital mobility, covered rates are relevant because that is what most capital responds to, but for domestic policy purposes local uncovered rates are required. Remember, however, that, if covered differentials are zero, the uncovered interest differential must equal the forward premium. That is, interest rate autonomy is bought at the price of compensating expected changes in the exchange rate.

A further complication arises over whether to use Euro-market or national interest rates. We look at the Euro-market in Chapter 29 below; here we need merely note that it comprises deposits (loans) placed (raised) in banks in a currency other than that of the country where the bank is situated (e.g. dollars lent in London, pounds lent in Paris). This reduces the chances that the loan will become subject to exchange restrictions, because the sovereign power where the loan is placed has no interest in another country's currency, while the issuer of the currency has no power over the loan. The Euro-market is also subject to fewer legal and administrative restrictions than are national banking systems. For these reasons we do not expect equality between, say, the Euro-sterling and London sterling rates of interest. Thus, although interest parity holds almost perfectly between the various Euro-currencies, imperfections between them and the national centres allows some scope for covered differentials between the latter.

The evidence   There are four approaches to measuring the degree of financial integration. First we can just compare interest rates across countries: if they are similar and move similarly we have found *prima facie* evidence for international integration. This approach avoids the problems over causation, but of course, by ducking that issue, it can give us no indication of how to manipulate interest rates if there is any scope for doing so. Nellis (1982) considered covered and uncovered interest rates in France, West Germany, the UK, Canada and the USA under both fixed exchange rates (1962–71) and floating (1973–80). His technique was to seek, statistically, a common factor that explained the evolution of all five interest rates. Under fixed rates, he found a factor to explain 71 per cent of the variance in uncovered rates and one to explain 72 per ent of that in covered rates, whereas with flexible rates the figures were 49 per cent and 75 per cent respectively. These figures indicate that, while interest rates do move together internationally, there is still an independent component. This is strongest for uncovered rates under floating, which suggests that floating has allowed greater (although far from complete) financial autonomy. The contrast with the results for covered rates – where floating has not changed the degree of integration – shows that the extra freedom over interest rates has been offset by a stronger degree of determination of forward premia and thus of exchange rates.

Once we recognise the possibility of interest rate independence, we need to ask what determines interest rates. This leads to the second approach to measuring integration, namely the estimation of equations explaining interest rates. A study of the UK over the 1970s (when exchange controls still existed) is Briault and Howson (1982). They used an asset markets approach to the exchange rate, and determined the London sterling rate, the Euro-sterling rate and the exchange rate simultaneously. They found strong evidence of imperfect substitutability between London and Euro-sterling markets, and also that, as before, financial independence comes at the expense of control of the exchange rate. Overall, a 1 percentage point increase in Euro-dollar rate generated a 0.4 percentage point increase in London rates, while a £1b. rise in the UK's net foreign assets would have increased London rates by 0.19 percentage points. A problem not considered by Briault and Howson is the authorities' role in capital markets. Herring and Marston (1977) argued that UK interest rates are determined directly by the government, but that the government is constrained in its choice by factors such as the balance of payments and foreign interest rates. They estimated (on data over 1961–71) that, in the long run, a 1 percentage point increase in the Euro-dollar rate raised London rates by 0.45–0.65 percentage points.

We now briefly consider direct studies of capital flows. If there is not perfect mobility we can consider capital flows as a function of interest rates. If, as we have argued, capital flows are a means of reallocating wealth over assets, and if the desired portfolio (stock) of assets is a function, *inter alia*, of relative interest rates, then capital *flows* should be related to *changes* in interest rates. Many researchers, however, related them to the level of interest rates, implying that the accumulation of assets could continue indefinitely. For short-run purposes the difference hardly matters, but it should be borne in mind for longer-term work. Typical estimates of the effects on UK capital inflows of a 1 per cent rise in the covered interest differential are £300m. (Beenstock and Bell, 1979) and £475m. (Hodjera, 1971). These are considerably reduced if we look at uncovered differentials (£48m. and £100m. respectively), suggesting a strong compensatory movement in the forward premium as interest rates change. These estimates refer to the 1960s when total current credits were only around £6–10b.; hence the inflows are relatively important, and one can only presume that increasing financial sophistication, and the abolition of exchange controls, increases their sensitivity to interest rates during the 1970s.

An alternative way of explaining capital flows eschews interest rates, and looks directly at the extent to which private capital flows offset domestic monetary changes and the extent to which the authorities sterilise reserve changes. Both offsets and sterilisation lead to a negative relationship between the domestic and foreign components of the money supply, and they are virtually impossible to tell apart. Kouri and Porter (1974) estimated offset coefficients of 40–80 per cent for certain European countries, whilst Argy and Kouri (1974) suggested similar or greater sterilisation coefficients. The estimates vary considerably over studies, and, of course, apply only if the authorities are intervening in the exchange markets; as with all the other approaches, however, they suggest substantial but incomplete integration.

The evidence suggests that international short-term capital is mobile – especially through covered arbitrage transactions; that countries still have some monetary autonomy via the restrictions and risks of their own markets; and that if they are not concerned to manage their exchange rates they could have considerably more control under floating rates than under fixed rates, via movements in the forward premium.

FURTHER READING

The use of simple policy models was pioneered by *Meade* (1951) and *Tinbergen* (1952), and first applied in our specific cases by *Swan* (1955) and *Mundell* (1962). Interesting recent extensions are *Meade* (1978) and *Argy* (1981, Part Six), both of whom consider recent history.

The *IS–LM* model is expounded in many textbooks: *Stern* (1973) is useful for the basic model, while both *Argy* (1981) and *Llewellyn* (1980) consider some variants. The developments in the text are taken mainly from *Branson and Buiter* (1984), but *Argy and Porter* (1972) were the first to introduce expectations into the model. *Branson* (1983) uses the Mundell–Fleming model as the basis of the portfolio model of exchange rates. *Llewellyn* (1980) considers the question of financial integration in depth from both theoretical and empirical standpoints, while *Hodjera* (1973) offers a survey of work on capital mobility until about 1972. *Goldstein* (1980) is a useful survey of flexible exchange rates and macro-economic policy.

KEY CONCEPTS

internal and external balance	targets and instruments
the assignment problem	capital mobility
BB locus	Mundell–Fleming model
capital movements – flows vs. stock adjustment	wealth accumulation
financial integration	offset coefficients

QUESTIONS FOR REVIEW

24.1 What is the assignment problem? What problems can arise if under a fixed exchange rate system there is no coordination between the fiscal and monetary authorities?

24.2 Show how incorporating (a) wealth and (b) expectations modifies the results of the Mundell–Fleming model.

24.3 Are the Mundell–Fleming results a sound basis for applying economic policy in an open economy?

24.4 How would one measure the degree of financial integration between open economies?

25 Two Case-Studies: Oil and the Dollar

This chapter pulls together the themes of Part II of this book to examine two major issues of recent economic history: the adjustment of the UK economy to the rises in oil price and the discovery of North Sea oil, and the huge appreciation of the US dollar over the first half of the 1980s. These problems are important in their own right, but they also help to cement our understanding of the theory discussed above. All the analysis used in this chapter has been described above; but, as well as rehearsing that work, the chapter will be useful in showing how the various arguments fit together to deal with two real world problems. Sections 25.1–25.3 deal with oil – the effects of a price rise, the effects of a discovery and, finally, their combination in the UK. Section 25.4 tackles the US dollar.

25.1 THE PRICE OF OIL

Pure theory We start with some simple trade theory, using a static, full employment and flexible-price model to explore the effects of an oil price rise. We compare the world economy at full equilibrium under two sets of circumstances differing only in the assumed price of oil. Imagine a world comprising just a group of oil producers (OPEC) and a group of oil importers (OECD). The oil importers use oil to produce both traded and non-traded goods, some of the former being exported to OPEC in return for oil. For simplicity we assume that OPEC has no non-traded sector. Imagine also that the world is in full equilibrium at some given price of oil and that suddenly and quite exogenously that price rises.

Assume that OECD's demand for oil is insensitive to price, and that OPEC always spends all its income on tradables. The price rise is then just equivalent to a transfer of income from OECD to OPEC (see Chapter 15). OECD reduces its expenditure and OPEC increases its by the same amount. However, the composition of their expenditure differs: OECD will cut back on both tradables and non-tradables, whereas OPEC will, by assumption, spend only on the former. The result is excess demand for tradables and excess supply of non-tradables. This will be eliminated by higher relative prices for tradables, and, assuming some mobility of factors of production between sectors, a shift in output away from non-tradables and towards tradables. If we identify tradables as manufactures and non-tradables as services, OECD is forced to *industrialise* to pay for the higher-priced oil.

Further price effects could arise if tradables and non-tradables use different amounts of oil: the oil-intensive good will rise in price relatively, which may either reinforce or reduce the original income effects. Also, if the demand for oil is price sensitive, the extent of the transfer would be reduced. Indeed, if demand for oil were price elastic, total OECD expenditure on oil would be reduced by the price rise, and, although OECD would suffer from having to find substitutes for oil, OPEC would also suffer to the extent that reduced current revenue was not offset by reduced costs (including the value of oil in the ground). In this case there would be no easily identified transfer.

The oil price rise represents a deterioration in OECD's terms of trade, which cuts its national income. It will not necessarily cut everybody's income, however, because relative factor rewards will be affected both via the factor intensities in tradable and non-tradable sectors (a Stolper–Samuelson result), and also via the substitutability of each factor for oil. For example, British coal miners almost certainly benefited from the higher price of oil.

Some Keynesian considerations

We now extend the simple model to account for various rigidities in the process of adjustment. First suppose the OPEC cannot spend all its extra income immediately. The price rise then transfers income from spenders (OECD) to savers (OPEC) and the result is a fall in demand. If prices are rigid – a Keynesian world – this has multiplier effects and reduces income, output and employment by a larger amount. It also, of course, has balance of payments consequences. OECD's exports no longer balance its imports, so it runs a current account deficit, whereas OPEC has an equal surplus. These imbalances can be financed only by corresponding capital flows. At first these may involve accumulating or decumulating reserves (national cash balances), but eventually they must involve OPEC lending its excess savings to OECD. This mitigates the decline in world demand and in OECD consumption, but only at the expense of substantial shifts in world wealth. Furthermore, such a situation cannot last indefinitely – the deficits and wealth transfer must eventually be corrected. Nevertheless, capital flows prolong and probably ease the period of adjustment.

The reduction in world income and the surplus of savings will probably combine to reduce the (real) rate of interest. This should encourage investment in OECD – especially in oil-substituting activities. It is most unlikely, however, given the fall in output and the general uncertainty surrounding an oil price rise, that such investment would approach the original loss of consumption in magnitude. This conclusion is reinforced once we observe that investment requires long-term finance whereas, over 1974–80, much of OPEC's lending was of a short-term nature.

A further complication involves adjustment within OECD countries. If wages and prices are rigid downwards, the required changes in relative prices can come about only through price rises. If there is additionally some element of real wage resistance – for instance, indexing money wages to compensate for price rises – adjustment would set off an inflationary spiral. Under these circumstances economic policy becomes important. If the government refuses to expand domestic demand to compensate for the demand lost through the transfer, and refuses to expand the money supply to validate the price rises in adjustment, the economy is doubly squeezed. There would be little inflation but a deep recession, although adjustment would be rapid. Alternatively, if the government pursued both compensating fiscal and monetary policy, this would postpone the decline in income but at the expense of inflation, a current deficit and prolonged disequilibrium. Roughly at these opposite poles were West Germany and Britain in 1974–5. The former adjusted quickly whereas the latter expanded her budget deficit and allowed the money supply to rise. Over 1974 Britain appeared to be weathering the OPEC storm better than most OECD countries, but by 1976 adjustment was forced on the country. Unfortunate though Britain's experience over the period 1975–85 may have been, however, we cannot be sure that a harsher response to the oil price rise would have improved it.

So far we have treated OECD as a single country. Once we relax this assumption there are several further complications. First, although OPEC is forced to lend its surplus to OECD, it is not forced to lend it to any particular OECD country. Hence, while for OECD as a whole the current deficit is balanced by a capital account surplus, this need not be so for every country. In fact, the countries with the worst deficits are likely to receive least OPEC funds. To some extent this is avoidable by 'recycling' OPEC funds among OECD countries; the burdens of adjustment will none the less fall with different speeds and severity on different OECD countries. Some capital-importing countries may even find themselves with appreciating exchange rates despite their long-run need for depreciation to stimulate industrialisation.

A related difficulty concerns the portfolio of assets chosen by OPEC. As wealth is transferred from OECD to OPEC it is shifted from OECD-preferred assets to OPEC-preferred assets. In 1974–5, this almost certainly appreciated sterling and depreciated the dollar relative to what they would have been. Possibly more serious is the relatively greater mobility of OPEC-owned funds. OPEC chose to lend on rather short maturities, which were easily switched between centres. The result was an increase in the potential volatility of exchange rates, which, even if it had never materialised, constrained governments in their policy-making.

Third, as OECD countries adjusted to their current deficits they reduced imports from each other as well as from OPEC; hence each country shifted some of its burden onto its fellow OECD members. The net result was a multiple contraction among OECD (see p. 257 above).

To conclude, therefore, an oil price rise involves a long-run process of industrialisation in OECD countries. The adjustment path is likely to be painful, involving recession and inflation, and is significantly complicated by the interactions between OECD countries.

25.2 THE DISCOVERY OF OIL

We now turn to the second oil shock experienced by Britain in the 1970s – the discovery and exploitation of North Sea oil. Although this was a boom, increasing incomes in Britain significantly, it was not without its attendant difficulties, most importantly the change it required in the structure of the economy. We concentrate on the British case, but it is not unique: similar natural resource discoveries have affected Australia (minerals), Holland (natural gas), Norway, Indonesia and Mexico (oil). We start, as before, with a simple trade model and gradually broaden out to a more realistic view.

Pure theory The most obvious theoretical approach to this problem is to apply the Rybczynski theorem (section 3.3 above). If we have two tradable sectors – oil and non-oil – an influx of the factors of production intensive in oil production (namely oil-fields) would indicate an expansion of oil and an absolute contraction of non-oil. This, however, is too simple and simple-minded. It requires that all prices are fixed by world trade, and it implies that non-oil must contract because it loses factors of production to oil. Since oil production requires few local factors, this is not a plausible view.

A more fruitful approach explicitly introduces demand, and recognises the role of the non-tradable sector as well as oil and non-oil tradables. The simplest model is from Forsyth and Kay (1980), on which the following example is based. Imagine a small, open economy with full employment, perfect competition, perfect information and a perfectly static environment. We examine it first with a small primary goods sector, and then with a large one, representing higher oil production. The economy's demand, supply and trade in the former case are described in part (A) of Table 25.1: a deficit (excess demand) in primary goods is balanced by a surplus (excess supply) in manufacturing; services are assumed to be entirely non-traded and therefore must have demand equal to supply.

Table 25.1 The effects of higher oil production

Actual income

	(A) *Without oil*			(B) *With oil*		
	Demand	Supply	Trade	Demand	Supply	Trade
Primary	10	5	− 5	12	25	+ 13
Manufacturing	40	45	+ 5	48	35	− 13
Services	50	50	0	60	60	0
Total	100	100	0	120	120	0

Permanent income

	(C) *Before/after oil*			(D) *During oil boom*		
	Demand	Supply	Trade	Demand	Supply	Trade
Primary	11	5	− 6	11	25	+ 14
Manufacturing	44	40	− 4	44	40	− 4
Services	55	55	0	55	55	0
Total	110	110	− 10	110	120	+ 10

Assume now that the net output of primaries rises by 20 units to 25. Assume also that the extra income is all spent and is allocated *pro rata* over the demand categories. The resulting demands are given in part (B) of Table 25.1. We can also immediately write in the output of primaries (25, by assumption), and the trade balances in primaries, services (zero by definition) and overall (zero because income and expenditure increase by equal amounts). Hence, we may simply deduce the trade balance in manufactures, and thence output in manufacturing and services. Services production must expand in line with demand, but that of manufactures declines, shifting that sector from surplus to deficit on the foreign account.

The mechanism by which these adjustments are achieved in a small, open economy is almost certainly via exchange rate appreciation. This reduces the relative price of tradable to non-tradable output. Depending on one's model of production, one can deduce from this the effects on factor rewards. In a Heckscher–Ohlin world, with manufactures as the labour-intensive good, real wages fall. In a factor-specific world, the rewards of factors tied to manufacturing fall by more than the price of manufactures, but the effects on the mobile factors are ambiguous. In either case, however, if wages are rigid, the fall in rewards tends to be reflected in a fall in employment.

Forsyth and Kay (1980) presented considerably more detail and derived their figures from the UK economy, but this simple comparative static exercise is the basis of their assertion that 'the contraction of manufacturing . . . [is] the only way [to] benefit from the North Sea'. However, while there is much force in their argument it is not unassailable.

The most significant criticism of the Forsyth and Kay argument is its static nature. By comparing two equilibria, they entirely ignored the feasibility and costs of moving from one to another. These are important in all analyses, but

S

for Britain and North Sea oil they are doubly so. Britain's period as a major oil producer will last, perhaps, thirty years. Hence, transition from equilibrium (A) to equilibrium (B) will inevitably be followed by transition back again – i.e. de-industrialisation followed by re-industrialisation. Such adjustment is costly: de-industrialisation causes hardship, and many would argue that re-industrialisation after twenty years of declining industrial output will be virtually impossible, because Britain will no longer have the skills or the technological infrastructure to compete. Hence, what may be sensible given perpetual oil production, may not be so for Britain.

One answer to this, which is consistent with Forsyth and Kay's analysis, is that Britain should not consume all the income from oil, but rather should invest it and consume only the interest. That is, we should look at the permanent income from oil, namely the increase in consumption that oil permits us to maintain for ever. Assuming the oil lasts twenty-five years and that a real rate of return of 3 per cent per annum is available on investment, the increase in permanent income is about half the annual increase in actual income while the oil flows. Looking at our illustrative economy, the situations with and without oil are given in parts (C) and (D) of Table 25.1. Consumption is now the same in the two cases, but of course production varies. Assume that the discovery of oil was entirely unexpected: the economy starts from the position (A) in Table 25.1 with a manufacturing surplus financing a primary deficit; it then evolves to (D), where oil exports finance both a manufacturing deficit and an outflow of investment abroad (the overall balance of trade surplus); finally it settles at (C), where the primary and manufacturing deficits are met by earnings on the earlier investment abroad. Compared with the previous scenario this pattern involves substantially less adjustment, although manufacturing still contracts somewhat.

In fact, of course, the oil and its contribution to permanent income will be anticipated, and so the economy will tend to shift from (A) to (C) prior to oil's coming on stream. In this case, borrowing is necessary to finance the payments deficit, but it is forthcoming given the collateral of future oil. In addition, the exchange rate starts to appreciate and manufacturing starts to decline even before the oil is physically available. There are strong reasons to believe that such anticipations affected Norway and Britain after 1975.

The picture just painted involves investing the oil revenues abroad. This helps to keep the exchange rate down while the oil is flowing, and provides the foreign exchange with which to maintain consumption afterwards. Forsyth and Kay preferred this policy to domestic investment in either non-tradables or tradables. To be invested at home, the oil needs to be converted into goods and services, and to the extent that these are non-traded this increases the squeeze on tradables. Furthermore, they argued, given its contraction, the returns on investment in the tradable manufacturing sector will be unreasonably low. However, although the private returns to foreign investment may exceed those of domestic investment, this is not necessarily so for the social returns. For example, private returns are reduced by taxes on profits, the risk of appropriation, externalities through raised employment and externalities from the dynamic effects of investment; however, whereas with foreign investment all these are lost to the investing nation, with home investment they accrue to it as social benefits (see p. 231 above). Hence it may conceivably pay Britain to invest her oil revenue in the expansion of the manufacturing sector: while the oil flows, manufacturing will be importing capital goods and probably making losses, but, when the oil has gone, the maintained manufacturing sector will still be healthy enough to earn the surplus necessary to finance the higher permanent consumption. Clearly the trade-off between foreign and domestic investment depends on the difference between private and social returns, the size of the transition costs in adjusting manufactures, and the extent to which local investment requires non-traded goods. Thus it is not possible to reject home investment *a priori* as Forsyth and Kay did. On the other hand, neither can one be confident that governments can identify and promote sectors of the economy that should be preserved for the sake of twenty years hence. Henderson (1977), for example, noted the British government's appalling record in this regard, while Gelb (1989) quoted several examples of inappropriate developing country responses to primary sector windfalls.

This section has argued that, if the benefits of an oil discovery are to be enjoyed, the revenue has to be spent, and this will inevitably lead to some structural change. We have analysed a very simple example of this change and shown that manufacturing must contract. This conclusion arises from nearly every analysis of this problem. Nevertheless, we have also argued that the extent and pattern of structural change is amenable to policy control, and that there may well be cases where it is beneficial to keep adjustment below the level implied by the free market.

Macro-economic adjustment

We now turn briefly to the macro-economics of adjustment to an oil discovery (following Eastwood and Venables, 1982). We take as given that the oil raises domestic demand, and that in the long run the relative price and output of non-tradables must rise. We shall assume that this implies an exchange rate appreciation. With perfect markets, flexible prices and rational expectations, adjustment would be instantaneous, but once we allow for sticky prices and wages there is a period of disequilibrium. We analyse this in the framework of a 'Dornbusch' economy assuming perfect capital mobility. With rational expectations, an oil discovery would lead to an immediate jump in demand to its new permanent income level and also to an immediate appreciation. This appreciation would not, however, reach the long-run equilibrium exchange rate or eliminate all the excess demand for domestic output; these are achieved only later, through further gradual appreciation. The reason for this undershooting is that the initial appreciation lowers import prices, which, by reducing the demand for money, lowers the domestic interest rate. This is consistent with foreign balance only if an anticipated appreciation equates the net return on domestic bills to the world rate of interest.

With rational expectations, the immediate jump in demand more than offsets the deflationary effects of the exchange rate appreciation, meaning that discovery is followed by excess, not deficient, demand for domestic output. However, if we assume that demand does not rise until residents actually receive the extra income, then there is a contraction, because the appreciation now reduces demand from the level that just matched pre-oil supply. Such a situation seems quite plausible. Most residents reap the benefits of an oil discovery only through tax cuts, and they are unlikely to be able to borrow or to reduce their savings by a corresponding amount just on the strength of expected future tax cuts. Hence, unless the government finances immediate tax cuts through its own borrowing, there will be a time lag between the oil discovery and the increase in demand. The result will be an exchange rate led depression, concentrated on the tradable goods sector.

Apart from government action, the only other possible relief of the

365

depression is that the investment programme to extract the oil raises demand. However, this is unlikely to offset the effects of appreciation entirely. In fact, if the programme were largely financed from abroad, it could exacerbate the appreciation, because, even if all physical equipment were imported, investment would still raise the demand for local goods and services such as construction. In addition, compared with domestic finance, foreign finance of the investment would reduce the long-term value of the exchange rate, because it would reduce local incomes and generate an outflow of profits. It seems possible, then, that under such circumstances some overshooting could occur.

There is one final consideration on the exchange rate. There was uncertainty surrounding the future price of oil over the 1970s and 1980s. Rises in the price hit industrial economies hard, and oil self-sufficiency reduces the impact of such shocks. This affects the risk properties of a self-sufficient country's currency, which will rise when 'oil-importer' currencies fall. Hence oil self-sufficiency provides an excellent hedge against oil price rises, and such 'portfolio' demand could lead to further appreciation. Few major currencies are 'backed by' oil self-sufficiency, so this may have been a major factor in the demand for sterling since the late 1970s.

25.3   THE BRITISH EXPERIENCE

British experience over the 1970s and 1980s appears to offer a classic testing ground for the theories of the previous two sections. As we saw in Chapter 17, sterling appreciated strongly in the early 1980s as the price of oil peaked and production of North Sea oil reached a plateau. Simultaneously the rest of the economy went into deep recession, led by the manufacturing sector, which accounts for most of UK tradable output: GDP fell by nearly 4 per cent and manufacturing output by 15 per cent between 1979 and 1981. Unfortunately, however, the test of the theories is less than complete, for the effects of the major oil shocks on output and the exchange rate are confounded by major changes in economic policy. The peak in the UK production and real price of oil coincided with a period of exceptionally tight monetary and fiscal policy, as the first Thatcher government introduced the Medium Term Financial Strategy, which supposedly committed it to a permanent reduction in money supply growth, and also a fierce constraint on government expenditure. Exchange rate theory suggests that these policies could explain the observed recession and appreciation of sterling just as easily as do the oil events of the period. Even worse from a scientific point of view, the mid-1980s saw the effects of both a major fall in real oil prices and a substantial relaxation of British monetary policy: so again we have two competing explanations of the mid-decade fall in sterling.

Several attempts have been made to disentangle the effects of oil and macro-economic policy on the British economy and sterling (see, for example, Forsyth and Kay, 1980, 1981, and Bank of England *Quarterly Bulletin*, December 1980 and March 1982). We consider a third study – Eastwood and Venables (1983). This concluded that policy rather than oil accounted for the large swings in sterling over the 1980s, a view which is corroborated by the evidence of the late-1980s when sterling continued to fluctuate despite very little significant change in the oil market.

Eastwood and Venables assessed the change in Britain's permanent income that accrued from the 'oil events' of the 1970s, and from this deduced the exchange rate effects. They identified four 'oil events':

- the discovery of North Sea oil,
- the 1973–4 price rise,
- the 1978–9 price rise, and
- revisions in expectations about the relative price of oil after 1980.

They calculated the effects of these events under two assumptions about expectations in 1970. Under 'perfect foresight', both oil price rises were assumed to be anticipated, hence perceived permanent income was already low in 1970 because people took into account the future high cost of oil. Under 'myopia', however, neither price rise was expected, and so permanent income was high in 1970 because people expected to continue consuming at the 1970 rate indefinitely. The oil price rises then came as a nasty surprise that cut perceived permanent income substantially.

The oil discovery, on the other hand, was assumed to be unexpected under both scenarios. It raised permanent income. With perfect foresight this was from a low base, whereas with myopia its positive impact was set against the permanent income loss that was incurred through the price rises. (Despite having local supplies, Britain still had to adjust to the new higher prices for oil.) Comparing 1970 and 1980, Eastwood and Venables tentatively suggested that, with perfect foresight, 'oil events' raised permanent income by 4.5 per cent, whereas with myopia they lowered it by 2 per cent. The latter result does not imply that Britain did not gain from North Sea oil, but merely that its unexpected benefits were more than offset by the unexpected loss from the price rises. Eastwood and Venables suggested that the myopic view is the more nearly correct,[1] and hence rejected Forsyth and Kay's approach based on Table 24.1, which is akin to the perfect foresight case (a straight injection of income).

The next step was to calculate the indirect income gains accruing through the change in the terms of trade of non-oil goods. Since Britain's non-oil trade was largely with other oil importers (OECD), the question concerned the impacts of the shocks on Britain relative to the rest of OECD. Eastwood and Venables argued that the oil price rises hit both equally, hence only the oil discovery could change the terms of trade between them. The resources devoted to oil were lost to other activities, and the authors estimated that the opportunity cost of oil was a loss of non-oil production of about 2 per cent of GDP. North Sea oil contributed about 4.5 per cent to GDP directly and this increased demand for local output by about 3 per cent of GDP. The fall in supply coupled with the rise in demand raised the relative price of UK non-oil goods. Assuming an infinite price elasticity of supply for imports, price elasticities of demand of $-2/3$ and $-4/3$ for imports and exports respectively, and an import/GDP ratio of $1/3$, the price elasticity of demand for UK output was $1/3$.[2] Assuming a zero price elasticity of supply for UK output, a 5 per cent cut in demand needed terms of trade change of 15 per cent, and this indirectly raised permanent income by a further 5 per cent of GDP.

Combining the direct and indirect benefits, Eastwood and Venables suggested a net gain in permanent income between 1970 and 1980 of about 7–9 per cent under perfect foresight and of around 0–2 per cent under myopia. The structural implications of these income and relative price effects are that the perfect foresight case suggests considerable growth of non-traded output and decline in manufacturing (cf. Forsyth and Kay), whereas the myopia case suggests little change or even a growth of manufacturing. Since the latter appears more realistic, there was probably little need for structural change between 1970 and 1980. On the other hand, appreciation was still necessary under myopia because the rest of OECD had to increase its volume of exports in response to the price rise, while the UK did not. In other words, the UK had to maintain her volume of exports while the rest of OECD expanded theirs; this still required a loss in Britain's share of world trade, but not the contraction of British manufacturing. The exchange rate change necessary to bring this about is not precisely estimable, but the evidence suggests it is considerably below the levels reached in 1980 and 1981.

Summary

We have applied some elementary economic theory and quantification to the very real problem of the oil shocks of the 1970s. The conclusions are as follows:

(i) The oil price rise substantially reduced OECD's real permanent income.
(ii) Britain is richer for having had North Sea oil. But
(iii) the benefits of North Sea oil only just, if at all, outweighed the costs of the higher oil price. 'Oil events' overall did little to boost income between 1970 and 1980.
(iv) If (i) had been anticipated and adjusted to by 1970, then (ii) would have required considerable readjustment: spending would have had to rise and non-traded sectors expand at the expense of traded good sectors. If, alternatively, (i) were not anticipated, the combination of (i) and (ii) would leave little room for a boom or structural change. The evidence suggests that the latter was the case.
(v) The discovery of North Sea oil significantly improved Britain's terms of trade. This involved appreciation, but probably not by the extent observed by the early 1980s. Thus the latter must be explained by monetary policy as well as by oil.

25.4 US POLICY AND THE DOLLAR

The appreciation of sterling described in the previous sections was dramatic and, some would argue, disastrous for the UK economy. It was dwarfed, however, by an even larger appreciation of the dollar around two years later. This not only squeezed the US tradables sector but, because of the USA's dominant position, sent shock waves through the whole world economy. Moreover, although the dollar has now returned to more normal levels, it is far from clear that the fundamental problem – the US budget deficit – is any closer to a solution. This section interprets the recent history of the dollar as no more than a simple application of the models that we have examined in the previous few chapters.

Reaganomics

As in the UK, the monetary squeeze in the USA started in the late 1970s. The role of the swing to the political right – Mrs Thatcher in 1979 and Mr Reagan in 1980 – was to intensify and give long-term credibility to the process. Both politicians accompanied their 'sound money' attitudes with a profound belief that the role of government in the economy should be reduced, and that doing so would unleash a burst of economic activity – a so-called supply-side revolution. Mrs Thatcher started mainly by cutting government expenditure, but Mr Reagan, hamstrung by election promises of no new taxes, a desire to raise defence spending and a political system in which the Congress (with its Democratic majority) exercised strong control over the budget, merely cut taxes. The theory was that tax cuts would stimulate activity and reduce tax evasion, and hence boost revenues.[3] They did not, and, as Table 25.2 shows, by 1984 the US government had slipped into heavy deficit.

Table 25.2 The US deficits and exchange rates, 1979–88

	IMF code[a]	1979	1980	1981	1982	1983	1984	1985	1986	1987	1988
Money supply (% increase in M2)	59mb	7.8	8.9	10.0	8.9	11.9	8.5	8.5	9.0	3.7	5.4
Long-term interest rate (%)	61	9.4	11.5	13.9	13.0	11.1	12.5	10.6	7.7	8.4	8.9
Inflation (% increase in GNP deflator)	99air	8.8	9.1	9.6	6.5	3.9	3.9	3.3	2.7	3.3	3.4
Effective exchange rate (index)	amx	67	67	75	84	89	96	100	82	72	68
Trade balance ($b.)	77acd	− 28	− 26	− 28	− 36	− 67	− 113	− 122	− 145	− 160	− 126
Current account ($b.)	77azd	− 1	2	6	− 9	− 47	− 106	− 116	− 139	− 152	− 135
Government deficit ($b.; year ending 30 September	80	− 36	− 76	− 79	− 126	− 203	− 178	− 212	− 212	− 148	− 150

Note:
[a] Code number from *International Financial Statistics*.
Source: IMF, *International Financial Statistics*, Annual Supplement 1989.

Appreciation,
1981–5

The history of the dollar may be broken up into three periods. The first, the appreciation of 1981 and 1982, reflects three factors: (a) the US monetary squeeze was tighter than those elsewhere and hence US interest rates rose relative to world averages; (b) the enhanced credibility of the tight money policy when Reagan became President improved the dollar's attractiveness as an asset both internally and externally; and (c) there may have been some anticipation of the fiscal pressures of later years – the first of Reagan's tax-cutting acts was dated 1981.

The second phase, 1982–5, was one of strong appreciation driven by fiscal expansion. The public deficit grew from 2.5 per cent of GNP in 1981 to 6 per cent in 1983,[4] and the resulting growth of government borrowing kept US real interest rates well above world average levels. At first the US private sector absorbed most of the government deficit, reducing investment and slightly raising savings. In the notation of equation (21.4), $(S - I)$ increased, so largely offsetting the increase in $(G - T)$, and in these circumstances the current account, $(X - M)$, did not come under much increased pressure. Very soon, however, US residents became reluctant to finance the deficit and a reduction in net exports became the only way of closing the resource gap. The mechanism was an appreciation of the dollar, the proximate cause of which was the huge inflow of capital into the USA attracted by high rates of return. There was some talk of overshooting and of the virtues of restricting capital mobility, but had the latter been effected the imbalance in the real economy would merely have resurfaced elsewhere.

The USA is the dominant force in the world economy, so the sudden increase in the US government's demands for resources affected the world's net savings balance. An increased flow of savings to the USA must be provided by a mixture of two effects: an increase in the world real interest rate or an appreciation of the dollar's real exchange rate. The former encourages net savings, $(S - I)$, world-wide, while the latter increases the share of a fixed pool of savings that the US can pre-empt.

Figure 25.1 The effects of the US budget deficit

Figure 25.1 considers equilibrium in the real economies of the USA and the rest of the world (RoW). Curve UU plots combinations of the real interest rate (i) and the dollar's real exchange rate (λ) that yield equilibrium in the USA. A higher interest rate must be offset by a depreciation of the dollar in order to maintain real equilibrium; since we are dealing with the dollar we use the US exchange rate convention, so that a depreciation is shown as an increase in λ. Hence UU slopes upwards to the right. If the US government increases its net expenditure, UU will shift upwards to $U'U'$: given the foreign balance, a higher interest rate is required to cut back on US private net investment. The curve RR represents a similar equilibrium in the rest of the world. Obviously a rise in its interest rate must be offset by an appreciation of the dollar to switch demand towards RoW goods.

If capital mobility forces the same real interest rate on both the USA and RoW, the initial equilibrium will be at A and the new one, after an increase in the US government deficit, at B. It is clear that, in the absence of other macro-economic shocks, a fiscal shock entails some combination of a rise in the world-wide real rate of interest and a dollar appreciation. The precise combination depends mainly on the slope of the RR curve. If RoW were large relative to USA, RR would be flat: very large changes in the exchange rate would be required to offset small interest-rate changes in the RoW, and the USA's fiscal shock would show up mainly in the exchange rate. The fact that the USA is fairly large relative to RoW, however, means that RR is steeper and the USA's policy does affect world interest rates.

Depreciation since 1985

During 1984 most economists believed that, at around 40 per cent above PPP, the dollar exchange rate was unsustainable. The pressures on the tradables sector were massive, and serious worries were raised about whether residents, and more importantly non-residents, would be willing to continue accumulating dollar assets. Still the dollar rose, however, possibly as the victim of a speculative bubble (see section 22.1). In early 1985, however, the trend reversed and the dollar started to depreciate, either because of portfolio pressures or because the US boom had eased somewhat. The depreciation was helped along by a change of mind by the US authorities, who recognised in 1985 that depreciation was necessary to head off the pressure for protection from the troubled tradables sector. The new view was embodied in the Plaza Agreement of September 1985 between the major economies, which attempted to 'talk down' the dollar. The fall in the dollar's effective exchange rate continued steadily until 1987, at which point a new agreement – the Louvre Agreement – sought to stabilise it at around its 1980 level. The attempt was unsuccessful at the time, although the dollar did settle down in 1988 after a further fall of about 10 per cent.

The decline in the exchange rate caused the dollar to lose none of its fascination for economists. Over 1984–6 the question was whether the dollar would achieve a soft-landing, i.e. fall to a sensible level without inducing a large recession (see Marris, 1985). By 1987 interest had focused on whether the rate had declined sufficiently for equilibrium, especially given that the current account deficit refused to disappear. Neither controversy is fully resolved yet, and to analyse them we start with the latter.

Since 1985 the US government has made some attempt to control its budget deficit – for instance, through the Gramm–Rudman Act – but it has been very half-hearted; hence the public sector deficit has continued largely unabated, and it is hardly surprising that as a result the current account deficit persists. Only if there were convincing reasons for private savings to increase could a growing and investing economy, such as the USA during this period, expect to cover such a large public deficit without recourse to foreign borrowing and a trade deficit. US private savings have remained stubbornly low, while investment has remained buoyant, so, at least on accounting grounds, the current account deficit is no surprise.

If we look inside the current account deficit we find examples of several of the phenomena noted above. The growth of imports and decline of exports during 1981–5 reflected both the USA's high economic growth rates relative to the rest of the world and her declining competitiveness. Relative import prices fell and relative export prices rose, both by about 20 per cent in response to the 25 per cent appreciation; that is, around 80 per cent of the effect of the appreciation was passed on to consumers. When the dollar depreciated, the situation was almost precisely reversed for exports: export prices fell in foreign currency terms and, before export volumes could respond favourably, revenues in 1985–6 were stagnant. For imports on the other hand, (foreign) producers absorbed about half of the exchange rate change in reduced profit margins, so that the prices of US imports had risen by only about 10 per cent by the end of 1987. As a result, import volumes and expenditure continued to rise significantly over 1985–7, and the current account displayed a deep and prolonged J-curve.

Several explanations were given for the apparently perverse behaviour of import prices. First, imports were coming increasingly from the NICs – expecially Korea and Taiwan – whose currencies moved very little against the dollar. Second, long-run hysteresis effects were blamed: the previous appreciation had damaged US import-competing industries beyond immediate repair, and so import demand could not contact very much (e.g. Baldwin, 1988). Third, a number of commentators noted that if industries were oligopolistic, profit-maximising producers would absorb certain shocks

371

themselves and the pass-through of exchange rate changes would be incomplete (e.g. Mann, 1989). This, however, does not really explain the asymmetry between appreciation and depreciation. Finally, and quite convincingly, Bhagwati (1988) noted that many US imports were subjected to VERs during the 1980s. VERs entail that the price of imports is determined solely by demand factors: it is the price at which the exogenously fixed volume of imports can be sold to consumers. The excess of this over the price at which producers would supply that quantity in a free market is pure rent – a return over and above that necessary to maintain supply. A depreciation raises the dollar supply price of US imports (which is the exporter's local currency price multiplied by the exchange rate), but hardly affects the dollar demand schedule at all. Thus, quite naturally, restricted import suppliers hardly altered their dollar prices at all, they absorbed the increase in the supply price that the depreciation induced in terms of reduced rents.

The persistence of the current account deficit makes its effect on wealth and portfolios ever larger. The USA is substantially the largest debtor nation in the world and her debts are increasing by well over $100b. per annum. Even if the rest of the world is willing to hold these debts, they require servicing by net exports. Hence in the long run the dollar will have to depreciate below its original equilibrium value in order to generate the trade surplus necessary for debt service. No one is really sure how large that further fall will have to be – it depends on the ultimate degree of pass-through and the effects of hysteresis – but it will probably have to go further than it had done by 1989. This then re-opens the question of the hard landing. Even though the USA has avoided recession until 1990, the increase in net exports required to service her debt may push her over the edge, particularly if there is ever a loss of confidence in dollar assets.

If the USA can restore fiscal and exchange stability without either a recession of inflation, she will have achieved a considerable policy coup. US economic growth has remained high by its own historical standards for most of the 1980s, even though a considerable degree of inflation had to be squeezed out of the economy early in the decade. Such success will be in marked contrast to Europe, and particularly the UK in which the so-called Thatcher miracle comprised mostly a recovery from a deep policy-induced slump (in 1980–2) and ended in inflation and recession (in 1989–90). If the USA is more successful, it will, ironically, be largely for Keynesian reasons – the fiscal relaxation kept the economy buoyant while the tight monetary stance squeezed out inflation. As noted above, however, it is not yet clear whether the USA will actually manage to avoid a recession.

FURTHER READING

Corden (1985) provides a simple analysis of the oil price rises of the 1970s. More formal approaches to oil as an intermediate good are *Dornbusch* (1980b) and *Findlay and Rodriguez* (1977) who consider the macro-economic implications. For a treatment of resource discoveries in the abstract, see *Corden and Neary* (1982) on trade theory, and *Eastwood and Venables* (1982) on macro-economics. *Corden* (1981) tackles the theoretical untangling of monetary policy and resource booms. Specific analyses of resource booms stretch back to *Gregory* (1976) – on Australia – and *Ellman* (1977) – on Holland; more recently they include – on Britain – *Forsyth and Kay* (1980, 1981), *Bank of England* (*Quarterly Economic Bulletin*, December 1980 and March 1982) and *Eastwood and Venables* (1983). The later Bank of England report is extremely clear and offers a thorough analysis of the costs of North Sea oil. *McCormick* (1982) and *Bean* (1987) analyse the UK, whilst *Barker and Brailovsky* (1981) offers a detailed and Keynesian approach to resource discovery in several countries. *Gelb* (1989) examines the effects of resource discoveries on developing country economies, including governments' policy responses, while *Neary and van Wijnbergen* (1986) contains some interesting analytical essays.

The dollar has attracted huge amounts of attention. *Blanchard* (1987) analyses US economic policy as a whole, while *Baldwin and Krugman* (1987) consider the persistence of the current account deficit, and *Marris* (1985) explores the hard-landing scenario. The OECD's *Economic Surveys* 1987/8 and 1988/9 offer useful data on the trade situation.

KEY CONCEPTS

industrialisation	non-tradables
permanent income	Dutch disease
myopia	net savings
net exports	pass-through

QUESTIONS FOR REVIEW

25.1 Why did the first oil price rise (1973–4) require Britain to industrialise while the second (1978–9) contributed to her de-industrialisation?

25.2 Can a country benefit from a resource boom without exchange rate appreciation?

25.3 Contrast the roles of fiscal policies in the appreciation of sterling and the dollar over the early 1980s.

25.4 What factors explain the persistence of the US current account deficit after the dollar depreciated?

NOTES

1 Their evidence comes from various pre-1973 writings, and the fact that the largest appreciation of sterling coincided with the 1978 oil price rise.

2 The calculation involves totally differentiating $Y = Q + pM$ and $S = Q + X$ holding $dY = 0$, where Y is income, Q local sales, M imports, X exports and p the price of foreign goods in terms of UK goods. S represents the demand for domestic output, the variable of interest.

3 Blanchard (1987) argued that Reagan was trying to bluff the Congress into reducing expenditure; Branson (1987), in his comment on this article, held that the exercise was simply a gross miscalculation.

4 Definitions of the deficit vary considerably between sources – a considerable difficulty in pinning down the US policy stance. The IMF figures quoted here are higher than most, but all sources agree on the rapid growth over 1981–4.

373

26 Exchange Rate Regimes and Optimum Currency Areas

We have considered the determinants of flexible exchange rates and their impact on economic policy. We now tackle the major normative issue in this area: what is the optimum degree and extent of exchange rate flexibility? Section 26.1 compares flexible and fixed exchange rate regimes in terms of their insulating properties, stability in the face of speculation, effects on world trade and a variety of other properties. Section 26.2 considers the international coordination of macro-economic policy; it describes several forms of coordination and then examines two proposals for policy coordination to increase the stability of exchange rates. The arguments for and against flexible exchange rates are specialised in section 26.3 in a discussion of the optimum currency area (the area within which exchange rates are fixed), and are made more concrete when we consider the European Monetary System in section 26.4.

26.1 FIXED VS. FLEXIBLE EXCHANGE RATES

This section considers the pros and cons of flexible exchange rates from the points of view of both individual countries and the world as a whole. It covers the insulating properties of flexible rates, the stabilising (or otherwise) effects of speculation, the effect of exchange rate fluctuations on trade, the ease of adjustment under different exchange rate regimes, and the possible inflationary biases of flexible exchange rates.

Transmission and insulation

In this sub-section we ask which exchange rate regime offers the domestic economy most insulation from unwanted economic shock. The latter may be of either domestic or foreign origin – they are deemed equally undesirable.

The simplest transmission mechanism for economic shocks is the international trade multiplier of Chapter 18. Assuming fixed exchange rates and ignoring all capital flows, it shows that economic activity in one country spills over (positively) to another via the trade balance. For example, an investment boom in France stimulates demand for both French and British output and causes expansion in both. Under fixed rates, therefore, British income is sensitive to activity in France. Now repeat the exercise with flexible rates. If the exchange rate always adjusts to keep the trade balance at zero, it would seem that Britain is insulated from France. Moreover, since Britain can no longer provide net resources to France (because trade is always balanced), all the extra investment must be supplied locally and so the expansion of French income will be correspondingly greater. Thus flexible rates, it seems, reduce the impact of foreign demand shocks and increase the effects of local demand shocks.

This result is broadly true, but the analysis is really too simple to be acceptable. The change in the exchange rate necessary to balance trade alters relative prices (because, in this Keynesian model, prices are fixed in local currency terms), and at the very least this should be taken into account. In the previous example, the French boom depreciates the franc and thus worsens

374

the French terms of trade. Conversely, of course, it improves Britain's terms of trade, and consequently makes her better off for any given level of output. Higher income normally entails proportionately higher savings, and since money income has not risen, higher savings involves lower money expenditure. Since the price of British output has not changed either, lower money expenditure means lower demand and output. Hence with flexibility a French boom reduces British output (though not her real income). This is known as the Laursen–Metzler effect (1950; and Behnke, 1980).

Even this is too simple, however, and we now turn to the full open *IS–LM* model to examine the impact of various shocks. The analysis is formally like that of Chapter 24, where we examined the effect of economic policy; however, there we asked whether (policy) shocks could shift income/output, whereas now we ask which regimes prevent shocks from influencing income. It could be argued that concern with insulation is misplaced, since shocks could always be met by countervailing policy shocks. This is forceful in theory, but not wholly convincing in practice, because it ignores the information and execution problems of conducting policy so precisely. In other words, an automatically stable regime is likely to save time, effort and mistakes.

Domestic expenditure shocks – e.g. investment booms – are precisely equivalent to fiscal policy in Chapter 24. With capital mobility, flexible rates offer more stability; in the simple model, flexible rates prevent any fiscal impact, but even in subtler models we would expect less than under fixed rates. With no capital mobility, however, fixed rates are more stable. Similarly, domestic monetary shocks are akin to monetary policy, and hence fixed rates are preferable regardless of the degree of capital mobility.

Consider now a foreign expenditure shock, raising the demand for local goods. This raises output and creates a current account surplus. Under flexible exchange rates, this surplus generates an appreciation that tends to offset the initial shock. Under fixed exchange rates, the surplus raises the money supply and this validates the output rise. Hence, flexible rates are more stable. A foreign monetary shock lowers the world rate of interest. Without capital mobility this presents no shock, but under perfect mobility it generates a huge potential inflow of funds. Under fixed rates, this expands the money supply (pushing the *LM* curve out) and raises income. With flexible rates, on the other hand, it produces an appreciation, dragging the *IS* curve back and reducing income. These two outcomes cannot strictly be ranked in terms of stability, but, since foreign monetary expansion is likely to be coupled with a foreign demand stimulus, it is likely that flexible rates result in less change in local incomes.

These simple exercises are not unambiguous, but they tend to confirm the earlier result that for foreign shocks flexible rates probably offer most insulation, whereas for domestic shocks fixed rates do. Intuitively, flexible rates bottle-up a disturbance in its country of origin, whereas fixed rates spread it around the world economy. Empirically, therefore, we would expect floating to be reflected in a weakening of the synchronisation of trade cycles around the world. In fact, synchronisation has increased since 1973 (Ripley, 1978), although this may well be due to economies experiencing common shocks (e.g. oil) rather than to causal links between them. Alternatively it may be that the exchange rate fluctuations necessary to ensure complete insulation were larger than governments could tolerate, and hence that only incomplete insulation was permitted. Recall from Chapters 18 and 19 how income effects tend to dominate short-term balance of payments behaviour. Hence, even relatively modest fluctuations in incomes may need large exchange rate changes to offset them.

Note finally that this section refers to income insulation: price insulation involves different issues. In particular, a flexible rate may allow a country to avoid importing inflation, via either the rising import prices or the pressures to cure payments surpluses that arise under fixed rates. On the other hand, the translation of random exchange rate fluctuations into local prices could increase the price variability associated with floating.

Speculation and intervention

This sub-section, which relates to section 22.2, asks whether speculation will tend to stabilise or de-stabilise the exchange rate, and (which is not quite the same thing) whether flexible rates are necessarily fluctuating rates. This is a critical matter in the argument over flexible exchange rates, because many of the objections to flexibility amount to a dislike of excess variation. We start by briefly considering speculation under fixed exchange rates.

Speculation can be profitable only if a change in the exchange rate occurs. Under a fixed rate system, the rate can fluctuate between the intervention points but not normally beyond. Provided the intervention points are close to parity, there is little scope for speculators because the size of any gain will be relatively small. The result is that a fixed rate system normally experiences little speculation, and the rate is stabilised by modest levels of official intervention. Occasionally, however, changes in the parity may be required – for instance, after a long period of inflation or the discovery of mineral resources. Then the speculators can have a field-day. The direction of change is obvious; the only uncertainty concerns the timing and the extent of the change. Suppose sterling is expected to depreciate: no one willingly holds sterling, and so the exchange rate falls to the lower intervention point. Here the Bank of England has to sell dollars to buy any sterling offered. This can go on only so long as the Bank has dollars to sell; when they run out, the exchange rate falls. The costs to speculators of backing such an outcome are very small. There is no prospect of an appreciation, so the only possible cost is the interest differential between holding dollars and sterling. If this were, say, 5 per cent per annum ($i_\pounds = i_\$ + 5\%$), it would still be profitable to speculate so long as sterling falls by 5 per cent within a year. Speculators face an almost sure thing. The pressure they put on the exchange rates can be massive and the costs of resisting it huge in terms of deflation and interest payments.

Under fixed rates, then, there is generally little speculation, but occasional periods of intense and destructive pressure. Under flexible rates on the other hand, there is always the prospect of significant changes in the rate and so speculation occurs most of the time; however, the fact that the rate responds to any pressure prevents the huge build-up of pressure. We now ask whether perpetual speculation could cause undue variability in exchange rates.

In the absence of speculation, the exchange rate would still fluctuate around its equilibrium path because, for example, trade may not be balanced every day. Would the addition of speculators to this market be stabilising, in the sense of moving the actual rate towards the equilibrium rate, or de-stabilising, moving it away? In terms of Figure 26.1, would speculation produce pattern (A) or pattern (B)?

The argument (due to Friedman, 1953) is that, if speculators push the rate out to (B), they will lose money, because they have to buy when the price is high (e.g. at T_1) and sell when it is low (T_2). Since people will not (indeed cannot) act persistently to make losses, Friedman argued, the great bulk of

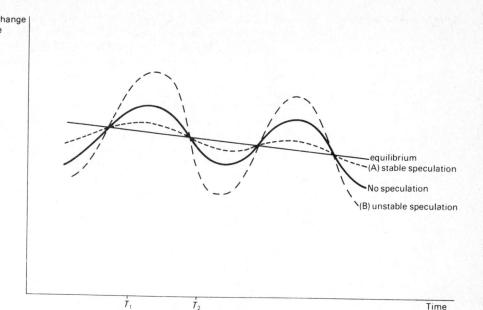

Figure 26.1 Speculation and the exchange rate

speculation must be stabilising. Within the context of a smoothly evolving equilibrium rate, an infinite time horizon and a fixed group of speculators, this argument has never been satisfactorily refuted. However, this is not really the relevant framework for exchange rates. First, anyone making a foreign transaction can speculate merely by slightly re-timing his payment, so the group of speculators is fluctuating. Second, it is not difficult to speculate when the equilibrium value is obvious; the difficulty and scope for error arise when the equilibrium changes. This is especially likely when there is only incomplete information (often only rumour) on which speculators can base their estimates. In such circumstances it is easy to envisage speculation pulling the actual rate away from the true equilibrium rate. Third, losses on speculation may be offset by earnings on trading margins, so inefficient trader–speculators may survive for years. Fourth, natural selection may take a very long time – for example, in section 22.2 we described two models in which speculative bubbles could persist. Finally, the eventual elimination of unprofitable speculators says nothing about the damage they can do as they make their losses. For instance, the profitability criterion did not prevent the Wall Street crash of 1929!

In the end, then, this is an empirical issue, and one that can be answered only by reference to actual exchange rate markets. The critical factor is the formation and precision of expectations. It is frequently argued that speculators, as professionals, will be better at this than other market participants. This is probably true, except compared with the central bank. It is hard to maintain that the bank could not out-predict speculators, for it has access to all the information they have plus some more. The issue then becomes whether or not the central bank would intervene only in the form that speculators would – to make profits – or whether it would use its position to try to exert a more far-reaching influence. If it did only the former – and

377

this was obvious publicly – the exchange market would be more stable with bank intervention than with speculation. None of this argues that speculation is not normally stabilising – it probably is – or that an exchange market with no intervention and no speculation would not be highly unstable. It merely says that, of the two, official intervention is probably more stable than speculation.

Consider, finally, a market with both speculation and intervention. The latter could obviously displace the former, but if there is a suspicion that the bank has objectives other than profit, or if it regularly forms different expectations from the speculators, then there is scope for trouble. With no intervention, private speculation is constrained by the possibility that the exchange rate could move in the direction opposite to that expected, producing large losses. If, however, the bank is in the market, and if the bank always gets its way over the rate (by virtue of its huge resources), then speculators who think they can second-guess the bank have nearly the 'sure-thing' found under fixed rates. In such circumstances the volume of speculation forthcoming could be huge and intervention a difficult and costly process. This so-called 'dirty float' – with intervention to influence the rate, but not around any announced parity, could be les desirable than either of the more extreme regimes.

There is virtually no empirical evidence on speculation alone, because it is impossible to disentangle it from other determinants of exchange rates. It clearly cannot be de-stabilising in all circumstances since there are plenty of examples of stable flexible rates, e.g. Canada in the 1950s (see Yeager, 1976). On the other hand, one has only to read the financial press to know that speculative sentiment can change very rapidly and greatly affect the exchange rate. It is difficult to believe that such jitters do not sometimes drive the rate away from equilibrium.

Uncertainty

Before the advent of floating it was frequently maintained that flexible exchange rates would increase the uncertainty involved in international economic transactions, and hence, by reducing them, harm international specialisation. There are several replies to this.

First, the conclusion is not inevitable, even in simple theoretical models. If the returns to exporting become less certain, some exporters may reduce average exports because exporting is less attractive, but others may increase them in order to keep down the probability that revenues fall short of some critical value. Second, traders may take forward cover in order to avoid exchange risk, although in truth, this is only part of the answer because forward markets are costly and incomplete. The cost is reflected by the spread between buying and selling prices that rewards forward dealers for their risk. Both spreads and forward risk – the average difference between the forward rate for delivery at a date and the spot rate at that date – have increased substantially since floating (Aliber, 1976; Crockett and Goldstein, 1976). Such costs, however, are so small absolutely (around 0.5 per cent of price in 1981 – International Monetary Fund, *Annual Report*, 1982) that they can hardly affect trade strongly.

A third reply is that flexible exchange rates, while increasing nominal exchange rate risk, may reduce other risks – especially on long-term transactions. For example, if one is contemplating direct investment, one is concerned about future costs in the host nation relative to the rest of the world. Flexible exchange rates may prevent large discrepancies in costs and real exchange rates, because the exchange rate would move to offset differences in local currency inflation. Also, governments sometimes adopt policies such as tariffs and exchange controls to defend fixed exchange rates; if flexible rates obviate the need for these, they further reduce uncertainty to private traders. In fact, neither of these arguments carries much conviction: since 1973 real exchange rate variability has increased, real exchange rate disequilibria have persisted, and trade restrictions have multiplied.

The fourth reply is empirical: how does exchange rate variability affect international trade flows? Early work, such as Hooper and Kolhagen (1978), found relatively little evidence of adverse consequences, but recently a more worrying picture had begun to emerge, e.g. de Grauwe (1987) and Perée and Steinherr (1989).

There are considerable practical difficulties in assessing the effects of exchange rate variability. For example, should one measure fluctuations in real or nominal exchange rates, and over what period – a quarter, a year, or a decade? It is *ex ante* uncertainty that matters, not *ex post* fluctuations, but how can the former be measured? How does one represent risk? Traditionally researchers have used the variance of the exchange rate (or its square-root – the standard deviation), but this treats positive and negative deviations symmetrically and fails to capture any effects due to other properties of the distribution of exchange rate changes. (For example, the very small probability of a very large loss may be far more influential on export behaviour than the variance allows.) Finally, research should allow for different industries to have different responses to a given level of fluctuations, and also for interactions between uncertainty in different markets; trade between countries A and B may increase despite an increase in the exchange rate uncertainty separating them if that increase is small relative to the increases in uncertainty for all other trade flows.

No study allows for all these complications, but Perée and Steinherr and de Grauwe generate some useful results. Perée and Steinherr presented two complex measures of nominal exchange rate uncertainty; both are based on the deviations of actual from equilibrium exchange rates, the first stressing the range of variation and the second the duration of deviations. The latter is as much a measure of exchange rate misalignment as of uncertainty, but that is just as important. Both measures suggest very considerable increases in uncertainty since 1973 (see Table 26.1 below). Perée and Steinherr then related aggregate exports to world demand, the real exchange rate, the relative prices of exports and home sales (to capture supply-side effects) and uncertainty. For Belgium, Germany, Japan and the UK, uncertainty seems to reduce exports, but for the USA it does not. The latter result probably reflects the fact that most US exports are invoiced in dollars and thus face no direct exchange risk; the risk – which is unavoidable – is borne by the buyers, who consequently demand lower prices, but that response is captured by Perée and Steinherr's relative price terms rather than their uncertainty measure.

De Grauwe (1987) considered both nominal and real exchange rate uncertainty, represented by the standard deviation of annual exchange rate changes. He analysed the effects on trade over very long time periods and estimated that since 1973 uncertainty has reduced the annual growth rate of trade between industrial countries by 1–1.5 per cent per year.

Adjustment

The obvious case for flexible exchange rates is that they ease the adjustment to economic shocks affecting foreign transactions. Rather than the authorities having to identify shifts in the equilibrium exchange rate and bring about the required change, a flexible exchange rate will find its way there automatically, responding only to the supply of and demand for currencies in the market. According to the advocates of flexible exchange rates, this is cheaper, more reliable, and avoids the long-lived disequilibria that characterised the fixed exchange rate period.

If all prices were perfectly flexible there would be no need for exchange rate changes. Any changes required between the relative prices of tradables and non-tradables could be achieved by changes in local currency prices. However, in practice this is actually a long and painful process (if it is possible at all), and it may be avoided by changing the exchange rate. As Friedman (1953) observed, it is more efficient to change the single price of foreign currency than to reprice every single good an economy produces, just as during summertime it is more efficient to alter the clocks to save daylight than to reschedule every activity by an hour.

This argument is, however, more a case against rigidly fixed rates than in favour of perfectly flexible rates. Provided governments do not persist too long with unrealistic rates, its main force may be accommodated by fixed but adjustable parities. Flexible exchange rates do not remove the external constraint; they merely translate it from a quantity dimension (balance of payments deficits) to a price dimension (depreciation). In fact, since 1973, disequilibria appear to have been just as persistent as before. West Germany and Switzerland, for instance, still show a strong tendency towards surplus and appreciation, while the USA shows the opposite.

A closely related issue is the ability of flexible rates to generate required structural change. A fluctuating exchange rate is constantly signalling the need for structural readjustment – towards tradables as the rate falls, and back again when it rises. Entrepreneurs obviously cannot follow each of these signals, and so they may, in fact, be rather slow to detect genuine indications for change. We do not, however, know of any evidence on this matter.

Inflationary bias

Implicit in the previous sub-section were the fears of the 1960s and 1970s that only the discipline of fixed exchange rates prevents governments from pursuing profligate policies of monetary expansion. This is a weak argument – it supposes that deficits provide greater discipline than depreciations – and it is readily dismissed by reference to the vicious deflations of 1980–2, e.g. in Britain, West Germany and the USA.

A more plausible ground for concern in the 1970s was the possibility that asymmetries in adjustment give a system of flexible rates an inflationary bias. If prices can adjust only upwards, a depreciation will raise the local currency prices of tradables, while the ensuing appreciation will raise the price of non-tradables. Either the government accommodates these price rises by expanding the money supply or it resists them and runs the risk of a depression as adjustment is thrown onto the quantity side of the economy. The latter is particularly likely if wages are inflexible downwards. If an appreciation reduces local currency tradable prices, but not labour costs, profits will be squeezed and this will eventually have repercussions on investment and output. This complaint against flexible rates is strengthened by comparison with the asymmetries of the fixed rate system. Since reserves are bounded below by zero, but not above, it is usually felt that fixed rates place greater burdens of adjustment on deficit countries than on surplus countries. Since the latter are obliged to pursue domestic deflation and anti-inflation policies, the system as a whole has a deflationary basis.

There was also a fear of the development of vicious circles of inflation and depreciation. If some exogenous shock required a depreciation of the currency, but this led to an equal amount of inflation via real wage and profit inflexibility coupled with an accommodating monetary policy, then one could envisage a vicious cycle. Each round of inflation would be offset by further depreciation, but this would generate further inflation, and so on. In most economies, however, there are lags in the adjustment of wages and only incomplete compensation for past inflation (as in Britain's 1973–4 indexation scheme). Furthermore, most tax systems exhibit fiscal drag, increasing their real tax-take in response to inflation, and most governments do not allow monetary policy to accommodate past price rises entirely. The result is that the inflation–depreciation cycle gradually squeezes real incomes and hence eventually collapses. Nevertheless, a shock requiring, say, a 5 per cent 'real' depreciation may involve a rather larger nominal depreciation.

This objection to flexible rates finds favour particularly with staunch monetarists like Mundell and Laffer. They argue that, since economies are homogeneous in prices, and domestic prices are perfectly flexible, exchange rate flexibility is unnecessary, and that, as it can exacerbate inflationary shocks, it is to be deplored.

A related but more recent concern (e.g. Giavazzi, 1989) is that the risk of inflation actually induces inflation. Modern macro-economic analysis holds that, while there may be no stable long-run trade-off between inflation and output, an unanticipated dose of inflation can temporarily raise output. If wages are fixed in nominal terms between wage rounds, inflation temporarily lowers real wages and thus increases employment and output. Of course, at the next wage round real wages and the previous real equilibrium will be restored, but at higher nominal prices. Under a fixed exchange rate regime this pattern of events would be impossible, because the inflation would put pressure on the exchange rate and would thus have to be reversed. Under flexible exchange rates, on the other hand, it *is* possible; and with rational expectations it will be partially anticipated in the form of higher nominal wage demands, which are, of course, potentially inflationary. The fixed rate is attractive in this case because it increases the government's anti-inflationary credibility – the government reaps benefits by tying its hands.

Finally we should note the possibility of an offsetting deflationary bias in the operation of a flexible exchange rates system (see Giavazzi, 1989). In controlling inflation, each government must make a trade-off between losses of output and the reductions in inflation that they induce. Under a flexible exchange rate regime, contractionary policies squeeze inflation both domestically and by appreciating the exchange rate, which reduces the internal prices of tradables. The former is absolute disinflation, but the latter is relative; it shifts the burden of inflation to other countries. Individual governments choose their degrees of deflation expecting to get both benefits but, if every country deflates, the relative components of disinflation roughly cancel out, and the reduction in inflation is less than was expected. That is, governments acting individually are over-optimistic about the returns to tight policy in terms of price stability, and consequently pursue tighter policies than their preferences really make optimal.

The evidence on inflation and floating exchange rates is ambiguous. That the level and dispersion of inflation rates have increased with floating is undeniable, but of itself this does not prove causation. Many would argue that the fixed exchange rate regime was abandoned *because* of the dispersion of inflation rates. Furthermore, even if flexible rates did exacerbate inflation levels and differences between countries, one cannot draw immediate welfare conclusions. In adjusting to the oil shocks, the ability of different economies to select different paths could have been beneficial.

Overall, flexible rates do seem to allow countries greater scope for inflation, but whether governments choose to exercise this freedom and whether such freedom is a 'bad thing', has not yet been determined.

Reserves

Perfect flexibility entails no official intervention in the exchange market. Apart from balances to fund official 'commercial' transactions, therefore, floating removes the need for foreign exchange reserves. Since reserves earn lower returns than longer-term investments (because of their greater liquidity), this represents a potential increase in income.

In practice, however, these savings are likely to be very small: earning, say, 2 per cent extra on 80 per cent of UK reserves in 1980 (a peak year) would have raised GNP by 0.1 per cent. Furthermore, there is doubt about whether floating has significantly reduced the use of (and demand for) foreign exchange reserves. The 1970s were a turbulent period and, of course, were mostly characterised by managed, rather than free floating; but Heller and Khan (1978) estimated that industrial countries (excluding the USA) reduced their reserve holdings by only 10–15 per cent relative to the pre-1972 era, while non-oil developing countries actually increased their holdings after 1972, probably reflecting their difficulties in pegging their exchange rates to major currencies that were themselves fluctuating.

Stability

It is frequently argued by advocates of flexible rates that instabilities in the exchange rate can only reflect instabilities in the economies they connect, and that it is better to let these instabilities work themselves out in the exchange rate where forward markets exist rather than elsewhere. For massive disequilibria, this statement is probably true (think how distorted East European economies became by eschewing the price mechanism), but for smaller, week-to-week, fluctuations there is no such presumption. For example, nearly all firms hold stocks of goods to smooth out demand fluctuations without resort to price changes, and there is no sound reason for denying such behaviour to countries in managing their foreign trade.

More significant still are the conclusions of Chapter 23. Price rigidities, volatile expectations and asset considerations combine to magnify real instabilities in the exchange market. Hence, although a perfectly stable environment may generate perfectly stable rates, ordinary economic fluctuations may generate great exchange rate volatility. Empirically, however, this has yet to be established, for the huge oil price rises, the massive monetary injection, and the conversion of many major governments to monetarism in the 1970s and 1980s hardly constituted 'ordinary' economic fluctuations.

Table 26.1 reports two measures of exchange rate stability over the fixed and floating periods. The first refers to monthly fluctuations in effective exchange rates. These understate the degree of bilateral variability, but show clearly that floating increased short-term fluctuation by around 200 per cent. The second reports Perée and Steinherr's measures: *V* measures the average range of uncertainty at any time, while *U* reflects the extent and duration of deviations from equilibrium. Both indicate substantial increases in uncertainty under floating rates, the latter showing in particular that floating did not avoid major exchange rate misalignments.

Table 26.1 Exchange rate variability under fixed and floating exchange rates: industrial countries

(A) *Month-to-month exchange rate changes*:[a]

	1961–70	1974–83
Nominal effective, absolute	0.20	1.18
Real effective, absolute	0.38	1.22
Nominal effective, relative to trend[b]	0.25	1.15

(B) *Uncertainty vis-à-vis the US dollar*[c]

		1961–70	1974–85
UK	V	1.17	1.73
	U	0.41	1.39
Germany	V	1.21	2.27
	U	0.22	4.30
Japan	V	1.02	1.86
	U	0.59	0.89

Notes:
[a] IMF (1984).
[b] Relative to 57-month moving average.
[c] Perée and Steinherr: average over annual values.

$$V_t = \frac{\max(X_{t-10}^t) - \min(X_{t-10}^t)}{\min(X_{t-10}^t)} + \left[1 + \frac{|X_t - X_t^*|}{X_t^*}\right]^2$$

$$U_t = \left[\sum_{i=t-10}^{t} \frac{|X_i - X_i^*|}{X_i^*}\right] \left[1 + \sum_{i=t-5}^{t} \frac{|X_i - X_i^*|}{X_i^*}\right]$$

where

X_t = nominal exchange rate in year t
$\max(X_{t-10}^t)$ = maximum value of X between year $(t-10)$ and t inclusive
$\min(X_{t-10}^t)$ = minimum value of X between year $(t-10)$ and t inclusive
X_t^* = equilibrium exchange rate in year t

V_t reflects the historical range of X and the deviation from equilibrium at one point of time. U_t reflects the extent of deviation *and* its duration. It weights recent deviations more heavily.

Sources: IMF (1984); Perée and Steinherr (1989).

26.2 INTERNATIONAL POLICY COORDINATION

One of the ironies of the late 1980s was that, despite the existence of flexible exchange rates, there was a growing interest in macro-economic policy coordination. National inflation and income levels are undoubtedly influenced by foreign conditions and increased financial integration is making the interrelationships between economies ever tighter and more immediate. As a result, governments often feel obliged to bring their policies into line with their neighbours' in order to avoid or to compensate for such external pressures. Thus, for example, tight money in Germany forces the British government to choose between raising British interest rates or suffering inflation as sterling depreciates. The exchange rate, as perhaps the most flexible economic variable, is the medium through which most such policy interactions are transmitted in the short run, and the existence in the 1980s of substantial and long-lived exchange rate misalignments raised the question of whether international policy coordination is desirable. This section considers some general issues of policy coordination and then examines two current proposals for coordination to stabilise exchange rates.

Types of coordination The possibility of beneficial coordination arises whenever there are policy spill-overs, i.e. wherever A's policy affects B. The international trade multiplier (section 18.3), the Laursen–Metzler effect (section 26.1), the deflationary bias of flexible exchange rates (section 26.1), and the $(n-1)$ problem (section 27.1) all offer scope for coordination, although it is not guaranteed that a mutually beneficial set of policy changes can always be negotiated. Thus, for example, the 'locomotives' of the mid-1970s never set off because the surplus countries declined to accept the inflation that deficit countries wished to force on them.

In thinking about coordination, a number of important distinctions should be noted (see the Group of Thirty, 1988). The first is *absolute vs. relative* coordination. Agreement to coordinate policies so that, say, global inflation is zero is absolute coordination; coordination to minimise inflation differentials across countries or to maintain a particular set of exchange rates is of the relative kind – it is as feasible at 10 per cent world inflation as at 0 per cent. Absolute coordination in a flexible exchange rate regime is sometimes referred to as defining a 'nominal anchor'.

The second distinction is between *global and regional* coordination. The latter is, say, coordination between members of the European Monetary System (see below): absolute regional coordination would concern the maintenance of the dollar: ECU exchange rate.

The third, and most crucial, distinction is between *rules and discretionary* (*ad hoc*) coordination. The latter occurs when sovereign countries meet and agree some course of action without any formal framework. Examples include the attempts to institute 'locomotive' growth in the mid-1970s, and the Plaza and Louvre Agreements about the dollar exchange rate in 1985 and 1987, respectively. Discretionary approaches to coordination have several attractions: they are flexible and so can address the issues of the moment; they are efficient in the sense that they are activated only when necessary; they respect sovereignty, because no country is obliged to act if it wishes not to, and so they seem likely to achieve only Pareto efficient outcomes;[1] and no effort is spent drawing up rules. The major disadvantage of discretionary coordination is that it is not automatic; agreement may take much effort to achieve; the nature of agreement is not known beforehand and, indeed, agreement may not be possible or even attempted. Rules, on the other hand, avoid these pitfalls, and can, therefore, instil much greater confidence in private agents' minds that coordination of a particular type will occur. Such confidence can be important in shaping private behaviour (e.g. the formation of inflationary expectations), but it comes at the cost of inflexibility and a loss of sovereignty.

The most obvious and important example of rules-based coordination is the fixed exchange rate system. The gold standard, whereby currencies were convertible into gold at a fixed rate, induced both absolute and relative coordination. The Bretton Woods system, whereby currencies were convertible into dollars at fixed rates, involved relative coordination. (These systems are discussed in Chapter 28 below.)

A further distinction concerns the *focus* of coordination: is it defined on outcomes or instruments? Fixed exchange rates fall in the former class: ruling out certain policies (e.g. import controls), countries are free to maintain their exchange rate how they will. Instrument-based coordination, on the other hand, sets acceptable levels for policy instruments, e.g. money supply growth or tariffs, without being directly concerned with their effects.

In reaching coordination agreements the parties have to agree fairly well over both the ultimate objective of coordination and the ways in which it can be achieved. Discussions between developing and industrial countries over commodity price agreements frequently fail because the former see the object as redistribution while the latter define it as stabilisation. Similarly, macro-economic coordination between the USA and the EC over the 1980s often foundered on disagreements about how the economy works and hence on what instruments to control.

A brief history of coordination

As noted above, the Bretton Woods system represented a strong form of policy coordination through its requirement to maintain exchange rates. When it collapsed in 1971, however, the widespread belief in the insulating properties of flexible exchange rates and the differences between countries' responses to the major macro-economic disturbances – the inflation of 1972–4 and the oil price rises – effectively precluded international coordination. The middle of the 1970s saw attempts to coordinate fiscal stances to restore growth, but the laboriously constructed agreement signed at the Bonn summit meeting of 1978 achieved relatively little. Renewed inflation over 1978–80 followed by vicious deflation in the early 1980s again drove coordination out of fashion. The USA's growing budget and current account deficit caused a sharp appreciation of the dollar but no willingness on the USA's part to undertake a cure.

The dollar peaked in 1985 and around the same time the US authorities decided that a depreciation was required in order to reduce the pressure for protection from their hard-pressed tradables sector. The result was the so-called Plaza Agreement of September 1985 which 'talked' the dollar down but entailed no new policy commitments, least of all about the US fiscal stance. The dollar fell almost continuously from September 1985, until by February 1987 it had returned to around its fundamental level. This was taken as a signal for a further effort at coordination. The Louvre Accord sought to persuade the markets that no further movement was required. In this it failed (the dollar kept on falling), but not because its objective was impossible. The problem was that governments neither declared firm limits beyond which they would prevent exchange rate fluctuations, nor made significant alterations in their policy stances. As a result the fundamental exchange rate continued to drift downwards, and the markets had no plausible reason to alter their behaviour.

Behind the failure of the Accord to attack fundamentals lay a strong disagreement about the nature of the problem and the measures necessary to address it. This clearly undermined its long-term credibility. On the other hand, the mere signing of the Accord showed that coordination was back in fashion, and since early 1987 central bank intervention on the foreign exchange markets has been more closely coordinated, which has probably curtailed day-to-day exchange rate fluctuations. It has also been argued (Group of Thirty, 1988) that the Louvre Accord lays the necessary foundations for future coordinations.

Plans for coordination

The shape of future policy coordination is very difficult to predict. Further *ad hoc* coordination seems quite likely, but we are probably a long way from formalising it into a set of rules. None the less economists have been busy designing systems and this section concludes with two such plans. Both propose rules for avoiding the gross exchange rate misalignments which, they say, have plagued the period of floating and distorted investment and growth. Their differences concern not ends, but means.

McKinnon

McKinnon's (1988) plan calls for rigidly fixed exchange rates with very small bands of variation, coupled with agreement by the three major players (USA, Japan and Germany) to control their money supplies to keep a price index for world tradable goods constant – the nominal anchor. The fixed rates would be maintained largely by monetary policy (interest rates), while the operation of PPP (in which McKinnon believes) would keep real exchange rates broadly constant. Given the resulting stable monetary policy, the current account would then have to be managed through fiscal policy. If short-term intervention was required, McKinnon argues that *all* countries (including the USA) should undertake *un*sterilised intervention in order that something like the specie flow mechanism should aid adjustment. If the fixed exchange rates were credible, McKinnon argues, speculation would not be worthwhile, for no changes would be anticipated; hence, given credibility, the world economy would proceed on a stable equilibrium path.

The McKinnon plan is very demanding. Governments surrender much autonomy: both fiscal and monetary policy have internationallly defined goals, and deviations from the appropriate stances would have to be corrected quickly in view of the rigid and narrow exchange rate bands. The scheme's rigidity would make adjustment to real shocks painful if nominal prices and wages were at all inflexible. One might also worry about the scheme's viability, for PPP is far from perfect and real exchange rates do affect current balances. Thus external shocks could place great strains on fiscal policy as governments fought to cure current account imbalances. Finally, it is not clear how the initial set of exchange rates would be chosen. The scheme might unkindly be held to have parallels with Britain's return to the gold standard in 1925, which many people, including Keynes, thought responsible for a decade of depression.

Williamson

Williamson (1987, 1988) offers a much less rigorous regime than McKinnon. He would allow very large exchange rate bands, ±10 per cent, and periodic realignments of central parities. Exchange rate parities would be set by reference to econometrically estimated fundamental equilibrium exchange rates (FEERs), and would be defended by monetary policy, intervention and 'talk'. International agreement would also fix targets for the growth of each country's nominal income; these would be determined as the sum of the country's expected real growth, a factor related to the previous year's inflation (to allow gradual disinflation) and a policy component to expand or contract demand cyclically. Williamson argues that the $2n$ targets – income for each of n countries plus $(n-1)$ exchange rates plus a nominal anchor – would be achieved by the following assignment: average nominal interest rates to world inflation – the nominal anchor; $(n-1)$ interest rate differentials to exchange rates; and n fiscal policies to national income objectives.

The Williamson model is Keynesian in approach (note the objective for fiscal policy) and politically pragmatic. It places very few constraints on governments' abilities to manipulate exchange rates or vary policy instruments. Williamson argues that exchange rate flexibility is necessary to cope with shocks and speculative pressures, and that the wide intervention bands allow the parity rate to be changed without the actual rate changing. He argues that policy flexibility is necessary to accommodate political pressures, and that the use of FEERs reflects the inadequacies of PPP as an exchange rate goal.

Two major criticisms beset Williamson's plan. First, determining FEERs would be almost impossible: economists do not agree on the model to use, let alone on the values of the crucial economic parameters; thus the whole exercise would become political rather than technical. Second, the plan imposes almost no constraints on official behaviour and thus would hardly differ from the present system. Since 1973 there have been few instances where exchange rates have differed by more than 10 per cent from reasonable FEERs, especially when one recognises the scope for discretion in fixing the latter. Thus while (unlike McKinnon's) Williamson's model is feasible, it is not obvious that it is useful.

26.3   OPTIMUM CURRENCY AREAS

Section 26.1 presented several strong arguments in favour of flexible exchange rates, and many economists are entirely convinced by them. However, if it is desirable for the UK to have a flexible exchange rate, why should Wales not have one, or Birmingham, or even Edgbaston within Birmingham? Evidently, as areas become smaller there is an increasing presumption that they will tie their currency to a larger neighbour's, and this section asks why. For simplicity's sake we compare a system of entirely flexible rates with a system of immutably fixed rates – indeed, rates fixed so firmly that the two currencies involved merge into one.

Adjustment   Suppose that Birmingham runs a deficit with the rest of the UK. Under flexible rates this would cause a depreciation of the Birmingham pound. As a small area, depreciation would not alter Birmingham's terms of trade, but rather alter the relative prices of tradable and non-tradable goods; for adjustment, resources would have to flow from non-tradables to tradable industries, and real absorption would have to decrease. But the non-traded sector in Birmingham is very small – in small-enough areas even hair-cuts become tradable (!) – and so, to generate a sufficient transfer of resources, a large exchange rate change would be necessary. However, if nearly all consumption is imported and if wages are fixed in local currency, exchange rate changes involve large switches in real income; such fluctuations are generally deemed undesirable, and more often than not they are resisted. The money illusion that allows depreciation to cut real incomes in larger economies is less likely to apply in smaller ones where the real income consequences are so obvious. Thus, unless the terms of trade can be changed, attempting to cure Birmingham's deficit by depreciation is likely to result in excessive fluctuations in prices and/or incomes.

Now contrast this with adjustment when the Birmingham pound is immutably tied to sterling, as in reality. To finance the deficit, private wealth has to be transferred from Birmingham to the rest of the UK. Since both areas use the same currency this is relatively straightforward and is, in fact, effected largely automatically through the banking system. When Birmingham residents' wealth has declined sufficiently, they will reduce their absorption. If Birmingham had an official institution responsible for managing the deficit, it would also probably help this process along with some expenditure-reducing policy. The more open the economy, the more effective (or less costly) is expenditure reduction as a method of curing deficits: the higher the marginal propensity to import, the smaller the proportion of any expenditure cut that

387

falls on domestic production and causes contraction via the multipler. In the limit, a completely open economy (all consumption imported) needs to reduce consumption by only £1 for every £1 fall in imports required.

The decline in local absorption will reduce demand for such non-tradable output as there is. This may reduce wages, improving competitiveness in tradables and hence taking the economy back to equilibrium. As we have observed many times already, if local currency prices are flexible there is no balance of payments problem. More likely, however, is that falling demand leads to unemployment. This will be alleviated, as will the deficit, if the unemployed move from Birmingham to the rest of the UK. To be sure, this is expensive both personally (financial and psychic costs) and socially (under-used infrastructure), but it is probably preferable to persistent unemployment. Hence another aid to adjustment under fixed rates is factor mobility.

Factor mobility cannot avoid all the consequences of depression in regions linked by a common currency, and within most countries a further element of adjustment (or finance) is introduced by government transfers. These may take the form of labour and investment subsidies to the regions or straightforward income transfer through unemployment benefits, etc. Hence, the willingness to transfer income between regions of a currency area is also an important part of its working.

Factor mobility and income transfers are particularly important when external shocks affect members of a currency union asymmetrically. For example, a rise in the price of oil would put upward pressure on sterling and downward pressure on the Deutschmark. Monetary union, however, would prevent such changes from occurring and thus push adjustment into the internal goods and factor markets, where it may be more painful.

To conclude, the exchange rate is less effective as an equilibrating mechanism in very open economies, whereas expenditure reduction is more effective. Adjustment under fixed rates is eased by the willingness to swap private assets, to move factors and to transfer income between different parts of a currency union. This suggests that regions/countries that have considerable mutual trade, compatible private and political institutions, and close cultural connections could benefit from forming a currency area.

Monetary factors

So far we have considered the real factors determining optimum currency areas, but there are also monetary considerations. First, the price fluctuations produced by exchange flexibility in a small, very open economy may reduce the 'moneyness' of the currency. Money is used as a store of value and a unit of deferred payment; to be effective it must be relatively stable in terms of the transactions it is used for. Flexible rates basically fix the price level in terms of domestic output, whereas fixed rates fix it in terms of foreign goods. Now, if consumers buy mostly foreign goods they will prefer to hold an asset and do their accounting in terms of foreign goods. Hence, domestic money will be unattractive unless there is a fixed exchange rate. In the limit, an attempt to float the rate may be greeted by a refusal to hold domestic currency and its displacement in internal circulation by the currency of a major supplier of imports. This argument is due to McKinnon (1963).

Clearly this argument is stronger the more open the economy. Clearly, also, it presupposes that the shocks that alter the exchange rate are domestic. If the foreign price level is fluctuating, a flexible rate may insulate domestic currency holdings by opposing movements, and render them more stable (in terms of foreign goods) than foreign currency. This counter had led many economists to reject McKinnon's (1963) argument, but it is not invincible. While fixing your currency to an unstable partner currency may not ensure stability, it is likely that, provided that that partner is a large and diversified economy, fluctuations in its price level will be smaller and less variable than the shocks that can hit a small economy. This is especially so if the latter's production is concentrated on a few primary products.

A second monetary factor concerns monetary policy. Obviously with only one money there can be only one monetary policy. Each region therefore loses the ability to pursue its own monetary policy and thus to choose its own rate of inflation. For a small open economy with no money illusion this hardly matters in the long run, because monetary policy does not affect the real side of the economy. However, if, for example, inflation causes short-term adjustment problems, joining an inflationary monetary union may be harmful. Similarly, if there is a short-run inflation–output trade-off or if there are public finance motives for favouring inflation, a forced reduction in inflation may be undesirable. Unanticipated inflation is an effective mode of taxation – it is universal, requires no legislation, and is cheap to collect. Moreover, if financial regulation forces residents to hold domestic money – e.g. through high bank reserve ratios and the prohibition on holding foreign currency – residents cannot fully avoid the inflation tax even if they see it coming. Giavazzi (1989) showed that the southern members of the EC raise revenues of between 3 and 5 per cent of GDP through inflationary finance.

Monetary union does not directly constrain member countries' fiscal autonomy, but it does oblige governments to finance their deficits through bond issues rather than by printing money. As their debts rise, however, governments will have to pay higher rates of interest and ultimately may be unable to borrow at all, so monetary union does ultimately impose a degree of fiscal responsibility. For example, the City of New York became technically bankrupt in this fashion in 1982, and had to undertake a fierce fiscal retrenchment.

In loose monetary unions where countries keep their separate currencies but are committed to particular rates of exchange, independent monetary policy is conceivable, but not very useful. If the union allows fairly free capital movement, any money created in one partner will rapidly flow out (as in Chapter 21), and the government will merely lose reserves as it fights to maintain the exchange rate.

This brings us to a third monetary factor. If two countries have substantial mutual trade and they elect to keep a fixed rate between their currencies, this rate has to be defended. If they then combined to have a single currency they would save on reserves. They may even find that the combined currency would be sufficiently attractive to third countries that they could earn seignorage by issuing it abroad. (Seignorage is the gain from creating and 'selling' money for goods – see Chapter 28.) In view of the comments above, the gains from reducing official reserves are likely to be small, although we have no estimate of the private gains from the corresponding reduction in private transaction balances.

Political factors

A currency area allows its participants to benefit from fixed exchange rates (certainty, etc.) on their mutual trade. Against this must be set the loss of exchange rate and monetary policies as means of adjustment. These costs will be minimised if there is agreement between the participants on the conduct and use of monetary policy and on making inter-partner transfers of incomes.

On the former, for example, a tight money regime and an inflation-prone regime (e.g. West Germany and the UK in the 1970s) are unlikely to make happy bed-fellows. Of course, if there are intentions of political integration, or even just of further economic integration involving tax harmonisation, etc., these will be very much more easily achieved with currency union than without. Indeed, once one gets above some relatively small minimum size it seems that the main advantages of currency union are political. This minimum size is contentious but almost certainly most European countries exceed it.

Some evidence

Table 26.2 shows the exchange rate regimes ruling in early 1988. The majority of countries pegged their rates to major partners' currencies or some basket of currencies for the reasons we have discussed. Many of the others had only limited flexibility, and indeed only eighteen admitted to independent floating. Despite this, however, 80 per cent of world trade takes place across a floating exchange rate (Emminger, 1979); for instance, Panamanian imports from Ireland cross a floating rate because the dollar, to which Panama pegs, floats against the European currency unit to which Ireland (loosely) pegs.

Table 26.2 Exchange rate arrangements, 31 March 1988[a]

			Examples
Pegged currencies:			
to	US dollar	39	Barbados, Zambia
	French franc	14	Congo, Mali
	Other single currency	5	Bhutan (Indian rupee), Swaziland (South African rand)
	SDR	7	Jordan, Seychelles
	Other basket	29	Algeria, Sweden
Restricted flexibility:			
EMS		8	France, West Germany
Relating to US dollar		4	Qatar, Saudi Arabia
Flexible currencies:			
Independent		18	UK,[b] USA
Adjusted by indicator		5	Brazil, Portugal
Other managed		21	Argentina, India

Note:
[a] Excludes Democratic Kampuchea.
[b] The UK joined the European Monetary System's Exchange Rate Mechanism in October 1990.
Source: IMF, *International Financial Statistics*, July 1988.

26.4 THE EUROPEAN MONETARY SYSTEM

Monetary unions stretch from immutable combinations (e.g. the states in the USA), through dominant/follower relationships (as the UK and Ireland were before 1979 when the Irish broke loose from sterling), to very loose associations seeking some exchange rate stability (the EC's European Monetary System). We conclude by briefly examining this weakest of approaches.

Monetary integration has always been one of the main aims of the European Community's 'integrationists'. The customs union was merely the first step towards further integration of laws, taxes, institutions and money.

Indeed, it was planned in the Werner Report of 1971 that monetary integration should occur hand-in-hand with othe other measures and be complete by 1980. The first step was the so-called 'snake in the tunnel' of 1972–8. This restricted movements between European currencies to tighter limits (the snake) than those permitted by the Smithsonian Agreement against other currencies (the tunnel). This was more wishful thinking than anything else. No steps were taken to bring the stability about and, in particular, each country had complete freedom over its own macro-ecomomic policy. The more independent nations rapidly dropped out – notably France and Britain – and the snake really became a Deutschmark area, comprising West Germany and her smaller dependent neighbours.

Monetary integration dropped quietly from view with all the other problems of the mid-1970s, but it was revived in 1979 as the European Monetary System (EMS) – an altogether more robust creature than the snake.

The Exchange Rate Mechanism

The EMS is built around the European Currency Unit (ECU), which is a composite of EC members' currencies backed by deposits of those currencies and of gold or dollars. The Exchange Rate Mechanism (ERM) defines members' exchange rate parities in terms of ECU and allows bands of 2.25 per cent (± 6 per cent for Spain and Britain) before defensive action is obligatory. The parities are subject to periodic renegotiation and had been changed twelve times by January 1990. The ERM contains a *divergence indicator*: when a currency diverges from its rates against other currencies by an average of more than three-quarters of the permitted amount, there is a presumption that corrective action will be taken. This comprises both intervention and, ultimately, policy change, and so the ERM should be seen as a means of regional policy coordination. The divergence indicators appears to place some discipline on governments, for most seek earnestly to avoid triggering it. The complexity of its formula was designed to ensure a degree of symmetry, whereby if most currencies fell against the Deutschmark, as they were expected to, it was the Germans who had to adjust. In fact during the 1980s sentiment was so anti-inflationary that most member governments welcomed the fixed parity with the non-inflating Deutschmark and generally adopted deflationary policy stances to avoid falling significantly below it. Nevertheless, the symmetry of adjustment may revive as an issue in future.

The EMS makes provision for a degree of reserve-pooling – to back the ECU – and for automatic short- and medium-term lending between members to help fund intervention. The EMS itself does not require the free circulation of capital, and indeed Italy, France and certain smaller members still operated capital controls at the beginning of 1990. The process of completing the internal market by 1992, however, does envisage the abolition of these controls and so will increase the degree of monetary integration. All EC members are members of the ERM except Portugal.

The effects of the ERM

The case for the ERM is basically the case for an optimum currency area – it trades the attractions of exchange rate stability against the loss of monetary autonomy. Of course, as presently constituted the EMS involves not very much of either, but the issue has aroused considerable interest and controversy, not least in the UK, which joined only in October 1990. We shall not rehearse the arguments for UK membership here, but rather examine the effects that ERM has had on its existing members.

It is sometimes argued that the EMS is a Deutschmark zone – that

391

Germany, the largest and least inflation-prone member, defines its own monetary policy and all others fall into line. There is obviously much to this argument, and indeed the link to the DM has been one of the attractions of ERM membership – it enhances other government's anti-inflationary reputations. The evidence, however, is that interactions flow both ways. De Grauwe (1989) and Cohen and Wyplosz (1989) showed that the German money supply and interest rates are influenced by, as well as influence, those variables in France, Italy and the Netherlands. Hence the EMS represents a pooling of monetary sovereignty not a surrender, which probably bodes well for its continuation and enhancement.

Another common argument is that commitment to the ERM reduces the interest rate premium in member countries by enhancing governments' anti-inflationary credibility. This obviously depends on what reputation the government had before entry and the probabilities that it will maintain its ERM parity. None the less, Cohen and Wyplosz (1989) suggested that French interest rate premia had not fallen since France joined the EMU in 1979, despite the large fall in inflation since then. They did find, however, that whereas prior to 1979 the premium responded to monetary factors, subsequently it depended only on fiscal effects. They attributed this to increased faith in the French monetary authorities, linked with a perception that the ERM parities are vulnerable to the asymmetric effects of real shocks which are reflected in differences between French and German fiscal stances.

A particular asymmetric shock which does strain the ERM is the substitutability between dollars and Deutschmark in world asset portfolios. Sentiment about the dollar is thus transmitted to the Deutschmark but not to the other ERM currrencies (which are not widely held abroad), and thus strains ERM parities (see Artis and Taylor, 1988).

Artis and Taylor (1988) conducted some sophisticated statistical tests on European exchange rates since 1979. They showed that ERM currencies have been less subject to major misalignment than the dollar or sterling; that ERM currencies have experienced declining volatility since 1979, while other currencies have become more volatile; that declining ERM exchange rate volatility has not been accompanied by increased interest rate volatility; that exchange rate predictability has improved for ERM currencies, but worsened for the dollar; and that, although the ERM has not prevented divergencies in members' competitiveness, it has reduced the rate of divergence and so made it more easily manageable. Overall, therefore, so far as exchange rate stability is concerned, the ERM of the EMS has been fairly successful.

The future

Several attempts have been made to move the EC beyond the loose exchange rate union of the EMS towards fuller monetary integration. They have foundered on the rocks of sovereignty and a feeling that the exchange rate is a necessary tool of economic policy. The latest attempt is part of the major process of 'completing the European internal market' (see section 14.3). It is argued that, as other frictions to intra-EC trade are reduced, variable exchange rates become an increasingly serious barrier to further economic integration: they create uncertainty and waste resources (*The Economist* calculated that, starting with £100 and converting it successively into each EC currency and back to sterling at retail rates, one would be left with only £48). It is also held that tighter monetary integration would ease other aspects of harmonisation – e.g. on taxes, banking regulations, and energy pricing.

In 1989, Jacques Delors, the President of the European Commission,

presented a report laying out a three-stage process towards full monetary
union. It was vigorously resisted by the UK authorities and certainly caused
some concern elsewhere. The issue became a touchstone of European good
faith, however, and eventually Mrs Thatcher conceded that the UK would go
along with stage I, which entailed UK accession to the ERM. Initially she
argued that this could occur only when UK inflation was approaching EC
levels and when all controls on intra-EC capital flows had been abolished, but
in the event Britain scrambled in with inflation at over 10 per cent per annum
in October 1990. The timing was largely political, hingeing, not least, around
a need to get interest rates down in time for a 1991 or early 1992 general
election. Stage I also entailed greater policy consultation and coordination,
and the establishment of an intergovernmental conference to agree the path for
stages II and III. This conference is scheduled for December 1990, but no
other timetable has been agreed for these stages, which are intended by Delors
to end in the creation of a single European currency, central bank and
monetary authority.

As with the EMS, the tools necessary to analyse the economics of full
monetary union have been described earlier in this chapter. Full integration is
not economically necessary – most EC members are perfectly viable currency
areas on their own – but it would offer some resource savings and would be an
obvious complement to economic and political unification.

FURTHER READING

Argy (1981) provides detail on the material in this chapter, *Tower and Willett* (1976)
adds further analysis on the transmission of disturbances, while the arguments over
speculation are summarised by *Stern* (1973) and *Lindert and Kindleberger* (1982). On
flexible exchange rates *Artus and Young* (1979) and *Dornbusch and Frankel* (1989) are
excellent, while *Yeager* (1976) gives a detailed account of the traditional case, along
with historical case studies. Classic references on this subject are *Friedman* (1953) and
Meade (1955). Further details of recent empirical evidence should be sought in the text
references. Statistical data and commentary on recent events may be found in
International Monetary Fund, *Annual Reports*.

Policy coordination is treated accessibly in the *Group of Thirty* (1988) and *Kenen*
(1988), and on a technical level by *Buiter and Marston* (1985) and *Bryant et al.* (1989).
Both *Williamson* and *McKinnon* should be read in the original.

The literature on monetary integration and currency unions is huge. *Corden* (1972b)
gives a balanced view, and *McKinnon* (1963) is a thought-provoking article. More
thorough and analytical is *Tower and Willett* (1976). Many of the theoretical arguments
are also dealt with in the literature on the EMS. The references in the text are
important and may be supplemented by *CEPR* (1989) and *Portes* (1989), which are
quite accessible, and two books *Giavazzi, Micossi and Miller* (1988) and *de Cecco and
Giovannini* (1989).

KEY CONCEPTS

insulation	stabilising speculation
exchange rate uncertainty	inflationary basis
rules vs. discretion	openness and policy effectiveness
Exchange Rate Mechanism	divergence indicator
asymmetric shocks	anti-inflationary credibility

QUESTIONS FOR REVIEW

26.1 For what shocks do flexible exchange rates offer greater insulation than fixed rates? Consider both income and price insulation.

26.2 What are the difficulties of establishing whether exchange rate uncertainty adversely affects world trade?

26.3 Contrast McKinnon's and Williamson's proposals for stabilising exchange rates.

26.4 In what ways might the loss of monetary autonomy harm an economy?

26.5 Does the ERM effectively constrain members' monetary and fiscal policies?

NOTES

1 Pareto efficient for the parities represented in the negotiations, that is.

Part III

27 The Demand for International Reserves

Part II of this book dealt with macro-economic aspects of the open economy from the viewpoint of a single country. We considered the deteminants of a country's balance of payments and/or exchange rate largely taking the rest of the world as given. We now examine the interactions of countries within the world economic system. The real aspects of this question are parallel to the single country results and were dealt with in Part II (e.g. the international multiplier, the transmission of fluctuations), but the monetary aspects raise new problems. These are the subject of this part of the book.

This chapter introduces the idea of the world as a single economic system. It considers what constitutes 'world money' and then discusses the public and private demand for that money. The next chapter considers the supply of world money. It takes a historical approach, describing the evolution of the world economy from a gold standard through to the present 'non-system' of payments. In the course of the history, however, the theoretical issues become perfectly plain. Chapter 29 deals briefly with private international capital markets, while Chapter 30 considers developing countries and the debt crisis.

27.1 WORLD MONEY AND THE WORLD ECONOMIC SYSTEM

Until we discover life elsewhere in the universe, the world is just a large, closed economy. All goods sold must be bought, and all paper money must be 'inside' money, i.e. must constitute a liability somewhere within the system as well as an asset.

The $(n - 1)$ problem Since it is closed, the world economy as a whole cannot run a balance of payments deficit or surplus. Thus one country's surplus *must* contribute to another's deficit and the sum of all countries' net payments positions *must* be zero. Therefore, if, out of n countries in the world, $(n - 1)$ have determined their balances of payments, that of the nth is determined automatically as minus the sum of the others. In other words, if all countries have payments objectives, the adding-up constraint implies that, except by chance, only $(n - 1)$ of them can possibly be successful. Exactly the same constraint applies to countries' stocks of assets. If the stock of assets is fixed and if $(n - 1)$ countries have determined their holdings, the nth is willy-nilly left with the remainder. Similarly, with exchange rates: the exchange rate is the price of one money relative to another, but with n currencies there can be only $(n - 1)$ independent relative prices.

There are several ways of coping with the '$(n - 1)$ problem'. At one extreme, one large country could agree to forgo any objectives over its balance of payments, assets and exchange rate, pursuing a policy of 'benign neglect'. (The nth country must be large enough to bear the surplus or deficit demanded by the other $(n - 1)$, however. For example, Chad's benign neglect would not grant OECD complete freedom over its balance of payments objectives.) At the other extreme, all countries could surrender a little sovereignty

397

by agreeing to operate according to some rule that ensured that their objectives were consistent with adding-up. In Chapter 28 we shall see how different institutional frameworks imply different solutions to this problem.

'World money' and international reserves

We are often told 'money is what money does'; although not very precise, this captures satisfactorily the notion that whatever fulfils the functions of money *is* money. Hence, anything that is used as a means of payment and a store of value in the international sphere might be called 'world money'. Official balances of 'world money' are known as international reserves.

Precise definitions vary, but most economists would treat holdings of the following as world money: gold, convertible foreign currencies, reserve positions with the International Monetary Fund (IMF), and holdings of Special Drawing Rights (SDRs). The latter pair are available only to official holders, and private gold is normally treated as non-money, but there are both private and official holdings of convertible currency.

The criteria that make these assets attractive to central bankers as reserves are their liquidity and their unconditional availability. Gold is always readily saleable. Foreign currencies are termed convertible if they may be exchanged on demand for gold or other currencies at their issuing central bank. We include officially held sight deposits, time deposits and short-term bills (e.g. Treasury bills) as part of reserves. IMF positions refer to potential borrowings from the IMF that are available automatically to the central bank. Beyond these, other credit is available but only on increasingly tight conditions. SDRs are basically an international paper money issued by the IMF. (Valued initially at SDR 1 = $1.00, their value in June 1990 was SDR 1 = $1.30; see section 28.1 for further discussion of SDRs.)

Figure 27.1(A) illustrates the growth of these four components of world reserves between 1950 and 1987. Gold is valued throughout at SDR35 per ounce. This was its value to central banks until 1974, but since then banks have been able to sell gold on the private market at substantially higher prices. At these prices, gold reserves amounted to SDR524 billion at end-1980, which would have more than doubled world reserves; however, any attempt to sell any but the slightest proportion of official gold would cause the price to collapse, so this is not a realistic estimate of world liquidity.

The figure illustrates the gradually increasing role of foreign currencies until 1970, after which holdings increased rapidly. IMF positions and SDRs contributed only slightly to world liquidity, while gold switched from a predominant to a subsidiary role.

Fierce though the increase in reserves over the 1970s appears, it did not keep pace with the value of world trade (see Figure 27.1(B)). In 1950, world reserves were around 80 per cent of annual imports, but this fell to 50 per cent in 1960, 31 per cent by 1970 and around 20 per cent by the 1980s. This reflects great improvements in the efficiency with which international money was used and also the declining role of official reserves under floating exchange rates. Private balances of foreign currencies compensated partially, growing significantly relative to trade over this period, although measurement difficulties preclude their precise quantification.

Table 27.1 gives the composition of foreign currency reserves. The dollar is completely dominant, with the Deutschmark gradually replacing sterling as the second currency. The period from 1950 to 1970 (for which comparable data are not available) was characterised by the rise of the dollar and the decline of sterling as reserve currencies. In 1950, sterling reserves were twice

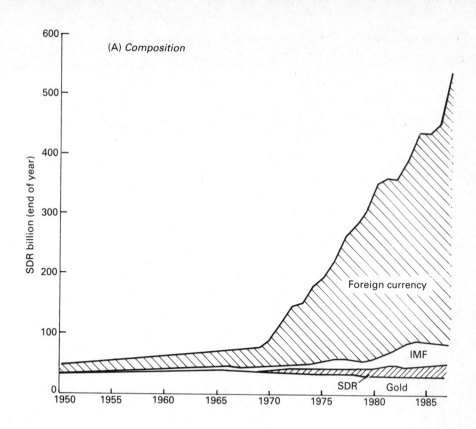

(A) *Composition*

SDR billion (end of year)

Foreign currency

IMF

SDR   Gold

%

(B) *Adequacy (ratio of reserves to annual world trade)*

Figure 27.1 World reserves, 1950–87. (A) Composition. (B) Adequacy

Source: International Monetary Fund, *International Financial Statistics* Yearbooks 1981 and 1987 and February 1989.

the size of dollar reserves, although restrictions on their use imposed by the British government limited their liquidity.

Supply and demand   A single small country's reserves are determined in level and composition by its demand for reserves. For the world as a whole, however, reserves are mainly determined by supply. In the short term, the supply of gold is virtually

399

Table 27.1 The share of national currencies in world foreign exchange reserves[a] (%, end of year)

	1970	1973	1976	1979	1982	1986
US dollar	83.3	76.1	76.5	73.2	70.7	66.6
Pound sterling	8.8	5.6	1.8	2.0	2.5	2.4
Deutschmark	2.1	7.1	9.0	12.5	12.7	14.8
French franc	0.1	1.1	1.6	1.3	1.3	1.3
Swiss franc		1.4	2.3	2.5	2.8	1.6
Dutch guilder	5.7	0.5	0.9	1.1	1.1	1.0
Japanese yen		0.1	2.0	3.6	4.7	6.9

Notes:
[a] All currencies measured in SDR; ignoring translation of certain EMS reserves into ECUs.
Sources: International Monetary Fund, *Annual Report* (1983, 1984, 1987); Heller and Knight (1978) for 1970.

fixed in quantity, and until recently in price. So too are IMF positions and SDR quotas. With foreign currencies, demands holds some sway if central banks will exchange their currency for other non-currency assets; then selling, say, sterling to the Bank of England for gold reduces the amount of sterling circulating (the supply of sterling), but merely redistributes holdings of gold. At present, however, one currency is convertible on demand only into another currency. Hence, the total level of currency reserves is basically supply determined, although there is scope for shifting currencies between official and private portfolios. By and large, however, the figures in Figure 27.1 reflect supply.

Foreign exchange reserves are created (supplied) by deficits on the basic balance of payments of reserve-currency countries. The USA may finance a deficit by either running down her assets (reserves) or increasing her liabilities. The latter involves creating a deposit of dollars in the name of the foreign country at a US bank. The foreign country now has more money and the world's supply of dollars has increased. Countries demanding more reserves acquire them by running a balance of payments surplus. The surfeit of currency they so earn is merely added to the reserves in some form or another. Clearly there is another face of the $(n-1)$ problem here. Unless new money is created, net acquisitions of reserve assets must sum to zero.

27.2 THE DEMAND FOR RESERVES

This section examines the overall demand for international reserves by national monetary authorities, ignoring, for now, their composition and the role of privately held assets. Nations hold stocks of money for basically the same reason as do individuals – to allow different time patterns for income and expenditure. If income and expenditure had to balance at each point of time, transactions would degenerate virtually to barter, but with money one can buy on one day and sell on another. This is especially necessary if there is uncertainty about the value or timing of transactions.

Finance and adjustment

Imagine an economy in perfect equilibrium that suddenly loses part of its income. In the absence of reserves it has immediately to undertake some form of adjustment. Either it must cut expenditure to balance income or it must run down its net worth by selling assets. The latter may be straightforward, but if its assets are illiquid the necessary rush may be expensive in terms of the price earned. The former – as we saw above – is likely to be painful. Now, if the loss of income were known to be permanent there would be a case for immediate adjustment – although economists frequently hold that adjustment costs rise with the speed as well as the extent of adjustment. If, on the other hand, the income loss were temporary there would be little case at all for adjustment, so long as it cost anything. An adequate stock of reserves allows a country to avoid real adjustment in response to temporary shocks, and to postpone – and thereby ease – adjustment in the case of permanent changes. Postponement could be overdone, but some will nearly always be desirable.

Clearly then, one determinant of the demand for reserves is the cost of adjusting to external shocks. If this is small, few reserves are necessary, whereas if it is large, more are. For real adjustment, three broad alternatives exist: one can cure a balance of payments deficit by deflation, depreciation or trade controls. For a given deficit, the costs of deflation decline relatively as the marginal propensity to import rises, because more of any expenditure reduction falls directly on imports. The costs of depreciation and trade controls probably increase with openness, because a proportionately greater switch of resources out of non-tradables production is necessary and this involves a greater shift in the terms of trade.

Which of the adjustment mechanisms is dominant – especially for relatively small and short-lived fluctuations – depends mainly on the exchange rate regime in operation. Fixed rates emphasise expenditure reduction, and floating rates expenditure switching visa depreciation. We might, therefore, expect that *ceteris paribus*, fixed rates would entail less open economies requiring relatively more reserves, while floating would entail the contrary. In fact the evidence is very mixed, probably because researchers tend to use the average rather than the marginal propensity to import to measure openness, and this could influence reserves through another channel (see p. 402 below). Heller and Khan (1978), however, found that a positive relationship between reserves and openness for industrial economies (see equation 27.1 below) became negative when data from the period of floating were included in estimation, and that floating reduced the mean level of reserves. Edwards (1983) found that, for those developing countries which traditionally kept exchange rates fixed over long periods of time, the demand for reserves increased with openness and the extent of economic shocks, while for those which were more willing to use depreciation as an adjustment tool neither openness nor variability significantly affected demand.

As well as possibly affecting the relationship between reserve demand and openness, the exchange rate regime has a more direct effect. Under fixed rates the authorities are obliged to intervene in the market to finance temporary disequilibria, and adjustment is discretionary. Under floating rates no obligation exists – indeed intervention may be prohibited – and adjustment is at least partly automatic. Hence reserve demands are likely to fall with the advent of floating. Heller and Khan confirmed this for developed countries since 1973, but not for non-oil developing countries. This is because the latter still pegged to the major currencies, a job made considerably more difficult by the disturbances of the 1970s.

Reserves are also influenced by the speed of adjustment: faster adjustment entails fewer reserves. We know of no empirical work on this question, however, although Clark (1970) has evidence of the equally plausible reverse relationship that countries with higher reserves can (and do) adjust more slowly.

401

Disturbances Our discussion of adjustment obviously presupposed the existence of economic shocks requiring finance or adjustment. If some finance is desirable, the amount depends on the size of the shock. Countries facing large and frequent payments shocks require greater reserves than more stable ones.

There are two sorts of shocks to consider. The first are temporary, reversible imbalances, i.e. the variability of net demands for foreign currency. Such random shocks are clear candidates for finance rather than adjustment, and the object must be to hold sufficient reserves to minimise the possibility of running out and having to adjust. Provided that the shocks really are random, the reserves will receive on average as many injections (via surpluses) as withdrawals; but this does not preclude there being a series of consecutive withdrawals. Clearly, the more reserves one has, the lower the probability of such a series exhausting them but, by the same token, the lower the probability of actually having to use the last unit of reserves. Hence the expected benefit of the marginal unit of reserves falls as the reserves grow, so, provided there is a cost to reserve holding, reserves will not be indefinitely high.

Just as obvious is that, if one can tolerate a given probability of reserve exhaustion, the greater the size of these random shocks, the greater the level of reserves required. There are many methods of measuring the variability of the balance of payments, but all confirm the theoretical result. Very roughly, a 10 per cent increase in the standard error of the shocks increases reserve holding by about 5–8 per cent under fixed rates and slightly less under floating rates.

A more contentious sort of shock is the permanent shock – for instance, the loss of an export market. Here adjustment is inevitable and finance can be justified only in terms of reducing costs by allowing a longer adjustment period. Again, the more likely and the larger these shocks, the greater the level of reserves required. It is obviously difficult to gauge the expected exposure to such shocks, but one measure of a country's vulnerability to foreign shocks is its average propensity to import. This argument predicts a positive relationship between reserves and the average propensity and clearly conflicts with the negative relationship predicted by the costs of adjustment argument. In general, the positive effect appears to dominate empirically.

Reserves and trade An important motive for individual cash holdings is the transactions motive – holding money to spend. Similarly with nations: the greater the volume of international trade, the greater the amount of reserves necessary to finance it. There are, however, economies of scale in cash use and so reserves appear to grow less than proportionately with trade. Estimates vary, but, for every 10 per cent rise in a country's imports, reserve demand probably increases by between 5–8 per cent.

Wealth Foreign exchange reserves are part of a nation's net wealth. They are unlikely to be inferior assets (in the technical sense) and so we would expect them to rise with wealth. This appears to be so empirically (Hipple, 1974), although the close relationship between wealth and imports makes it difficult to distinguish this and the previous explanation for reserve holdings.

Expectations In the face of a permanent shock, the decision to phase adjustment over several years represents an inter-temporal decision. Reserves expended this year are not available next year, and by using them now the government is implicitly stating that they are worth more now than later. This clearly involves a judgement about the future – i.e. expectations. These are impossible

402

to measure, but governments expecting large future adverse shocks or increased future variability are likely to hold higher reserves.

Alternatives to reserves

Owned reserves are often referred to as *unconditional liquidity*: there are no constraints at all on their use. A partial alternative is *conditional liquidity*, by which is meant certain borrowing from the IMF and other banks. It is conditional because increased resources are available only in return for promises, and eventually action, to implement an approved programme of recovery. These (often onerous) conditions and the time required for their negotiation clearly differentiate potential borrowing from reserves, but there is probably some degree of substitutability between them. Hence, a world system guaranteeing such borrowing would reduce reserve demand.

It is also possible to borrow from private capital markets. Increasingly over the 1970s, developing countries borrowed on the Euro-markets, and, as we saw in Chapter 17, the UK also visited this fount of beneficence, although mainly through the intermediation of various public non-monetary authorities. Although such finance is usually more expensive and of shorter maturity than official borrowing, at least for relatively small amounts it is unconditional. Sometimes, however, private bankers will not lend until the borrower has borrowed also from the IMF. This reflects not a lack of funds but a wish to impose some conditionality, and also the belief that countries with the 'IMF seal of approval' will not default on their other debts. Chapter 30 below explores these issues in more detail.

One final alternative for 'banker' countries is to issue their own debt. Instead of running down assets, they finance deficits by increasing liabilities; that is, they issue their own currency abroad in return for goods and assets. The USA and the UK have done this extensively in the past – hence the world's large holdings of their currencies. The rest of the world is willing to hold such currency so long as it pays a suitable rate of interest, is not likely to be devalued, and can obviously be converted into other currencies on demand. While this continues, such *liability settlement* is a profitable way of running an economy, since it permits deficits in excess of reserve (asset) levels. The problem arises, however, when there is doubt over the desirability of the currency; then the holders rush to convert it into other currencies and the reserves are instantly under pressure. Hence, issuing debt is an alternative to reserve holding, but, as liabilities rise, reserves must partly follow in order to maintain confidence in that debt.

The cost of reserves

All the previous points concern the benefits of reserve holding. There is also an opportunity cost, however, because wealth held as reserves cannot be invested in real capital or long-term financial assets. Most foreign currency reserves are, in fact, short-term deposits, so the opportunity cost is the difference between long and short-term rates of return. One should make some allowance for the higher variability of capital values on currency compared with real capital – especially since the latter may be invested at home – and also for the fact that gold earns no interest, but, all told, the opportunity costs of reserve holding are probably rather small.

The optimal reserve holding

Combining all the above arguments would allow us to calculate an optimal level of reserves for any country. It would, of course, be such that the marginal benefit of the last unit of reserves just equalled the marginal cost. No empirical work has successfully identified all the effects mentioned, but fairly typical equations are Heller and Khan's (1978), for the fixed-rate period 1964–72. For industrial countries (excluding the USA – the principal banker),

$$\log R_t = 1.38 + 0.44 \log m_t + 0.68 \log M_t + 0.66 \log \sigma_t \qquad (27.1)$$

and, for developing countries,

$$\log R_t = -1.86 - 0.61 \log m_t + 1.33 \log M_t + 0.33 \log \sigma_t \qquad (27.2)$$

where R_t is reserves in quarter t, M_t imports, m_t the average propensity to import and σ_t a measure of variability. The coefficients are all statistically significant at 5 per cent, except for those on m_t in (27.1) and σ_t in (27.2), and they largely accord with the arguments above.

Heller and Khan also estimated the speed with which actual reserves were adjusted towards their optimal level. Industrial countries took up about 30 per cent of the discrepancy per year and developing countries about 90 per cent. This probably indicates that poorer countries hold much smaller reserves relative to their shocks than rich countries. Bilson and Frenkel (1979), with very different methodology, found both groups adjusted by about 50 per cent of the discrepancy per year. Both sets of estimates imply rapid adjustment, which suggests that the equations above do represent some kind of desired long-run position.

The arguments so far refer to countries' own assessments of their reserve needs. The interrelationships of the world economy, however, also give countries interests in each other's holdings. For example, a country may have strong views about the appropriate level of reserves for countries owing it money; alternatively, if country A fears country B's deflation, it will wish B to have high reserves to induce a more relaxed domestic policy. The net effect of such interests is uncertain, but they illustrate that (a) the optimum level of world reserves is not necessarily just the sum of countries' own individually optimal levels, and (b) the optimum level of world reserves has a cosmopolitan as well as a nationalistic dimension.

27.3   PRIVATE vs. PUBLIC RESERVES

Exactly analogous arguments apply to private holdings of foreign exchange as to official reserves. Precise quantification is impossible, not least because it is so difficult to disentangle the figures for the Euro-dollar market (see Chapter 29), but it is beyond dispute that private balances have expanded rapidly, especially since the demise of the Bretton Woods system in 1971. The following figures probably define the minimum levels of private foreign exchange reserves. The Bank of England (*Quarterly Economic Review*, December 1982, 'Monetary Statistics') estimated that in March 1982 British private sector non-bank foreign currency deposits were £14.3b. (of which £11b. were with UK banks), compared with official reserves of £12b. in foreign currency and £7b. in other assets. Deutsche Bundesbank (*Monthly Review*, January 1989) estimated private balances at DM 64.6b. compared with reserves of DM 120.2b. at end 1987.

Since the incentives to hold cash are largely private, one may ask why official reserves are required at all. There are several explanations, of differing degrees of conviction. First, it is argued that pooling individual balances into a single holding yields economies of scale. This is certainly true, because balances grow less than proportionately with transactions and there will also be some offsetting between one person's surplus and another's deficit. Hence the combined reserves could be substantially smaller than the sum of the individual balances they replaced. However, if the economies of scale are so significant we would expect pooling to occur even in the absence of the monetary authority.

The second explanation of official reserves is as a 'war chest'. This amounts to their being no more than the government's own precautionary cash balance.

Third, reserves are the necessary concomitant of a fixed exchange rate. The government can maintain the exchange rate between narrow bands only if it has a means of buying and selling foreign exchange at the intervention prices. This is possible only if it owns some. Under a perfectly floating rate, intervention would not occur, so this explanation would not suffice. In the present managed float, reserves are required for management, and although they may not be used extensively their existence lends authority to the government's view of the correct exchange rate. Clearly there is no private substitute for this role for the reserves.

The fourth reason concerns power. One of the principal activities (if not functions) of governments is to define and enforce legal tender. This accords the government considerable power, and allows it to earn the seignorage from issuing its own money. If its money were displaced by foreign currency it would lose that income. It is, therefore, in the government's interest to prevent residents from using foreign money internally and this is most easily achieved by preventing them from holding it. Residents are required to deposit their foreign exchange at the central bank in return for domestic currency, and can withdraw it only in order to make transactions abroad. These deposits constitute the foreign exchange reserves.

Many countries still have exchange regulations of this kind, and often they are supplemented by restrictions on the purposes and extent to which withdrawals are possible. This is one way of trying to suppress an incipient deficit, and was pursued with increasing vigour in the UK until the mid-1970s. In 1979 exchange control was abolished. This presumably transferred some currency holdings from official to private hands. At the same time, however, by increasing the ease with which money could be shifted out of the country, it increased the size of the possible shocks that could hit the British economy. This increased the government's desire for reserves, thus offsetting the first effect.

27.4 THE COMPOSITION OF RESERVES

Section 27.2 discussed the costs and benefits of holding reserves in total. We now consider the composition of the reserves, and, since we argue that countries choose their portfolios to maximise the benefit from the reserves at least cost, we consider much the same factors as before.

Transactions costs and vehicle currencies

Suppose the only purpose of reserves were to finance the purchase of imports, and that the value and country of origin of all imports were known at the outset of the year. By matching the currencies in its reserves to the pattern of forthcoming transactions a country could (a) avoid the transactions costs of converting one currency to another during the year and (b) avoid any uncertainty about how many imports it could buy. Similarly, suppose the

405

reserves comprised only the receipts from the previous year's exports: they would then comprise the currencies of a country's trading partners. Obviously the real world is more complex than this, but we do nevertheless find a strong relationship between the geographical composition of a country's trade and the currency composition of its reserves.

This argument suggests that countries will hold many currencies in their reserves. In fact, though, there are economies from concentrating on relatively few. First, concentration allows smaller overall holdings: since reserves rise less than proportionately with the trade they finance, covering several countries' trade with the same currency will save reserves. For example, suppose we have 10 units of trade with countries A and B, and that to finance them we need 5 units of each currency in the reserves. If both were financed in A-currency, however, we would need no B-currency, but, from our estimate in section 27.2, doubling the trade denominated in A-currency would raise holdings of it by only 50–80 per cent. Hence, rather than hold 10 units of reserves we could manage with 7½–9 units.

Second, holding currency involves the risk of exchange rate changes. If we hold fewer currencies, there are fewer for which information and forecasts are required. Third, and closely related, the markets for the rarer currencies are rather thin – there are few buyers and sellers. Thus, their prices fluctuate more and any attempt to sell a significant amount could easily produce a price fall. Consequently, holding these rare currencies is riskier than holding others, and transacting in them more expensive. It was for this reason, we argued in Chapter 22, that trade between small economies is frequently conducted in a third or vehicle currency. The arguments about holding currencies reinforce this tendency towards a few world currencies. Furthermore, given the link between currency holding and trade, and given that a currency is in a sense backed up by the output of the country where it is legal tender, the vehicle currencies will tend to be those of the major economies. Such factors obviously contribute to the dominance of the dollar and the Deutschmark in reserve portfolios.

Financing trade is not the only function of foreign exchange reserves. They are also used to settle debts and support the exchange rate. Indeed, given the rough balance beween export and import flows with particular trading partners and the fact that most trade is financed privately, one might consider this the principal role for exchange reserves. Hence, the dominant transaction may well be exchange market intervention, and so the reserves will be heavily biased towards the intervention currency. For floating currencies this is not formally specified, but most countries intervene mainly in dollars. Where one currency is pegged to another, however, intervention almost always occurs in the latter. Holding reserves primarily in this currency not only avoids transaction costs but also avoids any uncertainty about the value of the reserves in terms of intervention.

Risk and return

Whatever their function, reserves represent a stock of wealth. We therefore expect that, consistent with fulfilling their purpose, they would be subject to the normal portfolio considerations of risk and return. For any degree of risk, reserve managers would maximise returns, and for any level of returns they would minimise risk. As we saw in section 22.1, the expected return from holding a short-term asset is the rate of interest plus the annual rate of change of capital value. The risks arise almost entirely from the latter – the value of foreign currencies (the exchange rate) cannot be perfectly foreseen. Central banks are probably more constrained in their portfolio management than private speculators, but nevertheless within limits these factors will be relevant.

The first prediction of this view is that, *ceteris paribus*, countries will prefer reserve assets paying higher rates of interest. The second is that very volatile currencies (or those expected to be volatile) will not be popular – another argument against holding 'minor' currencies. Third, currencies whose values are negatively correlated will be chosen together, because the risk of losses on one is offset by the chance of gains on the other. Fourth, and most important, if exchange rate changes are anticipated, central banks as well as private speculators will seek to move out of the currency whose depreciation is expected.

Constraints on reserve composition

If all countries were suddenly to try to liquidate their holdings of dollars, the price of dollars would slump and a huge crisis would emerge as the value of assets was slashed. To avoid this, some constraint on the freedom to swap between reserve assets is required. This is usually exercised by the major countries of the world by means of political agreement. It involves them in some loss of wealth or return, but is deemed to be worthwhile for the sake of preserving the system. Smaller countries, whose asset holdings are relatively small, are not normally party to such agreements. Political arrangements have in the past benefited both the UK and USA by stemming sales of their currencies, and at present operate to limit EMS countries from holding too many reserves of each other's currencies.

The evidence

Evidence on the determinants of the composition of reserves is hard to find because central banks are so coy about revealing their portfolios.

Chrystal (1977) examined total (private and official) holdings of dollars, sterling, Deutschmarks and francs over the 1960s by looking at the issuing countries' liabilities. He found strong evidence that holdings were influenced by rates of interest, some evidence that expected depreciation reduced holdings, and some evidence that currency holdings were related to the extent of the issuer's international trade.

Heller and Knight (1978) concentrated only on official reserves, looking at seventy-seven countries' reserves over 1973–6. They, too, found a link between currency holdings and trade, but they also found that countries pegging to sterling and the franc held more of those currencies than other countries. The shares of sterling and francs rose by 25 and 74 percentage points respectively.

Using the same data, Ben-Bassat (1980) calculated an optimal basket of reserve currencies for both industrial and developing countries. Optimality encompassed the return and risks of the reserve portfolio in terms of their purchasing power over countries' normal baskets of imports. For example, countries importing half from the USA and half from Britain were assumed to seek maximum returns in terms of a composite basket comprising half dollars and half sterling. He found that for developing countries the actual and predicted reserve portfolios matched fairly closely, whereas for industrial countries they did not. This suggests that portfolio considerations and international trade patterns do determine reserve composition, but that industrial countries have additional objectives and face constraints on the adjustment of their portfolios. Ben-Bassat also showed that, to reduce risk, portfolios should include substantial shares of both dollars and the European currencies since their fluctuations tend to be in opposite directions.

407

Dooley, Lizondo and Mathieson (1989) found quite strong evidence that transactions (trade, debt and intervention) are the dominant determinants of reserve composition. They attributed such dominance to the fact that these factors determine gross reserves directly, while portfolio influences affect net assets and may thus be addressed by altering lending and/or holdings of non-reserve assets. Like Ben-Basset they also found it easier to explain developing than industrial countries' reserves.

Gold and SDRs

Until relatively recently, gold was the predominant reserve asset. It is still held widely today, despite paying no rate of interest and despite no country being on a gold standard. Its sole attraction is the belief that it is a more secure store of value than paper currencies – that, while paper currencies depend on governments for their value, gold's almost universal acceptance guarantees its value under all circumstances. Gold is demanded particularly at times of general uncertainty – such as political crises – when the whole future of paper money may be questioned, but also as a refuge for funds removed from the dollar when the latter is under pressure. Its security is seen as compensation for its lack of earning power.

Over the 1960s, gold became very attractive relative to sterling and the dollar and it was only strong political pressure to avoid a crisis that prevented the wholesale conversion of currency balances (see section 28.3 below). One consequence of this incipient 'gold rush' was the introduction of a new reserve asset – the Special Drawing Right (SDR). Its value was defined in terms of gold, and guaranteed by the IMF, but by also paying a small rate of interest it was intended to be more attractive than gold. Since then it has been redefined in terms of a basket of five major currencies in both its value and its rate of interest. With its different characteristics from gold and currency, the SDR clearly has some role in diversified reserve portfolios. Indeed, Murphy and von Furstenberg (1981) found some evidence that non-oil developing countries find it a preferable asset to foreign exchange.

FURTHER READING

General references on the international monetary system include *Williamson* (1973), *Grubel* (1977), *Crockett* (1976), *McKinnon* (1979) and *Argy* (1981). Detailed accounts of the system in practice are available in International Monetary Fund, *Annual Reports*.

On the specific issues of this chapter, *Grubel* (1977) provides a more detailed introduction, and *Williamson* (1973) an excellent survey of older work. *Hipple* (1974) gives a thorough discussion of modelling the demand for reserves, while *Frenkel* (1978b), *Heller and Khan* (1978), and *Edwards* (1983, 1984) provide more recent estimates. *Clark* (1970) provides a formal model linking reserves to income, disturbances and the speed of adjustment, while *Bahmani-Oskooee* (1985) provides a comprehensive survey of the area.

The composition of currency reserves is well discussed in *Heller and Knight* (1978), *Ben-Bassat* (1980), and *Dooley et al.* (1989), while *Williamson* (1973) considers the gold/SDR/currency decision.

KEY CONCEPTS

$(n - 1)$ problem	benign neglect
unconditional liquidity	finance vs. adjustment
speed of adjustment	optimal reserve holdings
private balances	vehicle currency

QUESTIONS FOR REVIEW

27.1 Explain why the level and composition of Niger's international reserves reflects demand while those of the world's reserves reflect supply.

27.2 Why did sterling decline so much as a world reserve asset over the period 1950–80?

27.3 Does a regime of floating exchange rates economise on world reserves?

27.4 Many commentators find a positive relationship between countries' openness and their preferred level of reserves. What factors could explain this? Does it matter how openness is defined in these circumstances?

28 The Supply of International Money

This chapter analyses the supply of international money. We take a historical approach, starting with the gold standard of the late nineteenth century, at which time gold was the only source of international money. The gold standard was suspended during the First World War. It was reintroduced in the mid-1920s, but in the changed circumstances it proved inadequate and had collapsed by 1931, giving rise to a period of monetary disorder until 1939.

After the Second World War, the Western world, led by the USA, instituted a gold exchange standard where both gold and foreign exchange were used as world monies. We examine the negotiations over the new system culminating in the Bretton Woods Treaty establishing the International Monetary Fund. We then trace the history of the IMF and the Bretton Woods system until the latter's collapse in 1971. Over its lifetime the gold exchange standard was revealed to have critical shortcomings in both theory and practice; these are examined in section 28.3.

The collapse of the Bretton Woods system heralded a turbulent period for international monetary arrangements. The huge injections of liquidity in 1970–2 (see Figure 27.1) and the generally expansionary domestic policies caused unprecedented levels of inflation. These were exacerbated by a quadrupling of the price of oil, which placed great adjustment and financing burdens on all countries. The recycling of OPEC surpluses to the oil-deficit countries further raised liquidity and inflation in general, while different speeds of adjustment led to large divergencies between national inflation rates. Fixed exchange rates could not survive in these conditions, so the major currencies floated, and, as we have seen, fluctuated considerably.

Meanwhile, the IMF tried to adapt itself to the new circumstances. Unable to institute a fixed exchange rate system, it established rules for floating currencies and sought to smooth adjustment paths by providing new sources of finance. Most of these were aimed at developing countries, and provided extended credit for restructuring. In 1978–9 the price of oil rose again, plunging the world into another bout of inflation and stagnation, which in turn induced further policy change and institutional development. Section 28.4 looks at the creation and operation of Special Drawing Rights, while section 28.5 considers international monetary arrangements since 1971. The principal feature of the 1980s – the debt crisis – is postponed until Chapter 30.

28.1 GOLD AND THE GOLD STANDARD

The oldest form of money – international or domestic – is gold. Its attributes as money are well known: limited supply, durability, portability and, above all, almost universal acceptability. For centuries, gold tokens or coins circulated freely without regard to national boundaries – monarchs stamped the coins of their realms more to indicate purity than to claim jurisdiction. Provided none tried to debase or adulterate his coinage, the only difficulty of accepting another's coins was the inconvenience of different denominations. Gradually coins were supplemented by paper notes that indicated a claim over

410

gold, but provided repayment was guaranteed such notes were 'as good as gold'. At least this was so domestically, because the notes could easily be presented to their issuer, but holding foreign notes was less secure because the costs of presenting them were higher.

Hence, notes were not so mobile internationally, and it became normal to convert from one country's paper to another as one crossed national borders. Such conversion was quite simple, however, since each currency was fixed in terms of gold; with a little more expense one could always change pounds into gold and gold into francs, say, instead of converting pounds directly into francs. Thus the pound–franc exchange rate was determined by the currencies' gold values. In time, gold coinage became less popular but paper monies remained convertible into gold bars and so the principles of the system remained the same.

To illustrate the workings of the gold standard, consider a world economy of two countries operating with the circulation of gold coins but no other money. Starting from perfect equilibrium, suppose country A's aggregate demand rises. If output is fixed, A's absorption exceeds its income and it runs a balance of payments deficit. The excess expenditure is effected by buying goods in B *for gold coin*. Hence A's money supply decreases and B's rises. This could have any of three consequences: A's prices might fall, its income (and hence absorption) might fall, or its interest rate might rise. The first two cure the current account deficit, while the last finances it by an inflow of capital from abroad. Obviously B, whose money supply has risen, experiences the opposite effects.

The story of the previous paragraph is basically Hume's *Specie Flow Mechanism*.[1] It provides the intellectual basis of the monetary approach to the balance of payments: deficits lead to an outflow of cash and hence automatically correct themselves. It also schematically describes the operation of the gold standard. Provided that countries (i) maintain rigid links between their currencies and gold, (ii) allow gold to flow freely between themselves, and (iii) allow their money supplies to rise and fall with their stocks of gold, the same story applies whether gold or paper circulates domestically and whether or not domestic paper is fully or just partially backed by gold.

Observe in all this how the world supply of money – the stock of gold – is assumed exogenous. Applying the same principles to the world economy as to national economies, if gold supplies rise relative to demands, prices and/or incomes will rise and interest rates fall, whereas if they fall, prices and incomes will tend to fall or interest rates rise. Indeed, to the extent that the money supply affects anything, that thing will be beyond policy control under a gold standard.

Some history

Between 1880 and 1914 the industrialised world operated a gold standard satisfying the three conditions enumerated above. Although output was rather stagnant over the first part of the period (known as the Great Depression, until the 1930s outdid it), the gold standard was judged a success on the basis of this experience. It is not clear, however, that it was really tested. Economic and political conditions were very stable over the period, supplies of monetary gold were expanding, hence avoiding any deflationary strain, and economic management was very conservative. Furthermore, Britain – the centre of the world's financial system at that time – was persistently in current account surplus, so her only policy problem was to tailor her foreign investment to match her surplus. This was done via the interest rate and it obviated the

411

need for more fundamental domestic policy changes. Such behaviour suited Britain and the other industrialised countries well, but it caused some instability in the Empire and other 'peripheral' developing countries, as their sources of short-term finance periodically dried up as Britain cut back.

The second period of gold standard management was quite different. Gold convertibility was suspended during the First World War. The economic devastation prevented its immediate restoration in 1918, but its eventual re-establishment became an object of policy. Unfortunately, it was also held in Britain that it should be restored at pre-war exchange rates, and this involved undoing much of the inflation of the war and post-war boom. The result was vigorous deflation over the early 1920s, with prices and wages falling by up to 50 per cent. Even so, when Churchill restored convertibility in 1925 at the pre-war parity, Britain was still very uncompetitive, and the slump predicted by Keynes (1925) duly occurred. Most other major countries had followed Britain back to gold by 1927, but within five years the whole system had collapsed.

Several reasons have been advanced for this collapse. First, it has been suggested that wages and prices had become less flexible since the war and hence that adjustment laid more burden on incomes. This is not incontrovertible, but doubtless the General Strike of 1926 and its aftermath worsened the political environment for wage flexibility. Second, gold was unevenly distributed: France and the USA had excessive stocks, while the UK had too little. Coupled with the UK's relative economic weakening since 1913, her overvalued exchange rate and the amount of sterling held abroad, there was constant doubt about the ability of Britain to honour her debts in gold. The result was greater speculation than had previously been experienced and persistently tight domestic policies.

Third, whereas before 1913 Britain had acted as world banker, essentially running the gold standard via her interest rate policy, by 1926 she no longer had the economic power or the monopoly of financial expertise required to do so. Both New York and Paris challenged London's supremacy, but neither France nor the USA recognised any international role; besides, even if they had, it is not clear that three 'central banks' is a viable alternative to one. In other words, no country was willing or able to police the international monetary system for the common good.

Fourth, economic and political conditions were harsher than before the war. The reparations paid by Germany to her former enemies still distorted current account positions and contaminated the political atmosphere against cooperation. Business cycles were less synchronised and hence greater payments adjustment was necessary. There was a huge financial crisis in 1929–30, which destroyed both wealth and employment. This, in particular, turned countries inwards and heralded a decade of competitive depreciations and protectionism 'beggar-my-neighbour' policies. The cycles and the slump may, of course, have been caused by the inappropriate restoration of the gold standard – it is impossible to be sure; either way they certainly highlighted the system's shortcomings.

28.2 THE GOLD EXCHANGE STANDARD – THE PLANS

The gold exchange standard had its hey-day from the end of the Second World War to around 1970. Thus it has become closely identified with the

Bretton Woods system, but in fact the latter is just one (important) practical application of the general principle. We start by briefly examining the principle and then go on to look at the plans and practice of Bretton Woods.

Gold and paper money

Gold may have desirable properties as money, but its overriding disadvantage is its cost. Real resources are expended in mining and refining it, only for it eventually to be locked away underground again in the vaults of central banks. If a cheaper but equally desirable money could be found, these resources could be used productively. This is where paper currencies come in. We have already noted that paper replaced gold in circulation, and we know from domestic banking theory that paper need not be wholly backed by gold to be acceptable. So long as one is sure that if one tried to encash one's own paper it would be honoured, paper is acceptable; and, so long as everyone feels like that, the issuing central bank knows that not all its paper will be presented at once. Hence, it need hold gold only up to some fraction of its paper liabilities.

The gold exchange standard proper exists when central banks around the world are willing to hold some other central bank's paper (debt) instead of gold. Hence, paper not only circulates but enters asset portfolios. Obviously the system is unstable if every central bank issues its own debt, which is held by other central banks who then issue more of their own paper on the strength of it; but such circularity would quickly be recognised and rejected. However, if only one or two central banks with substantial reserves of gold issue paper, then the system may prove workable. Before 1913, some sterling was held in world reserves, backed by the gold and economic strength of the UK. After the First World War, exchange holdings rose at first, but after the instabilities reported above fell substantially. After the Second World War, the role of exchange reserves was recognised and formalised by the Bretton Woods agreement, and the US dollar became the principal asset.

Seignorage

If paper money saves resources, who benefits? This depends on the interest rate paid on paper money. In the domestic economy no interest is paid on cash and the whole of the benefit of creating cash accrues to the central bank, which lends it to the government. Assuming it costs virtually nothing to create paper money, the government benefits by £1 of resources for every £1 created. If that £1 were invested, it would earn, say i per cent per annum, so £i/100 represents the income flow generated by creating £1. If the government had to pay i per cent per annum on its created cash in order to persuade people to hold it, the government would gain nothing and the resources saved by using paper money would accrue entirely to the holders.

In the international monetary system, governments do pay interest on their debts, but, because these debts are short term and highly liquid, it is usually below the long-run rate of return on investment. If the latter is i_L per cent, but the government pays i per cent on its money debts, resources of i per cent accrue to the holders of foreign currencies and $(i_L - i)$ per cent to the issuers. Of course, both i_L and i must be measured as real rates of interest.

Seignorage is the term for the real resources that accrue to the issuers of money. In the case just discussed, this would be the present value of the income flow £$(i_L - i)$/100 per annum for every £1 issued.

Bretton Woods

Over the 1930s the USA maintained her traditional isolationist view of the world, but the Second World War made her realise that if the non-communist

413

world was to be successful and prosperous she would have to play a much more prominent part. Consequently, even as early as 1941 officials in both the UK and the USA were thinking about the shape of the post-war economy. There was general agreement that the flexible exchange rates and beggar-my-neighbour policies of the inter-war period were unacceptable. Beyond that, however, Britain, facing huge debts but still having an Empire, sought a liberal financial system offering plenty of credit but was less concerned with free trade. The USA, on the other hand, as the potential provider of credit, favoured a tighter financial system but more open trade and capital movements.

Britain's aspirations were embodied in the 'Keynes Plan'. This suggested the establishment of a world 'clearing union' at which all countries would hold accounts. These accounts would be denominated in a common unit – the 'bancor' – in terms of which exchange rates would be fixed; international imbalances would be settled by shifting bancor from one country's account to another. The extent to which balances could deviate from zero was to be limited, with both surplus and deficit (positive and negative balance) countries being obliged to adjust. Prominent among the methods of adjustment would be exchange rate changes. The limits on the bancor balances defined the extent of international credit, and this would be determined by the union to alleviate business cycles and promote world expansion.

The Keynes Plan was not a gold exchange system. Gold was not necessary and in general countries would not hold dollars or sterling; all reserves would be in terms of the new international paper money – the bancor. The world's money supply would be under international control, and used as a policy instrument. In fact, the system would closely mirror the domestic banking system, with a controllable paper money and a single central bank (the clearing union) at which separate money-issuing commercial banks (the national central banks) would hold deposits.

The actual outcome of the Bretton Woods Conference owed more to the American 'White plan' than to the Keynes Plan – reflecting the USA's greater power and influence. In terms of international monetary economics the most important institution established was the International Monetary Fund, which opened its doors in 1946 with thirty-five member countries. Each member was accorded a quota that determined its rights, obligations and voting powers. The quotas roughly reflected the members' levels of GNP and international trade, and voting was virtually in proportion to quotas.

Each country subscribed to the Fund reserves equal to its quota, 25 per cent in gold and 75 per cent in its own currency. In return it could borrow foreign currencies from the Fund up to 100 per cent of its quota. The first slice, or *tranche*, of 25 per cent corresponded to the country's gold subscription, and was available automatically. The remaining three tranches of 25 per cent, however, were to be available only on increasingly firm commitments to pursue policies to cure the balance of payments deficit. They also involved increasing service and interest charges. There were certain obligations on surplus countries, but since these were never implemented in practice, the Bretton Woods system placed all the adjustment burden on the borrowing, deficit countries.

The whole of the country's quota cannot be counted in its reserves because it is not available unconditionally (see Chapter 27), but, clearly, the larger the quotas the greater world liquidity. (Note (a) to Table 28.1 defines precisely

414

what is counted as reserves.) The IMF started with modest quotas ($8.8b. compared with Keynes' suggested $25b.); its articles made no recommendation for future growth, although quotas were to be reviewed at least every five years. It was generally expected that gold would provide for increases in world liquidity, and any general increase in quotas required an 80 per cent majority of votes.

The 80 per cent rule applied to virtually all issues at the Fund and it ensured that either the USA or the major European powers acting together could veto any change. This recognised the politics of the international economy, and, although frustrating to other nations, it has at least allowed the establishment and continuance of the institution itself. The Seventh General Review of Quotas in 1977 reduced the USA's share of votes below 20 per cent for the first time, and she agreed to accept the Review only on condition that the majority required for most proposals be raised from 80 per cent to 85 per cent, thus maintaining her veto.

Table 28.1 The IMF and world liquidity (SDR billion, end of year)

	1946	1960	1965	1970	1975	1980	1981	1984	1987
Total reserves	n.a.	60.0	71.2	93.3	194.4	354.5	376.1	440.2	538.9
of which: IMF reserve positions[a]	n.a.	3.6	5.4	7.7	12.6	16.8	21.3	41.6	31.5
borrowing from IMF[b]	n.a.	0.4	3.0	3.2	7.4	8.5	13.4	34.9	29.2
IMF statistics:									
Quotas[c]	7.5	14.7	16.0	28.4	29.2	59.6	60.7	90.0	90.0
SDRs allocations	—	—	—	3.4	9.3	17.4	21.4	21.4	21.4
Other facilities[d]	—	0.4	6.7	5.8	11.5	25.0	34.1	52.8	47.5
Shares of IMF quotas[e] (per cent):									
USA	36.8	28.1	25.8	23.6	22.9	21.2	20.8	19.9	19.9
UK	17.4	13.3	12.2	9.9	9.6	7.4	7.2	6.9	6.9
France	7.0	5.4	4.9	5.3	5.1	4.8	4.7	5.0	5.0
West Germany	—	5.4	4.9	5.6	5.5	5.4	5.3	6.0	6.0
Japan	—	3.4	3.1	4.2	4.1	4.2	4.1	4.7	4.7
Saudi Arabia	—	0.04	0.05	0.05	0.05	1.7	3.5	3.6	3.6

Notes:
[a] That part of IMF quotas and 'regular' borrowing counted as reserves. For any country this comprises its *gold* or *reserve tranche* (the first, unconditional, 25 per cent of its quota) plus total IMF lendings of its currency.
[b] Under all schemes except SDR facilities.
[c] Excluding quota of $1.3b. allocated to the USSR but never taken up.
[d] Total IMF resources under General Arrangement to Borrow, Oil Facility, Supplementary Financing Facility, Stand-by, Extended Arrangements and Medium Term Borrowing.
[e] A country's votes are calculated as 250 plus 1 for each SDR 100,000 of its quota.
Sources: 1960–87 – International Monetary Fund, *International Financial Statistics* (1982), Supplement No. 3 and February 1988; 1946 – IMF, *Report of the First Meeting of the Board of Governors.*

Table 28.1 traces the evolution of quotas, showing, first, the slightness of their contribution to world liquidity and, second, the relative roles of the various economies. Through time, the USA and the UK have lost influence, in keeping with their declining relative economic importance, displaced first by other industrial countries and latterly by OPEC countries such as Saudi Arabia. It also shows how various other IMF facilities have grown up in response to specific shortages of funds or adjustment.

The other major obligation of members of the IMF was to maintain their exchange rates within 1 per cent of their declared parity levels by means of intervention. Parities were declared relative to gold, but only the USA traded currency for gold; all other countries traded national currency for dollars. Hence, as the intervention and *de facto* peg currency, the dollar was given a unique and pivotal role. Although exchange rates were not immutably fixed, they were to be changed only in circumstances of '*fundamental disequilibrium*', and even then only after consultation or permission from the IMF. Fundamental disequilibrium was never defined, but it is clear that the Americans envisaged much less exchange rate flexibility than did Keynes.

The IMF also imposed obligations on members to abolish exchange controls on current account transactions (but not on capital transactions), to abolish any discrimination between trading partners, and to consult regularly. Over the years, several of the IMF's provisions have changed (see below), but the consultation has persisted and for this alone the IMF has been significant.

28.3 BRETTON WOODS IN PRACTICE

As we have seen, the Bretton Woods agreement favoured the more conservative American approach of a credit fund over Keynes' more radical banking solution. We now see how it performed, distinguishing three broad periods of history.

A quiet start, 1947–58

For the first eleven years of its life the IMF contributed little to world economic performance. Initially, its quotas were small and it interpreted conditionality very fiercely. (In fact, at first even gold tranche borrowings were conditional.) It also refused to make loans for reconstruction, which were seen as the province of the International Bank for Reconstruction and Development (IBRD) – the World Bank. As a result there was little borrowing.

This did not reflect a surplus of reserves, however. After the war the European economies were very weak and greatly in debt to the much stronger USA, who ran huge current account surpluses. Indeed, the problem was beyond the IMF and so, in order to stimulate European development, the USA instituted a system of unilateral transfers in 1948 – Marshall Aid. Over four years, nearly $12b. was transferred, plus $2b. in loans. This greatly helped the European economies and allowed the USA huge influence in the evolution of economic institutions in Europe and the world.

After 1950, however, the position changed. The exchange rate realignments in 1949 and the recovery programme stimulated European growth and competitiveness, and with increasing military expenditure abroad the US balance of payments slipped into deficit. This was financed by borrowing: the European nations took ownership of dollar deposits in New York. This was the start of the gold exchange standard, and it suited everybody well at first. The USA had no need to adjust and earned seignorage, spending it abroad in the form of her current deficit; meanwhile the emerging European economies were able to increase their low level of reserves. The dollars were fully backed and so commanded complete confidence: the ratio of US gold to official short-term dollar liabilities was 7.3 in 1949 and 2.1 in 1958. Over most of this period 'the' international monetary problem was generally perceived to be a shortage of liquidity (reserves), although by 1958 it was beginning to shift from being primarily a shortage of any liquidity towards being a shortage of liquidity with which to back the increasing stock of dollar debts.

The IMF became of age in 1956 when as a result of the Suez débâcle the UK was obliged to seek assistance, followed by France in 1957 and 1958.[2] Also in 1958, negotiations nearly doubled the effective level of quotas, and introduced convertibility for the major currencies. By this time, however, serious problems were beginning to emerge.

Most important was the issue of *confidence*. The US dollar had, in the absence of alternatives, become a major reserve asset abroad, but the USA's persistent and growing deficits were pushing the world to a state where dollar liabilities exceeded gold reserves. (This occurred in 1958 for total short-term liabilities and in 1964 for official short-term liabilities.) This raised questions of whether the fixed price of dollars in terms of gold could be maintained. Provided central banks abroad did not *all* try to cash in their dollars for gold, marginal transactions could be made at the official price, but a run on the dollar would be catastrophic. The European countries and Japan faced an impossible dilemma. Either they accepted poorly backed dollars or they cashed their dollars in, and, by causing a devaluation, brought about the very situation they feared. To quote a popular American saying, 'if a man owes you a thousand dollars, that's bad news for him; if he owes you a million dollars, that's bad news for you'.

The only solution to this was to substitute 'faith' for gold as the backing for the dollars, and accept them merely as paper money whose worth depended entirely on being able to pass them on to someone else. The problem then was how to stop the USA from just creating more dollars by running further deficits and absorbing real resources (the seignorage) in return. If one could not exercise the financial rein, only political agreement remained; that was of only limited effectiveness, however.

A closely related problem concerned *liquidity*. Since dollars were the only way of increasing world reserves, if the rest of the world desired more reserves it had to allow the USA's deficit, pay the seignorage and suffer the confidence problem that that entailed. If, on the other hand, it insisted on the USA curing her deficit, the resulting deflation or devaluation of the dollar would curtail the demand for its own goods and would be compounded by a shortage of international liquidity. Triffin (1960) first identified the horns of this dilemma: the world could cure its liquidity problem at the expense of its confidence problem, or its confidence problem at the expense of its liquidity problem – but not both together.

A further, and possibly more basic, problem was that of *adjustment*. Even for non-banker countries, exchange rate changes in either direction had not proved popular. Appreciation hit the tradables sector while depreciation hit incomes. Hence, balance of payments disequilibria tended to be persistent and foreign considerations dominated domestic policy-making. For example, the West Germans persistently ran surpluses and accumulated reserves (hence withdrawing liquidity from countries that required it), and faced almost constant pressure to inflate domestically to cure the situation. Conversely, the UK showed persistent deficits, reserve crises and domestic deflation.

For the banker country the situation was even more difficult. Few people favoured devaluing the dollar in terms of gold (see below), so there was nothing the USA could do about her exchange rate. Her trading partners, however, were constantly urging deflationary policy at home in order to cure the deficits for the sake of monetary stability abroad. This was resented in the USA, because it entirely subordinated domestic economic management to foreign considerations, when less than 10 per cent of GNP was traded.

Besides, the USA argued with some justification, as the owner of the peg currency she was the *n*th country (see section 27.1). Hence her deficits owed more to her partners' desire to acquire reserves than to her own profligacy; they should adjust, not she.

These problems were highlighted by a series of crises. In 1959–60 the US deficit had risen alarmingly and domestic measures were taken to reduce it. There was also a run on the dollar: as private holders switched into gold its price rose to $40 per ounce – well above the official price of $35. This was met by an agreement between major countries to form the 'Gold Pool', which sold (and could conceivably buy) official gold on the private market to maintain the price at $35.

Meanwhile, West Germany experienced the opposite trouble. With a strong balance of payments position she had accumulated substantial reserves. However, the domestic economy was already overheated so she rejected the possibility of reflation, and indeed pursued moderately deflationary policies over 1960–1. This raised interest rates and led to large inflows of capital, despite several policies designed to discourage or penalise foreign deposits. Eventually, the pressure became too great and to preserve her monetary autonomy Germany revalued the Mark by 4.5 per cent in March 1961.

Over this period Britain faced repeated sterling crises. The current account showed persistent weakness and official liabilities far outweighed liquid reserves. In 1964 the election of a Labour government led to an outflow of capital and, despite three years of increasing deflation, sterling had to be devalued in November 1967. During sterling crises, liquid funds migrated to New York and supported the dollar, but in general the USA's difficulties continued, and over 1962–7 increasingly strong measures were taken to reduce the dollar outflow and to maintain confidence in the dollar. These included strong political pressure on creditor nations not to convert dollars into gold – honoured by all major countries but France – and the raising of foreign loans denominated in foreign currency rather than dollars (known as Roosa Bonds, after a US official).

Some solutions

The problems of the international monetary system were a great preoccupation for economists – both official and academic – over this period. Many solutions were proposed and a few palliatives were adopted.

The price of gold was a major consideration. It was argued that raising it substantially (that is devaluing the dollar) would instantaneously cure the confidence and liquidity problems. World liquidity would rise as the gold component became more valuable, and the ratio of US liabilities (in dollars) to its assets (gold) would immediately be restored to a satisfactory level. Furthermore, the higher price would increase the supply of monetary gold in future both from private dishoarding and increased production; hence, it was said, liquidity would never be a problem again. Solving these two problems would also allow time and scope for fundamental adjustment to occur.

The counter-arguments were strong, however. The inefficiency of having to expend resources producing world money was noted. In addition, once confidence had been restored in the dollar it would (temporarily) be a more attractive asset than gold, because, by saving resources, it would be able to pay interest. Hence dollar debts would increase again, until suddenly confidence snapped and the crisis repeated itself. In other words, raising the gold price would not cure the fundamental instability of the gold exchange system. Furthermore, showing the gold price to be flexible would only exacerbate speculation in future, and the uncertainty of periodic jumps in its price would be very disruptive. Politically, it was felt, a price rise would mean the USA reneging on her promises to maintain the price and would also reward some very unpopular countries – South Africa and the USSR (the major producers), and France (the major hoarder), who had continued converting dollars into gold despite that fact that doing so weakened the backing of everybody else's dollars.

A second set of proposals suggested enhancing the IMF into something approaching a world central bank, along the lines of the Keynes Plan. This would involve converting gold and currency reserves into bancor. With the USA no longer responsible for providing liquidity, the monetary consequences of her curing her deficit would be ameliorated (although not the ensuing reduction of demand for other countries' exports). Equally radical – at least at the time – were proposals for flexible exchange rates. Advocates of this course argued that adjustment would become automatic and liquidity and confidence irrelevant since no one would require reserves. As we have now discovered, this was rather too simple a view.

A fourth solution to the liquidity problem was to allow other major currencies a reserve role. This would share the benefits of seignorage and break the world's dependence on the US deficit. However, in such a simple form it would probably create more confidence crises than before, because reserve holders could (and would) switch from one currency to another. To avoid this, some people suggested creating a composite reserve unit as a fixed bundle of major currencies, backed by deposits of those currencies at the IMF. This is similar to the way Special Drawing Rights (SDRs) have turned out, so we postpone discussion of it until the next section.

None of the above came about, but a final set of proposals did bear fruit: *extending IMF facilities*. In fact, the IMF had extended it facilities to members over the 1950s in two directions. First, it introduced *stand-by credits* in 1952. These were equivalent to overdraft facilities at the bank: countries negotiated the right to certain credit at the IMF but did not actually receive the money until they drew it. Stand-bys were still subject to conditionality and to the same limits as ordinary drawings, but their attraction was that they could instil confidence in the currency concerned without involving the interest charges of an actual loan. For the IMF, they supported members but used less resources than ordinary loans.

The second extension was the *General Arrangement to Borrow* (GAB), established in 1962. These are arrangements for mutual lending between the ten richest nations of the world – The Group of Ten. The Group decide the conditions and availability of their loans themselves, but the loans are administered by the IMF and any member of the Group who has made such a loan can, if needs be, borrow an equivalent amount from the IMF. The GAB was established with a view to supporting the US dollar, but in fact over 1964–6 Britain was the first and main beneficiary.

In 1963 a further development occurred – the *Compensatory Financing Facility* (CFF) – to allow countries to borrow if their export earnings fell below some 'normal' level through no fault of their own. Designed basically for primary producers, this at first merely defined the circumstances in which members could draw on their credit tranches unconditionally, and was limited to 25 per cent of quotas. By 1966, however, it had been extended to 50 per cent of quotas and was available additionally to normal borrowing. These arrangements were further modified over the 1970s (see section 28.4 and case-study

419

28.1). On a similar level was the *Buffer Stock Facility* under which the IMF would lend up to an additional 50 per cent of quota for the establishment of buffer stocks in critical primary export goods. This was introduced in 1969.

The final extension was the most radical – the introduction of *Special Drawing Rights* (SDRs), agreed in 1967 and implemented in 1970. SDRs were an unbacked international paper money. However, they were introduced too late and too cautiously to save the Bretton Woods system. We return to examine them in detail in section 28.4.

Collapse, 1967–71

The devaluation of sterling in November 1967 heralded the demise of the gold exchange standard. After a huge speculative attack, and despite a slight improvement in the current account, sterling was devalued by 14.3 per cent. This showed the power of capital movements and the fallibility of reserve currencies, and thus encouraged later speculation. Immediately after sterling, the dollar came under pressure. This was partly from European and Japanese governments, frustrated at the growing US deficits (especially military expenditure and long-term capital outflows) and the inflationary pressure they induced abroad, but mainly from private conversions into gold. Between September 1967 and March 1968, Gold Pool sales were $3.5b., of which $2.4b. came from the USA (nearly 20 per cent of her overall reserves). Eventually, therefore, the Gold Pool was abandoned, the private price cut free and agreement reached that official transactions would take place only at the official price of $35 per ounce. This essentially demonetised gold: no government would part with gold at $35 per ounce when the private price exceeded $150.

Next the European countries suffered pressure and hot money movements. France experienced outflows and eventual devaluation as a result of the political crisis of 1968, while Germany again faced domestic overheating and strong surpluses. The latter resulted in huge capital inflows – up to $4b. over three days in May 1969 – and eventually appreciation by 9.5 per cent in October.

During 1969, international capital migrated to the USA in response to tight monetary conditions and high rates of interest, but in 1970, as the US policy stance reversed, it flowed out again. By now the US trade balance had worsened significantly and military expenditure abroad continued unabated, with the result that US reserve liabilities rose by $7.5b. in 1970 and $27.5b. in 1971. As may be seen from Figure 27.1, these debts expanded world reserves massively (9.5 per cent and 30 per cent respectively), building up strong inflationary pressures throughout the international economy. By 1971, US gold reserves had fallen to $11.1b. – just 21 per cent of official liabilities and 16 per cent of total liquid liabilities.

In May 1971, West Germany, which was still facing overheating and huge capital inflows, finally gave up trying to sterilise or prevent the latter and floated the DM. The US deficit showed no sign of improving meanwhile, so on 15 August 1971 a new approach was unveiled: a domestic price freeze was announced, coupled with a 10 per cent import surcharge (tariff), export stimuli and controls on investment outflows. Most important formally, however, was the official suspension of dollar convertibility into gold. The world had had a *de facto* dollar system for several years – certainly since the two-tier gold market started in 1968 and really rather longer, because convertibility had been effectively ruled out since the mid-1960s. Now it was official. Over the next few weeks, as short-term capital rushed around the world, most countries abandoned their parities and floated their currencies.

The new policy was accompanied by US demands that other countries finance more of NATO's military expenditure abroad, liberalise their imports and, above all, revalue their currencies. The US object was to improve her current balance by about $13b. – about 25 per cent of total current credits! That substantial adjustment was necessary was universally agreed, but there was argument about how it should be achieved. The Europeans and Japanese argued that the dollar must be devalued, partly to increase the liquidity value of their gold (they expected to re-monetise gold sometime) and partly as a sign of some political contrition on the USA's part. The USA, on the other hand, wanted everyone else to revalue!

After six months the Smithsonian Agreement was signed in December 1971. This re-established fixed exchange rates, with an 8 per cent dollar devaluation relative to gold and revaluations of most other currencies relative to the dollar. Despite President Nixon's calling it 'the most significant monetary agreement in the history of the world', however, the Smithsonian arrangements had collapsed within fifteen months, leaving the world with the managed floating 'non-system' it has today.

The lessons   The lessons of the period 1950–71 are several.

First, an international monetary system must promote smooth adjustment.

Second, the optimum number of assets in a system is one: any more and there is scope for destabilising switching. The force of this is seen by considering domestic monetary history. Over 1973–7 sterling depreciated by 50 per cent in terms of goods, and yet there was no wholesale flight from domestic cash. Quite simply, there was nowhere to flee to. If there were only one international asset, the confidence problem would hardly exist.

Third, a system based on a key currency is viable only if there is the political will to make it work. This can come about by all countries pooling their sovereignty and agreeing to abide by a set of rules that might not always be immediately beneficial nationally. It is more likely, however, to be associated with the political hegemony of the key currency country. In this case, the key country sees some benefit in constraining its behaviour to maintain the system healthily, while the other countries lack the power to 'rock the boat'. Monetary difficulties have correlated perfectly with periods of political strain over the past century (1925–39, 1970–88), during which no single country has been able to unify the 'free world'.

28.4   SPECIAL DRAWING RIGHTS

Over the 1960s there was considerable debate – especially among the rich countries of the Group of Ten – about the problems of the international monetary system. Increasingly, the European nations objected to the flow of dollars into the world economy, but, as we saw in section 28.3, the only way that they could force adjustment on the USA without causing themselves a liquidity crisis was by replacing the dollar as the only expanding source of international reserves – that is, by finding a new asset. The USA also had some interest in a new asset for she hoped that it would supplement her gold reserves, thus alleviating the confidence problem. Discussions finally ended in 1967 with a proposal that the IMF should offer additional reserves to its members by means of *Special Drawing Rights* (SDRs).

Paper gold   Special Drawing Rights are quite unlike any other asset: they are an internationally created, unbacked, inconvertible paper money. Their value was initially defined as 1/35th of an ounce of gold – equivalent to US$1.00 – but they could not be encashed for gold. After agreeing on the extent of an SDR issue, each country receives SDRs in proportion to its IMF quota. They are unconditional reserves, but were (and are) subject to strict limitations on their usage. Countries receive (pay) interest on the excess (deficit) of their holdings over their SDR quota, but originally the interest rate was only 1.5 per cent per annum. SDRs can be created within the IMF's SDR accounts once every five years starting from 1967. They are then distributed to members over the following five years when they have been 'activated' by decision of the IMF. This decision must take account of (a) the need for additional reserves, (b) the improvement of balance of payments disequilibrium since 1967 (the world refused merely to finance US deficits indefinitely), and (c) the likelihood of extra SDRs aiding the adjustment process.

SDRs were invented as a substitute for gold rather than for dollars – hence the gold valuation and the low rate of interest. Their seignorage accrues mainly to the *users*. The IMF gives SDRs away and so gets nothing; neither does the country holding just its quota. The main gainers are countries that run down their SDR reserves in return for real goods and assets, because they can earn, say, i_L per cent per annum with these but pay only 1.5 per cent on their spending. SDR issues increment members' reserves but, unless explicit action is taken, not their internal money supply. This differs from 'earned' reserve increments, where the internal money supply rises in line with reserves unless policy action is taken. The quantity of SDRs is entirely within the control of the international community.

The issue of a new money is a risky business: one cannot tell whether it will be too popular, and hence drop out of circulation into national hoards (reserves), or unpopular, and hence circulate very fast as holders vie with each other to get rid of it. It was this uncertainty that led to the restrictions on SDR use. SDRs could be used only for transactions between official bodies, and then only for balance of payments settlement or in the light of a country's overall reserve policy; they were not available for shifting the composition of reserves between assets. Furthermore, each member was committed to hold an average of 30–300 per cent of its SDR issue over any quarter. When a country wished to use SDRs within the confines of these rules, it could ask the IMF to 'designate' a country that would swap SDRs for foreign currency. Designation was made with a view to the designatee's balance of payments, reserves and SDR holdings.

Between 1968 and 1969 the IMF studied the case for activation. The ratio of reserves to both imports and trade imbalances had been falling steadily over the 1950s and 1960s, and although these are not ideal indicators of reserve need – see Chapter 27 – this does suggest some tightening of liquidity. In addition, by this time the US deficit had contracted, both suggesting better adjustment and reducing reserve growth. Finally, there was evidence of increasing resort to restrictions on international transactions and requests for international financial support. Hence it was concluded that some increase in liquidity was required.

Deciding the amount of SDRs to issue was complex, however; while overall reserve demand might be estimable, the increase in the supply of other assets was not. The final decision was that reserves need would expand by $4–5b. per annum, while other reserves would grow at $1–1.5b. per annum – $0.5b.

in gold and Fund reserve positions and the remainder in US dollars. It was therefore decided to issue $3.5b. in 1970 and $3b. in each of 1971 and 1972 (the last year that SDRs created in 1967 could be issued). In the event, the predictions proved woefully wrong and the SDR issue just contributed to a glut of world liquidity: world reserves increased by $14.5b. (18.4 per cent) in 1970, $30.0b. (32.2 per cent) in 1971 and $23.6b. (19.2 per cent) in 1972. In the second quinquennium starting in 1972, therefore, no SDRs were created. In retrospect, it is clear that controlling just one source of reserves is useless if the requirement is to control liquidity.

Paper money? After 1971 there was little about international money that was systematic; exchange rates fluctuated violently and the gold market remained split, with the official price still a small fraction of the private price. It became increasingly anachronistic to value the SDR in terms of gold. In July 1974, therefore, the SDR was redefined to transform it more into a currency substitute than a gold substitute. Its value was fixed by a basket of the currencies of the sixteen countries with more than 1 per cent of world trade over 1968–72. The weights of this basket, which reflected each country's financial and commercial importance, are given in Table 28.2. The rate of interest was also raised – to 60 per cent of the average of the rates on the five major currencies. This increased SDR's attractiveness as an asset, but still left net holders subsidising net users.

The next stage in the SDR's development came with the Jamaica Agreement of 1976. This endorsed the Second Amendment to the IMF Articles, which became operational in March 1978. It legitimised the SDR as a peg for countries to define their exchange rates by, and reduced the restrictions on its use. In particular, the minimum holding was reduced from

Table 28.2 The value of the SDR

Date of basket currency	July 1974 Units	% weight	June 1978 Units	% weight	January 1981 Units	% weight	January 1986 Units	% weight
US dollar[a]	0.40	33	0.40	33	0.54	42	0.452	42
Deutschmark[a]	0.38	12½	0.32	12½	0.46	19	0.527	19
Pound sterling[a]	0.045	9	0.050	7½	0.071	13	0.0893	12
French franc[a]	0.44	7½	0.42	7½	0.74	13	1.02	12
Japanese yen[a]	26.00	7½	21.00	7½	34.00	13	33.4	15
Canadian dollar	0.071	6	0.070	5	—	—	—	—
Italian lira	47.00	6	52.00	5	—	—	—	—
Dutch guilder	0.14	4½	0.14	5	—	—	—	—
Belgian franc	1.60	3½	1.60	4	—	—	—	—
Swedish krona	0.13	2½	0.11	2	—	—	—	—
Australian dollar	0.012	1½	0.17	1½	—	—	—	—
Danish krone	0.11	1½	—	—	—	—	—	—
Norwegian krone	0.099	1½	0.10	1½	—	—	—	—
Spanish peseta	1.10	1½	0.15	1½	—	—	—	—
Austrian schilling	0.22	1	0.28	1½	—	—	—	—
South African rand	0.0082	1	—	—	—	—	—	—
Saudi Arabian riyal	—	—	0.13	3	—	—	—	—
Iranian rial	—	—	1.70	2	—	—	—	—

Note:
[a] The SDR interest rate is some fraction of the weighted average of short-term rates on these currencies in their issuing countries. The weights are proportional to the weights of the basket.
Sources: International Monetary Fund *Annual Reports*; Bank of England, *Quarterly Economic Review*, September 1974 and June 1979, *IMF Survey*, September 1988.

30 per cent to 15 per cent of quota, the interest rate was raised to 80 per cent of the average in the big five currencies, and permission was given for authorities to use SDRs for any transactions among themselves without IMF designation. These moves considerably enhanced the 'moneyness' of SDRs; they were supplemented by a redefinition of the basket in June 1978 based on trade statistics over 1972–6. SDRs took over many of the roles gold had played in transactions with the Fund – e.g. in depositing the first 25 per cent of the IMF quota and as a unit of account – and members reaffirmed their intention that the SDR should become the world's principal reserve asset. Finally, in each of 1979, 1980 and 1981 SDR 4b. were issued.

Development continued in 1981 with the abolition of the minimum holding, the extension of the list of official institutions accepting SDRs and a rise in the rate of interest to 100 per cent of the average in the big five currencies. The valuation calculation was also simplified to cover just the five major currencies (see Table 28.2). The valuation is reconsidered every five years to reflect changes in the roles of the major currencies. Table 28.2 reports the current position, which stems from January 1986. The last allocation of SDRs was in 1987, although the Interim Committee (see below) regularly reviews the case for a new issue.

The future of the SDR

Gold has finally dropped out of the international monetary scene, and the SDR is now firmly established as a money substitute. For official institutions it serves as a store of value, a unit of account and a medium of transaction. Unfortunately, however, it is not unique, or even predominant, in these roles, and there are reasons for believing that in its present form it never will be. That is, unless changes are made, we shall continue to live in a world of multiple reserve assets, with all its destabilising portfolio shifts and lack of control of international liquidity.

The interest rate on SDRs is now a market rate, so on that score it rivals and could displace currencies. Its value, too, is fixed as the average of several currencies, but this in fact is a mixed blessing. The SDR's value fluctuates with each of its five component currencies, although obviously only in proportion to that currency's weight in the basket. Consequently, its value is more stable in terms of goods than that of the most variable currency in the basket, but necessarily less stable than that of the least variable one. Hence, at any one time there will always be at least one more stable haven for funds than SDRs; if this one currency changes through time (e.g. sterling one year, dollars the next), the SDR may be acceptable on average, but there is a danger of destabilisation as reserve holders seek the currency that is expected to rise faster over the near future. If, on the other hand, one currency is persistently more stable than the SDR, it will displace the SDR as a store of wealth. The only ways around these problems are either to raise the SDR rate of interest above the market rate or to enact some self-denying ordinance by which authorities do not hold significant quantities of currency.

One could not ban all currency holding, however, because the SDR is not a universal money – in particular it is not used privately. (Some private transactions are now denominated in SDRs, but all settlement has to be effected in a national currency.) This highlights a further difficulty with SDRs – they usually have to be exchanged into currency before use, and this entails a cost. Furthermore, this cost is avoidable if, instead of holding SDRs, monetary authorities hold reserves of dollars, marks, francs, yen and sterling in just the proportions of the SDR basket. This portfolio would have just the same value and rate of interest as SDRs but would be freely and instantaneously usable in private markets. The obvious solution to this is to allow SDRs to be used in private settlements. In that case, however, since one could not prevent private transactors from also holding currency, there would be scope for private speculation against SDR–currency parities.

These problems are serious. Until the political will exists to make the SDR the true centre of the system, further developments are unlikely. Such will involves sacrificing the short-term national benefits of being able to switch assets in the reserve portfolio to the long-term cosmopolitan aim of a universal stable world money.

28.5 INTERNATIONAL MONEY SINCE 1972

The Committee of Twenty

The most lasting feature of the Smithsonian Agreement was the Committee of Twenty (C20) – the group set up to advise on the repair or replacement of the Bretton Woods system. It comprised representatives of the Group of Ten plus ten from the rest of the world. The developing countries were better represented than ever before in monetary discussions, largely at the instigation of the USA, which was anxious to dilute the wrath of Europe and Japan.

There was general agreement in C20 that liberal world trading and financial arrangements were desirable; that excessive capital movements were undesirable; that world liquidity should be controllable and controlled; and that excessive exchange rate movements (especially competitive ones) were to be avoided. Beyond that, however, there were differences. The USA advocated a system very like the Keynes Plan of 1944; symmetrical adjustment by deficit and surplus countries; exchange rate flexibility and restricted convertibility of dollars for gold. She was reluctant, however, to see the dollar displaced as a reserve asset, and opposed any moves towards compulsory asset settlement – that is, financing her deficit by selling reserve assets rather than by issuing dollar liabilities.

Europe and Japan, on the other hand, had a much more conservative approach. They favoured less exchange rate flexibility and stressed the role of 'responsible' internal policy as a means of producing adjustment. They were anxious to impose asset settlement on the USA (after all, everybody else already had it) and to dethrone the dollar as principal reserve asset. For this they suggested a 'substitution account' whereby the IMF converted dollar liabilities into SDRs and the USA gradually bought the dollars back from the IMF with SDRs earned from a balance of payments surplus. By 1974, however, the 'dollar overhang' of outstanding short-term liabilities exceeded one year's total current credits, so such repayments would have required a huge rise in US competitiveness over Europe and Japan. Besides, as we saw above, the SDR was most unlikely to have been an effective substitute for the dollar anyway. All told, it was probably a good thing that the substitution account was never born.

The third group – the developing countries (DCs) – supported fixed exchange rates (although, some commentators think, mistakenly), freedom over reserve composition, and an 'aid link' for SDRs (see p. 452 below).

While C20 worked towards a redesigned par value system, the world went the other way. In mid-1972, sterling and the French franc floated and by early 1973 all the major currencies had floated. With simultaneous upswings in most major countries, inflation rates grew alarmingly and their dispersion

Table 28.3 Current accounts, terms of trade and world prices, 1978–86

	1973	1974	1975	1976	1977	1978	1979	1980	1981	1982	1983	1984	1985	1986
Current account balances ($USb.):														
Industrial countries	20.3	−10.8	19.8	0.5	−2.2	15.1	−23.2	−60.5	−19.0	−22.4	−19.8	−58.3	−50.7	−19.0
Seven larger countries	14.8	−2.7	24.9	10.1	10.4	29.9	−10.8	−32.9	0.2	−6.8	−17.1	−62.0	−52.0	−19.6
Other industrial countries	5.5	−8.1	−5.1	−9.6	−12.6	−5.8	−12.5	−27.6	−19.2	−15.5	−2.7	3.7	1.3	0.5
Developing countries														
Oil-exporting countries	6.7	68.3	35.4	40.3	30.2	−6.1	51.4	95.9	34.8	−18.2	−19.3	−4.7	3.0	−37.1
Non-oil developing countries	−11.3	−37.0	−46.3	−32.6	−28.9	−29.3	−45.0	−65.5	−83.2	−68.8	−44.7	−28.4	−26.9	−9.2
Total[a]	15.7	20.5	8.9	8.2	−0.9	−29.0	−19.5	−29.2	−70.5	−107.1	−81.2	−86.5	−72.3	−65.5
Terms of trade (% change):														
Industrial countries	−1.8	−10.6	2.5	−1.0	−1.1	2.5	−2.9	−7.1	−1.8	1.9	1.4	0.3	0.8	0.0
Developing countries														
Oil-exporting countries	13.3	140.0	−5.1	5.8	0.8	−10.7	26.3	44.0	11.2	—	−8.5	0.7	−2.7	−47.4
Non-oil developing countries	5.3	−5.9	−8.5	5.9	−4.1	−1.6	−5.8	−4.2	−2.2	0.5	1.7	−1.2	1.1	−2.6p
World trade prices (in US dollar terms) for major commodity groups:														
Manufactures	17.7	21.8	12.3	1.0	9.0	15.3	13.6	10.4	−3.9	−2.1	−2.8	−3.0	1.21	7.9
Oil	40.0	225.8	5.1	6.3	9.3	0.4	46.0	63.6	9.8	−4.1	−11.7	−2.4	−4.8	−49.8
Non-oil primary commodities (market prices)	53.2	28.0	−18.2	13.3	20.7	−5.5	17.9	5.5	−13.5	−9.9	6.9	4.2	−12.9	−1.1

Note:
[a] Reflects errors, omissions and asymmetries in reported balance of payments statistics on current account, plus balance of listed groups with other countries (mainly the USSR and other non-IMF countries of Eastern Europe and, for years prior to 1977, China).
Sources: International Monetary Fund Annual Reports, 1983 for 1973–7, 1987 for 1978–86. Data revisions from year to year are large; there may be a discontinuity at the interface of the two sources; p provisional.

across countries increased, making fixed exchange rates quite infeasible. C20 reported in June 1974 with only minor repercussions on the world system. They recommended their own continuation as part of the IMF system – known as the Interim Committee – which is important for the politics of the IMF; they redefined the SDR; and they produced some rules for floating exchange rates. These were designed to prevent changes contrary to the requirements of orderly adjustment, and to encourage the smoothing of day-to-day fluctuations.

The oil price shock C20's reform plans were entirely swamped by the consequences of the rise in the price of oil. Between late 1973 and late 1974 the dollar price of crude oil quadrupled. We have discussed the real consequences of that already, but we now briefly consider its financial implications. Suddenly the OPEC oil producers found themselves with huge liquid resources – way beyond their spending capacity – while OECD and the non-oil DCs faced huge current account deficits requiring both short-term finance and medium-term adjustment. The extent of the current account and terms of trade changes are reported in Table 28.3.

The industrial countries' net payments for oil (oil payments less exports to OPEC) increased by about $55b. in 1974 (Organization for Economic Co-operation and Development, *Economic Outlook*, December 1978), but their combined current account worsened by only $32b. in 1974 and not at all in 1975 relative to 1973. Much of their adjustment fell on imports, which shifted the burden of the OPEC surpluses onto the non-oil DCs, whose combined current account deficits exceeded that of 1973 by $20–35b. in each of the succeeding four years. This partly reflected rising oil payments but mainly falling exports and primary export prices, caused by the sharp recession that the oil crisis induced in OECD. The DCs' response to this was partly real adjustment (output growth fell somewhat) but mainly to borrow extensively.

Borrowing was not difficult in 1974, because OPEC's profits were kept largely in liquid form in the international banking centres and the Euro-currency markets. For example, of its $55b. financial surplus in 1974,[3] OPEC deposited $23b. on the Euro-markets, $15b. in US and UK short-term assets, and $4b. with the IMF and World Bank (Argy, 1981). These funds were *recycled* to the DCs partly through increased official bilateral loans and aid from OECD and OPEC, and mostly through increased commercial loans – mainly from the Euro-markets – and export credit. The Euro-markets were also important for certain OECD countries. For example, the UK raised $5.7b., France $3.2b., and Italy $2.2b. in 1974. Japan, on the other hand, borrowed extensively in US domestic markets.

The contribution of official financial institutions to the alleviation of the oil crisis was modest but significant. The IMF's existing facilities were extensively used and two new facilities were developed. First, the *Extended Fund Facility* offered developing countries assistance to cure longer-run balance of payments problems. It involved both longer and larger loans than existing facilities (up to 140 per cent of quota over three years) and, although still conditional, it represented a step towards development or reconstruction finance. The second – the *Oil Facility* – was explicitly short term: for two years from May 1974 countries could borrow to finance balance of payments difficulties due to the oil price rise. This was additional to other facilities and there was no further conditionality. The loans lasted for three–seven years. To finance these loans the IMF borrowed from surplus countries – mainly OPEC – but, of course, it was able to do so more cheaply that the DC clients to which it re-lent the money, because it was itself underwriting the loans. As an addition to this scheme, certain rich donors agreed to subsidise the loans to the very poorest borrowers.

Figure 28.1 shows the use that was made of IMF facilities over 1972–87. Part (A) reports the drawings in each year – showing the sharp rise in the use of Fund credit and the roles of the Extended Facility (which is included under 'ordinary') and the Oil Facility. Over its short life-time the latter transferred about SDR 7b. from seventeen lenders to fifty-five borrowers.

The Second Amendment

The oil crisis dominated the international scene for several years. With countries seeking to adjust at different rates, the dispersion of inflation rates grew and there was no prospect of restoring a fixed-rate system. Besides, with widespread and deep recession, attention was focused primarily on providing stimulus and liquidity. The Interim Committee continued C20's deliberations and presented its proposals at a summit meeting in Jamaica in early 1976; these were adopted as the Second Amendment to the IMF Articles, to become operative in March 1978. Broadly speaking, the amendment legitimised

427

Figure 28.1 The use of IMF facilities, 1972–87. (A) Use of credit and reserves (drawings). (B) Use of credit (indebtedness)

Notes:
[a] Facilities are:

EAR	Enlarged Access Resources (on both Credit Tranche and Extended Facility).
SFF	Supplementary Financing Facility (on both Credit Tranche and Extended Facility).
Oil	Oil Facility.
CFF	Compensatory Financing Facility.

Ordinary Credit Tranche and Extended Facility from ordinary (non-borrowed) resources.
Reserve Reserve Tranche Drawings.

[b] At year end. Reserve Tranche Drawings are excluded, because they represent the recovery of a deposit rather than a credit facility.

Source: International Monetary Fund, *International Financial Statistics* (1982), Supplement No. 3 and February issues.

floating, officially demonetised gold, increased Fund resources, and redesigned the SDR.

The Second Amendment allows currencies either to float or to peg to any numeraire except gold. Members are obliged to foster exchange stability by appropriate domestic policies, and to this end are subject to Fund *surveillance* and must consult the Fund over exchange rate policies. Surveillance requires members to provide the IMF with information to ensure that exchange rate policy meets three basic rules: (a) manipulation must not prevent effective adjustment or be directed at gaining competitive advantages; (b) intervention is required to counteract disorderly market fluctuations; and (c) policies must take account of other members' interests. The IMF may institute discussions if a member appears to be in contravention of these rules, although in the end it has no sanction until the member seeks assistance.

The Second Amendment abolished the official price of *gold*. This completed the unfreezing of countries' gold reserves, which had begun in 1973 with permission to sell gold on the private market and continued in 1974 by allowing gold to be valued at private prices when it was used as collateral for official loans. More important, however, were the elimination of members' obligations to use gold in certain Fund transactions, and the decision to sell one-third of the IMF's gold. One-sixth was sold to members in proportion to their quotas at the old official price, while the other sixth was sold on the free market and the proceeds distributed to member DCs. This latter was one of the DCs' *quid pro quos* for agreeing the rest of the package (given the 80 per cent rule, DCs as a group had a blocking vote over the amendment).

The Jamaica Agreement was accompanied by the Sixth General Review of Quotas. Rises of about 35 per cent were agreed, but until these could be formally ratified (in 1978) the IMF agreed to raise all its borrowing limits correspondingly. The Compensatory Financing Facility was also liberalised. Both concessions were actively used (see Figure 28.1(A)), making an immediate contribution to world liquidity, and when the new quotas were ratified in 1978 there was a further surge in Reserve Tranche (unconditional) borrowing. Indeed, as case-study 28.1 argues, liquidity rather than the stabilization of foreign exchange receipts was the *CFF*'s principal contribution.

Despite this activity, however, IMF resources had still contracted as a proportion of total liquidity since the 1950s and 1960s (see Table 28.1). The DCs and deficit countries perceived this as a weakness, arguing that recovery from the post-oil slump could be thwarted by tight credit conditions, but a number of commentators viewed inflation as the major problem and advocated contractionary domestic policies and a reduction of world liquidity (e.g. Halm, 1977).

The IMF, 1977–89

By 1977 OPEC and OECD had largely re-established current account equilibrium. OPEC's surplus had been whittled away by strong increases in imports, a falling real price of oil and a fall in demand as non-OPEC sources of oil expanded and (minor) conservation measures occurred. The world economy began to expand and apart from rather large exchange rate fluctuations things seemed fairly healthy.

In 1978, however, revolution occurred in Iran, oil supplies fell and between 1978 and 1980 the price of oil rose by a further 150 per cent. This raised exactly the same problems as the previous oil crisis, but this time the DCs were already substantially in debt, and domestic policy in several OECD countries was less expansionary. The resulting recession was less deep but longer lived than 1974–5, with lower inflation but higher real and nominal interest rates. This last feature hit the developing countries particularly hard and their combined current account deficits worsened by nearly $20b. in each of 1979, 1980 and 1981. The deficit of $83b. in 1981 represented about 20 per cent of their total exports of goods and services and about 140 per cent of their foreign exchange reserves. By 1982, borrowing had become substantially more difficult as creditors worried about countries' ability to repay, and so adjustment was forced on these countries. This precipitated the debt crisis (the difficulties faced by many developing countries in servicing their debts to the rest of the world; see Chapter 30 below).

The response of the international community was also much as before, emphasising finance rather than adjustment. The existing facilities of the IMF were heavily drawn upon and further facilities introduced. A *Supplementary Financing Facility* was introduced in 1979. It was available only under Stand-by and Extended Arrangements, and like the Oil Facility was financed by borrowing from OECD and OPEC surplus countries. The IMF would lend up to 140 per cent of quota (conditionally), but the total facility was limited to SDR 7.6b., all of which was committed by March 1981. It was replaced by an *Enlarged Access* provision on similar terms, which offered borrowed and ordinary facilities up to 450 per cent of quota over three years. The *Compensatory Financing Facility* was also extended to cover rising import prices on cereals and expanded to 125 per cent of quota. Excluding Compensatory, Buffer Stock and Oil Finance, access is, however, generally limited to 600 per cent of quota. Finally, SDR issues were continued: the fourth quinquennium saw activation of SDR 4b. in each of 1979, 1980 and 1981.

No industrial country borrowed from the Fund during the 1980s, and international monetary affairs were dominated by the debt crisis. Thus the major recent developments in the IMF have concerned the provision of adjustment finance to developing countries. Several facilities were already aimed in their direction (e.g. the Buffer Stock and Compensatory Finance Facilities), but they were specific in their conditions of application and required relatively rapid repayment. The *Structural Adjustment Facility* (SAF) of March 1986 and the *Enhanced Structural Adjustment Facility* (ESAF) of December 1987, on the other hand, provide medium-term balance of payments lending to permit macro-economic stabilisation. Repayments are phased over the period five–ten years after disbursement and carry a very low rate of interest. Thus the facilities have a considerable element of aid in them and are financed by the Trust Fund and by related borrowing. SAF and ESAF are subject to fairly strict conditionally (see Chapter 30), but have been extensively used; SDR 2.26b. had been committed to thirty countries by June 1989. The ESAF closed in November 1989; like the Oil Facility it was a temporary response to a particular problem.

The menu of IMF facilities in 1989 is summarised in Table 28.4. To maximise access to Fund credit, a nation should be a cereal-importing, primary-producing deficit country, trying to establish an export buffer stock, undertaking long-term structural adjustment, and willing to cooperate with the Fund over policies to improve its balance of payments. Among the largest borrowers in March 1989 were: Sudan (with outstanding credit of 357 per cent of quota), Mexico (297 per cent) and Liberia (287 per cent).

Table 28.4 Potential cumulative disbursements under IMF arrangements and facilities, 1989

	Percentage of member quotas[a]
Under stand-by and extended arrangements:[b,c]	
Annual	90–110
Three-year	270–330
Cumulative	400–440
Special facilities:[c]	
Compensatory and contingency financing facility (CCFF)	
– Compensatory financing	40
– Contingency financing[d]	40
– Optional tranche[e]	25
– Excess cereal import costs	17
– Combined[f]	122
Buffer stock financing facility	45
Under SAF and ESAF arrangements:	
Structural adjustment facility[g]	
– First year	20
– Second year	30
– Third year	20
– Cumulative	70
Enhanced structural adjustment facility[h]	
– Cumulative	250

Notes:
[a] Under exceptional circumstances, the amounts disbursed may exceed the following limits.
[b] Excludes drawings on available reserve tranches (25 per cent).
[c] These arrangements and facilities are financed directly with Fund resources.
[d] Contingency financing may not exceed 70 per cent of access made under the associated arrangement, with a cumulative sublimit of 35 per cent of quota on account of deviations in interest rates.
[e] May be applied to supplement the amounts for compensatory financing, contingency financing, or excess in cereal import costs.
[f] Where a member has a satisfactory balance of payments position – except for the effect of an export shortfall or an excess in cereal costs – a limit of 83 per cent of quota applies to either the export or cereal element, with a combined limit of 105 per cent of quota.
[g] This facility is financed with the SDR 2.7b. in reflows from the Trust Fund.
[h] This facility is being financed with SAF resources and with special loan and grant contributions.
Source: IMF Survey, Supplement, September 1989.

CASE-STUDY 28.1: COMPENSATORY FINANCING FACILITY

The idea behind the IMF's Compensatory Financing Facility (CFF) was very simple. Some developing countries are heavily dependent on primary commodities for their export revenue and consequently experience major shocks when commodity prices or the quantities of commodities traded fall. Such fluctuations can cause balance of payments crises, which, if they cannot be financed, may induce quite unnecessary adjustment. Commodity price fluctuations may be mitigated either by operating a stabilising buffer stock scheme or by holding high levels of reserves, but simple borrowing facilities seem to be the cheapest way of tackling them.

The CFF scheme was introduced in 1963 but was not widely used until 1975 when, faced with collapsing commodity prices, the IMF liberalised its conditions. Members of the IMF could borrow to finance a shortfall in export earnings relative to trend provided that: the shortfall was temporary and not their fault; they had a balance of payments problem and were willing to cooperate with the IMF to find solutions; and they had not exceeded the current CFF borrowing limits. The shortfall was measured relative to a five-year average centred on the year of shortfall; i.e. relative to a magnitude that had partly to be forecast because it lay in the future.

The argument for using official finance for smoothing export fluctuations was that developing countries could not rely on always having access to private capital markets for such purposes. However, IMF loans were also made at below market rates, and, with three–five-year maturities, were longer term than most private facilities. Generous as these last two features appeared, they actually helped to undermine the CFF. Countries naturally preferred to repay non-concessionary loans before CFF finance, but this meant that when a shortfall arose they were often unable to borrow because they were already carrying the maximum permissible CFF debt from the previous shortfall.

There is strong evidence that the CFF had almost no stabilising effect on members' foreign exchange receipts. In an excellent and simple article, Finger and deRosa (1980) showed that CFF activities increased instability on over half the occasions they were used between 1963 and 1977, and Herrmann, Burger and Smit (1990) showed that the situation was no better over the 1980s. Among the possible explanations of this dismal performance are: (i) the lags between the shortfall arising and the CFF loan being received; (ii) repayments coinciding with subsequent shortfalls; (iii) the quota limits on borrowing; and (iv) bad forecasting. Finger and deRosa showed that (i) and (ii) were not important, that (iii) mattered for some countries, but that (iv) was a major problem: three-quarters of CFF drawings were for years in which the borrowers turned out to have excess not deficient export earnings! In the light of these findings, Finger and deRosa concluded that the real purpose of the CFF was to provide a relatively uncontentious way of increasing (certain) developing countries' access to IMF borrowing. The CFF may look perverse but it is politically much safer than an attempt to alter the quota rules in favour of poor primary commodity exporting countries.

The CFF scheme has evolved over the years. The borrowing limit relative to quota has been changed several times, and, most significantly, from 1981 excess cereal import expenditure as well as export shortfalls qualified for compensation. In 1988 the CFF was transformed into the CCFF – the Compensatory and Contingency Financing Facility. The compensatory element remains largely as before, but the new element – contingency finance – allows borrowing to cover a wide range of external shocks – e.g. oil price or interest rate rises – specifically so that these should not disturb previously agreed Fund programmes (see Pownall and Stuart, 1988).

FURTHER READING

For useful textbook treatments of the history of the international monetary system, see the first edition of this book, *Yeager* (1976), *Grubel* (1977, 1981), and *Argy* (1981). On post-war history alone, see also *MacBean and Snowden* (1981). Classic references include *Triffin* (1964) on the gold standard and *Keynes* (1980) on the establishment of the IMF. The latter gives a wealth of insight into both technicalities and politics, leaving strong impressions on Keynes' remarkable foresight and the enduring nature of economic problems. The analytical aspects of the gold exchange standard are covered in *Triffin*

(1960), *Johnson* (1967b) and *Williamson* (1973), while *Strange* (1971, especially ch. 1) treats political aspects of international money. *Williamson* (1977) gives a thorough and interesting account of the negotiations over the early 1970s, and the reasons for their failure, while *Bernstein et al.* (1976), *Kafka* (1976), and *Halm* (1977) explore the Jamaica Agreement. In fact, the *Princeton Essays in International Finance*, of which these are three, provide a useful and timely commentary on international financial matters in general.

On the SDR, *Chrystal* (1978) is stimulating (but slightly dated), and *Byrne* (1982) and *Coats* (1982) informative. Various issues of the International Monetary Fund's *Annual Reports* and the *Bank of England Quarterly Bulletin* provide details of the evolution of the SDR. Finally, details of the IMF's role in international finance are published in International Monetary Fund's *Annual Reports* and *IMF Survey* (especially the annual Supplement on the Fund, September), and discussed in many articles in the *IMF Staff Papers* – see the general index, November 1981.

KEY CONCEPTS

gold standard	specie flow
gold exchange standard	Bretton Woods
seignorage	IMF
confidence problem	liquidity problem
adjustment problem	compensatory finance
the SDR	international liquidity
recycling	surveillance

QUESTIONS FOR REVIEW

28.1 How does the gold standard solve the $(n - 1)$ problem? Is the solution automatic in (a) theory and (b) practice?

28.2 In what ways is the gold exchange system necessarily unstable?

28.3 Is control of the SDR issue sufficient to control international liquidity?

28.4 What conditions would be necessary for the SDR to become *the* world money?

28.5 Why has the IMF increased its menu of lending alternatives so much in the last two decades?

NOTES

1 Hume emphasised equilibration through prices.

2 The Suez crisis was an ill-advised and ill-executed attempt by the UK and France to invade Egypt to prevent the nationalisation of the Suez Canal. It resulted in a run on both currencies and a withdrawal of economic cooperation by the USA.

3 The financial surplus is the current account less export credits granted on oil.

29 The Euro-Currency Markets

We examined the causes and consequences of international capital mobility in Part II. We now turn to one important institutional aspect of the means by which capital moves – the Euro-currency markets. This chapter defines Euro-currencies and describes the mechanism by which they are created. It then considers the quantitative significance of the markets and the causes of their rapid growth since 1960. It considers whether they have had profound effects on the world liquidity, the new forms that Euro-transactions may take, and, finally, whether they should be subject to control.

On any measure the Euro-markets have grown prodigiously over the last thirty years. This has been partly due to a series of 'happy accidents' and partly due to the improvements they introduced in the efficiency of borrowing and lending money.

29.1 THE STRUCTURE OF THE EURO-MARKETS

A definition
The original Euro-currency was the *Euro-dollar*, which was a deposit (loan) of US dollars made at (by) a European bank. Since then, the definition has broadened to cover any deposit or loan made by a bank in a currency other than that of its country of residence. Most major currencies now have Euro-markets and significant markets exist in, for example, Singapore, Hong Kong, Rio de Janeiro and New York, as well as in European centres. Euro-banking should not be confused with multinational banking *per se*, which is merely banks owned in one country operating like local banks in another. While many actual banks fall into both categories, the two are logically distinct.

Recently a Eurobond market has also developed. This is similar to the Euro-currency market except that it deals in longer-term paper. It is now possible for large companies and official bodies to issue bonds in any of a number of currencies and in any of a number of centres. We consider these capital markets in section 29.4.

Some features of Euro-banking
Euro-banks accept deposits and make loans in a variety of currencies independently of their physical location. There are no formal restrictions on entry into Euro-banking, so many banks are involved and the market is highly competitive. Most major banks are involved to some extent. Transactions take the form of large sums ($1 m. and upwards) lent or borrowed for fixed periods of time. This 'wholesale' nature makes for great efficiency because the fixed costs of a transaction are spread over a large quantity of funds. The fixed time-periods mean that Euro-deposits are not primarily used for transactions balances, although obviously their existence allows such balances in domestic banks to be kept to a minimum. The geographical spread of the market is very wide. Over 1975–80, three-quarters of the business involved one non-European partner. As we saw in Chapter 28, the Euro-market is important in global intermediation – especially recycling OPEC surpluses to deficit countries. On the other hand, for European and American residents the Euro-market provides an alternative to the domestic banks for large transactions. In

this way its existence handicaps monetary policy, which depends primarily on government control of the domestic banking system.

Apart from the banks themselves, the principal agents in the Euro-markets are multinationals and the central banks of the developing countries. Both have extensive balances to be managed and the Euro-markets allow these to be invested at relatively high rates of interest, while still maintaining considerable liquidity and flexibility over their currencies of denomination.

An important feature of the Euro-system is the prevalence of inter-bank lending. About 70 per cent of gross transactions occur *between* banks. This provides an efficient 'invisible hand' to shift money from net lenders to net borrowers. The bank receiving a deposit does not itself have to know of a potential borrower, it merely re-lends to one that does. In fact, the typical Euro-loan has passed through several banks since it was originally deposited in the system. This phenomenon makes measuring the Euro-market very difficult, for one cannot just add all banks' balance sheets. It also means that, if banks can arbitrage between domestic and Euro-business, Euro interest rates are primarily determined by banks' behaviour rather than directly by the supply and demand for money by non-banks in the Euro-market. Finally, extensive inter-bank lending implies that difficulties for one Euro-bank could rapidly spread through the system and entail difficulties for many.

At the start of the era of floating exchange rates, several banks took open positions in currencies and a number suffered for it. In 1974, Lloyds Bank announced exchange losses of £33m. and Franklin National Bank, New York's largest commercial bank, also reported large losses. Most significant, however, the West German bank Herstatt went into liquidation owing over DM 2b. in deposits. This had several results. First, money flooded back from the Euro-markets to the domestic banks – although only temporarily. Second, Euro-banks were much more discriminating about potential bank borrowers, charging smaller and less well-known banks substantial premia. Third, considerable concern was expressed over the security of the Euro-market. Facing virtually no regulations, Euro-banks held few reserves and little capital and thus were vulnerable to default. Furthermore, since no overseeing body was responsible for the market, no lender of last resort was obvious. The Bank for International Settlements – a sort of central banks' bank situated in Basle – coordinated rescue-lending by national central banks in 1974, and drew up a rather weak agreement about future responsibilities: the Basle Concordat.

Table 29.1 The assets and liabilities of London-based Euro-banks, 15 August 1984 (US$b.)

Maturity	Total Liabilities	Assets	Inter-bank Liabilities	Assets	Non-bank Liabilities	Assets
< 8 days	143.1	109.5	101.9	96.8	41.2	12.6
8 days ≤ < 1 mth	130.6	102.7	87.9	88.4	42.7	14.3
1 mth ≤ < 3 mths	177.9	149.8	121.2	128.9	56.7	20.9
3 mths ≤ < 6 mths	115.5	97.2	82.0	82.3	33.6	14.9
6 mths ≤ < 1 yr	47.6	45.0	33.7	33.6	14.0	11.5
1 yr ≤ < 3 yrs	17.2	45.8	8.0	18.4	9.2	27.5
3 yrs ≤	18.9	107.3	11.2	23.1	7.8	84.1
Total	650.9	657.3	445.8	471.6	205.1	185.8

Note: Figures may not sum because of rounding.
Source: Bank of England Quarterly Bulletin, December 1984.

Finally, these bad experiences made banks much more cautious, and as a result they typically keep virtually closed positions in all currencies. That is, their assets and liabilities in each currency virtually match. This matching does not extend into maturities, however. Banks make money by borrowing short and lending long, since long-term interest rates generally exceed short. Table 29.1 shows the assets and liabilities of the London Euro-banks. It illustrates several points. First, London is a net borrower from non-banks and a net lender to the rest of the banking world. This largely reflects the UK's current surplus in 1984; it was not always the case. Second, Euro-banks are heavily concentrated in the short maturities. Third, while maturities with other banks are fairly well matched (the excess of long loans over deposits is proportionately great but quantitatively unimportant), considerable maturity transformation occurs with non-bank organisations. This suggests that the inter-bank market is merely a circulation of deposits looking for lending opportunities, whereas non-bank loans represent the *raison d'être* of the market. Fourth, like domestic banking lending, Euro lending is at variable rates of interest if it is other than very short term. This is usually accomplished by agreeing to renew (roll-over) a loan every few months at ruling rates of interest.

29.2 THE GROWTH OF THE EURO-CURRENCY MARKETS

Several different estimates exist of the size of the Euro-currency markets. The most popular is the Bank for International Settlement's *net* concept. This considers only banks physically situated in Europe, but nets out their inter-bank transactions. Since 1970 this has tended to understate expansion, however, because the non-European markets, especially those of the Far East, have tended to grow faster. Table 29.2 reports, therefore, both the BIS measure and a broader measure that allows for these other markets but cannot net out inter-bank transactions. Both measures, however, show clearly that the Euro-markets have grown prodigiously since the early 1960s, and it is to this that we now turn.

In asking why the Euro-currency markets have grown we are essentially asking (a) why non-Americans wish to hold dollars and not their own local currencies, and (b) why holders of dollars wish to deposit them outside America. Analogous questions may be posed about borrowers, although in general it has been pressure from lenders that has stimulated growth. The simple answer is, of course, that the Euro-markets offer a better combination of risk and return than local markets. But why? We should distinguish two classes of causes: natural economic advantages, and policy-induced and political factors.

Politics and policy   The origin of the Euro-dollar market is usually attributed to politics. During the early 1960s the Russians sold substantial amounts of gold for dollars. For reasons of ideological purity and fearing the possible confiscation of their assets, however, they wished to keep them outside the USA. Hence they deposited dollars in Europe – especially with the London banks. The banks found they could readily re-lend these dollars to the European and Japanese economies where rapid growth and tight money combined to produce credit shortages. In general, the dollars were converted to local currency and invested domestically.

Table 29.2 The growth of the Euro-currency markets, 1964–87 (US$b.)

Year	Net	Gross	World imports
1964	9	20	167
1965	12	24	182
1966	15	29	200.5
1967	18	36	209.7
1968	25	50	232.7
1969	44	85	264.8
1970	57	115	304.5
1971	71	150	339.8
1972	92	210	397.8
1973	160	315	549.1
1974	220	395	805.2
1975	255	485	837.8
1976	320	595	947.9
1977	390	740	1,085.7
1978	495	950	1,261
1979	590	1,235	1,584
1980	730	1,525	1,946
1981	1,018	1,954	1,928
1982	1,152	2,168	1,807
1983	1,237	2,278	1,752
1984	1,277	2,278	1,862
1985	1,480	2,846	1,895
1986	1,833	3,683	2,066
1987	2,221	4,509	2,404ᵖ

Sources: col. 1 – Bank for International Settlements, *Annual Reports*, and Levich (1989); change in definition, 1973; col. 2 – Morgan Guaranty Trust Co. and Levich (1989); col. 3 – IMF, *International Financial Statistics*; p provisional.

Growth was further stimulated by a piece of American legislation. During the late 1960s Regulation Q restricted the rate of interest US banks could pay on deposits. The British banks could easily out-bid this and so funds flowed into London. The resulting American credit shortage forced borrowers to Europe also, and this reverse flow rapidly became institutionalised as US banks established London branches to funnel funds back to New York.

A final political stimulus was the OPEC surpluses of 1974. OPEC too feared possible confiscation, but its surpluses were so huge that any means of recycling them to deficit countries would have been used. The Euro-markets, in fact, proved very efficient in this respect (see the following sub-section) and so underwent very considerable growth as OPEC prospered.

Related to these explanations is that of 'potential policy'. Many countries have established exchange controls at some time or another; these affect the terms on which money may be deposited in the country with respect to interest payments or the repatriation of capital. The attraction of the Euro-markets is that, say, sterling deposited in Paris is beyond the reach of the British authorities, while the French authorities have little interest in trying to control it since it has no implications for their currency. Hence Euro-markets allow depositors and borrowers to avoid one source of risk – namely, the possibility of restrictive action by the government in whose currency they are dealing.

Economic advantages These special factors undoubtedly stimulated the growth of the Euro-currency market, but, having been born, a number of sound economic reasons can be adduced as to why it has continued to thrive. These explain why it can handle funds more cheaply than domestic banking systems. 'Cheapness' involves lower dealing margins; that is, a lower spread between lending and borrowing rates of interest. Euro-deposit rates almost invariably lie above those of their corresponding domestic markets, whereas Euro-borrowing rates lie below.

The first economic consideration concerns *key currencies*. We have argued above that there are economies in both transactions and information costs if just a few currencies are used for international commerce. Coupled to this, companies benefit from dealing with *local banks*. A Belgian firm, for instance, is likely to wish to hold dollars in Belgium, and thus a Euro-market is born. In fact this argument suggests that Euro-markets would exist even if they had larger spreads than domestic markets. Nevertheless, the fact that they have smaller spreads is probably of some significance.

The second advantage the Euro-markets have is that of being free of the restrictive practices of domestic banking. It is difficult to avoid the conclusion that, at least until very recently, domestic banking systems were *oligopolistic*: there are generally few major banks, entry to the market is restricted (usually by legislation) and prices (rates of interest) are uniform across banks, although substantial non-price competition occurs. Hence, domestic margins tend to exceed the minimum required to survive, and there is room for a competitive institution – the Euro-market – to undercut local systems. This is especially so if it can bid away a section of business that is particularly cheap to service. In domestic banking, most customers pay an average charge, so that 'cheap' customers subsidise 'expensive' ones. By concentrating on large transactions, the Euro-market can service large 'cheap' customers at *their* marginal cost.

Allied to the lack of competition is the plethora of *controls* that domestic banks face. They are often obliged by the authorities to undertake particular types of business (e.g. rescuing ailing companies or financing exports) that are not in their immediate commercial interest, and they are subject to rigid restrictions on their balance sheets. To ensure the security and stability of the banking system, domestic banks in Britain are obliged to hold some minimum proportion of their deposits in non-interest-bearing central bank reserve assets and are also obliged to maintain minimal levels of capital to support their liabilities. This cuts the proportion of their funds that they can lend commercially and hence raises their prices (spreads). The Euro-banks are generally free from these restrictions and so can undercut local banks.

The reason that competition from off-shore banks suddenly blew up in the early 1960s is probably the huge improvements in communications technology. The Euro-markets are not physical institutions; rather they comprise separate bodies linked by telex and computer. Hence communication is a necessary condition for their existence.

A fourth advantage of the Euro-markets has already been mentioned. By restricting themselves to *wholesale transactions* the Euro-banks avoid providing expensive retail services (counter services, savings accounts, etc.), and are able to spread to fixed costs of transactions over large sums of money. Frequently, loans are too large for a single bank to cover alone, so syndicates are formed. In such *syndicated lending*, one bank conducts all the negotiations, receiving a fee, but the loan is then subscribed by several banks at the arranged rate of interest. The attraction to the banks of this procedure is that it allows a large loan to be issued without it dominating the balance sheet of any particular bank. As we saw above, a diversified portfolio is less risky than a concentrated one because it is highly unlikely that all borrowers will default at once. Hence, syndication reconciles large loans with risk spreading.

A final advantage for the Euro-system concerns *information*, as was noted by Niehans and Hewson (1976). Suppose a US bank has surplus funds and a Japanese bank has a potential borrower. If these two are to be matched without any mediation, the US bank has to know the Japanese bank and trust it enough to accept its assurances about its own and its client's creditworthiness. On a national level, if every US bank had to 'know' every Japanese bank the information requirement would be overwhelming. Now, however, introduce mediation by the Euro-banks. The Japanese Euro-banks know their local colleagues, as do US banks, but the Japanese and US Euro-banks also 'know' each other, if not directly then through a chain of other Euro-banks. Through this chain each bank need deal only with banks it knows, yet final borrowers and lenders quite unknown to each other can be put into contact. The system works because at each stage the Euro-bank borrows in its own name – thus guaranteeing its creditor repayment whether or not the ultimate borrower pays up. Hence, trust need never extend over more than one link of the chain.

Thus the Euro-market is an intermediary making money by economising on information. Each bank needs only relatively few contacts inside and outside the Euro-system, but through their mutual links the Euro-banks are able to connect final borrowers to final lenders. The mutual links are the inter-bank transactions, which are thus seen to be an essential part of the system. Notice that, in this role, no maturity transformation need occur at all. The whole string of loans would probably be liquidated at the same time.

29.3 THE CREATION OF LIQUIDITY

The ability of the Euro-markets to create international liquidity has been fiercely debated. There are basically two schools of thought: first, those who believe the Euro-system is analogous to the domestic banking system and that it could therefore create significant amounts of liquidity, and, second, those who believe it is merely an example of non-bank financial intermediation, with the power to raise the velocity of circulation modestly but little else. The former view generates a multiplier analysis of the market, while the latter produces a portfolio general equilibrium approach. Our own preference is for the latter.

A multiplier analysis This approach to Euro-markets is based on the analogy with a domestic banking system, so we start by briefly rehearsing a simple version of that analysis. Commercial banks are obliged to hold a proportion, r, of their deposits as reserves of non-interest-bearing cash. The remainder they lend out to the non-bank sector at positive rates of interest. Suppose we start from equilibrium, with total bank deposits (D) and reserves (R), where

$$R = rD. \tag{29.1}$$

Now suppose some additional cash (A) is deposited in the banking system (say via a balance of payments surplus). The banks keep rA of this as backing for A, but re-lend the remaining $(1-r)A$. The people who borrow this will spend it (assume at home) and the recipients will place most of what they receive back in their bank accounts in the commercial banking system: say they re-deposit proportion d, then $d(1-r)A$ will flow back to the banks. But this just provides more cash to the banks, so they keep r of it ($rd(1-r)A$ in all) and lend out the remaining $d(1-r)^2A$ of which $d^2(1-r)A$ returns, and so on. The total increase in money supply (M) from this process is the sum of all the increments to deposits: namely,

$$\Delta M = A + d(1-r)A + d^2(1-r)^2A + \ldots = \frac{1}{1 - d(1-r)}A. \qquad (29.2)^1$$

Hence the domestic money multiplier relating the increase in money supply to the initial impact is $1/[1 - d(1-r)]$. Clearly it is higher, the higher is d and the lower is r.

Now let us reinterpret this model in terms of Euro-currencies – specifically Euro-dollars. The reserves of the Euro-currency system are dollar deposits in New York; the analogue of the deposits above (the money supply) is Euro-deposits. The Euro-banks receive a deposit of A and lend out $\$(1-r)A$, keeping $\$rA$ back in reserves. Of the $\$(1-r)A$, $\$d(1-r)A$ is re-deposited in the Euro-system, and the story is just as before. The effect of the Euro-markets on world liquidity, therefore, seems to depend crucially on the reserve ratio (r) and the re-deposit ratio (d). We have already seen that Euro-bank reserves are very small: r is certainly below 0.05 and probably around only 0.01. Taken alone, the low r and the huge potential reserves (the whole of the domestic bank deposits in the US) would suggest an almost unlimited ability to create liquidity.

Now, however, consider the re-deposit ratio (d). Generally this is fairly low, because the Euro-loan is probably for transactions purposes (i.e. to spend) and Euro-markets are not designed primarily for holding that kind of balance. Hence the borrower is likely to keep the Euro-loan in a transactions account in some domestic banking system, as is the recipient of the money when it is spent. If this transaction account is in dollars in New York, nearly all the original dollar deposit (A) is passed from the Euro-market back to the US commercial system and no further Euro-creation occurs.

The alternative place to keep transaction balances is in local currency at non-US domestic banks. This involves swapping the dollars for local currency, which will normally entail their either returning to the USA (as above) or entering some country's official reserves. Since these, too, are generally held in American domestic banks, further Euro-dollar creation is stopped in this case too. If, however, central banks were to re-deposit their reserves on the Euro-markets, then d could rise substantially and multiple credit-creation could occur. This danger was recognised in the early 1970s when the Group of Ten agreed not to re-deposit, but it is still fairly significant today among developing countries. In 1988, about 30 per cent of their official foreign exchange reserves were in Euro-currencies (International Monetary Fund, *Annual Report*, 1989).

The *average* propensity to deposit on the Euro-markets is under 0.05 because Euro-deposits account for less than 5 per cent of world money supply (Johnston, 1983, p. 51). The *marginal* propensity is certainly higher, not least because much of the world money supply is not internationally mobile (because of exchange restrictions), so Euro-currencies account for a higher proportion of what is circulating freely in the international economy. Nevertheless, it is unlikely that d exceeds 0.20. Coupled with a minimum value of r of 0.01, the maximum multiplier is probably only 1.25.

Before leaving this analysis we should note that even with a relatively low multiplier the Euro-system could significantly raise the world money supply. The reserves for the Euro-system are deposits in the domestic banking systems of the Euro-currencies. Hence huge amounts are potentially available. Moreover, since the domestic deposits backing, say, Euro-dollars never leave the US banking system, the US money supply is not reduced by a shift into Euro-deposits, so any multiple Euro-creation represents a net gain in the world money supply.[2]

Portfolio analysis   The multiplier analysis just outlined depends on two crucial assumptions; (a) that whenever banks receive additional cash they wish to lend out as much as possible of it, and (b) that they can actually find borrowers at the ruling rate of interest. The latter is somewhat dubious even in a domestic system. The former, however, is ensured at home by the existence of legal reserve requirements in excess of those the banks would naturally choose, and the fact that reserves earn very low or even zero rates of interest. In the Euro-dollar market neither of these conditions holds: reserves are held at commercial short-term rates, and banks are entirely free to choose their own portfolios. Hence, at any set of ruling interest rates we must assume that the Euro-banks are content with their mix of reserves and commercial loans. Similarly, because there is no government 'advice' about whom banks may lend to, as there often tends to be at home, we might presume that all potential borrowers at the ruling rate of interest are actually satisfied. In other words, in the absence of any restrictions, the Euro-market is in competitive equilibrium, with the interest rate just balancing the supply of and demand for Euro-loans.

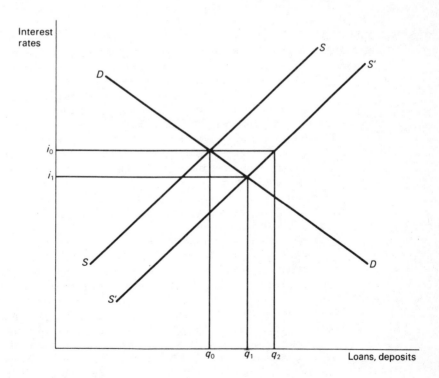

Figure 29.1 The Euro-dollar market in portfolio equilibrium

Let us represent the Euro-market in Figure 29.1. Ignoring the banks' spread between borrowing and lending rates, DD represents the (non-bank) demand for Euro-loans, while SS represents the (non-bank) supply of deposits to the Euro-market. Equilibrium is initially at (q_0, i_0), but suppose it is disturbed by a shift in the supply of deposits. Imagine this just represents a change in preferences such that, at any rate of interest, $q_0 q_2$, extra deposits are offered to the Euro-banks. The net result, of course, is a fall in the rate of interest and a net expansion of Euro-business by $q_0 q_1$; the 'multiplier' is $q_0 q_1 / q_0 q_2$, which is necessarily below unity.

The story behind Figure 29.1 is as follows. The Euro-banks, having received extra deposits, try to lend them out, but since at i_0 all demand has been met, this is only possible with a fall in the rate. The fall in the rate, however, makes re-lending less attractive relative to holding reserves – assuming that the reserve rate of interest remains unchanged – so only a fraction of the new deposits is lent out. Similarly, the falling rate of interest makes Euro-deposits less attractive to lenders relative to other assets, and so some deposits are withdrawn from the market. Hence, if the market is initially in full equilibrium, any change in deposits must be accompanied by interest rate changes, and these reduce the final increment to the Euro-market's total deposits below the size of the initial impact.

This model is simple but not fundamentally misleading. It is possible to add the national banking systems or differing maturities of loans to the general equilibrium system without altering the basic result (see, for instance, Freedman, 1977a, and Johnston, 1981). The result could be upset, however, by central bank re-depositing if this occurred independently of interest rates, but we have already seen that this is not prevalent among the major banks.

Liquidity creation in the portfolio model

The portfolio model just described treats Euro-banks as non-monetary financial intermediaries. It suggests that they cannot create credit (liquidity) because, given a stable demand and supply of deposits, their expansion is likely to be balanced by a contraction elsewhere. Although this is largely true at any one time, it is not true through time, however, because intermediaries are able to influence the scope of the market.

First, Euro-markets shift money from people who want to save to people who want to spend. Hence, they raise the velocity of circulation of any given money stock. Second, they may overcome restrictions and/or restrictive practices in other parts of the financial system, and hence increase the *effective* demand and/or supply of deposits overall. Third, and closely related, by competition they may improve the efficiency of the rest of the system, hence increasing its effectiveness and overall business.

These reasons suggest that even on the portfolio view Euro-markets may have added to the world money supply as they introduced new borrowing opportunities. For instance, they have probably increased the general efficiency of banking, they have almost certainly found customers who could not borrow on national systems (e.g. the developing countries), and they have shifted funds from countries where banks' reserves are excessive (surplus countries) to those where reserve shortage has constrained bank credit (deficit countries). However, not all Euro-business contributes additional liquidity – some of it merely displaces other national business. Furthermore, any such expansion is of a one-off nature. The market expands as the Euro-banks innovate but, once the supply of new customers is exhausted, growth is constrained by the rate at which existing customers raise their demand, which is normally much below that which can be achieved by broadening the market. In other words, the fact that the Euro-banks have found new borrowers for their deposits and hence raised world liquidity in the past does not mean that they will be able to do so for any future injection of funds.

'Net' vs. 'gross' liquidity

If all loans had the same maturity, financial institutions would be able to raise only the velocity of circulation. Someone who did not want his money for, say, three months would lend it to someone who did. The money would 'work harder', but little would be gained in terms of liquidity because the second person's (temporary) gain of purchasing power would be roughly balanced by the first's (equally temporary) loss. Thus, if Euro-banks' loans had identical maturity structure to their deposits, they would create little 'useful' or 'net' liquidity, regardless of the value of the multiplier.

Returning to Table 29.1, however, we see that Euro-banks do transform maturities and hence do create 'useful' liquidity. The lender of an eight-day deposit feels quite liquid – he will get his money back in a week – but so does the borrower of a three-year loan – he can spend extra cash over the next three years. The exact increase in 'net' liquidity depends on how we trade off one maturity against another; Johnston (1983) discussed two possible approaches, but we shall do no more than note that maturity transformation creates 'net' liquidity.

29.4 EURO-CAPITAL MARKETS

The purpose of banking is to collect idle balances in one area and translate them into active balances in another. Banks do this by offering three services: intermediation (linking borrowers to lenders), maturity transformation and insurance against default. The last arises because, for so long as the bank survives, depositors are guaranteed to get their money back regardless of whether it has been devoted to a good or a bad loan. The guarantee entails a process of aggregation whereby all the bank's deposit liabilities are backed by all its loans (assets), and it almost inevitably results in a degree of averaging in the rates of interest paid and charged. This is attractive to lenders in that it saves them from distinguishing good risks from bad (i.e. the banks economise on information requirements), but on the other side it means that at least to some extent very good (secure) borrowers are cross-subsidising poorer ones. This raises the possibility that, if no maturity transformation is required, and if a borrower can convince lenders of its high security, then it may be cheaper for very secure borrowers to borrow direct rather than via a bank.

The direct dealing between borrowers and lenders is what happens in capital markets, and such Euro-transactions have grown very rapidly in the 1980s. As the banks became troubled by potential defaults in the early 1980s – not least on loans to developing countries (see Chapter 30) – they became both less liquid and more expensive as a source of funds. As a result, major borrowers such as ICI and British Petroleum found it attractive to raise money directly, essentially because they were less likely to default than was the 'average' bank debtor. They still needed intermediation and, at times, maturity transformation, so there was still a role for international banks, even though they did not lend directly. This section sketches some of the major instruments for international capital transactions which have grown up recently. Like Euro-bank lending, these instruments increase the velocity of circulation and the effectiveness of capital markets, but do not directly create money.

Eurobonds are bonds that are issued and underwritten in a variety of national markets – usually through an international syndicate of banks. As with Euro-banking, the term 'Euro' denotes the decoupling of the countries and currencies involved. Eurobonds are to be contrasted with 'foreign bonds' by which non-residents borrow on a national capital market in that market's currency.

Most Eurobonds offer a fixed rate of interest, but some 20 per cent are *floating rate notes* (FRNs) with interest rates defined by a given margin over LIBOR (the London InterBank Offer Rate). In this respect they are like Euro-loans with a roll-over facility. FRNs attempt to shift the interest rate risk from lenders to borrowers, but rather tend to transform it from a capital risk to a default risk. A fixed-interest bond falls in value if the interest rate rises: the given stream of income is less valuable because it could be obtained by investing a smaller capital sum at the new, higher rate of interest. An FRN, on the other hand, maintains its capital value because interest receipts rise, but this increases the likelihood that the borrower will not be able to service his debt. The principal use of FRNs appears to be for inter-bank transactions; in 1986, 40 per cent of issues were made for banks, three-quarters of which were taken up by other banks.

Issuing debt requires reputation and a company's reputation in one type of market may be stronger than in another. In such cases, however, the company may still effectively be able to borrow advantageously in the latter market if it can arrange a swap. A *simple interest rate swap* occurs if, say, company A issues a fixed-rate bond and company B an FRN, but they agree to pay each other's interest. This would be advantageous if A could borrow relatively more cheaply in the fixed-interest market than B *and* had more optimistic expectations than B of a fall in interest rates. Note that, although interest payment liabilities are swapped, the liability to repay the capital of each issue stays with the issuers. Euro-banks are active in the swap markets both as intermediaries and by running their own books. Both interest rate and currency swaps have grown very rapidly since 1980; they account for a lot of Euro-business, and some 70 per cent of Eurobonds now have swaps of some kind attached to them.

Another instrument with characteristics intermediate to Eurobonds and Euro-loans is the *Euro-note*, which allows a form of maturity transformation. Euro-notes were first introduced in 1981 in the form of *Revolving Underwriting Facilities* (RUFs). An RUF is created when a bank agrees to underwrite a series of short-term note issues over a period of years: the maturity of the notes is, say, three months but the arrangement lasts for perhaps ten years. RUFs soon evolved into NIFs – *Note Issuance Facilities* – in which a syndicate of banks issues notes and agrees that, if it cannot place the notes with other lenders at less than some particular interest rate (usually variable), it will buy them itself. The banks earn an arrangement fee for setting up these deals plus an underwriting fee, and in return take on a contingent liability. In assessing the soundness of banks' operations it is very difficult to know how to treat such *off-balance sheet* liabilities. They are unlikely ever to be called upon and thus require relatively little capital backing, but, on the other hand, if they are ever required the bank has to find the money to honour them.

The market for NIFs has declined recently, largely to be replaced by *Euro-*

Commercial Paper (ECP) borrowing. Commercial paper is issued without underwriting, although issuers probably have a separate stand-by arrangement with a bank in case the issue fails; thus ECP makes no direct demands on the Euro-banks and consequently has no implications for the latter's capital adequacy. ECP is almost always denominated in dollars and traded in London. It is unsecured borrowing and is typically not rated by credit-rating agencies; thus only the very strongest of borrowers can operate in this market. Lesser companies are forced back into rated bonds or bank borrowing.

Capital markets vs. bank lending

The capital market instruments described in this section provide borrowers with cheap and flexible capital. They are, however, available only to top-grade borrowers and are both demanding and time-consuming to put together, with their requirements for issue prospectuses, etc. In addition, their terms, such as draw-down dates or currency of receipt, cannot be altered once fixed. Finally, capital instruments, especially ECP, are risky in the sense that no implicit commitment develops between borrower and lender such as often exists between banks and their clients: in hard times, capital markets may abandon a borrower entirely; banks rarely do. For all these reasons there remains a role for Euro-lending even with the growth of the capital market instruments, and, in fact, in 1987 and 1988 syndicated lending started to grow again, partly at the expense of FRN issues. Table 29.3 gives a break-down of new lending between capital markets and syndicated Euro-lending which serves much the same client base. Total Euro-lending, including that to smaller borrowers, exceeds syndicated lending by a factor of around two.

Table 29.3 International capital market and bank lending, 1973–86 (US$b.)

	1973	1980	1983	1984	1985	1986	1987	1988
International bank loans[a]	20.8	81.0	73.5	108.5	110.3	82.8	88.8	101.6
Capital market issues	4.2	20.4	59.6	110.1	204.0	279.2	218.5	240.1
of which								
bonds[b]	4.2	20.4	50.1	81.7	135.4	187.0	140.5	183.2
notes[c]	—	—	9.5	28.4	46.8	27.0	29.0	22.6
paper[d]	—	—	—	—	21.8	65.2	49.0	34.4

Notes:
[a] Wholly or partly in Euro-currency.
[b] Fixed and floating.
[c] NIFs plus other committed (i.e. underwritten) facilities.
[d] Non-underwritten facilities.
Sources: International Monetary Fund, *International Capital Markets: Developments and Prospects, 1989,* Tables 16, 17, 19, and Bank for International Settlements, *59th Annual Report,* 1989, pp. 102–129.

29.5 CONTROLLING THE EURO-MARKETS

Several arguments have been forwarded for controlling the Euro-markets. First, their ability to increase the velocity of circulation and (possibly) their ability to create credit have both been blamed for inflation. The former has occurred and may have raised inflation historically but, unless more financial innovations are forthcoming, velocity, and therefore inflation, will not rise in future. Credit creation has already been discussed and we have argued that the Euro-markets have little power to create credit themselves.

Second, there have been 'prudential' concerns. This argument states that unregulated banks tend to over-lend, and that they are consequently liable to crash. When this occurs they impose costs not only on themselves but also on depositors and the economy in general as economic activity slumps. Hence, it states, banks should be forced to keep larger reserve ratios and to behave in a 'responsible' way. This argument moves in and out of fashion. In 1974 and early 1983 it was popular because crashes seemed likely, but when times are easier most people are pleased to benefit from the economic stimulus that liberal lending induces.

A further argument for prudential control is that the volume of inter-bank lending transfers trouble from one bank to another, and makes it difficult for any particular bank to assess its true vulnerability. When Continental Illinois crashed in 1984, it threatened the stability of several off-shore banks whose reserves it held; this is sometimes said to be the reason why the Federal Reserve Board felt obliged to rescue it. Ironically it was the wholesale withdrawal of inter-bank reserve holdings by banks from Hong Kong and Singapore which triggered the critical run on Continental in the first place.

A degree of control of Euro-banks was exercised through the Basle Concordat and this was strengthened in 1983 after the failure of the Concordat to save, or even to identify who should save, Banco Ambrosiano, Italy's eleventh largest bank, which crashed in 1982. Broadly, the country of a bank's head office is responsible for its solvency world-wide, including its subsidiaries, and several national authorities now collect the consolidated accounting information necessary to allow such monitoring to be done. There remain many holes in the system, however, especially in the smaller off-shore centres.

Another argument for control has been antipathy towards international capital mobility. Capital mobility frustrates monetary policy and almost certainly exacerbates exchange rate variability (see Chapter 24). Since it is difficult to believe that short-term private mobility has many social benefits, it is argued, there would be net gains from reducing it; and since the Euro-markets have certainly permitted greater capital mobility, one way of achieving this would be to control them. However much one sympathises with the aim of this argument, it would be useless to control the Euro-banks without also controlling other channels of capital mobility.

Even if one accepts the case for control, it is not clear what controls should be enforced or how. The most obvious candidate is the enforcement of reserve ratios similar to domestic ones. This would reduce any multiplier and raise the Euro-banks' interest rate spreads, thus curtailing their level of operation and their power to generate expansion internally. Obviously, however, all countries would have to enforce the same ratio or banks would migrate to the 'lower-ratio' countries. Equally obvious are the incentives for countries to cheat.[3] Progress was made in this regard in 1987 when the UK and USA agreed common rules for banks' capital requirements, and other authorities, including the EC, subsequently fell into line with them. Yet again, however, relatively lax regulation by off-shore centres weakens the system considerably.

A further difficulty is where the reserves would be held. In domestic systems the central bank controls monetary policy and receives the reserves as subsidised loans. In return, it acts as lender of last resort, which involves periodically taking on commercially undesirable loans. On a world scale this role should ideally fall to some international institution, but one doubts the political feasibility of concentrating such power in any one place – *vide* the

446

IMF's laboured procedures. All told it will require greater political will than is presently evident to exercise effective control of the Euro-markets.

FURTHER READING

Crockett (1977), *McKinnon* (1979), *Llewellyn* (1980) and *Grubel* (1981) provide alternative textbook treatments of Euro-currency markets. *Johnston* (1983) provides a book-length introduction, while *Freedman* (1977b) describes the growth of the Euro-markets in terms of a series of happy accidents, and surveys some early references. On modelling the Euro-markets, *Niehans and Hewson* (1976) is excellent. *Crockett* (1976), *Johnston* (1981) and *Grabbe* (1981) also discuss the relationship between the multiplier and portfolio approaches, while *Hewson and Sakikabara* (1974), *Freedman* (1977a) and *Grabbe* (1981) present full general equilibrium models. *Lewis and Davis* (1987) and *Mullineux* (1987) fill in the banking and capital market details and *Gardener and Revell* (1987) describes the capital market instruments.

KEY CONCEPTS

Euro-dollar	inter-bank lending
maturity transformation	intermediation
syndicated lending	credit multiplier
portfolio model	Eurobond
FRN, NIF, ECP	prudential regulation

QUESTIONS FOR REVIEW

29.1   What is the role of intermediation in the Euro-banking system?
29.2   Contrast Euro-lending and Euro-capital market transactions. Why does the former persist?
29.3   Does the Euro-market increase world liquidity?
29.4   Appraise critically the case for regulating Euro-banking business in the same ways as domestic banking is regulated.

NOTES

1   The sum of an infinite series $1 + x + x^2 + \ldots$ is $1/(1 - x)$, provided $x < 1$.
2   This statement is rather over-simplified but it is nearly true. Of course, we have yet to conclude that multiple creation does actually occur.
3   It seems that one of the reasons for the switch from lending to capital market instruments (i.e. from banks earning profits via interest margins to preferring fees) after 1982 was the minimum capital requirements imposed on the former. That is, the attempt to avoid regulations can influence the nature, as well as the location, of business.

30 Developing Countries and the International Monetary System

Developing countries face the same problems and have the same economic concerns as industrial countries. In some cases, however, their poverty makes their problems more obvious and extreme and puts their solution into a different perspective. Thus, for example, the developing countries tend to place a greater weight on income growth and less on the dangers of inflation than most industrial countries. This chapter considers how the differences in perspective affect attitudes to the international monetary system and then analyses one particular issue of difference between industrial and developing countries – the debt crisis.

30.1 INTERNATIONAL MONEY AND DEVELOPMENT

Different objectives

In most respects the developing countries' (DCs) requirements of the international monetary system are the same as the industrial countries' (ICs): both desire smooth adjustment, strong economic activity and overall stability. However, within these broad objectives emphases differ. Like any poor person the DCs tend to hold relatively little by way of liquid reserves: any spare cash is quickly spent on the myriad pressing economic problems they face. Hence, in general DCs place less weight on money as a store of value than the rich. Conversely, of course, starting from a lower base, the DCs place a much greater emphasis on income growth.

The DCs feel a greater need for adjustment finance than the industrial countries, because holding relatively low reserves means that exogenous shocks impinge more readily on their domestic economies. If finance is not available, DCs are more frequently obliged to pursue domestic adjustment even in the face of clearly temporary deficits. Besides, since they are often more heavily specialised in primary goods, whose production and prices are less stable than those of manufactures, the DCs tend to suffer more shocks anyway. They also seek official adjustment finance more than ICs because they frequently do not have satisfactory access to private capital markets. This may be because of a lack of means to pay commercial rates of interest or because private markets, rightly or wrongly, suspect their creditworthiness.

The result of these different emphases is that DCs are persistently more expansionary in their international monetary aspirations than their richer partners, and typically keener to see surplus countries obliged to bear some of the adjustment burden.

International transfers

The major difference of opinion between the industrial and developing world, however, is one of substance not emphasis. The DCs hold that the international monetary system should be used to transfer resources from rich nations to poor. The reply from 'the North' – the industrial world – is that, although redistribution might be desirable, it would be wrong to confuse it with the logically separate issue of monetary control. For example, in Britain both controlling the money supply and providing social security payments are aims of policy, but the two are kept administratively separate. To establish

448

their case the DCs have to show either that transfers through the monetary system would be more efficient, or that monetary affairs frustrate other transfers.

The main instrument of transfer at present is international aid flows. These take the form of grants or concessionary loans and may be either bilateral (i.e. between two specific countries) or intermediated by one of the international agencies. The latter receive or raise money in the rich countries and distribute it to the poor. Generally, aid is granted for specific developmental purposes, but emergency food aid and large amounts of bilateral military aid also occur. In 1986, total receipts of aid by all DCs were $44.4b. This compared with direct investment inflows of $12.2b., private long-term loans of $13.9b. and official (non-concessional) long-term loans of $11.8b. Hence, aid amounted to 54 per cent of the long-term capital inflow.

Table 30.1 Resource flows to developing countries, 1979–86 (US$b.)

	1979	1980	1981	1982	1983	1984	1985	1986	Middle income	1986 Low income	Of which, least developed
Official development assistance	31.1	37.3	37.9	33.7	33.3	34.4	36.9	44.4	16.3	28.1	10.9
of which											
Bilateral	24.9	29.5	30.0	26.2	25.7	26.7	28.5	34.9	14.7	20.2	7.3
Multilateral	6.2	7.8	7.9	7.5	7.6	7.7	8.4	9.5	1.6	7.9	3.6
Other official finance	5.8	7.8	8.7	10.3	8.5	12.7	11.6	11.8	8.7	3.1	0.1
Export credit	13.5	17.0	17.2	13.6	7.4	7.1	4.6	−0.3	−2.6	2.3	0.2
Private flows	54.0	66.1	74.5	58.4	48.0	33.5	30.9	26.1	13.4	12.7	1.4
of which											
Direct investment	13.4	11.2	17.2	12.8	9.9	11.4	6.7	12.2	7.4	4.8	0.1
Bank lending	35.9	49.0	52.0	37.6	34.1	17.4	13.6	5.2	1.7	3.5	0.5
Other	4.7	5.9	5.3	8.0	4.0	4.7	9.6	8.7	4.3	4.4	0.8
Total	104.4	128.2	138.3	116.0	97.2	87.7	84.0	82.0	35.8	46.2	12.6
Total at 1986 prices	130.9	146.7	164.1	140.5	118.1	108.8	103.1	82.0	35.8	46.2	12.6

Source: OECD, *Financing and External Debt of Developing Countries, 1987 Survey.*

Table 30.1 gives further details of these flows. The most striking feature of the left-hand part of the table, on the total flows, is the 35 per cent decline in overall resource flows to the developing countries over the 1980s. This was almost entirely due to the fall in private sector lending – mainly bank lending and export credits. These fell from being the dominant form of resource transfer in the early 1980s to below 10 per cent in 1986. This was both the cause and the effect of the debt crisis, and is examined below. During the 1980s, foreign direct investment also declined somewhat, while official aid flows (assistance) and non-concessional lending (other official finance) grew, not least to compensate for the fall in private resources.

The right-hand side of the table gives a break-down of resource flows by class of recipient. The most notable, although not the most surprising, feature is the importance of official flows to the poorest countries. The forty-one least developed countries have very little commerce with which to attract private funds and consequently depend almost exclusively on official donors and charities, which are included under 'private: other'. When the other low-income countries are added in, the same traits are evident, although less markedly. Low-income countries have reached a stage of development at which some private lending/investment looks profitable, but are still heavily dependent on official sources. In more normal times than 1986 the middle-income countries would have had much greater private flows than the table shows. They receive little concessionary funding from multilateral agencies but still fairly significant amounts bilaterally, especially currently given the lack of private flows.

Bilateral flows give rise to one of the major complaints about current aid programmes – the political nature of many donations. For example, Egypt is the major recipient of international food aid, despite having the third highest per capita calorie intake in the Third World, while Israel receives more than twice as much aid per capita as any other country. These figures reflect the USA's – the major donor's – geo-political aims, but similar issues arise, for example, with Arab support for Jordan. Aid per capita is higher for lower-middle-income countries than for low-income ones, but it accounts for a higher proportion of the latter's GNP – 6.1 per cent in 1987 (excluding India and China, which receive only relatively small donations) compared with 1.8 per cent (*World Development Report*, 1989).

The UN has long held that the rich countries should aim to dispense at least 1 per cent of their GNP in financial transfers to developing countries, with at least 0.7 per cent in the form of official development assistance (i.e. concessionary aid). The major aid donors in 1987 were Saudi Arabia, Kuwait and Norway (3.4 per cent, 1.2 per cent and 1.1 per cent of GNP respectively); OECD managed 0.35 per cent overall, ranging from 1.1 per cent (Norway), and 0.98 per cent (the Netherlands), through 0.28 per cent (UK) to 0.17 per cent (Austria). These figures include tied aid – aid which may be spent only in the donor country. This is economically inefficient in the same way that barter trade is; it is better than nothing, but much less effective than a straight money transfer. The figures also include food aid, which, aside from humanitarian emergency aid, owes more to OECD countries' need to dispose of food surpluses than the to DC's need for food. For example, food aid shows a marked tendency to decline when food surpluses are low and commercial prices high, and can even be counter-productive in the long run, by driving recipient countries' local farmers out of business.

The World Bank

The principal multilateral agency concerned with transferring resources to the developing world is the World Bank (the International Bank for Reconstruction and Development) and its sister organisations. The Bank was created at the Bretton Woods Conference to fund and oversee post-war reconstruction. By the mid-1950s, however, it had become the development agency it now is. It raises its funds on world capital markets and its lending, which is devoted mostly to specific projects, must meet normal criteria of commercial viability. Although the grant element of Bank lending is small, borrowing governments get several advantages from using Bank funding. First, the Bank can borrow and on-lend more cheaply than they can borrow direct. Its borrowing is fully underwritten by its industrial country members and its lending 'programmes are important enough to guarantee it a very high priority in debtors' payment schedules. Consequently the Bank has always maintained its 'triple-A' credit rating despite lending to countries most of which do not. Second, the Bank has great expertise in proposing, assessing and managing projects. Hence Bank projects are usually commercially well conceived and fairly successful, although there are exceptions. Third, the Bank operates on longer time-horizons than most commercial lenders and is less likely to be panicked into withdrawing support if the economy under-performs.

The DCs' balance of payments problems of the late 1970s led the Bank to introduce a facility for making Structural Adjustment Loans (SALs) with up to 10 per cent of its portfolio. These were originally three–five-year loans to help economies adjust to the harsher economic conditions; they were not tied to specific projects but were general capital offered in return for commitments on macro-economic and structural (micro-economic) policies. Such loans were welcomed by client countries as well as the Bank, which was finding it difficult to lend on its usual criteria. SALs were subsequently extended to seven or more years, and in the fiscal year 1988 SALs accounted for 25 per cent of the Bank's new lending. SALs have been subject to the same criticisms as IMF lending and conditionality (see below), and there has been opposition to the rigour of the policies called for by the Bank. A recent study (World Bank, 1989), however, suggested that, despite having more severe than average economic shocks, countries using SALs have shown slightly better than average balance of payments and economic growth performance. It also suggested that adherence to the conditions of the loans had been quite good, with around 80 per cent of countries achieving or making 'substantial progress' towards the agreed policies and goals. The policies typically called for include reduced public sector deficits, changes in public sector management (sometimes privatisation) and international trade liberalisation.

The World Bank has four affiliated organisations. The oldest is the International Development Association (IDA) founded in 1962 to make 'soft loans' to the poorest countries. It still applies strict criteria of viability to the schemes that it will finance, but it charges below market rates of interest and offers very long maturities. It is financed by donations from the richer members of the World Bank. The International Finance Corporation (IFC) – the Bank's private capital arm – lends to and takes equity in private sector companies on a commercial basis. It also offers intermediation and advice to middle-income countries in their relations with private lenders, including funding the set-up costs associated with establishing a company.

The Multilateral Investment Guarantee Association (MIGA) was formed in 1988 to offer guarantees to foreign direct investment against armed conflict, expropriation and difficulties in repatriating earnings. In accordance with our theories above, MIGA addresses a market failure directly rather than by trying to compensate for it by lending in its own name. A major worry for potential investors is security, and nothing a borrowing country government can do in isolation can really guarantee that next year it, or its successor, will not expropriate an investment. However, by signing a pledge with an organisation which could cut off much of its capital inflow should it go back on its word, the DC government can make a credible commitment to 'good' behaviour. In theory this should unlock a stream of private investment, although it is too early to be sure in practice. The last affiliate is the International Convention on the Settlement of Investment Disputes (ICSID), whose role is obvious from its name.

In the fiscal year 1987–8 the World Bank made new commitments of $14.8b., the IDA made new commitments of $4.5b., and the IFC approved investments of $1.3b. (World Bank, *Annual Report*, 1988).

451

With IMF votes proportional to quotas and quotas proportional to economic size, the IMF is quite clearly controlled by the rich countries of 'the North'. It has not ignored the developing countries, however; most of its borrowers are DCs and it has gradually introduced measures to meet their requirements. Nevertheless, the DCs feel that it has been less beneficent than it might have been, criticising it on two major issues: the size and distribution of resources and conditionality.

DCs have persistently called for greater Fund resources. They have also argued that rather than expand every country's borrowing rights roughly proportionately, as has tended to happen, new resources should be concentrated on those most in need – the poor deficit countries. At first the DCs protested in vain, but in 1973 the success of OPEC encouraged DCs to act in concert and this considerably increased their political effectiveness. The DCs were well represented on the Committee of Twenty – nine out of twenty places – and held a blocking minority of votes on the IMF Board. Thus they could effectively frustrate any plans the North might form, so their agreement was necessary for the Second Amendment.

The issue the DCs fought most vigorously was the *SDR–aid link*. This suggested that SDRs should be issued solely to DCs, which, by spending them, would rapidly put them into general circulation. Provided the rate of interest was below commercial rates (as applied to the DCs) this would grant the DCs seignorage – a form of painless (and invisible?) aid. The North objected on many grounds: not confusing money creation and aid; that 'the link' would encourage the over-creation of SDRs and hence inflation; that it would freeze the interest rate below market rates; and that if aid were given via SDRs it would just be withdrawn from other channels. Also, one suspects, a mere unwillingness to give away resources was present. In the event the link was squashed.

In compensation, however, the DCs were granted several other concessions. Resources – especially the special funds – were expanded and the proceeds of the gold sales were distributed to the DCs. Special arrangements were also made for countries with small quotas.

Conditionality

The need for conditionality of some sort is rarely questioned. The IMF exists to provide short-term circulating balance of payments finance; it therefore needs to ensure that repayments will be made on time so that resources are always available for new borrowers. Compensatory, Buffer Stock and First Credit Tranche finance are available on uncontentious 'low conditionality': borrowers are requested to take reasonable steps to balance their payments. Upper Credit Tranches, Extended Enlarged and Structural facilities, on the other hand, require agreement with the IMF over economic policies and macro-economic performance. These are enshrined in a 'letter of intent', and credit, which is always paid in instalments, is available only if the conditions are met. These conditions are the contentious issue, the argument frequently being made by developing countries that they are unnecessary for short-term stabilisation and deleterious to long-run growth.

There are three methods of trying to isolate the effects of a Fund programme. First, a *positive* approach compares economic indicators during a Fund programme with those observed before the programme or observed in similar non-programme countries during the programme period. The difficulties of this approach are those of ensuring genuine comparability: before-and-after studies are distorted by shocks during the programme and the fact that performance prior to the programme is unsustainable; cross-country comparisons ignore differences between countries and also the fact that going to the Fund indicates the seriousness of the problems and/or a willingness to pursue Fund-type policies. The *normative* approach compares economic indicators with the values prescribed in the letter of intent. This too cannot take account of new shocks. Third, the *conjectural* approach attempts to compare outcomes under the Fund programme with those of an alternative sustainable economic policy; this is the ideal approach, but is very difficult to implement. Finally, we should note that assessing the effects of a Fund programme is logically different from assessing the contribution of the conditionality attached to it; however, economists have made no progress at all on the latter issue.

Economic stabilisation is greatly complicated by the existence of a large volume of outstanding debt – see page 465 below. Hence it is useful to divide Fund programmes into pre- and post-1982 sets before analysing their effects. Important studies of the earlier period include Donovan (1982), Goldstein and Montiel (1986) and Pastor (1987). The results of such studies are mixed; the balance of payments effects of a programme are commonly positive, but few other indicators show consistent responses. Bird (1982b) offered a useful summary of the pre-1982 debate, despite pre-dating some of the quantitative analysis. He identified eight areas of complaint and reply over conditionality:

- The IMF is hard-line and doctrinaire, considering only monetary solutions and ignoring structural elements of DCs' balance of payments problems. This is denied, the Fund claiming to be pragmatic and pointing to the Extended and Structural Facilities as evidence of its concern for structural adjustment.
- The IMF emphasises short-term balance of payments correction at the expense of longer-run development. This is justified by the Fund, arguing that its Articles oblige it to act only for short-term finance; nevertheless, lending periods were significantly extended over the 1970s and 1980s.
- The IMF assumes that payments difficulties always arise from internal mismanagement rather than from external shock. The Fund, however, claims that the causes of a disequilibrium are of secondary importance; if it is permanent, balance of payments adjustment must occur and this usually involves domestic policy regardless of cause.
- The IMF is inflexible in its choice of performance criteria. This is denied, mainly on the grounds that the few broad criteria chosen cover very many different specific indicators.
- Conditions far exceed those necessary to guarantee the repayment of the small amounts of IMF lending. This is explained by (a) the fact that application to the Fund is often postponed until a crisis has arisen, and hence urgent action is actually necessary; and (b) Fund conditions are often necessary to attract the additional private finance needed for adjustment.
- The fund frequently ignores domestic political and institutional constraints. This is denied – the 1979 Guidelines on Conditionality expressly enjoin the Fund to take these into account.
- The Fund is biased: it favours the rich – especially banker – countries and, among the others, free market economies. This is countered by pointing to the Fund's successful relationship with certain socialist states.
- Conditionality achieves little success. Balance of payments positions may

be improved, but inflation and income inequalities are often worsened while there are no detectable effects on economic growth. This is denied: the Fund argues that most of the shortfall between the conditions and the actual outcome is due to external shocks and/or a lack of political commitment to cure the problems.

Bird then analysed ten IMF recovery programmes in each of the periods 1964–9, 1970–3 and 1974–9. His principal conclusions were:

- The IMF must encourage private finance by taking a firm line on conditionality. Its own resources are inadequate to the DCs' needs.
- The IMF does emphasise credit control – nineteen out of twenty arrangements since 1970 involved credit ceilings. However, different parts of credit are specified for different countries to control, allowing considerable tailoring of conditionality to individual countries' circumstances.
- The IMF is not doctrinally committed to the monetary theory of the balance of payments. Many of its conditions – e.g. devaluation – are contrary to the prescriptions of these theories.
- The IMF did not insist unduly on devaluation. Only about one-quarter to one-third of all arrangements involve devaluation. Trade liberalisation figures about as frequently. Devaluation is quite frequently contractionary, however (see Chapter 20 above).
- The IMF does tend to emphasise demand over supply considerations, but given its short time-horizon an alternative approach is not obvious. The Structural Facilities and cooperation with the World Bank now tend to weaken this conclusion.
- The IMF is not even-handed in its treatment of borrowers; it is subject to political influences, especially via the nationally appointed Executive Directors. However, it is not overtly anti-socialist.
- The IMF has had mixed success with its programmes.

Many of Bird's points carry over to the 1980s, when conditionality was probably less successful than previously. Edwards (1989) showed that the content of conditionality has changed somewhat: every programme over 1983–5 imposed credit ceilings and 80 per cent required devaluation; there was a larger selection of other measures such as fiscal changes than previously, and a slightly greater insistence on trade and/or financial liberalisation. Before-and-after assessments are inappropriate over 1983–5, because nearly every developing country had to make significant current account improvements as international lending dried up. Edwards showed that few programmes actually achieved their targets, however, probably due to the terms of trade shocks and debt problems of the period. It is also plain that IMF programmes, while keeping debtor countries afloat, have singularly failed to solve the debt crisis, although it is not clear that this can be laid at the door of conditionality (see section 30.3 below).

A conceptual criticism of current conditionality was made by Spraos (1986). He argued that the Fund confuses targets and instruments. Its Articles of Agreement specify a concern only with the balance of payments and exchange convertibility. Thus for the Fund to be prescriptive about internal matters such as fiscal stances is inappropriate. Rather, Spraos argued, it should insist on certain balance of payments criteria and leave the rest to the country's discretion. This is a perfectly logical position, although it ignores possible difficulties over the sustainability of clients' economic programmes and the role of the IMF in facilitating private as well as official lending.

To conclude, there is clearly some room for DC dissatisfaction with the IMF. It is not, however, nearly as clear-cut as some critics claim. Given the IMF's role as a world monetary institution rather than a development agency, it would be unrealistic to expect it to funnel large amounts of low-condition finance to the DCs. Moreover, the DCs do not always capitalise on their moral case for increased transfers. Too frequently, resources are devoted to expensive military or prestige programmes rather than to unglamorous but basic economic development, and donors frequently express concern about the honesty and efficiency with which DCs' domestic policies are administered. While these views often amount to the pot calling the kettle black, there is no doubt that they contribute to a reluctance by the North to transfer resources to the South, be it through aid or by redesigning the IMF.

30.2 THE DEBT CRISIS

Everyone has heard about the debt crisis. Crudely, it exists because certain developing countries have borrowed more than they can repay on time, with the result that they are suffering years of austerity as they try to meet their obligations, while their creditors suffer the uncertainty of not knowing when or whether they will be repaid. A common reaction to such crises is 'a plague on both your houses', 'neither a borrower nor lender be'. Such views tend to gain particular currency after periodic financial crises (the 1980s were certainly not the first) as both borrowers and lenders recover their equilibrium; they also characterised the reaction of the Romanian government, which paid off all its foreign debt over the 1980s. In general, however, such isolationism is not a sensible response, for borrowing has an important role in economic development, as a glance at Australian or American economic history amply illustrates. This section briefly explores the simple economics of borrowing before considering the origins and consequences of the current debt crisis.

The analytics of borrowing

Like individuals, countries borrow in order to sever the link between current consumption and current income: if, in any period, consumption is to exceed income, borrowing (or at least dissaving) must occur. Thus borrowing is an issue of inter-temporal optimisation, and by this stage in the book it will be no surprise that its analysis involves social welfare functions and budget constraints.

When we consider foreign borrowing, the simplest form of the budget constraint is that the cumulated value of imports (current debits) discounted to a point in time cannot exceed the cumulated value of exports (credits); that is, all debits must eventually be paid for by credits. This requirement may be written as:

$$\sum_{\tau=0}^{\infty} (1+i)^{-\tau} X_\tau - \sum_{\tau=0}^{\infty} (1+i)^{-\tau} M_\tau \geq 0, \qquad (30.1)$$

where i is the rate of interest, M_τ is 'imports' in year τ and X_τ 'exports' in year τ.

If we consider an arbitrary year, t, (30.1) tells us that any excess of imports over exports up to t must be balanced by trade surpluses after t. The cumulated excess of past imports over exports is just the value of debt outstanding in t, so that we can write

$$D_t \leq \sum_{\tau = t}^{\infty} (1 + i)^{-\tau} B_\tau \qquad (30.2)$$

where D_t is debt outstanding at the beginning of year t and B_τ the trade balance $(X - M)$ in year τ. Note that (30.2) involves future values of B_τ and the implicit assumption that i is constant. Thus if ever it is used as the basis of actual lending or borrowing decisions, expectations about these magnitudes will be critical. Ignoring the government, we may write $B_\tau = Y_\tau - I_\tau - C_\tau$ where Y is national income, I investment and C consumption, so that

$$D_t \leq \sum_{\tau = t}^{\infty} (1 + i)^{-\tau} (Y_\tau - I_\tau) - \sum_{\tau = t}^{\infty} (1 + i)^{-\tau} C_\tau. \qquad (30.3)$$

Optimal borrowing will be determined to maximise an inter-temporal welfare function defined over the stream of consumption, C_t, C_{t+1}, ... C_∞, subject to (30.3).

Most developing countries will want to borrow during the course of development because, being poor, they place a high value on present rather than future consumption, and, at least in theory, because, being capital-scarce, they have good investment opportunities. Sound investment stimulates future income, and so relaxes the borrowing constraint (30.3). Indeed, if investment opportunities allow net income $(Y - I)$ to grow at an annual rate g, we can write the first term of (30.3) as

$$\sum_{\tau = t}^{\infty} (1 + i)^{-\tau} (1 + g)^{\tau} (Y_t - I_t); \qquad (30.4)$$

if the growth rate exceeds the rate of interest this term is infinite, and there is no limit to borrowing! That is, each year's borrowing can be more than repaid out of the future stream of income it generates, and so causes no reduction in future consumption.

We can use (30.2) and (30.3) to see what went wrong in the debt crisis. At any time the nominal value of debt, D_t, is given. If a country gets into a situation whereby the inequalities in (30.2) and (30.3) are reversed it cannot honour its debt. It is *insolvent* and the true value of its debt (the present value of the stream of repayments it can make) falls below its face value. This might happen for either or both of two reasons: first, ill-informed lenders might just have lent too much, and, second, lending that looked sound when it was made has ceased to be so because some of the elements of the borrowing constraint have changed unexpectedly. Thus a rise in the interest rate, i, would reduce the present value of future trade balances, as would a decline in the growth of exports or export prices. Similarly, a disruption of economic growth would reduce national income and thus future trade surpluses.

In fact countries are unlikely to become technically insolvent because they are unlikely to wish to borrow up to the point where future consumption is at minimum subsistence levels for ever. Thus adverse external shocks could almost always be compensated by squeezing future consumption further. However, if there are political or humanitarian constraints on doing so, it is possible that countries become effectively insolvent.

Suppose that the solvency constraint is satisfied. A crisis is still possible if borrowers face *liquidity constraints* – the absence of sufficient income or lending to make debt payments in a particular year. In these circumstances further borrowing to finance the debt service would be justified by the solvency criterion, but it is possible that it would not be forthcoming. There are good commercial reasons for banks to ration customers' borrowing, and prudential regulations about the share of any one customer in a bank's portfolio may actually forbid further lending. Moreover, there is also an externality. Suppose that the banking system could provide sufficient funds to solve a country's liquidity crisis, but that no single bank acting alone could do so. If each bank believes that the others will not lend, it has no incentive to do so itself. If it were the only lender, the liquidity crisis would still occur and creditors would receive only, say, x per cent of which they were due. That means they would take a loss of $(100 - x)$ per cent on their assets. Lending just before such a crisis unfolded would increase the value of the assets on which losses were taken, and so would not be rational. Thus no bank would lend and they would all make losses, even though, had they all lent, none of them would have made losses. Organising collective lending under such circumstances has been a major theme of the management of the debt crisis.

The origins, 1973–9

It is not correct to think of the debt crisis as having a single cause or even necessarily a single set of causes. Rather, it arose from the interaction of a number of factors, none of which alone was sufficient to cause serious economic difficulties.

The seeds of the debt crisis were sown in the 1970s. As we saw above, the oil-importing developing countries borrowed heavily during that period in order to finance their oil imports without curtailing aggregate expenditure. The 1970s did not represent the nirvana of economic development, but on most criteria it was a fairly good decade for developing countries, with reasonable rates of income growth, strong export growth, and steady commodity prices. The last two statistics suggested that high borrowing could be easily managed; debt/export and debt/GDP ratios were no higher at the end than at the beginning of the decade. The 1970s also seemed pretty good for the banks. The recycling of the OPEC surpluses had been generally praised and was certainly profitable. Lending to developing countries allowed the major banks to diversify their portfolios and to break free of the constraints on domestic expansion: economic growth was sluggish throughout OECD, while in the USA regulation prohibited inter-state banking and thus curtailed economies of scale and portfolio diversification.

Three features of the recycling were to store up problems for the future, however. First, it was predominantly bank lending. Foreign direct investment is obviously not an appropriate medium for the general balance of payments finance that developing countries required, but in the past they had issued bonds rather than borrowed from banks for general finance. Bond finance was scarce in the 1970s, however, ironically partly because the Council of Foreign Bondholders – an institution established in the 1930s in response to the bond defaults of that decade – discouraged issues by countries which had not previously reached agreement with their creditors over previous defaults. The attraction of bond finance for the system as a whole is that, although default is painful for the individuals who lose their money, it does not undermine the payments system in the way that a major default on bank lending might.

Second, much of the lending was at variable interest rates, that is at, say,

LIBOR plus y per cent. This was attractive to banks because it shifted all the interest rate risk onto the borrowers, and, when in later years interest rates rose, that risk proved a grievous burden for them to bear. We should note, however, that the fundamental problem was not the variable rates *per se*, but the fact that they allowed banks effectively to borrow short and lend long with impunity. If such maturity transformation had been undertaken with fixed-rate loans and the interest rate had risen, the banks would have been squeezed directly; but, of course, foreseeing this possibility the banks would never have got into such a position in the first place. Thus the variable rates shifted risk from a party which was not prepared to accept it to one which, possibly through ignorance, was. Without such a shift, however, the 1970s would probably not have seemed such a success at recycling.

The third latent problem of the 1970s was that the loans were mostly to governments or at least guaranteed by them. There was a view among bankers that 'countries can't go bust', from which they concluded that such sovereign lending was inherently safe, and that, of course, is why the developing country governments' guarantees helped to increase the flow of lending. Such a view is basically sound – it is very unlikely that a country could accumulate debts in excess of the value of all its future foreign earnings – but it is also naive. A government faces constraints on repayments far in advance of the point at which the whole of its foreign exchange is devoted to them, and it is that point at which default becomes a possibility. Public guarantees have the effect of socialising the repayments (all society pays) and of greatly increasing the pressure not to default. It is unfortunate if a private firm goes broke and a foreign bank loses its money, but there is no legal case for any sanctions to be imposed other than on the directors of the firm. If, on the other hand, a government repudiates a debt because it is unwilling or unable to tax its subjects any further, that is an overt and political act and may attract all sorts of retribution.

The second oil crisis, 1979–81

The year 1979 brought the second oil crisis in which crude oil prices increased by a further 150 per cent. It had the same impact on the world economy as the first crisis, with soaring balance of payments deficits and increased borrowing among both developed and developing oil importers. Moreover, by this time several developing countries were already heavily in debt and had become dependent on overseas borrowing to maintain overvalued exchange rates and large public sector deficits. Thus the new shock was superimposed on an existing need for economic adjustment. However, there was, and still is, good reason to believe that, if the global economic environment had remained the same as in the 1970s, all that would have been required was a mild slow-down in economic growth rather than a full-blown crisis.

The final ingredient of the crisis was the change in OECD countries' macro-economic policies in 1979. After nearly a decade of lax monetary and fiscal policies, several OECD countries embarked on programmes of economic retrenchment – for example, 'Thatcherism' and 'Reagonomics' in the UK and USA. The growth rate of nominal demand fell sharply, but because both programmes were more successful in imposing monetary squeezes than in their control of fiscal policy, real interest rates rose to unprecedented levels. After several years of negative rates, the real rate of interest rose to 3.5 per cent in 1979 and double that in 1987 (Corbo, 1989). These changes meant that interest rates now exceeded the growth rate of foreign exchange revenues, a recipe for long-run debt disaster. Table 30.2 quantifies the changes in

Table 30.2 Export earnings of developing countries and interest rates, 1976–87

	1976	1977	1978	1979	1980	1981	1982	1983	1984	1985	1986	1987
Change in $ export earnings (%)	15.2	18.2	13.6	30.4	30.0	5.1	−5.6	−1.4	7.7	−2.7	−2.6	16.6
Nominal LIBOR (%)	6.1	6.4	8.3	12.0	14.2	16.5	13.3	9.8	11.2	8.6	6.7	7.3
World inflation (%)	7.6	7.6	7.7	8.1	9.4	8.8	7.2	5.0	4.2	3.8	3.4	2.9
Real LIBOR (%)	−1.4	−1.1	0.6	3.6	4.3	7.1	5.6	4.6	6.7	4.7	3.2	4.3

Sources: World Bank, *World Debt Tables 1988–89*, and Corbo (1989).

interest rates and export earnings; Corbo (1989) calculated that for heavy borrowers the increase in the interest rate and the decline in the terms of trade were equivalent to a 6 per cent reduction in GDP in 1981–2 relative to 1978–80.

The financial pressure was felt first by private firms that had borrowed abroad heavily. Many of them suffered acute distress and, rather than let them fail, governments tended to take over or subsidise their debt service payments. This 'socialisation' of private debt was doubly costly. First, it lost the opportunity for 'natural' default through bankruptcy and thus kept up the level of debt outstanding, and, second, it greatly increased the fiscal burden of servicing the country's debt.

In retrospect, 1980–1 was the crucial period in the creation of the debt crisis. It is now clear that immediate and vigorous adjustment was called for to stimulate non-traditional export earnings, to curtail borrowing, and, in OECD, to control the US budget deficit. At the time, however, expectations were that the policies of the 1970s would soon be restored and thus that rationality required increased borrowing to tide countries over the period of temporary difficulty. Consequently gross borrowing continued to grow vigorously – by 24 per cent in 1980 and 18 per cent in 1981. In fairness, however, we should note that some mild economic adjustment was undertaken, that banks began to shorten the maturities on which they would lend – a sure sign of nervousness – and that, according to some figures, net transfers to developing countries (new lending minus repayments and interest) started to fall.

Much of the lending over 1980–1 was directed towards the less credit-worthy countries – those undertaking least by way of adjustment. Mexico, Brazil and Argentina (the *MBA* countries) nearly doubled their liabilities over the two-year period, from $57b. at the end of 1979 to $105b. at the end of 1981 (Sachs, 1989b), while the seventeen highly indebted countries (HICs)[1] accounted for over 60 per cent of the increase in developing country debt over the period (*World Bank Debt Tables, 1988–89*).

The crisis breaks, 1982

By 1982 the austere macro-economic environment was beginning to look permanent and the flow of new lending came to an abrupt halt. After two years of rapidly rising debt/export and debt/GDP ratios, the banks suddenly wanted out. The suddenness of this reversal created problems for many borrowing countries: some could cope, but others could not, and it rapidly became evident that, while lending to the former would soon return to normal, that to the latter would not. That is, banks would lend to countries which could adjust to the new environment but not to those which could not. Prominent among the latter group was Mexico – a prolific borrower which was not only running a profligate and inappropriate macro-economic policy but

459

also had to cope with a sudden deterioration in her terms of trade as the price of oil fell. The debt crisis proper is frequently dated from 18 August 1982 when Mexico announced that she could no longer honour her debts. This was not the first debt service problem of the period; Turkey, Costa Rica, Peru and Zaire had all had problems and required help during the previous decade. They had had smaller debts, however, and had sought help during a period of general buoyancy. The problem with Mexico was that she confirmed the bad news that the banks already knew was due.

Several features distinguished the countries which suffered most from the dramatic fall in borrowing. Sachs (1989b) argued that in particular they had inappropriate fiscal policies and trade regimes. Some countries, particularly in Latin America, have long traditions of large budget deficits – mainly because public funds are used heavily to address income distribution issues and it is politically easier to give rather than take money. Foreign borrowing provided a simple solution to these political dilemmas by financing the resulting deficits in a relatively non-inflationary way. Once it had dried up, however, governments were unable to solve all their distributive conflicts immediately and so resorted to printing money to fund the deficit. A related phenomenon was so-called *capital flight* by which, fearing depreciation and/or increased taxes, the well-heeled parts of the private sector sent their assets abroad while the government borrowed them back from foreign banks to finance the resulting decline in reserves. This essentially traded public liabilities for private assets and was a serious problem over the early 1980s. It is dealt with in case-study 30.1.

CASE-STUDY 30.1: CAPITAL FLIGHT

So-called 'capital flight' was a major feature of the early 1980s, as residents in certain indebted countries exported capital nearly as fast as governments imported it. In fact, capital flight is difficult to define, let alone measure with any accuracy, so we should be cautious of the statement in the previous sentence. The simplest definition is merely that it represents capital flows abroad made by domestic residents. Some commentators, however, are more restrictive, and talk of capital flight as being just abnormal flows or of being motivated by placing assets beyond the reach of national authorities. However, it is not easy to see why it is that, when an American firm puts 30 per cent of its equity abroad, that is 'strategic diversification', while when a Bolivian businessman puts 4 per cent abroad that is capital flight.

Using the simple definition, Cumby and Levich (1987) reported capital flight over 1980–1 of:

	$b.	*as % of change in debt*
Argentina	10.8	84
Brazil	1.9	10
Mexico	15.6	44
Venezuela	13.0	167
Philippines	2.9	39

These figures suggest that a substantial proportion of the increase in official debt among the worst-hit countries was offset by accumulations of assets in private hands.

460

The causes of capital flight may be divided into two groups. First, unsustainable macro-economic policies (e.g. high inflation, public sector deficit, accumulation of debt) can make devaluation seem almost inevitable. While the government resists it – perhaps to help control inflation – rational agents will seek foreign assets as a hedge. A typical chain of events might be that the government finances a transfer to the private sector by printing money. The additional cash leads the private sector to seek foreign goods and assets, whereupon the government, intent on maintaining the exchange rate, sells foreign exchange from the reserves in return for domestic currency. To replenish its reserves the government then borrows abroad. This is no more than the monetary theory of the balance of payments (see section 21.1 above) and implies no sinister intent. Indeed, capital flight may even be beneficial in preventing the government from pursuing inappropriate macro-economic policies indefinitely.

Capital flight can also occur if governments discriminate against resident capital through taxes, regulations on interest rates or preventing exchange into foreign assets. Residents will then naturally seek capital havens abroad, especially if they fear the onset of a financial crisis, because governments typically favour non-resident over resident capital in such situations. Both sets of causes suggest strong incentives for capital flight from the heavily indebted countries in 1980–1. The different intensities recorded above probably reflect differences in the ability to flee – i.e. exchange controls – rather than in the incentives for it.

Many commentators have argued that capital flight is anti-social and economically harmful – that it shows the better-off avoiding the burdens and responsibilities of economic adjustment. Williamson and Lessard (1987) argued that necessarily it either curtails the supply of investible funds or leads to increased gross borrowing abroad with the increased risk exposure that that entails. They also claimed that it can stultify the domestic financial system and lead to large redistributions of income. Cuddington (1986) added that capital flight causes macro-econoimic disruption and uncertainty, particularly to exchange rates and interest rates, and that it causes fiscal strains by eroding the tax base. If the marginal social return to investment exceeds the marginal private return, capital outflows will be inefficient socially, although, as we noted in section 16.3 above, such an argument implicitly assumes that investment at home is the alternative to an outflow. Finally, capital flight will complicate the politics of introducing austerity measures, for it implies that some people can avoid the associated costs.

The principal solution to capital flight is responsible macro-economic policy, but a pragmatic use of capital controls could be advantageous in certain circumstances.

The trade regime also affected countries' exposure to borrowing crises. Outward-oriented regimes such as Korea's provided robust and diversified export revenues on which to borrow. Such regimes typically induce considerable economic flexibility, as firms are used to responding to market signals, and encourage capital accumulation in a range of industries which can earn foreign exchange. Inward-looking regimes, on the other hand, tend to be rigid and inefficient. Overvalued exchange rates concentrate investment in non-tradable industries, which cannot readily start to earn foreign exchange when depreciation occurs.

Corbo (1989) identified several further characteristics of the subsequently debt-stressed economies. He compared the seventeen HICs with a sample of previously heavy borrowers which none the less managed to keep open their access to international capital markets after 1982. The two groups were similar in many respects prior to 1982, but the HICs had, on average, a higher proportion of floating-rate debt, higher real exchange rates (i.e. lower export competitiveness), worse inflation, larger public sector deficits and much more rapid debt accumulation over 1980–1.

The creditors

It would be unfair to blame the banks for the debt crisis – after all, you cannot force countries to borrow. However, one may ask whether they acted entirely prudently. During the boom of the 1970s there was little to indicate any difficulty over sovereign lending, although perhaps they should have considered whether borrowers' policies were such that they could have serviced their debt out of their own resources rather than new borrowing. In 1980 and 1981, however, the acceleration in lending was remarkable. It was true that each bank was ignorant of how much was being lent by other banks and so could not satisfactorily assess the overall picture, but developing country lending was imprudent by other criteria. Safe banking depends on diversification – to ensure that only a few loans will go wrong at once – but certain major US banks became heavily dependent on particular countries. True, they had many separate loans in each country, but if the danger was macro-economic or, even worse, political, all those loans would go wrong together.

By 1982 the nine major overseas lending ('money-centre') banks in the US held assets in developing countries worth nearly 300 per cent of their capital; over half of these were in Latin America, especially the *MBA* countries. Even one major default would have threatened bank insolvency – that is, where liabilities (deposits) exceeded assets (loans plus capital) – and even the threat of insolvency is sufficient to cause a run on a bank as depositors clamour to get their money out. Thus in August 1982 there was a real threat of global financial collapse if Mexico could not be persuaded to honour her debt.

The same argument was made about voluntarily writing off some of the debt. When a bank writes off or writes down (reduces the value of) a debt, its capital is absorbed in covering the lost assets. This leaves it more vulnerable to other default and is anyway limited by the extent of available capital balances. In 1982, capital balances were so small and the extent of possible default so large that it would have been highly risky to have even contemplated starting along this route.

The American banks faced these problems in a particularly acute form. They are legally required to take loans off their books almost as soon as they become non-performing, i.e. as soon as interest payments fall into arrears. Thus for the sake of the solvency of the financial system, as well as of the banks' managements, it was important to keep interest payments up to date. Thus the early management of the debt crisis required the maintenance of both current interest payments and the capital value of the debt. These twin objectives have continued to colour the attitudes of the USA and international institutions in later years, although with rather less justification. Most banks have now built up their capital reserves, written down some of their developing country debt, and assessed the true value of the remainder. As we shall see below, selective debt write-offs are now quite possible for most banks.

In deciding its lending policy to a country in trouble, a bank must consider not only the objective facts of the country's economic position, but also the attitudes of other banks. Solvency is a public good. As one bank recalls its loans, or refuses to renew them, the value of all other banks' loans declines because there are fewer resources left over to service them. Thus individual rationality dictates that each bank rush to get its own loans repaid in full before other banks undermine the country's ability to do so. In private affairs bankruptcy law exists to stop this rush – it makes all creditors wait and treats them equally – but countries cannot go bankrupt. Thus in sovereign lending creditors must find other ways of ensuring that they act in their collective interest, and the difficulties of doing so can provide a serious obstacle to agreements between creditors and debtors.

30.3 RESOLVING THE DEBT PROBLEM

This section discusses some of the components of a solution to the debt crisis. The ultimate objective is to get the highly indebted countries (HICs) growing again, so that they may resume their economic development and repay at least a fair proportion of their debt. This requires, above all, reopening their access to capital markets. At first the problem was seen as one of liquidity, so that rescheduling debt repayments into the future looked sufficient. Now, however, more fundamental solutions seem necessary. This section does not discuss the various plans proposed for resolving the debt crisis – e.g. the Baker Plan, the Bradley Plan, the Brady Plan – for no plan has yet shown much sign of permanence. Rather it discusses the basic principles, which will allow students to assess the various plans for themselves. We start by considering how the HICs themselves have fared under debt.

Adjustment to debt   Initial reactions to the debt crisis were that, provided the banking system could be preserved, the developing country debtors would be able to adjust to their new circumstances without undue hardship. Given steady growth in OECD countries, a gentle decline in real interest rates and reasonable commodity prices, developing countries would resume their export growth, and, with mild and temporary austerity at home, could convert this into declining debt/export and debt/GDP ratios. The first two conditions have broadly been met and yet the HICs are further in debt now than ever. In part this might be due to falling real commodity prices, but more likely it reflects the failure of the early prognoses to take account of the *internal* corollaries of balance of payments adjustment.

The early 1980s brought three shocks: rising interest rates, falling export prices and critically, a cessation of lending. The last entailed moving almost overnight from a situation in which government expenditure and investment exceeded taxes and savings – recall tht $(X - M) = (S - I) + (T - G)$ – to one of balance or even surplus. Investment slumped, with inevitable consequences for future growth and exports, and the public budget came under intense pressure. Most governments cut non-interest public expenditure vigorously, but were unable to achieve the required level of net savings quickly enough. Consequently they had to find new means of finance. Bond finance drove domestic real interest rates up (this was the mechanism for cutting investment), while money finance just created inflation. These consequences in turn fed back adversely onto the public deficit by respectively increasing interest costs and reducing the real value of tax receipts.

463

Public infrastructural investment was one of the major casualties of the public sector squeeze, especially in countries such as Brazil where reducing public sector wages or transfer payments was politically so difficult. The lack of investment hindered adjustment, for, as traditional commodity export prices fell or remained low, the natural switch to new sectors was hampered by the lack of facilities. Coupled with the absence of critical imported intermediate inputs as imports were compressed, this problem has resulted in disappointing export growth over recent years.

The theory of Chapter 20 tells us correctly that an adverse external shock requires a shift in the real exchange rate to favour tradables over non-tradable production. The HICs experienced this as their nominal exchange rates depreciated after the onset of the crisis. Unfortunately, however, many non-traded industries had previously borrowed in foreign currency terms – or, at least, domestic banks had borrowed dollars to lend on to them in local currency. Depreciation increased the local currency costs of repaying and servicing these debts, with the result that many firms and local banks became insolvent. The collapse of domestic banking systems would have further hindered adjustment, so in several cases governments took them over, but of course in doing so increased the public deficit and debt burdens. Even where collapse was avoided, weakness in the non-traded sector further eroded the tax base.

Once the public finances are under threat, fears of a crisis can become self-fulfilling. The high deficit leads residents to anticipate inflation; this drives up interest rates, increases the deficit and so increases the chances of inflation. Such a vicious cycle may explain the persistence of the public sector difficulties in the Latin American HICs.

The final link in the vicious cycle of debt and decline has been the failure of the financial community to resume lending to the indebted countries. Adjustment takes time and the arguments of this section suggest that attempting too rapid a pace of change actually worsens the position. On the other hand, offering more money to countries in such trouble looks to the lenders like throwing good money after bad; all their incentives are to restrict the flow. The next sub-section considers lending in more detail. First, however, we consider the present situation of the HICs quantitatively.

Table 30.3 summarises the recent history of the highly indebted countries. The gravity of the shocks they faced in the early 1980s is evident from rows (1)–(3) and (13): low world growth, collapsing terms of trade and, in 1982, a cut in private lending. The immediate consequences for their economies are evident in rows (4)–(8). Exports fell in 1981 followed by GDP, investment, imports and consumption. The duration of the difficulties is obvious, and it is worth noting (although it is not evident from the table) that the HICs under-performed relative to other developing countries in almost all respects. Rows (9)–(13) show the striking failure of new lending to pick up. Net capital flows (disbursements less repayments) fell from over $40b. in 1981 to around $6b. a year in the late 1980s. Net resource transfers (net flows less interest payments) have been negative since 1983 and falling. They represent the rate at which the rest of the world is extracting claims over resources from the HICs. Such reverse flows are unprecedented and are a serious barrier to the HICs' attempts to grow out of their debt.

We should remember that there are differences between the individual HICs, and that, although they account for the preponderance of world debt, they are not necessarily the worst-hit countries. Sub-Saharan Africa (of which

Table 30.3 Highly indebted countries and the world economy, 1980–8

	1980	1981	1982	1983	1984	1985	1986	1987
The world economy (% change):								
(1) Industrial country output	1.3	2.0	−0.4	2.8	4.5	3.1	2.7	3.3
(2) World trade (volume)	1.3	2.4	−1.0	3.0	9.9	4.0	2.6	4.3
(3) Commodity prices	5.5	−13.9	−10.1	7.1	3.7	−12.9	−1.2	3.4
The HICs' economies (% change):								
(4) GDP	5.6	0.6	−0.4	−2.9	1.9	3.7	3.4	1.7
(5) Investment	9.4	0.4	−13.1	−21.0	−2.1	4.5	1.9	0.8
(6) Per capita consumption	3.4	0.3	−2.2	−4.1	−1.7	0.2	2.6	−1.4
(7) Exports	1.1	−6.6	0.0	5.0	9.3	2.2	0.7	0.4
(8) Imports	8.2	2.3	−14.1	−20.4	−1.1	−1.6	4.0	−1.7
The HICs' debt (US$b.)								
(9) Total external debt stock	289.0	351.0	391.0	422.0	438.0	454.0	482.0	527.0
(10) Net flows	28.6	43.7	34.6	19.1	13.3	6.0	4.5	6.2
(11) Net resource transfers	8.8	18.3	3.7	−9.9	−19.9	−26.5	−25.8	−21.8
(12) Debt: new commitments	37.2	55.3	50.6	37.6	26.2	23.0	17.9	24.3
(13) of which: private lending	27.3	41.4	37.4	23.9	16.1	12.3	3.7	11.7
(14) Debt/exports (%)	171	203	259	295	277	296	353	357
(15) debt/GNP (%)	33	36	45	57	57	59	62	63

Sources: World Bank, *World Debt Tables 1988–89;* IMF, *International Financial Statistics*, for commodity prices.

only two countries are in the HIC group) claims that distinction, with worse growth, debt ratios and prospects than the HICs in general. The sub-Saharan countries are quite possibly insolvent, but since their debt is much smaller than that of the HICs they are less of a threat to the banking system and less important politically; on the other hand, for these very reasons, they may be more easily forgiven their debt.

Debt rescheduling   The joint perceptions that the world financial system was under threat but that the developing countries would soon grow out of trouble led Western governments to see the avoidance of debt relief (i.e. reduction) as among their highest priorities in the early 1980s. Hence they put great pressure on debtors to keep up with interest payments in order that the banks could pretend that the loans were still 'good', and so keep them on their books at full value. If debt relief was ruled out, and yet there was no money for current payments, rescheduling was the only option (except, perhaps, sending in the marines!). Mexico's announcement of difficulties in August 1982 was followed by several forms of emergency financing, and by November she had agreed a deal with the IMF. Despite the speed with which it was composed, this deal provided a framework for many agreements over the next two years. Sachs (1989b) lists five important characteristics:

(1)   The IMF offered high-conditionality loans, but only if the HIC government and its commercial bank creditors agreed a rescheduling agreement.

(2)   The commercial banks rescheduled their claims by extending maturities, but without reducing the present value of their loans. (For Mexico this was achieved by raising the interest rate!)

(3)   The HICs agreed to maintain full and prompt debt servicing.

(4)   The rescheduling was contingent on an agreement with the IMF being signed.

465

(5)   Official creditors rescheduled their loans on similar conditions to the private sector.

Implicit in this structure is that no creditor receives more favourable treatment than any other, and that the package depends on the IMF 'seal of approval'. The latter reflected a view that only the Fund could insist on the conditionality required to make the loans eventually repayable.

Another novel feature of the Mexican deal was the so-called 'concerted lending', by which the IMF declared that it would lend new money only if all or nearly all the commercial creditors did likewise. This was intended (a) to prevent the commercial banks from creating a worse crisis by scrambling to get their money out – the externality problem, (b) to prevent new official money from merely being recycled via the HICs into the commercial banks' vaults, and (c) to maintain a reasonable flow of finance during the adjustment period. In the first two senses the emergency programmes have achieved some success, although smaller banks have reduced their exposure to the HICs; in the last sense, however, they have been a complete failure, mostly because concerted lending has been much less common than anticipated. Only the large (*MBA*) debtors have received significant amounts. The negotiating costs of putting together concerted lending programmes are worthwhile only for large packages and only large borrowers have sufficient debt outstanding to persuade banks that a concerted package is better than the alternative of default.

Debt default

The statistics of Table 30.3 and the difficulties of making rescheduling agreements raise the issue of why the debtors do not default on their loans – just refuse to pay them. A common answer is that default would close them off from new money. There is some truth in this argument, but it is easily exaggerated. First, most HICs are making negative transfers every year at present – i.e. the policy of not defaulting has not generated any new money, so default can hardly lose it. Second, historical experience suggests that in the aftermath of a debt crisis – and there have been several before now – all potential borrowers find credit tight, not just the defaulters. Third, recent temporary defaulters (e.g. Peru) have found that at least short-term trade credits have remained available after default.

Finally, suppose that indeed there were some new money available now. For any finite stream of borrowing the debtor would, at some point in the future, reach the maximum of its cumulated inflow, and would face net outflows from that point on. At that point, there is no net inflow with which to prevent default, and, if the 'new money' argument were the only reason for not defaulting, default would occur. If creditors foresaw this maximum, however, they would not lend the last few units that achieved the maximum, because, anticipating default, they would not expect to get them back. This would bring the point of maximum inflow back towards the present. But the same argument would apply at the new maximum, so bringing the maximum further back, and so on. Thus if the promise of new money was all that prevented default, no one would ever lend in the first place. Bulow and Rogoff (1989), whose sophisticated argument this is, suggest that we should, therefore, look elsewhere for sanctions against default.

It is here that the involvement of debtor governments in foreign borrowing is important. Official default is an explicit and political act. Not only would it cut the defaulter off from other borrowing (e.g. from the IMF or the World

466

Bank), but it might induce other retaliation in trade policy or even foreign policy spheres. Several industrial countries, most notably the USA, have made quite explicit their disapproval of default, and have sought to reprimand defaulters severely. The ruling and financial elites in most developing countries do not relish taking on the might of Uncle Sam, and thus seek earnestly to avoid default.

Several governments have unilaterally rescheduled their debt service (i.e. defaulted in one way or another) over the 1980s, but most have been brought back into the fold by subsequent rescheduling and relief arrangements. In part, the severity with which they have been treated has depended on their size, strategic importance and international political profile. The main pressure to come back into the system, however, has arisen from the economic chaos that has followed default. Since default is so political an act, it must be accompanied by a good deal of drum-banging to persuade the population that any privations that it causes are worthwhile for the sake of sovereignty, freedom from foreign oppression, etc. Unfortunately, these are exactly the sentiments which encourage loose fiscal and monetary policies, so default has usually been followed by a major macro-economic collapse.

Debt relief

Even if they are willing to undertake domestic adjustment, the HICs have been hamstrung by their inability to borrow new money. Even when they have an investment project offering very high rates of return, lenders will not support it because they fear that, when it comes to repayment, the new loans will be aggregated with existing ones and thus become part of the general low-quality debt stock. They would be prepared to lend if their new loans could be granted *seniority* – i.e. given precedence in repayment over existing debt – but this raises huge legal problems. Besides, it could be done only occasionally because, once it is possible that a loan can be 'bounced' down the queue by a subsequent one, no one wants to make the first one. The near-impossibility of distinguishing new private loans from old ones is one of the major ways in which a *debt overhang* – a large nominal stock of outstanding debt – curtails lending and economic growth. Such a situation suggests that relief from existing debt commitments may be necessary before lending can resume.

The difficulties of obtaining new money (from either existing or new lenders) while there are still problems over old money are not new. Past experience suggests that troubled debtors usually need a period of significantly reduced debt-service burden in which to stabilise their economies and start adjustment. Such periods may be engendered by interest holidays, negotiated debt reductions, increased lending or unilateral suspension of debt-service payments. Lindert and Morton in Sachs (1989a) showed that a partial write-down of debt during a crisis is the norm, not the exception, and that it used typically to be achieved by bilateral negotiations between debtors and their creditors. It may well be, they suggested, that the active role of creditor governments and international institutions, an innovation of the 1980s, has hindered the process of recovery by complicating the mechanisms and disturbing the relative bargaining powers of the parties.

The apparent inability of the HICs to resolve their problems has led recently to increased interest in plans involving some degree of write-off, although the banks, official institutions and creditor governments are still very wary of such schemes. These parties no longer comprise a single homogeneous coalition, however. There is a growing exasperation in official circles with the commercial banks' refusal to resume lending and there has long been a strong

467

political sentiment, especially in the USA, that debt relief must not take the form of recycling money from official coffers through the HICs and into the banks' vaults. In other words, official thinking increasingly looks for real concessions from private creditors.

The possibility of debt relief raises serious problems of moral hazard in sovereign lending – the worry that agents will act irresponsibly because they believe that in a crisis they will be bailed out. On the banks' side this may take the form of high risk, high return sovereign lending with insufficient monitoring; when things go well the high profits accrue privately to bank shareholders and managers, but the worst risks are socialised when governments have to support ailing banks in order to prevent a collapse – i.e. when there is 'lending of last resort'. Such support has occurred in the last decade, but in general the authorities have tried to ensure that, although bank depositors are protected, those who profited through the 1970s should now bear the costs. Indeed, there is scope for considerable debt write-off before the returns to sovereign lending over the 1970s and 1980s are reduced to normal levels. In fact, however, for so long as governments are committed to preserving ailing banks, it is not clear that they can entirely overcome the moral hazard problem, and there is a growing tacit realisation that practical debt relief schemes will have to relieve the banks as well as the HICs.

The original objection to debt relief – namely that major banks might fold – almost certainly no longer holds. Since 1982 the banks have made major additions to their capital and reserves against developing country loans, and have reduced their outstanding loans to the HIC private sector significantly. Thus between 1982 and 1986 the exposure of the nine major US banks to developing countries fell from 288 per cent of capital to 173 per cent (177 per cent to 120 per cent for exposure to Latin America) and has probably fallen further since then. Other banks in the USA and abroad were less exposed in the first place. Huizinga (1989) argues that banks' share prices now reflect the quality of their Third World portfolios as measured by the prices of their debt on the secondary market (see below). Thus, he argues, shareholders have already borne the capital losses implicit in losing some of the HICs' debt, and yet still consider their banks still solvent. A partial write-off of the debt overhang would merely regularise this situation.

A perverse consequence of the banks' strengthening position is that they now feel less pressure to continue lending to the HICs. When they were highly exposed, fresh lending was necessary to avert the threat of default which would have brought them down. Now, however, they could withstand any but the largest default, and so can find safer uses for their money, especially if they feel that new lending will either be spent repaying competitors' loans or be squandered by continuing poor economic management.

A large debt overhang also introduces a moral hazard for the debtor governments (see Krugman, 1989b). Imagine that a country owes more than it could ever reasonably pay off, but that it has no idea of how much relief it may be able to negotiate. Firm economic management in the form of a stabilisation programme will merely serve to increase the proportion of the debt that can eventually be paid off, and thus reduce the degree of relief. In these circumstances, the local population may receive no return at all for the economic hardships of stabilisation, and thus the government might, quite rationally, decide not to impose any. The result is that the world is poorer, because, although the HIC incomes will be the same with or without the austerity measures, the creditors have received less. The arguments of both this and the previous paragraph suggest a serious need for debt relief, and the sooner the better.

The simplest and most obvious form of debt relief is debt forgiveness – creditors writing down the face value of their debt. Official lenders have done this for some African countries, but commercial lenders have been reluctant to do so. To them it looks like merely exchanging possible losses for certain ones. It also raises the externality problem if not all creditors write down at the same time or rate. An individual lender wishes everyone except himself to reduce their claims: the general reduction in debt will strengthen the borrowing country's economy and increase the probability that any remaining debt will be paid off in full. Thus, even if creditors recognise the collective advantages of debt reduction, none has an individual interest in starting it off. This externality – that the value of one loan depends on the terms for another – appears regularly in discussions of debt relief and has led Sachs, among others, to claim that 'concerted debt reduction' orchestrated by the IMF and the World Bank is the only viable form of relief.

The argument above about the debt overhang suggests that a write-down could even increase the repayments on HIC debts by breaking down the moral hazard problem. General forgiveness, however, raises huge political problems as debtors have to be sorted into deserving and less deserving cases and creditors (both official and private) organised. Some economists advocate it strongly (e.g. Sachs, 1989b) – at least on a selective basis – but many are still cautious. Cohen (1989), for example, shows that few debtors face serious 'overhang' problems and that, while relief on debt service would be appropriate, capital write-offs are not yet necessary. More significantly, there is still a marked reluctance by official institutions to contemplate simple forgiveness on a wide scale.

Voluntary debt reduction

The official institutions' alternative to forgiveness is voluntary debt reduction, by which creditors agree to reduce the notional value of outstanding debt individually. Not surprisingly, such schemes mostly amount to rescheduling or repackaging rather than relieving debt, for they ignore the externality issue. Among the best known are *debt–equity swaps* whereby creditors are invited to convert their debt into equity in local business; unless this is done at a discount, the expected value of repayments is the same. It is attractive to the lenders because it reschedules payments to periods of success (i.e. when dividends are high) and overcomes the moral hazard dilemma in economic policy. Borrowers have found it less attractive, on the other hand, because it provides little net relief and raises concerns about widespread foreign ownership. Only Chile has made much use of debt–equity swaps. Other similar schemes involve converting debt into *local currency bonds*, but since these are usually index-linked against inflation there is again little direct benefit to the debtor.

Exit bonds are different from local currency bonds. They convert debt into long-maturity dollar bonds and exempt their holders from any further responsibilities in concerted lending. This allows smaller banks to buy their way out of the debt bind at a discount, but, of course, does nothing for the borrowers. Similarly, sales and purchases of debt instruments on the *secondary market* merely redistribute existing claims. The prices of loans on the secondary market offer some indication of expectations about repayments and consequently of the true value of Third World debt to creditors. The discounts are high for the HICs, with prices ranging from 10¢ per dollar for Bolivia, 22¢ for

Argentina, 46¢ for Brazil and Mexico to 99¢ for Turkey in September 1988.

The secondary market raises an interesting possibility for debt relief – a *buy-back*, whereby the debtor country buys back its own debt at a discount. This is a form of voluntary debt reduction because buy-backs are forbidden under most rescheduling agreements unless the creditors agree, and once a buy-back is allowed there is no compulsion on particular creditors to sell their debt. Despite its apparent attractions, however, the buy-back is not a panacea and indeed has been described by Bulow and Rogoff (1988) as a 'boondoggle' which transfers resources to the creditors. Their argument is explored in case-study 30.2.

CASE-STUDY 30.2: THE BOLIVIAN BUY-BACK BOONDOGGLE

In 1988 Bolivia had $670m. of commercial debt valued at 6¢ per dollar on the secondary market. Thus its value to creditors was $40m. Complete repayment looked quite impossible, so the $40m. represented the most that the creditors thought they could get their hands on – that indeed is how the 6¢ came about. Bolivia then spent $34m. buying back $300m. of debt (approximately 11¢ per dollar); the secondary price of the remaining $368m. rose to 11¢, valuing it at very nearly $40m. The end result was that Bolivia was still expected to repay the equivalent of about $40m.! Thus, unless they got something else out of the buy-back, the Bolivians were just $34m. worse off.

The logic of this incident is spelt out in Bulow and Rogoff (1988) and its related commentary. For so long as full repayment is not possible, the price of a country's debt is the maximum repayment that can be expected of it divided by the face value of the debt. Since a buy-back hardly affects the maximum possible repayment, it cannot alone generate a net improvement for the country; it just wastes money raising the price of the remaining debt. The buy-back price must equal the post-buy-back price, because once a buy-back has been agreed that is the value of the marginal unit of debt to its holder.

In the Bolivian case a number of special factors mean that, the analysis above notwithstanding, Bolivia was probably a net gainer. The resources for the buy-back were provided specially by official donors on concessionary terms; Bolivia's deal with the IMF was the first *not* to require full payment of interest arrears to private creditors – the buy-back was a substitute; new World Bank loans were provided in 1988; there is reportedly an agreement that all commercial debt will be cleared at 11¢ – that is, the next buy-back will not be at its post buy-back price; and Bolivia is not being pressed on other loans.

Sachs, the principal author of the buy-back, argued in his reply to Bulow and Rogoff that it was a huge success. He believed that it had brought political and economic stability to what, in the early 1980s, was the world's worst 'basket case'. He attributed the success to the realism of the IMF and US governments in recognising that full repayment was impossible, and to their provision of a framework in which Bolivia could negotiate with her creditors. He held that such realism provides the key to future solutions to the debt problem. Bulow and Rogoff implicitly agreed, arguing that the Bolivian success stemmed solely from the concessions that were associated with the buy-back.

Sachs (1989b) suggests several reasons why voluntary debt reduction is unlikely ever to allow the HICs to return to financial security and normal borrowing:

- *The externality problem.* To join a voluntary debt reduction scheme a creditor must believe that he will do better by joining than by holding on to his loans. Thus the scheme must pay a price for debt instruments equal to that which will rule *after* the scheme has been implemented. For example, suppose a scheme left only $1 of outstanding debt; this would be worth $1 because it could certainly be repaid in full, thus no one will sell their last unit for less than face value. Case-study 30.2 suggests that this problem beset the Bolivia buy-back, albeit at a much lower price than dollar-for-dollar.

- *Precedent.* Banks will not offer generous terms to small borrowers, no matter how bad their condition, for fear of establishing precedents for large borrowers. The banks can afford to be hawkish about small loans because they could absorb a total default. Thus small borrowers are worth more as examples than as customers *per se*. This argument illustrates the old adage: 'If you owe your banker a thousand dollars, that's bad news for you; if you owe him a million, it's bad news for him.'

- *Official money.* Official institutions – especially the World Bank and the IMF – have a large stake in the stability of the debtor governments. Thus if private creditors refuse to reduce debt, the institutions are likely to increase their lending somewhat. This reduces the probability of default if the banks hang out for a better deal. Evidence of this effect is that official creditors have now virtually stopped collecting money from the HICs.

- *The role of the large banks.* In normal commerce the largest lenders take the lead in arranging terms for distressed debtors. In the debt crisis the opposite has occurred for four reasons. First, the large banks claim that debt reduction would undermine their long-term relationships with the debtor countries. Second, their high exposure makes it more difficult for them to accept formal write-downs (for capital adequacy reasons). Third, because of their dominant position, they have greater access than smaller banks to debt–equity swaps, which are more favourable than other voluntary debt reduction schemes. Finally, as the small banks get out at a discount, the value of the large banks' debts rises. Thus delay is privately rational. It was only the large banks which failed to take part in the Bolivia buy-back.

- *The negotiating cycle.* In nearly all cases, official institutions insist that debtor governments negotiate agreements with private creditors before they can have access to official funds (e.g. IMF programmes). Since debtor governments can scarcely afford to drop out of the official system, the requirement greatly weakens them in their private sector negotiations.

These reasons all suggest that significant debt reduction will occur only in a concerted rather than voluntary (i.e. individual) fashion. And indeed developments in 1989 were moving in that direction. The Brady Plan – named after US Secretary of the Treasury, Nicholas Brady – offers official money to stabilise the HIC debt situation if the banks will accept some write-down. The promise is backed up by an implicit threat that if the banks refuse to cooperate the IMF will undermine the legality of their claims. International law requires private debts to be paid provided that doing so does not contravene a greater

471

legal principle. Case law recognises the IMF as the arbiter of 'legal' exchange controls; if a country introduced exchange controls preventing outflows of foreign currency for capital purposes, and if the IMF recognised these as legal, this would take precedence over foreign debt commitments in dollars. Debtors would still have to repay their debts, but in their own, inconvertible, currencies. This would be little hardship and would in many cases allow inflation rapidly to devalue (i.e. relieve) the real debt burden. Despite the threat, there is still an element of voluntariness in the Brady scheme; negotiations are conducted between debtors and creditors, who then collectively request official support. By June 1990 four agreements had been reached under the Brady Plan. The first, and most contentious, was with Mexico: $48.5b. of debt was offered capital and partial interest guarantees, provided that each bank agreed to one of the following adjustments to its debt: a write-down of existing debt by 35 per cent (chosen by banks holding 41 per cent of the debt), an interest cap on existing debt of 6.25 per cent (47 per cent of the debt) or making new loans equal to 25 per cent of existing debt (12 per cent). These terms represented a good deal for the banks – especially the second alternative – and overall, despite the rhetoric, the plan has a strong element of bailing the banks out. Moreover, the small amount of new money, coupled with the clause of the agreement that prevents the renegotiation of the new or restructured debt, means that the Mexicans gained relatively little from the arrangement, especially if times get hard again. Further deals with slightly different details have been signed by Costa Rica, the Philippines and Venezuela (see the Bank for International Settlements, *Annual Report, 1990*).

Official creditors and conditionality

Official creditors have played a crucial role in the management of the debt crisis. Governments and the IMF and the World Bank have increased their lending to the HICs, often being the only lenders, and have also frequently rescheduled their debts. Both institutions have introduced new facilities designed to get money to the HICs and African debtors, and the IMF has been crucial in organising concerted lending by private creditors. It is highly likely that but for its efforts the 1980s would have witnessed a massive financial collapse.

None the less the IMF has attracted a good deal of criticism for its efforts. Sachs has argued that the Bank's and the Fund's intervention have prolonged the crisis. Their requirement for negotiated deals with private creditors has effectively prevented the HICs from settling with their creditors on realistic terms. Other commentators have argued that their fault lies in inappropriate conditionality. The general conditionality issue has been explored above and it must be admitted that conditionality has been almost wholly unsuccessful with the HICs. Time and again its requirements have been violated and have needed renegotiation. In part this may be a general failing of the Bank–Fund model of the economy, but more probably it reflects the special circumstances of the HICs.

First, IMF programmes are almost always designed on the assumption of full and timely debt service. This has made them very burdensome for the debtors, so there are clearly strong incentives to find alternative paths of development. Second, official lending helps to offset the negative resource transfer to private lenders, but rarely reverses it. Thus the financial squeeze continues during a Fund programme. Third, the supply-side adjustments implicit in Fund–Bank stabilisation programmes take time and, frequently, investment. The HICs have little of either. Fourth, experience of trade liberalisation – an important component of the programmes – suggests that gradual change under a stable macro-economic regime is the route to success, as Korea has shown since 1962. The relatively short duration of stabilisation programmes tends to rush the task.

There may be a case for modifying conditionality somewhat: perhaps stressing macro-economic goals prior to international trade goals, and writing programmes for longer periods. Few economists, however, would dispense with it altogether. Any long-term lending, let alone recovery from a debt crisis, raises time-consistency problems: how can debtors be made to deliver on the policies required to make debt repayment feasible? Only an institution like the IMF has the authority and a sufficiently long time-horizon to impose such consistency. Moreover, although imposing time-consistency sounds dictatorial, it is in fact to the debtors' advantage, for at least in theory it unlocks the flow of private finance (see the discussion of the MIGA on page 451 above). Besides, countries that have tried to adjust without conditonality have generally got into serious problems, not least in Latin America where, in the absence of Fund pressure, there is little bulwark against short-term populist economic policies.

Conditionality would look a good deal more attractive and effective if it were linked to a degree of debt relief. The IMF has the means to pursue case-by-case debt relief through the arrangements it makes with debtors and so could relieve some of the pressure on the worst-hit countries. Moreover, creditor banks and governments are far more likely to agree debt relief schemes if they believe that the IMF can ensure that its benefits are not frittered away, but are used to stimulate economic recovery to the joint advantage of both creditors and debtors. Thus IMF conditionality is an important part of debt management.

FURTHER READING

International aid is discussed in *Mosley* (1987). *Bird* (1982a,b) provides a useful summary of the traditional position of developing countries on international monetary affairs and *Nowzad* (1981) describes the IMF response. On the effectiveness of Bank–Fund programmes see *Donovan* (1981, 1982), *Goldstein and Montiel* (1986), *Pastor* (1987) and *World Bank* (1989). Conditionality is discussed simply by *Crockett* (1982), at length by *Williamson* (1983), and critically by *Spraos* (1986). More general radical critiques of the IMF treatment of DCs include *Hayter* (1971) and *Payer* (1974).

The literature on the debt crisis is massive. The best single reference is *Sachs* (1989a), but *Smith and Cuddington* (1985) is good on some of the analytical issues. The *Brookings Papers on Economic Activity* provide a regular and accessible commentary on debt issues, as does the World Bank's *World Development Report, 1985*. The IMF's *Annual Report* and Occasional Papers on *International Capital Markets: Developments and Prospects* and the World Bank's *World Debt Tables* provide studied official accounts of events. *Eichengreen and Portes* (1986, 1987) make fascinating historical comparisons.

KEY CONCEPTS

tied aid	official development assistance
conditionality	sovereign lending
free-riding	net resource transfers
capital flight	concerted lending

bank capital adequacy
debt overhang
voluntary debt reduction

liquidity vs. solvency
structural adjustment
debt rescheduling vs. relief
buy-backs

QUESTIONS FOR REVIEW

30.1 What are the difficulties of assessing the success of a Fund programme?

30.2 Why have conditionality? What factors should be subject to conditions?

30.3 Was recycling OPEC's surpluses bound to lead to problems?

30.4 What features distinguished the HICs from other countries before 1982? What has done so since?

30.5 Can voluntary debt reduction make a major contribution to solving the debt crisis?

30.6 'The objective of debt management is to open the HICs up to normal capital market borrowing as soon as possible.' Why? Why has this not happened yet?

NOTE

1 'Highly indebted countries' is an analytical grouping designated by the World Bank. It comprises Argentina, Bolivia, Brazil, Chile, Colombia, Costa Rica, Côte d'Ivoire, Ecuador, Jamaica, Mexico, Morocco, Nigeria, Peru, Philippines, Uruguay, Venezuela and Yugoslavia – the countries with the largest debts.

Bibliography

Adelman, I. (1979), *Economic Growth and Resources*, vol. 4, Macmillan, London.

Ahmed, J. (1978), 'Tokyo Round of trade negotiations and the generalised system of preferences', *Economic Journal*, vol. 88, pp. 285–97.

Aitken, N. D. (1973), 'The effects of the EEC and EFTA on European trade: a temporal cross-section analysis', *American Economic Review*, vol. 63, pp. 881–92.

Aitken, N. D. and Obutelewicz, R. S. (1976), 'A cross-sectional study of EEC trade with the association of African countries', *Review of Economics and Statistics*, vol. 58, pp. 425–33.

Alexander, S. S. (1952) 'The effects of devaluation on a trade balance', *IMF Staff Papers*, pp. 263–78.

Aliber, R. Z. (1974), *National Monetary Policies and the International Financial System*, Chicago University Press, Chicago.

Aliber, R. Z. (1976), 'The firm under pegged and floating exchange rates', *Scandinavian Journal of Economics*, vol. 78, pp. 309–22.

Amacher, R. C., Haberler, G. and Willet, T. D. (1979), *Challenges to a Liberal International Economic Order*, American Enterprise Institute, Washington, DC.

Aquino, A. (1981), 'Changes over time in the pattern of comparative advantage in manufactured goods', *European Economic Review*, vol. 15, pp. 41–62.

Argy, V. (1981), *The Postwar International Money Crisis*, Allen & Unwin, London.

Argy, V. and Kouri, P. (1974), 'Sterilization policies and the volatility in international reserves', in Aliber (1974), pp. 209–30.

Argy, V. and Porter, M. G. (1972), 'The forward exchange market and the effects of domestic and external disturbances under alternative exchange', *IMF Staff Papers*, vol. 19, pp. 503–28.

Armington, P. S. (1977), 'The role of "non-price competitiveness" in exporting', *The Banker*, August.

Arndt, S. W. and Richardson, J. D. (1987), *Real–Financial Linkages among Open Economies*, MIT Press, Cambridge, Mass.

Arrow, K. (1962), 'The economic implications of learning-by-doing', *Review of Economic Studies*, vol. 29, pp. 153–77.

Artis, M. J. and Taylor, M. P. (1988), 'Exchange rates and the EMS: assessing the track record', Discussion Paper No. 250, Centre for Economic Policy Research, London.

Artus, J. R. (1970), 'The short-run effects of domestic demand on pressure on British export performance', *IMF Staff Papers*, vol. 17, pp. 247–74.

Artus, J. R. (1973), 'The short-run effects of domestic demand pressure on export delivery delays for machinery', *Journal of International Economics*, vol. 3, pp. 21–36.

Artus, J. R. (1975), 'The 1967 devaluation of the pound sterling', *IMF Staff Papers*, vol. 22, pp. 595–640.

Artus, J. R. and Rhomberg, R. R. (1973), 'A multi-lateral exchange rate model', *IMF Staff Papers*, vol. 20, pp. 591–611.

Artus, J. R. and Young, J. H. (1979), 'Fixed and flexible exchange rates: a renewal of the debate', *IMF Staff Papers*, vol. 26, pp. 654–98.

Aw, B. Y. and Roberts, M. J. (1986), 'Measuring quantity change in quota-constrained import markets', *Journal of International Economics*, vol. 21, pp. 45–60.

Aw, B. Y. and Roberts, M. J. (1988), 'Price and quality level comparisons for US footwear imports: an application of multilateral index numbers', Chapter 10 of Feenstra (1988b), pp. 257–75.

Bacharach, M. (1976), *Economics and the Theory of Games*, Macmillan, London.

Bacon, R., Godley, W. A. H. and McFarquhar, A. (1978), 'The direct costs to Britain of belonging to the EEC', *Cambridge Economic Policy Review*, vol. 4, pp. 44–9.

Bahmani-Oskooee, M. (1985), 'Demand for international reserves: survey of recent empirical studies', *Applied Economics*, vol. 17, pp. 359–75.

Baillie, R. and McMahon, P. (1989), *The Foreign Exchange Market: Theory and Econometric Evidence*, Cambridge University Press, Cambridge.

Baillie, R. and Selover, D. D. (1987), 'Co-integration and models of exchange rate determination', *International Journal of Forecasting*, vol. 3, pp. 43–52.

Balassa, B. (1964), 'The purchasing power parity doctrine: a reappraisal', *Journal of Political Economy*, vol. 72, pp. 584–96.

475

Balassa, B. (1971), *The Structure of Protection in Developing Countries*, Johns Hopkins Press, Baltimore, Md.

Balassa, B. (1975), *European Economic Integration*, North Holland, Amsterdam.

Balassa, B. (1979), 'A stages approach to comparative advantage', in Adelman (1979), vol. 4, pp. 121–36.

Balassa, B. (1981), 'Adjustment to external shocks in developing countries', Staff Working Paper, No. 472, World Bank, Washington, DC.

Balassa, B. and Bauwens, L. (1987), 'Intra-industry specialisation in a multi-country and multi-industry framework', *Economic Journal*, vol. 97, pp. 923–39.

Balassa, B. and Bauwens, L. (1988), 'Inter-industry and intra-industry specialisation in manufactured goods', *Weltwirtschaftliches Archiv*, vol. 124, pp. 1–13.

Baldwin, J. R. and Gorecki, P. K. (1983), 'Trade tariffs and relative plant scale in Canadian manufacturing industries: 1970–79', Discussion Paper 232, Economic Council of Canada, Ottawa.

Baldwin, R. A. (1988), 'Hysteresis in import prices: the beach head effect', *American Economic Review*, vol. 78, pp. 773–85.

Baldwin, R. A. (1989), 'The growth effects of 1992', *Economic Policy*, vol. 9, pp. 247–82.

Baldwin, R. A. and Flam, H. (1989), 'Strategic trade policies in the market for 30–40 seat commuter aircraft', *Weltwirtschaftliches Archiv*, vol. 125, pp. 484–500.

Baldwin, R. A. and Krugman, P. R. (1987), 'The persistence of the US trade deficit', *Brookings Papers in Economic Activity*, no. 1, pp. 1–43.

Baldwin, R. A. and Krugman, P. R. (1988), 'Market access and international competition: a simulation study of 16k random access memories', Chapter 7 of Feenstra (1988b), pp. 171–97.

Baldwin, R. E. (1969), 'The case against infant industry protection', *Journal of Political Economy*, vol. 77, pp. 295–305.

Baldwin, R. E. (1970), *Non-Tariff Distortions of International Trade*, Allen & Unwin, London.

Baldwin, R. E. (1971), 'Determinants of the commodity structure of US trade', *American Economic Review*, vol. 61, pp. 126–46.

Baldwin, R. E. (1976), 'Trade and employment effects in the US multilateral tariff reductions', *American Economic Review*, vol. 56, pp. 142–8.

Baldwin, R. E. (1979), 'Determinants of trade and investment: further evidence', *Review of Economics and Statistics*, vol. 61, pp. 40–8.

Baldwin, R. E. (1984), 'Rent-seeking and trade policy: an industry approach', *Weltwirtschaftliches Archiv*, vol. 112, pp. 613–23.

Baldwin, R. E. (1985), *The Political Economy of US Import Trade Policy*, MIT Press, Cambridge, Mass.

Baldwin, R. E. (1988), *Trade Policy Issues and Empirical Analysis*, Chicago University Press, Chicago.

Baldwin, R. E. (1989), 'The political economy of trade protection', *The Journal of Economic Perspectives*, vol. 3(4), pp. 119–36.

Baldwin, R. E. and Murray, T. (1977), 'MFN tariff reductions and LDC benefits under the GSP', *Economic Journal*, vol. 87, pp. 30–46.

Baldwin, R. E. *et al.* (1965), *Trade Growth and the Balance of Payments*, North Holland, Amsterdam.

Bale, M. D. and Lutz, E. (1981), 'Price distortions in agriculture and their effects: an international comparison', *American Journal of Agricultural Economics*, vol. 63, pp. 7–22.

Ball, R. J. (1973), *The International Linkage of National Economic Models*, North Holland, Amsterdam.

Balogh, T. (1963), *Unequal Partners*, Basil Blackwell, Oxford.

Balogh, T. and Streeten, P. (1960), 'Domestic versus foreign investment', *Bulletin of Oxford Institute of Economics and Statistics*, vol. 23, pp. 213–24.

Bark, T. and de Melo, J. (1987), 'The effects of non-tariff barriers in footwear trade: preliminary evaluation', Discussion Paper, No. 298, Economic and Research Staff, World Bank, Washington, DC.

Barker, T. S. (1968), 'Devaluation and the rise in UK prices', *Bulletin of the Oxford University Institute of Economics and Statistics*, vol. 30, pp. 129–41.

Barker, T. S. (1970), 'The determinants of Britain's visible imports 1949–66', no. 10 of *A Programme for Growth*, Chapman & Hall, London.

Barker, T. S. (1977), 'International trade and economic growth: an alternative to the neo-classical approach', *Cambridge Journal of Economics*, vol. 1, pp. 153–72.

Barker, T. S. and Brailovsky, V. (1981), *Oil or Industry*, Academic Press, New York.

Barker, T. S. (1979), 'The identification of activity effects, trends and cycles in import demand', *Oxford Bulletin of Economics and Statistics*, vol. 41, pp. 63–8.

Barker, T. S. and Brailovsky, V. (1981), *Oil or Industry*, Academic Press, New York.

Batchelor, R. A. (1977), 'Sterling exchange rates 1951–1976: a Casselian analysis', *National Institute Economic Review*, no. 81, pp. 41–66.

Bibliography

Batchelor, R. (1979), 'Must floating exchange rates be unstable', *Annual Monetary Review*, vol. 1, City University, London.

Batchelor, R. and Horne, J. (1979), 'Money, the balance of payments, and the exchange rate', *Annual Monetary Review*, vol. 1, City University, London.

Bator, F. M. (1957), 'The simple analytics of welfare maximisation', *American Economic Review*, vol. 47, pp. 22–59.

Bean, C. (1987), 'The impact of North Sea oil', Chapter 3 of Dornbusch and Layard (1987), pp. 64–96.

Becker, G. S. (1983). 'A theory of competition among pressure groups for political influence', *Quarterly Journal of Economics*, vol. 98, pp. 371–400.

Beckerman, W. (1974), *In Defence of Economic Growth*, Cape, London.

Beenstock, M. and Bell, S. (1979), 'A quarterly econometric model of the capital account in the UK balance of payments', *Manchester School*, vol. 47, pp. 33–62.

Behnke, E. A. (1980), 'International transmission of business cycles – the Sohmen–Laursen–Metzler effect', in Chipman and Kindleberger (1980), pp. 257–66.

Ben-Bassat, A. (1980), 'The optimal composition of foreign-exchange reserves', *Journal of International Economics*, vol. 10, pp. 285–96.

Bernstein, E. M. *et al.* (1976), *Reflections on Jamaica*, Princeton Essay in International Finance No. 115, University Press, Princeton, NJ.

Bhagwati, J. N. (1964), 'The pure theory of international trade: a survey', *Economic Journal*, vol. 74, pp. 1–84.

Bhagwati, J. N. (1968a), *The Theory and Practice of Commercial Policy: Departures from Unified Exchange Rates*, Special paper in International Economics No. 8, Princeton University Press, Princeton, NJ.

Bhagwati, J. N. (1968b), 'Distortions and immiserizing growth: a generalisation', *Review of Economic Studies*, vol. 35, pp. 481–5.

Bhagwati, J. N. (1969a), *Trade, Tariffs and Growth*, Weidenfeld & Nicolson, London.

Bhagwati, J. N. (1969b), 'On the equivalence of tariffs and quotas', Chapter 12 of Bhagwati (1986c).

Bhagwati, J. N. (1969c), *International Trade: Selected Readings*, Penguin, Harmondsworth, Middx.

Bhagwati, J. N. (1971) 'The generalised theory of distortions and welfare', in Bhagwati *et al.* (1971), pp. 69–90.

Bhagwati, J. N. (1980), 'Lobbying and welfare', *Journal of Public Economics*, vol. 14, pp. 355–63.

Bhagwati, J. N. (1981), *International Trade: Selected Readings*, 1st edn, MIT Press, Cambridge, Mass.

Bhagwati, J. N. (1982a), 'Directly unproductive, profit-seeking (DUP) activities', *Journal of Political Economy*, vol. 90, pp. 988–1002.

Bhagwati, J. N. (1982b), *Import Competition and Response*, University of Chicago Press, Chicago.

Bhagwati, J. N. (1983a), *International Economic Theory, vol. I The Theory of Commercial Policy*, MIT Press, Cambridge, Mass.

Bhagwati, J. N. (1983b), *International Economic Theory, vol. II International Factor Mobility*, MIT Press, Cambridge, Mass.

Bhagwati, J. N. (1986), 'Export promoting trade strategy: issues and evidence', Development Policy Issues, No. 7, World Bank, Washington DC.

Bhagwati, J. N. (1988), *Protectionism*, MIT Press, Cambridge, Mass.

Bhagwati, J. N. and Brecher, R. A. (1987), 'Voluntary export restraints vs import restrictions: A welfare theoretic comparison', in Kierzkowski (1987), pp. 41–53.

Bhagwati, J. N. and Ramaswami, V. K. (1963), 'Domestic distortions, tariffs and the theory of optimum subsidy', *Journal of Political Economy*, vol. 72, pp. 44–50.

Bhagwati, J. N. and Srinivasan, T. N. (1969), 'Optimal intervention to achieve non-economic objectives', *Review of Economic Studies*, vol. 36, pp. 27–38.

Bhagwati, J. N. and Srinivasan, T. N. (1980), 'Revenue-seeking: a generalisation of the theory of tariffs', *Journal of Policial Economy*, vol. 88, pp. 1069–87.

Bhagwati, J. N. and Srinivasan, T. N. (1982), 'The welfare consequences of directly-unproductive profit-seeking (DUP) lobbying activities: price versus quantity distortions', *Journal of International Economics*, vol. 13, pp. 33–44.

Bhagwati, J. N. and Srinivasan, T. N. (1983), *Lectures on International Trade*, MIT Press, Cambridge, Mass.

Bhagwati, J. N., Ramaswami, V. K. and Srinivasan, T. N. (1969), 'Domestic distortions, tariffs and the theory of optimum subsidy: some further results', *Journal of Political Economy*, vol. 77, pp. 1005–10.

Bhagwati, J. N. *et al.* (1971), *Trade, Balance of Payments and Growth*, North Holland, Amsterdam.

Bhandari, J. S. and Putnam, P. H. (1984), *Economic Interdependence and Flexible Exchange Rates*, MIT University Press, Cambridge, Mass.

477

Bilson, J. F. O. and Frenkel, J. A. (1979), 'International reserves: adjustment dynamics', *Economics Letters*, vol. 4, pp. 267–70.

Bird, G. (1982a), *The International Monetary System and the Less Developed Countries*, 2nd edn, Macmillan, London.

Bird, G. (1982b), 'The International Monetary Fund and developing countries: retrospect and prospect', mimeo.

Black, J. (1989), 'The gains from intra-industry trade', mimeo, Gregynog Hall, University of Wales, April.

Black, J. and Hindley, B. (1980), *Current Issues in Commercial Policy and Diplomacy*, Macmillan, London.

Black, J. and MacBean, A. I. (1989), *Causes of Changes in the Structure of International Trade 1960–85*, Macmillan, London.

Black, J. and Winters, L. A. (1983), *Policy and Performance in International Trade*, Macmillan, London.

Blackaby, F. (1979), *De-Industrialisation*, Heinemann, London.

Blake, D., Beenstock, M. and Brasse, V. (1986), 'The performance of UK exchange rate forecasters', *Economic Journal*, vol. 96, pp. 986–99.

Blanchard, O. J. (1987), 'Reaganomics', *Economic Policy*, vol. 5, pp. 15–56.

Blaug, M. (1980), *The Methodology of Economics*, Cambridge University Press, Cambridge.

Bloch, H. (1974), 'Prices, costs and profits in Canadian manufacturing: the influence of tariffs and concentration', *Canadian Journal of Economics*, vol. 7, pp. 594–610.

Bond, M. E. (1979), 'The world trade model: invisibles', *IMF Staff Papers*, vol. 26, pp. 257–333.

Bond, M. E. (1987), 'An econometric study of primary commodity exports from developing country regions of the world', *IMF Staff Papers*, vol. 34, pp. 191–227.

Borner, S. (1989), *Survival and Growth in a Polycentric World Economy*, Macmillan, London.

Bowen, H. P., Leamer, E. E. and Sveikauskas, L. (1987), 'Multi-country, multi-factor tests of the factor abundance theory', *American Economic Review*, vol. 77, pp. 791–809.

Brander, J. A. and Krugman, P. R. (1983), 'A reciprocal dumping model of international trade', *Journal of International Economics*, vol. 15, pp. 313–21.

Brander, J. A. and Spencer, B. J. (1981), 'Tariffs and the extraction of foreign monopoly rents under potential entry', *Canadian Journal of Economics*, vol. 14, pp. 371–89.

Brander, J. J. and Spencer, B. J. (1985), 'Export subsidies and international market share rivalry', *Journal of International Economics*, vol. 18, pp. 83–100.

Branson, W. H. (1977), 'Asset markets and relative prices in exchange rate determination', *Sozialwissenschaftliche Annalen*, vol. 1, pp. 69–89.

Branson, W. H. (1980), 'Comment' on Dornbusch (1980a), *Brookings Papers in Economic Activity*, vol. 10, pp. 87–194.

Branson, W. H. (1981), 'Comment' on Frenkel (1981), *European Economic Review*, vol. 16, pp. 167–71.

Branson, W. H. (1983), 'Macroeconomic determinants of real exchange rates', Chapter 1 of Herring (1983), pp. 33–84.

Branson, W. H. (1987), 'Discussion' (on Blanchard 1987), *Economic Policy*, no. 5, pp. 48–52.

Branson, W. H. and Buiter, W. H. (1984), 'Monetary and fiscal policy with flexible exchange rates', Chapter 9 of Bhandari and Putnam (1984), pp. 251–85.

Branson, W. H., Halttunen, H. and Masson, P. (1977), 'Exchange rates in the short-run, the dollar-deutschmark rate', *European Economic Review*, vol. 10, pp. 303–24.

Brech, M. J. and Stout, D. K. (1981), 'The rate of exchange and non-price competitiveness: a provisional study within UK manufactured exports', *Oxford Economic Papers*, vol. 33, Supplement, pp. 268–81.

Brecher, R. A. and Bhagwati, J. N. (1981), 'Foreign ownership and the theory of trade and welfare', *Journal of Political Economy*, vol. 89, pp. 497–511.

Brecher, R. A. and Bhagwati, J. N. (1982), 'Immiserising transfers from abroad', *Journal of International Economics*, vol. 13, pp. 353–64.

Brechling, F. and Wolfe, J. N. (1965), 'The end of stop–go', *Lloyds Bank Review*, no. 75, pp. 22–30.

Briault, C. B. and Howson, S. K. (1982), *A Portfolio Model of Domestic and External Financial Markets*, Discussion Paper, No. 20, Bank of England, London.

Brooman, F. S. (1970), *Macroeconomics*, 3rd edn, Allen & Unwin, London.

Brown, R. N., Enoch, C. A. and Mortimer-Lee, P. D. (1980), *The Interrelationships Between Costs and Prices in the United Kingdom*, Discussion Paper, No. 8, Bank of England, London.

Bryant, R. C. *et al.* (1989), *Macroeconomic Policies in an Interdependent World*, International Monetary Fund, Washington, DC.

Buiter, W. H. and Marston, R. C. (1985), *International Economic Policy Co-ordination*, Cambridge University Press, Cambridge.

478

Bibliography

Buiter, W. H. and Miller, M. H. (1981a), 'The Thatcher experiment: the first two years', *Brookings Papers in Economic Activity*, vol. 11, pp. 315–79.

Buiter, W. H. and Miller, M. H. (1981b), 'Monetary policy and international competitiveness: the problem of adjustment', *Oxford Economic Papers*, vol. 33, Supplement, pp. 143–75.

Bulow, J. and Rogoff, K. (1988), 'The buyback boondoggle', *Brookings Papers in Economic Activity*, No. 2, pp. 675–715.

Bulow, J. and Rogoff, K. (1989), 'Sovereign debt: is to forgive to forget?', *American Economic Review*, vol. 79, pp. 43–50.

Byrne, W. J. (1982), 'Evolution of the SDR, 1974–81', *Finance and Development*, vol. 19(3), pp. 31–5.

Calvo, G. A. and Rodriguez, C. A. (1977), 'A model of exchange rate determination under currency substitution and rational expectations', *Journal of Political Economy*, vol. 85, pp. 617–25.

Capie, F. (1983), 'Tariff protection and economic performance in the nineteenth century', in Black and Winters (1983), pp. 1–24.

Capie, F. (1988), 'Trade policies and economic recession', Paper given to International Economics Study Group Conference, University of Sussex.

Carse, S., Williamson, J. and Wood, G. E. (1980), *The Financing Procedure of British Foreign Trade*, Cambridge University Press, London.

Caves, R. E. (1974a), 'The causes of direct investment: foreign firms' shares in Canadian and UK manufacturing industry', *Review of Economics and Statistics*, vol. 56, pp. 279–93.

Caves, R. E. (1974b), 'Multinational firms, competition, and productivity in host country markets', *Economica*, vol. 41, pp. 176–93.

Caves, R. E. (1981), 'Intra-industry trade and market structure in the industrial countries', *Oxford Economic Papers*, vol. 33, pp. 203–23.

Caves, R. E. (1982), *Multinational Enterprise and Economic Analysis*, Cambridge University Press, Cambridge.

Caves, R. E. and Johnson, H. G. (1968), *Readings in International Economics*, Allen & Unwin, London.

Caves, R. E. and Jones, R. W. (1981), *World Trade and Payments*, 3rd edn, Little Brown, Boston.

Caves, R. E. and Krause, L. B. (1980), *Britain's Economic Performance*, Brookings Institution, Washington, DC.

Caves, R. E. *et al.* (1980), *Competition in the Open Economy*, Harvard University Press, Cambridge, Mass.

Cecchini, P. (1988), *The Costs of non-Europe*, Wildwood House, London.

Centre for Economic Policy Research (1989), *The European Monetary System in Transition*, CEPR, London.

Chacholiades, M. (1981), *Principles of International Economics*, McGraw Hill, New York.

Chappell, H. W. Jr (1982), 'Campaign contributions and congressional voting: a simultaneous probit–tobit model', *Review of Economics and Statistics*, vol. 64, pp. 77–83.

Cheh, J. (1974), 'United States concessions in the Kennedy Round and short-run labour adjustment costs', *Journal of International Economics*, vol. 4, pp. 323–40.

Chipman, J. S. (1966), 'A survey of the theory of international trade', Part III, 'The modern theory', *Econometrica*, vol. 34, pp. 18–76.

Chipman, J. S. and Kindleberger, C. P. (eds) (1980), *Flexible Exchange Rates and the Balance of Payments*, Studies in International Economics No. 7, North Holland, Amsterdam.

Chrystal, K. A. (1977), 'Demand for international media of exchange', *American Economic Review*, vol. 67, pp. 840–50.

Chrystal, K. A. (1978), *International Money and the Future of the SDR*, Princeton Essay in International Finance, No. 128, Princeton University Press, Princeton, NJ.

Clark, P. B. (1970), 'Demand for international reserves: a cross-country analysis', *Canadian Journal of Economics*, vol. 3, pp. 577–894.

Cline, W. *et al.* (1978), *Trade Negotiations in the Tokyo Round: A Quantitative Assessment*, Brookings Institution, Washington, DC.

Coase, R. H. (1937), 'The nature of the firm', *Economica*, vol. 4, pp. 386–405.

Coats, W. L. Jr (1982), 'The SDR as a means of payments', *IMF Staff Papers*, vol. 29, pp. 422–36.

Cohen, B. J. (1969), *Balance of Payments Policy*, Penguin, Harmondsworth, Middx.

Cohen, D. (1989), 'Debt relief and secondary market discount', Discussion Paper, No. 312, Centre for Economic Policy Research, London.

Cohen, D. and Wyplosz, C. (1989), 'The European Monetary Union: an agnostic evaluation', Chapter 8 of Bryant *et al.* (1989), pp. 311–37.

Collie, D. and de Meza, D. (1986), 'Inadequacies of the strategic rational of export subsidies', *Economics Letters*, vol. 22, pp. 369–72.

Commission of the European Communities (1988), 'The economics of 1992', *The European Economy*, no. 35.

479

Commission of the European Communities (1989), 'First Survey on State Aids in the European Community', EC, Brussels.

Connell, D. (1979), *The UK's Performance in Export Markets – Some Evidence from International Trade Data*, NEDO, London.

Cooper, C. A. and Massell, B. F. (1965a), 'A new look at customs union theory', *Economic Journal*, vol. 75, pp. 742–7.

Cooper, C. A. and Massell, B. F. (1965b), 'Towards a general theory of customs unions for developing countries', *Journal of Political Economy*, vol. 73, pp. 461–76.

Cooper, R. N. (1971), *Currency Devaluation and Developing Countries*, Princeton Essay in International Finance, No. 86, Princeton University, Princeton, NJ.

Corbet, H. (1979), 'The importance of being earnest about further GATT negotiations', *The World Economy*, vol. 3, pp. 319–42.

Corbo, V. (1989), 'A re-examination of a decade of debt crisis: origin and adjustment', mimeo, World Bank.

Corden, W. M. (1957), 'Tariffs, subsidies and the terms of trade', *Economica*, vol. 24, pp. 235–42.

Corden, W. M. (1966), 'The structure of a tariff system and effective protective rate', *Journal of Political Economy* vol. 74, pp. 221–37.

Corden, W. M. (1971), *The Theory of Protection*, Oxford University Press, Oxford.

Corden, W. M. (1972a), 'Economies of scale and customs union theory', *Journal of Political Economy*, vol. 80, pp. 465–75.

Corden, W. M. (1972b), *Monetary Integration*, Essay in International Finance, No. 93, Princeton University, Princeton, NJ.

Corden, W. M. (1974), *Trade Policy and Economic Welfare*, Oxford University Press, Oxford.

Corden, W. M. (1977), *Inflation, Exchange Rates and the World Economy*, Oxford University Press, Oxford.

Corden, W. M. (1981), 'The exchange rate monetary policy and North Sea oil the economic theory of the squeeze on tradables', *Oxford Economic Papers*, vol. 33, Supplement, pp. 23–46.

Corden, W. M. (1984), *The Revival of Protectionism*, Group of Thirty, New York.

Corden, W. M. (1985), *Inflation, Exchange Rates and the World Economy*, Oxford University Press, Oxford.

Corden, W. M. and Jones, R. W. (1976), 'Devaluation, non-flexible prices, and the trade balance for a small country', *Canadian Journal of Economics*, vol. 9, pp. 150–61.

Corden, W. M. and Neary, J. P. (1982), 'Booming sector and de-industrialisation in a small open economy', *Economic Journal*, vol. 92, pp. 825–48.

Cornwall, J. (1977), *Modern Capitalism*, Martin Robertson, Oxford.

Cournot, A. (1838), *Researches into the Mathematical Principles of the Theory of Wealth*; translated by N. T. Bacon, Macmillan, New York, 1897.

CPRS (1975), *The Future of the British Car Industry*, HMSO, London.

Crafts, N. E. R. (1991), 'Economic growth', Chapter 9 of Crafts and Woodward (1991).

Crafts, N. E. R. and Woodward, N. W. C. (1991), *The British Economy since 1945*, Oxford University Press, Oxford.

Cripps, T. F., Godley, W. A. H. and Fetherston, M. J. (1974), *Evidence to the Select Committee on Public Expenditure*, 9th Report, HC328.

Crockett, A. D. (1976), 'The Euro-currency markets: an attempt to clarify some basic issues', *IMF Staff Papers*, vol. 23, pp. 375–86.

Crockett, A. D. (1977), *International Money: Issues and Analysis*, Nelson, London.

Crockett, A. D. (1982), 'Issues in the use of fund resources', *Finance and Development*, vol. 19(2), pp. 10–15.

Crockett, A. D. and Goldstein, M. (1976), 'Inflation under fixed and flexible exchange rates', *IMF Staff Papers*, vol. 23, pp. 509–44.

Cuddington, J. T. (1986), *Capital Flight: Estimates, Issues and Explanations*, Princeton Studies in International Finance, No. 58, Princeton University, Princeton, NJ.

Cumby, R. and Levich, R. M. (1987), 'On the definition and magnitude of recent capital flight', Chapter 3 of Williamson and Lessard (1987), pp. 27–78.

Currie, D., Peel, D. and Peters, W. (1981), *Micro Economic Analysis*, Croom Helm, London.

Daltung, S., Eskeland, G. and Norman, V. D. (1988), *Optimum Trade Policy towards Imperfectly Competitive Industries: Two Norwegian Examples*, Discussion Paper No. 218, Centre for Economic Policy Research, London.

Dam, K. (1970), *The Gatt*, Chicago University Press, Chicago.

Davenport, M. (1990), 'The Charybdis of anti-dumping: a new form of EC industrial policy', Discussion Paper No. 22, Royal Institute of International Affairs, London.

de Cecco, M. and Giovannini, A. (1989), *A European Central Bank? Perspectives on Monetary Unification after Ten Years of the EMS*, Cambridge University Press, Cambridge.

480

de Grauwe, P. (1987), 'Exchange rate variability and the slow down of international trade', *IMF Staff Papers*, vol. 35, pp. 63–84.

de Grauwe, P. (1989), 'Is the European Monetary System a DM-zone?', Discussion Paper No. 297, Centre for Economic Policy Research, London.

de Marchi, N. B. (1976), 'Anomaly and the development of economics: the case of the Leontief paradox', in Latsis (1976), pp. 109–27.

de Melo, J. and Winters, L. A. (1989), 'Price and quality effects of VERs revisited: a case study of Korean footwear exports', PPR Discussion Paper, No. 216, World Bank, April.

de Meza, D. (1986), 'Export subsidies and high productivity: cause or effect?', *Canadian Journal of Economics*, vol. 19, pp. 347–50.

de V. Graaff, J. (1957), *Theoretical Welfare Economics*, Cambridge University Press, Cambridge.

Deardorff, A. V. (1979), 'Weak links in the theory of comparative advantage', *Journal of International Economics*, vol. 9, pp. 197–210.

Deardorff, A. V. (1980), 'The general validity of the law of comparative advantage', *Journal of Political Economy*, vol. 88, pp. 941–57.

Deardorff, A. V. (1982), 'The general validity of the Heckscher–Ohlin Theorem', *American Economic Review*, vol. 72, pp. 683–94.

Deardorff, A. V. (1983), 'Testing trade theories and predicting trade flows', Chapter 10 of Jones and Kenen (1983), vol. 1, pp. 467–518.

Deardorff, A. V. (1989), 'Empirical research on trade liberalisation with imperfect competition: a survey', *OECD Economic Studies*, no. 12, pp. 7–50.

Deardorff, A. V. and Stern, R. M. (1983a), 'The effects of domestic tax/subsidies and import tariffs on the structure of protection in US, UK and Japan', in Black and Winters (1983), pp. 43–64.

Deardorff, A. V. and Stern, R. M. (1983b), 'Economic effects of the Tokyo Round', *Southern Economic Journal*, vol. 49, pp. 605–24.

Department of Trade and Industry (1983), 'Memorandum to Select Committee on the European Communities', House of Lords, session 1983–4, 7th report, pp. 1–41.

Destler, I. M. and Odell, J. S. (1987), *Anti-protection: Changing Forces in United States Trade Politics*, Policy Analysis in International Economics, Institute for International Economics, Washington, DC.

Dixit, A. K. (1979), 'A model of duopoly suggesting a theory of entry barriers', *Bell Journal of Economics*, vol. 10, pp. 20–32.

Dixit, A. K. (1984), 'International trade policy for oligopolistic industries', *Economic Journal – Supplement*, vol. 94, pp. 1–16.

Dixit, A. K. (1987), 'How should the US respond to other countries' trade policies?', in Stern (1987), pp. 245–82.

Dixit, A. K. (1988), 'Optimal trade and industrial policies for the US automobile industry', Chapter 6 of Feenstra (1988b), pp. 141–65.

Dixit, A. K. (1990), 'Trade policy with imperfect information', Chapter 1 of Jones and Krueger (1990), pp. 9–24.

Dixit, A. K. and Grossman, G. M. (1986), 'Targetted export promotion with several oligopolistic industries', *Journal of International Economics*, vol. 21, pp. 233–49.

Dixit, A. K. and Kyle, A. S. (1985), 'The use of protection and subsidies for entry promotion and deterrence', *American Economic Review*, vol. 75, pp. 139–52.

Dixit, A. K. and Norman, V. D. (1980), *Theory of International Trade*, Nisbet/Cambridge University Press, London.

Dixit, A. K. and Norman, V. D. (1986), 'Gains from trade without lump-sum compensation', *Journal of International Economics*, vol. 21, pp. 111–22.

Dixit, A. K. and Woodland, A. (1982), 'The relationship between factor endowments and commodity trade', *Journal of International Economics*, vol. 13, pp. 201–14.

Donovan, D. J. (1981), 'Real responses associated with exchange rate action in selected upper credit tranche stabilisation progs', *IMF Staff Papers*, vol. 28, pp. 697–727.

Donovan, D. J. (1982), 'Macro economic performance and adjustment under fund supported progams: the experience of the seventies', *IMF Staff Papers*, vol. 29, pp. 171–203.

Dooley, M. P., Lizondo, J. S. and Mathieson, D. J. (1989), 'The currency composition of reserves', *IMF Staff Papers*, vol. 36, pp. 385–434.

Dore, R. P. (1982), 'Adjustment in process: a Lancashire town', Chapter 11 in Bhagwati (1982b), pp. 295–317.

Dornbusch, R. (1975a), 'Exchange rates and fiscal policy in a popular model of international trade', *American Economic Review*, vol. 65, pp. 859–71.

Dornbusch, R. (1975b), 'Alternative price stabilization rules and the effects of exchange rate changes', *Manchester School*, vol. 43, pp. 275–97.

481

Dornbusch, R. (1976), 'Expectations and exchange rate dynamics', *Journal of Political Economy*, vol. 84, pp. 1161–76.

Dornbusch, R. (1980a), 'Exchange rate economics: where do we stand?', *Brookings Papers in Economic Activity*, vol. 10(1), pp. 143–85.

Dornbusch, R. (1980b), *Open Economy Macro-economics*, Basic Books, New York.

Dornbusch, R. (1986), *Dollars, Debts and Deficits*, MIT Press, Cambridge, Mass.

Dornbusch, R. (1987), 'Exchange rates and prices', *American Economic Review*, vol. 17, pp. 93–106.

Dornbusch, R. and Fischer, S. (1980), 'Sterling and external balance', in Caves and Krause (1980), pp. 21–71.

Dornbusch, R. and Frankel, J. (1989), 'The flexible exchange rate system: experience and alternatives', in Borner (1989).

Dornbusch, R. and Frenkel, J. A. (1979), *International Economic Policy: Theory and Evidence*, Johns Hopkins University Press, Baltimore , Md.

Dornbusch, R. and Layard, R. (1987), *The Performance of the British Economy*, Oxford University Press, London.

Dunning, J. H. (1972), *International Investment*, Penguin, Harmondsworth, Middx.

Dunning, J. H. (1974), *Economic Analysis and the Multinational Enterprise*, Allen & Unwin, London.

Dunning, J. H. (1979), 'Explaining changing patterns of international investment: in defence of the eclectic theory', *Oxford Bulletin of Economics and Statistics*, vol. 41, pp. 269–96.

Dunning, J. H. (1988), *Explaining International Production*, Unwin Hyman, London.

Dunning, J. H. and McQueen, M. (1981), 'The eclectic theory of international production: a case study of the international hotel industry', *Managerial and Decision Economics*, vol. 2, pp. 197–210.

Dunning, J. H. and Pearce, R. D. (1981), *The World's Largest Industrial Enterprises*, Gower, Farnborough.

Eastman, H. C. and Stykolt, S. (1960), 'A model for the study of protected oligopolies', *Economic Journal*, vol. 70, pp. 336–47.

Eastwood, R. K. and Venables, A. J. (1982), 'The macro economic implications of a resource discovery in an open economy', *Economic Journal*, vol. 92, pp. 285–99.

Eastwood, R. K. and Venables, A. J. (1982), 'Oil sector shocks and the UK economy 1970–80: a macro economic appraisal', mimeo, University of Sussex.

Eaton, J, and Grossman, G. M. (1986), 'Optimal trade and industrial policy under oligopoly', *Quarterly Journal of Economics*, vol. 101, pp. 383–406.

Eaton, J. and Panagariya, A. (1982), 'Growth and welfare in a small, open economy', *Economica*, vol. 49, pp. 409–19.

Edwards, S. (1983), 'The demand for international reserves and exchange rate adjustments: the case of LDCs, 1964–72', *Economica*, vol. 50, pp. 269–80.

Edwards, S. (1984), 'The demand for international reserves and monetary equilibrium: some evidence from developing countries', *Review of Economics and Statistics*, vol. 66, pp. 495–500.

Edwards, S. (1989), 'The International Monetary Fund and the developing countries: a critical evaluation', Working Paper, No. 2909, National Bureau of Economic Research, Cambridge, Mass.

Eichengreen, B. and Portes, R. (1986), 'Debt and default in the 1930s: causes and consequences', *European Economic Review*, vol. 30, pp. 599–640.

Eichengreen, B. and Portes, R. (1987), 'The anatomy of financial crises', Chapter 1 of Portes and Swoboda (1987), pp. 10–57.

Ellman, M. (1977), 'Report from Holland: the economics of North Sea hydrocarbons', *Cambridge Journal of Economics*, vol. 1, pp. 281–90.

Emminger, O. (1979), 'The exchange rate as an instrument of policy', *Lloyds Bank Review*, no. 133, July, pp. 1–22.

Ennew, R., Greenway, D. and Reed, G. (1990), 'Further evidence of effective tariffs and effective protection in the UK', *Oxford Bulletin of Economics and Statistics*, vol. 52, pp. 69–78.

Esty, D. C. and Caves, R. E. (1983), 'Market structure and political influence: new data on political expenditures, activity and success', *Economic Inquiry*, vol. 21, pp. 24–38.

Ethier, W. (1982), 'National and international returns to scale in the modern theory of international trade', *American Economic Review*, vol. 72, pp. 389–405.

Ethier, W. J. (1983), 'Higher dimensional issues in trade theory', Chapter 3 of Jones and Kenen (1983), pp. 131–84.

Ethier, W. and Horn, H. (1984), 'A new look at economic integration', in Kierzkowski (1984), pp. 207–29.

Falvey, R. E. (1981), 'Commercial policy and intra-industry trade', *Journal of International Economics*, vol. 11, pp. 495–512.

Feder, G. (1983), 'On exports and economic growth', *Journal of Development Economics*, vol. 12, pp. 59–74.

Feenstra, R. C. (1988a), 'Quality change under trade restrictions in Japanese quotas', *Quarterly Journal of Economics*, vol. 103, pp. 131–46.

Feenstra, R. C. (1988b), *Empirical Methods of International Trade*, MIT Press, Cambridge, Mass.

Feinstein, C. H. and Reddaway, W. B. (1978), 'Open surpluses, the world recession and the UK economy', *Midland Bank Review*, Spring, pp. 7–19.

Findlay, R. (1970a), *Trade and Specialisation*, Penguin, Harmondsworth, Middx.

Findlay, R. (1970b), 'Factor proportions and comparative advantage in the long-run', *Journal of Political Economy*, vol. 78, pp. 27–34.

Findlay, R. and Rodriguez, C. A. (1977), 'Intermediate imports and macro-economic policy under flexible exchange rates', *Canadian Journal of Economics*, vol. 10, pp. 208–17.

Finger, J. M. (1975), 'Trade overlap and intra-industry trade', *Economic Inquiry*, vol. 13, pp. 581–9.

Finger, J. M. (1979), 'Trade liberalisation: a public choice perspective', in Amacher, Haberler and Willet (1979), pp. 421–61.

Finger, J. M. (1981), 'The industry-country incidence of "less than fair value" cases in US import trade', *Quarterly Review of Economics and Business*, Summer, pp. 260–79.

Finger, J. M. and DeRosa, D. (1980), 'The Compensatory Finance Facility and export instability', *Journal of World Trade Law*, vol. 14, pp. 14–22.

Finger, J. M. and Olechowski, A. (1987), *The Uruguay Round: A Handbook*, World Bank, Washington, DC.

Finger, J. M., Hall, K. H. and Nelson, D. R. (1982), 'The political economy of administered protection', *American Economic Review*, vol. 72, pp. 452–66.

Fleming, J. M. (1962), 'Domestic financial policies under fixed and under floating exchange rates', *IMF Staff Papers*, vol. 9, pp. 369–79.

Forsyth, P. J. and Kay, J. A. (1980), 'The economic implications of North Sea oil revenues', *Fiscal Studies*, vol. 1, July, pp. 1–28.

Forsyth, P. J. and Kay, J. A. (1981), 'Oil revenues and manufacturing output', *Fiscal Studies*, vol. 2, July, pp. 9–17.

Frankel, J. A. (1979), 'On the mark: a theory of floating exchange rates based on real interest differentials', *American Economic Review*, vol. 69, pp. 610–22.

Freedman, C. (1977a), 'A model of the Eurodollar market', *Journal of Monetary Economics*, vol. 3, pp. 139–61.

Freedman, C. (1977b), 'The Euro-dollar market: a review of five recent studies', *Journal of Monetary Economics*, vol. 3, pp. 467–78.

Freeman, C. (1979), 'Technical innovation and British trade performance', in Blackaby (1979), pp. 56–78.

Freeman, C. and Young, A. (1965), *The Research and Development Effort in Western Europe, North America and the Soviet Union*, OECD, Paris.

Frenkel, J. A. (1976), 'A monetary approach to the exchange rate: doctrinal aspects and empirical evidence', *Scandinavian Journal of Economics*, vol. 78, pp. 200–24.

Frenkel, J. A. (1978a), 'Purchasing power parity: doctrinal perspective and evidence from the 1920s', *Journal of International Economics*, vol. 8, pp. 169–92.

Frenkel, J. A. (1978b), 'International reserves: pegged exchange rates and managed float', *Carnegie–Rochester Conference Series on Public Policy*, no. 9, pp. 111–40.

Frenkel, J. A. (1981), 'The collapse of purchasing power parities during the 1970s', *European Economic Review*, vol. 16, pp. 145–65.

Frenkel, J. A. and Goldstein, M. (1986), 'A guide to target zones', *IMF Staff Papers*, vol. 33, pp. 633–73.

Frenkel, J. A. and Johnson, H. G. (1976), *The Monetary Approach to the Balance of Payments*, Allen & Unwin, London.

Frenkel, J. A. and Johnson, H. G. (1978), *The Economics of Exchange Rates*, Addison Wesley, Reading, Mass.

Frenkel, J. A. and Rodriguez, C. A. (1982), 'Exchange rate dynamics and the overshooting hypothesis', *IMF Staff Papers*, vol. 29, pp. 1–30.

Friedman, M. (1953), 'The case for flexible exchange rates', *Essays in Positive Economics*, University of Chicago Press, pp. 157–203.

Fukuda, H. (1973), *Britain in Europe: Impact on the Third World*, Macmillan, London.

Gardener, E. P. M. and Revell, J. (1987), *Securitisation: History, Forms and Risk*, Research Monograph, No. 5, Institute of European Finance, University College of North Wales, Bangor.

GATT (1979), *The Tokyo Round of Multilateral Trade Negotiations*, Report by the Director General, GATT, Geneva.

Bibliography

Gelb, A. (1989), *Oil Windfalls: Blessing or Cure?*, Oxford University Press, Oxford.

Genberg, H. (1978), 'Purchasing power parity under fixed and flexible exchange rates', *Journal of International Economics*, vol. 8, pp. 247–76.

Geroski, P. and Jacquemin, A. (1986), 'Industrial change, barriers to mobility, and European industrial policy', *Economic Policy*, no. 1, pp. 169–205.

Giavazzi, F. (1989), 'The exchange rate question in Europe', Chapter 7 of Bryant *et al.* (1989), pp. 283–304.

Giavazzi, F., Micossi, S. and Miller, M. (1988), *The European Monetary System*, Cambridge University Press, Cambridge.

Giersch, H. (1974), *The International Division of Labour: Problems and Prospects*, JCB Mohr, Tübingen.

Giovannini, A. (1988), 'Exchange rates and traded goods prices', *Journal of International Economics*, vol. 24, pp. 45–68.

Goldstein, M. (1980), *Have Flexible Exchange Rates Handicapped Macro Economic Policy?*, Special Paper in International Economics, No. 14, Princeton University, Princeton, NJ.

Goldstein, M. and Khan, M. S. (1976), 'Large versus small price changes and the demand for imports', *IMF Staff Papers*, vol. 23, pp. 200–25.

Goldstein, M. and Khan, M. S. (1978), 'The supply and demand for exports: a simultaneous approach', *Review of Economics and Statistics*, vol. 60, pp. 275–86.

Goldstein, M. and Montiel, D. (1986), 'Evaluation of Fund stabilisation programs with multi-country data. Some methodological pitfalls', *IMF Staff Papers*, vol. 33, pp. 304–44.

Goodhart, C. (1988), 'The foreign exchange market: a random walk with a dragging anchor', *Economica*, vol. 55, pp. 437–60.

Gordon, R. J. (1982), 'Why US wage and employment behaviour differs from that in Britain and Japan', *Economic Journal*, vol. 92, pp. 13–44.

Goto, J. (1989), 'The Multifibre Arrangement and its effects on developing countries', *World Bank Research Observer*, vol. 4, pp. 203–27.

Grabbe, J. O. (1981), 'Liquidity creation and maturity transformation in the Euro-dollar markets', *Journal of Monetary Economics*, vol. 10, pp. 39–72.

Greenaway, D. (1983), *International Trade Policy: From Tariffs to the New Protectionism*, Macmillan, London.

Greenaway, D. (1985), *Current Issues in International Trade*, Macmillan, London.

Greenaway, D. (1988), *Economic Development and Intenational Trade*, Macmillan, London.

Greenaway, D. and Hindley, B. (1985), *What Britain Pays for Voluntary Export Restraints*, Thames Essay No. 43, Trade Policy Research Centre, London.

Greenaway, D. and Milner, C. R. (1983), 'On the measurement of intra-industry trade', *Economic Journal*, vol. 93, pp. 900–8.

Greenaway, D. and Milner, C. R. (1986), *The Economics of Intra-Industry Trade*, Blackwell, Oxford.

Greenaway, D. and Nam, C. H. (1988), 'Industrial and macroeconomic performance in developing countries under alternative trade strategies', *Kyklos*, vol. 41, pp. 419–35.

Greenaway, D. and Sapsford, D. (1987), 'Further econometric analysis of the relationship between fiscal dependence on trade taxes and economic development', *Public Finance*, vol. 42, pp. 309–19.

Greene, M. L. (1975), *Waiting Time: A Factor in Export Demand for Manufactures*, Princeton Study in International Finance, No. 37, Princeton University, Princeton, NJ.

Greenhalgh, C. (1990), 'Innovation and trade performance in the United Kingdom', *Economic Journal Supplement*, vol. 100, pp. 105–18.

Gregory, R. G. (1976), 'Some implications of the growth of the mineral sector', *Australian Journal of Agricultural Economics*, vol. 20, pp. 71–91.

Gribbin, J. D. (1971), *The Profitability of UK Exports*, Government Economic Service Occasional Paper, No. 1, HMSO, London.

Grilli, E. R. and Yang, M. C. (1988), 'Primary commodity prices, manufactured goods prices, and the terms of trade of developing countries', *World Bank Economic Review*, vol. 2, pp. 1–48.

Grinols, E. L. (1984), 'A thorn in the lion's pay: has Britain paid too much for Common Market membership?', *Journal of International Economics*, vol. 16, pp. 271–93.

Grinols, E. L. (1989), 'Procedural protectionism: the American Trade Bill and the new interventionist mode', *Weltwirtschaftliches Archiv*, vol. 125, pp. 501–21.

Grossman, G. M. (1983), 'Partially mobile capital: a general approach to two-sector trade theory', *Journal of International Economics*, vol. 15, pp. 1–17.

Grossman, G. M. and Horn, H. (1988), 'Infant industry protection reconsidered: the case of informational barriers to entry', *Quarterly Journal of Economics*, vol. 103, pp. 767–87.

Group of Thirty (1988), *International Macroeconomic Policy Co-ordination*, Group of Thirty, New York.

Grubel, H. G. (1977), *The International Monetary System*, 3rd edn, Penguin, Harmondsworth, Middx.

Grubel, H. G. (1981), *International Economics*, 2nd edn, Irwin, Homewood, Ill.

Grubel, H. G. and Lloyd, P. J. (1975), *Intra-Industry Trade: The Theory and Measurement of International Trade in Differentiated Products*, Macmillan, London.

484

Haberler, G. (1936), *The Theory of International Trade with its Applications to Commercial Policy*, W. Hodge and Co., London.

Haberler, G. (1949), 'The market for foreign-exchange and the stability of the balance of payments: a theoretical analysis', *Kyklos*, vol. 3, pp. 193–218.

Haberler, G. (1950), 'Some problems in the pure theory of international trade', *Economic Journal*, vol. 60, pp. 223–40.

Hacche, G. and Townend, J. (1981a), 'A broad look at exchange rate movements for eight currencies 1972–80', *Bank of England Quarterly Review*, vol. 21, pp. 489–507.

Hacche, G. and Townend, J. (1981b), 'Exchange rates and monetary policy: modelling sterling's effective exchange rate', *Oxford Economic Papers: Supplement*, vol. 33, pp. 201–47.

Hahn, F. H. (1977), 'The monetary approach to the balance of payments', *Journal of International Economics*, vol. 7, pp. 231–50.

Halm, G. N. (1977), *Jamaica and the Bar-Value System*, Princeton Essay in International Finance, No. 120, Princeton University, Princeton, NJ.

Hamilton, A. (1790), *Report of Manufactures 1790*; *Papers on Public Credit Commerce and Finance*, Columbia University Press, New York, 1934.

Hamilton, C. B. (1981), 'A new approach to estimation of the effects of non-tariff barriers to trade: an application to the Swedish textile and clothing industry', *Weltwirtschaftliches Archiv*, vol. 117, pp. 298–324.

Hamilton, C. B. (1986), 'The upgrading effect of voluntary export restraints', *Weltwirtschaftliches Archiv*, vol. 122, pp. 358–63.

Hamilton, C. B. (1990), *Textiles Trade and the Developing Countries: Eliminating the Multifibre Arrangement in the 1990s*, World Bank, Washington, DC.

Harris, R. G. and Cox, D. (1984), *Trade, Industrial Policy, and Canadian Manufacturing*, Ontario Economic Council, Toronto.

Havrylyshyn, O. (1984), 'The direction of developing country trade: empirical evidence of differences between South–South and North–South Trade', World Bank Conference Series, World Bank, Washington, DC.

Havrylyshyn, O. and Civan, E. (1983), 'Intra-industry trade and the stage of development', Chapter 5 of Tharakan (1983), pp. 111–40.

Hawkins, C. and McKenzie, G. (eds) (1982), *The British Economy: What Will Our Children Think?* Macmillan, London.

Hayter, T. (1971), *Aid as Imperialism*, Penguin, Harmondsworth, Middx.

Helleiner, G. K. (1973), 'Manufactured exports from less developed countries and multinational firms', *Economic Journal*, vol. 83, pp. 21–47.

Helleiner, G. K. (1976), *A World Divided*, Cambridge University Press, London.

Helleiner, G. K. (1977), 'Transnational enterprises and the new political economy of US trade policy', *Oxford Economic Papers*, vol. 29, pp. 102–16.

Heller, H. R. and Khan, M. S. (1978), 'The demand for international reserves under fixed and floating exchange rates', *IMF Staff Papers*, vol. 25, pp. 623–49.

Heller, H. R. and Knight, M. (1978), *Reserve Currency Preferences of Central Banks*, Princeton Essay in International Finance, No. 131, Princeton University, Princeton, NJ.

Heller, P. S. (1976), 'Factor endowment change and comparative advantage: the case of Japan, 1956–1969', *Review of Economics and Statistics*, vol. 58, pp. 283–92.

Helpman, E. (1981), 'International trade in the presence of product differentiation, economies of scale and monopolistic competition: a Chamberlin–Heckscher–Ohlin approach', *Journal of International Economics*, vol. 11, pp. 305–40.

Helpman, E. (1983), 'Increasing returns, imperfect markets and trade theory', Chapter 7 of Jones and Kenen (1983), pp. 325–65.

Helpman, E. (1987), 'Imperfect competition and international trade: evidence from fourteen industrial countries', *Journal of the Japanese and International Economies*, vol. 1, pp. 62–81.

Helpman, E. and Krugman, P. (1985), *Market Structure and Foreign Trade: Increasing Returns, Imperfect Competition and the International Economy*, MIT Press, Cambridge, Mass.

Helpman, E. and Krugman, P. R. (1989), *Trade Policy and Market Structure*, MIT Press, Cambridge, Mass.

Henderson, P. D. (1977), 'Two British errors: their probable size and some possible lessons', *Oxford Economic Papers*, vol. 29, pp. 159–205.

Henry, G. B. (1970), 'Domestic demand pressure and short-run export fluctuations', *Yale Economic Essays*, vol. 10, pp. 43–81.

Henry, S. G. B., Sawyer, M. C. and Smith, P. (1976), 'Models of inflation in the United Kingdom', *National Institute Economic Review*, no. 77, pp. 60–71.

Herrmann, R., Burger, K. and Smit, H. P. (1990), 'Commodity policy: price stabilization versus financing', Chapter 10 of Winters and Sapsford (1990), pp. 240–89.

Herring, R. C. (1983), *Managing Foreign Exchange Risk*, Cambridge University Press, Cambridge.

Herring, R. J. and Marston, R. C. (1977), *National Monetary Policies and International Financial Markets*, North Holland, Amsterdam.

Hewson, J. and Sakikabara, E. (1974), 'The Euro-dollr deposit multiplier: a portfolio approach', *IMF Staff Papers*, vol. 21, pp. 307–28.

Hindley, B. (1980), 'Voluntary export restraints and Article XIX of the GATT', in Black and Hindley (1980), pp. 52–72.

Hindley, B. (1983), 'Trade policy, economic performance, and Britain's economic problems', in Black and Winters (1983), pp. 25–42.

Hindley, B. (1988), 'Dumping and the Far East trade of the European Community', *The World Economy*, vol. 11, pp. 445–64.

Hindley, B. (1990), 'The economics of dumping and anti-dumping action: is there a baby in the bathwater?', mimeo, London School of Economics.

Hindley, B. and Smith, A. (1984), 'Comparative advantage and trade in services', *The World Economy*, vol. 7, pp. 369–90.

Hipple, F. S. (1974), *The Disturbances Approach to the Demand for International Reserves*, Study in International Finance, No. 35, Princeton University, Princeton, NJ.

Hirsch, S. (1967), *Location of Industry of International Competitiveness*, Oxford University Press, Oxford.

Hirsch, S. (1974), 'Hypotheses regarding trade between developing and industrial countries', in Giersch (1974), pp. 65–82.

Hirsch, S. (1975), 'The product cycle model of international trade – a multi-country cross section', *Oxford Bulletin of Economics and Statistics*, vol. 37, pp. 305–17.

Hirsch, S. (1976), 'An international trade and investment theory of the firm', *Oxford Economic Papers*, vol. 28, pp. 258–70.

Hocking, R. D. (1980), 'Trade in motor cars between the major European producers', *Economic Journal*, vol. 90, pp. 504–25.

Hodjera, Z. A. (1971), 'Short-run capital movements of the United Kingdom 1963–1967', *Journal of Political Economy*, vol. 79, pp. 739–75.

Hodjera, Z. A. (1973), 'International short term capital movements: a survey of theory and empirical analysis', *IMF Staff Papers*, vol. 20, pp. 683–740.

Hood, N. and Young, S. (1979), *The Economics of Multinational Enterprise*, Longman, London.

Hooper, P. and Kolhagen, S. W. (1978), 'The effect of exchange rate uncertainty on the price and volume of international trade', *Journal of International Economics*, vol. 8, pp. 483–511.

Horst, T. (1972), 'Firm and industry determinants of the decision to invest abroad: an empirical study', *Review of Economics and Statistics*, vol. 54, pp. 258–66.

Horstmann, I. and Markusen, J. R. (1986), 'Up the average cost curve: inefficient entry and the new protectionism', *Journal of International Economics*, vol. 20, pp. 225–48.

Hudec, R. E. (1987), *Developing Countries in the GATT Legal System*, Gower, Aldershot.

Hufbauer, G. C. (1970), 'The impact of national characteristics and technology on the commodity composition of trade in manufactured goods', in Vernon (1970), pp. 145–232.

Hufbauer, G. C. and Chilas, J. G. (1974), 'Specialisation by industrial countries: extent and consequences', in Giersch (1974), pp. 3–38.

Hufbauer, G. C., Berliner, D. T. and Elliott, K. A. (1986), *Trade Protection in the United States: 31 Case Studies*, Institute for International Economics, Washington, DC.

Hughes, J. J. and Thirlwall, A. P. (1977), 'Trends and cycles in import penetration in the UK', *Oxford Bulletin of Economics and Statistics*, vol. 39, pp. 301–18.

Hughes, K. S. (1986), *Exports and Technology*, Cambridge University Press, Cambridge.

Huizinga, H. (1989), *How Has the Debt Crisis Affected Commercial Banks?* Policy, Planning and Research Working Paper, No. 195, World Bank, Washington, DC.

Hunter, L. and Markusen, J. R. (1988), 'Per-capita income as a determinant of trade', Chapter 4 of Feenstra (1988b), pp. 89–109.

Hymer, S. H. (1979), *The Multinational Corporation: A Radical Approach*, Cambridge University Press, Cambridge.

IMF (1984), *Exchange Rate Volatility and World Trade*, Occasional Paper No. 19, IMF, Washington, DC.

IMF (1987), *Report on the World Current Account Discrepancy*, IMF, Washington, DC.

Imlah, A. H. (1958), *Economic Elements in the Pax Britannica*, Harvard University Press, Cambridge, Mass.

Isard, P. (1977), 'How far can we push the law of one price?', *American Economic Review*, vol. 67, pp. 942–8.

Isard, P. (1978), *Exchange Rate Determination: A Survey of Popular Views and Recent Models*, Princeton Study in International Finance, No. 42, Princeton University, Princeton, NJ.

Jacquemin, A. and Sapir, A. (1989), *The European Internal Market*, Oxford University Press, Oxford.

Jacquemin, A. and Sapir, A. (1991), 'Competition and imports in the European market', in Venables and Winters (1991).

Johnson, H. G. (1953), 'Optimum tariffs and retaliation', *Review of Economic Studies*, vol. 22, pp. 142–53.

Johnson, H. G. (1958a), 'Towards a general theory of the balance of payments', Chapter 6 of Johnson (1958b), pp. 153–68.

Johnson, H. G. (1958b), *International Trade and Economic Growth*, Allen & Unwin, London.

Johnson, H. G. (1965a), 'Optimal trade intervention in the presence of domestic distortions', in Baldwin *et al.* (1965), pp. 3–34.

Johnson, H. G. (1965b), 'An economic theory of protectionism, tariff bargaining and the formation of customs union', *Journal of Political Economy*, vol. 73, p. 256–83.

Johnson, H. G. (1967a), *Economic Policies towards Less Developed Countries*, Allen & Unwin, London.

Johnson, H. G. (1967b), 'Theoretical problems of the international monetary system', *Pakistan Development Review*, vol. 7, pp. 1–28.

Johnson, H. G. (1971), *Aspects of the Theory of Tariffs*, Allen & Unwin, London.

Johnston, R. B. (1981), *Theories of the Growth of the Euro-Currency Market: A Review of the Euro-Currency Deposit Multiplier*, BIS Economic Paper, No. 4, BIS, Basle.

Johnston, R. B. (1983), *The Economics of the Euro-Market: History, Theory and Policy*, Macmillan, London.

Jones, R. W. (1956), 'Factor proportions and the Heckscher–Ohlin Theorem', *Review of Economic Studies*, vol. 24, pp. 1–10.

Jones, R. W. (1971), 'A three factor model in theory, trade and history', Chapter 1 of Bhagwati *et al.* (1971), pp. 3–21.

Jones, R. W. (1974), 'The small country in a many-commodity world', *Australia Economic Papers*, vol. 13, pp. 225–36.

Jones, R. W. (1975), 'Presumption and the transfer problem', *Journal of International Economics*, vol. 5, pp. 263–74.

Jones, R. W. (1976), *Two-ness in Trade Theory: Costs and Benefits*, Princeton Special Paper in International Economics, No. 12, Princeton University Press, Princeton, NJ.

Jones, R. W. and Kenen, P. B. (1983), *Handbook of International Economics, International Trade Theory*, two vols, North Holland, Amsterdam.

Jones, R. W. and Krueger, A. O. (1990), *The Political Economy of International Trade*, Basil Blackwell, Oxford.

Kafka, A. (1976), *The International Monetary Fund: Reform with Reconstruction?*, Princeton Essay in International Finance, No. 118, Princeton University Press, Princeton, NJ.

Katrak, H. (1973), 'Human skills, R and D and scale economies in the exports of the United Kingdom and the United States', *Oxford Economic Papers*, vol. 25, pp. 337–60.

Katrak, H. (1982), 'Labour skills, R and D and capital requirements in the international trade and investment of UK, 1968–78', *National Institute Economic Review*, no. 101, pp. 38–47.

Katseli-Papaefstratiou, L. T. (1979), *The Re-emergence of the Purchasing Power Parity Doctrine in the 1970s*, Princeton Special Papers in International Finance, No. 13, Princeton University, Princeton, NJ.

Keesing, D. B. and Wolf, M. (1980), *Textile Quotas against Developing Countries*, Thames Essay, No. 23, Trade Policy Research Centre, London.

Kelly, M. *et al.* (1988), *Issues and Developments in International Trade Policy*, Occasional paper, No. 63, IMF, Washington, DC.

Kemp, M. C. and Wan, H. (1976), 'An elementary proposition concerning the formation of customs unions', *Journal of International Economics*, vol. 6, pp. 95–7.

Kenen, P. B. (1975), *International Trade and Finance*, Cambridge University Press, Cambridge.

Kenen, P. B. (1988), *Managing Exchange Rates*, Chatham House Paper, Routledge, London.

Keynes, J. M. (1925), *The Economic Consequences of Mr Churchill*, Hogarth Press, London.

Keynes, J. M. (1929), 'The German transfer problem', *Economic Journal*, vol. 39, pp. 1–7.

Keynes, J. M. (1931), 'Mitigation by tariff'; *Essays in Persuasion*, vol. 9, J. M. Keynes, *Collected Writings*, Macmillan, London, 1972, pp. 231–44.

Keynes, J. M. (1980), *Collected Writings, Activities, Shaping the Post War World, vol. XXV*, Moggridge, Macmillan for the Royal Economic Society, London.

Khan, M. S. and Ross, K. Z. (1975), 'Cyclical and secular income elasticities of the demand for imports', *Review of Economics and Statistics*, vol. 59, pp. 357–61.

Kierzkowski, H. (1984), *Monopolistic Competition in International Trade*, Oxford University Press, Oxford.

Kierzkowski, H. (1987), *Protection and Competition in International Trade*, Blackwell, Oxford.

Knetter, M. M. (1989), 'Price discrimination by US and German exporters', *American Economic Review*, vol. 79, pp. 198–210.

Komiya, R. (1980), 'Is international co-ordination of national economic policies necessary?' in Oppenheimer (1980), pp. 16–33.

Kopits, G. F. (1976), 'Intra-firm royalites crossing frontiers and transfer pricing behaviour', *Economic Journal*, vol. 86, pp. 781–805.

Kouri, P. and Porter, M. (1974), 'International capital flows and portfolio equilibrium', *Journal of Political Economy*, vol. 82, pp. 443–67.

Krause, M. B. (1972), 'Recent developments in customs union theory: an interpretive survey', *Journal of Economic Literature*, vol. 10, pp. 413–36.

Kravis, I. B. (1970), 'Trade as the handmaiden of growth: similarities between the nineteenth and twentieth centuries', *Economic Journal*, vol. 80, pp. 850–72.

Kravis, I. B. and Lipsey, R. E. (1971), *Price Competitiveness in World Trade*, National Bureau of Economic Research, New York.

Kravis, I. B. and Lipsey, R. E. (1978), 'Price behaviour in the light of balance of payments theories', *Journal of International Economics*, vol. 8, pp. 193–246.

Kravis, I. B. and Lipsey, R. E. (1982), 'Prices and market shares in international machinery trade', *Review of Economics and Statistics*, vol. 64, pp. 110–16.

Kravis, I. B., Heston, A. and Summers, R. (1982), *World Product and Income. International Comparisons of Real Gross Product*, Johns Hopkins University Press, Baltimore, Md.

Kreinin, M. E. and Officer, L. H. (1978), *The Monetary Approach to the Balance of Payments*, Princeton Studies in International Finance, No. 43, Princeton University, Princeton, NJ.

Krueger, A. O. (1974), 'The political economy of the rent-seeking society', *American Economic Review*, vol. 64, pp. 291–303.

Krueger, A. O. (1983a), 'The effects of trade strategies on growth', *Finance and Development*, vol. 20(2), pp. 6–8.

Krueger, A. O. (1983b), *Exchange Rate Determination*, Cambridge University Press, Cambridge.

Krueger, A. O. and Tuncer, B. (1982), 'An empirical test of the infant industry argument', *American Economic Review*, vol. 72, pp. 1142–52.

Krugman, P. R. (1979), 'Increasing returns, monopolistic competition, and international trade', *Journal of International Economics*, vol. 9, pp. 469–79.

Krugman, P. R. (1981), 'Intra-industry specialisation and the gain from trade', *Journal of Political Economy*, vol. 89, pp. 959–73.

Krugman, P. R. (1984), 'Import protection as export promotion', Chapter 11 of Kierzkowski (1984), pp. 180–93.

Krugman, P. R. (1987a), 'Is free trade passé?', *Journal of Economic Perspectives*, vol. 1, Fall, pp. 131–44.

Krugman, P. R. (1987b), *Strategic Trade Policy and the New International Economics*, MIT Press, Cambridge, Mass.

Krugman, P. R. (1987c), 'Pricing to market when the exchange rate changes', in Arndt and Richardson (1987).

Krugman, P. R. (1989a), 'Differences in income elasticities and trends in real exchange rates', *European Economic Review*, vol. 33, pp. 1031–54.

Krugman, P. R. (1989b), 'Private capital flows to problem debtors', Chapter 15 of Sachs (1989a), pp. 285–98.

Krugman, P. R. and Taylor, L. (1978), 'Contractionary effects of devaluation', *Journal of International Economics*, vol. 8, pp. 445–56.

Laidler, D. (1981), 'Some policy implications of the monetary approach to the balance of payments and exchange rate analysis', *Oxford Economic Papers*, vol. 33, Supplement, pp. 70–84.

Laird, S. and Yeats, A. (1988), 'Trends in non-tariff barriers of developed countries 1966–1986', PPR Working Paper WPS 137, World Bank, Washington, DC.

Laird, S. and Yeats, A. (1990), *Quantitative Methods for Trade Barrier Analysis*, Macmillan, London.

Lall, S. (1973), 'Transfer pricing by multi-national manufacturing firms', *Oxford Bulletin of Economics and Statistics*, vol. 35, pp. 173–95.

Lall, S. (1980), 'Monopolistic advantages and foreign investment by US manufacturing industry', *Oxford Economic Papers*, vol. 32, pp. 102–22.

Lall, S. and Streeten, P. (1977), *Foreign Investment, Transnationals and Developing Countries*, Macmillan, London.

Lancaster, K. J. (1957), 'The Heckscher–Ohlin trade model: a geometric treatment', *Economica*, vol. 24, pp. 19–39.

Lancaster, K. J. (1966), 'A new approach to consumer theory', *Political Economy*, vol. 74, pp. 132–57.

Lancaster, K. J. (1969), *Introduction to Modern Micro-economics*, Rand McNally, Chicago.

Lancaster, K. J. (1980), 'Intra-industry trade under perfect monopolistic competition', *Journal of International Economics*, vol. 10, pp. 151–75.

Lancaster, K. J. (1982), 'Comment' on Krugman, in Bhagwati (1982b), pp. 208–16.

Landesmann, M. and Snell, A. (1989), 'The consequences of Mrs. Thatcher for UK manufacturing exports', *Economic Journal*, vol. 99, pp. 1–27.

Langhammer, R. J. and Sapir, A. (1987), *Economic Impact of Generalized Tariff Preferences*, Gower, Aldershot.

Latsis, S. J. (1976), *Method and Appraisal in Economics*, Cambridge University Press, Cambridge.

Laursen, S. and Metzler, L. A. (1950), 'Flexible exchange rates and the theory of employment', *Review of Economics and Statistics*, vol. 32, pp. 281–99.

Lavergne, R. P. (1983), *The Political Economy of US Tariffs: an Empirical Analysis*, Academic Press, London.

Layard, P. R. G. and Walters, A. A. (1978), *Micro-economic Theory*, McGraw-Hill, New York.

Leach, D. and Cubbin, J. (1978), 'Import penetration in the UK passenger car market: a cross-section study', *Applied Economics*, vol. 10, pp. 289–303.

Leamer, E. E. (1974), 'The commodity composition of international trade in manufactures: an empirical analysis', *Oxford Economic Papers*, vol. 26, pp. 350–74.

Leamer, E. E. (1980), 'The Leontief Paradox reconsidered', *Journal of Political Economy*, vol. 88, pp. 495–503.

Leamer, E. E. (1984), *Sources of International Comparative Advantage*, MIT Press, Cambridge, Mass.

Leibenstein, H. (1966), 'Allocative efficiency v x-efficiency', *American Economic Review*, vol. 56, pp. 392–415.

Leontief, W. A. (1954), 'Domestic production and foreign trade: the American capital position re-examined', *Economia Internazionale*, vol. 7, pp. 3–32.

Lerner, A. (1936), 'The symmetry between import and export taxes', *Economica*, vol. 3, pp. 306–13.

Levačić, R. and Rebmann, A. (1982), *Macro-Economics, An Introduction to Keynesian and Neo-Classical Controversies*, 2nd edn, Macmillan, London.

Levich, R. M. (1989), *The Euromarkets after 1992*, Working Paper No. 3003, National Bureau of Economic Research, Cambridge, Mass.

Levinsohn, J. and Feenstra, R. (1990), 'Identifying the competition', *Journal of International Economics*, vol. 28, pp. 199–216.

Lewis, M. K. and Davis, K. T. (1987), *Domestic and International Banking*, Philip Allen, Deddington.

Lewis, W. A. (1954), *The Theory of Economic Growth*, Allen & Unwin, London.

Lewis, W. A. (1980), 'The slowing down of the engine of growth', *American Economic Review*, vol. 70, pp. 555–64.

Lim, D. (1976), 'Export instability and economic growth: a return to fundamentals', *Oxford Bulletin of Economics and Statistics*, vol. 38, pp. 311–22.

Linder, S. B. (1961), *An Essay on Trade and Transformation*, John Wiley, New York.

Lindert, P. H. and Kindleberger, C. P. (1982), *International Economics*, 7th edn, Irwin, Homewood, Ill.

Lipsey, R. E. and Weiss, M. Y. (1981), 'Foreign production and exports in manufacturing industries', *Review of Economics and Statistics*, vol. 63, pp. 488–94.

Lipsey, R. G. (1960), 'The theory of customs unions: a general survey', *Economic Journal*, vol. 70, pp. 496–513.

Lipsey, R. G. and Lancaster, K. (1956), 'The general theory of second-best', *Review of Economics Studies*, vol. 24, pp. 11–32.

List, E. (1841), *The National System of Political Economy*; reprinted by Longmans Green, New York, 1904.

Little, I. M. D. (1957), *A Critique of Welfare Economics*, Oxford University Press, Oxford.

Little, I., Scitovsky, T. and Scott, M. (1970), *Industry and Trade in Some Developing Countries: A Comparative Study*, Oxford University Press, Oxford.

Llewellyn, D. T. (1980), *International Financial Integration: The Limits of Sovereignty*, Macmillan, London.

Lloyd, P. J. (1982), '3 × 3 theory of customs unions', *Journal of International Economics*, vol. 12, pp. 41–64.

Loertscher, R. and Wolter, F. (1980), 'Determinants of intra-industry trade: among countries and across industries', *Weltwirtschaftliches Archiv*, vol. 116, pp. 280–93.

Lund, P. J. and Miner, D. A. (1973), *An Econometric Study of the Machine-tool Industry*, Government Economic Service Occasional Paper, No. 4, HMSO, London.

Lynn, J. and Jay, A. (1981), *The Complete 'Yes Minister'*, BBC Books, London.

Lyons, B. (1981), 'Price cost margins, market structure, and international trade', in Currie, Peel and Peters (1981), pp. 276–95.

MacBean, A. I. (1966), *Export Instability and Economic Development*, Allen & Unwin, London.

MacBean, A. I. and Nguyen, D. T. (1987), *Commodity Policies: Problems and Prospects*, Croom Helm, London.

MacBean, A. I. and Snowden, P. N. (1981), *International Institutions in Trade and Finance*, Allen & Unwin, London.

McCormick, B. (1982), 'North Sea oil: what will our children think?', in Hawkins and McKenzie (eds) (1982), pp. 187–212.

MacDonald, R. (1988), *Floating Exchange Rates: Theories and Evidence*, Unwin Hyman, London.

MacDonald, R. and Torrance, T. S. (1988), 'Expectations formation and risk in four foreign exchange markets', Discussion Paper 88/01, Department of Economics, University of Aberdeen.

MacDougall, G. D. A. (1951), 'British and American exports: a study suggested by the theory of comparative costs', *Economic Journal*, vols 61, 62, pp. 697–724, and 487–521.

Machlup, F. (1943), *International Trade and the National Income Multiplier*, Blakiston, Philadelphia.

Machlup, F. (1966), *International Monetary Economics*, Allen & Unwin, London.

McKinnon, R. I. (1963), 'Optimum currency areas', *American Economic Review*, vol. 53, pp. 717–24.

McKinnon, R. I. (1979), *Money in International Exchange*, Oxford University Press, Oxford.

McKinnon, R. I. (1980), 'Exchange-rate instability, trade imbalances and monetary policies in Japan and the United States', in Oppenheimer (1980), pp. 225–50.

McKinnon, R. I. (1981), 'The exchange rate and macro-economic policy: changing postwar perceptions', *Journal of Economic Literature*, vol. 19, pp. 531–57.

McKinnon, R. I. (1988), 'Monetary and exchange rate policies for international financial stability: a proposal', *Journal of Economic Perspectives*, vol. 2, pp. 83–104.

Magee, S. P. (1972), 'Welfare efects of restrictions on US trade', *Brookings Papers in Economic Activity*, vol. 3, pp. 645–701.

Magee, S. P. (1973a), 'Factor market distortions, production and trade: a survey', *Oxford Economic Papers*, vol. 25, pp. 1–43.

Magee, S. P. (1973b), 'Currency contracts, pass-through, and devaluation', *Brookings Papers in Economic Activity*, vol. 3, pp. 303–23.

Magee, S. P. (1975), 'Prices, incomes and foreign trade', in Kenen (1975), pp. 175–253.

Magee, S. P. (1976), 'The empirical evidence on the monetary approach to the balance of payments and exchange rates', *American Economic Review. Papers and Proceedings*, vol. 66, pp. 163–70.

Magee, S. P. (1980), 'Three simple tests of the Stolper–Samuelson theorem', in Oppenheimer (1980), pp. 138–53.

Magee, S. P., Brock, W. A. and Young, L. (1990), *Black Hole Tariffs and Endogenous Policy Theory*, Cambridge University Press, London.

Maizels, A. (1965), *Industrial Growth and World Trade*, Cambridge University Press, London.

Mann, C. L. (1989), 'The effects of exchange rate trends and volatility on export prices: industry examples from Japan, Germany and the United States', *Weltwirtschaftliches Archiv*, vol. 125, pp. 588–618.

Mansell, K. (1980), 'UK visible trade in the post-war years', *Economic Trends*, October, pp. 136–50.

Markusen, J. R. and Melvin, J. R. (1981), 'Trade, factor prices and the gains from trade with increasing returns to scale', *Canadian Journal of Economics*, vol. 14, pp. 450–69.

Markusen, J. R. and Venables, A. J. (1988), 'Trade policy with increasing returns and imperfect competition: contradictory results from competing models', *Journal of International Economics*, vol. 24, pp. 299–316.

Marquez, J. (1988), *Income and Price Elasticities of Foreign Trade Flows: Econometric estimation and analysis of the US trade deficit*, International Finance Discussion Paper, No. 324, Board of Governors of the Federal Reserve System, Washington, DC.

Marris, S. (1985), *Deficits and the Doillar: The World Economy at Risk*, Policy Analyses in International Economics, No. 14, Institute for International Economics, Washington, DC.

Marsden, J. S. and Hollander, G. (1983), 'Floating exchange rates, inflation and selective protectionism; their effects on the competitiveness of Australian industry', in Black and Winters (1983), pp. 92–129.

Marston, R. C. (1986), 'Real exchange rates and productivity growth in the United States and Japan', Working Paper 1922, National Bureau of Economic Research, Boston, Mass.

Martin, J. P. *et al.* (1990), 'Economy-wide effects of agricultural policies in OECD countries: simulation results with WALRAS', *OECD Economic Studies*, No. 13, pp. 131–72.

Marvel, H. P. and Ray, E. J. (1987), 'Intra-industry trade: sources and effects on protection', *Journal of Political Economy*, vol. 95(6), pp. 1278–91.

Mayer, W. (1974), 'Short-run and long-run equilibrium for a small open economy', *Journal of Political Economy*, vol. 82, pp. 955–68.

Mayer, W. (1984), 'Endogenous tariff formation', *American Economic Review*, vol. 74, pp. 970–85.

Mayes, D. G. (1978), 'The effects of economic integration on trade', *Journal of Common Market Studies*, vol. 17, pp. 1–25.

Meade, J. E. (1951), *The Theory of International Economic Policy. Volume 1: The Balance of Payments*, Oxford University Press, Oxford.

Meade, J. E. (1955), 'The case for variable exchange rates', *Three Banks Review*, no. 27, September, pp. 3–28.

Meade, J. E. (1978), 'The measuring of "internal balance"', *Economic Journal*, vol. 88, pp. 423–35.

MEDC (1968), *Market – the world*, NEDO, London.

Meese, R. A. and Rogoff, K. (1983), 'Empirical exchange rate models of the seventies: do they fit out of sample?', *Journal of International Economics*, vol. 14, pp. 3–24.

Meese, R. A. and Rogoff, K. (1988), 'Was it real? The exchange rate–interest differential relation over the modern floating-rate period', *Journal of Finance*, vol. 43, pp. 933–48.

Melvin, J. R. (1969), 'Increasing returns to scale as a determinant of trade', *Canadian Journal of Economics*, vol. 3, pp. 389–402.

Melvin, J. R. (1986), 'The non-equivalence of tariffs and import quotas', *American Economic Review*, vol. 76, pp. 1131–4.

Melvin, J. R. (1989), 'Trade in producer services: a Heckscher–Ohlin approach', *Journal of Political Economy*, vol. 97, pp. 1180–96.

Messerlin, P. A. (1983), 'Bureaucracies and the political economy of protection, reflections of a continental European', *Weltwirtschaftliches Archiv*, vol. 117, pp. 461–96.

Messerlin, P. A. (1989), 'The EC anti dumping regulations: a first economic appraisal 1980–85', *Weltwirtschaftliches Archiv*, vol. 125, pp. 563–87.

Messerlin, P. A. (1990), 'Anti-dumping regulations or pro-cartel law? The EC chemicals case', mimeo, World Bank, February.

Metzler, L. A. (1950), 'A multiple region theory of income and trade', *Econometrica*, vol. 18, pp. 329–54.

Metzler, L. A. (1951), 'A multiple country theory of income transfers', *Journal of Political Economy*, vol. 59, pp. 14–29.

Miles, M. A. (1979), 'The effects of devaluation on the trade balance and the balance of payments: some new results', *Journal of Political Economy*, vol. 87, pp. 600–20.

Miller, M. H. (1971), 'Estimates of the static balance of payments and welfare costs of UK entry into the Common Market', *National Institute Economic Review*, no. 57, pp. 69–83.

Miller, M. H. and Spencer, J. E. (1977), 'The static economic effects of the UK joining the EEC: a general equilibrium approach', *Review of Economic Studies*, vol. 44, pp. 71–93.

Milner, C. (1988), 'Trade strategies and economic development: theory and evidence', Chapter 4 of Greenaway (1988), pp. 55–76.

Minhas, B. S. (1963), *An International Comparison of Factor Costs and Factor Use*, North Holland, Amsterdam.

Mishan, E. J. (1967), *The Costs of Economic Growth*, Staples Press, London.

Moran, C. (1988), 'A structural model of developing countries' manufactured exports', *World Bank Economic Review*, vol. 2, pp. 321–40.

Morton, K. and Tulloch, P. (1977), *Trade and Developing Countries*, Croom Helm, London.

Mosley, P. (1987), *Overseas Aid: Its Defence and Reform*, Wheatsheaf, Brighton.

Mullineux, A. (1987), *International Money and Banking: The Creation of a New Order*, Wheatsheaf, Brighton.

Mundell, R. A. (1957), 'International trade and factor mobility', *American Economic Review*, vol. 47, pp. 321–35.

Mundell, R. A. (1960), 'The pure theory of international trade', *American Economic Review*, vol. 50, pp. 67–110.

Mundell, R. A. (1962), 'The appropriate use of monetary and fiscal policy for internal and external balance', *IMF Staff Papers*, vol. 9, pp. 70–9.

Mundell, R. A. (1963), 'Capital mobility and stabilization policy under fixed and flexible exchange rates', *Canadian Journal of Economics and Political Science*, vol. 29, pp. 475–85.

Mundell, R. A. (1964), 'Tariff preferences and the terms of trade', *Manchester School of Economic and Social Studies*, vol. 32, pp. 1–13.

Murphy, R. G. and von Furstenberg, G. M. (1981), 'An analysis of factors influencing the level of SDR holdings in non-oil developing countries', *IMF Staff Papers*, vol. 28, pp. 310–37.

Murray, T. (1977), *Trade Preferences for Developing Countries*, Macmillan, London.

Mussa, M. (1979), 'The two-sector model in terms of its dual: a geometric exposition', *Journal of International Economics*, vol. 9, pp. 513–26.

Muth, J. E. (1961), 'Rational expectations and the theory of price movements', *Econometrica*, vol. 29, pp. 313–35.

National Consumer Council (1990), *International Trade and the Consumer: Working Paper 1: Textiles and Clothing*, National Consumer Council, London.

National Institute (1971), 'Entry into the EEC: a comment on some of the economic issues', *National Institute Economic Review*, no. 57, pp. 35–61.

Neary, J. P. (1978), 'Short-run capital specificity and the pure theory of international trade', *Economic Journal*, vol. 88, pp. 488–510.

Neary, J. P. (1985), 'Two-by-two international trade theory with many goods and factors', *Econometrica*, vol. 53, pp. 1233–47.

Neary, J. P. and van Wijnbergen, S. (1986), *Natural Resources and the Macroeconomy*, Basil Blackwell, Oxford.

NEDC (1965), *Investment in Machine-tools: a survey by the management consultants' association'*, HMSO, London.

NEDO (1977), *International Price Competitiveness, Non-price Factors and Export Performance'*, NEDO, London.

Nellis, J. G. (1982), 'A principal components analysis of international financial integration under fixed and floating exchange', *Applied Economics*, vol. 14, pp. 339–54.

Nelson, R. R. (1962), *The Rate and Direction of Inventive Activity*, Princeton University Press, Princeton, NJ.

Newbery, D. M. G. and Stiglitz, J. E. (1984), 'Pareto inferior trade', *Review of Economic Studies*, vol. 51, pp. 1–12.

Newlyn, W. (1965), 'Gains and losses in the East African Common Market', *Yorkshire Bulletin*, vol. 17, pp. 130–8.

Niehans, J. (1980), 'Purchasing power parity under flexible rates, in Oppenheimer (1980), pp. 255–72.

Niehans, J. and Hewson, J. (1976), 'The Eurodollar market and monetary theory', *Journal of Money, Credit and Banking*, vol. 1, pp. 1–27.

Niskanen, W. (1971), *Bureaucracy and Representative Government*, Aldine-Atherton, Chicago.

Nogues, J. J., Olechowski, A. and Winters, L. A. (1986), 'The extent of industrial countries' non-tariff barriers to trade', *World Bank Economic Review*, vol. 1, pp. 181–99.

Norall, C. (1986), 'New trends in antidumping practice in Brussels', *The World Economy*, vol. 9, pp. 97–112.

Nowzad, B. (1981), *The IMF and its Critics*, Princeton Essay in International Finance, No. 146, Princeton University Press, Princeton, NJ.

Nurkse, R. (1959), *Patterns of Trade and Development*, Alonquist & Wiksell, Stockholm.

OECD (1979), *The OECD Linkage Model*, OECD Economic Outlook Occasional Papers, January.

OECD (1987a), *Structural Adjustment and Economic Performance*, OECD, Paris.

OECD (1987b), *International Investment and Multinational Enterprises: Recent Trends in International Direct Investment*, OECD, Paris.

OECD (1989), *Agricultural Polices, Markets and Trade*, OECD, Paris.

Officer, L. H. (1976a), 'The purchasing power parity theory of exchange rate: a review article', *IMF Staff Papers*, vol. 23, pp. 1–60.

Officer, L. H. (1976b), 'The productivity bias in purchasing power parity: an econometric investigation', *IMF Staff Papers*, vol. 23, pp. 545–79.

Ohlin, B. (1929), 'The reparations problem: a discussion', *Economic Journal*, vol. 39, pp. 172–3.

Ohlin, B. (1933), *Inter-regional and International Trade*, Harvard University Press, Cambridge, Mass.

Okun, A. M. (1981), *Prices and Quantities: a Macro-economic Analysis*, Basil Blackwell, Oxford.

Olsen, M. (1965), *The Logic of Collective Action*, Harvard University Press, Cambridge, Mass.

Oppenheimer, P. (1980), *Issues in International Economics*, Oriel Press, Oxford.

Oppenheimer, P. *et al.* (1978), *Business Views on Exchange Rate Policy*, Confederation of British Industry, London.

Orcutt, G. H. (1950), 'Measurement of price elasticities in international trade', *Review of Economics and Statistics*, vol. 32, pp. 117–32.

Oxley, L. T. and George, D. A. R. (1989), 'The scientific content of the new classical orthodoxy', Discussion Paper No. XIV, Department of Economics, University of Edinburgh.

Page, S. A. B. (1977), 'Currency of invoicing in merchandise trade', *National Insitute Economic Review*, no. 81, pp. 77–81.

Panagariya, A. (1980), 'Variable returns to scale in general equilibrium theory once again', *Journal of International Economics*, vol. 10, pp. 499–526.

Panić, M. (1975), 'Why the UK's propensity to import is high', *Lloyds Bank Review*, no. 115, January, pp. 1–12.

Panić, M. and Joyce, P. L. (1980), 'UK manufacturing industry: international integration and trade performance', *Bank of England Quarterly Review*, no. 1, pp. 42–55.

Panić, M. and Rajan, A. (1971), *Product Changes in Industrial Countries' Trade: 1955–68*, National Economic Development Office, London.

Pastor, M. Jnr (1987), 'The effects of IMF programs in the third world: debate and evidence from Latin America', *World Development*, vol. 15, pp. 249–62.

Pavitt, K. (1980), *Technical Innovation and British Economic Performance*, Macmillan, London.

Payer, C. (1974), *The Debt Trap*, Penguin, Harmondsworth, Middx.

Pearce, I. F. (1961), 'The problem of the balance of payments', *International Economic Review*, vol. 1, pp. 1–21.

Pearce, I. F. (1970), *International Trade*, Macmillan, London.

Pelcovits, M. D. (1976), 'Quotas versus tariffs', *Journal of International Economics*, vol. 6, pp. 363–70.

Pelkmans, J. and Winters, L. A. (1988), *Europe's Domestic Market*, Chatham House Paper, No. 43, Routledge, London.

Peltzman, S. (1985), 'An economic interpretation of the history of congressional voting in the twentieth century', *American Economic Review*, vol. 75, pp. 657–75.

Perée, E. and Steinherr, A. (1989), 'Exchange rate uncertainty and foreign trade', *European Economic Review*, vol. 33, pp. 1241–64.

Petit, M. (1985), *Determinants of Agricultural Policies in the United States and the European Community*, Research Report, No. 51, International Food Policy Research Institute, Washington, DC.

Pincus, J. J. (1975), 'Pressure groups and the pattern of tariffs', *Journal of Political Economy*, vol. 85, pp. 757–78.

Pomfret, R. (1987), *Unequal Trade*, Basil Blackwell, Oxford.

Portes, R. (1989), *Macro Economic Policy Coordination and the European Monetary System*, Discussion Paper No. 342, Centre for Economic Policy Research, London.

Portes, R. and Swoboda, A. (1987), *Threats to International Financial Stability*, Cambridge University Press, Cambridge.

Posner, M. V. (1961), 'International trade and technical change', *Oxford Economics Papers*, vol. 13, pp. 323–41.

Pownall, R. and Stuart, B. (1988), 'The IMF's Compensatory and Contingency Financing Facility', *Finance and Development*, December, pp. 9–11.

Prais, S. J. and Wagner, K. (1988), 'Productivity and management: the training of foremen in Britain and Germany', *National Institute Economic Review*, no. 123, pp. 34–49.

Pratten, C. F. (1971), *Economies of Scale in Manufacturing Industry*, Cambridge University Press, Cambridge.

Pratten, C. F. (1976), *Labour Productivity Differentials within International Companies*, Cambridge University Press, Cambridge.

Preeg, E. H. (1970), *Traders and Diplomats*, Brookings Institution, Washington, DC.

Ray, G. F. (1966), *The Competitiveness of British Industrial Products: A round up*, Woolwich Economic Papers, No. 10, London.

Ray, G. F. (1979), 'Comment', in Blackaby (1979), pp. 73–7.

Reddaway, W. B. (1968), *Effects of United Kingdom Direct Investment Overseas*, Cambridge University Press, Cambridge.

Ricardo, D. (1817), *Principles of Political Economy*; reprinted as vol.1 of P. Sraffa (ed.), *The Works and Correspondence of David Ricardo*, Cambridge University Press, London, 1951.

Richardson, J. D. (1978), 'Some empirical evidence of commodity arbitrage and the law of one price', *Journal of International Economics*, vol. 8, pp. 341–52.

Riedel, J. (1984), 'Trade as the engine of growth in developing countries, revisited', *Economic Journal*, vol. 94, pp. 56–73.

Riedel, J. (1988), 'Trade as an engine of growth: theory and evidence', Chapter 3 of Greenaway (1988), pp. 25–54.

Ripley, D. M. (1978), 'The transmissions of fluctuations in economic activity: some recent evidence', in *Managed Exchange-Rate Flexibility Conference Series*, No. 20, Federal Reserve Bank of Boston, Boston.

Robinson, J. (1937), 'The foreign exchanges', in *Essays in the Theory of Employment*, Basil Blackwell, Oxford.

Robson, P. (1987), *The Economics of International Integration*, 3rd edn, Allen & Unwin, London.

Rodriguez, C. A. (1974), 'The non-equivalence of tariffs and quotas under retaliation', *Journal of International Economics*, vol. 41, pp. 295–8.

Rodrik, D. (1988), 'Imperfect competition, scale economies and trade policy in developing countries', in Baldwin (1988), pp. 109–37.

Rothwell, R. (1980), 'Innovation in textile machinery', in Pavitt (1980), pp. 125–41.

Russell, R. R. and Wilkinson, M. (1979), *Microeconomics: A Synthesis of Modern and Neo-classical Analysis*, John Wiley, New York.

Ryan, C. (1988), 'Trade in services: An introductory survey', *Economic and Social Review*, vol. 20, pp. 37–48.

493

Rybczynski, T. (1955), 'Factor endowments and relative commodity prices', *Economica*, vol. 22, pp. 336–41.

Sachs, J. D. (1989a), *Developing Country Debt and the World Economy*, Chicago University Press, Chicago.

Sachs, J. D. (1989b), *Efficient Debt Reduction*, Policy, Planning and Research Working Paper, No. 194, World Bank, Washington, DC.

Salter, W. E. G. (1959), 'Internal and external balance: the role of price and expenditure effects', *Economic Record*, vol. 35, pp. 226–58.

Samuelson, P. A. (1948), 'International trade and the equalisation of factor prices', *Economic Journal*, vol. 58, pp. 163–84.

Samuelson, P. A. (1949), 'International factor-price equalisation once again', *Economic Journal*, vol. 59, pp. 181–97.

Samuelson, P. A. (1952), 'The transfer problem and transport costs: the terms of trade when impediments are absent', *Economic Journal*, vol. 62, pp. 278–304.

Samuelson, P. A. (1954), 'The transfer problem and transport costs II: analysis of effects of trade impediments', *Economic Journal*, vol. 64, pp. 264–89.

Samuelson, P. A. (1962), 'The gains from trade once again', *Economic Journal*, vol. 72, pp. 820–9.

Samuelson, P. A. (1981), 'Bertil Ohlin 1899–1979', *Journal of International Economics Supplement*, vol. 11, pp. 147–64.

Sapir, A. (1990), 'Does 1992 come before or after 1990? On regional versus multi-lateral integration', Chapter 11 of Jones and Krueger (1990), pp. 197–221.

Sapir, A. and Lutz, E. (1981), *Trade in Services: Economic Determinants and Development Related Issues*, World Bank Staff Working Paper, No. 480, World Bank, Washington, DC.

Sapsford, D. R. (1988), 'The debate over trends in the terms of trade', Chapter 7 of Greenaway (1988), pp. 117–31.

Schadler, S. (1977), 'Sources of exchange rate variability: theory and empirical evidence', *IMF Staff Papers*, vol. 24, pp. 253–96.

Scherer, F. M. (1980), *Industrial Market Structure and Economic Performance*, 2nd edn, Rand McNally, Chicago.

Shepsle, K. A. and Weingast, B. R. (1981), 'Political preferences for the pork barrel: a generalisation', *American Journal of Political Science*, vol. 25, pp. 96–111.

Silberston, Z. A. (1989), *The Future of the Multifibre Arrangement: Implications for the UK Economy*, HMSO, London.

Smallwood, C. (1975), 'Economic growth and the pure theory of international trade', *Scottish Journal of Political Economy*, vol. 22, pp. 135–59.

Smith, A. (1776), *An Inquiry into the Nature and Causes of the Wealth of Nations*; reprinted by Methuen, London, 1961, ed. E. Cannan.

Smith, A. (1982), 'Some simple results on the gains from trade, from growth and from public production', *Journal of International Economics*, vol. 13, pp. 215–30.

Smith, A. (1989), *The Market for Cars in the Enlarged European Community*, Discussion Paper No. 360, Centre for Economic Policy Research, London.

Smith, A. and Venables, A. J. (1986), 'Trade and industrial policy under imperfect competition', *Economic Policy*, no. 3, pp. 621–60.

Smith, A. and Venables, A. J. (1988), 'Completing the internal market in the European Community', *European Economic Review*, vol. 32, pp. 1501–25.

Smith, G. W. and Cuddington, J. T. (1985), *International Debt and the Developing Countries*, World Bank, Washington, DC.

Smith, S. T. *et al.* (1983), *UK Trade in Manufacturing: The Pattern of Specialisation during the 1970s*, Government Economic Service Working Paper, HMSO, London.

Snape, R. H. (1963), 'Some effects of protection in the world sugar industry', *Economica*, vol. 30, pp. 63–73.

Soete, L. L. G. (1981), 'A general test of technological gap trade theory', *Weltwirtschaftliches Archiv*, vol. 117, pp. 638–60.

Solomon, R. F. and Ingham, K. P. D. (1977), 'Discriminating between MNC subsidiaries and indigenous companies: a comparative analysis of British mechanical engineering', *Oxford Bulletin of Economics and Statistics*, vol. 39, pp. 127–38.

Spencer, G. H. (1984), 'The World Trade Model: revised estimates', *IMF Staff Papers*, vol. 31, pp. 469–98.

Spraos, J. (1986), *IMF Conditionality; Ineffectual, Inefficient, Mistargeted*, Essay in International Finance, No. 166, International Finance Section, Princeton University, Princeton, NJ.

Stern, R. M. (1973), *The Balance of Payments: Theory and Economic Policy*, Macmillan, London.

Stern, R. M. (1975), 'Testing trade theories', in Kenen (1975), pp. 3–49.

Stern, R. M. (1987), *US Trade Policies in a Changing World Economy*, MIT Press, Cambridge, Mass.

494

Bibliography

Stern, R. M. and Maskus, K. E. (1981), 'Determinants of the structure of US foreign trade, 1958–76', *Journal of International Economics*, vol. 11, pp. 207–24.

Stern, R. M., Francis, J. and Schumacher, B. (1976), *Price Elasticities in International Trade*, Macmillan, London.

Stern, R.M. *et al.* (1977), *The Presentation of the US Balance of Payments: A Symposium*, Essay in International Finance, No. 123, Princeton University, Princeton, NJ.

Steuer, M. D. (1973), *The Impact of Foreign Direct Investment on the United Kingdom*, HMSO, London.

Steuer, M. D., Ball, R. J. and Eaton, J. R. (1966), 'The effect of waiting times on foreign orders for machine tools', *Economica*, vol. 33, pp. 387–403.

Stevens, C. (1981), *The EEC and the Third World: A Survey*, ODI/IDS, London.

Stolper, W. F. and Samuelson, P. A. (1941), 'Protection and real wages', *Review of Economic Studies*, vol. 9, pp. 58–73.

Strange, S. (1971), *Sterling and British Policy*, Oxford University Press, London.

Swan, T. W. (1955), 'Longer run problems of the balance of payments', Chapter 27 of Caves and Johnson (1968), pp. 455–64.

Swann, D. (1988), *The Economics of the Common Market*, 7th edn, Penguin, Harmondsworth, Middx.

Takacs, W. E. (1978), 'The non-equivalence of tariffs, import quotas and voluntary export restraints', *Journal of International Economics*, vol. 8, pp. 565–74.

Takacs, W. E. and Winters, L. A. (1990), *Labour Adjustment Costs and British Footwear Protection*, Discussion Paper 376, Centre for Economic Policy Research, London.

Taplin, G. R. (1973), 'A model of world trade', in Ball (1973), pp. 177–223.

Tarr, D. G. (1979), 'Cyclical dumping: the case of steel products', *Journal of International Economics*, vol. 9, pp. 57–64.

Tarr, D. G. and Morkre, M. E. (1984), *Aggregate Costs to the United States of Tariffs and Quotas on Imports*, Federal Trade Commission, Washington, DC.

Taylor, M. P. (1987), 'Covered interest parity: a high frequency, high quality data study', *Economica*, vol. 54, pp. 429–38.

Tharakan, P. K. M. (1983), *Intra-Industry Trade, Empirical and Methological Aspects*, North Holland, Amsterdam.

Thirlwall, A. P. (1980), *Balance of Payments Theory and the United Kingdom Experience*, Macmillan, London.

Tilton, J. E. (1971), *International Diffusion of Technology: The Case of Semi-conductors*, Brookings Institution, Washington, DC.

Tinbergen, J. (1952), *On the Theory of Economic Policy*, North Holland, Amsterdam.

Tower, E. and Willett, T. D. (1976), *The Theory of Optimum Currency Areas and Exchange Rate Flexibility*, Special Paper in International Economics, No. 11, Princeton University, Princeton, NJ.

Trades Union Congress, *Economic Review*, annual, TUC, London.

Trela, I. and Whalley, J. (1990), 'Unravelling the threads of the MFA', Chapter 2 of Hamilton (1990), pp. 11–45.

Triffin, R. (1960), *Gold and the Dollar Crisis*, Yale University Press, New Haven, Conn.

Triffin, R. (1964), *The Evolution of the International Monetary System: Historical reappraisal and future perspectives*, Princeton Study in International Finance, No. 12, Princeton University Press, Princeton, NJ.

Truman, E. M. (1975), 'The effects of European economic integration in the production and trade of manufactured product', in Balassa (1975), pp. 3–40.

Tyers, R. and Anderson, K. (1988), 'Liberalising OECD agricultural policies in the Uruguay Round: Effects on trade and welfare', *Journal of Agricultural Economics*, vol. 39, pp. 197–216.

Tyler, W. G. (1981), 'Growth and export expansion in developing countries, some empirical evidence', *Journal of Development Economics*, vol. 9, pp. 121–30.

United Nations (1978), *Transnational Corporations in World Development*, Commission on Transnational Corporations, E/C 10/38, UN, New York.

United Nations (1981), *Commodity Indexes for the Standard International Trade Classification, Revision*, Statistical Paper Series M, No. 38 Rev., UN, New York.

Utton, M. A. and Morgan, A. D. (1983), *Concentration and Foreign Trade*, Cambridge University Press, Cambridge.

Vaitsos, C. V. (1974), *Intercountry Income Distribution and Transnational Enterprises*, Oxford University Press, Oxford.

Vaitsos, C. V. (1976), 'Power, knowledge and development policy', in Helleiner (1976), pp. 113–46.

495

Vanek, J. (1959), 'The natural resource content of foreign trade, 1870–1955, and the relative abundance of natural resources in the United States', *Review of Economics and Statistics*, vol. 41, pp. 146–53.

Varian, H. R. (1989), 'Measuring the deadweight costs of DUP and rent-seeking activity', *Economics and Politics*, vol. 1, pp. 81–95.

Venables, A. J. (1984), 'Multiple equilibria in the theory of international trade with monopolistically competitive commodities', *Journal of International Economics*, vol. 16, pp. 103–22.

Venables, A. J. (1985), 'Trade and policy with imperfect competition: the case of identical products and free entry', *Journal of International Economics*, vol. 19, pp. 1–19.

Venables, A. J. and Winters, L. A. (1991), *'1992': Trade and Industry*, Cambridge University Press, London.

Vernon, R. (1966), 'International investment and international trade in the product cycle', *Quarterly Journal of Economics*, vol. 80, p. 190–207.

Vernon, R. (1970), *The Technology Factor in International Trade*, National Bureau of Economic Research, New York.

Viner, J. (1937), *Studies in the Theory of International Trade*, Allen & Unwin, London.

Viner, J. (1950), *The Customs Union Issue*, Carnegie Endowment for International Peace, New York.

Walker, W. B. (1979), *Industrial Innovation and International Trade Performance*, JAI Press, Greenwich, Conn.

Wells, J. D. and Imber, J. C. (1977), 'The home and export performance of UK industries', *Economic Trends*, August, pp. 78–89.

Wells, L. T. (1969), 'Test of a product cycle model of international trade: US exports of consumer durables', *Quarterly Journal of Economics*, vol. 82, pp. 152–62.

Wells, S. J. (1964), *British Export Performance: A Comparative Study*, Cambridge University Press, London.

Weston, A. (1981), 'Who is more preferred? An analysis of the new Generalised System of Preferences', in Stevens (1981), pp. 73–86.

Whalley, J. (1985), *Trade Liberalization among Major World Trading Areas*, MIT Press, Cambridge, Mass.

Whalley, J. *et al.* (1989), *The Uruguay Round and Beyond*, Macmillan, London.

Whitley, J. D. and Wilson, R. A. (1979), 'Trends and cycles in import penetration in the UK: a comment', *Oxford Bulletin of Economics and Statistics*, pp. 69–77.

Whitman, M. von (1975), 'Global monetarism and the monetary approach to the balance of payments', *Brookings Papers in Economic Activity*, vol. 5, pp. 491–536.

Williamson, J. and Lessard, D. R. (1987), *Capital Flight and Third World Debt*, Institute for International Economics, Washington, DC.

Williamson, J. H. (1971), *On Estimating the Income Effects of British Entry to the EEC*, Surrey Paper in Economics, No. 6, Surrey University Press, Guildford.

Williamson, J. H. (1973), 'International liquidity: a survey', *Economic Journal*, vol. 83, pp 685–746.

Williamson, J. H. (1977), *The Failure of World Monetary Reform 1971–74*, Nelson, Sunbury-on-Thames.

Williamson, J. H. (1983), *IMF Conditionality*, MIT Press, Cambridge, Mass.

Williamson, J. H. (1987), 'Exchange management: the role of target zones', *American Economic Review, Papers and Proceedings*, pp. 200–4.

Williamson, J. H. (1988), 'Comment on McKinnon's monetary rule', *Journal of Economic Perspectives*, vol. 2, pp. 113–19.

Williamson, J. H. and Bottrill, A. (1969), 'The impact of customs unions on trade in manufactures', *Oxford Economic Papers*, vol. 23, pp. 323–51.

Winch, D. M. (1971), *Analytical Welfare Economics*, Penguin, Harmondsworth, Middx.

Winham, G. R. (1986), *International Trade and the Tokyo Round Negotiation*, Princeton University Press, Princeton, NJ.

Winters, L. A. (1974), 'United Kingdom exports and the pressure of demand: a note', *Economic Journal*, vol. 84, pp. 623–8.

Winters, L. A. (1978), 'The accounting framework of certain balance of payments theories: a didactic note', *Journal of Economic Studies*, vol. 5, pp. 31–6.

Winters, L. A. (1981), *An Econometric Model of the Export Sector: UK Visible Exports and their Prices, 1955–1973*, Cambridge Studies in Applied Econometrics, No. 4, Cambridge University Press, London.

Winters, L. A. (1982), 'Britain's trade patterns since joining the Common Market', *British Review of Economic Issues*, vol. 4, pp. 17–46.

Winters, L. A. (1983a), 'The consequences of devaluing sterling', in *International Monetary Arrangements*, Fourth Report of Treasury and Civil Service Committee, vol. III, House of Commons paper 21–III, Session 1982–83, pp. 96–136.

Winters, L. A. (1983b), 'Memorandum', *House of Lords, 7th Report of the Select Committee on the European Communities: The UK's Changing Trade Patterns Subsequent to Membership of the European Community*, HMSO, London, pp. 369–87.

Winters, L. A. (1984a), 'The patterns of international trade 1950–1980', *Economic Review*, vol. 1, pp. 33–8.

Winters, L. A. (1984b), 'British imports of manufactures and the Common Market', *Oxford Economic Papers*, vol. 36, pp. 103–18.

Winters, L. A. (1985), 'Separability and the modelling of international economic integration', *European Economic Review*, vol. 27, pp 335–53.

Winters, L. A. (1987a), 'The economic consequences of agricultural support: a survey', *OECD Economic Studies*, no. 9, pp. 7–54.

Winters, L. A. (1987b), 'Negotiating the abolition of non-tariff barriers', *Oxford Economic Papers*, vol. 39, pp. 465–80.

Winters, L. A. (1987c), 'The political economy of the agricultural policy of industrial countries', *European Review of Agricultural Economics*, vol. 14, pp. 285–304.

Winters, L. A. (1987d), 'Britain in Europe: a survey of quantitative trade studies', *Journal of Common Market Studies*, vol. 25, pp. 315–35.

Winters, L. A. (1988), 'Completing the European internal market: some notes on trade policy', *European Economic Review*, vol. 32, pp. 1477–99.

Winters, L. A. (1989a), 'Patterns of world trade in manufactures: does trade policy matter?', Chapter 3 of Black and MacBean (1989), pp. 24–59.

Winters, L. A. (1989b), 'The so-called Non-Economic Objectives of agricultural policy', *OECD Economic Studies*, no. 13, pp. 237–66.

Winters, L. A. (1990a), 'The national security argument for agricultural protection', *The World Economy*, vol. 13, pp. 170–90.

Winters, L. A. (1990b) 'The Road to Uruguay', *The Economic Journal*, vol. 100, pp. 1288–1303.

Winters, L. A. and Sapsford, D. (1990), *Primary Commodity Prices: Economic Models and Policy*, Cambridge University Press, Cambridge.

Winters, L. A. and Yu, K. (1988), 'A simple financial model of developing countries' imports', *Journal of Foreign Exchange and International Finance*, vol. 2, pp. 44–56.

Wolf, B. M. (1977), 'Industrial diversification and internationalisation: some empirical evidence', *Journal of Industrial Economics*, vol. 26, pp. 177–91.

Wonnacott, P. and Wonnacott, R. (1981), 'Is unilateral tariff reduction preferable to a customs union? The curious case of the missing foreign tariff', *American Economic Review*, vol. 71, pp. 704–14.

World Bank (1989), *Adjustment Lending: An Evaluation of Ten Years of Experience*, Policy and Research Series Paper, No. 1, World Bank, Washington, DC.

Yang, B. M. (1987), 'The supply and demand for exports from industrialised countries: a disequilibrium analysis', *Applied Economics*, vol. 19, pp. 1137–48.

Yarrow, G. (1987), 'Economic aspects of anti-dumping policies', *Oxford Review of Economic Policy*, vol. 3, pp. 66–79.

Yeager, L. B. (1976), *International Monetary Relations: Theory, History and Policy*, 2nd edn, Harper & Row, New York.

Yeats, A. J. (1979), *Trade Barriers Facing Developing Countries*, Macmillan, London.

Yeomans, K. A. (1968), *Applied Statistics, Volume Two*, Penguin, Harmondsworth.

Author Index

Subject Index

absolute advantage 15, 16
absorption approach 289, 309
adjustment 379, 387, 400, 402, 417, 431, 459
adjustment costs 168
administered protection 168
adverse selection 146
African, Caribbean and Pacific Countries 188
agricultural protection 117, 128, 129, 186
anti-dumping duties 140, 168, 198
anti-monde 190
arbitrage 313, 314, 329
assignment problem 345

balance of payments 237ff
balancing item 241
Baldwin envelope 132, 205
basic balance 240
Bertrand assumption 151
Bank for International Settlements (BIS) 435, 436
Brady plan 471
Bretton Woods system 384, 385, 413ff, 416, 425
bubbles 320

calibration 154, 155, 195
Cambridge Economic Policy Group 260
Common Agricultural Policy (CAP) 186
capital account 240, 309
    flight 460
    markets 143
    mobility 333, 347, 348
Compensatory Financing Facility 419, 429, 430, 431
Committee of Twenty 425, 452
common external tarriff 176
common market 176
commonwealth preference 176
community indifference curves 84
comparative advantage 17, 123, 168
competitiveness, 269, 281ff
    non-price 266, 280, 282
concerted lending 466
conditionality 451, 452ff, 472, 473
cone of diversification 38
conjectural variation 59, 152
consumer surplus 91
consumption feasibility locus 14, 132
consumption set 14, 81
consumption tax 95, 125
convoy theory 257, 258
Costs of non-Europe 194
cost reduction 182
countervailing duties 168
Cournot assumption 58, 147, 158
coverage ratio 112
covered interest arbitrage 315
crowding-out 350
currency substitution 334
current account 239, 240, 242, 269, 289, 309, 329

customs unions 176ff

debt buy-back 470
    crisis 449, 455ff
    default 466
    forgiveness 469
    overhang 467, 468
    relief 465, 467, 468, 473
    rescheduling 465
debt-equity swaps 469
Delors report 392
devaluation 136, 137, 269, 270, 274, 289, 295, 297, 299, 302, 306
directly unproductive profit-seeking activities (DUPs) 108, 160ff
discrimination 176, 181
dollar 368ff
domestic distortions 82, 123ff, 160, 205, 230
dumping 140ff
    counter-cyclical 141
    margin 141, 142
    predatory 140

East African Common Market 179
eclectic theory 220, 226
economic growth 201ff, 203
    export-led 208
economic integration 176ff
    dynamic effects 183, 197
economic unions 176
economies of scale 57ff, 62, 74, 98, 99, 145, 147, 182, 195, 197, 208, 213, 218, 224
economies of scale, external 52, 144
ECU 391ff
effective protection 95ff
efficiency, semi-strong 318
    weak-form 318
efficient markets 318, 319, 340
elasticities approach 269ff 309
embargo 129
employment 127, 136
Euratom 186
euro-bonds 144
euro-capital markets 443ff
euro-commercial paper 445
euro-dollar 357, 358, 404, 434
euro-markets 403, 427, 434ff
European Coal and Steel Community 185
European Communities 72, 176, 183ff
European Economic Community 186
European Free Trade Association (EFTA) 72, 176, 187, 190
European Internal Market 193ff, 392
European Monetary System 384, 390ff, 407
exchange rate 248ff, 269, 312ff, 328, 344
    effective 249
    nominal 249
    real 249
    regimes 374ff

Subject Index

68   9